AA007899

21st International Conference on Spoken Language Translation (IWSLT 2024)

Bangkok, Thailand
15-16 August 2024

ISBN: 979-8-3313-0131-6

Printed from e-media with permission by:

Curran Associates, Inc.
57 Morehouse Lane
Red Hook, NY 12571

CURRAN ASSOCIATES INC. proceedings.com

Some format issues inherent in the e-media version may also appear in this print version.

Copyright© (2024) by the Association for Computational Linguistics
All rights reserved.

Printed with permission by Curran Associates, Inc. (2024)

For permission requests, please contact the Association for Computational Linguistics
at the address below.

Association for Computational Linguistics
209 N. Eighth Street
Stroudsburg, Pennsylvania 18360

Phone: 1-570-476-8006
Fax: 1-570-476-0860

acl@aclweb.org

Additional copies of this publication are available from:

Curran Associates, Inc.
57 Morehouse Lane
Red Hook, NY 12571 USA
Phone: 845-758-0400
Fax: 845-758-2633
Email: curran@proceedings.com
Web: www.proceedings.com

IWSLT 2024

The 21st International Conference on Spoken Language Translation

Proceedings of the Conference

August 15-16, 2024

The IWSLT 2024 organizers gratefully acknowledge the support from our Diamond sponsor Apple.

Diamond

©2024 Association for Computational Linguistics

Introduction

The International Conference on Spoken Language Translation (IWSLT) is the premiere annual scientific conference for the study, development and evaluation of spoken language translation technology. Launched in 2004 and spun out from the C-STAR speech translation consortium before it (1992-2003), IWSLT is the main venue for scientific exchange on all topics related to speech-to-text translation, speech-to-speech translation, simultaneous and consecutive translation, speech dubbing, cross-lingual communication including all multimodal, emotional, paralinguistic, and stylistic aspects and their applications in the field. The conference organizes evaluations around challenge areas, and presents scientific papers and system descriptions. IWSLT is organized by the Special Interest Group on Spoken Language Translation (SIGSLT), which is supported by ACL, ISCA and ELRA.

This year, IWSLT featured spoken language translation shared tasks organized into seven distinct tracks: (i) speech-to-speech translation, (ii) simultaneous speech translation, (iii) subtitling, (iv) offline speech translation, (v) dubbing, (vi) low resource, and (vii) indic speech translation. Each track was coordinated by one or more chairs. The resulting evaluation campaigns attracted a total of 18 teams, from academia, research centers and industry. System submissions resulted in 26 system papers that will be presented at the conference. Following our call for papers, this year we received 10 submissions of research papers, 7 of which were accepted for oral presentation through a double-blind review process. The proceedings also include a survey paper summarizing recent research highlights, 2 test suite papers, which were peer-reviewed consistently with scientific and system papers respectively. In addition, the conference program is enriched by the presentation of 2 speech translation papers published in the Findings of the ACL over the past year.

The program committee is excited about the quality of the accepted papers and expects lively discussion and exchange at the conference. The conference chairs and organizers would like to express their gratitude to everyone who contributed and supported IWSLT. In particular, we wish to thank our Diamond sponsor Apple. We thank the shared tasks chairs, organizers, and participants, the program committee members, as well as all the authors that went the extra mile to submit system and research papers to IWSLT, and make this year's conference a big success. We also wish to express our sincere gratitude to ACL for hosting our conference and for arranging the logistics and infrastructure that allow us to hold IWSLT 2024 as a hybrid conference.

Welcome to IWSLT 2024, welcome to Bangkok!

Marine Carpuat, Program Chair
Marcello Federico and Alex Waibel, Conference Chairs

Organizing Committee

Conference Chairs

Marcello Federico, AWS AI Labs, USA
Alex Waibel, CMU, USA

Program Chair

Marine Carpuat, UMD, USA

Sponsorship Chair

Sebastian Stüker, Zoom, Germany

Evaluation Chair

Jan Niehues, KIT, Germany

Website and Publication Chair

Elizabeth Salesky, JHU, USA

Publicity Chair

Atul Kr. Ohja, University of Galway, Ireland

Program Committee

Program Committee

Milind Agarwal, GMU
Ibrahim Said Ahmad, Northeastern University
Md Mahfuz Ibn Alam, GMU
Antonios Anastasopoulos, GMU
Laurent Besacier, Naver Labs, France
Mauro Cettolo, FBK, Italy
Lizhong Chen, Oregon State University
William Chen, CMU
Josep Maria Crego, Systran, France
Anna Currey, AWS AI Labs
Qianqian Dong, ByteDance AI Lab, China
Akiko Eriguchi, Microsoft, USA
HyoJung Han, UMD
Benjamin Hsu, Amazon
Hirofumi Inaguma, Meta AI, USA
Takatomo Kano, NTT
Philipp Koehn, JHU
Surafel Melaku Lakew, Amazon AI, USA
Yves Lepage, Waseda University, Japan
Evgeny Matusov, AppTek, Germany
Chandresh Maurya, IIT Indore
Paul McNamee, JHU
Jan Niehues, KIT
Atul Kr. Ojha, U. Galway
John E. Ortega, Northeastern University
Sara Papi, FBK
Kumar Rishu, Charles University
Matthias Sperber, Apple, USA
Sebastian Stüker, Zoom, Germany
Katsuhito Sudoh, NAIST, Japan
Yun Tang, Meta AI, USA
Brian Thompson, AWS AI Labs, USA
Ioannis Tsiamas, Polytechnic University of Catalonia (UPC)
Marco Turchi, Zoom, Germany
David Vilar, Google, Germany
Yogesh Virkar, Amazon
Matthew Wiesner, JHU
Krzystof Wolk, Polish-Japanese Academy of Information Technology, Poland
Tong Xiao, Northeastern University
Rodolfo Zevallos, Universitat Pompeu Fabra

Table of Contents

Program

Thursday, August 15, 2024

09:00 - 09:15	*Welcome Remarks*
09:15 - 10:30	*Findings of the IWSLT 2024 Evaluation Campaign*
10:30 - 11:00	*Coffee Break*
11:00 - 12:00	*Findings of the IWSLT 2024 Evaluation Campaign*
12:00 - 12:30	*Oral Session A: Test Suite Papers (2)*
12:30 - 14:00	*Lunch Break*
14:00 - 15:30	*Poster Session I: System Papers for Low-Resource and Indic Tracks (13)*
15:30 - 16:00	*Coffee Break*
16:00 - 16:30	*Oral Session B: Scientific Papers (1) and Highlight Papers (1)*
16:30 - 17:30	*Panel Discussion*

Friday, August 16, 2024

09:00 - 10:30	*Oral Session C: Scientific Papers (6)*
10:30 - 11:00	*Coffee Break*
11:00 - 12:30	*Poster Session II: Findings Papers (1) and System Papers for Speech-to-Speech, Simultaneous, Subtitling, Offline & Dubbing tracks (12)*
12:30 - 14:00	*Lunch Break*
14:00 - 14:15	*Oral Session D: Findings Papers (1)*
14:15 - 15:30	*Planning Session for 2025*
15:30 - 16:00	*Coffee Break*
16:00 - 16:15	*Closing Remarks*

FINDINGS OF THE IWSLT 2024 EVALUATION CAMPAIGN

Ibrahim Said Ahmad[16] **Antonios Anastasopoulos**[1] **Ondřej Bojar**[4] **Claudia Borg**[5]
Marine Carpuat[2] **Roldano Cattoni**[3] **Mauro Cettolo**[3] **William Chen**[7] **Qianqian Dong**[9]
Marcello Federico[8] **Barry Haddow**[11] **Dávid Javorský**[4] **Mateusz Krubiński**[4]
Tsz Kin Lam[11] **Xutai Ma**[6] **Prashant Mathur**[8] **Evgeny Matusov**[13]
Chandresh Kumar Maurya[20] **John P. McCrae**[14] **Kenton Murray**[10] **Satoshi Nakamura**[12]
Matteo Negri[3] **Jan Niehues**[15] **Xing Niu**[8] **Atul Kr. Ojha**[14] **John E. Ortega**[16]
Sara Papi[3] **Peter Polák**[4] **Adam Pospíšil**[4] **Pavel Pecina**[4] **Elizabeth Salesky**[10]
Nivedita Sethiya[20] **Balaram Sarkar**[20] **Jiatong Shi**[7] **Claytone Sikasote**[21]
Matthias Sperber[17] **Sebastian Stüker**[18] **Katsuhito Sudoh**[22,12] **Brian Thompson**[8]
Alex Waibel[7] **Shinji Watanabe**[7] **Patrick Wilken**[13] **Petr Zemánek**[4] **Rodolfo Zevallos**[19]
[1]GMU [2]UMD [3]FBK [4]Charles U. [5]U. Malta [6]Meta [7]CMU [8]Amazon [9]ByteDance
[10]JHU [11]U. Edinburgh [12]NAIST [13]AppTek [14]U. Galway [15]KIT [16]Northeastern U.
[17]Apple [18]Zoom [19]U. Pompeu Fabra [20]IIT Indore [21]U. Zambia [22]Nara Women's U.

Abstract

This paper reports on the shared tasks organized by the 21st IWSLT Conference. The shared tasks address 7 scientific challenges in spoken language translation: simultaneous and offline translation, automatic subtitling and dubbing, speech-to-speech translation, dialect and low-resource speech translation, and Indic languages. The shared tasks attracted 18 teams whose submissions are documented in 26 system papers. The growing interest towards spoken language translation is also witnessed by the constantly increasing number of shared task organizers and contributors to the overview paper, almost evenly distributed across industry and academia.

1 Introduction

The International Conference on Spoken Language Translation (IWSLT) is the premier annual scientific conference for all aspects of spoken language translation (SLT). IWSLT is organized by the Special Interest Group on Spoken Language Translation (SIGSLT), which is supported by ACL, ISCA and ELRA.

Like in all the previous 20 editions, this year's conference was preceded by an evaluation campaign featuring shared tasks addressing scientific challenges in SLT. This paper reports on the 2024 IWSLT Evaluation Campaign, which offered the following 7 shared tasks:

- **Offline SLT**, with focus on speech-to-text translation of recorded conferences and interviews from English to German, Japanese and Chinese.
- **Simultaneous SLT**, focusing on speech-to-text translation of streamed audio of conferences and interviews from English to German, Japanese and Chinese.
- **Automatic Subtitling**, with focus on speech-to-subtitle translation of audio-visual documents from English to German and Spanish and on compression of pregenerated German and Spanish subtitles.
- **Speech-to-speech Translation**, focusing on natural-speech to synthetic-speech translation of recorded utterances from English to Chinese.
- **Automatic Dubbing**, focusing on dubbing of production quality videos from English to Chinese.
- **Low-resource SLT**, focusing on the translation of recorded speech from Bhojpuri to Hindi, Irish to English, Marathi to Hindi, Maltese to English, North Levantine Arabic to English, Pashto to French, Tamasheq to French, Quechua to Spanish, and Bemba to English.
- **Indic Languages Track**, with focus on Speech-to-Text translation of TED talk audios from English to Indic languages including Hindi, Tamil, and Bengali.

The shared tasks attracted 18 teams (see Table 1) representing both academic and industrial organizations. The following sections report on

Proceedings of the 21st International Conference on Spoken Language Translation (IWSLT 2024), pages 1–59
August 15-16, 2024 ©2024 Association for Computational Linguistics

Team	Organization
ALADAN	Vocapia, France, Lingea and Charles U., Czechia, Crowdee, Germany (Kheder et al., 2024)
APPTEK	Applications Technology (AppTek), Germany
CMU	Carnegie Mellon University, USA (Xu et al., 2024; Yan et al., 2024)
FBK	Fondazione Bruno Kessler, Italy (Papi et al., 2024; Gaido et al., 2024a)
HW-TSC	Huawei Translation Services Center, China (Wu et al., 2024; Wei et al., 2024) (Jiawei et al., 2024; Li et al., 2024a; Xie et al., 2024; Li et al., 2024b)
JHU	Johns Hopkins University, USA (Robinson et al., 2024)
KIT	Karlsruhe Institute of Technology, Germany (Koneru et al., 2024; Li et al., 2024c)
NAIST	Nara Institute of Science and Technology, Japan (Ko et al., 2024)
NICT	Nat. Inst. of Information and Comm. Technology, Japan (Dabre and Song, 2024)
NITKKR	National Institute of Technology Kurukshetra, India (Singh et al., 2024)
NYA	NetEase YiDun AI Lab, Hangzhou, China (Zhang et al., 2024)
QUESPA	Northeastern U, USA, U. de Pompeu Fabra, Spain, CMU, USA (Ortega et al., 2024)
RACAI	Romanian Academy, Romania (Gasan and Păiș, 2024)
SETU-DCU	SETech U, Ireland Unive di Pisa, Italy ADAPT, DCU, Ireland (Zafar et al., 2024)
UM,UOM	University of Malta, Malta (Nabhani et al., 2024; Abela et al., 2024)
UOM-DFKI	University of Malta, Malta, DFKI, Germany (Rishu et al., 2024)
BITSP	Birla Institute of Technology And Science - Pilani, India (Anand et al., 2024)
YMOSLEM	Independent Researcher, Ireland (Moslem, 2024)

Table 1: List of participants to the IWSLT 2024 shared tasks

each shared task in detail. Each section includes a description of the proposed challenge, the data and evaluation metrics used for training and testing systems, the received submissions, and finally a summary of the results. Detailed results for some of the shared tasks are reported in a corresponding appendix.

2 Offline SLT

Recent advances in deep learning are providing the opportunity to address traditional NLP tasks in new and completely different ways. One of these tasks is spoken language translation (SLT), an overarching problem that can be cast in various manners, ranging from offline to simultaneous processing, to produce either textual or speech outputs under both unconstrained and constrained conditions. This section reports on the 2024 round of the IWSLT Offline Speech Translation Track, which consists of translating audio speech from one language into text in a different target language without any specific time or structural constraints, different from the simultaneous (see §3), subtitling (§4), speech-to-speech (§5), and dubbing (§7) tasks. Under this general problem definition, the goal of the offline SLT track—the one with the longest tradition at IWSLT—is to continuously challenge this rapidly evolving technology by gradually introducing novel aspects that raise the difficulty bar.

2.1 Challenge

For years, SLT has been addressed by cascading an automatic speech recognition (ASR) system with a machine translation (MT) system. More recent trends involve using a single neural network to directly translate the input audio signal in one language into text in another language, bypassing intermediate symbolic representations such as transcriptions. In light of this evolution, the challenges addressed by the 2024 round of the offline track stem from the following considerations. **(1)** Although the results of the recent IWSLT campaigns have confirmed that the performance of end-to-end models is approaching that of cascade solutions, it is currently not clear which of the two technologies is more effective. Moreover, **(2)** all recent evaluations have been based on test sets extracted from TED talks, which represent a relatively simpler application scenario compared to the variety of potential deployments of SLT technology. In this controlled scenario, a single speaker delivers a prepared speech without background noise or interaction with other speakers. Finally, **(3)** last year's edition showed that introducing complexity to the scenario (e.g., including spontaneous speech, terminology, and dialogues) resulted in a clear performance degradation compared to using the classic TED talk test set.

Therefore, in addition to addressing the question of whether the cascade solution remains the dominant technology, this year we focused on understanding whether current state-of-the-art solutions can handle more complex scenarios (e.g., spontaneous speech, terminology, different accents, background noise, and dialogues). To shed light on these aspects, participants were challenged with data representative of different domains and conditions, namely:

- **TED Talks**[1] – the classic IWSLT evaluation material, for which fresh test data were collected also this year;
- **TV series** from ITV Studios[2] – data featuring multiple individuals interacting in various scenarios. The speech translation system needs to deal with overlapping speakers, different accents, and background noise;
- **Physical training videos** offered by Peloton[3] – data featuring individuals exercising in the gym. The speech translation system needs to deal with with background noise and an informal speaking style;
- **Accented English conversations** – data featuring conversations, each containing two friends interacting on a daily topic, such as hobbies and vacation. The speakers were selected to cover a wide range of English speakers around the globe. In addition to the variety of accents, another major challenge is the presence of spontaneous speech.

In continuity with the last two years, three language directions were proposed. Depending on the evaluation scenario, the language conditions covered are:

- English → German: TED talks, TV series, physical training videos, and accented English conversations;
- English → Japanese: TED talks.
- English → Chinese: TED talks.

[1]https://www.ted.com/

[2]https://www.itvstudios.com/

[3]https://www.onepeloton.com/

2.1.1 Test Suites

To further broaden the scope of evaluation conditions and explore specific aspects relevant to SLT, this year we provided participants with the option to submit additional test suites alongside the standard evaluation setting described above. The purpose of a test suite is to assess an SLT system on particular aspects that are generally hidden or overlooked by the classic evaluation frameworks. While the official evaluation relies solely on the designated official test sets, these supplementary test suites offer a valuable means to enhance system testing across a wider spectrum of phenomena. They also provide an opportunity to pinpoint specific and challenging issues that impact SLT performance. The particular test suite composition and its evaluation were fully delegated to the interested test suite provider.

2.2 Data and Metrics

Training and development data. Similar to the 2023 edition, participants were offered the possibility to submit systems built under three training data conditions:

1. **Constrained**: the allowed training data is limited to a medium-sized framework in order to keep the training time and resource requirements manageable. The complete list[4] of allowed training resources (speech, speech-to-text-parallel, text-parallel, text-monolingual) does not include any pre-trained language model.
2. **Constrained with large language models** (constrained^{+LLM}): in addition to all the constrained resources, a restricted selection[4] of large language models is allowed to give participants the possibility to leverage large language models and medium-sized resources. We reproduce the list of allowed LLMs in Table 2.
3. **Unconstrained**: any resource, pre-trained language models included, can be used with the exception of evaluation sets. This setup is proposed to allow the participation of teams equipped with high computational power and effective in-house solutions built on additional resources.

[4]See the IWSLT 2024 offline track web page: https://iwslt.org/2024/offline

LLM	Source
Wav2vec 2.0	https://github.com/pytorch/fairseq/blob/main/examples/wav2vec/README.md
Hubert	https://github.com/pytorch/fairseq/tree/main/examples/hubert
WavLM	https://github.com/microsoft/unilm/tree/master/wavlm
SpeechLM	https://github.com/microsoft/unilm/tree/master/speechlm
data2vec	https://github.com/facebookresearch/fairseq/tree/main/examples/data2vec
MBART	https://github.com/pytorch/fairseq/blob/main/examples/mbart/README.md
MBART50	https://github.com/pytorch/fairseq/tree/main/examples/multilingual#mbart50-models
M2M100	https://github.com/pytorch/fairseq/tree/main/examples/m2m_100
Delta LM	https://github.com/microsoft/unilm/tree/master/deltalm
T5	https://github.com/google-research/text-to-text-transfer-transformer
BLOOM	https://huggingface.co/bigscience/bloom-560m#model-details
(Note: only the small 560M parameter version)	
Mistral 7B Instruction Fine-tuned	https://huggingface.co/mistralai/Mistral-7B-Instruct-v0.1
Mistral 7B Base Model	https://huggingface.co/mistralai/Mistral-7B-v0.1
LLama2 7B Chat Model	https://huggingface.co/meta-llama/Llama-2-7b-chat-hf
Llama2 7B base model	https://huggingface.co/meta-llama/Llama-2-7b-hf
NLLB 3.3B	https://huggingface.co/facebook/nllb-200-distilled-1.3B
NLLB 1.3B	https://huggingface.co/facebook/nllb-200-3.3B
NLLB 600M	https://huggingface.co/facebook/nllb-200-distilled-600M
Seamless Models (SeamlessM4T/Streaming/Expressive)	https://github.com/facebookresearch/seamless_communication

Table 2: List of LLMs allowed in the constrained^{+LLM} training data condition.

The development data allowed under the constrained condition consists of the dev set from IWSLT 2010, as well as the test sets used for the 2010, 2013-2015 and 2018-2020 IWSLT campaigns. Besides this TED-derived material, additional development data were released to cover the three new scenarios included in this round of evaluation.

Test data. As in previous rounds of the offline track, the collection of new test data for the **TED talks** scenario started by isolating a set of talks (41 in total) that are not included in the current public release of MuST-C (Cattoni et al., 2021). Starting from this material, which was used to build the initial English-German test set, the talks for which Japanese and Chinese translations are available were selected to build the English-Japanese and English-Chinese test sets. Since further checks revealed a partial overlap between the selected talks and the TED2020 corpus[5] (Reimers and Gurevych, 2020) a final cleaning step had to be applied to remove the overlapping talks (4 for en-de, 4 for en-ja, none for en-zh). After this removal, the final test sets comprise 37 talks for English-German (corresponding to a total duration of 3h:07m:14s), 30 talks for English-Japanese (2h:14m:11s), and 30 talks for English-Chinese (3h:20m:19s).

For the **TV series** scenario, the 7 TV series for a total duration of 06h:01m are offered by ITV Studios.[6] Each series includes multiple speakers, background noise, and different audio conditions.

For the **Physical training** scenario, the 9 physical training videos for a total duration of 03h:59m are offered by Peloton.[7] Each video includes a single speaker in a room practicing sports activities with, often, background music and breathy voice.

For the **Accent challenge** scenario, the test set has 1,448 utterances that are sampled from 76 conversations in the Edinburgh International Accents of English Corpus (EdAcc, Sanabria et al., 2023). In total, the test set contains about 3.5 hours of audio data, 34k English words, 25.2k German words and 33 accents. The German translations are created from the English transcripts by our professional translators who are paid at a rate of 0.095 GBP per word. The translators, with access to the aligned audio files, were required to translate the transcripts in a fluent and faithful manner while allowing punctuation and casing. For example, hesitation tokens like "ACH" and "HMM" in the transcripts are not included in the translation. The complete translation guidelines are attached in Appendix B.1.

Metrics. Systems were evaluated with respect to their capability to produce translations similar to the target-language references. The similarity was measured in terms of multiple automatic met-

[5]https://opus.nlpl.eu/TED2020/en&de/v1/TED2020

[6]https://www.itvstudios.com

[7]https://www.onepeloton.com

rics: COMET[8] (Rei et al., 2020), BLEU[9] (Papineni et al., 2002a), chrF (Popović, 2015). Among them, this year COMET was chosen as the primary evaluation metric based the findings of Macháček et al. (2023) and Sperber et al. (2024), which indicate its highest correlation with human judgements. The submitted runs were therefore ranked based on the COMET calculated on the test set by using automatic resegmentation of the hypothesis based on the reference translation by mwerSegmenter,[10] using a detailed script accessible to participants.[11] Moreover, similar to last year's round, a human assessment was performed on the best-performing submission of each participant in order to enhance the soundness and completeness of the evaluation.

2.3 Submissions

This year, 4 teams participated in the offline task, submitting a total of 38 runs. Table 3 provides a breakdown of the participation in each subtask showing, for each training data condition, the number of participants, the number of submitted runs and, for each training data condition (constrained, constrained^{+LLM}, unconstrained), the number of submitted runs obtained with cascade and direct systems. Notably, no direct system was submitted this year.

- CMU (Yan et al., 2024) participated with cascade en-de, en-ja, en-zh systems trained under the unconstrained condition. Their model consists of an ASR system based on Whisper and an MT system based on fine-tuned NLLB models. The ASR system is enhanced by the application of a specific fine-tuning to process unsegmented recordings without the need for a separate voice-activity detection stage. The MT systems generate a set of candidate translations via epsilon-sampling that are then pooled and the 1-best translation is selected using COMET-based Minimum Bayes-Risk decoding.

- HW-TSC (Wu et al., 2024) participated with cascade en-de, en-ja, en-zh systems trained under the constrained, constrained with Large Language Models, and unconstrained conditions. The authors used different training strategies for each different condition. Under the *constrained* condition, an ASR is trained from scratch testing Conformer and U2. All audio inputs are augmented with spectral augmentation), and Connectionist Temporal Classification (CTC) is added to make the model converge better. The MT system takes advantage of the Deep Transformer-Big model structure, R-Drop and data selection to identify in-domain data from a large pool of parallel data. Under the *constrained + LLM* condition, the ASR system is a combination of the wav2vec2 encoder and mBART50 decoder, where the self-attention of the encoder and decoder are frozen and all constrained are used for fine-tuning. The MT system is based on Llama2-7B fine-tuned with parallel data and source language consistent instructions, and applying CPO. Under the *unconstrained* condition, the ASR system is based Whisper fine-tuned and MuST-C, while the MT model selects the 1-best translation from a pool of candidates generated both with NMT and LLM using COMET. Audio segmentation is performed using SHAS.

- KIT (Koneru et al., 2024) participated with a cascade en-de system trained under the constrained with Large Language Models condition. This submission is based on a four-step approach. The audio is first transcribed by a fine-tuned ASR, the n-best list is then processed by an LLM to generate the best hypothesis. The final transcripts is translated to generate the text in the target language. The transcript and the translation are then paired and document- level automatic post-editing is applied to improve the coherence of the translations. The ASR is based on the combination of WavLM encoder and mBART50 decoder fine-tuned on the task data. Audio segmentation is based on SHAS, but a longformer technique is also tested to use context better. The ASR refiner and the MT post-editor are fine-tuned versions of Mistral 7B Instruction-tuned LLM using QLoRA, while

[8] Unbabel/wmt22-comet-da

[9] BLEU+case.mixed+numrefs.1+smooth.exp+tok.13a +version.1.4.14

[10] https://www-i6.informatik.rwth-aachen.de/web/Software/mwerSegmenter.tar.gz

[11] https://github.com/isl-mt/SLT.KIT/blob/master/scripts/evaluate/Eval.sh

English-German										
Participants	**Runs**	**Constrained**			**Constrained^{+LLM}**			**Unconstrained**		
4	14	2	Cascade	2	3	Cascade	3	9	Cascade	9
			Direct	-		Direct	-		Direct	-
English-Chinese										
Participants	**Runs**	**Constrained**			**Constrained^{+LLM}**			**Unconstrained**		
3	13	2	Cascade	2	2	Cascade	2	9	Cascade	9
			Direct	-		Direct	-		Direct	-
English-Japanese										
Participants	**Runs**	**Constrained**			**Constrained^{+LLM}**			**Unconstrained**		
3	11	2	Cascade	2	2	Cascade	2	4	Cascade	4
			Direct	-		Direct	-		Direct	-

Table 3: Breakdown of the participation in each sub-task (English→German, English→Chinese, English→Japanese) of the IWSLT offline ST track. For each language direction, we report the number of participants, the number of submitted runs and, for each training data condition (constrained, constrained^{+LLM}, unconstrained), the number of submitted runs obtained with cascade and direct systems.

NLLB 200 3.3B is used as the MT system. The post-editing step showed to be less effective when the ASR quality is low. For this reason, LLM refinement is not used for the EPTV and ITV datasets.

- NYA (Zhang et al., 2024) participated with cascade en-de, en-ja, en-zh systems trained under the unconstrained condition. The ASR is based on Whisper-v3-large, while the MT system is a wider and deeper Transformer model. The MT model is enhanced by leveraging several techniques such as R-Drop, data augmentation with backward translations, domain adaptation via data filtering, and ASR output adaptation where the human-quality transcript in the SLT data is replaced with the automatic transcript. The final MT model is an ensemble of two/three models. The audio is segmented using SHAS.

2.4 Results

We will analyse the different aspects of the results by language pair.

2.4.1 English to German

Correlation between BLEU, COMET and DA scores Table 25 shows the aggregated result of the participated systems on the four test sets. In terms of ranking based on the BLEU score, NYA wins 3 out of 4 test sets, except on ITV which CMU and HW-TSC(U) have a tie. However, the ranking is substantially changed when COMET is used. In this case, CMU is the winning system in all conditions, indicating that this submission achieves the best performance. But in contrast to last year when the human evaluation validated the automatic metric rankings, the correlation between the automatic rankings and the human ranking is not as good as shown in Table 18. (More details on our human evaluation using DA are provided in Appendix A.2.1.) For the human evaluation, HW-TSC(C+) achieves the best performance overall and has the best DA ranking on 3 out of four test sets. Only on the accent test set, NYA has better scores. However, it is worth noticing that no system performs significantly better than HW-TSC(C+) on any dataset.

The results show that it is essential to perform a human evaluation since no automatic metric, at the moment, can predict the performance of the individual systems well. Furthermore, additional research on performing reliable automatic metrics for speech translation would be very valuable.

It is interesting to note that all the submissions are based on the cascade architecture this year. This is an important change compared to previous editions where the end-to-end architectures competed with the cascade ones.

Context Beyond Segment Level One of the participating teams, KIT, used document-level post-editing to improve the coherence of translation. We note that while document-level consistency is a critical feature of text and speech translation, our evaluation this year does not reflect it yet. All used automatic metrics are segment-oriented. As detailed in Appendix A.2.1 also the particular setup of DA this year did not allow the annotators to consider longer context because the segments were shuffled for DA. (Two neighbouring segments were provided but only to account for segmentation errors, not for assessment of context-level phenomena.) It is therefore conceivable that the outputs of the KIT system were somewhat penalized.

Domains Similar to last year's edition, we evaluated each submitted system on different domains. First of all, the results show that the systems perform very differently in the different domains. When looking at the human ranking, the best quality is achieved in the TED domain. This is not surprising, since research has focused on this for many years and a significant amount of training resources exist. The performance on ITV and Peloton is lower, and the Accent data set appears to be the most challenging condition, indicating that speech translation remains an unsolved problem.

The availability of human rankings of the same systems across different domains allows us also to analyse whether automatic scores can be used to assess the quality of SLT system across domains. When ranking the difficulty level of different domains, we see that COMET ranks them similar than the human ranking except that COMET shows overall lower scores for Peloton, identifying Peloton as more challenging than Accent. In contrast, string-based metrics like BLEU are not able to do this. This also shows that additional metrics might be needed to measure the quality across domains.

Data conditions On top of the above, we can also observe the improvement in both BLEU and COMET scores caused by using an additional large language model or additional data. HW-TSC submitted three primary systems for each data condition, and both the unconstrained (U) and the constrained^{+LLM} (C^{+}) models have a noticeable gain over the constrained model (C). The two better models perform similarly in both BLEU and COMET. Interestingly, additional training data beyond the language model data does not significantly improve. In terms of DA score, the constrained^{+LLM} model is >0.6 points better than the other models in different data conditions.

Progress compared to last year We also performed an automatic evaluation of the system on the test sets from last year from the domains TED, EMPAC, and ACL. The results are summarized in Table 26. Although the participants optimized for different domains, for each domain and each metric this year's submissions achieved the best performance. When comparing the best submission from this year and last year, this year's submission is between 4.4 and 1.5 BLEU points better and 1.1 to 2.7 COMET percent points better than the best system from last year.

Performance by accents For the accent test set, we performed an additional details analysis for the different accents.

Figure 1 shows the BLEU and COMET of each system across the 33 accents. The numbers in parenthesis are audio duration in the format of "minutes:seconds". We use the self-reported labels from the original work as the prior choice for accent labeling. Since accents could be loosely defined (e.g., multi-class), subjective, and most speakers in the annotation are not the related experts, we thus derive the labels from other attributes, such as the first language of the speaker, if necessary and refine the labels to country-level. There is one speaker who declares his accent as "Trans-Atlantic" and speaks multiple first languages. We assign this special case as "Mixed".

The aggregated result on Table 25 shows that CMU is the winning system on Accent when COMET is used for ranking, whereas NYA would be the winner if BLEU is used instead. Does this winning situation occurs on a wide range of accents or on a small subset? The breakdown on Figure 1 shows that CMU (the blue-diamond points) has better COMET scores, especially relative to NYA, and is within Top-2 on a wide range of accents. Similar observations are found in the better BLEU scores of NYA (the yellow-star points).

For the three primary systems submitted by HW-TSC (the red points), their performances are rather consistent across the 2 metrics and the accents. In most cases, both the constrained^{+LLM} (the circles) and the unconstrained models (the squares) perform similarly, while the constrained model (the triangles) falls slightly behind. In the North Macedonian and the Pakistani accents, the constrained model seems to be better in both BLEU and COMET, but their data sizes are rather small, i.e. <1 minute. In the constrained LLM setting, the HW-TSC system in general performs better than the KIT system in a wide range of accents, but the KIT system has a slight edge in Indonesian,

Israeli and Japanese accents.

The macro-average across accents are 18.7 BLEU and 0.679 COMET. Despite their fairly large test sizes, French, Irish, Jamaican, Kenyan and Vietnamese are below average. In Brazilian, German, Mexican and South African accents, all systems perform rather poorly, i.e., <10 BLEU. Potential causes are the train-test mismatch in accents, their small test sizes and the resegmentation error in the short utterances. Additionally, these speeches contain a mix of disfluencies and named entities, e.g., food ingredients, imposing further translation challenges.

2.4.2 English to Japanese

For the English to Japanese direction, we only have one test condition, the TED domain. In this case, the HW-TSC is the winner in all metrics, BLEU, COMET, and human ranking. However, the order of the submissions from HW-TSC varies across different metrics. Furthermore, the other two participants perform similarly on human ranking, but CMU is clearly better on COMET and NYA is clearly better on BLEU. This again suggests that the automatic metrics do not perform sufficiently well on speech translation tasks yet. Similar to the En-De language direction, all the submitted systems are based on the cascade architecture.

When comparing the submissions from this year and last year on the two progress test sets (TED and ACL), we again see a clear improvement compared to last year's best systems.

For the data conditions, we see again a better performance of the unconstrained (U) and the constrained^{+LLM} (C^{+}) submissions from HW-TSC compared to the system using only constrained data. However, this does not hold for the BLEU metric and the human evaluation. In these metrics, we see no clear benefit from using more data.

2.4.3 English to Chinese

For the English to Chinese direction, we also have only one test condition, the TED domain. In this case, the HW-TSC is the best system in human evaluation and COMET, while NYA performed best in BLEU. While this could indicate a good correlation between human evaluation and COMET, NYA actually serves as a counterexample: it performed worst in COMET and second best in human evaluation. This again suggests that the automatic metrics do not work reliably on speech translation tasks yet. Similar to the other language directions, all the submitted systems are based on the cascade architecture.

When comparing the submissions from this year and last year on the two progress test sets (TED and ACL), we again see a clear improvement compared to the best systems of last year.

For the data conditions, we see again a better performance of the unconstrained (U) and the constrained^{+LLM} (C^{+}) submissions from HW-TSC compared to the system using only constrained data, when considering the COMET metric and the human evaluation.

3 Simultaneous SLT

Simultaneous speech translation focuses on translating speech in real-time, in manner vaguely similar to simultaneous interpreting. The system is designed to begin translating before the speaker has finished their sentence. This technology is particularly useful in scenarios such as international conferences, personal travel, or public emergency events.

This year, the task included two tracks: speech-to-text and speech-to-speech, covering four language directions: English to German, English to Chinese, English to Japanese, and Czech to English—a new language direction added this year.

3.1 Challenge

We have retained the settings from last year's shared task. A single latency constraint is introduced for each of the tracks:

- An average lagging of 2 seconds for the speech-to-text track.
- A starting offset of 2.5 seconds for the speech-to-speech track.

Participants are allowed to submit no more than one system per track and language direction, provided the system's latency remains within the specified constraints. The latency performance of the systems is evaluated using the open MuST-C tst-COMMON test set (Di Gangi et al., 2019). Submissions were accepted only in the form of Docker images, which were later executed by the organizers on the blind-test set in a controlled environment. An example implementation was

set	domain	#utter.	#words/ utter.	duration (min)
dev	ParCzech	276	24	56
	ELITR	314	13	28.6
test	MockConf	1113	14	129.5

Table 4: Statistics of the dev and test sets for the Czech-English simultaneous task.

provided using the SimulEval toolkit (Ma et al., 2020).

3.2 Data

To simplify the setting and allow participants to focus on the new modeling aspects of simultaneous translation, we adhere to the constraints with large language models as defined for the offline SLT task, see Section 2.2 above. This is the sole data condition for the task. The test data differ across different language pairs:

English to German, Chinese, and Japanese Common TED Talks, which are the same as those used in the Offline task, as described in Section 2.2.

Czech to English The devset was created from two sources:

- A subset called "context" was taken from ParCzech 3.0 (Kopp et al., 2021), consisting of consecutive recordings of Parliament of the Czech Republic.
- An entire recording of a debate about AI from the ELITR test set (Ansari et al., 2021).[12]

The reference translations of the devset were done by students of translation studies from the Faculty of Arts at Charles University.

The testset was gathered from mock conferences that were part of the interpreting curriculum of the Faculty of Arts at Charles University. A speaker pretends to be a celebrity or an interesting person and delivers a made-up speech on a predetermined topic. We included 13 such speeches. The reference translations were provided by professional translators. Due to confidentiality of recordings, the testset is not released to the community. The statistics of the data are displayed in Table 4.

[12]`https://github.com/ELITR/elitr-testset/tree/master/documents/2021-theaitre-related/robothon-debate`

3.3 Evaluation

We evaluate two aspects of the model: quality and latency.

Quality We conducted both automatic and human evaluation. BLEU score (Papineni et al., 2002b) is used for automatic quality evaluation. For speech output, the BLEU score is computed on the transcripts from Whisper (Radford et al., 2023) ASR model. The ranking of the submission is based on the BLEU score on the Common blind test set. The human evaluation was conducted in English-to-German/Chinese/Japanese, as described in A.1.

Latency We only conducted automatic evaluation. We report the following metrics for each speech-to-text systems.

- Average Lagging (AL; Ma et al., 2019)
- Length Adaptive Average Lagging (LAAL; Polák et al., 2022; Papi et al., 2022a)
- Average Token Delay (ATD; Kano et al., 2023)
- Differentiable Average Lagging (DAL; Arivazhagan et al., 2019)

For speech-to-speech systems, we report start-offset, end-offset and Average Token Delay. The latency metrics will not be used for ranking.

3.4 Submissions

Four teams in total submitted systems this year, with all teams participating in at least one language direction in the speech-to-text track. All teams entered the English-to-German track; three teams entered the English-to-Chinese and English-to-Japanese tracks; and two teams entered the Czech-to-English track, to which we added a Whisper-based benchmark. For the speech-to-speech track, two teams submitted systems, with one team submitting for all language directions and the other only in the English-to-Japanese direction.

CMU **(Xu et al., 2024)** participated in the speech-to-text track for the English-to-German direction. Their system integrates the WavLM-based speech encoder (Chen et al., 2021), a modality adapter, and the Llama2-7B-based decoder (Touvron et al., 2023). The training is conducted in two stages: modality alignment and full fine-tuning, both performed on MuST-C v2 data (Cattoni et al., 2021). The two-stage training results in an offline speech translation model, which is then adapted to a simultaneous speech translation model with a simple fixed hold-n policy.

FBK **(Papi et al., 2024)** participated in all language directions of the speech-to-text track. Their system is a unified multilingual simultaneous speech translation system, combining AlignAtt (Papi et al., 2023b) and SeamlessM4T-medium (Seamless Communication et al., 2023). The SeamlessM4T model is directly used in its streaming mode without additional retraining. The generated hypotheses are further processed through AlignAtt for policy learning. Based on diverse training sources, the model can translate into approximately 200 target languages from 143 source languages.

HW-TSC **(Li et al., 2024a)** participated in all language directions of both the speech-to-text and speech-to-speech tracks. Except for the Czech-to-English direction, all other models utilize cascaded simultaneous speech translation approaches by combining offline speech recognition, machine translation, and text-to-speech. For the Czech-to-English direction, they utilize the offline SeamlessM4T (Seamless Communication et al., 2023) as the backbone for speech-to-text translation, combined with a text-to-speech system. They followed their last year's submissions as the base setting (Guo et al., 2023). Additionally, they applied online voice-activity-detection-oriented segmentation, chunk padding in the speech recognition system to achieve smaller delays, and added an ensemble strategy for machine translation to achieve better stability. For end-to-end speech-to-text translation, they fine-tuned the SeamlessM4T model using the suggested data in the simultaneous SLT shared task.

NAIST **(Ko et al., 2024)** participated in three language directions of the speech-to-text track. Their speech-to-text system combined HuBERT (Hsu et al., 2021) and mBART (Liu et al., 2020b) in an end-to-end fashion, with a local agreement policy (Liu et al., 2020a; Polák et al., 2022). Their speech-to-speech system further applied an incremental text-to-speech module tuned with AlignAtt policy (Papi et al., 2023b).

ORGANIZER'S BENCHMARK by Charles University was prepared for the Czech-to-English direction. The system is based on Whisper (Radford et al., 2023) version `large-v2`. We applied an onlinization technique (Polák et al., 2022, 2023a,b) to utilize the offline Whisper model in the simultaneous regime, and applied prompting to leverage the translation history from previous segments. Due to organizational reasons, the benchmark was run on different hardware so the comparison of computationally-aware latency with other systems is not possible.

3.5 Results

We rank the system performance based on BLEU scores. The detailed results can be found in the respective tables in Appendix A.2.3.

Speech-to-Text The ranking of the speech-to-text track is as follow

- English to German (Table 29):
  HW-TSC, CMU, NAIST, FBK
- English to Chinese (Table 30):
  HW-TSC, NAIST, FBK
- English to Japanese (Table 31):
  HW-TSC, NAIST, FBK
- Czech to English (Table 32):
  ORGANIZER'S BENCHMARK (with context of 2 segments), FBK, HW-TSC

Speech-to-Speech As mentioned in Section 3.4, two teams submitted speech-to-speech track this year. HW-TSC submitted systems on all language directions and NAIST submitted on English to Japanese Direction. We only rank the English to Japanese Direction. The rank is: HW-TSC, NAIST. See Table 33 for more details.

3.6 Conclusions

Over the past four years, the IWSLT has consistently featured simultaneous translation tasks, reflecting a growing interest and impressive progress in this area. The shared task also brings the establishment of standardized evaluation protocols for simultaneous translation research. The recent integration of foundation models has further expanded the potential of this task. All teams integrated such models into their submissions using different approaches. CMU and NAIST teams combined two foundation models each specialized in one modality (speech encoder and text decoder) together using fine-tuning, while others chose existing ST models such as SeamlessM4T or Whisper and modified them for simultaneous use. Surprisingly, even large models (e.g., the CMU's Llama2-7B-based decoder) achieved competitive computationally-aware latencies.

The only cascaded system in the competition (HW-TSC) was consistently rated first in three language pairs. Nevertheless, according to all latency measurements, this system also exhibited the highest computationally-aware latencies.

One of the interesting points this year is the newly-added Czech-to-English translation direction where we included our Whisper-based benchmark. When operating at the segment level, this benchmark performed worse than participants' systems, but given one or two of its previous translation outputs, it improved over them. This confirms that the role of context is very important in speech translation task and the best uses of LLMs for this task are still to be found.

Several promising directions for future improvements remain. Investigating downstream tasks such as cross-lingual dialogues could provide deeper insights into practical applications of simultaneous translation. Developing more interactive evaluation methods could enhance the understanding and effectiveness of these systems. Lastly, optimizing the evaluation procedure to expedite the process remains crucial, as the current system managed by the organizers can be time-consuming.

4 Automatic Subtitling

In recent years, the task of automatically creating subtitles for audiovisual content in another language has gained a lot of attention due to the rapid increase in the global distribution and streaming of movies, series, and user-generated videos. Reflecting these trends, the automatic subtitling track was introduced for the first time in 2023 as part of the IWSLT Evaluation Campaigns. Given the growing interest in this area, the task has been continued this year with the addition of a new subtrack, **subtitle compression**, alongside the existing **automatic subtitling** sub-task from the previous edition.

In the automatic subtitling task, participants were asked to generate subtitles in German and/or Spanish from English speech in audiovisual documents. In the new subtitle compression task, participants were required to automatically rephrase subtitles that did not comply with the reading speed constraint (i.e., subtitles exceeding a certain length/time ratio given in characters per second) to ensure they met the required standards.

The decision to have works focusing on this specific aspect of subtitling is highly motivated by the existing requirements posed by subtitles providers (Papi et al., 2023a). In fact, the constraint on the reading speed is a commonly adopted standard to ensure that viewers can enjoy audiovisual content without experiencing fatigue or distraction due to excessive reading demands (Kruger, 2001). Therefore, adhering to this limit is crucial, making the development of ad-hoc methods to improve automatically generated subtitles that exceed this threshold of particular interest.

4.1 Challenge

Automatic Subtitling. The task of automatic subtitling is multifaceted: starting from speech, not only must the translation be generated, but it must also be segmented into subtitles that comply with constraints ensuring a high-quality user experience. These constraints include proper reading speed, synchrony with the voices, the maximum number of subtitle lines, and characters per line. Most audio-visual companies define their own subtitling guidelines, which can slightly differ from each other. In the case of IWSLT participants, we asked to generate subtitles according to specific guidelines provided by TED, including:

- The maximum subtitle reading speed is 21 characters per second;
- lines cannot exceed 42 characters, including white spaces;
- Subtitles cannot exceed 2 lines.

Participants were expected to use only the audio track from the provided videos (dev and test sets), the video track was of low quality and primarily meant to verify time synchronicity and other aspects of displaying subtitles on screen. That being said, the exploitation of the video was permitted.

The subtitling sub-track required participants to automatically subtitle audio-visual documents in German and/or Spanish, where the spoken language is always English. These documents were collected, similarly to last year, from the following sources:

- TED talks;[13]
- Physical training videos offered by Peloton;[14]
- TV series from ITV Studios.[15]

Subtitle Compression. The objective of the subtitle compression sub-track was to engage teams interested in the subtitling task but unable to build a complete automatic subtitling system. Participants were provided with automatic subtitles (in German and Spanish) generated by a non-participating system, namely the system presented in (Papi et al., 2023a), and asked to rephrase those that exceeded the reading speed constraint (more than 21 characters per second) to make them compliant. Time boundaries were to remain unchanged: only the text within a given time span had to be compressed when necessary. The original audiovisual documents (from the ITV test24 set of the subtitling sub-track) were also provided.

Although the subtitle compression task may appear simpler than subtitling, and it certainly is from the point of view of architectural complexity, it still presents its own difficulties. These challenges include those inherent in *text summarization*, such as identifying the main content of the original text, which must be preserved, and distinguishing accessory information, which can be omitted if necessary. Additionally, a peculiar challenge is that the text that needs to be reformulated is potentially error-prone and often does not consist of well-formed sentences but rather spans of text representing portions of sentences or words spanning contiguous phrases. It is expected that the most effective solutions are those capable of looking at the context, in an attempt to recover as much as possible the missing information in the text being processed.

4.2 Data and Metrics

4.2.1 Automatic subtitling

Data. This sub-track proposed two training data conditions:

- **Constrained**: the official training data condition, in which the allowed training data is limited to a medium-sized framework[16] to keep the training time and resource requirements manageable;
- **Unconstrained**: a setup without data restrictions (any resource, pre-trained language models included, can be used) to allow also the participation of teams equipped with high computational power and effective in-house solutions built on additional resources.

domain	set	AV docs	hh::mm	ref subtitles de	ref subtitles es
TED	dev	17	04:11	4906	4964
	test23	14	01:22	1375	1422
	test24	16	01:50	1832	1826
Peloton	dev	9	03:59	4508	4037
	test23	8	02:43	2700	2661
	test24	4	01:40	1418	1574
ITV	dev	7	06:01	4489	4762
	test23	7	05:08	4806	4896
	test24	7	05:54	4564	4528

Table 5: Statistics of the dev and evaluation sets for the subtitling task.

For each language and domain, a development set and two test sets were released, that of the 2023 evaluation (**tst2023**), used for measuring progress over years, and a new one (**tst2024**). Table 5 provides some statistics on these sets.

Metrics. The evaluation was carried out from three perspectives, subtitle quality, translation quality, and subtitle compliance, through the following automatic measures:

- Subtitle quality vs. reference subtitles:
  - **SubER**, primary metric, used also for ranking (Wilken et al., 2022);[17]
- Translation quality vs. reference translations:
  - **BLEU**[18] and **CHRF**[19] via sacreBLEU;
  - **BLUERT** (Sellam et al., 2020).

  Automatic subtitles are realigned to the reference subtitles using mwerSegmenter (Matusov et al., 2005)[20] before running sacreBLEU and BLEURT.

[13] https://www.ted.com/
[14] https://www.onepeloton.com
[15] https://www.itvstudios.com
[16] https://iwslt.org/2024/subtitling#training-data-allowed-for-constrained-conditions
[17] https://github.com/apptek/SubER
[18] sacreBLEU signature: nrefs:1|case:mixed|eff:no|tok:13a|smooth:exp|version:2.0.0
[19] sacreBLEU signature: nrefs:1|case:mixed|eff:yes|nc:6|nw:0|space:no|version:2.0.0
[20] https://www-i6.informatik.rwth-aachen.de/web/Software/mwerSegmenter.tar.gz

- Subtitle compliance:[21]
  - rate of subtitles with more than 21 characters per second (**CPS**);
  - rate of lines longer than 42 characters, white spaces included (**CPL**);
  - rate of subtitles with more than 2 lines (**LPB**).

4.2.2 Subtitle compression

Data. No specific training data was released for this sub-track. Any solution was allowed, without limitations on the training data, including the use of LLM prompted for text compression (e.g. chatGPT). The original audio, though potentially helpful, could either be used or not by participants; its transcription with external tools (e.g. Whisper) was also permitted.

As a development set, a minimal example taken from the EuroParl Interviews benchmark (Papi et al., 2023a)[22] was released, where the non-participating subtitling system introduced in (Papi et al., 2023a)[23] was employed to generate automatic, sometimes non-compliant subtitles, which were associated with corresponding compliant reference subtitles.

The test set consists of German and Spanish automatic subtitles for the audiovisual documents defining the ITV test24 set of the subtitling sub-track; the same non-participating subtitling system was employed to generate the subtitles to be corrected.

Metrics. Since the text in subtitles has to be compressed to fulfill the CPS requirement, but at the same time its meaning should be preserved as best as possible, both **CPS** and **BLEURT** are considered primary metrics in the evaluation of compression quality.

4.3 Submissions

4.3.1 Automatic subtitling

The subtitling sub-track saw the participation of three teams: APPTEK, the MT unit of Fondazione Bruno Kessler (FBK) with two different systems, and Huawei Translation Service Center (HW-TSC). The details about the participants' systems are provided below:

AppTek: the cascade-based subtitling system developed by APPTEK[24] leveraging their in-production automatic captioning and translation offerings. A pipeline of in-house hybrid ASR, punctuation and inverse text normalization models is used to create English captions, which are segmented into blocks and lines via a neural segmentation model in combination with hard subtitling constraints, similar to Matusov et al. (2019). Time stamps follow from the HMM alignment of the first and last word in a block. In a second step, the generated source template is translated with customized transformer-based NMT models, for which full sentences are extracted and translations are reinserted into the template using a variant of the source-side segmentation method that enforces splitting into the existing blocks. The NMT models make use of preceding sentence context, and prefix tokens are used to provide genre and formality information (e.g. "talks" + "formal" for TED) and to control the length of the translation (Matusov et al., 2020). For the primary submission, the MT component is fine-tuned on high quality media and entertainment customer data. In addition, the following newly developed features are employed: automatic MT length token selection to condense translation only where necessary due to space constraints; extension of subtitle timings for lower reading speed; improved Spanish MT model. The contrastive submissions do not use these upcoming features. The second contrastive submission is created using APPTEK's general domain MT models, which are trained on publicly available data.

FBK-AI4C$_{\text{DIR}}$ (Gaido et al., 2024a): the FBK's direct subtitling system is based on the transcription-free novel architecture, SBAAM or Speech Block Attention Area Maximization, introduced in (Gaido et al., 2024b). SBAAM leverages cross-attention scores to retrieve the timestamp information and is the first fully direct solution capable of producing automatic subtitles by eliminating any dependence on intermediate transcripts. It is the only system trained under constrained conditions, utilizing only the limited data provided by the IWSLT 2024 organizers. This includes non-subtitle material, which was automatically segmented into subtitles using the multimodal segmenter by Papi et al. (2022b). SBAAM is also employed as a reference system in the

[21] https://github.com/hlt-mt/FBK-fairseq/blob/master/examples/speech_to_text/scripts/subtitle_compliance.py

[22] https://mt.fbk.eu/europarl-interviews/

[23] https://github.com/hlt-mt/FBK-fairseq/blob/master/fbk_works/DIRECT_SUBTITLING.md

[24] https://www.apptek.com/

AI4Culture EU project[25] and is available at: https://github.com/hlt-mt/FBK-fairseq/blob/master/fbk_works/SBAAM.md.

FBK-AI4C$_{CSC}$ (Gaido et al., 2024a): the FBK's cascade subtitling system, developed by FBK within the AI4Culture project, exploiting pre-trained language models and, therefore, participating under the unconstrained conditions. The system is a cascade solution with Whisper (Radford et al., 2023) as the ASR model, and Helsinki Opus-MT (Tiedemann and Thottingal, 2020) as the MT model, together with additional components developed in-house. The cascade solution is publicly available at: https://github.com/hlt-mt/FBK-subtitler.

HW-TSC (Xie et al., 2024): the unconstrained cascade solution developed by HW-TSC, which relies on Whisper (Radford et al., 2023) to estimate both transcripts and word-level timestamps, on Bert-restore-punctuation[26] for retrieving punctuation and sentence segmentation, and on wav2vec2-large-960h-lv60[27] for the CTC-based force alignment between transcripts and translations, obtained by in-house MT models. The MT models (English to German and English to Spanish) were directly employed on the sentence-level ASR transcripts while the timestamps were left unchanged between transcripts and translations. Moreover, they are the only models among all participants that were specifically adapted to the domains of the audiovisual documents through ad-hoc domain adaptation.

4.3.2 Subtitle compression

Three teams participated in the sub-track: the FBK MT unit, the Huawei Translation Service Center (HW-TSC), and the Research Institute for Artificial Intelligence *Mihai Drăgănescu*, Romanian Academy (RACAI). The solutions they proposed differ from each other, although they share the use of Large Language Models as a common trait. Specifically:

FBK (Gaido et al., 2024a): the primary submission exploited GPT-4 (Achiam et al., 2023), which was prompted in zero-shot mode with an instruction asking the model to shorten the input text using the maximum number of characters compatible with the subtitle duration (value computed offline and passed as a parameter) while preserving the original words as much as possible. In the two contrastive runs, non-compliant subtitles were compressed by deleting function words from lists of different lengths.

HW-TSC (Xie et al., 2024): the subtitle compression method for the primary run is based on MT models, which are first employed for back-translating the non-compliant subtitles into English, and then to re-translate English into the original language (either German or Spanish) by setting a large beam size and a high length penalty, so that short translations are generated and rewarded. The still non-compliant subtitles are rewritten using the LLM Llama2 (Touvron et al., 2023), instructed with few-shot prompts to condense the input text. The two contrastive runs are variants of the primary one: in the first, the LLM is not applied and the compression is carried out only by the translation models; in the second, the subtitles of the primary run rewritten by either the MT model or the LLM which are still non-compliant are replaced by the original text.

RACAI (Gasan and Păiș, 2024): the submission involves generating multiple alternatives for the original non-compliant subtitle and selecting the one that maximizes both reading speed compliance (measured by CPS), and content similarity with the original subtitle (measured by ROUGE (Lin, 2004)). The alternatives are generated by i) rephrasing the subtitles using LLMs, specifically T5 (Raffel et al., 2020) and BART (Lewis et al., 2020), which were fine-tuned for the text summarization task, and ii) generating new subtitles through the automatic transcription of the original English audio using Whisper, translating them with NLLB (Costa-jussà et al., 2022), and then applying the LLMs as in the first method.

4.4 Results

The performance of runs for the two sub-tracks is presented and discussed separately in the following two subsections.

4.4.1 Automatic subtitling

Scores on tst2024 of all runs calculated using automatic metrics are shown in Tables 34 and 35, while Tables 37 and 38 refer to tst2023, where cumulative scores of runs submitted to the 2023 edi-

[25] https://pro.europeana.eu/project/ai4culture-an-ai-platform-for-the-cultural-heritage-data-space

[26] Bert-restore-punctuation1

[27] https://huggingface.co/felflare/bert-restore-punctuation

tion are also reported to allow the quantification of progresses.[28]

This year, unlike in the last edition, only one team (**FBK-AI4C**$_{\text{DIR}}$) participated with a system trained under constrained data conditions. Consequently, comparing its results with those of other participants is inherently unfair, and must be acknowledged if any comparisons are made. Notably, **FBK-AI4C**$_{\text{DIR}}$ is also the only direct system in the competition, highlighting that, despite advancements in direct approaches to spoken language processing, constructing cascade subtitling systems remains prevalent.

tst2024: Looking at performance in both German and Spanish, APPTEK achieved the best compromise between translation quality and subtitle compliance, as attested by the SubER values. It is interesting to note that their primary and contrastive1 systems provide better subtitle quality than contrastive2, especially on Spanish; since the first two systems featured fine-tuning on proprietary data, it can be hypothesized that such data is somehow "close" to the domains proposed in this evaluation campaign and therefore that the adaptation has rewarded these models. Overall, the new APPTEK systems (primary and contrastive1) surpass the one currently in production (contrastive2), although surprisingly the latter shows the best global SubER on German.

Focusing on the quality of the translation, in particular in terms of BLEURT, which better correlates with humans compared to BLEU and ChrF, the performance of HW-TSC's system is superior, likely because it is the only system explicitly fine-tuned on in-domain data. However, this system has not been optimized in terms of compliance, resulting in the lowest CPL score and, consequently, in high SubER scores.

The FBK cascade system, based mainly on pre-trained general-purpose models, shows high translation quality, especially in Spanish, and an acceptable conformity of subtitles. This proves the feasibility of building effective subtitling systems by appropriately assembling off-the-shelf models.

The FBK direct system, the only one based on a direct architecture and trained in constrained conditions, generated German subtitles with a surprisingly competitive overall SubER, despite the quality of the translation of the ITV and Peloton documents being lower compared to other systems. The good SubER probably derives from the ability of this system to satisfy subtitle compliance, which demonstrates the potential of the innovative approach it is based on. On the other hand, the gap in terms of translation quality on the two more challenging domains is in line with what already happened last year and with expectations, since unconstrained training allows building models on data more representative of real-life content.

tst2023: On German, the best systems are those by APPTEK which however did not improve the SubER score of the last year; in fact, there is an improvement in the quality of the translation which is counterbalanced by a worst CPS. Moreover, we note that the CPS of 4 out of 5 submissions from last year is better than any 2024 primary submission.

On Spanish, the improvements in the quality of the translations and of the SubER scores are generalized, while the CPS values worsen.

The progress made by the FBK team over the past year with their direct approach is notable in various aspects and for both languages, demonstrating the potential of end-to-end solutions for automatic subtitling.

4.4.2 Human evaluation

This year's edition of the automatic subtitling subtrack introduces the human evaluation of the primary submissions for **tst2024** en→de. Table 24 shows the direct assessment scores obtained on a sample of 1000 subtitles randomly selected from the whole test set. The ranking differs from the automatic one based on SubER, particularly for the HW-TSC system which achieves the best DA value but the worst SubER score. This can be explained by the design of the human evaluation, which was focused on assessing the translation quality while segmentation and subtitle compliance were not directly considered. In fact, the human ranking closely agrees with the pure translation quality metrics, in particular BLEURT (see Table 24 vs. column Bleurt of Table 34). While this reassures the validity of using automatic MT metrics also for the domain of subtitle translation, in future evaluations we see the need to provide the evaluators with subtitles instead of plain text sentences so that subtitle compliance, segmentation and timing errors can be accounted for.

[28] In 2023, the evaluation was done on the three domains still proposed here plus one additional domain, EPTV; for the sake of comparability, in the computation of the cumulative scores of the 2023 runs, EPTV has been excluded.

4.4.3 Subtitle compression

Table 36 shows the results of the submissions to the subtitle compression sub-track in terms of BLEURT, computed against the reference subtitles and in charge of quantifying the translation quality, and CPS, as a measure of reading speed compliance. For the sake of discussion, the table also includes the results of a simple `Baseline` (id=[1]) and those of the provided subtitles to compress (id=[0]). In the baseline method, the original subtitles with a non-compliant reading speed were cut at the maximum number of characters compatible with the subtitle duration and without regard to maintaining the integrity of the words, which therefore may be incomplete.

The results indicate that the participants designed methods aimed to find a trade-off between translation quality and CPS compliance, standing the working point of their systems in the area between the two extremes represented by subtitles [0] and [1], which is highlighted in Figure 2.

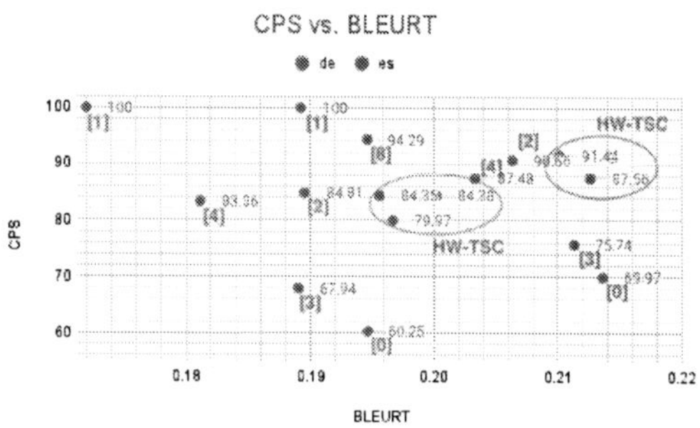

Figure 2: Scatter plot of compression results from Table 36.

Between [0] and [1], the subtitles generated by the contrastive **FBK** ([3,4]) and by the **RACAI** ([8]) systems are placed according to a nearly linear relationship. **HW-TSC**'s and, at a lesser extent, primary **FBK** ([2]) submissions differ markedly from this trend, thus demonstrating that it is possible to obtain a better compromise between the two contrasting features. In particular, the family of **HW-TSC** solutions is the most effective, approaching (in Spanish) or even overcoming (in German) the translation quality of the original subtitles, while achieving compliance for even more than 90% of the original subtitles. However, the noteworthy result of the **FBK** primary run shows the potential of prompting a generative LLM (GPT-4) to shorten subtitles; considering that it was done in zero-shot modality, there should be room for further improvements.

4.5 Conclusions

Overall, the second edition of the subtitling track continues to highlight the challenges and particularities of the automatic subtitling task. As in the previous edition, a clear gap in subtitle quality can be observed between the well-recorded, single-speaker, mostly formal style TED talk content that has traditionally been used for SLT evaluation at IWSLT, as opposed to the variety of audio conditions, dialog settings, language styles and speaking rates encountered in other types of content such as TV shows and sport videos. While no clear advancement in terms of best achieved translation quality or subtitle compliance compared to last year can be reported, remarkable improvements were achieved in the direct approach, which due to access to audio information during translation such as prosody, speaker changes and even speaker age/gender seems especially promising for subtitling of dialogs. The aspect of high speaking rates and the resulting necessity to condense subtitles down to a comfortable reading speed has been addressed and analyzed in isolation by the introduction of the subtitle compression task. Here, using LLMs for rephrasing has emerged as one of the promising approaches which was used by all participants.

5 Speech-to-Speech Translation

Speech-to-speech translation (S2ST) is a highly complex process involving the conversion of audio signals from one language to another. In offline translation, the system assumes that the entire audio is available before the translation process begins. This approach allows the translation system to process the audio input as a whole, enabling more effective speech recognition, semantic comprehension, and translation.

The main objective of this task is to encourage the development of automated methods for speech-to-speech translation that can perform efficiently and accurately in offline settings. Achieving this goal will not only advance the field but also contribute to improving access to information and communication across different languages and cultures.

5.1 Challenge

Participants built speech-to-speech translation systems from English into Chinese using any possible method, for example with a cascade system (ASR + MT + TTS or end-to-end speech-to-text translation + TTS) or an end-to-end or direct speech-to-speech system. Participants can use any techniques to boost the system performance.

5.2 Data and Metrics

Data. This task allowed the same training data from the Offline task on English-Chinese speech-to-text translation. More details are available in Sec. 2.2. In addition to the Offline task data, the following training data was allowed to help build English-Chinese speech-to-speech models and Chinese text-to-speech systems:

- **GigaS2S**, target synthetic speech for the Chinese target text of GigaST (Ye et al., 2023) that was generated with an in-house single-speaker TTS system;
- **aishell 3** (Shi et al., 2020), a multi-speaker Chinese TTS dataset.

Metrics. Since there was only one participant this year, we only conducted automatic evaluation in order to save resources.

Automatic metrics. To automatically evaluate translation quality, the speech output was automatically transcribed with a Chinese ASR system[29] (Yao et al., 2021), and then **BLEU**[30] (Papineni et al., 2002b), **chrF**[31] (Popović, 2015), and **COMET**[32] (Rei et al., 2022) were computed between the generated transcript and the human-produced text reference. BLEU and chrF were computed using SacreBLEU (Post, 2018).

5.3 Submissions

We only received submissions from one participant this year.

- HW-TSC (Wu et al., 2024) submitted three cascaded systems corresponding to three scenarios: constrained, constrained with large language models, unconstrained. All three scenarios employ a cascaded system that consists of an Automatic Speech Recognition (ASR) model, a translation model, and a Text-to-Speech (TTS) model. In the constrained scenario, the ASR model is trained on WeNet using constrained data. The translation model is a Transformer model trained using constrained data, with data enhancement, data denoising, and domain adaptation strategies applied, followed by model ensemble. The TTS model uses the VITS architecture. In the LLM constrained scenario, the ASR model is the same as in the constrained scenario. The translation model uses multiple LLMs for model ensemble, which are fine-tuned on llama2-13b using different strategies. The TTS model is the same as above. In the unconstrained scenario, the ASR model uses Whisper. The translation model employs multiple NMT models and LLMs for model ensemble. The TTS model remains the same as in the previous scenarios.

5.4 Results

Results by automatic metrics are shown in Table 39 in the Appendix.

6 Low-resource SLT

The 4th edition of the Low-resource Spoken Language Translation track focused on the translation of speech from a variety of data-scarce languages. The target language is typically a higher-resource one, generally of similar geographical or historical linkages. The goal of this shared task is to benchmark and promote speech translation technology for a diverse range of dialects and low-resource languages. While significant research progress has been demonstrated recently, many of the world's languages and dialects lack the parallel data at scale needed for standard supervised learning.

6.1 Challenge

This year's task significantly expanded the typological and geogrpahical diversity of the languages, language families, and scripts represented. The eight subtasks were:

- Bhojpuri → Hindi
- Marathi → Hindi
- Irish → English

[29] `https://github.com/wenet-e2e/wenet/blob/main/docs/pretrained_models.en.md`

[30] sacreBLEU signature: `nrefs:1|case:mixed|eff:no|tok:zh|smooth:exp|version:2.3.1`

[31] sacreBLEU signature: `nrefs:1|case:mixed|eff:yes|nc:6|nw:0|space:no|version:2.3.1`

[32] `https://huggingface.co/Unbabel/wmt22-comet-da`

- Maltese → English
- Bemba → English
- North Levantine Arabic → English
- Tamasheq → French
- Quechua → Spanish

Teams were allowed to submit to as few as one language pair, up to all eight. Both constrained and unconstrained submissions were allowed, to be separately ranked. For the constrained scenario, teams were only allowed to submit systems using the data provided by the shared task. For the unconstrained systems, teams were allowed to use any data as well as any pre-trained models.

6.2 Data and Metrics

Table 6 provides a summary of the training data that were part of the shared task. We describe in more detail the data for each language pair below.

North Levantine Arabic–English (apc-eng) Levantine Arabic, a well-established unit within the Arabic dialectal continuum, can be divided into at least three regional variants (Al-Wer and de Jong, 2017). *North* Levantine Arabic (also known as Syrian or Shami, ISO code: `apc`) is based on the urban speech of mainly Beirut and Damascus and is perceived as a separate linguistic unit (Ghobain, 2017).

Participants were provided with the UFAL Parallel Corpus of North Levantine 1.0 (Sellat et al., 2023), which includes about 120k lines of multi-parallel North Levantine-Modern Standard Arabic-English textual data, that can be downloaded from the LINDAT/CLARIAH-CZ Repository.[33] For additional speech data in North Levantine Arabic, participants were pointed to two LDC resources: the BBN/AUB DARPA Babylon Levantine corpus (Makhoul et al., 2005) and the Levantine Arabic QT Training Data Set 5 corpus (Maamouri et al., 2006).

Participants were also encouraged to use the Tunisian Arabic training data used in the last two years' shared task (LDC2022E01). This three-way parallel data corresponds to 160 hours and 200k lines of aligned audio in Tunisian speech, Tunisian transcripts, and English translations. Additionally, a number of OpenSLR resources in Modern Standard Arabic were highlighted: Tunisian Modern Standard Arabic speech and transcriptions[34], the MADCAT Arabic LDC corpus (Lee et al., 2012), the Arabic portion of theMediaSpeech corpus (Kolobov et al., 2021), and the Arabic speech to text Quran data.[35]

Overall, the provided resources were supposed to help participants, but only the unconstrained scenario was considered within this year's initial run of the apc-eng language pair.

The development[36] and test[37] data consist of recordings of native speakers of the dialect and is a mix of spontaneous monologues and dialogues on the topics of everyday life (health, education, family life, sports, culture), living abroad, and everyday life in Syria. The transcription and translation team consisted of students of Arabic at Charles University, with an additional quality check provided by the native speakers of the dialect.

Bemba–English (bem-eng) Bemba (also known as IciBemba) is a Bantu language (ISO code: `bem`), spoken predominantly in Zambia and other parts of Africa by over 10 million people. It is the most populous indigenous language spoken by over 30% of the population in Zambia where English is the lingua franca and official high-resourced language of communication. Bemba is native to the people of Northen, Luapula and Muchinga provinces of Zambia but also spoken in other parts of the country including urban areas such as Copperbelt, Central and Lusaka provinces by over 50% of the population (ZamStats, 2012).

The provided Bemba-English corpus (Sikasote et al., 2023a) consists of over 180 hours of Bemba audio data, along with transcriptions and translations in English. The dataset is comprised of recorded multi-turn dialogues between native Bemba speakers grounded on images.

In addition, we provided transcribed (28 hours) and untranscribed (60 hours) monolingual Bemba speech from Zambezi Voice (Sikasote et al., 2023b) and BembaSpeech (Sikasote and Anastasopoulos, 2022) datasets.

Bhojpuri–Hindi (bho-hin) Bhojpuri (ISO code: `bho`) belongs to the Indo-Aryan language group. It is dominantly spoken in India's western part of Bihar, the north-western part of Jharkhand,

[33] `http://hdl.handle.net/11234/1-5033`

[34] `https://www.openslr.org/46/`

[35] `https://www.openslr.org/132/`

[36] `http://hdl.handle.net/11234/1-5518`

[37] `http://hdl.handle.net/11234/1-5519`

and the Purvanchal region of Uttar Pradesh. As per the 2011 Census of India, it has around 50.58 million speakers (Ojha and Zeman, 2020). Bhojpuri is spoken not just in India but also in other countries such as Nepal, Trinidad, Mauritius, Guyana, Suriname, and Fiji. Since Bhojpuri was considered a dialect of Hindi for a long time, it did not attract much attention from linguists and hence remains among the many lesser-known and less-resourced languages of India.

The provided Bhojpuri–Hindi corpus consists of 22.77 hours of Bhojpuri speech data (see Table 6) from the news domain, extracted from News On Air[38] and translated into Hindi texts.[39] Additionally, the participants were directed that they may use monolingual Bhojpuri audio data (with transcription) from ULCA-asr-dataset-corpus[40] as well as Bhojpuri Language Technological Resources (BHLTR) (Ojha et al., 2020; Ojha, 2019)[41] and Bhojpuri-wav2vec2 based model.[42]

Irish–English (gle-eng) Irish (also known as Gaeilge; ISO code: `gle`) has around 170,000 L1 speakers and 1.85 million people (37% of the population) across the island (of Ireland) claim to be at least somewhat proficient with the language. In the Republic of Ireland, it is the national and first official language. It is also one of the official languages of the European Union (EU) and a recognized minority language in Northern Ireland with the ISO `ga` code.

The provided Irish audio data were compiled from the news domain, Common Voice (Ardila et al., 2020),[43] and Living-Audio-Dataset.[44] The Irish–English corpus consists of 12 hours of Irish speech data (see Table 6), translated into English texts.

Maltese–English (mlt-eng) Maltese (ISO code: `mlt`) is a Semitic language, with a heavy influence from Italian and English. It is spoken mostly in Malta, but also in migrant communities abroad, most notably in Australia and parts of America and Canada.

The data release for this shared task consists of over 14 hours (split into dev and train) of audio data, together with their transcription in Maltese and translation into English. Participants were also allowed to use additional Maltese data including the text corpus used to train BERTu (Micallef et al., 2022), a Maltese BERT model, the MASRI Data speech recognition data (Hernandez Mena et al., 2020), and any data available at the Maltese Language Resource Server.[45]

Marathi–Hindi (mar-hin) Marathi (ISO code: `mar`) is an Indo-Aryan language and is dominantly spoken in the state of Maharashtra in India. It is one of the 22 scheduled languages of India and the official language of Maharashtra and Goa. As per the 2011 Census of India, it has around 83 million speakers which covers 6.86% of the country's total population.[46] Marathi is the third most spoken language in India.

The provided Marathi–Hindi corpus consists of 24.58 hours of Marathi speech data (see Table 6) from the news domain, extracted from News On Air[47] and translated into Hindi texts.[48] The dataset was manually segmented and translated by Panlingua.[49] Additionally, the participants were directed that they may use monolingual Marathi audio data (with transcription) from Common Voice (Ardila et al., 2020),[50] as well as the corpus provided by He et al. (2020)[51] and the Indian Language Corpora (Abraham et al., 2020).[52]

Quechua–Spanish (que-spa) Quechua (macrolaguage ISO code: `que`) is an indigenous language spoken by more than 8 million people in South America. It is mainly spoken in Peru, Ecuador, and Bolivia where the official high-resource language is Spanish. It is a highly inflective language based on its suffixes which agglutinate and are found to be similar to other languages

[38] `https://newsonair.gov.in`
[39] `https://github.com/panlingua/iwslt2024_bho-hi`
[40] `https://github.com/Open-Speech-EkStep/ULCA-asr-dataset-corpus`
[41] `https://github.com/shashwatup9k/bho-resources`
[42] `https://www.openslr.org/64/`
[43] `https://commonvoice.mozilla.org/en/datasets`
[44] `https://github.com/Idlak/Living-Audio-Dataset`
[45] `https://mlrs.research.um.edu.mt/`
[46] `https://censusindia.gov.in/nada/index.php/catalog/42561`
[47] `https://newsonair.gov.in`
[48] `https://github.com/panlingua/iwslt2023_mr-hi`
[49] `http://panlingua.co.in/`
[50] `https://commonvoice.mozilla.org/en/datasets`
[51] `https://www.openslr.org/64/`
[52] `https://www.cse.iitb.ac.in/~pjyothi/indiccorpora/`

Language Pairs		Train Set	Dev Set	Test Set	Additional Data
Bhojpuri–Hindi	bho–hi	19.88	2.07	0.82	Monolingual audio with transcription (ASR) and monolingual text
Irish–English	ga–eng	9.46	1.03	0.69	IWSLT 2023 test set (with references) and MT data (monolingual and parallel corpora)
Marathi–Hindi	mr–hi	15.88	3.66	0.61	Monolingual audio with transcriptions (ASR), IWSLT 2023 test set (with references) and monolingual text
Maltese–English	mlt–eng	10	2	2	Monolingual audio with transcriptions (ASR), monolingual text
North Levantine–English	apc–eng	-	2.5	1.85	-
Tamasheq–French	tmh–fra	17	-	-	Untranscribed audio, data in other regional languages
Quechua–Spanish	que–spa	1.60	1.03	1.03	48 hours of monolingual audio with transcriptions (ASR) and MT data (not transcribed)
Bemba–English	bem–eng	167.17	5.89	5.83	28.12 hours of monolingual audio with transcriptions (ASR) and 60 hours of untranscribed audio data.

Table 6: Training, development and test data details (in hours) for the language pairs of the low-resource shared task.

like Finnish. The average number of morphemes per word (synthesis) is about two times larger than in English. English typically has around 1.5 morphemes per word and Quechua has about 3 morphemes per word.

There are two main regional divisions of Quechua known as Quechua I and Quechua II. This data set consists of two main types of Quechua spoken in Ayacucho, Peru (Quechua Chanka ISO: `quy`) and Cusco, Peru (Quechua Collao ISO: `quz`) which are both part of Quechua II and, thus, considered a "southern" languages. We label the data set with `que` - the ISO norm for Quechua II mixtures.

The constrained setting allowed a Quechua-Spanish speech translation dataset along with the additional parallel (text-only) data for machine translation compiled from previous work (Ortega et al., 2020). The audio files for training, validation, and test purposes consisted of excerpts of the Siminchik corpus (Cardenas et al., 2018) that were translated by native Quechua speakers. For the unconstrained setting, participants were directed to another larger data set from the Siminchik corpus which consisted of 48 hours of fully transcribed Quechua audio (monolingual).

Tamasheq–French Tamasheq is a variety of Tuareg, a Berber macro-language spoken by nomadic tribes across North Africa in Algeria, Mali, Niger and Burkina Faso. It accounts for approximately 500,000 native speakers, being mostly spoken in Mali and Niger. This task is about translating spoken Tamasheq into written French. Almost 20 hours of spoken Tamasheq with French translation are freely provided by the organizers. A major challenge is that no Tamasheq transcription is provided, as Tamasheq is a traditionally oral language.

The provided corpus is a collection of radio recordings from Studio Kalangou[53] translated to French. It comprises 17 hours of clean speech in Tamasheq, translated into the French language. The organizers also provided a 19-hour version of this corpus, including 2 additional hours of data that was labeled by annotators as potentially noisy. Both versions of this dataset share the same validation and test sets. Boito et al. (2022) provides a thorough description of this dataset.

In addition to the 17 hours of Tamasheq audio data aligned to French translations, and in light of recent work in self-supervised models for speech processing, we also provide participants with unlabeled raw audio data in the Tamasheq language,

[53]`https://www.studiokalangou.org/`

as well as in other 4 languages spoken from Niger: French (116 hours), Fulfulde (114 hours), Hausa (105 hours), Tamasheq (234 hours) and Zarma (100 hours). All this data comes from the radio broadcastings of Studio Kalangou and Studio Tamani.[54]

Note that this language pair is a continuation of last year's shared task, using the same test set as last year.

6.2.1 Metrics

We use standard lowercase BLEU with no punctuation to automatically score all submissions. Additional analyses for some language pairs are provided below. Were applicable, we also report chrF++ (Popović, 2015).

6.3 Submissions

The Shared Task received a record 69 submissions (for speech translation) from 12 teams for all 8 language pairs. The Shared Task also received 15 submissions for the speech recognition task of transcribing the input audio. They are described in detail below.

ALADAN (Kheder et al., 2024) provided a submission for the apc-eng direction, building upon a cascade of ASR and MT systems. The authors propose a character-level and word-level normalization process to handle the orthographic inconsistency between Arabic Dialects, merging words based on a combination of weighted Levenshtein distance and similarity of embeddings, as computed with a task-specific Word2vec model. Both ASR and MT systems are trained on a combination of public (e.g., IWSLT22 data, GALE speech corpus[55] for ASR, and, e.g., the UFAL parallel dataset provided by the organizers, Global Voices, LDC2012T09 for MT) and internal data (a combination of crowd-sourced and web-scrapped resources). For ASR, TDNN-F (Povey et al., 2018) and Zipformer (Yao et al., 2023) models are considered, that are firstly trained on a generic Arabic data, and then fine-tuned on a dialect-specific speech. For MT, both encoder-decoder models and instruction-following LLMs are explored. The primary solution uses both ASR systems combined with the ROVER (Fiscus, 1997) algorithm, with the MT step performed by the fine-tuned Command-R[56] LLM, enhanced by MBR decoding and checkpoint averaging. Contrastive submissions differ in the MT step, with the first one using the final checkpoint of the fine-tuned LLM, and the second one using a Transformer-based NLLB model.

BITSP (Anand et al., 2024) submitted systems for the Bhojpuri to Hindi and Marathi to Hindi tasks. Their approach relied on cascading transcriptions which were piped into translation systems. They used a fine-tuned Whisper model for Marathi-Hindi and an vakyansh-wav2vec model for Bhojpuri-Hindi (Chadha et al., 2022; Gupta et al., 2021). Translation was done using fine-tuned NLLB for both tasks (NLLB Team et al., 2022). They also looked at using sentence-embeddings generated using the MuRIL (Multilingual Representations for Indian Languages) (Khanuja et al., 2021) model for the Marathi-Hindi task.

HW-TSC (Jiawei et al., 2024) participated in the apc-eng direction with a cascade solution based on the off-the-shelf Whisper (Radford et al., 2022) model for ASR combined with a Transformer-based MT model trained from scratch for Arabic-to-English translation. The MT system (35 encoder layers, 3 decoder layers, with d_{hidden} = 512 and d_{FFN} = 2048) was trained on the mix of publicly available (e.g., OpenSubtities, GlobalVoices, TED) and in-house corpora, both filtered based on sentence embeddings extracted with LaBSE (Feng et al., 2022). No dialect-specific datasets were used for training directly. Instead, an in-domain model was fine-tuned on the validation set to score the training samples using domain features (Wang et al., 2020c), with the highest-scoring subset explored for the final fine-tuning.

JHU (Robinson et al., 2024) provided systems for all eight language pairs. The main effort of their work revolved around fine-tuning large and publicly available models in three proposed systems, one cascaded and two end-to-end. For the cascaded system, they proposed fine-tuning Whisper transcription (not translation) and then piping that output to a fine-tuned NLLB model. For the end-to-end systems, they fine-tuned for translation directly on SEAMLESS4MT v2 and Whisper translation (not transcription). In addition, they

[54] `https://www.studiotamani.org/`

[55] `https://arabicspeech.org/resources`

[56] `https://cohere.com/command`

Team Name	Language Pairs							
	apc-eng	bem-eng	bho-hin	gle-eng	mlt-eng	mar-hin	que-spa	tmh-fra
SETU-DCU (Zafar et al., 2024)				✓	✓			
UM (Nabhani et al., 2024)	✓				✓			
UoM (Abela et al., 2024)					✓			
QUESPA (Ortega et al., 2024)							✓	
JHU (Robinson et al., 2024)	✓	✓	✓	✓	✓	✓	✓	✓
HW-TSC (Jiawei et al., 2024)	✓							
ALADAN (Kheder et al., 2024)	✓							
KIT (Li et al., 2024c)	✓	✓	✓		✓			
BITSP (Anand et al., 2024)			✓			✓		
YMoslem (Moslem, 2024)				✓				
UoM-DFKI (Rishu et al., 2024)			✓					
Total Teams per Lang Pair:	5	2	4	3	5	2	2	1

Table 7: Breakdown of the teams and the language pairs subtasks that they participated in for the Low-Resource Shared Task.

looked at a variety of different training paradigms such as intra-distillation (Xu et al., 2022), joint training, multi-task learning, curriculum learning, and pseudo-translation. The best-performing approach, similar to the broader results of this shared task differed for different language pairs. However, fine-tuned SEAMLESSM4T v2 tends to perform best for source languages on which it was pre-trained. Additionally, while multi-task training helps Whisper fine-tuning, in general cascaded systems with Whisper and NLLB tend to outperform Whisper alone. Finally, intra-distillation was shown to help NLLB fine-tuning.

KIT (Li et al., 2024c) participated in the Maltese-to-English, Bemba-to-English, North Levantine Arabic-to-English tasks in the unconstrained condition. They leveraged pretrained multilingual models by fine-tuning them for the target language pairs, looking at SeamlessM4T, NLLB (NLLB Team et al., 2022), and MMS (Pratap et al., 2024). Due to the large size of the models, they experimented with adapter fine-tuning to reduce the number of trainable parameters using LORA (Hu et al., 2021) and package PEFT (Mangrulkar et al., 2022). They were also able to show that Minimum Bayes Risk is effective in improving speech translation performance by combining systems in all of their language pairs.

SETU-DCU (Zafar et al., 2024) presented systems for two language pairs, Irish–English and Maltese–English. Both of their submissions, despite lower performance on the Irish (GA) task, were on the unconstrained condition configuration. There were two submissions to the Maltese (MLT) task ranging from 44.7 to 52.6 BLEU and one submission to the GA task at 0.6 BLEU.

The MLT results of 52.6 BLEU were favorable due to SETU-DCU's primary submission based on a cascaded (ASR to MT) setup of a Whisper (Radford et al., 2022) ASR system used in conjunction with an MT system based on the NLLB (NLLB Team et al., 2022) where both systems were fine-tuned on the Maltese–English data provided. Additionally, their cascaded Contrastive 1 system which used mBart-50 for decoding, scored 44.7 BLEU showing that the use of the NLLB system augmented performance by nearly 8 BLEU points. Further results can be attributed to data preparation such as removing unnecessary data chunks from the dataset, eliminating special characters, and converting the sentences to lowercase along with the following hyper-parameter configuration: batch size of 16, learning rate of 1e-5, 500 warmup steps, 30,000 max steps, per-device eval batch size of 8, generation max length of 225, and intervals of 1,000 steps for saving and evaluating, and 25 steps for logging.

SETU-DCU's submission for the unconstrained GA task performed poorly compared to other systems submitted. It consisted of a direct speech translation system using the Whisper *small* model by first resampling data at 16 khz and using the following hyper-parameter configuration: batch size of 16, learning rate of 1e-5, 500 warmup steps, 1 gradient accumulation steps, generation max length of 225, and intervals of 500 steps for saving and evaluating. The model was fine-tuned over three epochs. Their only submission used Whisper for fine-tuning; however, their claim is that since the data Whisper was trained on did not contain GA at the time of fine-tuning, generation was inconsistent.

UoM-DFKI (Rishu et al., 2024) participated in the Maltese to English shared task using two popular end-to-end pretrained models, Whisper and wav2vec 2.0. They hypothesised that Maltese shares lots of vocabulary with Arabic and Italian and would therefore have good cross-lingual transfer ability due to pretraining data in those models. In addition, they investigated other popular neural models, BERT (Devlin et al., 2019) which they decided against making a formal submission, and mBART (Liu et al., 2020b) which was used as their contrastive submission. Overall, the end-to-end system performed much better than the contrastive submission.

UoM (Abela et al., 2024) participated in the constrained task of the Maltese to English translation language pair. Their approach relied on a cascaded system consisting of a pipeline containing: a DeepSpeech 1 ASR system (Hannun et al., 2014), a KenLM model to optimise the transcriptions (Heafield, 2011), and finally an LSTM machine translation model. For their ASR system, they trained using the MASRI dataset and CommonVoice and used a much smaller layer size (64) than normal due to the lack of large amounts of data. These outputs were then used to decode using a 3-gram statistical language model trained on Malti v4.0. The translation system was implemented using fairseq (Ott et al., 2019) comparing both transformer and LSTM architectures, with their best performing system using LSTMs. The authors hypothesize that this was due to the very small amount of data available as a bitext.

UM (Nabhani et al., 2024) competed in the unconstrained task for Maltese-English and North Levantine Arabic-English spoken language translation using a pipeline approach. For the ASR component of their systems, they relied on fine-tuning XLS-R using 50 hours of Maltese speech data. To correct outputs, they relied on the statistical toolkit KenLM (Heafield, 2011). Machine translation was then done using a fine-tuned version of the 1.3B parameter NLLB model (NLLB Team et al., 2022). They experimented with a variety of data sources such as CommonVoice, MASRI, and OPUS-100.

YMoslem (Moslem, 2024) The Yasmin Moslem team (independent researcher) presented an end-to-end approach for speech translation from spoken Irish to written English. Their models are based on Whisper, utilizing small, medium, and large versions. The primary system employs Whisper-large, which has been fine-tuned using the official training data, supplemented with synthetic audio data and the data augmentation technique involving white noise and voice activity detection.

The synthetic audio data was generated using Azure's text-to-speech service, applied to the Wikimedia dataset comprising 7,545 text segments. The resulting synthetic audio dataset consists of two parts: one featuring a female voice (OrlaNeural) and the other a male voice (ColmNeural). This resulted in a total of 15,090 utterances, with each text segment used to generate a synthetic speech segment for each voice. The same approach has been applied to 3,966 text segments coming from the SpokenWords dataset.

In addition to the official IWSLT-2023 training dataset and the aforementioned synthetic audio dataset, the Irish portion of the FLEURS dataset, the Bitesize dataset, and the SpokenWords dataset were utilized to fine-tune the Whisper-Large model. Note that the Irish portion of the Spoken Words dataset has been translated into English using the Google Translation API.

QUESPA (Ortega et al., 2024) submitted six total systems consisting of three *constrained* and three *unconstrained* systems. Team QUESPA were able to improve the previous year's results despite the data remaining the same as last year's ranging from 1.4 to 2.0 BLEU for the constrained task and 11.1 to 19.7 BLEU for the unconstrained one. This year QUESPA provided developmental results on several models that used mel-filter bank (MFB) features extracted using Fairseq (Wang et al., 2020a) were included that show the effect of the *s2t transformers* model type size ranging from extra-small to large.

QUESPA's *Constrained* systems did not vary

Language Pair	Winning Team	System	Constrained?	BLEU
apc-eng	ALADAN	primary	no	28.71
bem-eng	JHU	primary	no	32.60
bho-hin	JHU	primary	no	24.40
gle-eng	JHU	contrastive1	no	16.00
mlt-eng	KIT	primary	no	58.90
mar-hin	IITM	primary	no	47.20
que-spa	QUESPA	contrastive1	no	19.70
tmh-fra	baseline	primary	no	8.83

Table 8: Winning submissions for each language pair of the Low-Resource Shared Task.

much from last year's systems as far as system architecture is concerned. However, they were able to identify a caveat in the training data set which contains audio wav files of lengths from 1 to 30 seconds while the developmental and test sets were all of 30 seconds in length. Their opinion is that the varied length warranted a severe hyper-parameter empirical search resulting in a Primary system that scored 2.0 BLEU with the following configuration of a Fairseq (Wang et al., 2020a) speech translation model based on mel-Filter Bank features: extra-small transformer, 6 encoder layers, 3 decoder layers, Adam optimization, 500 epochs and a learning rate of .0002 while using an average of the last 10 checkpoints which outperformed the same model with other hyper-parameters from last year. Their Contrastive 1 system, similar to the primary system, introduced a new concept of data augmentation in combination with a medium transfomer (s2t_transformer), 12 encoder layers, 6 decoder layers, and 8 attention heads and 200 epochs. More importantly, in Contrastive 1 they introduced audio augmentation via LibRosa[57] where the translation was the same but four audio techniques were introduced: *Noise* (0.009 aggregation), *Roll* ($sr/10$), *Time*(0.4), and *Pitch* (-5) to create 4-fold sets of the original. Additionally, QUESPA's Contrastive 1 system removed SpecAugment as an audio augmentation technique. Finally, the Contrastive 2 system from Team QUESPA were identical to the primary system with the change of epochs to 400 and model type to a medium-size (s2t_transformer).

QUESPA's *Unconstrained* systems were a novel introduction for the QUE–SPA task and outperformed last year's best systems. Their primary system introduced the SpeechT5 (Ao et al., 2022) ASR PLM which consists of 12 Transformer encoder blocks and 6 Transformer decoder blocks, with a model dimension of 768, an internal dimension (FFN) of 3,072, and 12 attention heads. It used normalized training text from the LibriSpeech language model as unlabeled data, which consisted of 400 million sentences and fine-tuned on the competition data while optimizing with Adam and a learning rate maximum of 0.0002. Fine-tuning was performed using the SpeechT5 fine-tuning recipe[58] for Speech-Translation with the same hyperparameter settings. Additionally, their primary system used a data augmentation technique (noise, distortion, duplication)[59] (Ma, 2019) for total of 120h: 60h original + 60h synthetic data scoring 16.0 BLEU, higher than previous year's results. For Contrastive 1, QUESPA introduced a combination of more data by manually translating Quechua to Spanish 55 hours of the total set along with an additional 19 minutes of Guarani and 29 minutes of Bribiri from the AmericasNLP[60] shared task. On top of that, they applied two data augmentation techniques: (1) *nlpaug* (Ma, 2019) and (2) DA-TTS (Zevallos et al., 2022), which involves generating synthetic text and audio using a de-lexicalization algorithm and a TTS system for the source language (Quechua). These two data augmentation techniques generated 62 hours and 50 hours respectively. Altogether, they used a total of 167h and 48 min: 55h (new dataset) + 48 min (ANLP dataset) + 62h nlpaug + 50h DA-TTS. The Contrastive 1 system was QUESPA's best system scoring 19.7 BLEU. The Contrastive 2 system was also newly

[57] `https://librosa.org/`

[58] `https://github.com/microsoft/SpeechT5/tree/main/SpeechT5`

[59] `https://github.com/makcedward/nlpaug`

[60] `https://turing.iimas.unam.mx/americasnlp/2022_st.html`

introduced with the use of Whisper medium-size, multi-lingual model for ASR in a cascade approach basically replacing last year's "fleurs" ASR system. The MT system was identical to the one they used last year called FloresMT (Ortega et al., 2023). QUESPA's Contrastive 2 system resulted in a score of 11.1 BLEU.

6.4 Results

Table 8 summarizes the winning submissions for each language pair. Detailed results for all teams' systems and settings are available in Appendix B.5.

Of the 8 language pairs, 5 different teams had the top performing system on at least one language pair. This shows how competitive the shared task was, and that a multitude of approaches are helpful for low-resource speech translation. Additionally, no team was able to beat the baseline on the Tamasheq-French direction (which corresponds to last year's best system). This suggests that there continues to be lots of room for improvement and that this remains an active area of research.

Compared to previous iterations of the shared task, many of the language pairs had marked improvements with large gains in the official automatic metrics. For example, BLEU scores for Maltese-English and Marathi-Hindi are in the 40s and 50s. Furthermore, for North Levantine Arabic-English, Bemba-English, and Bhojpuri-Hindi are above 20 BLEU points. Even for Quechua-Spanish, the least resourced language pair, the best submission's BLEU score is almost 20 points.

This marks stark improvements from last year's shared task systems for some language pairs. In Marathi-Hindi, the best system in 2023 achieved a BLEU score of 39.7, with this year's best system improving by more than 7 BLEU points. Similarly, the improvements in the quality and quantity of the Maltese data lead to a more than 50 BLEU points improvement compared to last year. For Irish and Tamasheq, the performance increases are more modest, about 1 to 2 BLEU points in each, compared to the 2023 Shared Task.

For the language pairs included for the first time in the shared task, we find that Bemba-English and Bhojpuri-Hindi end up with decent systems, a result of high-quality data availability: for instance, Bemba-English has an order of magnitude more training data –167h– than any other language pair in our shared task); and Bhojpuri is the second most "high-resourced" language in our set, with almost 22 hours of speech translation data.

Within the systems submitted to the initial run of the North Levantine Arabic-English language pair, all of the primary submissions are based on a pipeline approach exploring ASR and MT, with a single submission combining E2E and cascaded systems. Since the popular NLLB model explored by several submissions supports an input/output combination of dialectical Arabic/English and a large-scale, parallel textual dataset of Levantine Arabic was provided, the participating teams mainly struggled with the ASR component. The winning submission by ALADAN, which outperformed a second-place team by over 8 BLEU points, uses an internal dataset of Levantine speech to boost the performance of their ASR component. While the data used for fine-tuning the MT system is comparable between the submissions, ALADAN explored a much larger, prompt-driven LLM compared to the 600M/1.3B NLLB variants explored by other teams.

We note that almost all submissions followed the unconstrained setting – a clear indication that pre-trained multilingual systems seem to be the best option for building ST for low-resource languages, at least under the current data, architectural, and compute constraints.

7 Automatic Dubbing

7.1 Challenge and Test Sets

Dubbing is a form of speech translation where the user can not only hear the translated speech, but also can often see the original speaker. This adds numerous challenges and constraints, including isochrony (does the new translation respect the timing of the original speech), phonetic synchrony or lip sync (is the new speech compatible with the mouth movements of the original speaker, if visible), kinesic synchrony (is the new speech consistent with visible body movements of the original speakers), and others (Mayoral et al., 1988; Chiaro, 2009; Chaume, 2020; Brannon et al., 2023).

For English→Chinese, we use the ITV test set from subtitle task. We manually selected 10min sections from each of clip 15, 16, 18, 19, and 21. The 10min sections were manually selected with several goals:

1. Speech is fairly clear

2. A mix of on-/off-screen dialogues
3. A diverse set of genders and accents
4. Avoid excessive profanity
5. Avoid opening/closing credits

German→English followed the same setup as the submissions from last year (Chronopoulou et al., 2023; Pal et al., 2023; Rao et al., 2023)

7.2 Submissions

This task received a total of four English→Chinese submissions (see Table 9): one end-to-end dubbing submission and three participants in the offline speech translation task (speech to text) scored our challenge set (set5). For the offline submissions, we utilized the provided translations to generate dubs.

We also received one submission (Li et al., 2024b) for German→English. We chose to focus on English→Chinese for evaluation due to the availability of the offline speech systems to compare against, which should represent strong speech translation models (but not dubbing specific models).

The process of generating dubs from text translations involved several steps. First, due to the absence of source language subtitles, we downloaded subtitles from an open-source website and manually time align the five clips. Each time aligned sentence was then split at commas and full stops to create manageable segments for processing, while keeping a track of original sentences and time-stamps.

Similarly, the translations from the three submissions were also split at commas and full stops. We used Vecalign (Thompson and Koehn, 2019, 2020) a tool for sequence alignment, in conjunction with LASER-2 embeddings (Heffernan et al., 2022), to align the source language with the target language. This ensured that the meaning and context of the translated text matched the original as closely as possible. Timestamps were then projected from the source to the target language, providing a temporal map for the dubbing process.

For each sentence, we employed Amazon Polly, a text-to-speech service, to generate the corresponding speech. We also used the duration of the source speech segment as a constraint to generate target speech with Polly. Polly allowed this by adding a flag with $max\_durations$, where the generated speech cannot go beyond maximum duration. We used Zhiyu standard voice as that allowed use of this flag via SSML wrapper. Adding duration constraint essentially ensured that the target speech did not exceed the length of the source speech. Typically, the target speech was shorter than the source speech, so we filled the remaining portion with silences to maintain synchronization.

We synchronized the start time of the target speech with the source speech using the previously obtained timestamps to ensure that the dialogue matched the visual cues accurately. Finally, we concatenated the target speech segments to form the complete clip.

7.3 Metrics and Results

We report speech overlap (between the original audio and the dubbed audio) in Table 10. For reference, in a large corpus of professionally dubbed media, human speech overlap between original and dubbed speech is about 0.658 (mean) and 0.731 (median) (Brannon et al., 2023). The dubbing submission HWTSC-Dubbing is similar to the human statistics, while the cascaded systems generated in part by the task organizers perform substantially worse.

We report PEAVS (Perceptual Evaluation of Audio-Visual Synchrony) score (Goncalves et al., 2024), an automatic metric with a 5-point scale that evaluates the quality of audio-visual synchronization, in Table 12. PEAVS is the only AV sync evaluation metric that is grounded in human judgements as it is trained on a large Audio-Visual synchrony benchmark for "in-the-wild" videos. In our case, we use PEAVS for evaluating the quality of synchrony in the generated dubs. As expected for a system optimized with speech timing in mind, HWTSC-Dubbing performs best here.

Table 12 also reports BLASER 2.0-QE scores. BLASER 2.0-QE is a reference-free modality-agnostic automatic metric for speech translation quality (Seamless Communication et al., 2023). It only supports short-form speech, so we segment the full speech into sentences as mentioned in Section 7.2 and report average scores. Surprisingly, the dubbing submission performs the best at this metric, even though it is optimized for both translation quality and timing. It is worth noting that the segments being evaluated are quite short, often much shorter than typical sentences in written text, and lack of domain context has been shown

Submission	Submission Type
HWTSC-Dubbing (Li et al., 2024b)	Dubbing
HWTSC-Offline (Wu et al., 2024)	Offline Speech Translation Challenge Set
NYA-Offline (Zhang et al., 2024)	Offline Speech Translation Challenge Set
CMU-Offline (Yan et al., 2024)	Offline Speech Translation Challenge Set

Table 9: Submissions to the Dubbing Track

to be problematic in machine translation metrics even for normal length sentences (Läubli et al., 2018; Toral et al., 2018; Vernikos et al., 2022). BLASER 2.0-QE is not trained on dubbing data, so there is likely degradation due to domain mismatch (Zouhar et al., 2024).

We report two measures of lip sync, both from Prajwal et al. (2020): LSE-D (lip-sync error distance) and LSE-C (Lip Sync Error - Confidence) (see Table 13). LSE-D measures the accuracy of audio-visual synchronization by identifying the offset with the smallest distance between audio and video features. LSE-C measures the confidence in this synchronization by comparing the best match's distance to those of adjacent offsets, with higher values indicating greater confidence. In essence, LSE-D tells us how well the audio and video are synchronized, while LSE-C tells us how sure the model is about that synchronization. HWTSC-Dubbing performs the best at LSE-D on average, although one strange result is that the metric prefers HWTSC-Dubbing to the original audio in two of the test sets, which does not make sense. Another surprise is that CMU-Offline slightly outperforms HWTSC-Dubbing on the LSE-C metric.

We also conduct human judgements to evaluate translation quality and naturalness. We evaluate the first 20 sentences of each clip based on the rubric (Table 11), and report the average score for each submission in Table 12. In general, the dubbing system produces more natural speech but sometimes less accurate translation than the offline systems. The offline systems oftentimes have to speed up the speech synthesis to match the original duration of a sentence, leading to hard-to-recognize speeches.

8 Indic Languages Track

In the realm of spoken language processing, speech-to-text translation (ST) holds a crucial role at the intersection of natural language processing. The primary aim of ST is to convert spoken language from one linguistic context into written text in another language. This typically involves using Automatic Speech Recognition (ASR) to convert speech in the source language into text, followed by Machine Translation (MT) to translate the source language text into the target language. ST is a multimodal task that takes speech input and produces output in text format. Furthermore, it is inherently multilingual, taking speech input in one language and generating text output in another. Traditionally, human language translators proficient in both the source and target languages have handled this task. However, the scarcity of translators fluent in multiple languages has created a pressing need for a dedicated model tailored to excel in the unique realm of ST tasks across diverse languages. Recent advancements in ST have predominantly focused on high-resource languages, leaving a significant gap for low-resource languages that face a substantial catch-up journey. The attention imbalance is primarily due to the scarcity of data for low-resource languages, as most deep-learning models depend on data abundance. Acquiring such data for low-resource languages poses a formidable challenge.

While a considerable body of research is dedicated to ST across diverse language families, a noticeable gap exists in investigating this domain concerning low-resource Indian languages. Currently, there are no datasets specifically designed for the ST task in Indian languages, covering both the Indo-Aryan and the Dravidian language families. This research aims to create either an End-to-End (E2E) or a Cascaded ST model

This Indic track aims to establish an ST translation model that spans a diverse array of dialects and low-resource languages originating from the Indo-Aryan and Dravidian language families in India. Given that a significant portion of the data is sourced from very low-resource languages, these languages remain largely unexplored in the realm of speech translation. Compounding this challenge is the fact that many of the target languages are distantly related to English. Consequently, we anticipate that relying solely on pre-trained

Test Set	15	16	18	19	21	Average
HWTSC-Dubbing	0.721	0.585	0.718	0.749	0.715	0.698
HWTSC-Offline	0.281	0.228	0.277	0.374	0.238	0.280
NYA-Offline	0.316	0.194	0.274	0.385	0.225	0.279
CMU-Offline	0.365	0.206	0.323	0.372	0.253	0.304

Table 10: Speech Overlap (↑), computed on speech segments as detected by silero-vad (Silero Team, 2021).

Score	Description
1	Speech is not natural at all and/or the translation has nothing to do with the source.
2	Speech is not natural but you can understand why some of the words in the translation are there.
3	Speech is partially matching speakers lips and/or is a bit natural as well as the meaning of the source sentence are adequately transferred into the target language.
4	Speech naturalness is of acceptable quality and the meaning of the source sentence is mostly preserved.
5	Speech is mostly natural and the translation is almost perfect or is a good paraphrase of reference.
6	Speech looks completely natural and the translation is perfect in every sense of the word.

Table 11: Dubbing human evaluation rubric.

Model	PEAVS (↑)	BLASER-QE (↑)	Human Evaluation (↑)
Original	3.82 ±0.41	–	–
HWTSC-Dubbing	3.05 ±0.45	3.25	3.9
HWTSC-Offline	1.33 ±0.37	3.07	3.5
NYA-Offline	1.28 ±0.31	3.03	3.3
CMU-Offline	1.28 ±0.31	3.07	3.2

Table 12: PEAVS (Perceptual Evaluation of Audio-Visual Synchrony) score (Goncalves et al., 2024), BLASER 2.0-Q, a reference-free modality-agnostic automatic metric for speech translation quality (Seamless Communication et al., 2023), and human evaluation results.

Test Set	15	16	18	19	21	Average
Original	8.220	7.258	11.553	9.311	10.197	9.308
HWTSC-Dubbing	11.969	5.398	11.341	11.887	11.200	10.359
HWTSC-Offline	13.596	12.219	12.024	12.748	8.437	11.805
NYA-Offline	14.094	11.539	10.488	12.833	8.409	11.473
CMU-Offline	14.793	12.834	12.499	12.817	7.933	12.175

Table 13: Lip sync error distance (LSE-D, ↓) (Prajwal et al., 2020) at clip level.

Test Set	15	16	18	19	21	Average
Original	3.714	0.656	1.190	3.340	1.443	2.069
HWTSC-Dubbing	0.638	1.011	1.463	1.185	0.893	1.038
HWTSC-Offline	0.477	0.834	1.095	1.355	0.849	0.922
NYA-Offline	0.674	0.567	1.153	0.944	0.697	0.807
CMU-Offline	0.706	0.971	2.143	1.019	0.718	1.112

Table 14: Lip-sync error confidence (LSE-C, ↑) (Prajwal et al., 2020) at clip level.

models may encounter numerous obstacles. The dataset provided will serve as the inaugural benchmark and gold standard dataset, encompassing all Indian languages. We aspire for participants to develop systems capable of real-world deployment in the future.

8.1 Challenge

The Indic shared task consists of ST for three language pairs from English (en) to Hindi (hi), Tamil (ta), and Bengali (bn). The ST data for all these three language pairs is derived from the Indic-TEDST dataset (Sethiya et al., 2024). The submissions are allowed for both the constrained and the unconstrained cases. The constrained case involves only the data provided in the task. The unconstrained case can utilize either the data provided in the challenge or any external data, along with any pre-trained models. The submissions are also allowed for the cascade and end-to-end models for all the language pairs. Thus, the task accepts the following cases for all three language pairs (en-hi, en-ta, and en-bn):

- End-to-end + Constrained
- End-to-end + Unconstrained
- Cascade + Constrained
- Cascade + Unconstrained

8.2 Data and Metrics

The ST task data for the Indic track encompasses three Indian languages representing diverse language families. The languages included in this shared task are Hindi (hi), Bengali (bn), and Tamil (ta), originating from the Indo-Aryan and Dravidian language families. The dataset includes speech and text (transcriptions) in English (source language) and text (translations) in Hindi, Bengali, and Tamil (target languages).

The data for this Indic track comprises a ST corpus that includes 3 low-resource Indian languages. The data is curated from the TED talks with Indic translations, usually a talk spans from 3 minutes to 15 minutes. A segmentation of the audio files in the form of YAML is provided with the data. Table 15 illustrates the consistency maintained across all corpora, with an equal number of lines in their .en, .lang, and .yaml files. However, due to inherent linguistic differences, the number of tokens in the .en and .lang files varies. The count of audio files corresponds to the number of distinct talks, each delivered by an individual speaker. Additionally, the speech hours indicate the cumulative speech duration in a given language. Each parameter is meticulously categorized into test, train, and valid subsets, establishing a comprehensive and structured dataset.

Lang en→	Split	#Lines	#Tokens (en)	#Tokens (lang)	#Audio files	#Speech (hrs)
bn	test	1.1	19.3	17.3	15	2.09
	train	5.1	89.4	80.4	106	9.20
	valid	1.3	22.1	20.4	30	2.30
hi	test	7.2	118.6	138.0	75	13.52
	train	45.8	752.6	890.5	528	76.46
	valid	7.6	130.3	158.5	150	13.52
ta	test	2.2	38.9	28.0	20	4.04
	train	8.0	135.1	101.5	145	14.41
	valid	2.1	35.4	27.3	42	3.56

Table 15: Statistics of Indic track dataset. #Lines and #Tokens (.en & .lang) are in terms of thousands(K). All the data in the above table is approximated.

English-Hindi: Hindi is the third most spoken language in the world, with 615 million speakers. It belongs to the Indo-Aryan language family, mainly spoken in India. It is also the official language of India, written in devanagiri script. The data contains English speech, English text (transcripts), and Hindi text (translations). The speech in English language is 103.5 hours and the text in Hindi language is 37K lines.

English-Bengali: Bengali is the 7th most spoken language in the world, with 228 million speakers. It belongs to the Indo-Aryan language family, spoken in the Bengal region of South Asia. It is also the official language of Bangladesh, written in Bengali-Assamese script. The data contains English speech, English texts (transcripts), and Bengali texts (translations). The speech in English language is 13.59 hours and the text in Bengali language is 6.9K lines.

English-Tamil: Tamil is one of the classical languages of India, spoken by 90.8 million speakers. It belongs to dravidian language family, spoken by the tamil people of South Asia. It is the official language of Tamil Nadu state of India, written in Brahmi script. The data contains English speech, English texts (transcripts), and Tamil texts (translations). The speech in English language is 22.01 hours and the text in Tamil language is 8K lines.

Metrics: Case-sensitive detokenized BLEU using sacreBLEU (Post, 2018) is used to report the performance of all the submissions.

8.3 Submissions

There were four teams participating in this inaugural task: Research team from National Institute of Information and Communications Technology of Japan (NICT) , the Voice Intelligence Team of Samsung (SRI-B), the Huawei Translation Service Center (HW-TSC), and a team from National Institute of Technology Kurukshetra, India (NITKKR). The participants submitted their result under various constraints, including end-to-end constrained, unconstrained, cascaded end-to-end, and unconstrained approaches. Below, we provide an overview of each team's approach and their results.

NICT: Their submission included cascaded and end-to-end approach in unconstrained setting for all the language pairs. The cascaded system involves fine-tuning the Whisper model for ASR and fine-tuning the IndicTrans2 model for MT. This dual fine-tuning aimed to address the format mismatch between spoken and written language. For the end-to-end syatem, the IndicTrans2 model is used to generate pseudo translation data, which replaced the gold transcription data for fine-tuning the Whisper model. This strategy aimed to distill knowledge from a stronger translation model and ensure consistent formatting. In stage 1, Whisper is fine-tuned using English transcription and Indic language translation. Stage 2 involves generation of pseudo translations for all English transcriptions, and fine-tuning Whisper using English audio and the pseudo translations. During inference, the fine-tuned Whisper model performed direct end-to-end speech translation.

HW-TSC: The submission included implementation of cascaded approach in the unconstrained setting. It involves Whisper-large-v3 model for Automatic Speech Recognition (ASR) and a Transformer model for Machine Translation (MT). For MT, strategies like LaBSE for parallel corpus filtering, data diversification using multiple model predictions, forward and back translation for data augmentation, domain fine-tuning with scored data selection, and regularized dropout for enhanced training efficiency are used. The base architecture is from FAIRSEQ toolkit (Wang et al., 2020b) with hyperparameters of 2048 as batch size, learning rate of 5e-4, label-smoothing-cross-entropy loss with label smoothing of 0.1, 4000 warmup steps, and Adam optimizer settings (ß1 = 0.9, ß2 = 0.98). During inference, a beam size of 4 and length penalties of 1.0 is applied to optimize translation outputs.

SRI-B: The submission included end-to-end approach in both constrained and unconstrained setting. In the constrained setting the base architecture used is from FAIRSEQ toolkit (Wang et al., 2020b). Pre-processing involves the extraction of 80 channel log mel-filter bank features with a window size of 25ms and SpecAugment for data augmentation. The s2t_conformer among fairseq's built-in architectures for speech-to-text translation is used. It consist of 16 encoder layers and 6 decoder layers with label-smoothed cross-entropy loss and the Adam optimizer with a learning rate of 2e-3 to train the models. Under the unconstrained setting, the method involves using the pre-trained SeamlessM4T v2 from Meta, a multi-lingual end-to-end model designed for various languages. The pre-trained multi-lingual model is used to directly generate text in Indic languages directly from English for evaluation.

NITKKR: The submission adopts cascaded approach in unconstrained setting to solve the task. It begins with audio preprocessing and transcription, utilizing ResembleAI for noise reduction, distortion restoration, and speech bandwidth enhancement. The processed audio is then fed into OpenAI's Whisper model for real-time ASR. Subsequently, MT models are applied: Helsinki-NLP's OPUS-MT for translating English to Hindi, and Facebook's Multilingual BART (MBART) for both English to Tamil and English to Bengali translations.

8.4 Results

Scores on the test set of all submissions are calculated using automatic metrics and the respective settings are presented in Table 16. In the following section, we discuss results from each direction of languages.

8.4.1 En-Hi

Unconstrained Setting: In the E2E approach, NICT achieved a BLEU score of 33.02, significantly outperforming SRI-B, which scored 21.63. This superior performance by NICT can be attributed to their robust use of pseudo translation data aimed to distill knowledge from a stronger

Language	Setting	Approach	Team ID	BLEU
En-Hi	Unconstrained	E2E	NICT	33.02
			SRI-B	21.63
		Cascaded	NICT	**60.54**
			HW-TSC	47.14
			NITKKR	19.77
	Constrained	E2E	SRI-B	29.76
En-Bn	Unconstrained	E2E	NICT	10.79
			SRI-B	18.13
		Cascaded	NICT	**52.63**
			HW-TSC	35.04
			NITKKR	4.46
	Constrained	E2E	SRI-B	2
En-Ta	Unconstrained	E2E	NICT	13.46
			SRI-B	11.93
		Cascaded	NICT	**39.84**
			HW-TSC	30.79
			NITKKR	11.76
	Constrained	E2E	SRI-B	0.81

Table 16: Results on all language pairs and setting from all the submissions.

translation model to ensure consistent formatting. In the cascaded approach, NICT again led with a remarkable 60.54 BLEU score, significantly higher than HW-TSC at 47.14 and NITKKR at 19.77. The cascaded approach by NICT utilized the strengths of pretraining the ASR and MT model to address the format mismatch problem which leads to maximizing the performance.

Constrained: In the E2E approach, there was one submission by SRI-B, which achieved a BLEU score of 29.76.

8.4.2 En-Bn

Unconstrained: SRI-B with a BLEU score of 18.13 beats NICT which scored 10.79 when implementing the E2E approach. In the cascaded approach, NICT scored the highest with 52.63 BLEU, compared to HW-TSC at 35.04 and NITKKR at 4.46. The same strategy from En-Hi allowed NICT to excel in this category, demonstrating the effectiveness of their cascaded approach.

Constrained: For the E2E approach, SRI-B scored a BLEU of 2 demonstrating the challenges of the constrained setting in this language pair.

8.4.3 En-Ta

Unconstrained: NICT led with a BLEU score of 13.46, while SRI-B scored 11.93 for the models using E2E approach. NICT's consistent use of Whisper for ASR and their robust translation models contributed to their leading position. For teams using the cascaded approach, NICT again achieved the highest BLEU score of 39.84, followed by HW-TSC at 30.79 and NITKKR at 11.76. The result could be explained due to the method of addressing the format mismatch problem by NICT already mentioned above.

Constrained: In this setting there is one submission using the E2E approach, by SRI-B. They achieve a score of 0.81, which shows the limitations on this setting and language pair. The low score could be explained due to limited data and the morphologically complex structure of the Tamil language.

8.5 Conclusion

This is the first time that a speech-to-translation task is presented for the Indic track as one of the IWSLT tasks. The results presented in the work establish an important benchmark for the end-to-end as well as cascade models for both the constrained and unconstrained conditions. This work highlights a major performance gap between the end-to-end and the cascade models. Also, a noteworthy gap is seen in the performance with the unconstrained data and pretrained models are used. We plan to include more data and more Indic languages in the next edition.

Acknowledgements

The FBK team (Roldano Cattoni, Mauro Cettolo, Matteo Negri and Sara Papi) is co-funded by the European Union under the project *AI4Culture: An AI platform for the cultural heritage data space* (Action number 101100683).

Atul Kr. Ojha and John P. McCrae would like to thank Science Foundation Ireland (SFI) under Grant Number SFI/12/RC/2289_ P2 Insight_2 and thanks to RTÉ/TG4 for sharing the Irish speech data. We would also like to thank Panlingua Language Processing LLP for providing the Marathi-Hindi, and Bhojpuri-Hindi speech translation data and for their support.

The work by Tsz Kin Lam and Barry Haddow was funded by UK Research and Innovation (UKRI) under the UK government's Horizon Europe funding guarantee (grant number 10039436: UTTER).

The work by Mateusz Krubiński, Petr Zemánek, Adam Pospíšil, and Pavel Pecina was funded by the European Commission via its H2020 Program (contract no. 870930: WELCOME).

The work by University of Malta was supported through H2020 EU Funded LT-Bridge Project (GA 952194) and DFKI for access to the Virtual Laboratory.

Brian Thompson's contributions to this work were conducted outside of, and are unrelated to, his employment at Amazon.

Ondřej Bojar would like to acknowledge the support from the 19-26934X (NEUREM3) grant of the Czech Science Foundation. The work of Peter Polák has been supported by the Ministry of Education, Youth and Sports of the Czech Republic, Project No. LM2023062 (LINDAT/CLARIAH-CZ). Dávid Javorský has been supported by the grant 272323 of the Grant Agency of Charles University.

References

Kurt Abela, Md Abdur Razzaq Riyadh, Melanie Galea, Alana Busuttil, Roman Kovalev, Aiden Williams, and Claudia Borg. 2024. UOM-Constrained IWSLT 2024 Shared Task Submission - Maltese Speech Translation. In *Proceedings of the 21th International Conference on Spoken Language Translation (IWSLT)*.

Basil Abraham, Danish Goel, Divya Siddarth, Kalika Bali, Manu Chopra, Monojit Choudhury, Pratik Joshi, Preethi Jyoti, Sunayana Sitaram, and Vivek Seshadri. 2020. Crowdsourcing speech data for low-resource languages from low-income workers. In *Proceedings of the 12th Language Resources and Evaluation Conference*, pages 2819–2826.

Josh Achiam, Steven Adler, Sandhini Agarwal, Lama Ahmad, Ilge Akkaya, Florencia Leoni Aleman, Diogo Almeida, Janko Altenschmidt, Sam Altman, Shyamal Anadkat, et al. 2023. Gpt-4 technical report. *arXiv preprint arXiv:2303.08774*.

Farhad Akhbardeh, Arkady Arkhangorodsky, Magdalena Biesialska, Ondřej Bojar, Rajen Chatterjee, Vishrav Chaudhary, Marta R. Costa-jussa, Cristina España-Bonet, Angela Fan, Christian Federmann, Markus Freitag, Yvette Graham, Roman Grundkiewicz, Barry Haddow, Leonie Harter, Kenneth Heafield, Christopher Homan, Matthias Huck, Kwabena Amponsah-Kaakyire, Jungo Kasai, Daniel Khashabi, Kevin Knight, Tom Kocmi, Philipp Koehn, Nicholas Lourie, Christof Monz, Makoto Morishita, Masaaki Nagata, Ajay Nagesh, Toshiaki Nakazawa, Matteo Negri, Santanu Pal, Allahsera Auguste Tapo, Marco Turchi, Valentin Vydrin, and Marcos Zampieri. 2021. Findings of the 2021 conference on machine translation (WMT21). In *Proceedings of the Sixth Conference on Machine Translation*, pages 1–88, Online. Association for Computational Linguistics.

Enam Al-Wer and Rudolf de Jong. 2017. *Dialects of Arabic*, chapter 32. John Wiley & Sons, Ltd.

Harpreet Singh Anand, Amulya Ratna Dash, and Yashvardhan Sharma. 2024. Empowering Low-Resource Language Translation: Methodologies for Bhojpuri-Hindi and Marathi-Hindi ASR and MT. In *Proceedings of the 21th International Conference on Spoken Language Translation (IWSLT)*.

Ebrahim Ansari, Ondřej Bojar, Barry Haddow, and Mohammad Mahmoudi. 2021. SLTev: Comprehensive Evaluation of Spoken Language Translation. In *Proceedings of the 16th Conference of the European Chapter of the Association for Computational Linguistics: Demo Papers*, Kyiv, Ukraine. Association for Computational Linguistics.

Junyi Ao, Rui Wang, Long Zhou, Chengyi Wang, Shuo Ren, Yu Wu, Shujie Liu, Tom Ko, Qing Li, Yu Zhang, Zhihua Wei, Yao Qian, Jinyu Li, and Furu Wei. 2022. SpeechT5: Unified-modal encoder-decoder pre-training for spoken language processing. In *Proceedings of the 60th Annual Meeting of the Association for Computational Linguistics (Volume 1: Long Papers)*, pages 5723–5738, Dublin, Ireland. Association for Computational Linguistics.

Rosana Ardila, Megan Branson, Kelly Davis, Michael Henretty, Michael Kohler, Josh Meyer, Reuben Morais, Lindsay Saunders, Francis M Tyers, and Gregor Weber. 2020. Common voice: A massively-multilingual speech corpus. In *LREC*.

Naveen Arivazhagan, Colin Cherry, Wolfgang Macherey, Chung-Cheng Chiu, Semih Yavuz, Ruoming Pang, Wei Li, and Colin Raffel. 2019. Monotonic infinite lookback attention for simultaneous machine translation. In *Proceedings of the 57th Annual Meeting of the Association for Computational Linguistics*, pages 1313–1323, Florence, Italy. Association for Computational Linguistics.

Marcely Zanon Boito, Fethi Bougares, Florentin Barbier, Souhir Gahbiche, Loïc Barrault, Mickael Rouvier, and Yannick Estéve. 2022. Speech resources in the tamasheq language. *Language Resources and Evaluation Conference (LREC)*.

William Brannon, Yogesh Virkar, and Brian Thompson. 2023. Dubbing in practice: A large scale study of human localization with insights for automatic dubbing. *Transactions of the Association for Computational Linguistics*, 11:419–435.

Ronald Cardenas, Rodolfo Zevallos, Reynaldo Baquerizo, and Luis Camacho. 2018. Siminchik: A speech corpus for preservation of southern quechua. *ISI-NLP 2*, page 21.

Roldano Cattoni, Mattia Antonino Di Gangi, Luisa Bentivogli, Matteo Negri, and Marco Turchi. 2021. Must-c: A multilingual corpus for end-to-end speech translation. *Computer Speech & Language*, 66:101155.

Mauro Cettolo, Marcello Federico, Luisa Bentivogli, Jan Niehues, Sebastian Stüker, K. Sudoh, K. Yoshino, and Christian Federmann. 2017. Overview of the IWSLT 2017 Evaluation Campaign. In *Proceedings of the 14th International Workshop on Spoken Language Translation (IWSLT 2017)*, pages 2–14, Tokyo, Japan.

Harveen Singh Chadha, Anirudh Gupta, Priyanshi Shah, Neeraj Chhimwal, Ankur Dhuriya, Rishabh Gaur, and Vivek Raghavan. 2022. Vakyansh: Asr toolkit for low resource indic languages. *arXiv preprint arXiv:2203.16512*.

Frederic Chaume. 2020. *Audiovisual translation: dubbing*. Routledge.

Sanyuan Chen, Chengyi Wang, Zhengyang Chen, Yu Wu, Shujie Liu, Zhuo Chen, Jinyu Li, Naoyuki Kanda, Takuya Yoshioka, Xiong Xiao, Jian Wu, Long Zhou, Shuo Ren, Yanmin Qian, Yao Qian, Micheal Zeng, and Furu Wei. 2021. Wavlm: Large-scale self-supervised pre-training for full stack speech processing. *IEEE Journal of Selected Topics in Signal Processing*, 16:1505–1518.

Delia Chiaro. 2009. Issues in audiovisual translation. In *The Routledge companion to translation studies*, pages 155–179. Routledge.

Alexandra Chronopoulou, Brian Thompson, Prashant Mathur, Yogesh Virkar, Surafel M Lakew, and Marcello Federico. 2023. Jointly optimizing translations and speech timing to improve isochrony in automatic dubbing. *arXiv preprint arXiv:2302.12979*.

Marta R Costa-jussà, James Cross, Onur Çelebi, Maha Elbayad, Kenneth Heafield, Kevin Heffernan, Elahe Kalbassi, Janice Lam, Daniel Licht, Jean Maillard, et al. 2022. No language left behind: Scaling human-centered machine translation. *arXiv preprint arXiv:2207.04672*.

Raj Dabre and Haiyue Song. 2024. NICT's Cascaded and End-To-End Speech Translation Systems using Whisper and IndicTrans2 for the Indic Task. In *Proceedings of the 21th International Conference on Spoken Language Translation (IWSLT)*.

Jacob Devlin, Ming-Wei Chang, Kenton Lee, and Kristina Toutanova. 2019. BERT: Pre-training of deep bidirectional transformers for language understanding. In *Proceedings of the 2019 Conference of the North American Chapter of the Association for Computational Linguistics: Human Language Technologies, Volume 1 (Long and Short Papers)*, pages 4171–4186, Minneapolis, Minnesota. Association for Computational Linguistics.

Mattia A. Di Gangi, Roldano Cattoni, Luisa Bentivogli, Matteo Negri, and Marco Turchi. 2019. MuST-C: a Multilingual Speech Translation Corpus. In *Proceedings of the 2019 Conference of the North American Chapter of the Association for Computational Linguistics: Human Language Technologies, Volume 1 (Long and Short Papers)*, pages 2012–2017, Minneapolis, Minnesota.

Fangxiaoyu Feng, Yinfei Yang, Daniel Cer, Naveen Arivazhagan, and Wei Wang. 2022. Language-agnostic BERT sentence embedding. In *Proceedings of the 60th Annual Meeting of the Association for Computational Linguistics (Volume 1: Long Papers)*, pages 878–891, Dublin, Ireland. Association for Computational Linguistics.

Jonathan Fiscus. 1997. A post-processing system to yield reduced word error rates: Recognizer output voting error reduction [rover].

Markus Freitag, George Foster, David Grangier, Viresh Ratnakar, Qijun Tan, and Wolfgang Macherey. 2021a. Experts, errors, and context: A large-scale study of human evaluation for machine translation. *Transactions of the Association for Computational Linguistics*, 9:1460–1474.

Markus Freitag, Ricardo Rei, Nitika Mathur, Chi-kiu Lo, Craig Stewart, George Foster, Alon Lavie, and Ondřej Bojar. 2021b. Results of the WMT21 metrics shared task: Evaluating metrics with expert-based human evaluations on TED and news domain. In *Proceedings of the Sixth Conference on Machine Translation*, pages 733–774, Online. Association for Computational Linguistics.

Marco Gaido, Sara Papi, Mauro Cettolo, Roldano Cattoni, Andrea Piergentili, Matteo Negri, and Luisa Bentivogli. 2024a. Automatic Subtitling and Subtitle Compression: FBK at the IWSLT 2024 Subtitling track. In *Proceedings of the 21th International Conference on Spoken Language Translation (IWSLT)*.

Marco Gaido, Sara Papi, Matteo Negri, Mauro Cettolo, and Luisa Bentivogli. 2024b. SBAAM! Eliminating Transcript Dependency in Automatic Subtitling. In *Proceedings of the 62nd Annual Meeting of the Association for Computational Linguistics (Volume 1: Long Papers)*, Bangkok, Thailand.

Carol-Luca Gasan and Vasile Păiș. 2024. Multi-Model System for Effective Subtitling Compression. In *Proceedings of the 21th International Conference on Spoken Language Translation (IWSLT)*.

Elham Abdullah Ghobain. 2017. Dubbing melodramas in the arab world: between the standard language and colloquial dialects. *The Arabic Language and Literature*, 2:49.

Lucas Goncalves, Prashant Mathur, Chandrashekhar Lavania, Metehan Cekic, Marcello Federico, and Kyu J. Han. 2024. Peavs: Perceptual evaluation of audio-visual synchrony grounded in viewers' opinion scores.

Yvette Graham, Timothy Baldwin, Alistair Moffat, and Justin Zobel. 2013. Continuous measurement scales in human evaluation of machine translation. In *Proceedings of the 7th Linguistic Annotation Workshop and Interoperability with Discourse*, pages 33–41, Sofia, Bulgaria. Association for Computational Linguistics.

Jiaxin Guo, Daimeng Wei, Zhanglin Wu, Zongyao Li, Zhiqiang Rao, Minghan Wang, Hengchao Shang, Xiaoyu Chen, Zhengzhe Yu, Shaojun Li, Yuhao Xie, Lizhi Lei, and Hao Yang. 2023. The HW-TSC's Simultaneous Speech-to-Text Translation system for IWSLT 2023 evaluation. In *Proceedings of the 20th International Conference on Spoken Language Translation (IWSLT)*.

Anirudh Gupta, Harveen Singh Chadha, Priyanshi Shah, Neeraj Chhimwal, Ankur Dhuriya, Rishabh Gaur, and Vivek Raghavan. 2021. Clsril-23: Cross lingual speech representations for indic languages. *arXiv preprint arXiv:2107.07402*.

Awni Hannun, Carl Case, Jared Casper, Bryan Catanzaro, Greg Diamos, Erich Elsen, Ryan Prenger, Sanjeev Satheesh, Shubho Sengupta, Adam Coates, et al. 2014. Deep speech: Scaling up end-to-end speech recognition. *arXiv preprint arXiv:1412.5567*.

Fei He, Shan-Hui Cathy Chu, Oddur Kjartansson, Clara Rivera, Anna Katanova, Alexander Gutkin, Isin Demirsahin, Cibu Johny, Martin Jansche, Supheakmungkol Sarin, and Knot Pipatsrisawat. 2020. Open-source multi-speaker speech corpora for building Gujarati, Kannada, Malayalam, Marathi, Tamil and Telugu speech synthesis systems. In *Proceedings of the Twelfth Language Resources and Evaluation Conference*, pages 6494–6503, Marseille, France. European Language Resources Association.

Kenneth Heafield. 2011. KenLM: Faster and smaller language model queries. In *Proceedings of the Sixth Workshop on Statistical Machine Translation*, pages 187–197, Edinburgh, Scotland. Association for Computational Linguistics.

Kevin Heffernan, Onur Çelebi, and Holger Schwenk. 2022. Bitext mining using distilled sentence representations for low-resource languages. In *Findings of the Association for Computational Linguistics: EMNLP 2022*, pages 2101–2112, Abu Dhabi, United Arab Emirates. Association for Computational Linguistics.

Carlos Daniel Hernandez Mena, Albert Gatt, Andrea DeMarco, Claudia Borg, Lonneke van der Plas, Amanda Muscat, and Ian Padovani. 2020. Masriheadset: A maltese corpus for speech recognition. In *Proceedings of The 12th Language Resources and Evaluation Conference*, pages 6381–6388, Marseille, France. European Language Resources Association.

Wei-Ning Hsu, Benjamin Bolte, Yao-Hung Hubert Tsai, Kushal Lakhotia, Ruslan Salakhutdinov, and Abdelrahman Mohamed. 2021. Hubert: Self-supervised speech representation learning by masked prediction of hidden units. *IEEE/ACM Trans. Audio, Speech and Lang. Proc.*, 29:3451–3460.

Edward J Hu, Yelong Shen, Phillip Wallis, Zeyuan Allen-Zhu, Yuanzhi Li, Shean Wang, Lu Wang, and Weizhu Chen. 2021. Lora: Low-rank adaptation of large language models. *arXiv preprint arXiv:2106.09685*.

Zheng Jiawei, Hengchao Shang, Zongyao Li, Zhanglin Wu, Daimeng Wei, Zhiqiang Rao, Shaojun Li, Jiaxin Guo, Bin Wei, Yuanchang Luo, and Hao Yang. 2024. HW-TSC's Submissions To the IWSLT2024 Low-resource Speech Translation Tasks. In *Proceedings of the 21th International Conference on Spoken Language Translation (IWSLT)*.

Japan Translation Federation JTF. 2018. JTF Translation Quality Evaluation Guidelines, 1st Edition (in Japanese).

Yasumasa Kano, Katsuhito Sudoh, and Satoshi Nakamura. 2023. Average Token Delay: A Latency Metric for Simultaneous Translation. In *Proc. INTERSPEECH 2023*, pages 4469–4473.

Simran Khanuja, Diksha Bansal, Sarvesh Mehtani, Savya Khosla, Atreyee Dey, Balaji Gopalan, Dilip Kumar Margam, Pooja Aggarwal, Rajiv Teja Nagipogu, Shachi Dave, et al. 2021. Muril: Multilingual representations for indian languages. *arXiv preprint arXiv:2103.10730*.

Waad Ben Kheder, Josef Jon, André Beyer, Abdel Messaoudi, Rabea Affan, Claude Barras, Maxim Tychonov, and Jean-Luc Gauvain. 2024. ALADAN at IWSLT24 Low-resource Arabic Dialectal Speech Translation Task. In *Proceedings of the 21th International Conference on Spoken Language Translation (IWSLT)*.

Yuka Ko, Ryo Fukuda, Yuta Nishikawa, Yasumasa Kano, Tomoya Yanagita, Kosuke Doi, Mana Makinae, Haotian Tan, Makoto Sakai, Sakriani Sakti,

Katsuhito Sudoh, and Satoshi Nakamura. 2024. NAIST Simultaneous Speech Translation System for IWSLT 2024. In *Proceedings of the 21th International Conference on Spoken Language Translation (IWSLT)*.

Rostislav Kolobov, Olga Okhapkina, Andrey Platunov Olga Omelchishina, Roman Bedyakin, Vyacheslav Moshkin, Dmitry Menshikov, and Nikolay Mikhaylovskiy. 2021. Mediaspeech: Multilanguage asr benchmark and dataset.

Sai Koneru, Thai Binh Nguyen, Ngoc-Quan Pham, Danni Liu, Zhaolin Li, Alexander Waibel, and Jan Niehues. 2024. Blending LLMs into Cascaded Speech Translation: KIT's Offline Speech Translation System for IWSLT 2024. In *Proceedings of the 21th International Conference on Spoken Language Translation (IWSLT)*.

Matyáš Kopp, Vladislav Stankov, Ondřej Bojar, Barbora Hladká, and Pavel Straňák. 2021. ParCzech 3.0. LINDAT/CLARIAH-CZ digital library at the Institute of Formal and Applied Linguistics (ÚFAL), Faculty of Mathematics and Physics, Charles University.

Helena Kruger. 2001. The creation of interlingual subtitles: Semiotics, equivalence and condensation. *Perspectives*, 9(3):177–196.

Samuel Läubli, Rico Sennrich, and Martin Volk. 2018. Has machine translation achieved human parity? a case for document-level evaluation. In *Proceedings of the 2018 Conference on Empirical Methods in Natural Language Processing*, pages 4791–4796, Brussels, Belgium. Association for Computational Linguistics.

D Lee, S Ismael, S Grimes, D Doermann, S Strassel, and Z Song. 2012. Madcat phase 1 training set. *LDC2012T15. DVD. Philadelphia: Linguistic Data Consortium*.

Mike Lewis, Yinhan Liu, Naman Goyal, Marjan Ghazvininejad, Abdelrahman Mohamed, Omer Levy, Veselin Stoyanov, and Luke Zettlemoyer. 2020. BART: Denoising sequence-to-sequence pretraining for natural language generation, translation, and comprehension. In *Proceedings of the 58th Annual Meeting of the Association for Computational Linguistics*, pages 7871–7880, Online. Association for Computational Linguistics.

Shaojun Li, Zhiqiang Rao, Bin Wei, Yuanchang Luo, Zhanglin Wu, Zongyao Li, Hengchao Shang, Jiaxin Guo, Daimeng Wei, and Hao Yang. 2024a. HW-TSC's Simultaneous Speech Translation System for IWSLT 2024. In *Proceedings of the 21th International Conference on Spoken Language Translation (IWSLT)*.

Yuang Li, Jiaxin GUO, Min Zhang, Ma Miaomiao, Zhiqiang Rao, Weidong Zhang, Xianghui He, Daimeng Wei, and Hao Yang. 2024b. Pause-Aware Automatic Dubbing using LLM and Voice Cloning. In *Proceedings of the 21th International Conference on Spoken Language Translation (IWSLT)*.

Zhaolin Li, Enes Yavuz Ugan, Danni Liu, Carlos Mullov, Tu Anh Dinh, Sai Koneru, Alexander Waibel, and Jan Niehues. 2024c. The KIT Speech Translation Systems for IWSLT 2024 Dialectal and Low-resource Track. In *Proceedings of the 21th International Conference on Spoken Language Translation (IWSLT)*.

Chin-Yew Lin. 2004. ROUGE: A package for automatic evaluation of summaries. In *Text Summarization Branches Out*, pages 74–81, Barcelona, Spain. Association for Computational Linguistics.

Danni Liu, Gerasimos Spanakis, and Jan Niehues. 2020a. Low-latency sequence-to-sequence speech recognition and translation by partial hypothesis selection. In *Proceedings of Interspeech 2020*, pages 3620–3624.

Yinhan Liu, Jiatao Gu, Naman Goyal, Xian Li, Sergey Edunov, Marjan Ghazvininejad, Mike Lewis, and Luke Zettlemoyer. 2020b. Multilingual denoising pre-training for neural machine translation. *Transactions of the Association for Computational Linguistics*, 8:726–742.

Arle Lommel, Hans Uszkoreit, and Aljoscha Burchardt. 2014. Multidimensional Quality Metrics (MQM): A Framework for Declaring and DescribingTranslation Quality Metrics. *Revista Tradumàtica: tecnologies de la traducció*, 12:455–463.

Edward Ma. 2019. Nlp augmentation. https://github.com/makcedward/nlpaug.

Mingbo Ma, Liang Huang, Hao Xiong, Renjie Zheng, Kaibo Liu, Baigong Zheng, Chuanqiang Zhang, Zhongjun He, Hairong Liu, Xing Li, Hua Wu, and Haifeng Wang. 2019. STACL: Simultaneous translation with implicit anticipation and controllable latency using prefix-to-prefix framework. In *Proceedings of the 57th Annual Meeting of the Association for Computational Linguistics*, pages 3025–3036, Florence, Italy. Association for Computational Linguistics.

Xutai Ma, Mohammad Javad Dousti, Changhan Wang, Jiatao Gu, and Juan Pino. 2020. SIMULEVAL: An evaluation toolkit for simultaneous translation. In *Proceedings of the 2020 Conference on Empirical Methods in Natural Language Processing: System Demonstrations*, pages 144–150, Online. Association for Computational Linguistics.

Mohamed Maamouri, Tim Buckwalter, David Graff, and Hubert Jin. 2006. Levantine arabic qt training data set 5. *Speech Linguistic Data Consortium, Philadelphia*.

Dominik Macháček, Ondřej Bojar, and Raj Dabre. 2023. MT Metrics Correlate with Human Ratings of Simultaneous Speech Translation. In *Proceedings of the 20th International Conference on Spoken Language Translation (IWSLT)*.

John Makhoul, Bushra Zawaydeh, Frederick Choi, and David Stallard. 2005. Bbn/aub darpa babylon levantine arabic speech and transcripts. *Linguistic Data Consortium (LDC), LDC Catalog No.: LDC2005S08*.

Sourab Mangrulkar, Sylvain Gugger, Lysandre Debut, Younes Belkada, Sayak Paul, and B Bossan. 2022. Peft: State-of-the-art parameter-efficient fine-tuning methods. *URL: https://github.com/huggingface/peft*.

Evgeny Matusov, Gregor Leusch, Oliver Bender, and Hermann Ney. 2005. Evaluating machine translation output with automatic sentence segmentation. In *Proc. of the International Workshop on Spoken Language Translation (IWSLT)*, pages 138–144.

Evgeny Matusov, Patrick Wilken, and Yota Georgakopoulou. 2019. Customizing neural machine translation for subtitling. In *Proceedings of the Fourth Conference on Machine Translation (Volume 1: Research Papers)*, pages 82–93, Florence, Italy. Association for Computational Linguistics.

Evgeny Matusov, Patrick Wilken, and Christian Herold. 2020. Flexible customization of a single neural machine translation system with multi-dimensional metadata inputs. In *Proceedings of the 14th Conference of the Association for Machine Translation in the Americas (Volume 2: User Track)*, pages 204–216, Virtual. Association for Machine Translation in the Americas.

Roberto Mayoral, Dorothy Kelly, and Natividad Gallardo. 1988. Concept of constrained translation. non-linguistic perspectives of translation. *Meta*, 33(3):356–367.

Kurt Micallef, Albert Gatt, Marc Tanti, Lonneke van der Plas, and Claudia Borg. 2022. Pre-training data quality and quantity for a low-resource language: New corpus and BERT models for Maltese. In *Proceedings of the Third Workshop on Deep Learning for Low-Resource Natural Language Processing*, pages 90–101, Hybrid. Association for Computational Linguistics.

Yasmin Moslem. 2024. Leveraging Synthetic Audio Data for End-to-End Low-Resource Speech Translation. In *Proceedings of the 21th International Conference on Spoken Language Translation (IWSLT)*.

Sara Nabhani, Aiden Williams, Miftahul Jannat, Kate Rebecca Belcher, Melanie Galea, Anna Taylor, Kurt Micallef, and Claudia Borg. 2024. UM IWSLT 2024 Low-Resource Speech Translation: Combining Maltese and North Levantine Arabic. In *Proceedings of the 21th International Conference on Spoken Language Translation (IWSLT)*.

NLLB Team, Marta R. Costa-jussà, James Cross, Onur Çelebi, Maha Elbayad, Kenneth Heafield, Kevin Heffernan, Elahe Kalbassi, Janice Lam, Daniel Licht, Jean Maillard, Anna Sun, Skyler Wang, Guillaume Wenzek, Al Youngblood, Bapi Akula, Loic Barrault, Gabriel Mejia-Gonzalez, Prangthip Hansanti, John Hoffman, Semarley Jarrett, Kaushik Ram Sadagopan, Dirk Rowe, Shannon Spruit, Chau Tran, Pierre Andrews, Necip Fazil Ayan, Shruti Bhosale, Sergey Edunov, Angela Fan, Cynthia Gao, Vedanuj Goswami, Francisco Guzmán, Philipp Koehn, Alexandre Mourachko, Christophe Ropers, Safiyyah Saleem, Holger Schwenk, and Jeff Wang. 2022. No language left behind: Scaling human-centered machine translation. *arXiv preprint*.

Atul Kr. Ojha. 2019. English-Bhojpuri SMT System: Insights from the Kāraka Model. *arXiv preprint arXiv:1905.02239*.

Atul Kr. Ojha, Valentin Malykh, Alina Karakanta, and Chao-Hong Liu. 2020. Findings of the LoResMT 2020 shared task on zero-shot for low-resource languages. In *Proceedings of the 3rd Workshop on Technologies for MT of Low Resource Languages*, pages 33–37, Suzhou, China. Association for Computational Linguistics.

Atul Kr. Ojha and Daniel Zeman. 2020. Universal Dependency treebanks for low-resource Indian languages: The case of Bhojpuri. In *Proceedings of the WILDRE5– 5th Workshop on Indian Language Data: Resources and Evaluation*, pages 33–38, Marseille, France. European Language Resources Association (ELRA).

John E Ortega, Richard Castro Mamani, and Kyunghyun Cho. 2020. Neural machine translation with a polysynthetic low resource language. *Machine Translation*, 34(4):325–346.

John E. Ortega, Rodolfo Zevallos, and William Chen. 2023. QUESPA Submission for the IWSLT 2023 Dialect and Low-resource Speech Translation Tasks. In *Proceedings of the 20th International Conference on Spoken Language Translation (IWSLT)*.

John E. Ortega, Rodolfo Joel Zevallos, Ibrahim Said Ahmad, and William Chen. 2024. QUESPA Submission for the IWSLT 2024 Dialectal and Low-resource Speech Translation Task. In *Proceedings of the 21th International Conference on Spoken Language Translation (IWSLT)*.

Myle Ott, Sergey Edunov, Alexei Baevski, Angela Fan, Sam Gross, Nathan Ng, David Grangier, and Michael Auli. 2019. fairseq: A fast, extensible toolkit for sequence modeling. In *Proceedings of NAACL-HLT 2019: Demonstrations*.

Proyag Pal, Brian Thompson, Yogesh Virkar, Prashant Mathur, Alexandra Chronopoulou, and Marcello Federico. 2023. Improving Isochronous Machine Translation with Target Factors and Auxiliary Counters. In *Proc. INTERSPEECH 2023*, pages 37–41.

Sara Papi, Marco Gaido, Alina Karakanta, Mauro Cettolo, Matteo Negri, and Marco Turchi. 2023a. Direct Speech Translation for Automatic Subtitling. *Transactions of the Association for Computational Linguistics*, 11:1355–1376.

Sara Papi, Marco Gaido, Matteo Negri, and Luisa Bentivogli. 2024. SimulSeamless: FBK at IWSLT 2024 Simultaneous Speech Translation. In *Proceedings of the 21th International Conference on Spoken Language Translation (IWSLT)*.

Sara Papi, Marco Gaido, Matteo Negri, and Marco Turchi. 2022a. Over-generation cannot be rewarded: Length-adaptive average lagging for simultaneous speech translation. In *Proceedings of the Third Workshop on Automatic Simultaneous Translation*, pages 12–17, Online. Association for Computational Linguistics.

Sara Papi, Alina Karakanta, Matteo Negri, and Marco Turchi. 2022b. Dodging the data bottleneck: Automatic subtitling with automatically segmented ST corpora. In *Proceedings of the 2nd Conference of the Asia-Pacific Chapter of the Association for Computational Linguistics and the 12th International Joint Conference on Natural Language Processing (Volume 2: Short Papers)*, pages 480–487, Online only. Association for Computational Linguistics.

Sara Papi, Marco Turchi, Matteo Negri, et al. 2023b. AlignAtt: Using attention-based audio-translation alignments as a guide for simultaneous speech translation. In *Proceedings of Interspeech 2023*. ISCA.

Kishore Papineni, Salim Roukos, Todd Ward, and Wei-Jing Zhu. 2002a. BLEU: a Method for Automatic Evaluation of Machine Translation. In *Proceedings of the 40th Annual Meeting of the Association for Computational Linguistics (ACL)*, pages 311–318, Philadelphia, USA.

Kishore Papineni, Salim Roukos, Todd Ward, and Wei-Jing Zhu. 2002b. Bleu: a method for automatic evaluation of machine translation. In *Proceedings of the 40th annual meeting on association for computational linguistics*. Association for Computational Linguistics.

Peter Polák, Danni Liu, Ngoc-Quan Pham, Jan Niehues, Alexander Waibel, and Ondřej Bojar. 2023a. Towards efficient simultaneous speech translation: CUNI-KIT system for simultaneous track at IWSLT 2023. In *Proceedings of the 20th International Conference on Spoken Language Translation (IWSLT 2023)*, pages 389–396, Toronto, Canada (in-person and online). Association for Computational Linguistics.

Peter Polák, Ngoc-Quan Pham, Tuan Nam Nguyen, Danni Liu, Carlos Mullov, Jan Niehues, Ondřej Bojar, and Alexander Waibel. 2022. CUNI-KIT system for simultaneous speech translation task at IWSLT 2022. In *Proceedings of the 19th International Conference on Spoken Language Translation (IWSLT 2022)*, pages 277–285, Dublin, Ireland (in-person and online). Association for Computational Linguistics.

Peter Polák, Brian Yan, Shinji Watanabe, Alex Waibel, and Ondřej Bojar. 2023b. Incremental Blockwise Beam Search for Simultaneous Speech Translation with Controllable Quality-Latency Tradeoff. In *Proc. INTERSPEECH 2023*, pages 3979–3983.

Maja Popović. 2015. chrf: character n-gram f-score for automatic mt evaluation. In *Proceedings of the tenth workshop on statistical machine translation*, pages 392–395.

Matt Post. 2018. A call for clarity in reporting BLEU scores. In *Proceedings of the Third Conference on Machine Translation: Research Papers*, pages 186–191, Brussels, Belgium. Association for Computational Linguistics.

Daniel Povey, Gaofeng Cheng, Yiming Wang, Ke Li, Hainan Xu, Mahsa Yarmohammadi, and Sanjeev Khudanpur. 2018. Semi-orthogonal low-rank matrix factorization for deep neural networks. In *19th Annual Conference of the International Speech Communication Association, Interspeech 2018, Hyderabad, India, September 2-6, 2018*, pages 3743–3747. ISCA.

K R Prajwal, Rudrabha Mukhopadhyay, Vinay P. Namboodiri, and C.V. Jawahar. 2020. A lip sync expert is all you need for speech to lip generation in the wild. In *Proceedings of the 28th ACM International Conference on Multimedia*, MM '20, page 484–492, New York, NY, USA. Association for Computing Machinery.

Vineel Pratap, Andros Tjandra, Bowen Shi, Paden Tomasello, Arun Babu, Sayani Kundu, Ali Elkahky, Zhaoheng Ni, Apoorv Vyas, Maryam Fazel-Zarandi, et al. 2024. Scaling speech technology to 1,000+ languages. *Journal of Machine Learning Research*, 25(97):1–52.

Alec Radford, Jong Wook Kim, Tao Xu, Greg Brockman, Christine McLeavey, and Ilya Sutskever. 2022. Robust Speech Recognition via Large-Scale Weak Supervision.

Alec Radford, Jong Wook Kim, Tao Xu, Greg Brockman, Christine McLeavey, and Ilya Sutskever. 2023. Robust speech recognition via large-scale weak supervision. In *International Conference on Machine Learning*, pages 28492–28518. PMLR.

Colin Raffel, Noam Shazeer, Adam Roberts, Katherine Lee, Sharan Narang, Michael Matena, Yanqi Zhou, Wei Li, and Peter J. Liu. 2020. Exploring the limits of transfer learning with a unified text-to-text transformer. *Journal of Machine Learning Research*, 21(140):1–67.

Zhiqiang Rao, Hengchao Shang, Jinlong Yang, Daimeng Wei, Zongyao Li, Jiaxin Guo, Shaojun Li, Zhengzhe Yu, Zhanglin Wu, Yuhao Xie, Bin

Wei, Jiawei Zheng, Lizhi Lei, and Hao Yang. 2023. Length-aware NMT and adaptive duration for automatic dubbing. In *Proceedings of the 20th International Conference on Spoken Language Translation (IWSLT 2023)*, pages 138–143, Toronto, Canada (in-person and online). Association for Computational Linguistics.

Ricardo Rei, José GC de Souza, Duarte Alves, Chrysoula Zerva, Ana C Farinha, Taisiya Glushkova, Alon Lavie, Luisa Coheur, and André FT Martins. 2022. Comet-22: Unbabel-ist 2022 submission for the metrics shared task. In *Proceedings of the Seventh Conference on Machine Translation (WMT)*, pages 578–585.

Ricardo Rei, Craig Stewart, Ana C Farinha, and Alon Lavie. 2020. Comet: A neural framework for mt evaluation. *arXiv preprint arXiv:2009.09025*.

Nils Reimers and Iryna Gurevych. 2020. Making monolingual sentence embeddings multilingual using knowledge distillation. In *Proceedings of the 2020 Conference on Empirical Methods in Natural Language Processing (EMNLP)*, pages 4512–4525, Online. Association for Computational Linguistics.

Kumar Rishu, Aiden Williams, Claudia Borg, and Simon Ostermann. 2024. UoM-DFKI submission to the low resource shared task. In *Proceedings of the 21th International Conference on Spoken Language Translation (IWSLT)*.

Nathaniel Romney Robinson, Kaiser Sun, Cihan Xiao, Niyati Bafna, Weiting Tan, Haoran Xu, Henry Li Xinyuan, Ankur Kejriwal, Sanjeev Khudanpur, Kenton Murray, and Paul McNamee. 2024. JHU IWSLT 2024 Dialectal and Low-resource System Description. In *Proceedings of the 21th International Conference on Spoken Language Translation (IWSLT)*.

Ramon Sanabria, Nikolay Bogoychev, Nina Markl, Andrea Carmantini, Ondrej Klejch, and Peter Bell. 2023. The edinburgh international accents of english corpus: Towards the democratization of english asr. In *ICASSP 2023-2023 IEEE International Conference on Acoustics, Speech and Signal Processing (ICASSP)*, pages 1–5. IEEE.

Seamless Communication, Loïc Barrault, Yu-An Chung, Mariano Cora Meglioli, David Dale, Ning Dong, Paul-Ambroise Duquenne, Hady Elsahar, Hongyu Gong, Kevin Heffernan, John Hoffman, Christopher Klaiber, Pengwei Li, Daniel Licht, Jean Maillard, Alice Rakotoarison, Kaushik Ram Sadagopan, Guillaume Wenzek, Ethan Ye, Bapi Akula, Peng-Jen Chen, Naji El Hachem, Brian Ellis, Gabriel Mejia Gonzalez, Justin Haaheim, Prangthip Hansanti, Russ Howes, Bernie Huang, Min-Jae Hwang, Hirofumi Inaguma, Somya Jain, Elahe Kalbassi, Amanda Kallet, Ilia Kulikov, Janice Lam, Daniel Li, Xutai Ma, Ruslan Mavlyutov, Benjamin Peloquin, Mohamed Ramadan, Abinesh Ramakrishnan, Anna Sun, Kevin Tran, Tuan Tran, Igor Tufanov, Vish Vogeti, Carleigh Wood, Yilin Yang, Bokai Yu, Pierre Andrews, Can Balioglu, Marta R. Costa-jussà, Onur Celebi, Maha Elbayad, Cynthia Gao, Francisco Guzmán, Justine Kao, Ann Lee, Alexandre Mourachko, Juan Pino, Sravya Popuri, Christophe Ropers, Safiyyah Saleem, Holger Schwenk, Paden Tomasello, Changhan Wang, Jeff Wang, and Skyler Wang. 2023. Seamlessm4t: Massively multilingual & multimodal machine translation.

Thibault Sellam, Dipanjan Das, and Ankur Parikh. 2020. BLEURT: Learning robust metrics for text generation. In *Proceedings of the 58th Annual Meeting of the Association for Computational Linguistics*, pages 7881–7892, Online. Association for Computational Linguistics.

Hashem Sellat, Shadi Saleh, Mateusz Krubiński, Adam Pospíšil, Petr Zemánek, and Pavel Pecina. 2023. UFAL parallel corpus of north levantine 1.0. LINDAT/CLARIAH-CZ digital library at the Institute of Formal and Applied Linguistics (ÚFAL), Faculty of Mathematics and Physics, Charles University.

Nivedita Sethiya, Saanvi Nair, and Chandresh Maurya. 2024. Indic-TEDST: Datasets and baselines for low-resource speech to text translation. In *Proceedings of the 2024 Joint International Conference on Computational Linguistics, Language Resources and Evaluation (LREC-COLING 2024)*, pages 9019–9024, Torino, Italia. ELRA and ICCL.

Yao Shi, Hui Bu, Xin Xu, Shaoji Zhang, and Ming Li. 2020. Aishell-3: A multi-speaker mandarin tts corpus and the baselines. *arXiv preprint arXiv:2010.11567*.

Claytone Sikasote and Antonios Anastasopoulos. 2022. BembaSpeech: A speech recognition corpus for the Bemba language. In *Proceedings of the Thirteenth Language Resources and Evaluation Conference*, pages 7277–7283, Marseille, France. European Language Resources Association.

Claytone Sikasote, Eunice Mukonde, Md Mahfuz Ibn Alam, and Antonios Anastasopoulos. 2023a. BIG-C: a multimodal multi-purpose dataset for Bemba. In *Proceedings of the 61st Annual Meeting of the Association for Computational Linguistics (Volume 1: Long Papers)*, pages 2062–2078, Toronto, Canada. Association for Computational Linguistics.

Claytone Sikasote, Kalinda Siaminwe, Stanly Mwape, Bangiwe Zulu, Mofya Phiri, Martin Phiri, David Zulu, Mayumbo Nyirenda, and Antonios Anastasopoulos. 2023b. Zambezi Voice: A Multilingual Speech Corpus for Zambian Languages. In *Proc. INTERSPEECH 2023*, pages 3984–3988.

Silero Team. 2021. Silero vad: pre-trained enterprise-grade voice activity detector (vad), number detector and language classifier. `https://github.com/snakers4/silero-vad`.

Deepanjali Singh, Ayush Anand, Abhyuday Chaturvedi, and Niyati Baliyan. 2024. IWSLT 2024 Indic Track system description paper: Speech-to-Text Translation from English to multiple Low-Resource Indian Languages. In *Proceedings of the 21th International Conference on Spoken Language Translation (IWSLT)*.

Matthias Sperber, Ondřej Bojar, Barry Haddow, Dávid Javorský, Xutai Ma, Matteo Negri, Jan Niehues, Peter Polák, Elizabeth Salesky, Katsuhito Sudoh, and Marco Turchi. 2024. Evaluating the IWSLT2023 speech translation tasks: Human annotations, automatic metrics, and segmentation. In *Proceedings of the 2024 Joint International Conference on Computational Linguistics, Language Resources and Evaluation (LREC-COLING 2024)*, pages 6484–6495, Torino, Italia. ELRA and ICCL.

Brian Thompson and Philipp Koehn. 2019. Vecalign: Improved sentence alignment in linear time and space. In *Proceedings of the 2019 Conference on Empirical Methods in Natural Language Processing and the 9th International Joint Conference on Natural Language Processing (EMNLP-IJCNLP)*, pages 1342–1348, Hong Kong, China. Association for Computational Linguistics.

Brian Thompson and Philipp Koehn. 2020. Exploiting sentence order in document alignment. In *Proceedings of the 2020 Conference on Empirical Methods in Natural Language Processing (EMNLP)*, pages 5997–6007, Online. Association for Computational Linguistics.

Jörg Tiedemann and Santhosh Thottingal. 2020. OPUS-MT — Building open translation services for the World. In *Proceedings of the 22nd Annual Conferenec of the European Association for Machine Translation (EAMT)*, Lisbon, Portugal.

Antonio Toral, Sheila Castilho, Ke Hu, and Andy Way. 2018. Attaining the unattainable? reassessing claims of human parity in neural machine translation. In *Proceedings of the Third Conference on Machine Translation: Research Papers*, pages 113–123, Brussels, Belgium. Association for Computational Linguistics.

Hugo Touvron, Louis Martin, Kevin Stone, Peter Albert, Amjad Almahairi, Yasmine Babaei, Nikolay Bashlykov, Soumya Batra, Prajjwal Bhargava, Shruti Bhosale, et al. 2023. Llama 2: Open foundation and fine-tuned chat models. *arXiv preprint arXiv:2307.09288*.

Giorgos Vernikos, Brian Thompson, Prashant Mathur, and Marcello Federico. 2022. Embarrassingly easy document-level MT metrics: How to convert any pretrained metric into a document-level metric. In *Proceedings of the Seventh Conference on Machine Translation (WMT)*, pages 118–128, Abu Dhabi, United Arab Emirates (Hybrid). Association for Computational Linguistics.

Changhan Wang, Yun Tang, Xutai Ma, Anne Wu, Dmytro Okhonko, and Juan Pino. 2020a. fairseq s2t: Fast speech-to-text modeling with fairseq. *arXiv preprint arXiv:2010.05171*.

Changhan Wang, Yun Tang, Xutai Ma, Anne Wu, Dmytro Okhonko, and Juan Pino. 2020b. Fairseq S2T: Fast speech-to-text modeling with fairseq. In *Proceedings of the 1st Conference of the Asia-Pacific Chapter of the Association for Computational Linguistics and the 10th International Joint Conference on Natural Language Processing: System Demonstrations*, pages 33–39, Suzhou, China. Association for Computational Linguistics.

Wei Wang, Ye Tian, Jiquan Ngiam, Yinfei Yang, Isaac Caswell, and Zarana Parekh. 2020c. Learning a multi-domain curriculum for neural machine translation. In *Proceedings of the 58th Annual Meeting of the Association for Computational Linguistics*, pages 7711–7723, Online. Association for Computational Linguistics.

Bin Wei, Zongyao Li, Jiaxin Guo, Daimeng Wei, Zhanglin Wu, Xiaoyu Chen, Zhiqiang Rao, Shaojun Li, Yuanchang Luo, Hengchao Shang, Hao Yang, and Yanfei Jiang. 2024. HW-TSC's Speech to Text Translation System for IWSLT 2024 in Indic track. In *Proceedings of the 21th International Conference on Spoken Language Translation (IWSLT)*.

Patrick Wilken, Panayota Georgakopoulou, and Evgeny Matusov. 2022. SubER - a metric for automatic evaluation of subtitle quality. In *Proceedings of the 19th International Conference on Spoken Language Translation (IWSLT 2022)*, pages 1–10, Dublin, Ireland (in-person and online). Association for Computational Linguistics.

Zhanglin Wu, Jiaxin Guo, Daimeng Wei, Zongyao Li Zhiqiang Rao, Hengchao Shang, Yuanchang Luo, Shaojun Li, and Hao Yang. 2024. Improving the Quality of IWLST 2024 Cascade Offline Speech Translation and Speech-to-Speech Translation via Translation Hypothesis Ensembling with NMT models and Large Language Models. In *Proceedings of the 21th International Conference on Spoken Language Translation (IWSLT)*.

Yuhao Xie, Yuanchang Luo, Zongyao Li, Zhanglin Wu, Xiaoyu Chen, Zhiqiang Rao, Shaojun Li, Hengchao Shang, Jiaxin Guo, Daimeng Wei, and Hao Yang. 2024. HW-TSC's submission to the IWSLT 2024 Subtitling track. In *Proceedings of the 21th International Conference on Spoken Language Translation (IWSLT)*.

Haoran Xu, Philipp Koehn, and Kenton Murray. 2022. The importance of being parameters: An intra-distillation method for serious gains. In *Proceedings of the 2022 Conference on Empirical Methods in Natural Language Processing*, pages 170–183.

Xi Xu, Siqi Ouyang, and Lei Li. 2024. CMU's IWSLT 2024 Simultaneous Speech Translation System. In

Proceedings of the 21th International Conference on Spoken Language Translation (IWSLT).

Brian Yan, Patrick Fernandes, Jinchuan Tian, Siqi Ouyang, William Chen, Karen Livescu, Lei Li, Graham Neubig, and Shinji Watanabe. 2024. CMU's IWSLT 2024 Offline Speech Translation System: A Cascaded Approach For Long-Form Robustness. In *Proceedings of the 21th International Conference on Spoken Language Translation (IWSLT)*.

Zengwei Yao, Liyong Guo, Xiaoyu Yang, Wei Kang, Fangjun Kuang, Yifan Yang, Zengrui Jin, Long Lin, and Daniel Povey. 2023. Zipformer: A faster and better encoder for automatic speech recognition. *CoRR*, abs/2310.11230.

Zhuoyuan Yao, Di Wu, Xiong Wang, Binbin Zhang, Fan Yu, Chao Yang, Zhendong Peng, Xiaoyu Chen, Lei Xie, and Xin Lei. 2021. Wenet: Production oriented streaming and non-streaming end-to-end speech recognition toolkit. *arXiv preprint arXiv:2102.01547*.

Rong Ye, Chengqi Zhao, Tom Ko, Chutong Meng, Tao Wang, Mingxuan Wang, and Jun Cao. 2023. Gigast: A 10,000-hour pseudo speech translation corpus. In *Interspeech 2023*.

Maria Zafar, Antonio Castaldo, Prashanth Nayak, Rejwanul Haque, Neha Gajakos, and Andy Way. 2024. The SETU-DCU Submissions to IWSLT 2024 Low-Resource Speech-to-Text Translation Tasks. In *Proceedings of the 21th International Conference on Spoken Language Translation (IWSLT)*.

ZamStats. 2012. 2010 census of population and housing - national analytical report.

Rodolfo Zevallos, Nuria Bel, Guillermo Cámbara, Mireia Farrús, and Jordi Luque. 2022. Data augmentation for low-resource quechua asr improvement. *arXiv preprint arXiv:2207.06872*.

Yingxin Zhang, Guodong Ma, and Binbin Du. 2024. The NYA's Offline Speech Translation System for IWSLT 2024. In *Proceedings of the 21th International Conference on Spoken Language Translation (IWSLT)*.

Vilém Zouhar, Shuoyang Ding, Anna Currey, Tatyana Badeka, Jenyuan Wang, and Brian Thompson. 2024. Fine-tuned machine translation metrics struggle in unseen domains. In *Proceedings of the 61nd Annual Meeting of the Association for Computational Linguistics*, Bangkok, Thailand. Association for Computational Linguistics.

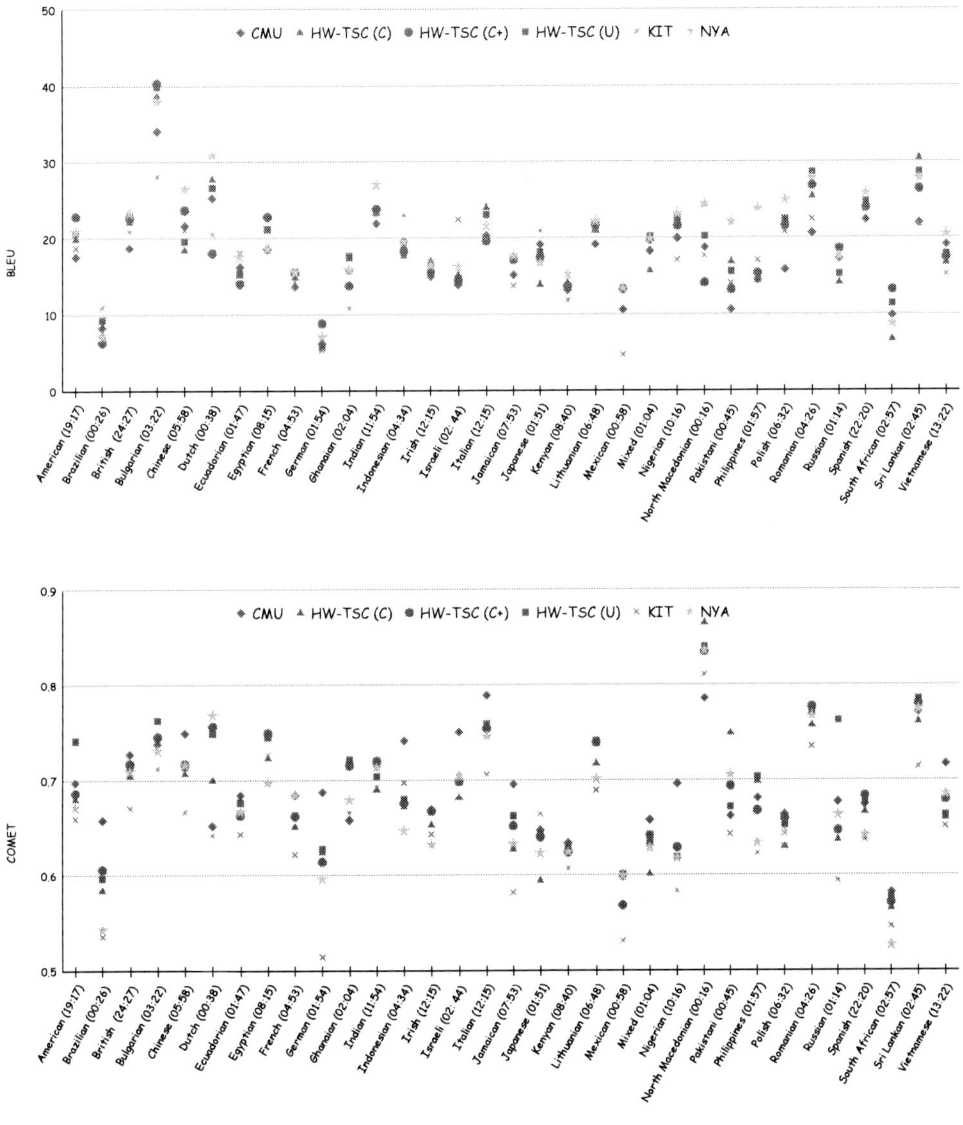

Figure 1: Performance in BLEU (up) and COMET (down) across a wide range of accents. The audio duration for each accent is denoted in a "(minutes:seconds)" format. The macro-average across accents are 18.7 BLEU and 0.679 COMET.

Appendix A. Human Evaluation

A Human Evaluation

Human evaluation included MQM for the English-to-Japanese simultaneous speech translation task (A.1), as well as direct assessment for offline, simultaneous, and subtitling tasks (A.2).

A.1 MQM-based Human Evaluation for the English-to-Japanese Simultaneous Task

For the English-to-Japanese Simultaneous Translation Task, we conducted a human evaluation using a variant of Multidimensional Quality Metrics (MQM; Lommel et al., 2014). MQM has been used in recent MT evaluation studies (Freitag et al., 2021a) and WMT Metrics shared task (Freitag et al., 2021b). For the evaluation of Japanese translations, we used *JTF Translation Quality Evaluation Guidelines* (JTF, 2018), distributed by Japan Translation Federation (JTF). The guidelines are based on MQM but include some modifications in consideration of the property of the Japanese language.

We hired a Japanese-native professional interpreter as the evaluator. The evaluator checked translation hypotheses along with their source speech transcripts and chose the corresponding error category and severity for each translation hypothesis on a spreadsheet. Here, we asked the evaluator to focus only on *Accuracy* and *Fluency* errors, because other types of errors in Terminology, Style, and Locale convention would not be so serious in the evaluation of simultaneous translation. Finally, we calculated the cumulative error score for each system based on the error weighting presented by Freitag et al. (2021a), where *Critical* and *Major* errors have the same level of error scores. The results are shown in Table 17.

A.2 Direct Assessment

For the offline translation track (Section 2), simultaneous translation track (Section 3), and subtitling track (Section 4), we conducted a human evaluation of primary submissions based on a random selection of 1000 segments from each test set. Human graders were asked for direct assessment (DA) (Graham et al., 2013; Cettolo et al., 2017; Akhbardeh et al., 2021), expressed through scores between 0 and 100.

A.2.1 Automatic Segmentation

In the case of offline and subtitling tracks, we collected segment-level annotations based on the resegmentated test data (see Section 2). Because we did not want issues from the segmentation to influence scores negatively, we followed Sperber et al. (2024) and provided translators not only with the source sentence and system translation, but also with the system translation of the previous and following segments. Annotators were then instructed as follows: *"Sentence boundary errors are expected and should not be factored in when judging translation quality. This is when the translation appears to be missing or adding extra words but the source was segmented at a different place. To this end, we have included the translations for the previous and next sentences also. If the source and translation are only different because of sentence boundary issues, do not let this affect your scoring judgement. Example for a clear case for a good translation suffering only from sentence boundary issues that should not result in a poor score:*
*Source: *you'll see that there's actually* a sign near the road.*
Translation: ein Schild neben der Straße gibt.

Team	BLEU (on three talks)	Error score	# Errors		
			Critical	Major	Minor
NAIST	17.2	27.4	0	3	16
HW-TSC	20.6	50.2	0	8	12
FBK	11.4	130.5	1	21	25

Table 17: Human evaluation results on two talks (107 lines) in the English-to-Japanese Simultaneous speech-to-text translation task. Error weights are 5 for Critical and Major errors and 1 for Minor errors.

*Previous sentence: Ich bin mir sicher, dass Sie nicht wissen, dass, wenn Sie weiter weitergehen, *Sie sehen – (Gelächter) – dass es tatsächlich**
Next sentence: ...."
No video or audio context was provided. Segments were shuffled and randomly assigned to annotators to avoid bias related to the presentation order. Annotation was conducted by professional translators fluent in the source language and native in the target language.

A.2.2 Subtitling Constraints

The subtitling task (Section 4) includes cases where systems compress translations in order to match subtitling constraints, e.g. filtering out non-relevant information present in the source. This is desired in subtitling and should therefore not be penalized in human evaluation. To this end, we provided annotators with the following instructions: *"When judging the translations, please consider that these are subtitles which are compressed translations of the original speech, not the translations of the subtitles in the source language. Thus, there may be significant differences in how the source and the target sentences are formulated. Subtitles are created independently for each language with the goal of good readability during the short time period when they are displayed on screen. Readability in terms of number of characters per second may differ between the source (English) and target (German). Please take this into account. The translation should convey the same meaning as the source sentence but may omit information that is not very important for getting the main message of the sentence across. It is OK if the sentence is shortened this way in order to fulfil the readability constraints."*

A.2.3 Computing rankings

System rankings are produced from the average DA scores computed from the average human assessment scores according to each individual annotator's mean and standard deviation, similarly to Akhbardeh et al. (2021). Ranks are established according to Wilcoxon rank-sum statistical significance test with $p < 0.05$. The below tables show the DA scores and rankings. Note that the guidelines are different for offline, simultaneous, and subtitling tasks. This makes results not directly comparable across tasks, and we consequently only present within-task rankings here. Within each of the tasks (only the offline and subtitling English-to-German have more domains), all the outputs were assessed in one annotation run, distributing the scoring items randomly to annotators across domains, with all annotators most likely seeing all the domains. This allows us to treat the DA scores across domains in a given task as comparable, so we present them in the same table.

Table 18: Offline task, **English to German**

	All		TED		ITV		Accent		Peloton	
System	Rank	DA	Rank	DA	Rank	DA	Rank	DA	Rank	DA
HWTSC-LLM	1	84.8	1-2	94.9	1-2	84.7	1-4	76.1	1-4	82.6
HWTSC	2-3	84.2	3-5	92.8	1-3	84.0	1-4	76.8	1-4	81.6
CMU	2-4	83.3	3-5	92.5	2-3	83.1	1-4	75.4	1-4	81.2
NYA	3-4	81.0	1-2	94.7	4	73.9	1-4	77.9	1-4	80.2
KIT	5	76.7	3-5	91.8	5	69.3	5	72.8	5	74.6

Table 19: Offline task, **English to Japanese**

System	TED Rank	TED DA
HWTSC	1-3	75.4
HWTSC-LLM	1-2	74.7
NYA	2-4	72.8
CMU	3-4	72.9

Table 20: Offline task, **English to Chinese**

System	TED Rank	TED DA
HWTSC-LLM	1	78.9
NYA	2-3	77.2
HWTSC	2-4	76.5
CMU	3-4	75.8

Table 21: Simultaneous task, English to German

System	TED Rank	TED DA
CMU	1	87.3
HWTSC	2	86.0
FBK	3-4	84.2
NAIST	3-4	83.4

Table 22: Simultaneous task, English to Japanese

System	TED Rank	TED DA
NAIST	1	77.4
HWTSC	2	75.4
FBK	3	71.7

Table 23: Simultaneous task, English to Chinese

System	TED Rank	TED DA
HWTSC	1-2	80.0
NAIST	1-2	79.2
FBK	3	76.1

Table 24: Subtitling task, English to German. *All* combines the ITV and Peloton DA scores

System	All		ITV		Peloton	
	Rank	DA	Rank	DA	Rank	DA
HWTSC	1	72.2	1	73.0	1-2	71.3
AppTek	2-3	68.2	2	69.3	3	67.3
FBK-cascade	2-3	66.3	3	62.2	1-2	71.5
FBK-direct	4	52.8	4	46.5	4	61.2

Appendix B. Automatic Evaluation Results and Details

B.1 Offline SLT

- Systems are ordered according to the COMET score (denoted by COMET, the third column).
- The "Joint" column is computed by averaging the scores of the 4 test sets, aka macro-averaging.
- The "D" column indicates the data condition in which each submitted run was trained, namely: Constrained (C), Constrained^{+LLM} (C$^+$), Unconstrained (U).
- All systems are based on cascade architecture.

System	D	Joint		TED 2024		ITV		Peloton		Accent	
		COMET	BLEU	COMET	BLEU	COMET	BLEU	COMET	BLEU	COMET	BLEU
CMU	U	0.743	18.3	0.862	25.7	0.735	17.3	0.670	11.5	0.705	18.5
HW-TSC	C$^+$	0.731	19.3	0.851	27.4	0.728	17.2	0.652	11.9	0.691	20.7
HW-TSC	U	0.727	19.1	0.849	27.1	0.723	17.3	0.646	11.0	0.690	20.8
HW-TSC	C	0.717	18.5	0.841	26.6	0.712	16.7	0.637	10.4	0.678	20.2
NYA	U	0.695	19.5	0.837	28.1	0.648	15.8	0.616	12.2	0.677	21.7
KIT	C$^+$	0.677	17.5	0.832	27.5	0.618	13.2	0.600	10.2	0.656	19.1

Table 25: Official results of the automatic evaluation for the Offline Speech Translation Task, **English to German**.

System	D	TED 2023		EMPAC		ACL	
		COMET	BLEU	COMET	BLEU	COMET	BLEU
CMU	U	0.858	27.2	0.820	16.2	0.837	31.5
HW-TSC	U	0.849	32.6	0.799	17.4	0.823	38.3
HW-TSC	C$^+$	0.844	29.0	0.802	18.4	0.825	38.2
HW-TSC	C	0.843	32.8	0.792	17.1	0.808	37.0
NYA	U	0.837	29.8	0.756	17.2	0.826	45.5
KIT	C$^+$	0.831	28.7	0.723	15.2	0.781	35.1
Best 2023		0.821	30.2	0.382	16.9	0.801	41.1

Table 26: Official results of the automatic evaluation for the Offline Speech Translation Task on progress test sets, **English to German**.

System	D	TED 2024		TED 2023		ACL	
		COMET	BLEU	COMET	BLEU	COMET	BLEU
HW-TSC	U	0.853	23.6	0.856	23.1	0.868	31.8
HW-TSC	C$^+$	0.851	23.1	0.856	22.2	0.839	32.5
CMU	U	0.841	18.3	0.850	17.9	0.849	19.1
HW-TSC	C	0.839	23.9	0.831	24.3	0.839	28.0
NYA	U	0.812	20.1	0.822	21.0	0.861	39.9

Table 27: Official results of the automatic evaluation for the Offline Speech Translation Task on official test set and progress test sets, **English to Japanese**.

System	D	TED 2024		TED 2023		ACL	
		COMET	BLEU	COMET	BLEU	COMET	BLEU
HW-TSC	U	0.845	37.0	0.834	36.3	0.857	50.8
HW-TSC	C^+	0.842	36.2	0.831	35.8	0.855	49.8
CMU	U	0.834	31.5	0.827	30.6	0.853	43.1
HW-TSC	C	0.824	38.3	0.810	37.3	0.833	52.4
NYA	U	0.823	40.4	0.814	39.1	0.855	59.1

Table 28: Official results of the automatic evaluation for the Offline Speech Translation Task on official test set and progress test sets, **English to Chinese**.

Translation Guidelines

In this task, we aim to obtain high quality German translations of the English transcripts. The transcripts (inside the "transcripts.txt" file) contain conversations between friends talking about a daily topic, e.g. hobbies and vacation. There are **76** conversations (recordings) in total. In each conversation, there are only two speakers, but the same pair of speakers may appear in another set(s) of conversations, see the list below. **The content of each recording is independent of each other, so they could be translated independently**. For each source sentence (line) to be translated, we provide metadata, such as the recording id, speaker id, the audio file and the utterance number. The utterance number indicates its order in the conversation. It begins from 0 (which is not included in the transcripts required for translation) and stands for the beginning of the conversation. In general, most recordings start from an utterance number of 15.

The general translation guidelines are:

- All translations should be **"from scratch", without post-editing from Machine Translation.** We can detect post editing so will reject translations that are post-edited.
- Translators should **preserve the line structure of the source file**. By this we mean that they should not add or remove line-breaks , and each line is English should correspond to a line of German. Note that each line of the source file corresponds to one audio file.
- We need the **translations to be returned in the same format**. If you prefer to receive the text in a different format, then please let us know as we may be able to accommodate it.
- Translators should **avoid inserting parenthetical explanations** into the translated text and obviously **avoid losing any pieces of information from the source text**. We will check a sample of the translations for quality, and we will check the entire set for evidence of post-editing.

Since it is a conversation between friends, please pay attention to the below:

- You might need to use the context before and/or after the utterance to translate.
- **[Important]** There are disfluencies in the transcripts, including but not limited to, hesitation, repetitions, and correction. **We expect to have fluent and faithful translations. These disfluencies in the transcripts might be helpful for your translation, but they are not required as long as the meaning is clear. Please avoid word-by-word translation of them.**
    a. In general, please focus on the core meaning in the translation. You might rephrase or remove the redundant parts in the transcripts if necessary, e.g., repetitions.
    b. For Hesitation, some examples are below, please do **NOT** include them in the translation. We keep them on the transcripts as it might help signal a "pause" in the utterance.

Examples of disfluencies:

- Hesitation:
    a. List of possible tokens: {"ACH", "AH", "EEE", "EH", "ER", "EW", "HA", "HEE","HM", "HUH", "MM", "OOF", "UH", "UM", "HMM"}
    b. Example: "YEAH I KNOW ~~UM~~ WAIT WHAT WAS I GONNA SAY ~~UM~~ SO DO YOU WANNA ASK THE QUESTION NOW"?
- Repetitions:

a. "WELL ACTUALLY ARE THEY LIKE ALL THESE ~~ALL THESE ALL THESE~~ DUMPLINGS OF EASTERN EUROPEAN ORIGIN"

A note on the recording_id

There are 76 conversations / recordings in total, but the same pair of speakers may show up in another conversation(s) (122 speakers in total). In spite of the same pair of speakers, the contents in each of these conversations are also independent of each other. These conversations have their id extended by "_PX" where "X" is a number. Below is the list of recodings that have "_PX" in their names:

- EDACC-C23_P1, EDACC-C23_P2
- EDACC-C32_P1, EDACC-C32_P2
- EDACC-C33_P1
- EDACC-C40_P1, EDACC-C40_P2, EDACC-C40_P3
- EDACC-C43_P1
- EDACC-C46_P1, EDACC-C46_P2
- EDACC-C05_P0, EDACC-C05_P1
- EDACC-C29_P1, EDACC-C29_P2
- EDACC-C31_P1, EDACC-C31_P2
- EDACC-C38_P1, EDACC-C38_P2
- EDACC-C35_P1, EDACC-C35_P2, EDACC-C35_P3
- EDACC-C36_P1, EDACC-C36_P2
- EDACC-C37_P1, EDACC-C37_P2
- EDACC-C47_P1, EDACC-C47_P2
- EDACC-C57_P1, EDACC-C57_P2

B.2 Simultaneous SLT

Team	BLEU	LAAL	AL	AP	DAL	ATD
HW-TSC	26.39	2.17 (4.19)	1.92 (4.07)	0.919 (1.66)	3.10 (7.37)	2.18 (5.31)
CMU	24.65	2.21 (3.57)	2.01(3.45)	0.87 (1.24)	3.04 (4.73)	2.22 (3.22)
NAIST	23.37	2.30 (3.33)	2.05 (3.17)	0.91 (1.22)	3.03 (4.53)	2.23 (3.12)
FBK	21.18	2.00 (3.03)	1.71 (2.84)	0.92 (1.24)	2.52 (3.77)	2.02 (2.49)

Table 29: Simultaneous Speech-to-Text Translation, English to German. Except for AP, the latency is measured in seconds. Numbers in brackets are computation aware latency.

Team	BLEU	LAAL	AL	AP	DAL	ATD
HW-TSC	34.23	2.10 (3.93)	2.00 (3.89)	0.78 (1.42)	3.05 (7.45)	0.94 (4.24)
NAIST	29.33	2.36 (3.19)	2.24 (3.11)	0.79 (1.06)	3.01 (4.51)	1.04 (1.81)
FBK	25.20	2.73 (4.43)	2.61 (4.16)	0.84 (1.17)	3.61 (5.44)	1.09 (2.42)

Table 30: Simultaneous Speech-to-Text Translation, English to Chinese. Except for AP, the latency is measured in seconds. Numbers in brackets are computation aware latency.

Team	BLEU	LAAL	AL	AP	DAL	ATD
HW-TSC	19.394	2.44 (4.10)	2.39 (4.01)	0.77 (1.28)	3.35 (7.03)	0.74 (3.44)
NAIST	17.954	2.39 (3.41)	2.31 (3.37)	0.79 (1.14)	3.08 (5.21)	0.56 (1.68)
FBK	12.136	2.15 (3.74)	2.07 (3.70)	0.72 (1.18)	2.85 (5.53)	0.59 (2.25)

Table 31: Simultaneous Speech-to-Text Translation, English to Japanese. Except for AP, the latency is measured in seconds. Numbers in brackets are computation aware latency.

Team	BLEU	LAAL	AL	AP	DAL	ATD
BENCH-2	29.93	2.28	1.95	0.78	3.03	2.75
BENCH-1	29.43	2.35	2.02	0.82	3.13	2.78
FBK	29.20	2.55 (3.92)	2.14 (3.65)	0.93 (1.24)	3.20 (4.67)	2.75 (3.29)
HW-TSC	27.11	2.00 (5.11)	1.53 (4.86)	0.89 (2.28)	3.27 (11.03)	2.63 (8.38)
BENCH-0	26.85	3.34	3.09	0.75	3.99	3.39

Table 32: Simultaneous Speech-to-Text Translation, Czech to English. Except for AP, the latency is measured in seconds. Numbers in brackets are computationally-aware latency. BENCH-N represents ORGANIZER'S BENCHMARK, with N indicating the number of previously translated segments used as a Whisper prompt to provide the model with the context.

Target Language	Team	ASR BLEU	Start Offset	End Offset	ATD
English to German	HW-TSC	23.33	2.00	4.30	3.22
English to Japanese	HW-TSC	17.37	2.36	3.41	3.31
	NAIST	14.35	2.39	4.20	4.18
English to Chinese	HW-TSC	28.97	2.04	2.99	3.11
Czech to English	HW-TSC	25.93	1.58	3.52	3.67

Table 33: Simultaneous Speech-to-Speech from English Speech. The latency is measured in seconds. The BLEU scores are computed based on transcript from the default Whisper (Radford et al., 2023) ASR model (large) for each language direction.

B.3 Automatic Subtitling

Team	Condition	System	Domain	Subtitle quality SubER	Translation quality Bleu	Translation quality ChrF	Translation quality Bleurt	Subtitle compliance CPS	Subtitle compliance CPL	Subtitle compliance LPB
APPTEK	U	cntrstv2	ALL	70.34	17.45	41.77	.4746	73.25	100.00	98.78
			ted	60.55	24.70	53.00	.5823	86.89	100.00	97.27
			itv	72.19	16.47	39.12	.4575	65.46	100.00	99.18
			pltn	77.68	10.22	32.38	.3910	83.70	100.00	99.14
APPTEK	U	prmry	ALL	71.01	17.54	42.82	.4842	73.94	100.00	99.78
			ted	63.03	23.35	54.03	.5904	79.67	100.00	99.33
			itv	72.38	16.98	40.42	.4683	69.23	100.00	99.92
			pltn	77.45	10.17	32.46	.3981	83.03	100.00	99.80
APPTEK	U	cntrstv1	ALL	71.52	17.48	43.28	.4874	67.18	100.00	96.73
			ted	63.97	23.13	55.09	.6024	73.91	100.00	91.81
			itv	72.79	16.88	40.62	.4689	61.24	100.00	97.88
			pltn	77.64	10.26	32.70	.3987	79.17	100.00	98.40
FBK-AI4C$_{DIR}$	C	prmry	ALL	73.99	13.48	36.12	.3775	76.19	88.86	99.99
			ted	57.50	25.79	54.78	.6114	83.10	83.69	100.00
			itv	78.90	9.67	28.43	.2911	70.45	90.04	99.97
			pltn	80.68	7.71	30.45	.3542	82.16	92.77	100.00
HW-TSC	U	cntrstv2	ALL	74.44	16.70	41.78	.5008	86.40	60.18	100.00
			ted	69.44	22.40	50.60	.5513	93.98	37.83	100.00
			itv	74.72	16.08	40.18	.5031	82.84	65.55	100.00
			pltn	80.26	11.11	32.89	.4284	90.62	66.12	100.00
FBK-AI4C$_{CSC}$	U	prmry	ALL	75.56	16.23	40.10	.4503	64.64	91.79	100.00
			ted	63.26	22.94	53.70	.5872	79.99	89.52	100.00
			itv	79.92	14.86	35.16	.4048	54.20	91.12	100.00
			pltn	78.34	11.30	34.13	.4202	76.52	96.99	100.00
HW-TSC	U	prmry	ALL	75.60	16.62	42.64	.5066	67.92	57.34	100.00
			ted	70.27	22.09	50.97	.5556	80.09	36.44	100.00
			itv	76.04	16.09	41.34	.5098	61.72	61.80	100.00
			pltn	81.35	11.13	33.56	.4332	76.40	64.93	100.00
HW-TSC	U	cntrstv1	ALL	77.11	16.52	43.00	.5148	28.67	62.64	100.00
			ted	70.48	22.06	51.00	.5559	46.25	36.66	100.00
			itv	78.04	16.07	41.80	.5194	19.80	66.38	100.00
			pltn	83.09	10.93	34.25	.4467	40.61	74.57	100.00

Table 34: Subtitling Task: automatic evaluation scores on tst2024 en→de. *C* and *U* stand for *constrained* and *unconstrained* training condition, respectively; *prmry* and *cntrstv* for *primary* and *contrastive* systems. Ranking based on SubER scores on ALL domains.

Team	Condition	System	Domain	Subtitle quality SubER	Translation quality Bleu	ChrF	Bleurt	Subtitle compliance CPS	CPL	LPB
AppTek	U	prmry	ALL	62.02	25.59	49.75	.5268	82.42	100.00	99.94
			ted	45.73	39.29	63.86	.6995	88.05	100.00	99.76
			itv	66.80	21.37	44.35	.4761	79.18	100.00	99.98
			pltn	73.55	15.45	41.43	.4728	86.83	100.00	100.00
FBK-AI4C$_{CSC}$	U	prmry	ALL	63.01	26.60	49.64	.5174	69.97	93.28	100.00
			ted	40.75	45.69	69.20	.7500	83.42	90.31	100.00
			itv	70.82	18.92	40.17	.4262	60.85	93.46	100.00
			pltn	74.17	16.18	44.42	.5108	80.24	97.03	100.00
AppTek	U	cntrstv1	ALL	63.65	24.33	48.63	.5152	75.98	100.00	98.52
			ted	47.71	37.61	62.68	.6892	85.50	100.00	96.60
			itv	67.85	20.37	43.44	.4668	70.82	100.00	98.98
			pltn	76.72	13.70	39.75	.4533	82.37	100.00	99.14
HW-TSC	U	cntrstv2	ALL	63.77	26.92	50.09	.5453	91.43	62.67	100.00
			ted	49.64	42.35	64.55	.6859	94.97	38.82	100.00
			itv	67.57	21.39	43.94	.5045	90.09	69.19	100.00
			pltn	75.08	16.79	43.95	.4999	92.26	66.20	100.00
HW-TSC	U	prmry	ALL	64.18	27.38	51.50	.5554	74.80	60.42	100.00
			ted	48.93	44.20	66.12	.6953	81.48	37.43	100.00
			itv	68.42	22.10	45.46	.5159	71.28	66.28	100.00
			pltn	75.83	16.97	44.84	.5071	79.90	65.38	100.00
HW-TSC	U	cntrstv1	ALL	64.87	27.25	51.58	.5583	33.42	66.14	100.00
			ted	49.02	44.18	66.11	.6951	47.70	38.24	100.00
			itv	69.50	22.01	45.56	.5183	25.92	71.22	100.00
			pltn	76.17	16.84	45.07	.5150	44.09	75.58	100.00
AppTek	U	cntrstv2	ALL	66.25	22.25	47.74	.4985	73.47	100.00	98.61
			ted	46.82	38.63	64.18	.6853	84.53	100.00	96.48
			itv	72.12	17.40	41.15	.4440	66.82	100.00	99.10
			pltn	79.46	12.60	39.25	.4391	83.03	100.00	99.33
FBK-AI4C$_{DIR}$	C	prmry	ALL	67.13	22.03	44.69	.4277	76.00	90.35	100.00
			ted	39.86	45.63	69.63	.7441	82.43	86.59	100.00
			itv	77.00	11.91	31.95	.2986	70.61	92.60	100.00
			pltn	79.70	11.88	40.05	.4329	82.26	89.58	100.00

Table 35: Subtitling Task: automatic evaluation scores on tst2024 en→es. *C* and *U* stand for *constrained* and *unconstrained* training condition, respectively; *prmry* and *cntrstv* for *primary* and *contrastive* systems. Ranking based on SubER scores on ALL domains.

id	Team	System	de Bleurt	de CPS	es Bleurt	es CPS
0	subtitles to compress		.1946	60.25	.2136	69.97
1	baseline		.1720	100.00	.1892	100.00
2	FBK	primary	.1895	84.81	.2063	90.66
3	FBK	contrastive 1	.1890	67.94	.2113	75.74
4	FBK	contrastive 2	.1811	83.36	.2033	87.48
5	HW-TSC	primary	.1956	84.35	.2101	91.42
6	HW-TSC	contrastive 1	.1967	79.97	.2126	87.56
7	HW-TSC	contrastive 2	.2002	84.38	.2102	91.44
8	RACAI	primary	not submitted		.1946	94.29

Table 36: Compression Task: automatic evaluation scores on German and Spanish subtitles.

Team	Con-di-tion	System	Domain	Subtitle quality SubER	Translation quality Bleu	ChrF	Bleurt	Subtitle compliance CPS	CPL	LPB
AppTek	U	cntrstv2	ALL	70.05	16.51	40.51	.4730	70.46	100.00	98.87
			ted	60.38	23.58	50.67	.5808	82.29	100.00	97.50
			itv	69.09	16.97	39.90	.4718	65.00	100.00	99.03
			pltn	78.02	9.96	34.41	.4217	75.58	100.00	99.22
AppTek	U	prmry	ALL	70.29	17.24	41.77	.4813	72.13	100.00	99.84
			ted	61.46	24.22	52.85	.6012	77.30	100.00	99.45
			itv	69.21	17.97	41.27	.4790	67.64	100.00	99.96
			pltn	77.99	10.46	34.67	.4262	78.62	100.00	99.80
AppTek	U	cntrstv1	ALL	70.88	17.16	42.08	.4846	65.08	100.00	97.13
			ted	62.59	24.08	53.51	.6097	70.12	100.00	92.51
			itv	69.70	18.04	41.56	.4818	59.96	100.00	97.91
			pltn	78.45	10.29	34.76	.4276	72.92	100.00	97.85
HW-TSC	U	cntrstv2	ALL	72.37	17.69	41.75	.5064	85.10	58.39	100.00
			ted	62.79	26.33	52.40	.5916	93.56	32.02	100.00
			itv	71.35	18.10	41.39	.5139	82.01	65.86	100.00
			pltn	80.40	10.86	34.74	.4508	88.04	54.55	100.00
HW-TSC	U	prmry	ALL	73.10	17.92	43.00	.5156	65.44	55.51	100.00
			ted	62.90	26.79	53.56	.6013	78.54	30.30	100.00
			itv	72.16	18.35	42.95	.5244	60.15	62.37	100.00
			pltn	81.38	10.91	35.46	.4577	71.22	52.55	100.00
FBK-AI4C$_{CSC}$	U	prmry	ALL	73.78	16.46	39.07	.4454	61.44	93.04	100.00
			ted	62.86	22.44	51.88	.5910	76.28	90.67	100.00
			itv	74.91	16.19	35.91	.3996	54.70	92.97	100.00
			pltn	78.38	10.59	36.09	.4550	65.10	94.66	100.00
FBK-AI4C$_{DIR}$	C	prmry	ALL	74.26	13.08	34.77	.3742	72.75	89.35	99.96
			ted	59.06	24.41	52.05	.5996	79.52	83.97	99.94
			itv	77.15	10.40	29.13	.2939	68.73	91.00	99.97
			pltn	78.03	9.41	33.39	.4059	74.84	90.14	99.96
HW-TSC	U	cntrstv1	ALL	74.34	17.80	43.57	.5279	27.53	61.69	100.00
			ted	63.21	26.61	54.29	.6148	41.37	36.08	100.00
			itv	74.12	18.23	43.42	.5335	18.37	67.29	100.00
			pltn	81.77	10.85	36.12	.4751	41.44	61.99	100.00
Submissions 2023 (here ALL={ted,itv,pltn}, while last year *eptv* was considered as well):										
AppTek	U	prmry	ALL	70.23	15.10	37.39	.4291	87.87	100.00	100.00
MateSub	U	prmry	ALL	74.00	14.92	38.92	.4579	84.47	99.26	100.00
AppTek	C	prmry	ALL	77.14	12.40	33.17	.3300	93.01	100.00	100.00
FBK	C	prmry	ALL	79.70	10.77	31.99	.3016	69.23	83.72	99.99
AppTek	C	cntrstv	ALL	83.75	9.33	29.28	.2790	88.90	100.00	100.00

Table 37: Subtitling Task: automatic evaluation scores on tst2023 en→de. *C* and *U* stand for *constrained* and *unconstrained* training condition, respectively; *prmry* and *cntrstv* for *primary* and *contrastive* systems. Ranking based on SubER scores on ALL domains.

Team	Condition	System	Domain	Subtitle quality SubER	Translation quality Bleu	ChrF	Bleurt	Subtitle compliance CPS	CPL	LPB
AppTek	U	prmry	ALL	63.97	23.25	47.46	.5121	80.98	100.00	99.98
			ted	46.75	36.33	61.47	.6889	88.92	100.00	99.84
			itv	66.39	22.17	45.42	.4881	77.61	100.00	100.00
			pltn	71.61	15.47	40.75	.4646	83.82	100.00	100.00
HW-TSC	U	cntrstv2	ALL	64.72	25.00	49.02	.5480	90.78	62.45	100.00
			ted	44.98	43.71	66.71	.7240	94.76	33.30	100.00
			itv	67.35	22.17	45.13	.5213	89.53	71.44	100.00
			pltn	73.73	17.20	43.05	.5059	91.66	56.41	100.00
AppTek	U	cntrstv1	ALL	65.37	22.27	46.61	.5007	74.41	100.00	98.91
			ted	48.98	34.49	60.17	.6758	85.26	100.00	97.19
			itv	67.29	21.55	44.82	.4784	69.77	100.00	99.17
			pltn	73.36	14.37	39.76	.4510	78.35	100.00	99.26
HW-TSC	U	prmry	ALL	65.41	25.29	50.38	.5579	72.10	59.42	100.00
			ted	44.50	44.83	68.02	.7326	82.83	31.93	100.00
			itv	68.20	22.60	46.72	.5319	68.95	67.58	100.00
			pltn	74.95	17.21	44.07	.5152	73.94	54.50	100.00
HW-TSC	U	cntrstv1	ALL	65.97	25.21	50.49	.5612	33.25	66.05	100.00
			ted	44.45	44.63	68.08	.7353	48.76	38.26	100.00
			itv	69.27	22.56	46.84	.5338	25.02	72.91	100.00
			pltn	74.95	17.19	44.22	.5213	44.16	64.58	100.00
FBK-AI4C$_{CSC}$	U	prmry	ALL	66.02	23.87	46.53	.4811	67.56	94.25	100.00
			ted	40.81	43.11	68.20	.7408	81.79	92.20	100.00
			itv	71.62	19.18	39.70	.4019	62.11	94.22	100.00
			pltn	73.16	16.19	42.78	.4921	69.30	95.60	100.00
AppTek	U	cntrstv2	ALL	68.69	19.83	45.46	.4817	71.43	100.00	99.00
			ted	48.14	35.78	62.51	.6681	82.76	100.00	97.74
			itv	71.58	17.85	42.21	.4572	66.60	100.00	99.25
			pltn	77.76	12.62	38.75	.4301	75.54	100.00	99.14
FBK-AI4C$_{DIR}$	C	prmry	ALL	70.09	19.16	41.58	.3972	73.08	91.64	99.97
			ted	40.45	42.09	67.76	.7224	82.59	89.77	99.93
			itv	78.20	12.09	31.50	.2827	70.11	92.89	100.00
			pltn	75.52	13.20	40.33	.4389	72.01	90.84	99.96
Submissions 2023 (here ALL={ted,itv,pltn}, while last year *eptv* was considered as well):										
MateSub	U	prmry	ALL	67.29	22.54	46.40	.4993	85.51	99.53	100.00
AppTek	C	prmry	ALL	72.33	17.72	38.49	.3467	95.30	100.00	100.00
FBK	C	prmry	ALL	73.93	16.70	37.68	.3217	76.57	91.84	99.99

Table 38: Subtitling Task: automatic evaluation scores on tst2023 en→es. *C* and *U* stand for *constrained* and *unconstrained* training condition, respectively; *prmry* and *cntrstv* for *primary* and *contrastive* systems. Ranking based on SubER scores on ALL domains.

B.4 Speech-to-Speech Translation

System Ref	D	Test BLEU	 chrF	 COMET
Cascade Systems				
HW-TSC	U	33.6	29.4	74.79
	C+	31.8	28.1	74.41
	C	31.4	28.5	73.65

Table 39: Official results of the **automatic evaluation** for the English to Chinese Speech-to-Speech Translation Task. The "D" column indicates the data condition in which each submitted run was trained, namely: Constrained (C), Constrained^{+LLM} (C^{+}), Unconstrained (U).

B.5 Low-Resource SLT

North Levantine Arabic→English (Unconstrained Condition)

Team	System	BLEU↓	chrF2	COMET
ALADAN	primary	28.71	52.25	0.7763
ALADAN	contrastive1	28.50	52.12	0.7706
ALADAN	contrastive2	22.12	46.38	0.7296
KIT	primary	20.86	44.54	0.7013
KIT	contrastive1	19.73	45.43	0.7098
JHU	primary	15.95	38.89	0.6951
JHU	contrastive1	14.74	37.27	0.6775
HW-TSC	primary	13.64	33.31	0.5877
KIT	contrastive2	11.87	34.76	0.6064
UM	contrastive1	5.09	24.50	0.5378
UM	primary	4.74	24.10	0.5369
UM	contrastive2	3.53	21.56	0.5196

Table 40: Automatic evaluation results for the North Levantine Arabic to English task, unconstrained Condition. A lowercase, no punctuation variant of chrF2 is reported. The `Unbabel/wmt22-comet-da` model was used for COMET computation, with the source side (Arabic transcript) unmodified and the target side lowercased and with removed punctuation.

Bemba→English (Unconstrained Condition)

Team	System	BLEU
JHU	primary	32.6
KIT	primary	28.8
KIT	contrastive2	28.1
JHU	contrastive1	27.0
KIT	contrastive1	27.0
JHU	contrastive2	26.7

Team	System	WER
KIT ASR	primary	33.2
JHU ASR	primary	35.7

Table 41: Automatic evaluation results for the Bemba to English task, unconstrained Condition.

Bhojpuri→Hindi (Unconstrained Condition)

Team	System	BLEU	chrF2
JHU	primary	24.4	49.5
JHU	contrastive1	23.9	48.7
JHU	contrastive2	12.2	39.1
BITSP	primary	12.9	41.1
DFKI_MLT	primary	0.1	6.1

Table 42: Automatic evaluation results for the Bhojpuri to Hindi task, unconstrained Condition.

Irish→English (Unconstrained Condition)

Team	System	BLEU	chrF2
JHU	contrastive1	16.0	39.0
JHU	primary	15.3	38.3
Ymoslem	primary	7.6	27.6
Ymoslem	contrastive1	7.4	26.5
Ymoslem	contrastive2	5.1	24.7
SETU-DCU	primary	0.6	15.4

Table 43: Automatic evaluation results for the Irish to English task, unconstrained Condition.

Maltese→English (Unconstrained Condition)

Team	System	BLEU	chrF2
KIT	primary	58.9	76.5
SETU-DCU	primary	56.7	81.9
KIT	contrastive2	56.2	75.0
KIT	contrastive1	55.2	74.4
SETU-DCU	contrastive1	52.6	72.1
UoM	primary	52.4	72.3
UoM	contrastive1	52.4	72.3
UoM	contrastive2	52.3	72.1
SETU-DCU	contrastive2	44.7	65.5
JHU	primary	41.4	68.6
JHU	contrastive1	36.5	64.2
UoM-DFKI	primary (e2e)	35.1	59.0
JHU	contrastive2	24.8	55.8
UoM-DFKI	contrastive1 (e2e)	18.5	42.0

Table 44: Automatic evaluation results for the Maltese to English task, Unconstrained Condition. e2e denotes end-to-end system.

Maltese→English (Constrained Condition)

Team	System	BLEU	chrF2
UoM	primary	0.5	15.6

Table 45: Automatic evaluation results for the Maltese to English task, Constrained Condition.

Marathi→Hindi (Unconstrained Condition)

Team	System	BLEU	chrF2
IITM	primary	47.2	70.1
JHU	primary	37.7	62.7
JHU	contrastive1	37.3	62.4
JHU	contrastive2	28.5	55.0
BITSP	contrastive1	25.0	50.1
BITSP	primary	21.3	48.1
BITSP	contrastive2	19.0	44.8

Team	System	WER	CER
IITm ASR	primary	22.8	7.3
JHU ASR	primary	26.7	8.9
BITSP ASR	contrastive1	62.9	17.5
BITSP ASR	primary	69.3	21.2
BITSP ASR	contrastive2	69.3	21.2

Table 46: Automatic evaluation results for the Marathi to Hindi task, Unconstrained Condition.

Quechua→Spanish (Constrained Condition)

Team	System	BLEU	chrF2
QUESPA	contrastive2	1.3	30.9
QUESPA	contrastive1	1.4	30.3
QUESPA	primary	2.0	30.0

Table 47: Automatic evaluation results for the Quechua to Spanish task, Constrained Condition. ChrF2 scores were only taken into account for those systems that scored less than 5 points BLEU.

Quechua→Spanish (Unconstrained Condition)

Team	System	BLEU	chrF2
QUESPA	contrastive1	19.7	43.1
QUESPA	primary	16.0	52.2
JHU	primary	12.5	49.7
QUESPA	contrastive2	11.1	44.6
JHU	contrastive1	6.4	39.5
JHU	contrastive2	0.9	13.0

Table 48: Automatic evaluation results for the Quechua to Spanish task, Unconstrained Condition.

Tamasheq→French (Unconstrained Condition)

Team	System	BLEU
Organizer Baseline	primary	8.83
JHU	primary	6.07
JHU	contrastive	0.50

Table 49: Automatic evaluation results for the Tamasheq to French task, Unconstrained Condition.

Pause-Aware Automatic Dubbing using LLM and Voice Cloning

Yuang Li, Jiaxin Guo, Min Zhang, Miaomiao Ma, Zhiqiang Rao
Weidong Zhang, Xianghui He, Daimeng Wei, Hao Yang
Huawei Translation Services Center, China
{liyuang3, guojiaxin1, zhangmin186, mamiaomiao, raozhiqiang, zhangweidong17, hexianghui, weidaimeng, yanghao30}@huawei.com

Abstract

Automatic dubbing aims to translate the speech of a video into another language, ensuring the new speech naturally fits the original video. This paper details Huawei Translation Services Center's (HW-TSC) submission for IWSLT 2024's automatic dubbing task, under an unconstrained setting. Our system's machine translation (MT) component utilizes a Transformer-based MT model and an LLM-based post-editor to produce translations of varying lengths. The text-to-speech (TTS) component employs a VITS-based TTS model and a voice cloning module to emulate the original speaker's vocal timbre. For enhanced dubbing synchrony, we introduce a parsing-informed pause selector. Finally, we rerank multiple results based on lip-sync error distance (LSE-D) and character error rate (CER). Our system achieves LSE-D of 10.75 and 12.19 on subset1 and subset2 of DE-EN test sets respectively, superior to last year's best system.

1 Introduction

The task of automatic dubbing is to translate spoken language in a video into another language such that the translated speech can be seamlessly blended with the original video. A unique aspect of dubbing is isochrony, which refers to the property that the speech translation is time-aligned with the original speaker's visual cues. The spoken words should match the speaker's lip movements, ensuring the audio is heard when the lips move and is silent when they don't.

To address this challenge, a unified model that simultaneously processes translations and speech timing is optimal, allowing for adjustments in translation to fit timing constraints. Chronopoulou et al. (2023) accomplish this by simply binning target phoneme durations and interleaving them with target phonemes during training and inference. Pal et al. (2023) enhance this approach by predicting the durations of phonemes as target factors. However, these methods fail to utilize pre-trained machine translation (MT) models and large language models (LLM) that are trained on massive text corpora. Moreover, constructing large-scale datasets with phoneme duration labels is challenging, thus limiting the translation quality. Therefore, a disentangled approach that considers MT and dubbing synchrony separately can achieve better results. Our system (Rao et al., 2023) from last year first generated a set of translation candidates and later reranked them based on speech overlaps, achieving better mean opinion scores (MOS) than the baseline systems. Therefore, this year we extend last year's system by using more advanced pre-trained models and a more sophisticated pause-aware dubbing pipeline.

Specifically, our method comprises the following key components:

- A Transformer-based MT (Machine Translation) model, which is a fine-tuned version of NLLB-1.3B on the CoVoST2 dataset (Changhan Wang, 2020).
- An LLM-based post-editor that modifies the lengths of translations.
- A VITS-based (Kong et al., 2023) TTS model that is non-autoregressive and supports speed control.
- A voice cloning (VC) module based on OpenVoice (Qin et al., 2023), ensuring that the input speech and output speech share the same tone color.
- A pause-aware dubbing pipeline that identifies potential split points using sentence parsing.
- A reranking method based on LSE-D and CER.

In this paper, we provide detailed analyses of the components mentioned above. Our system

Proceedings of the 21st International Conference on Spoken Language Translation (IWSLT 2024), pages 60–64
August 15-16, 2024 ©2024 Association for Computational Linguistics

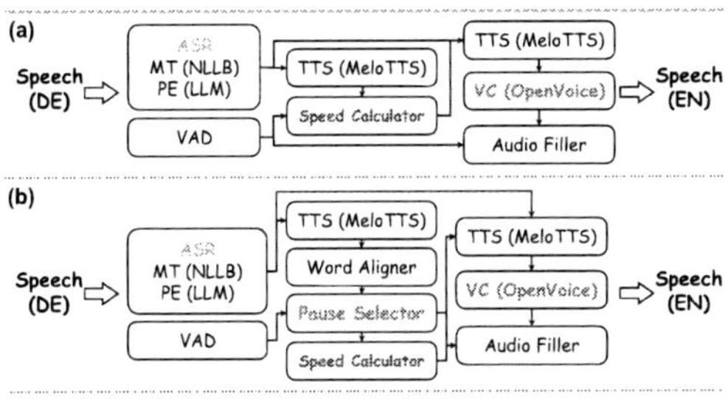

Figure 1: Diagram illustrating the process of automated dubbing: (a) without accounting for pauses; (b) with consideration of pauses. (Note that the ASR results are provided by the organizer in this track.)

achieves an LSE-D of 10.75 on subset1 and 12.19 on subset2 of the DE-EN test sets, respectively, outperforming last year's best system. Additionally, we take into account the vocal timbre of the speech, which can enhance the perceptual quality.

2 Methods

2.1 System Design

Figure 1 (a) shows the naive automatic dubbing system which assumes that the speech of the video does not have obvious pauses. First, an automatic speech recognition (ASR) model transcribes the source speech. The result of this step is provided by the organizer. Then, an MT model translates the source German (DE) text into the target English (EN) text, followed by an LLM that is prompted to change the length of the translation. Utilizing MeloTTS [1], the target speech is synthesized and its duration is compared with the original speech to determine the speed factor. Finally, we regenerate the target speech, convert the tone color, and fill the audio into the original video based on timestamps from the voice activity detection (VAD) [2] system.

Figure 1 (b) illustrates the pause-aware dubbing system. Unlike the naive system, it integrates a pause selector. This selector generates an index of potential word positions that best align with the pauses in the original speech. To avoid unnatural sentence breaks, sentence parsing is employed to determine groups of words that should remain together. Finally, the TTS model is utilized to produce audio clips for each text segment, with the speed factor calculated for each independently.

[1]https://github.com/myshell-ai/MeloTTS

[2]https://github.com/snakers4/silero-vad

Algorithm 1 Pause Selector

Require: t_{pause}, $\textbf{text}_{MT} = \{w_1, ..., w_n\}$
$\textbf{split} = \{t_1, ..., t_{n-1}\}, T_{src}, T_{tts}$

$PP, VP, NP = Parsing(\textbf{text}_{MT})$

$\textbf{index} = SplitPoint(PUNC, PP, VP, NP)$

$i = argmin(abs(\frac{t_{pause}}{T_{src}} - \frac{\textbf{split}_i}{T_{tts}}))\quad i \in \textbf{index}$

return i

2.2 Pause Selector

Algorithm 1 provides the details of the pause selector. Given the time of the pause (t_{pause}) predicted by VAD, the translation ($\textbf{text}_{MT}$), the word-level timestamps (**split**) of synthetic speech predicted by a CTC-based aligner from WhisperX (Bain et al., 2023), and the duration of source and generated speech (T_{src}) and (T_{tts}), we first use sentence parsing [3] to obtain the prepositional phrases (PP), verb phrases (VP), and noun phrases (NP). The possible split index can be only after these phrases and punctuations. Then, we select the best index that minimizes the distance between the normalized word time by duration and the normalized time of the pause.

2.3 LLM-based Post-Editor

You are a professional German-English translator and skilled proofreader. Now you are given the original German text and its English translation. Please improve the translation and make it more **complex/simple** without explaining. Source (German): "{DE}" Initial Translation (English): "{EN}" Revised Translation (English):

Table 1: Prompt for LLM-based post-editor.

LLM (Touvron et al., 2023; Zeng et al., 2023) is known for its exceptional zero-shot and few-shot capabilities, meaning it can perform downstream tasks using a prompt that describes the task or a few examples. In the context of automatic dubbing, we use LLM to generate translations with different lengths so that we can select the one that results in the best lip-sync accuracy. The input prompt for the LLM is shown in Table 1. We first describe

[3]https://github.com/Halvani/Constituent-Treelib

the task and the role of the LLM as a translator and a proofreader. Then, we instruct it to make the translation more complex or simple. Finally, we provide the source and translated text. We use "complex" and "simple" as indicators of output length as they contribute to better stability than "longer" and "shorter".

2.4 TTS and VC

We use MeloTTS, which is based on the architecture of VITS (Kim et al., 2021; Kong et al., 2023). VITS leverages variational autoencoder, adversarial learning, normalizing flow, and stochastic duration predictor to generate realistic speech in an end-to-end manner without relying on external word alignment and a vocoder. To convert the voice into the desired tone color, we adopt OpenVoice (Qin et al., 2023), which disentangles the tone color information in the encoder. The target speaker embedding is integrated into the decoder.

2.5 Rerank

We use LSE-D and CER to select the final synthetic speech from multiple candidates. The CER is computed between the original ASR transcription and the transcription of the generated speech. For subset1, there are no obvious pauses, so we only use system (a) as shown in Figure 1. For subset2, which contains notable pauses, we use both systems (a) and (b) in Figure 1. For the same translation, we only use system (b) if we do not observe a decline in CER and note an improvement in LSE-D compared to system (a). To rank multiple translations of different lengths, we use the average rank determined by LSE-D and CER and select the translation with the lowest rank. Note that we use CER rather than word error rate to mitigate the influence of the ASR model's limited ability to recognize out-of-vocabulary words. During rerank, we considered four translations: the original translation, the translation using LLM-based post editor without indicating the output length, the "complex" translation, and the "simple" translation.

3 Experimental Setups

We fine-tuned the NLLB-1.3B [4] model for 20 epochs on the CoVoST2 (Changhan Wang, 2020) DE-EN subset, using a learning rate of 3×10^{-5} and a batch size of 512. For the LLM-based post-editor, when employing the “complex” indicator, we sampled three answers and selected the one with the highest Comet score (Rei et al., 2020) compared to the original translation. For the “short” indicator, we sampled only once. When adjusting the speech speed, we set the lower bound to $0.75\times$ and the upper bound to $2.5\times$. We adopted several evaluation metrics: the BLEU score and the Comet score to evaluate MT quality, and the lip-sync error distance (LSE-D) (Chung and Zisserman, 2017) [5] and ASR character error rate (CER) to measure dubbing performance. We used the Wav2Vec2-base model [6], fine-tuned on LibriSpeech, as the ASR model, which utilizes a character-level vocabulary. We opted not to use a more advanced ASR model since the less robust model is more sensitive to speech quality. During rerank, we considered four translations: the original translation, the translation using LLM-based post editor without indicating the output length, the "complex" translation, and the "simple" translation. Additionally, we attempted to enhance the speech by applying denoising and audio super-resolution techniques [7], which remove noise and upscale the audio from 16kHz to 44.1kHz.

4 Experimental Results

4.1 Performance of MT and LLM-based Post-Editor

As shown in Table 2, the NLLB-1.3B model, fine-tuned on the target-domain CoVoST2 dataset, achieves high translation quality with BLEU scores of 46.37 and 44.03 on subset1 and subset2, respectively, and Comet scores of 89.29 and 88.01, respectively. When using an LLM to post-process the translations, we observe a decrease in BLEU scores, especially for longer translations. However, we find that the Comet scores are similar to those of the unmodified translations, indicating that the LLM effectively performs paraphrasing without changing the meaning of the translations.

4.2 Results for Pause-Aware Automatic Dubbing

For subset2, we observe that the pause-aware automatic dubbing pipeline (Dubbing (b)) contributes

[4]https://huggingface.co/facebook/nllb-200-distilled-1.3B

[5]When computing LSE-D, we used the video with subtitles.

[6]https://huggingface.co/facebook/wav2vec2-base-960h

[7]https://github.com/resemble-ai/resemble-enhance

	Subset1				Subset2							
	MT		Dubbing (a)		MT		Dubbing (a)		Dubbing (b)		Dubbing (a + b)	
Method	BLEU↑	Comet↑	LSE-D↓	CER↓	BLEU↑	Comet↑	LSE-D↓	CER↓	LSE-D↓	CER↓	LSE-D↓	CER↓
NLLB (fine-tune)	46.37	89.29	10.92	5.68	44.03	88.01	13.88	3.93	12.27	4.47	12.39	3.59
LLM-PE	43.03	89.42	11.03	5.78	40.75	88.00	12.90	3.97	12.25	4.21	12.46	3.51
LLM-PE (simple)	44.50	88.01	10.97	6.35	43.88	87.98	12.89	4.47	12.22	4.61	12.38	3.93
LLM-PE (complex)	19.67	84.08	11.12	4.75	18.88	83.74	13.05	3.60	12.35	4.46	12.73	3.28
Rerank (LSE-D)	41.18	88.15	10.62	5.70	39.13	87.79	/	/	/	/	11.96	3.76
Rerank (CER)	29.42	85.88	11.05	3.76	29.32	85.03	/	/	/	/	12.62	2.36
Rerank (LSE-D&CER)	38.13	87.91	10.75	4.62	38.60	87.13	/	/	/	/	12.19	3.02
+ Enhance	/	/	11.18	5.39	/	/	/	/	/	/	12.52	4.07
- VC	35.10	87.91	10.86	4.08	39.09	87.28	/	/	/	/	12.14	2.73

Table 2: Performance of MT and dubbing measured by BLEU score, Comet score, LSE-D, and ASR-CER (%). Rerank is applied to the results that correspond to the first four rows.

to a significantly lower LSE-D than the naive pipeline (Dubbing (a)). For instance, with pause-aware dubbing, the LSE-D decreases from 13.88 to 12.27 for the original translation. However, there is an increase in CER. The possible reason could be that the pauses in the translation may be unnatural, or the TTS model's ability to generate speech for incomplete sentences is limited. Therefore, we combine the two systems. For the same translation, we only use system (b) if we do not observe a decline in CER and note an improvement in LSE-D compared to system (a). This combination method (Dubbing (a + b)) results in the lowest CERs, and the LSE-D is also notably better than the naive system (a).

4.3 Results for Rerank

LSE-D measures the synchronization of speech with video, while CER assesses speech intelligibility. Employing either metric for reranking could enhance the results according to their respective evaluations. Using their average rank can achieve a balance between them. For subset1 and subset2, the final dubbed videos achieve LSE-D scores of 10.75 and 12.19, respectively, and CERs of 4.62% and 3.02%, respectively. It is worth noting that the CER for longer speeches tends to be lower due to more contextual information, while the LSE-D tends to be higher as it is more difficult to align the pauses.

4.4 Alternative Systems

We carried out ablation studies and provided alternative systems in our submission. When VC is not used, the LSE-D is similar to the complete system. The CER is notably lower because the sole TTS model provides better speech quality, whereas the VC model can introduce some noise. However, without VC, using a female's voice for a male speaker is unreasonable. Our TTS model operates at a sample rate of 16kHz. To improve the subjective listening experience, we adopted an audio super-resolution model to enhance it to 44.1kHz. Perceptually, higher frequencies contribute to better quality. However, we found that audio super-resolution negatively impacts the LSE-D and CER, although we do not observe noticeable distortion in the audio samples.

5 Discussion

Compared to last year's system, which utilized a length-aware MT system that employed a length tag to indicate the desired output length, this year's approach aims to enhance translation quality by fine-tuning a pre-trained MT model rather than training one from scratch. Although we attempted to incorporate length tags in the fine-tuning process, we found that they failed to produce translations with varying lengths due to the limited number of epochs and fine-tuning data. Consequently, we used an LLM which has robust rewriting capabilities.

We submitted a single entry for the English-Chinese subtask, which presents significantly greater challenges than the German-English subtask due to factors such as long-form video, speaker changes, and background music. To address these challenges, we enhanced our automatic dubbing system with an open-source diarization model (Desplanques et al., 2020), a source separation tool (Takahashi and Mitsufuji, 2017), and a TTS API [8]. However, given the complexity of the task and the lack of labeled test set, we have not provided a detailed analysis. In movie dub-

[8] https://github.com/rany2/edge-tts

bing, it is crucial that the emotion of the dubbed speech matches that of the original speech, therefore, expressive TTS models are preferred. We evaluated the Seamless Expressive model (Barrault et al., 2023), however, we observed that the speech quality was inconsistent, and for non-English languages, the speech did not sound native.

6 Conclusion

In this paper, we propose a novel pause-aware automatic dubbing system that ensures translated speech signals are not only accurate but also maintain the timbre of the original speech. The key components involve a novel pause selector, informed by parsing, to align dubbing with the video's pace, a VC model to convert the tone color, and an LLM to provide translation candidates. For future work, we plan to carry out more systematic experiments on long-form, movie-like videos and provide more expressive dubbed videos.

References

Max Bain, Jaesung Huh, Tengda Han, and Andrew Zisserman. 2023. Whisperx: Time-accurate speech transcription of long-form audio. *Proc. InterSpeech.*

Loïc Barrault, Yu-An Chung, Mariano Coria Meglioli, David Dale, Ning Dong, Mark Duppenthaler, Paul-Ambroise Duquenne, Brian Ellis, Hady Elsahar, Justin Haaheim, et al. 2023. Seamless: Multilingual expressive and streaming speech translation. *arXiv preprint arXiv:2312.05187.*

Juan Pino Changhan Wang, Anne Wu. 2020. Covost2 and massively multilingual speech-to-text translation.

Alexandra Chronopoulou, Brian Thompson, Prashant Mathur, Yogesh Virkar, Surafel M Lakew, and Marcello Federico. 2023. Jointly optimizing translations and speech timing to improve isochrony in automatic dubbing. *arXiv preprint arXiv:2302.12979.*

Joon Son Chung and Andrew Zisserman. 2017. Out of time: automated lip sync in the wild. In *Proc. ACCV Workshop*, pages 251–263. Springer.

Brecht Desplanques, Jenthe Thienpondt, and Kris Demuynck. 2020. Ecapa-tdnn: Emphasized channel attention, propagation and aggregation in tdnn based speaker verification. *arXiv preprint arXiv:2005.07143.*

Jaehyeon Kim, Jungil Kong, and Juhee Son. 2021. Conditional variational autoencoder with adversarial learning for end-to-end text-to-speech. In *Proc. ICML*, pages 5530–5540.

Jungil Kong, Jihoon Park, Beomjeong Kim, Jeongmin Kim, Dohee Kong, and Sangjin Kim. 2023. Vits2: Improving quality and efficiency of single-stage text-to-speech with adversarial learning and architecture design. *arXiv preprint arXiv:2307.16430.*

Proyag Pal, Brian Thompson, Yogesh Virkar, Prashant Mathur, Alexandra Chronopoulou, and Marcello Federico. 2023. Improving isochronous machine translation with target factors and auxiliary counters. *arXiv preprint arXiv:2305.13204.*

Zengyi Qin, Wenliang Zhao, Xumin Yu, and Xin Sun. 2023. Openvoice: Versatile instant voice cloning. *arXiv preprint arXiv:2312.01479.*

Zhiqiang Rao, Hengchao Shang, Jinlong Yang, Daimeng Wei, Zongyao Li, Jiaxin Guo, Shaojun Li, Zhengzhe Yu, Zhanglin Wu, Yuhao Xie, et al. 2023. Length-aware nmt and adaptive duration for automatic dubbing. In *Proc. IWSLT*, pages 138–143.

Ricardo Rei, Craig Stewart, Ana C Farinha, and Alon Lavie. 2020. Comet: A neural framework for mt evaluation. *arXiv preprint arXiv:2009.09025.*

Naoya Takahashi and Yuki Mitsufuji. 2017. Multi-scale multi-band densenets for audio source separation. In *Proc. WASPAA*, pages 21–25. IEEE.

Hugo Touvron, Thibaut Lavril, Gautier Izacard, Xavier Martinet, Marie-Anne Lachaux, Timothée Lacroix, Baptiste Rozière, Naman Goyal, Eric Hambro, Faisal Azhar, et al. 2023. LLaMA: Open and efficient foundation language models. *arXiv preprint arXiv:2302.13971.*

Aohan Zeng, Xiao Liu, Zhengxiao Du, Zihan Wang, Hanyu Lai, Ming Ding, Zhuoyi Yang, Yifan Xu, Wendi Zheng, Xiao Xia, Weng Lam Tam, Zixuan Ma, Yufei Xue, Jidong Zhai, Wenguang Chen, Peng Zhang, Yuxiao Dong, and Jie Tang. 2023. Glm-130b: An open bilingual pre-trained model. *Proc. ICLR.*

NICT's Cascaded and End-To-End Speech Translation Systems using Whisper and IndicTrans2 for the Indic Task

Haiyue Song and **Raj Dabre**
National Institute of Information and Communications Technology (NICT)
Hikaridai 3-5, Seika-cho, Soraku-gun, Kyoto, Japan
{haiyue.song,raj.dabre}@nict.go.jp

Abstract

This paper presents the NICT's submission for the IWSLT 2024 Indic track, focusing on three speech-to-text (ST) translation directions: English to Hindi, Bengali, and Tamil. We aim to enhance translation quality in this low-resource scenario by integrating state-of-the-art pre-trained automated speech recognition (ASR) and text-to-text machine translation (MT) models. Our cascade system incorporates a Whisper model fine-tuned for ASR and an IndicTrans2 model fine-tuned for MT. Additionally, we propose an end-to-end system that combines a Whisper model for speech-to-text conversion with knowledge distilled from an IndicTrans2 MT model. We first fine-tune the IndicTrans2 model to generate pseudo data in Indic languages. This pseudo data, along with the original English speech data, is then used to fine-tune the Whisper model. Experimental results show that the cascaded system achieved a BLEU score of 51.0, outperforming the end-to-end model, which scored 19.1 BLEU. Moreover, the analysis indicates that applying knowledge distillation from the IndicTrans2 model to the end-to-end ST model improves the translation quality by about 0.7 BLEU.

1 Introduction and Related Work

Speech-to-text translation is crucial for breaking the language barriers during international activities, such as translating diverse languages in online meetings. Although high-resource language pairs often achieve excellent results, the performance for low-resource language pairs remains unsatisfactory (Radford et al., 2023; Joshi et al., 2020), such as English to Indic languages. This paper presents NICT's submission to the Indic Track of IWSLT 2024, which includes translation directions from English to Hindi, Bengali, and Tamil. An overview of the cascade and end-to-end systems is illustrated in Figure 1.

Data scarcity is a significant challenge for the English to Indic languages ST task due to its low-resource scenario and we are using data-driven neural models. Data augmentation on speech and text data is an efficient way to address this challenge (Shanbhogue et al., 2023; Mi et al., 2022). Assisting information such as phonetic information (Cheng et al., 2021) and spectral features (Berrebbi et al., 2022), or knowledge transferred from related languages (Anastasopoulos et al., 2022; Gow-Smith et al., 2023; Song et al., 2020) can also enhance the performance. To this end, we use data combined data from three directions rather than using them separately.

Cascade and end-to-end (E2E) systems are two popular paradigms in ST with their advantages. In general, cascaded systems show higher translation quality (Agarwal et al., 2023) and end-to-end systems usually show lower latency and less modeling burden (Xu et al., 2023). To maximize the translation quality, we adopt the cascaded way and attempt to make full use of the recent advancements in ASR and MT fields (Sperber and Paulik, 2020). Following preliminary experiments, we decided to participate in the **unconstrained** setting, where we leverage pre-trained models such as Whisper and IndicTrans2 to develop our cascaded and E2E systems. Although additional datasets like IndicVoices are available for Indic languages (Javed et al., 2024), we refrain from using them due to concerns about test set overlap.

We use Whisper (Radford et al., 2023) as our ASR system. Unlike previous work (Wang et al., 2023a) who prompt Whisper without fine-tuning, we fine-tune Whisper-medium on the training data. Our results demonstrate significant improvements through fine-tuning. Although other ASR systems such as HuBERT (Hsu et al., 2021), wav2vec 2.0 (Baevski et al., 2020) and others (Communication et al., 2023; Wang et al., 2023b) exist, we adopt Whisper for its ease of use and its ability to deliver

Proceedings of the 21st International Conference on Spoken Language Translation (IWSLT 2024), pages 65–70
August 15-16, 2024 ©2024 Association for Computational Linguistics

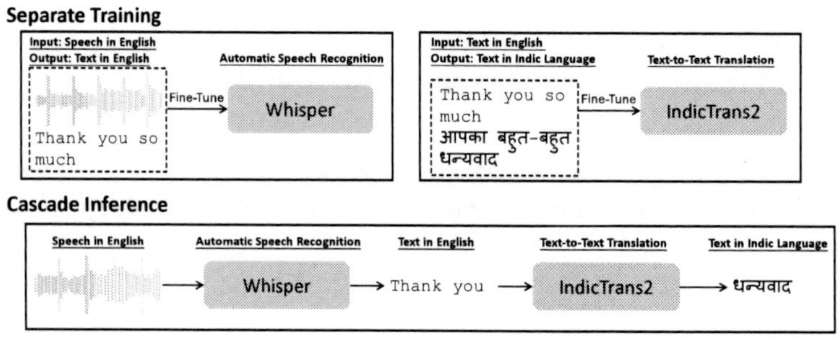

(a) Cascaded system training and inference process.

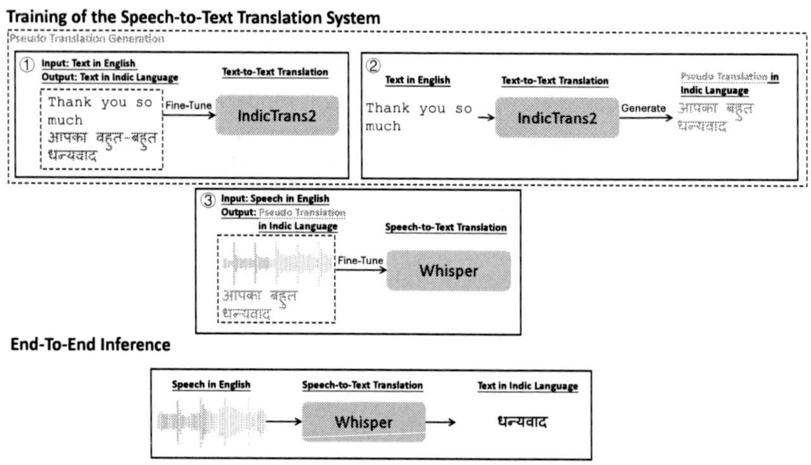

(b) End-To-End system training and inference process.

Figure 1: Comparison of Cascaded and End-To-End systems.

high-quality transcriptions of English speech. We then cascade Whisper with IndicTrans2 (Gala et al., 2023) as our MT system. It supports high-quality translations across 22 popular Indic languages and outperforms the mBART50 model (Liu et al., 2020) and the M2M-100 model (Fan et al., 2020) in directions involving Indic language. Additionally, we explore the potential of the E2E system by employing knowledge distillation from the IndicTrans2 model into the Whisper model. Experimental results show that our cascaded systems are about 32 BLEU better than the E2E systems. Furthermore, E2E systems trained with distilled translations, which are obtained by translating English transcripts to Indic languages via IndicTrans2, tend to be about 0.7 BLEU points better than those using the originally provided gold standard translations.

The remainder of this paper is structured as follows: Section 2 describes the datasets and data preprocessing. Section 3 introduces our cascade and end-to-end models. Section 4 presents the experimental settings, results, and analysis. Lastly, Section 5 concludes the paper.

2 Data

We show the statistics of the original corpora and how we pre-process the raw data in this section.

2.1 Dataset

Direction	Train	Dev	Test	Total Speech Hours
en → hi	44,538	7,612	7,044	95.70
en → bn	5,138	1,344	1,170	16.44
en → ta	7,950	2,139	2,194	22.15

Table 1: Statistics of the datasets showing the number of sentences in the training, development, and test sets alongside total speech hours.

We use only the corpus provided on the official site, with statistics shown in Table 1. We do not leverage any extra data, although our systems are built under the *unconstrained* condition. In the table, *en*, *hi*, *bn*, and *ta* represent English, Hindi, Bengali, and Tamil, respectively. We obtain the audio segments of textual sentences from the original files according to the offset and duration information. After segmentation, each data sample contains an audio segment in English, its transcription, and a translation in one of the three Indic languages. We observed that the data belongs to the spoken language domain, where the sentences are shorter compared to sentences in written texts. Moreover, there is almost no punctuation in English transcriptions and Indic language translations.

2.2 Pre-processing

To fine-tune a more robust Whisper model, we combine data from three English datasets as they belong to the same distribution.

3 Method

We describe the training and inference processes of the cascaded and E2E systems.

3.1 Cascaded System

The training and inference phases of the cascaded system are shown in Figure 1a. During training, we fine-tune the Whisper model using English audio paired with its English transcription. We then fine-tune the IndicTrans2 model using the English transcriptions and their corresponding translations in the Indic language. Although the Whisper model without fine-tuning can achieve reasonable performance, we found the format mismatch problem as presented in Figure 2. It is a type of domain mismatch between spoken language and written language, where there is less punctuation in the spoken language. However, this is prevalent in the training and development datasets, so we do not bother processing this further.

Transcription	And its only 30 years old
Whisper output w/o fine-tuning	and it's only 30 years old.
Whisper output w/ fine-tuning	And its only 30 years old

Figure 2: We fine-tune Whisper to address the format mismatch problem.

During inference, the English transcription generated by the fine-tuned Whisper model is input into the fine-tuned IndicTrans2 model, which then produces the final output in the Indic language.

3.2 End-to-end System

The training and inference phases of the E2E Whisper model are shown in Figure 1b. During training, we first generate pseudo translation data using the IndicTrans2 model. We then use this pseudo data, instead of the gold transcription, to fine-tune the Whisper model. The motivation is to distill knowledge from a stronger translation model. The outputs of IndicTrans2, which are in a more consistent format, are easier for the Whisper model to learn than the human-annotated transcriptions. As shown in stage 1, we fine-tune the IndicTrans2 using English transcriptions and their translations in the Indic language. In stage 2, we generate pseudo translations for all English transcriptions in the dataset. Finally, we fine-tune the Whisper model using English audio data and these pseudo translations. During inference, we solely rely on the fine-tuned Whisper model to perform E2E ST.

4 Experiments

4.1 Settings

All our models are multilingual, achieved by combining all data into a single collection and using language indicator tokens to indicate the target language, as is the common practice. For the ASR module, we used the medium architecture of Whisper (Radford et al., 2023), which showed higher performance compared to the tiny, base, and small architectures. During fine-tuning, we set the learning rate to $1e-5$, batch size to 16, and epoch size to 50. We allocated 10% of the total training steps for warmup and implemented early stopping if there was no improvement in loss after $1,000$ steps, with evaluations every 100 steps on the development set. For the MT part of our experiments, we used the IndicTrans2 (Gala et al., 2023) model. We fine-tuned using the scripts provided in the IndicTrans2 library[1] including data preparation[2] and fine-tuning[3]. Using our fine-tuned IndicTrans2 model, we performed standard beam search decoding with a beam of size 5.

[1]https://github.com/AI4Bharat/IndicTrans2

[2]https://github.com/AI4Bharat/IndicTrans2/blob/main/prepare_data_joint_finetuning.sh

[3]https://github.com/AI4Bharat/IndicTrans2/blob/main/finetune.sh

4.2 Main Results: Submitted Systems

Table 2 presents the results of our cascaded and E2E systems on the test set.

Direction	Cascaded	E2E	Δ
English→ Bengali	52.6	10.8	41.8
English→ Hindi	60.5	33.0	27.5
English→ Tamil	39.9	13.5	26.4
Average	51.0	19.1	31.9

Table 2: BLEU scores on the test set.

Direction	Cascaded	E2E
English→ Bengali	50.0	7.9
English→ Hindi	64.1	32.1
English→ Tamil	41.7	12.1

Table 3: BLEU scores on the first 500 sentences from the dev set.

The scores are provided by the organizers, who do not provide a comparison with other participants at the time of writing this paper. Nevertheless, it is evident that cascaded systems outperform E2E systems by a wide margin. This indicates that data scarcity is a major problem limiting E2E system development for English to Indic language speech translation. We also provide scores for the same languages on 500 development set samples in Table 3, where we can see that there are similar trends as observed for the test set.

4.3 Impact of Distillation on E2E Systems

In Table 4, we present the differences between an E2E system trained on original translations and those trained on distilled translations. It is clear that distillation, performed by translating English transcriptions into Indic language sentences used as references for E2E systems, leads to a reasonable improvement of 0.7 BLEU.

Direction	E2E-Dist	E2E-Orig	Δ
English→ Bengali	7.9	7.6	0.3
English→ Hindi	32.1	31.2	0.9
English→ Tamil	12.1	11.2	0.9
Average	17.4	16.7	0.7

Table 4: BLEU scores comparison of E2E systems on the first 500 sentences from the dev set. E2E-Dist represents an E2E system trained on translated (distilled) Indic languages references, whereas E2E-Orig refers to when original references are used.

5 Conclusion

This paper presented NICT's submission to the IWSLT 2024 English to Indic speech-to-text translation task. We took advantage of the advancements in ASR and MT where we combined the Whisper model and IndicTrans2 model in our cascaded system. In our end-to-end system, we further utilize the pseudo translation data technique, also known as knowledge distillation, to empower the Whisper model. Future work will focus on combining Whisper with IndicTrans2 jointly to train an even stronger speech translation system.

References

Milind Agarwal, Sweta Agrawal, Antonios Anastasopoulos, Luisa Bentivogli, Ondřej Bojar, Claudia Borg, Marine Carpuat, Roldano Cattoni, Mauro Cettolo, Mingda Chen, William Chen, Khalid Choukri, Alexandra Chronopoulou, Anna Currey, Thierry Declerck, Qianqian Dong, Kevin Duh, Yannick Estève, Marcello Federico, Souhir Gahbiche, Barry Haddow, Benjamin Hsu, Phu Mon Htut, Hirofumi Inaguma, Dávid Javorský, John Judge, Yasumasa Kano, Tom Ko, Rishu Kumar, Pengwei Li, Xutai Ma, Prashant Mathur, Evgeny Matusov, Paul McNamee, John P. McCrae, Kenton Murray, Maria Nadejde, Satoshi Nakamura, Matteo Negri, Ha Nguyen, Jan Niehues, Xing Niu, Atul Kr. Ojha, John E. Ortega, Proyag Pal, Juan Pino, Lonneke van der Plas, Peter Polák, Elijah Rippeth, Elizabeth Salesky, Jiatong Shi, Matthias Sperber, Sebastian Stüker, Katsuhito Sudoh, Yun Tang, Brian Thompson, Kevin Tran, Marco Turchi, Alex Waibel, Mingxuan Wang, Shinji Watanabe, and Rodolfo Zevallos. 2023. FINDINGS OF THE IWSLT 2023 EVALUATION CAMPAIGN. In *Proceedings of the 20th International Conference on Spoken Language Translation (IWSLT 2023)*, pages 1–61, Toronto, Canada (in-person and online). Association for Computational Linguistics.

Antonios Anastasopoulos, Loïc Barrault, Luisa Bentivogli, Marcely Zanon Boito, Ondřej Bojar, Roldano Cattoni, Anna Currey, Georgiana Dinu, Kevin Duh, Maha Elbayad, Clara Emmanuel, Yannick Estève, Marcello Federico, Christian Federmann, Souhir Gahbiche, Hongyu Gong, Roman Grundkiewicz, Barry Haddow, Benjamin Hsu, Dávid Javorský, Věra Kloudová, Surafel Lakew, Xutai Ma, Prashant Mathur, Paul McNamee, Kenton Murray, Maria Nădejde, Satoshi Nakamura, Matteo Negri, Jan Niehues, Xing Niu, John Ortega, Juan Pino, Elizabeth Salesky, Jiatong Shi, Matthias Sperber, Sebastian Stüker, Katsuhito Sudoh, Marco Turchi, Yogesh Virkar, Alexander Waibel, Changhan Wang, and Shinji Watanabe. 2022. Findings of the IWSLT 2022 evaluation campaign. In *Proceedings of the 19th International Conference on Spoken Language Translation (IWSLT 2022)*, pages 98–157, Dublin, Ireland (in-person and online). Association for Computational Linguistics.

Alexei Baevski, Henry Zhou, Abdelrahman Mohamed, and Michael Auli. 2020. wav2vec 2.0: A framework for self-supervised learning of speech representations.

Dan Berrebbi, Jiatong Shi, Brian Yan, Osbel Lopez-Francisco, Jonathan D. Amith, and Shinji Watanabe. 2022. Combining spectral and self-supervised features for low resource speech recognition and translation.

Yao-Fei Cheng, Hung-Shin Lee, and Hsin-Min Wang. 2021. Allost: Low-resource speech translation without source transcription.

Seamless Communication, Loïc Barrault, Yu-An Chung, Mariano Coria Meglioli, David Dale, Ning Dong, Mark Duppenthaler, Paul-Ambroise Duquenne, Brian Ellis, Hady Elsahar, Justin Haaheim, John Hoffman, Min-Jae Hwang, Hirofumi Inaguma, Christopher Klaiber, Ilia Kulikov, Pengwei Li, Daniel Licht, Jean Maillard, Ruslan Mavlyutov, Alice Rakotoarison, Kaushik Ram Sadagopan, Abinesh Ramakrishnan, Tuan Tran, Guillaume Wenzek, Yilin Yang, Ethan Ye, Ivan Evtimov, Pierre Fernandez, Cynthia Gao, Prangthip Hansanti, Elahe Kalbassi, Amanda Kallet, Artyom Kozhevnikov, Gabriel Mejia Gonzalez, Robin San Roman, Christophe Touret, Corinne Wong, Carleigh Wood, Bokai Yu, Pierre Andrews, Can Balioglu, Peng-Jen Chen, Marta R. Costa-jussà, Maha Elbayad, Hongyu Gong, Francisco Guzmán, Kevin Heffernan, Somya Jain, Justine Kao, Ann Lee, Xutai Ma, Alex Mourachko, Benjamin Peloquin, Juan Pino, Sravya Popuri, Christophe Ropers, Safiyyah Saleem, Holger Schwenk, Anna Sun, Paden Tomasello, Changhan Wang, Jeff Wang, Skyler Wang, and Mary Williamson. 2023. Seamless: Multilingual expressive and streaming speech translation.

Angela Fan, Shruti Bhosale, Holger Schwenk, Zhiyi Ma, Ahmed El-Kishky, Siddharth Goyal, Mandeep Baines, Onur Celebi, Guillaume Wenzek, Vishrav Chaudhary, Naman Goyal, Tom Birch, Vitaliy Liptchinsky, Sergey Edunov, Edouard Grave, Michael Auli, and Armand Joulin. 2020. Beyond english-centric multilingual machine translation.

Jay Gala, Pranjal A Chitale, A K Raghavan, Varun Gumma, Sumanth Doddapaneni, Aswanth Kumar M, Janki Atul Nawale, Anupama Sujatha, Ratish Puduppully, Vivek Raghavan, Pratyush Kumar, Mitesh M Khapra, Raj Dabre, and Anoop Kunchukuttan. 2023. Indictrans2: Towards high-quality and accessible machine translation models for all 22 scheduled indian languages. *Transactions on Machine Learning Research.*

Edward Gow-Smith, Alexandre Berard, Marcely Zanon Boito, and Ioan Calapodescu. 2023. NAVER LABS Europe's multilingual speech translation systems for the IWSLT 2023 low-resource track. In *Proceedings of the 20th International Conference on Spoken Language Translation (IWSLT 2023)*, pages 144–158, Toronto, Canada (in-person and online). Association for Computational Linguistics.

Wei-Ning Hsu, Benjamin Bolte, Yao-Hung Hubert Tsai, Kushal Lakhotia, Ruslan Salakhutdinov, and Abdelrahman Mohamed. 2021. Hubert: Self-supervised speech representation learning by masked prediction of hidden units. *IEEE/ACM Trans. Audio, Speech and Lang. Proc.*, 29:3451–3460.

Tahir Javed, Janki Nawale, Eldho Ittan George, Sakshi Joshi, Kaushal Bhogale, Deovrat Mehendale, Ishvinder Virender Sethi, Aparna Ananthanarayanan, Hafsah Faquih, Pratiti Palit, Sneha Ravishankar, Saranya Sukumaran, Tripura Panchagnula, Sunjay Murali, Kunal Sharad Gandhi, R Ambujavalli, M ManickamK, C Venkata Vaijayanthi, Krishnan Srinivasa Raghavan Karunganni, Pratyush Kumar, and Mitesh M. Khapra. 2024. Indicvoices: Towards building an inclusive multilingual speech dataset for indian languages. *ArXiv*, abs/2403.01926.

Pratik Joshi, Sebastin Santy, Amar Budhiraja, Kalika Bali, and Monojit Choudhury. 2020. The state and fate of linguistic diversity and inclusion in the NLP world. In *Proceedings of the 58th Annual Meeting of the Association for Computational Linguistics*, pages 6282–6293, Online. Association for Computational Linguistics.

Yinhan Liu, Jiatao Gu, Naman Goyal, Xian Li, Sergey Edunov, Marjan Ghazvininejad, Mike Lewis, and Luke Zettlemoyer. 2020. Multilingual denoising pre-training for neural machine translation. *Transactions of the Association for Computational Linguistics*, 8:726–742.

Chenggang Mi, Lei Xie, and Yanning Zhang. 2022. Improving data augmentation for low resource speech-to-text translation with diverse paraphrasing. *Neural Networks*, 148:194–205.

Alec Radford, Jong Wook Kim, Tao Xu, Greg Brockman, Christine McLeavey, and Ilya Sutskever. 2023. Robust speech recognition via large-scale weak supervision. In *International Conference on Machine Learning*, pages 28492–28518. PMLR.

Akshaya Vishnu Kudlu Shanbhogue, Ran Xue, Soumya Saha, Daniel Zhang, and Ashwinkumar Ganesan. 2023. Improving low resource speech translation with data augmentation and ensemble strategies. In *Proceedings of the 20th International Conference on Spoken Language Translation (IWSLT 2023)*, pages 241–250, Toronto, Canada (in-person and online). Association for Computational Linguistics.

Haiyue Song, Raj Dabre, Zhuoyuan Mao, Fei Cheng, Sadao Kurohashi, and Eiichiro Sumita. 2020. Pre-training via leveraging assisting languages for neural machine translation. In *Proceedings of the 58th Annual Meeting of the Association for Computational*

Linguistics: Student Research Workshop, pages 279–285, Online. Association for Computational Linguistics.

Matthias Sperber and Matthias Paulik. 2020. Speech translation and the end-to-end promise: Taking stock of where we are. In *Proceedings of the 58th Annual Meeting of the Association for Computational Linguistics*, pages 7409–7421, Online. Association for Computational Linguistics.

Minghan Wang, Yinglu Li, Jiaxin Guo, Zongyao Li, Hengchao Shang, Daimeng Wei, Min Zhang, Shimin Tao, and Hao Yang. 2023a. The HW-TSC's speech-to-speech translation system for IWSLT 2023. In *Proceedings of the 20th International Conference on Spoken Language Translation (IWSLT 2023)*, pages 277–282, Toronto, Canada (in-person and online). Association for Computational Linguistics.

Tianrui Wang, Long Zhou, Ziqiang Zhang, Yu Wu, Shujie Liu, Yashesh Gaur, Zhuo Chen, Jinyu Li, and Furu Wei. 2023b. Viola: Unified codec language models for speech recognition, synthesis, and translation.

Chen Xu, Rong Ye, Qianqian Dong, Chengqi Zhao, Tom Ko, Mingxuan Wang, Tong Xiao, and Jingbo Zhu. 2023. Recent advances in direct speech-to-text translation. In *Proceedings of the Thirty-Second International Joint Conference on Artificial Intelligence, IJCAI-23*, pages 6796–6804. International Joint Conferences on Artificial Intelligence Organization. Survey Track.

Transforming LLMs into Cross-modal and Cross-lingual Retrieval Systems

Frank Palma Gomez[1] **Ramon Sanabria**[2] **Yun-hsuan Sung**[4]
Daniel Cer[4] **Siddharth Dalmia**[3‡] **Gustavo Hernandez Abrego**[4‡]
[1]Boston University [2]The University of Edinburgh [3]Google DeepMind
[4]Google Research
fpg@bu.com*

Abstract

Large language models (LLMs) are trained on text-only data that go far beyond the languages with paired speech and text data. At the same time, Dual Encoder (DE) based retrieval systems project queries and documents into the same embedding space and have demonstrated their success in retrieval and bi-text mining. To match speech and text in many languages, we propose using LLMs to initialize multi-modal DE retrieval systems. Unlike traditional methods, our system doesn't require speech data during LLM pre-training and can exploit LLM's multilingual text understanding capabilities to match speech and text in languages unseen during retrieval training. Our multi-modal LLM-based retrieval system is capable of matching speech and text in 102 languages despite only training on 21 languages. Our system outperforms previous systems trained explicitly on all 102 languages. We achieve a 10% absolute improvement in Recall@1 averaged across these languages. Additionally, our model demonstrates cross-lingual speech and text matching, which is further enhanced by readily available machine translation data.

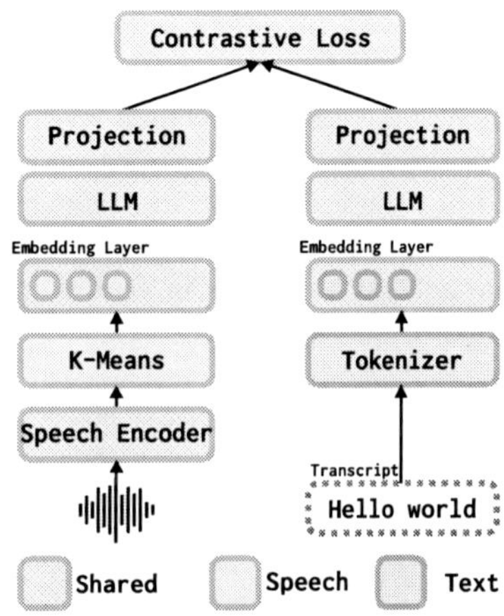

Figure 1: **Our dual encoder architecture and training pipeline**. We expand the embedding layer of our backbone LLM to support the additional discretized speech tokens, that are extracted from a pre-trained speech encoder. At the same time, we tokenize the corresponding transcripts with the LLM tokenizer. We encode the speech tokens and transcripts separately and train the model with a contrastive loss over the dot product between speech and transcript embeddings.

1 Introduction

LLMs have demonstrated their effectiveness in modelling textual sequences to tackle various downstream tasks (Brown et al., 2020; Hoffmann et al., 2022; Chowdhery et al., 2023). This effectiveness has led to the development of powerful LLMs capable of modelling text in a wide range of languages. The abundance of textual data in different languages across the internet has fueled the progress of multi-lingual models (Johnson et al., 2017; Xue et al., 2020; Siddhant et al., 2022). On the other hand, speech technologies are prevalent in smartphones and personal assistants, but their language availability is relatively limited compared to the languages that LLMs support (Baevski et al., 2020; Radford et al., 2023).

Various efforts have explored solutions to the speech-text data scarcity problem (Duquenne et al., 2021; Ardila et al., 2019; Wang et al., 2020). Works such as SpeechMatrix (Duquenne et al., 2022) use separate speech and text encoders to mine semantically similar utterances that are neighbors in an embedding space. However, these approaches are limiting because they require speech and text encoders that have aligned representation spaces.

We posit that we can retrieve speech and text utterances by aligning both modalities within the embedding space built from a single pre-trained LLM. We take inspiration from previous works

*Work done by Frank and Ramon during their internship in Google Research and Google DeepMind respectively.

‡ Equal Advising Contributions.

Proceedings of the 21st International Conference on Spoken Language Translation (IWSLT 2024), pages 71–80
August 15-16, 2024 ©2024 Association for Computational Linguistics

that use pre-trained LLMs to perform automatic speech recognition (ASR) and automatic speech translation (AST) (Rubenstein et al., 2023; Wang et al., 2023; Hassid et al., 2023; Gong et al., 2023; Peng et al., 2023). Our intuition is that we can perform the speech and text alignment leveraging the capabilities of text-only LLMs without requiring two separate models.

In this paper, we propose converting LLMs into speech and text DE retrieval systems without requiring speech pre-training and outperform previous methods with significantly less data. By discretizing speech into acoustic units (Hsu et al., 2021), we extend our LLMs embedding layer and treat the acoustic units as ordinary text tokens. Consequently, we transform our LLM into a retrieval system via a contrastive loss allowing us to match speech and text utterances in various languages. Our contributions are the following:

1. We build a speech-to-text symmetric DE from a pre-trained LLM. We show that our retrieval system is effective matching speech and text in 102 languages of FLEURS (Conneau et al., 2023) despite only training on 21 languages.
2. We show that our model exhibits cross-lingual speech and text matching without training on this type of data. At the same time, we find that cross-lingual speech and text matching is further improved by training on readily available machine translation data.

2 Method

We train a transformer-based DE model that encodes speech and text given a dataset $D = \{(x_i, y_i)\}$, where x_i is a speech utterance and y_i is its transcription. We denote the speech and text embeddings as $\boldsymbol{x_i} = E(x_i)$ and $\boldsymbol{y_i} = E(y_i)$, respectively, where E is a transformer-based DE that encodes speech and text.

2.1 Generating Audio Tokens

We convert raw speech into discrete tokens using the process in Lakhotia et al. (2021); Borsos et al. (2023). The process converts a speech query x_i into an embedding using a pre-trained speech encoder. The output embedding is then discretized into a set of tokens using k-means clustering. We refer to the resulting tokens as *audio tokens*. We use the 2B variant of the Universal Speech Model (USM) encoder (Zhang et al., 2023) as the speech encoder and take the middle layer as the embedding for x_i. Additionally, we generate audio tokens at 25Hz using k-means clustering [1]. We will refer to this as our *audio token vocabulary*.

2.2 Supporting Text and Audio Tokens

To support text and audio tokens in our LLM, we follow the formulation of Rubenstein et al. (2023). We extend the embedding layer of a transformer decoder by a tokens, where a represents the size of our audio token vocabulary. This modification leads to an embedding layer with size $(t + a) \times m$, where t is the number of tokens in the text vocabulary and m is the dimensions of the embedding vectors. In our implementation, the first t tokens represent text and the remaining a tokens are reserved for audio. We initialize the embeddings layer from scratch when training our model.

3 Data and Tasks

Appendix A.3 details our training and evaluation datasets along with the number of languages in each dataset, the split we used, and the size of each dataset. We focus on the following retrieval tasks:

Speech-to-Text Retrieval (S2T) involves retrieving the corresponding transcription from a database given a speech sample. In S2T, we train on CoVoST-2 (Wang et al., 2021) speech utterances and their transcriptions. CoVoST-2 is a large multilingual speech corpus derived from Wikipedia expanding over 21 languages and provides translation to and from English. We use FLEURS (Conneau et al., 2023) to evaluate S2T performance on 102 languages. FLEURS is an n-way parallel dataset containing speech utterances from FLoRES-101 (Goyal et al., 2021) human translations. To evaluate S2T, we report recall at 1 ($R@1$) rates for retrieving the correct transcription for every speech sample and word error rate (WER).

Speech-to-Text Translation Retrieval (S2TT) attempts to retrieve the corresponding text translation of a speech sample. We use S2TT to measure the cross-lingual capabilities of our multi-modal DE retrieval system. We evaluate this capability zero-shot on X $\rightarrow$ En S2TT data of FLUERS and explore if we can further improve this capability by training on readily-available machine translation data from WikiMatrix (Schwenk et al., 2019). We pick French, German, Dutch, and Polish to English

[1]We use the **USM-v2** audio tokenizer from Rubenstein et al. (2023)

	R@1 ↑	*WER* ↓
mSLAM DE (Conneau et al., 2023)	76.9	14.6
PaLM 2 DE (Proposed Model)	86.7	13.4

Table 1: PaLM 2 DE results for *R@1* and WER compared against the mSLAM DE on 102 languages from FLEURS for speech-to-text retrieval (S2T).

that are common across WikiMatrix and FLEURS and further discuss the amount of machine translation data used in Appendix A.3. For S2TT, we report 4-gram corpusBLEU (Post, 2018).

4 Model

Figure 1 shows an illustration of our model. We initialize our dual encoder from PaLM 2 XXS (Google et al., 2023) and append a linear projection layer after pooling the outputs along the sequence length dimension. The embedding and linear projection layers are initialized randomly. After initializing our model from PaLM 2, we use a contrastive loss (Hadsell et al., 2006). Appendix A.1 includes more details on our training setup. We will refer to our proposed model as PaLM 2 DE.

5 Experiments

We train our DE model to perform S2T, where the task is to retrieve the corresponding transcription given a speech sample. We train on the 21 languages from CoVoST-2 and evaluate our model using the S2T portion of FLEURS in 102 languages.

5.1 Speech-to-Text Retrieval

Table 1 shows the average *R@1* and WER for S2T for 102 languages from FLEURS. We compare against the mSLAM DE model from Conneau et al. (2023), a model trained on 426k hours of S2T data in 51 languages and fine-tuned on FLEURS training data. Our model significantly outperforms the mSLAM DE baseline in *R@1* and WER metrics despite being trained with only 1/10 of the data and having been initialized from a text-only LLM. More importantly, our model was only trained on the 21 languages in CoVoST-2 and never fine-tuned on the FLEURS training data.

5.1.1 Seen-Unseen Breakdown

In Figure 2 we break down the *R@1* scores based on seen and unseen languages during training. We find that our model performs best on the 20 languages that are within the training and evaluation

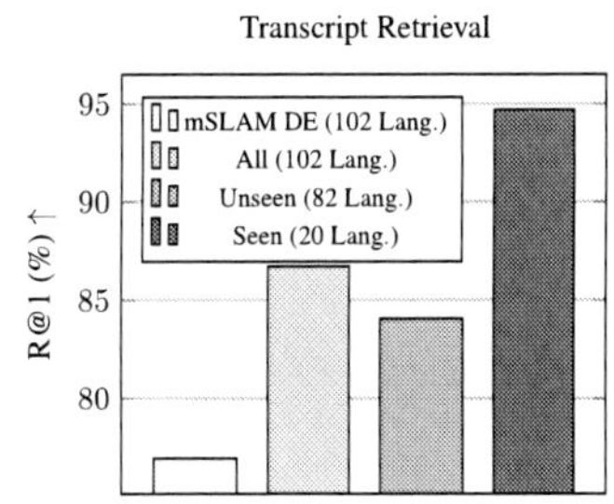

Figure 2: *R@1* transcription retrieval for seen and unseen languages in the training set.

Language Group (#)	*R@1* ↑ mSLAM DE (Conneau et al., 2023)	*R@1* ↑ PaLM 2 DE (Proposed Model)	# Wins
Afro-Asiatic (7)	73.67	**84.22**	5
Atlantic-Congo (14)	**86.77**	70.41	1
Austro-Asiatic (2)	**47.90**	34.42	0
Austronesian (6)	75.50	**90.73**	6
Dravidian (4)	65.70	**92.06**	4
Indo-European (51)	84.62	**95.32**	49
Japonic (1)	5.80	**91.54**	1
Kartvelian (1)	70.50	**82.92**	1
Koreanic (1)	5.20	**52.36**	1
Kra-Dai (2)	3.20	**22.09**	1
Mongolic (1)	70.70	**99.89**	1
Nilo-Saharan (1)	91.00	**92.52**	1
Sino-Tibetan (3)	3.40	**90.66**	3
Turkic (5)	81.28	**92.86**	4
Uralic (3)	91.40	**99.04**	3
All (102)	76.90	**86.72**	81

Table 2: FLEURS S2T (*R@1*) performance by language groups. Bold represents better performance. Numbers in parenthesis are the number of languages within the language group. # Wins is the number of languages where PaLM 2 DE outperforms mSLAM in the language group.

data, but still perform well on the remaining 82 unseen languages. We hypothesize this is due to the vast textual multilingual data our backbone LLM has seen during pre-training.

5.1.2 Language Group Breakdown

Table 2 shows the *R@1* language group breakdown for S2T on FLEURS. We find that although we only trained on 21 languages, our model significantly outperforms mSLAM DE in 13 of the 15 language groups. These results are consistent with the experiments in Hassid et al. (2023) which explore the effect of initializing speech language models from pre-trained LLMs.

5.2 Evaluating on Cross-Modal and Cross-Lingual Tasks

We evaluate on S2TT to gauge the cross-modal and cross-lingual capabilities of our model. We show we can improve S2TT by simply combining S2T

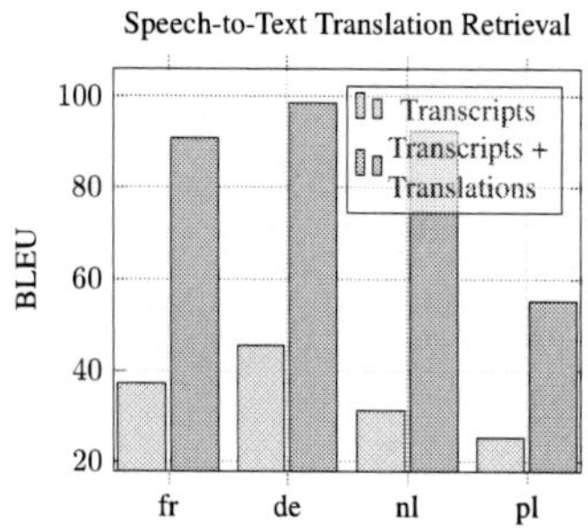

Figure 3: BLEU scores for FLEURS zero-shot S2TT when training on **Transcripts** or **Transcripts + Translations** for PaLM 2 DE. Combining transcripts and translation data improves zero-shot S2TT retrieval.

and translation data without S2TT training data.

5.2.1 Zero-Shot S2TT

Given the multi-lingual capabilities of our backbone language model, we explore if these capabilities are transferred after training our model contrastively on the S2T task. We hypothesize that our model should showcase cross-lingual and cross-modal capabilities due to the cross-modal training task and the cross-lingual capabilities of the backbone LLM. We evaluate S2TT in a zero-shot setting to assess our model's performance retrieving English translations given a speech sample in another language. Using the FLEURS S2TT portion, we evaluate S2TT X $\rightarrow$ En in 4 languages: German, Polish, French, and Dutch.

Figure 3 shows BLEU S2TT performance using S2T CoVoST-2 in 21 languages. We call this setup **Transcripts** in Figure 3. Our results demonstrate that even when only training our model on speech and transcriptions, we can achieve some zero-shot S2TT performance and We find that S2TT BLEU scores are considerably higher for languages present S2T training data. For example, Polish was not in the S2T training therefore its BLEU scores are the lowest.

5.2.2 Improving S2TT with MT Data

To further improve our model's cross-lingual performance, we add readily available translation data from Schwenk et al. (2019) to improve S2TT. For each batch, we combine 25% translation and 75% S2T data. Figure 3 shows comparison of only training on S2T (**Transcripts**) and combining S2T and translation data (**Transcriptions + Translations**). We find that combining S2T and translation data significantly improves the S2TT BLEU scores in all 4 languages without training on S2TT data. This finding demonstrates that we can improve our models cross-lingual performance with highly accessible translation data without needing scarce and often expensive speech-to-text translation training data.

6 Related Work

The success of pre-trained LLMs have motivated the application of these models in different modalities. Lakhotia et al. (2021) transformed speech into pseudo-text units to introduce the task of generative spoken language modeling. Borsos et al. (2023) introduced a framework to generate audio with long-term consistency. Consequently, Hassid et al. (2023) showed that SpeechLMs benefit from being initialized from pre-train LLMs while Rubenstein et al. (2023) demonstrated that pre-trained LLMs can be adapted to various tasks that required text and speech understanding.

On the other hand, several works aim to build joint speech and text representations (Khurana et al., 2022; Gow-Smith et al., 2023). Chung et al. (2021) introduced w2v-bert which combines masked language modeling and contrastive learning to create speech representations. Bapna et al. (2022) jointly pre-trains on speech and text from unsupervised speech and text data. Recently, Duquenne et al. (2023) employed separate speech and text encoders to generate embeddings in over 200 languages. Nevertheless, there is still a lack of understanding of whether joint speech and text representations can be built from a single encoder. We fill this gap by using pre-trained LLMs to jointly train on speech samples and their transcriptions to show that our approach is capable of speech-text matching in 102 languages.

7 Conclusion

We present an effective approach to developing a speech-to-text DE from a text-only LLM. Our findings suggest that by using a text-only LLM as a backbone model, we can drastically outperform previous approaches using considerably less speech-to-text training data. Additionally, we find that we can improve zero-shot speech translation by simply combining readily available translation and S2T data. We showcase our findings in 102 languages for S2T and 4 languages in S2TT; opening up the possibility of using speech-to-text DE's in different cross-model and cross-lingual settings.

8 Acknowledgements

We would like to thank Shankar Kumar, Ankur Bapna, and the anonymous reviewers for the valuable feedback on the draft of the paper. Chris Tar, Mario Guajardo-Céspedes, and Jason Riesa for the early experiment discussions and feedback. Christian Frank, Duc Dung Nguyen, Alex Tudor, and Dalia El Badawy for helping answer questions about AudioPaLM.

References

Rosana Ardila, Megan Branson, Kelly Davis, Michael Henretty, Michael Kohler, Josh Meyer, Reuben Morais, Lindsay Saunders, Francis M Tyers, and Gregor Weber. 2019. Common voice: A massively-multilingual speech corpus. *arXiv preprint arXiv:1912.06670.*

Alexei Baevski, Yuhao Zhou, Abdelrahman Mohamed, and Michael Auli. 2020. wav2vec 2.0: A framework for self-supervised learning of speech representations. *Advances in neural information processing systems*, 33:12449–12460.

Ankur Bapna, Colin Cherry, Yu Zhang, Ye Jia, Melvin Johnson, Yong Cheng, Simran Khanuja, Jason Riesa, and Alexis Conneau. 2022. mslam: Massively multilingual joint pre-training for speech and text. *arXiv preprint arXiv:2202.01374.*

Zalán Borsos, Raphaël Marinier, Damien Vincent, Eugene Kharitonov, Olivier Pietquin, Matt Sharifi, Dominik Roblek, Olivier Teboul, David Grangier, Marco Tagliasacchi, et al. 2023. Audiolm: a language modeling approach to audio generation. *IEEE/ACM Transactions on Audio, Speech, and Language Processing.*

Tom Brown, Benjamin Mann, Nick Ryder, Melanie Subbiah, Jared D Kaplan, Prafulla Dhariwal, Arvind Neelakantan, Pranav Shyam, Girish Sastry, Amanda Askell, et al. 2020. Language models are few-shot learners. *Advances in neural information processing systems*, 33:1877–1901.

Aakanksha Chowdhery, Sharan Narang, Jacob Devlin, Maarten Bosma, Gaurav Mishra, Adam Roberts, Paul Barham, Hyung Won Chung, Charles Sutton, Sebastian Gehrmann, et al. 2023. Palm: Scaling language modeling with pathways. *Journal of Machine Learning Research*, 24(240):1–113.

Yu-An Chung, Yu Zhang, Wei Han, Chung-Cheng Chiu, James Qin, Ruoming Pang, and Yonghui Wu. 2021. W2v-bert: Combining contrastive learning and masked language modeling for self-supervised speech pre-training. In *2021 IEEE Automatic Speech Recognition and Understanding Workshop (ASRU)*, pages 244–250. IEEE.

Alexis Conneau, Min Ma, Simran Khanuja, Yu Zhang, Vera Axelrod, Siddharth Dalmia, Jason Riesa, Clara Rivera, and Ankur Bapna. 2023. Fleurs: Few-shot learning evaluation of universal representations of speech. In *2022 IEEE Spoken Language Technology Workshop (SLT)*, pages 798–805. IEEE.

Paul-Ambroise Duquenne, Hongyu Gong, Ning Dong, Jingfei Du, Ann Lee, Vedanuj Goswani, Changhan Wang, Juan Pino, Benoît Sagot, and Holger Schwenk. 2022. Speechmatrix: A large-scale mined corpus of multilingual speech-to-speech translations. *arXiv preprint arXiv:2211.04508.*

Paul-Ambroise Duquenne, Hongyu Gong, and Holger Schwenk. 2021. Multimodal and multilingual embeddings for large-scale speech mining. *Advances in Neural Information Processing Systems*, 34:15748–15761.

Paul-Ambroise Duquenne, Holger Schwenk, and Benoît Sagot. 2023. Sentence-level multimodal and language-agnostic representations. *arXiv preprint arXiv:2308.11466.*

Yuan Gong, Alexander H Liu, Hongyin Luo, Leonid Karlinsky, and James Glass. 2023. Joint audio and speech understanding. In *2023 IEEE Automatic Speech Recognition and Understanding Workshop (ASRU)*, pages 1–8. IEEE.

Google, Rohan Anil, Andrew M Dai, Orhan Firat, Melvin Johnson, Dmitry Lepikhin, Alexandre Passos, Siamak Shakeri, Emanuel Taropa, Paige Bailey, Zhifeng Chen, et al. 2023. Palm 2 technical report. *arXiv preprint arXiv:2305.10403.*

Edward Gow-Smith, Alexandre Berard, Marcely Zanon Boito, and Ioan Calapodescu. 2023. NAVER LABS Europe's multilingual speech translation systems for the IWSLT 2023 low-resource track. In *Proceedings of the 20th International Conference on Spoken Language Translation (IWSLT 2023)*, pages 144–158, Toronto, Canada (in-person and online). Association for Computational Linguistics.

Naman Goyal, Cynthia Gao, Vishrav Chaudhary, Peng-Jen Chen, Guillaume Wenzek, Da Ju, Sanjan Krishnan, Marc'Aurelio Ranzato, Francisco Guzmán, and Angela Fan. 2021. The flores-101 evaluation benchmark for low-resource and multilingual machine translation. *Transactions of the Association for Computational Linguistics*, 10:522–538.

Raia Hadsell, Sumit Chopra, and Yann LeCun. 2006. Dimensionality reduction by learning an invariant mapping. *2006 IEEE Computer Society Conference on Computer Vision and Pattern Recognition (CVPR'06)*, 2:1735–1742.

Michael Hassid, Tal Remez, Tu Anh Nguyen, Itai Gat, Alexis Conneau, Felix Kreuk, Jade Copet, Alexandre Defossez, Gabriel Synnaeve, Emmanuel Dupoux, et al. 2023. Textually pretrained speech language models. *arXiv preprint arXiv:2305.13009.*

Jordan Hoffmann, Sebastian Borgeaud, Arthur Mensch, Elena Buchatskaya, Trevor Cai, Eliza Rutherford, Diego de Las Casas, Lisa Anne Hendricks, Johannes Welbl, Aidan Clark, et al. 2022. Training compute-optimal large language models. *arXiv preprint arXiv:2203.15556*.

Wei-Ning Hsu, Benjamin Bolte, Yao-Hung Hubert Tsai, Kushal Lakhotia, Ruslan Salakhutdinov, and Abdelrahman Mohamed. 2021. Hubert: Self-supervised speech representation learning by masked prediction of hidden units. *IEEE/ACM Transactions on Audio, Speech, and Language Processing*, 29:3451–3460.

Melvin Johnson, Mike Schuster, Quoc V Le, Maxim Krikun, Yonghui Wu, Zhifeng Chen, Nikhil Thorat, Fernanda Viégas, Martin Wattenberg, Greg Corrado, et al. 2017. Google's multilingual neural machine translation system: Enabling zero-shot translation. *Transactions of the Association for Computational Linguistics*, 5:339–351.

Sameer Khurana, Antoine Laurent, and James Glass. 2022. Samu-xlsr: Semantically-aligned multimodal utterance-level cross-lingual speech representation. *IEEE Journal of Selected Topics in Signal Processing*, 16(6):1493–1504.

Diederik P. Kingma and Jimmy Ba. 2014. Adam: A method for stochastic optimization. *CoRR*, abs/1412.6980.

Kushal Lakhotia, Eugene Kharitonov, Wei-Ning Hsu, Yossi Adi, Adam Polyak, Benjamin Bolte, Tu-Anh Nguyen, Jade Copet, Alexei Baevski, Abdelrahman Mohamed, and Emmanuel Dupoux. 2021. On generative spoken language modeling from raw audio. *Transactions of the Association for Computational Linguistics*, 9:1336–1354.

Jianmo Ni, Gustavo Hernandez Abrego, Noah Constant, Ji Ma, Keith Hall, Daniel Cer, and Yinfei Yang. 2022. Sentence-t5: Scalable sentence encoders from pre-trained text-to-text models. In *Findings of the Association for Computational Linguistics: ACL 2022*, pages 1864–1874, Dublin, Ireland. Association for Computational Linguistics.

Puyuan Peng, Brian Yan, Shinji Watanabe, and David Harwath. 2023. Prompting the hidden talent of web-scale speech models for zero-shot task generalization. *arXiv preprint arXiv:2305.11095*.

Matt Post. 2018. A call for clarity in reporting BLEU scores. In *Proceedings of the Third Conference on Machine Translation: Research Papers*, pages 186–191, Brussels, Belgium. Association for Computational Linguistics.

Alec Radford, Jong Wook Kim, Tao Xu, Greg Brockman, Christine McLeavey, and Ilya Sutskever. 2023. Robust speech recognition via large-scale weak supervision. In *International Conference on Machine Learning*, pages 28492–28518. PMLR.

Paul K Rubenstein, Chulayuth Asawaroengchai, Duc Dung Nguyen, Ankur Bapna, Zalán Borsos, Félix de Chaumont Quitry, Peter Chen, Dalia El Badawy, Wei Han, Eugene Kharitonov, et al. 2023. Audiopalm: A large language model that can speak and listen. *arXiv preprint arXiv:2306.12925*.

Holger Schwenk, Vishrav Chaudhary, Shuo Sun, Hongyu Gong, and Francisco Guzmán. 2019. Wikimatrix: Mining 135m parallel sentences in 1620 language pairs from wikipedia. *ArXiv*, abs/1907.05791.

Aditya Siddhant, Ankur Bapna, Orhan Firat, Yuan Cao, Mia Xu Chen, Isaac Caswell, and Xavier Garcia. 2022. Towards the next 1000 languages in multilingual machine translation: Exploring the synergy between supervised and self-supervised learning. *arXiv preprint arXiv:2201.03110*.

Changhan Wang, Anne Wu, Jiatao Gu, and Juan Miguel Pino. 2021. Covost 2 and massively multilingual speech translation. In *Interspeech*.

Changhan Wang, Anne Wu, and Juan Pino. 2020. Covost 2 and massively multilingual speech-to-text translation. *arXiv preprint arXiv:2007.10310*.

Chengyi Wang, Sanyuan Chen, Yu Wu, Ziqiang Zhang, Long Zhou, Shujie Liu, Zhuo Chen, Yanqing Liu, Huaming Wang, Jinyu Li, Lei He, Sheng Zhao, and Furu Wei. 2023. Neural codec language models are zero-shot text to speech synthesizers.

Linting Xue, Noah Constant, Adam Roberts, Mihir Kale, Rami Al-Rfou, Aditya Siddhant, Aditya Barua, and Colin Raffel. 2020. mt5: A massively multilingual pre-trained text-to-text transformer. *arXiv preprint arXiv:2010.11934*.

Yinfei Yang, Gustavo Hernandez Abrego, Steve Yuan, Mandy Guo, Qinlan Shen, Daniel Cer, Yun-Hsuan Sung, Brian Strope, and Ray Kurzweil. 2019. Improving multilingual sentence embedding using bi-directional dual encoder with additive margin softmax. *arXiv preprint arXiv:1902.08564*.

Xu Zhang, Felix X. Yu, Sanjiv Kumar, and Shih-Fu Chang. 2017. Learning spread-out local feature descriptors. *2017 IEEE International Conference on Computer Vision (ICCV)*, pages 4605–4613.

Yu Zhang, Wei Han, James Qin, Yongqiang Wang, Ankur Bapna, Zhehuai Chen, Nanxin Chen, Bo Li, Vera Axelrod, Gary Wang, et al. 2023. Google usm: Scaling automatic speech recognition beyond 100 languages. *arXiv preprint arXiv:2303.01037*.

A Appendix

A.1 Training Setup

Ni et al. (2022) showed that applying a contrastive loss to sentence encoders leads to improved retrieval performance in downstream tasks. After

Input Type	Before Tokenization	Input Ids
Speech	`[English Speech]` **`50,210,245,`** `...`	`240, 503,` **`32050, 32210, 32245,`** `...`
Transcription	`[English Text] Hello World .`	`59, 294, 691, ...`

Table 3: Example of the speech and transcript inputs given to our model. The speech input is composed of a prefix containing the language and the input modality. Text will be tokenized using the LLMs tokenizer and an offset will be applied to the audio token to match the tokens that were reserved within the audio token vocabulary. Bold numbers represent the audio tokens before tokenization and after the offset is applied to the audio tokens.

initializing our model from the PaLM 2, we use a contrastive loss (Hadsell et al., 2006).

$$L = -\frac{1}{N}\sum_{i=1}^{N}\frac{e^{\text{sim}(\boldsymbol{x}_i,\boldsymbol{y}_i)}}{\sum_{j=1}^{N}e^{\text{sim}(\boldsymbol{x}_i,\boldsymbol{y}_j)}} \quad (1)$$

Using equation 1, our multi-modal DE will learn from paired speech and text embeddings $(\boldsymbol{x}_i, \boldsymbol{y}_i)$, where $\boldsymbol{y}_i$ is considered as a positive example to $\boldsymbol{x}_i$ while all other examples where $i \neq j$ are negative ones. The model should learn to bring the positive transcriptions closer to the corresponding speech sample, while pushing away all the other negative transcriptions. In our training, the positive and negative distinction is done within the training batch. Hence, we apply an in-batch softmax as part of our loss computation. Lastly, *sim()* is a similarity function formulated as the dot product between the speech sample and the transcription embeddings.

To train our model, we use the sum of a contrastive loss with a spreadout loss (Zhang et al., 2017) of both the speech and text embeddings. We calculate the contrastive loss (Yang et al., 2019) in a bidirectional way, by adding the loss in the speech-to-text and the text-to-speech direction.

We use the Adam (Kingma and Ba, 2014) optimizer with a learning rate of 1.0×10^{-3} with linear ramp cosine decay scheduler with 2.5k warm up steps. We use a dropout probability of 0.1 and train for 100k steps with a batch size of 1024.

A.2 Expressing Tasks

For training and inference, we found that using a prefix improves speech-to-text retrieval performance. Therefore, we pre-pend a prefix containing the language and modality shown in in Table 3. In the case of a speech utterance, the prefix will be tokenized with the LLMs tokenizer and the remaining will be converted to audio tokens.

A.3 Data

Table 4 shows the training and evaluation datasets we used through out our experiments. We used 21 languages CoVoST-2 to train our model on speech-to-text retrieval which amounts to approximately 900 hours of speech. To evaluate our models speech-to-text retrieval capabilities, we evaluate on FLEURS speech-to-text test split on 102 languages. We use FLEURS speech-to-text translation test split to evaluate our models abilities on tasks that require cross-lingual and cross-modal knowledge. We evaluate of 4 different languages: German, Polish, French, and Dutch.

Dataset	Type	Task	Langs.	Split	Size
CoVoST-2	Speech	S2T	21	Train	900 h.
FLEURS	Speech	S2T	102	Test	283 h.
FLEURS	Speech	S2TT	102	Test	283 h.
Wikimatrix	Text	MT	4	Train	9M sents.

Table 4: Training and evaluation datasets. CoVoST-2 is used for speech-to-text retrieval (S2T), Wikimatrix is for machine translation retrieval (MT), and FLEURS is for evaluating X → En speech-to-text translation retrieval (S2TT) and also speech-to-text retrieval (S2T).

	# Sents. X → En
German (de)	6.2M
Polish (pl)	2.1M
French (fr)	705k
Dutch (nl)	570k

Table 5: Number of parallel sentences used in the machine translation mixture from Wikimatrix corpus.

We find that combining speech-to-text retrieval data and readily available translation data improves our models cross-lingual and cross-modal abilities. Table 5 shows the number of parallel sentences we used during training from X → En.

A.4 Performance Breakdown By Language

Table 6 includes the PaLM 2 DE *R@1* for each language found in FLEURS. We also include the language group from Table 2 and the number of examples found within each S2T test set.

Idx	Language Name	Code	Family	# Examples	*R@1*	
					mSLAM	PaLM 2 DE
1	Afrikaans	af	Indo-European	414	90.1	99.3
2	Amharic	am	Afro-Asiatic	516	34.1	69.6
3	Arabic	ar	Afro-Asiatic	427	82.7	98.8
4	Armenian	hy	Indo-European	929	50.3	89.7
5	Assamese	as	Indo-European	980	81.5	87.4
6	Asturian	ast	Indo-European	946	90.1	100.0
7	Azerbaijani	az	Turkic	918	83.0	98.4
8	Belarusian	be	Indo-European	955	90.2	97.2
9	Bengali	bn	Indo-European	911	83.5	84.6
10	Bosnian	bs	Indo-European	923	95.5	99.8
11	Bulgarian	bg	Indo-European	657	95.1	100.0
12	Burmese	my	Sino-Tibetan	870	2.4	19.3
13	Cantonese	yue	Sino-Tibetan	819	2.4	83.6
14	Catalan	ca	Indo-European	938	93.2	100.0
15	Cebuano	ceb	Austronesian	532	79.8	94.9
16	Croatian	hr	Indo-European	914	98.0	99.8
17	Czech	cs	Indo-European	720	98.1	99.6
18	Danish	da	Indo-European	929	94.1	99.9
19	Dutch	nl	Indo-European	364	95.3	100.0
20	English	en	Indo-European	647	96.0	99.1
21	Estonian	et	Uralic	892	95.6	99.9
22	Filipino	fil	Austronesian	928	73.1	89.1
23	Finnish	fi	Uralic	916	93.0	98.9
24	French	fr	Indo-European	675	90.7	100.0
25	Fula	ff	Atlantic-Congo	649	81.4	81.7
26	Galician	gl	Indo-European	927	90.9	100.0
27	Ganda	lg	Atlantic-Congo	705	90.7	75.7
28	Georgian	ka	Kartvelian	978	70.5	82.9
29	German	de	Indo-European	841	91.2	100.0
30	Greek	el	Indo-European	649	81.2	73.2
31	Gujarati	gu	Indo-European	1000	77.0	95.9
32	Hausa	ha	Afro-Asiatic	557	84.5	83.1
33	Hebrew	he	Afro-Asiatic	792	64.0	76.0
34	Hindi	hi	Indo-European	417	78.0	83.7
35	Hungarian	hu	Uralic	902	85.3	98.3
36	Icelandic	is	Indo-European	46	71.7	97.8
37	Igbo	ig	Atlantic-Congo	869	85.8	64.9
38	Indonesian	id	Austronesian	684	79.6	99.4
39	Irish	ga	Indo-European	829	55.1	69.5
40	Italian	it	Indo-European	857	93.5	100.0
41	Japanese	ja	Japonic	650	5.8	91.5
42	Javanese	jv	Austronesian	722	78.0	97.0
43	Kabuverdianu	kea	Indo-European	859	95.4	99.9

Idx	Language Name	Code	Family	# Examples	R@1	
					mSLAM	PaLM 2 DE
44	Kamba	kam	Atlantic-Congo	798	89.7	81.5
45	Kannada	kn	Dravidian	831	69.0	88.8
46	Kazakh	kk	Turkic	841	88.7	83.1
47	Khmer	km	Austro-Asiatic	765	42.1	20.3
48	Korean	ko	Koreanic	382	5.2	52.4
49	Kyrgyz	ky	Turkic	974	84.3	88.6
50	Lao	lo	Kra-Dai	399	37.0	23.3
51	Latvian	lv	Indo-European	848	97.4	100.0
52	Lingala	ln	Atlantic-Congo	440	91.2	76.4
53	Lithuanian	lt	Indo-European	985	96.8	98.2
54	Luo	luo	Nilo-Saharan	254	91.0	92.5
55	Luxembourgish	lb	Indo-European	929	80.5	74.6
56	Macedonian	mk	Indo-European	967	96.1	98.8
57	Malay	ms	Austronesian	749	77.7	98.7
58	Malayalam	ml	Dravidian	944	62.3	88.3
59	Maltese	mt	Afro-Asiatic	918	92.7	76.0
60	Mandarin	cmn	Sino-Tibetan	944	5.4	100.0
61	Maori	mi	Austronesian	890	64.7	65.3
62	Marathi	mr	Indo-European	1005	69.8	82.4
63	Mongolian	mn	Mongolic	949	70.7	99.9
64	Nepali	ne	Indo-European	724	66.1	89.6
65	Northern-Sotho	nso	Atlantic-Congo	738	80.8	70.3
66	Norwegian	nb	Indo-European	357	91.9	100.0
67	Nyanja	ny	Atlantic-Congo	745	85.5	63.6
68	Occitan	oc	Indo-European	968	77.4	99.4
69	Oriya	or	Indo-European	875	15.7	95.1
70	Oromo	om	Afro-Asiatic	41	92.7	100.0
71	Pashto	ps	Indo-European	510	84.8	91.0
72	Persian	fa	Indo-European	858	85.4	100.0
73	Polish	pl	Indo-European	758	95.8	99.3
74	Portuguese	pt	Indo-European	914	91.9	99.9
75	Punjabi	pa	Indo-European	574	70.6	96.7
76	Romanian	ro	Indo-European	882	92.0	100.0
77	Russian	ru	Indo-European	774	93.2	100.0
78	Serbian	sr	Indo-European	700	97.7	99.1
79	Shona	sn	Atlantic-Congo	920	84.1	53.9
80	Sindhi	sd	Indo-European	977	71.8	85.4
81	Slovak	sk	Indo-European	791	97.6	99.5
82	Slovenian	sl	Indo-European	834	97.4	100.0
83	Somali	so	Afro-Asiatic	1007	68.7	86.0
84	Sorani-Kurdish	ckb	Indo-European	918	80.8	96.7
85	Spanish	es	Indo-European	907	69.6	100.0
86	Swahili	sw	Atlantic-Congo	487	91.2	86.2

Idx	Language Name	Code	Family	# Examples	*R@1*	
					mSLAM	PaLM 2 DE
87	Swedish	sv	Indo-European	758	94.2	100.0
88	Tajik	tg	Indo-European	590	76.3	92.7
89	Tamil	ta	Dravidian	582	58.0	98.1
90	Telugu	te	Dravidian	471	73.5	93.0
91	Thai	th	Kra-Dai	1011	3.2	20.9
92	Turkish	tr	Turkic	742	84.5	100.0
93	Ukrainian	uk	Indo-European	750	93.5	99.3
94	Umbundu	umb	Atlantic-Congo	264	77.3	62.1
95	Urdu	ur	Indo-European	299	70.6	91.3
96	Uzbek	uz	Turkic	861	67.6	94.2
97	Vietnamese	vi	Austro-Asiatic	850	64.5	48.6
98	Welsh	cy	Indo-European	1002	82.3	96.1
99	Wolof	wo	Atlantic-Congo	351	90.6	87.5
100	Xhosa	xh	Atlantic-Congo	1034	90.9	30.2
101	Yoruba	yo	Atlantic-Congo	816	92.4	84.6
102	Zulu	zu	Atlantic-Congo	822	85.5	67.2
	All (102)				76.9	86.7

Table 6: Language name, code, family, and number of examples for each test set found in FLEURS. We report *R@1* for mSLAM and PaLM 2 DE.

Conditioning LLMs with Emotion in Neural Machine Translation

Charles Brazier and **Jean-Luc Rouas**
Univ. Bordeaux, CNRS, Bordeaux INP, LaBRI, UMR 5800, F-33400 Talence, France
charles.brazier@u-bordeaux.fr jean-luc.rouas@labri.fr

Abstract

Large Language Models (LLMs) have shown remarkable performance in Natural Language Processing tasks, including Machine Translation (MT). In this work, we propose a novel MT pipeline that integrates emotion information extracted from a Speech Emotion Recognition (SER) model into LLMs to enhance translation quality. We first fine-tune five existing LLMs on the Libri-trans dataset and select the most performant model. Subsequently, we augment LLM prompts with different dimensional emotions and train the selected LLM under these different configurations. Our experiments reveal that integrating emotion information, especially arousal, into LLM prompts leads to notable improvements in translation quality.

1 Introduction

Large Language Models (LLMs) are transformer-based (Vaswani et al., 2017) deep learning models designed to understand and generate natural language text by predicting the probability of the next token in a sequence. LLMs excel across various Natural Language Processing (NLP) tasks, such as information retrieval (Zhu et al., 2023b), instruction following (Ouyang et al., 2022), or engaging in chatbot discussions (OpenAI, 2022).

Among NLP tasks, LLMs have shown great capacities in Machine Translation (MT) (Zhu et al., 2023a), the task of translating a text from one language to another. Previous research has enhanced LLM performance in MT through various strategies, including optimized prompting techniques (Zhang et al., 2023), in-context learning features (Brown et al., 2020) to improve translation quality over time (Moslem et al., 2023a,b), and a two-stage fine-tuning method composed of a first fine-tuning on monolingual data to learn general linguistic knowledge followed by a second fine-tuning on parallel data (Xu et al., 2023) that establishes the current state-of-the-art method in MT.

Apart from LLMs, previous works in MT have demonstrated the possibility of controlling the translation by adding extra information to the model that is not explicitly specified in the source sentence to be translated, and that can influence the translation. Existing works in that direction focused on the control of politeness (Sennrich et al., 2019), gender (Vanmassenhove et al., 2018; Gaido et al., 2023), or emotion (Brazier and Rouas, 2024) of the translation and showed that this extra information helps improve translation quality.

In this work, we propose to improve translation performances of an LLM-based model by adding emotion as extra information in the prompt of the model to condition the translation. This work relies on the fact that words can be classified into emotion categories, leading to affective word lists (Pennebaker et al., 2001). Thus, conditioning the translation with a specific emotion would use a suitable vocabulary in the translation. In Brazier and Rouas (2024), authors showed that adding arousal information, reflecting the level of stimulation (ranging from calm to excited), extracted from the voice and added at the start of each input text sentence, helps improve translation performances. In the following, we study the behavior of several LLMs for the task of MT when emotion dimensions are added to input prompts.

To address this problem, we first fine-tune several existing LLMs for the task of English-to-French text-to-text translation. Then, after selecting the best model as baseline for our experiments, we compute for each input sentence its emotional dimensions with the help of a state-of-the-art Speech Emotion Recognition (SER) model applied to audio recordings. Finally, we compare translation performance with and without the addition of each emotional dimension as extra information added to each input prompt. We show that emotion improves translation (BLEU and COMET), especially in the case of arousal.

Proceedings of the 21st International Conference on Spoken Language Translation (IWSLT 2024), pages 81–86
August 15-16, 2024 ©2024 Association for Computational Linguistics

2 Related works

In this work, we aim at combining an LLM-based MT model with emotion information to improve translation performances. In the following, we first describe a close work that performs this combination without the use of an LLM. Then, we list several existing LLMs that can be used as a baseline for our MT task.

2.1 Machine Translation with Emotion

To our knowledge, the only work that combines an MT model with emotion information is described in Brazier and Rouas (2024). In this study, the authors utilize a state-of-the-art Speech Emotion Recognition (SER) model (Wagner et al., 2023) to automatically estimate dimensional emotion values, including arousal, dominance, and valence, for each audio recording associated with text sentence. These values are then transformed into unique emotion tokens, either positive or negative, which are added at the beginning of tokenized input text sentences. The authors report an increase in translation BLEU score, especially when adding arousal tokens at the start of input sentences.

The MT model used for their experiments is a transformer-based encoder-decoder architecture, comprising 6 layers for the encoder, 6 layers for the decoder, and 4 attention heads in each self-attention layer. The model is trained on the Libri-trans dataset (Kocabiyikoglu et al., 2018), which includes triplets of English recordings, English texts, and French texts, totaling 235 hours of data (230h for train, 2h for dev, and 3.5h for test). The model performs English-to-French translation.

In this work, we propose to use the same translation pipeline, but instead of using a specific MT model, we replace it with a fine-tuned LLM. Since LLMs have more trainable parameters, we anticipate improved translation performances. However, our objective is to observe how LLMs behave when augmented with emotion information in the input prompt.

2.2 LLM selection for MT

Recent advances in Large Language Modeling have significantly expanded the capabilities of LLMs across various tasks, such as reasoning, coding, or mathematics. Among the numerous existing LLMs (Chiang et al., 2024), the best-performing models are GPT-4 (OpenAI, 2023), LLaMA 3 (AI@Meta, 2024), Gemini 1.5 (Team, 2024), or Claude 3 (Anthropic, 2024).

For the task of MT, we restrict our LLM selection to models that are open-source, promising (high rank in the LLM arena[1], or already fine-tuned to the MT task), and that only contain 7 billion (7B) of parameters. We select 5 different models that are described in the following.

The first selected LLM is *Mistral-7B-v0.1*[2], an open-source model (Jiang et al., 2023) which ranks among the best 7B-parameter models.

As the second model, we select *Mistral-7B-Instruct-v0.2*[3]. The model is similar to the previous model but has been fine-tuned to follow instructions.

Our third selected model is *TowerBase-7B-v0.1*[4]. This model (Alves et al., 2024) is based on LLaMA 2 (AI@Meta, 2023) and its training has been continued on multilingual data (including English and French monolingual data, as well as bilingual data).

Similarly to Mistral, we select *TowerInstruct-7B-v0.2*[5] as our fourth model. This model is a variant of the previous one that has been fine-tuned to follow instructions including translations.

Finally, as our fifth model, we select the SOTA MT model *ALMA-7B-R*[6], which is based on LLaMA 2 (AI@Meta, 2023), and fine-tuned on monolingual and parallel data. However, the data used for fine-tuning does not include French.

3 Experiments and results

In this section, we describe our experiments for the task of English-to-French text-to-text translation. We conduct two successive experiments. Firstly, we fine-tune five existing LLMs on the Libri-trans dataset (Kocabiyikoglu et al., 2018) and consider the best model as a foundation for our second experiment. Secondly, we fine-tune the selected LLM on the same task but under different configurations. Henceforth, prompts used for translation include each emotion dimension that is automatically estimated from the SER model.

3.1 Fine-tuning LLMs on Libri-trans

To perform MT with LLMs, the task needs to be converted into a language modeling problem with

[1]http://chat.lmsys.org/?leaderboard
[2]http://huggingface.co/mistralai/Mistral-7B-v0.1
[3]http://huggingface.co/mistralai/Mistral-7B-Instruct-v0.2
[4]http://huggingface.co/Unbabel/TowerBase-7B-v0.1
[5]http://huggingface.co/Unbabel/TowerInstruct-7B-v0.2
[6]http://huggingface.co/haoranxu/ALMA-7B-R

Model	BLEU		COMET	
	dev	test	dev	test
Mistral	16.4	16.7	73.2	72.5
MistralInstruct	16.0	17.9	72.1	71.9
TowerBase	**24.0**	**20.6**	**73.8**	**72.9**
TowerInstruct	6.4	6.1	35.5	35.5
ALMA	7.1	7.5	52.1	52.8

Table 1: BLEU and COMET scores of our five selected LLMs on dev and test sets of Libri-trans.

the use of prompts. In this work, we perform zero-shot prompting and follow two different templates. The first template will be applied to *Mistral-7B-v0.1* and *TowerBase-7B-v0.1*:

```
English: <src txt> \n French: <tgt txt>
```
(1)

where `<src txt>` and `<tgt txt>` refer to the English source sentence and the French target sentence respectively.

The second template will be applied to models that follow instructions, namely *Mistral-7B-Instruct-v0.2*, *TowerInstruct-7B-v0.2*, and *ALMA-7B-R*:

```
[INST] Translate from English to French: <src txt> [/INST] \n <tgt txt>
```
(2)

To fine-tune LLMs, we employ QLoRA (Hu et al., 2022; Dettmers et al., 2023), a Parameter Efficient Fine-Tuning method (Mangrulkar et al., 2022) that allows training with significantly fewer parameters. Additionally, we apply a 4-bit quantization to reduce memory usage while maintaining 16-bit precision during computation.

We provide two distinct metrics to evaluate our MT models. The first metric is the BLEU score computed using sacrebleu (Post, 2018). It reflects the degree of lexical matches (number of common n-grams) between the proposed translation and its corresponding reference. The second metric is the COMET score [7] (Rei et al., 2022). It is computed from a trained model and reflects translation quality between translation, reference, and also the source sentence. According to the metric ranking presented in Freitag et al. (2022), we rely more on the COMET score than on the BLEU score.

Table 1 showcases the results of our first experiment. In this table, we report BLEU and COMET scores of the five selected LLMs on both the dev and test sets of the Libri-trans dataset.

[7] https://huggingface.co/Unbabel/wmt22-comet-da

The table highlights three models, *Mistral-7B-v0.1*, *Mistral-7B-Instruct-v0.2*, and *TowerBase-7B-v0.1*, that attain high BLEU and COMET scores. They obtain COMET scores ranging from 72.1 to 73.8 on the dev set and from 71.9 to 72.9 on the test set. Additionally, their BLEU scores ranged from 16.0 to 24.0 on the dev set and from 16.7 to 20.6 on the test set. While COMET scores are not meant to be interpretable (but enable the comparison between models), BLEU scores indicate, on average, a translation that is more or less clear with numerous grammatical errors. These low BLEU scores are comparable to performances of previous works on this dataset (Zhao et al., 2021; Brazier and Rouas, 2024) and are mainly caused by the nature of the data (audiobooks with literary vocabulary).

Also, it is worth noting that two models, *TowerInstruct-7B-v0.2* and *ALMA-7B-R*, exhibit poor performances in MT when fine-tuned on Libri-trans. In the case of *ALMA-7B-R*, this can be explained by the fact that French is not among the languages included in the data used to pre-train the model. Thus, the model fails at predicting French text.

As additional training information, all LLMs have obtained their optimal state in a maximum of 5 epochs. This represents a training time of 3 hours on a GPU NVIDIA A100 for each model. This fast fine-tuning time is due to QLoRA and 4-bit quantization strategies.

To summarize, the best machine translation performances were achieved with the *TowerBase-7B-v0.1*. This LLM serves as a baseline and foundation model for the following experiment.

3.2 Fine-tuning LLMs with Emotion

The second experiment aims at observing the behavior of our LLM-based *TowerBase-7B-v0.1* model on the task of English-to-French Machine Translation when emotion information is added to the prompt before translation.

As a first step, we estimate the emotion of each English recording present in the Libri-trans dataset. Following the same methodology as Brazier and Rouas (2024), we compute dimensional emotion values for arousal, dominance, and valence with the help of a trained SER model (Wagner et al., 2023). Emotion values range between 0 and 1 and are correctly balanced (medians between 0.4 and 0.6, see Brazier and Rouas (2024)).

As a second step, we create specific prompts that include the emotion information in the text. For this purpose, we propose 3 different templates. The first template adds emotion information before the source sentence:

English <status> <emotion>: <src txt> \n French: <tgt txt> (3)

where status is replaced by either *with* or *without* if the emotion value is higher or lower than 0.5 respectively, emotion is replaced by either *arousal*, *dominance*, or *valence*, src txt represents the English source sentence, and tgt txt represents the French target translation.

The second template adds emotion information before the target sentence:

English: <src txt> \n French <status> <emotion>: <tgt txt> (4)

The third template is inspired from Brazier and Rouas (2024), where emotion information is added as a discrete token at the start of the source sentence:

English: [<emotion> <polarity>] <src txt> \n French: <tgt txt> (5)

where polarity is replaced by either *positive* or *negative* if the emotion value is higher or lower than 0.5 respectively.

In this experiment, the *TowerBase-7B-v0.1* model is retrained from its initial state and not from the training checkpoint obtained after the previous experiment. In the following, all models obtain their best performances in less than 5 training epochs.

Table 2 showcases the results of our second experiment. It reports BLEU and COMET scores of the selected *TowerBase-7B-v0.1* model on the dev and test sets of the Libri-trans dataset under different configurations. The first line mentions the score of the LLM obtained in the previous experiment and serves as a baseline for the second experiment. The other lines correspond to the model trained with different emotions (arousal, dominance, or valence), and with different prompts (the numbers 3, 4, and 5 refer to their equation number).

We first remark that, except in the case of *dominance5*, all COMET scores improved, compared to their baseline. This reflects a better translation quality when adding emotion information to the prompts. The best COMET scores are obtained when arousal information is added to the prompt using Equation 3. In this configuration, COMET scores are increased by +1.1 and +1.4 for the dev and test sets of Libri-trans respectively.

Model	**BLEU**		**COMET**	
	dev	**test**	**dev**	**test**
TowerBase	24.0	20.6	73.8	72.9
+arousal3	22.1	21.8	**74.9**	**74.3**
+arousal4	**25.6**	**24.1**	74.8	73.9
+arousal5	19.3	19.2	74.2	73.4
+dominance3	19.9	19.4	74.4	73.5
+dominance4	18.9	20.9	**74.9**	74.0
+dominance5	16.5	20.1	73.4	73.0
+valence3	21.5	18.9	74.1	73.5
+valence4	18.3	21.2	74.6	73.9
+valence5	17.2	16.0	74.5	73.6

Table 2: BLEU and COMET scores of the TowerBase model on dev and test sets of Libri-trans. First line: baseline score. Other lines: score when trained with emotion in the prompt.

Secondly, we observe that BLEU scores show improvements only for specific models. The best BLEU scores are obtained when arousal information is added to the prompt using Equation 4. In this configuration, BLEU scores increase by +1.6 and +3.5 for the dev and test sets of Libri-trans respectively. However, due to the low ranking of BLEU (Freitag et al., 2022), we do not conduct further analysis based on this metric.

In summary, incorporating emotion information into the translation process appears to enhance translation quality. The highest scores are achieved when utilizing the arousal dimension with Equation 3 or 4. This finding aligns with the results reported in Brazier and Rouas (2024).

4 Conclusion

We proposed a new MT pipeline that combines an LLM-based model and emotion information extracted from a SER model to improve translation performances. We obtain the best performances when the arousal value is added to the LLM prompt.

As future work, we will apply our method to other multilingual datasets including Must-C (Di Gangi et al., 2019). Unlike the Libri-trans dataset, which consists of literary text read by speakers, Must-C encompasses various speech types, such as TED talks, which can offer more emotional variability and therefore further enhance translation performance. We also plan to extend our method to the speech-to-text task, also known as Speech translation.

5 Acknowledgements

The research presented in this paper is conducted as part of the project FVLLMONTI, which has received funding from the European Union's Horizon 2020 Research and Innovation action under grant agreement No 101016776.

References

AI@Meta. 2023. LLaMA 2: Open Foundation and Fine-tuned Chat Models. *Preprint*, arXiv:2307.09288.

AI@Meta. 2024. LLaMA 3 Model Card.

Duarte M. Alves, José Pombal, Nuno M. Guerreiro, Pedro H. Martins, João Alves, Amin Farajian, Ben Peters, Ricardo Rei, Patrick Fernandes, Sweta Agrawal, Pierre Colombo, José G.C. de Souza, and André F.T. Martins. 2024. Tower: An Open Multilingual Large Language Model for Translation-Related Tasks. *Preprint*, arXiv:2402.17733.

Anthropic. 2024. Claude 3: Introducing the Next Generation of Claude.

Charles Brazier and Jean-Luc Rouas. 2024. Usefulness of Emotional Prosody in Neural Machine Translation. In *Proc. of the International Conference on Speech Prosody (SP)*, Leiden, The Netherlands.

Tom B. Brown, Benjamin Mann, Nick Ryder, Melanie Subbiah, Jared Kaplan, Prafulla Dhariwal, Arvind Neelakantan, Pranav Shyam, Girish Sastry, Amanda Askell, Sandhini Agarwal, Ariel Herbert-Voss, Gretchen Krueger, Tom Henighan, Rewon Child, Daniel M. Ramesh, Aditya ans Ziegler, Jeffrey Wu, Clemens Winter, Christopher Hesse, Mark Chen, Eric Sigler, Mateusz Litwin, Scott Gray, Benjamin Chess, Jack Clark, Christopher Bernet, Sam McCandlish, Alec Radford, Ilya Sutskever, and Dario Amodei. 2020. Language Models are Few-shot Learners. In *Proc. of the Annual Conference on Neural Information Processing Systems (NeurIPS)*, volume 33, pages 1877–1901, Virtual.

Wei-Lin Chiang, Lianmin Zheng, Ying Sheng, Anastasios Nikolas Angelopoulos, Tianle Li, Dacheng Li, Hao Zhang, Banghua Zhu, Michael Jordan, Joseph E. Gonzalez, and Ion Stoica. 2024. Chatbot Arena: An Open Platform for Evaluating LLMs by Human Preference. *Preprint*, arXiv:2403.04132.

Tim Dettmers, Artidoro Pagnoni, Ari Holtzman, and Luke Zettlemoyer. 2023. Qlora: Efficient Finetuning of Quantized LLMs. In *Proc. of the Annual Conference on Neural Information Processing Systems (NeurIPS)*, volume 36, New Orleans, LA, USA.

Mattia Antonino Di Gangi, Roldano Cattoni, Luisa Bentivogli, Matteo Negri, and Marco Turchi. 2019. MuST-C: a Multilingual Speech Translation Corpus. In *Proc. of the Conference of the North American Chapter of the Association for Computational Linguistics: Human Language Technologies (NAACL-HLT)*, pages 2012–2017, Minneapolis, MN, USA.

Markus Freitag, Ricardo Rei, Nitika Mathur, Chi-kiu Lo, Craig Stewart, Eleftherios Avramidis, Tom Kocmi, George Foster, Alon Lavie, and André F. T. Martins. 2022. Results of WMT22 Metrics Shared Task: Stop Using BLEU – Neural Metrics Are Better and More Robust. In *Proc. of the Conference on Machine Translation (WMT)*, pages 46–68, Abu Dhabi, United Arab Emirates.

Marco Gaido, Dennis Fucci, Matteo Negri, and Luisa Bentivogli. 2023. How to Build Competitive Multi-gender Speech Translation Models for Controlling Speaker Gender Translation. In *Proc. of the Italian Conference on Computational Linguistics (CLiC-it)*.

Edward J. Hu, Yelong Shen, Phillip Wallis, Zeyuan Allen-Zhu, Yuanzhi Li, Shean Wang, Lu Wang, and Weizhu Chen. 2022. LoRA: Low-Rank Adaptation of Large Language Models. In *Proc. of the International Conference on Learning Representations (ICLR)*, Virtual.

Albert Q. Jiang, Alexandre Sablayrolles, Arthur Mensch, Chris Bamford, Devendra Singh Chaplot, Diego de las Casas, Florian Bressand, Gianna Lengyel, Guillaume Lample, Lucile Saulnier, Lélio Renard Lavaud, Marie-Anne Lachaux, Pierre Stock, Teven Le Scao, Thibaut Lavril, Thomas Wang, Timothée Lacroix, and William El Sayed. 2023. Mistral 7B. *Preprint*, arXiv:2310.06825.

Ali Can Kocabiyikoglu, Laurent Besacier, and Olivier Kraif. 2018. Augmenting Librispeech with French Translations: A Multimodal Corpus for Direct Speech Translation Evaluation. In *Proc. of the International Conference on Language Resources and Evaluation (LREC)*, Miyazaki, Japan.

Sourab Mangrulkar, Sylvain Gugger, Lysandre Debut, Younes Belkada, Sayak Paul, and Benjamin Bossan. 2022. PEFT: State-of-the-art Parameter-Efficient Fine-Tuning methods. `https://github.com/huggingface/peft`.

Yasmin Moslem, Rejwanul Haque, John D. Kelleher, and Andy Way. 2023a. Adaptive Machine Translation with Large Language Models. In *Proc. of the Annual Conference of the European Association for Machine Translation (EAMT)*, pages 227–237, Tampere, Finland.

Yasmin Moslem, Rejwanul Haque, and Andy Way. 2023b. Fine-tuning Large Language Models for Adaptive Machine Translation. *Preprint*, arXiv:2312.12740.

OpenAI. 2022. `https://chat.openai.com/`.

OpenAI. 2023. GPT-4 Technical Report. *Preprint*, arXiv:2303.08774.

Long Ouyang, Jeffrey Wu, Xu Jiang, Diogo Almeida, Carroll L. Wainwright, Pamela Mishkin, Chong Zhang, Sandhini Agarwal, Katarina Slama, Alex Ray, John Schulman, Jacob Hilton, Fraser Kelton, Luke Miller, Maddie Simens, Amanda Askell, Peter Welinder, Paul F. Christiano, Jan Leike, and Ryan Lowe. 2022. Training Language Models to Follow Instructions with Human Feedback. In *Proc. of the Annual Conference on Neural Information Processing Systems (NeurIPS)*, volume 35, pages 27730–27744, New Orleans, LA, USA.

J.W. Pennebaker, M.E. Francis, and R.J. Booth. 2001. Linguistic Inquiry and Word Count: LIWC 2001. *Mahway: Lawrence Erlbaum Associates*, 71.

Matt Post. 2018. A Call for Clarity in Reporting BLEU Scores. In *Proc. of the Conference on Machine Translation: Research Papers (WMT)*, pages 186–191, Brussels, Belgium.

Ricardo Rei, José G. C. de Souza, Duarte M. Alves, Chrysoula Zerva, Ana C Farinha, Taisiya Glushkova, Alon Lavie, Luisa Coheur, and André F. T. Martins. 2022. COMET-22: Unbabel-IST 2022 Submission for the Metrics Shared Task. In *Proc. of the Conference on Machine Translation (WMT)*, pages 578–585, Abu Dhabi, United Arab Emirates.

Rico Sennrich, Barry Haddow, and Alexandra Birch. 2019. Controlling Politeness in Neural Machine Translation via Side Constraints. In *Proc. of the Conference of the North American Chapter of the Association for Computational Linguistics: Human Language Technologies (NAACL-HLT)*, pages 35–40, San Diego, USA.

Gemini Team. 2024. Gemini 1.5: Unlocking Multimodal Understanding across Millions of Tokens of Context. *Preprint*, arXiv:2403.05530.

Eva Vanmassenhove, Christian Hardmeier, and Andy Way. 2018. Getting Gender Right in Neural Machine Translation. In *Proc. of the Conference on Empirical Methods in Natural Language Processing (CEMNLP)*, pages 3003–3008, Brussels, Belgium.

Ashish Vaswani, Noam Shazeer, Niki Parmar, Jakob Uszkoreit, Llion Jones, Aidan N Gomez, Łukasz Kaiser, and Illia Polosukhin. 2017. Attention is All you Need. In *Proc. of the Annual Conference on Neural Information Processing Systems (NIPS)*, pages 5998–6008, Long Beach, USA.

Johannes Wagner, Andreas Triantafyllopoulos, Hagen Wierstorf, Maximilian Schmitt, Felix Burkhardt, Florian Eyben, and Björn W Schuller. 2023. Dawn of the Transformer Era in Speech Emotion Recognition: Closing the Valence Gap. *IEEE Transactions on Pattern Analysis and Machine Intelligence*, 45:10745–10759.

Haoran Xu, Young Jin Kim, Amr Sharaf, and Hany Hassan Awadalla. 2023. A Paradigm Shift in Machine Translation: Boosting Translation Performance of Large Language Models. *Preprint*, arXiv:2309.11674.

Biao Zhang, Barry Haddow, and Alexandra Birch. 2023. Prompting Large Language Model for Machine Translation: A Case Study. In *Proc. of the International Conference on Machine Learning (ICML)*, pages 41092–41110, Edinburgh, Scotland.

Chengqi Zhao, Mingxuan Wang, Qianqian Dong, Rong Ye, and Lei Li. 2021. NeurST: Neural speech translation toolkit. In *Proc. of the Joint Conference of the Annual Meeting of the Association for Computational Linguistics and the International Joint Conference on Natural Language Processing (ACL)*, pages 55–62, Online.

Wenhao Zhu, Hongyi Liu, Qingxiu Dong, Jingjing Xu, Shujian Huang, Lingpeng Kong, Jiajun Chen, and Lei Li. 2023a. Multilingual Machine Translation with Large Language Models: Empirical Results and Analysis. *Preprint*, arXiv:2304.04675.

Yutao Zhu, Huaying Yuan, Shuting Wang, Jiongnan Liu, Wenhan Liu, Chenlong Deng, Zhicheng Dou, and Ji-Rong Wen. 2023b. Large Language Models for Information Retrieval: A Survey. *Preprint*, arXiv:2308.07107.

The NYA's Offline Speech Translation System for IWSLT 2024

Yingxin Zhang, Guodong Ma, Binbin Du
NetEase YiDun AI Lab, Hangzhou, China
{zhangyingxin03,maguodong,dubinbin}@corp.netease.com

Abstract

This paper reports the NYA's submissions to IWSLT 2024 Offline Speech Translation (ST) task on the sub-tasks including English to Chinese, Japanese, and German. In detail, we participate in the unconstrained training track using the cascaded ST structure. For the automatic speech recognition (ASR) model, we use the Whisper large-v3 model. For the neural machine translation (NMT) model, the wider and deeper Transformer is adapted as the backbone model. Furthermore, we use data augmentation technologies to augment training data and data filtering strategies to improve the quality of training data. In addition, we explore many MT technologies such as Back Translation, Forward Translation, R-Drop, and Domain Adaptation. Moreover, our model is a one-to-many ST system that utilizes flags for different tasks. Experimental results on the tst2022 test set demonstrate that our model achieves 36.37, 20.92, and 24.28 BLEU in En2Zh, En2Ja, and En2De, respectively.

1 Introduction

The Offline Speech Translation (ST) Task translates the source audio into target text. Currently, there are two leading solutions for ST. The first is the traditional cascade system (Matusov et al., 2005a), which decouples the ST task into an automatic speech recognition (ASR) and a neural machine translation (NMT) task. In the traditional cascade system, when translating, the source speech is recognized into source text, and then the NMT model is used to translate the source text into target text. However, it often leads to higher architectural complexity and error propagation (Duong et al., 2016), affecting subsequent NMT tasks. In order to alleviate this problem, the end-to-end (E2E) ST architecture (Bérard et al., 2016) is proposed. The E2E ST combines ASR and NMT modeling to establish the map between the source audio and the target text.

For the E2E ST architecture, one disadvantage is the lack of parallel training data. For the traditional cascade ST system, sufficient training can obtain high-accuracy ASR and MT systems due to the large ASR and MT datasets. Therefore, the traditional cascade ST system generally achieves better performance than the E2E ST. At the same time, in the recent offline track of IWSLT evaluation (Anastasopoulos et al., 2021, 2022; Agarwal et al., 2023), we can see that the cascade ST system is better than the E2E ST system. Thus, in this work, we use the traditional cascaded ST scheme.

Specifically, in the ASR task, we directly adopt the Whisper (Radford et al., 2023) large-v3 model, which can achieve a strong comprehensive ASR performance. We also explore sharding strategies, such as Supervised Hybrid Audio Segmentation (SHAS) (Tsiamas et al., 2022), to segment the source audio for better ST results. In the MT task, we use the Transformer architecture (Vaswani et al., 2017) as the backbone model. To ensure the MT model is fully trained, we meticulously collect a large amount of parallel data and monolingual data from various data sources. Furthermore, we delve into many MT technologies such as Back Translation (Sennrich et al., 2016), Forward Translation, R-Drop (Wu et al., 2021), Domain Adaptation, and Ensemble (Ganaie et al., 2022). Moreover, we compare the two solutions: one-to-one and one-to-many ST, and we find that one-to-many is better.

Through the above explorations, our model finally achieves good ST performance. In detail, experimental results on the tst2022 test set demonstrate that our model achieves 36.37, 20.92, and 24.28 BLEU in En2Zh, En2Ja, and En2De, respectively.

The rest of this paper is organized as follows. Section 2 describes the datasets and data preprocessing. Section 3 describes our speech translation system, which includes ASR and MT models.

Proceedings of the 21st International Conference on Spoken Language Translation (IWSLT 2024), pages 87–93
August 15-16, 2024 ©2024 Association for Computational Linguistics

Corpus	En2Zh	En2Ja	En2De
CoVoST (Wang et al., 2020)	171K	191K	220K
MuST-C v3 (Cattoni et al., 2021)	296K	251K	238K
NewsCommentary (Tiedemann, 2012)	400K	-	345K
OpenSubtitles (Lison and Tiedemann, 2016)	4.9M	832K	12M
Tatoeba (Tiedemann, 2012)	-	193K	302K
GigaST (Ye et al., 2023)	6.2M	-	6.3M
JParaCrawl (Morishita et al., 2020)	-	6.4M	-
Total	12M	8.2M	19.5M

Table 1: Data statistics on MT datasets.

Section 4 reports the experimental results. Finally, we conclude in Section 5.

2 Dataset

2.1 Text Data

The dataset used for machine translation is shown in Table 1, which contains both speech-to-text-parallel and text-parallel data types of all language pairs allowed by IWSLT 2024. Additionally, we employ the GigaST dataset to expand our text training data. sBERT (Reimers and Gurevych, 2019, 2020) is used for calculating sentence representations. We compute sentence embeddings for all parallel text data and remove sentences pairs that lower than 0.7 cosine similarity. The data statistics in table represent the number of sentences remaining in each dataset after sBERT filtering.

2.2 Data pre-processing

We perform the following preprocessing steps to filter all text-parallel data:

- Remove empty sentences and duplicate sentences.
- Remove sentences containing invalid characters and HTML tags.
- Remove sentences longer than 200 tokens or shorter than 3 tokens.
- Remove sentences with unbalanced source-target token ratio.
- Remove sentences with too much punctuation.
- Remove sentences where the source or target language constitutes a low percentage.
- Remove sentences with mismatched punctuation marks, such as quotation marks.

Then we apply mosesdecoder toolkits[1] (Koehn et al., 2007) for punctuation, space and case normalization. The sentences are then tokenized using joint SentencePiece model (SPM) (Kudo and Richardson, 2018). The vocabulary size of joint SPM is about 130,000, with 40k in English, 40k in Chinese, 30k in German, and 20k in Japanese, both source and target side share the same dictionary.

3 Speech translation system

3.1 ASR model

Whisper[2] (Radford et al., 2023) is an excellent multilingual ASR system trained on 680,000 hours of multilingual and multitask supervision data. It still shows strong robustness in various audio scenes, such as accent speech and background noise, and achieves good recognition results. It adopts the Encoder-Decoder architecture (Dong et al., 2018), and the training data has an extraordinarily structured design. In addition, it uses a method similar to prompt during the training process. The open-source Whisper models have five sizes of models: tiny, base, small, medium, and large. It is worth noting that the OpenAI has recently updated the Whisper large model to form a more effective large-v3 version model. In this work, we adopt the Whisper large-v3 version as the ASR part of our ST system.

3.2 MT model

3.2.1 Model structure

We adopt Transformer model (Vaswani et al., 2017) to build our machine translation system and implemente them on Fairseq toolkits (Ott et al., 2019). More specifically, we adopt a wider and deeper Transformer model which contains 18-layer encoder, 6-layer decoder, 16 self-attention heads and

[1]https://github.com/moses-smt/mosesdecoder
[2]https://github.com/openai/whisper

Language	Raw data	Filter data
Chinese	22M	9M
Japanese	30M	15M
English	8M	4.1M

Table 2: Data statistics on monolingual corpus.

FFN with 4096 dimensions. We utilize all provided parallel data from three language directions (En2Zh, En2De, En2Ja) for model training, and derived a one-to-many MT model.

3.2.2 R-Drop

The Dropout method (Srivastava et al., 2014; Gao et al., 2022) is an influential strategy for the regularization of deep neural networks. While it enhances the efficacy of the training process, the stochastic nature of dropouts might result in discrepancies between the training and inference phases. R-Drop, as introduced by Wu et al. (2021), ensures consistency among the output distributions of the sub-models generated by dropout. To enhance the consistency within our model, we implement the R-Drop algorithm and set weight factor α to 5. Consequently, the R-Drop training strategy significantly improves the performance of our baseline model.

Furthermore, when using the R-drop mechanism to train models, the model computation increases exponentially, which will consume more training time and GPU resources. Given the limitation of time and resources, we adopt it solely for our foundational model, and integrate the R-Drop-augmented model into ST system by using model ensemble approach during the evaluation stage.

3.2.3 Data Augmentation

Previous works (Edunov et al., 2018) has demonstrated that the incorporation of synthetic data can significantly enhance the efficacy of machine translation systems. We implement following data augmentation methodologies to further refine our translation models.

Forward translation (FT) is a process of transforming source language into target language using MT model. On the contrary, backward translation (BT) (Sennrich et al., 2016) is the translation of target language back into source language, forcing the model to learn a more robust representation of the source language. Both methods use additional monolingual resources to create bilingual data.

As shown in Table 2, we select 22M sentences of Chinese, 8M sentences of English and 30M sentences of Japanese of monolingual data from public datasets, such as Common Crawl and News Crawl corpus. Moreover, to make our MT model have better results in ACL scenarios, we adopt the scientific English monolingual corpus from Rohatgi et al. (2023). After data pre-processing pipeline mentioned above, approximately 40%-50% of the sentences from the original data are retained for each language. BT model is trained separately for each language pair, and then the monolingual data is used for backward translation. We employ an iterative forward-backward translation approach to progressively enhance the translation quality of both the FT model and BT model. As shown in figure 1, the FT model and BT model generated pseudo-labels *target'* and *source'* respectively. We mix them with labelled text pairs *(source, target)* to update our BT model and FT model. As the BLEU scores of BT model increased, the positive impact of the back-translated data on the FT model also becomes more pronounced.

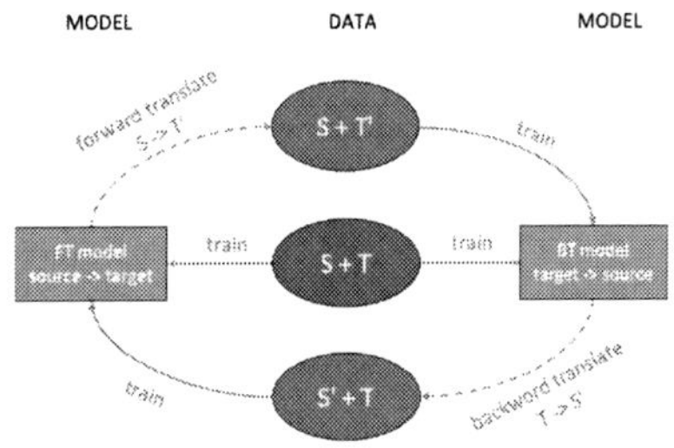

Figure 1: The iterative updating process for FT and BT model.

When using data generated by BT model, we refer to the tagged BT method (Caswell et al., 2019), adding a special token <BT> at the beginning of source sentence.

We also convert numerical expressions in English sentences into forms that more closely match the ASR transcription results, e.g., converting '21' to 'twenty-one', '2018' to 'two thousand and eighteen'. Additionally, we randomly discard punctuation marks within sentences to enable the model to generalize well across varying punctuation styles. These transformed sentences are merged with the original sentences to obtain an augmented dataset.

3.2.4 Domain adaptation

Considering the quality of machine translation models is easily influenced by specific domain, we also select in-domain data and fine-tune the model

	System	En2Zh	En2Ja	En2De
1	Baseline model	35.04	18.75	23.14
2	+ R-drop	35.67	19.36	23.71
3	+ GigaST	35.42	19.21	23.70
4	+ Backward translation	35.71	19.77	23.94
5	+ Domain adaptation	35.44	19.90	23.97
	Ensemble(2,4)	36.33	20.90	24.26
	Ensemble(2,4,5)	**36.37**	**20.92**	**24.28**

Table 3: Main results with BLEU scores on IWSLT tst2022 datasets

System	En2Zh	En2Ja
one-to-one	32.77	18.38
one-to-many	**35.04**	**18.75**

Table 4: BLEU scores on IWSLT tst2022 datasets (one-to-one vs. one-to-many ST)

System	En2Zh	En2Ja	En2De
Baseline	35.42	19.21	23.70
+ BT-Ja	35.37	19.71	**24.00**
+ BT-Zh	**35.71**	**19.77**	23.94

Table 5: BLEU scores on IWSLT tst2022 datasets with different BT data

to enhance in-domain performance. We use MUST-C data (Cattoni et al., 2021) as domain-specific dataset to train monolingual language models separately, and then use them to score all language pairs. We set specific thresholds to filter parallel data closer to the domain, with higher scores implying better quality, and train incrementally to get domain-specific model. The filtered in-domain data is about 5-10% of the total data.

3.2.5 ASR output adaptation

For ST dataset, we use ASR models to transcribe the audio data and replace their source side label with ASR recognition results, and finally obtain an augmented dataset containing ASR noise. ASR model may produce incorrect transcriptions for words with similar pronunciations, which, despite reducing the quality of MT training dataset, also bolster the robustness of the ST system. For this part of data, we also add a special tag <ASR> at the beginning of source sentence.

4 Experiments and results

All models are implemented on Fairseq toolkits (Ott et al., 2019) and trained on four NVIDIA A100 GPUs. The IWSLT test sets of tst2022 are used to evaluate the translation performance at sentence level. The mwerSegmenter toolkit[3] (Matusov et al., 2005b) is used to resegment and align translation results and then SacreBLEU[4] (Post, 2018) is used to compute BLEU scores. For the Japanese text, tokenization is performed using the Mecab, while for the Chinese text, tokenization is executed at character level. We apply SHAS[5] (Tsiamas et al., 2022) for audio segmentation and try a variety of combinations for min and max segment length, the optimal parameters is 5-30 secs for TED domain.

The table 4 presents a comparative analysis between the one-to-one and the one-to-many systems, specifically their performance on En2Zh and En2Ja. In the one-to-one system, each source language corresponds to only one target language, with BLEUs of 32.77 in En2Zh and 18.38 in En2Ja. In the one-to-many system, a source language text can correspond to multiple target language texts. The system trains data from English to three target languages (En2Zh , En2Ja , En2De) simultaneously and distinguishes the target language type by adding <zh>/<ja>/<de> tags. The performance of the one-to-many system improves to 35.04 in En2Zh and 18.75 in En2Ja. These scores indicate that one-to-many system outperforms the one-to-one system.

For the one-to-many system in Table 3, we first train a baseline model with all constrained data. We find that introducing R-drop mechanism positively affects model performance. Then, we add GigaST dataset for incremental training, which enriches the data diversity but also leads to a dramatic increase in the training data. We observe that as the amount of training data increases, R-drop no longer benefits model performance while consuming more training time, so we remove the R-drop mechanism

[3]https://www-i6.informatik.rwth-aachen.de/web/Software/mwerSegmenter.tar.gz
[4]https://github.com/mjpost/sacrebleu
[5]https://github.com/mt-upc/SHAS

in subsequent stages.

In the forth stage, we collect monolingual data in Chinese and Japanese and perform back translation. As shown in table 5, the model performance is incrementally enhanced by incorporating back translation data into training dataset. Specifically, after adding BT-Ja data, the BLEU score for En2Ja improves significantly from 19.21 to 19.71, while En2Zh slightly decreases to 35.37. The addition of BT-Zh data enhances En2Zh to 35.71 and En2Ja to 19.77. Notably, although no BT data is added for En2De, its BLEU score still improves by 0.24, demonstrating a positive impact of back translation data on the overall model performance. Finally, domain adaptation brings some improvements in En2Ja and En2De.

Finally, we integrate the baseline model, which is enhanced by the R-drop mechanism, with fine-tuned models that leverage additional data, backward translation, and adaptation techniques. The ensemble of model (2, 4) achieves notable improvements, with BLEU scores of 36.33 for En2Zh, 20.90 for En2Ja, and 24.26 for En2De. Furthermore, the ensemble of model (2, 4, 5) slightly surpasses the ensemble of model (2, 4), reaching scores of 36.37 for En2Zh, 20.92 for En2Ja, and 24.28 for En2De. This indicates the effectiveness of model ensemble in boosting translation quality.

5 Conclusion

This paper describes our submission to the IWSLT24 offline speech translation task. We collect a large amount of parallel and monolingual data from the public data sources and adopt the traditional cascade ST architecture for the unconstrained training track. For the ASR model, we use the excellent Whisper large-v3 model, which is trained on 680,000 hours of multilingual and multitask supervision data. It shows strong robustness in various audio scenes. For the MT model, we explore a wider and deeper Transformer model using Fairseq tookit. To make the model fully trained, we carefully experiment many MT technologies, such as Back Translation, Forward Translation, Domain Adaptation, and R-Drop. Experimental results on the tst2022 test set show that our model achieves 36.37, 20.92, and 24.28 BLEU in En2Zh, En2Ja, and En2De, respectively.

References

Milind Agarwal, Sweta Agrawal, Antonios Anastasopoulos, Luisa Bentivogli, Ondřej Bojar, Claudia Borg, Marine Carpuat, Roldano Cattoni, Mauro Cettolo, Mingda Chen, William Chen, Khalid Choukri, Alexandra Chronopoulou, Anna Currey, Thierry Declerck, Qianqian Dong, Kevin Duh, Yannick Estève, Marcello Federico, Souhir Gahbiche, Barry Haddow, Benjamin Hsu, Phu Mon Htut, Hirofumi Inaguma, Dávid Javorský, John Judge, Yasumasa Kano, Tom Ko, Rishu Kumar, Pengwei Li, Xutai Ma, Prashant Mathur, Evgeny Matusov, Paul McNamee, John P. McCrae, Kenton Murray, Maria Nadejde, Satoshi Nakamura, Matteo Negri, Ha Nguyen, Jan Niehues, Xing Niu, Atul Kr. Ojha, John E. Ortega, Proyag Pal, Juan Pino, Lonneke van der Plas, Peter Polák, Elijah Rippeth, Elizabeth Salesky, Jiatong Shi, Matthias Sperber, Sebastian Stüker, Katsuhito Sudoh, Yun Tang, Brian Thompson, Kevin Tran, Marco Turchi, Alex Waibel, Mingxuan Wang, Shinji Watanabe, and Rodolfo Zevallos. 2023. FINDINGS OF THE IWSLT 2023 EVALUATION CAMPAIGN. In *Proceedings of the 20th International Conference on Spoken Language Translation (IWSLT 2023)*, pages 1–61, Toronto, Canada (in-person and online). Association for Computational Linguistics.

Antonios Anastasopoulos, Loïc Barrault, Luisa Bentivogli, Marcely Zanon Boito, Ondřej Bojar, Roldano Cattoni, Anna Currey, Georgiana Dinu, Kevin Duh, Maha Elbayad, Clara Emmanuel, Yannick Estève, Marcello Federico, Christian Federmann, Souhir Gahbiche, Hongyu Gong, Roman Grundkiewicz, Barry Haddow, Benjamin Hsu, Dávid Javorský, Věra Kloudová, Surafel Lakew, Xutai Ma, Prashant Mathur, Paul McNamee, Kenton Murray, Maria Nădejde, Satoshi Nakamura, Matteo Negri, Jan Niehues, Xing Niu, John Ortega, Juan Pino, Elizabeth Salesky, Jiatong Shi, Matthias Sperber, Sebastian Stüker, Katsuhito Sudoh, Marco Turchi, Yogesh Virkar, Alexander Waibel, Changhan Wang, and Shinji Watanabe. 2022. Findings of the IWSLT 2022 evaluation campaign. In *Proceedings of the 19th International Conference on Spoken Language Translation (IWSLT 2022)*, pages 98–157, Dublin, Ireland (in-person and online). Association for Computational Linguistics.

Antonios Anastasopoulos, Ondřej Bojar, Jacob Bremerman, Roldano Cattoni, Maha Elbayad, Marcello Federico, Xutai Ma, Satoshi Nakamura, Matteo Negri, Jan Niehues, Juan Pino, Elizabeth Salesky, Sebastian Stüker, Katsuhito Sudoh, Marco Turchi, Alexander Waibel, Changhan Wang, and Matthew Wiesner. 2021. FINDINGS OF THE IWSLT 2021 EVALUATION CAMPAIGN. In *Proceedings of the 18th International Conference on Spoken Language Translation (IWSLT 2021)*, pages 1–29, Bangkok, Thailand (online). Association for Computational Linguistics.

Alexandre Bérard, Olivier Pietquin, Laurent Besacier, and Christophe Servan. 2016. Listen and translate: A proof of concept for end-to-end speech-to-text translation. In *NIPS Workshop on end-to-end learning for speech and audio processing*.

Isaac Caswell, Ciprian Chelba, and David Grangier. 2019. Tagged back-translation. *arXiv preprint arXiv:1906.06442*.

Roldano Cattoni, Mattia Antonino Di Gangi, Luisa Bentivogli, Matteo Negri, and Marco Turchi. 2021. Must-c: A multilingual corpus for end-to-end speech translation. *Computer speech & language*, 66:101155.

Linhao Dong, Shuang Xu, and Bo Xu. 2018. Speech-transformer: A no-recurrence sequence-to-sequence model for speech recognition. In *2018 IEEE International Conference on Acoustics, Speech and Signal Processing (ICASSP)*, pages 5884–5888.

Long Duong, Antonios Anastasopoulos, David Chiang, Steven Bird, and Trevor Cohn. 2016. An attentional model for speech translation without transcription. In *Proceedings of the 2016 Conference of the North American Chapter of the Association for Computational Linguistics: Human Language Technologies*, pages 949–959, San Diego, California. Association for Computational Linguistics.

Sergey Edunov, Myle Ott, Michael Auli, and David Grangier. 2018. Understanding back-translation at scale. *arXiv preprint arXiv:1808.09381*.

Mudasir A Ganaie, Minghui Hu, Ashwani Kumar Malik, Muhammad Tanveer, and Ponnuthurai N Suganthan. 2022. Ensemble deep learning: A review. *Engineering Applications of Artificial Intelligence*, 115:105151.

Pengzhi Gao, Zhongjun He, Hua Wu, and Haifeng Wang. 2022. Bi-simcut: A simple strategy for boosting neural machine translation. In *Proceedings of the 2022 Conference of the North American Chapter of the Association for Computational Linguistics: Human Language Technologies*, pages 3938–3948.

Philipp Koehn, Hieu Hoang, Alexandra Birch, Chris Callison-Burch, Marcello Federico, Nicola Bertoldi, Brooke Cowan, Wade Shen, Christine Moran, Richard Zens, Chris Dyer, Ondřej Bojar, Alexandra Constantin, and Evan Herbst. 2007. Moses: Open source toolkit for statistical machine translation. In *Proceedings of the 45th Annual Meeting of the Association for Computational Linguistics Companion Volume Proceedings of the Demo and Poster Sessions*, pages 177–180, Prague, Czech Republic. Association for Computational Linguistics.

Taku Kudo and John Richardson. 2018. SentencePiece: A simple and language independent subword tokenizer and detokenizer for neural text processing. In *Proceedings of the 2018 Conference on Empirical Methods in Natural Language Processing: System Demonstrations*, pages 66–71, Brussels, Belgium. Association for Computational Linguistics.

Pierre Lison and Jörg Tiedemann. 2016. Opensubtitles2016: Extracting large parallel corpora from movie and tv subtitles. In *Proceedings of the Tenth International Conference on Language Resources and Evaluation (LREC'16)*, pages 923–929.

E. Matusov, S. Kanthak, and Hermann Ney. 2005a. On the integration of speech recognition and statistical machine translation. In *Proc. Interspeech 2005*, pages 3177–3180.

Evgeny Matusov, Gregor Leusch, Oliver Bender, and Hermann Ney. 2005b. Evaluating machine translation output with automatic sentence segmentation. In *Proceedings of the Second International Workshop on Spoken Language Translation*, Pittsburgh, Pennsylvania, USA.

Makoto Morishita, Jun Suzuki, and Masaaki Nagata. 2020. JParaCrawl: A large scale web-based English-Japanese parallel corpus. In *Proceedings of The 12th Language Resources and Evaluation Conference*, pages 3603–3609, Marseille, France. European Language Resources Association.

Myle Ott, Sergey Edunov, Alexei Baevski, Angela Fan, Sam Gross, Nathan Ng, David Grangier, and Michael Auli. 2019. fairseq: A fast, extensible toolkit for sequence modeling. In *Proceedings of the 2019 Conference of the North American Chapter of the Association for Computational Linguistics (Demonstrations)*, pages 48–53, Minneapolis, Minnesota. Association for Computational Linguistics.

Matt Post. 2018. A call for clarity in reporting BLEU scores. In *Proceedings of the Third Conference on Machine Translation: Research Papers*, pages 186–191, Belgium, Brussels. Association for Computational Linguistics.

Alec Radford, Jong Wook Kim, Tao Xu, Greg Brockman, Christine McLeavey, and Ilya Sutskever. 2023. Robust speech recognition via large-scale weak supervision. In *International Conference on Machine Learning*, pages 28492–28518. PMLR.

Nils Reimers and Iryna Gurevych. 2019. Sentence-bert: Sentence embeddings using siamese bert-networks. In *Proceedings of the 2019 Conference on Empirical Methods in Natural Language Processing*. Association for Computational Linguistics.

Nils Reimers and Iryna Gurevych. 2020. Making monolingual sentence embeddings multilingual using knowledge distillation. In *Proceedings of the 2020 Conference on Empirical Methods in Natural Language Processing*. Association for Computational Linguistics.

Shaurya Rohatgi, Yanxia Qin, Benjamin Aw, Niranjana Unnithan, and Min-Yen Kan. 2023. The acl ocl corpus: Advancing open science in computational linguistics. In *Proceedings of the 2023 Conference on Empirical Methods in Natural Language Processing*, pages 10348–10361.

Rico Sennrich, Barry Haddow, and Alexandra Birch. 2016. Improving neural machine translation models with monolingual data. In *Proceedings of the 54th Annual Meeting of the Association for Computational Linguistics (Volume 1: Long Papers)*, pages 86–96.

Nitish Srivastava, Geoffrey Hinton, Alex Krizhevsky, Ilya Sutskever, and Ruslan Salakhutdinov. 2014. Dropout: a simple way to prevent neural networks from overfitting. *The journal of machine learning research*, 15(1):1929–1958.

Jörg Tiedemann. 2012. Parallel data, tools and interfaces in OPUS. In *Proceedings of the Eighth International Conference on Language Resources and Evaluation (LREC'12)*, pages 2214–2218, Istanbul, Turkey. European Language Resources Association (ELRA).

Ioannis Tsiamas, Gerard I. Gállego, José A. R. Fonollosa, and Marta R. Costa-jussà. 2022. SHAS: Approaching optimal Segmentation for End-to-End Speech Translation. In *Proc. Interspeech 2022*, pages 106–110.

Ashish Vaswani, Noam Shazeer, Niki Parmar, Jakob Uszkoreit, Llion Jones, Aidan N Gomez, Łukasz Kaiser, and Illia Polosukhin. 2017. Attention is all you need. *Advances in neural information processing systems*, 30.

Changhan Wang, Anne Wu, and Juan Pino. 2020. Covost 2 and massively multilingual speech-to-text translation. *arXiv preprint arXiv:2007.10310.*

Lijun Wu, Juntao Li, Yue Wang, Qi Meng, Tao Qin, Wei Chen, Min Zhang, Tie-Yan Liu, et al. 2021. R-drop: Regularized dropout for neural networks. *Advances in Neural Information Processing Systems*, 34:10890–10905.

Rong Ye, Chengqi Zhao, Tom Ko, Chutong Meng, Tao Wang, Mingxuan Wang, and Jun Cao. 2023. GigaST: A 10,000-hour Pseudo Speech Translation Corpus. In *Proc. INTERSPEECH 2023*, pages 2168–2172.

Improving the Quality of IWLST 2024 Cascade Offline Speech Translation and Speech-to-Speech Translation via Translation Hypothesis Ensembling with NMT models and Large Language Models

Zhanglin Wu, JiaXin Guo, Daimeng Wei, Zhiqiang Rao,
Zongyao Li, Hengchao Shang, Yuanchang Luo, Li ShaoJun, Hao Yang
Huawei Translation Service Center, Beijing, China
{wuzhanglin2,guojiaxin1,weidaimeng,raozhiqiang,
lizongyao,shanghengchao,luoyuanchang1,lishaojun18,yanghao30}@huawei.com

Abstract

This paper presents HW-TSC's submission to the IWSLT 2024 Offline Speech Translation Task and Speech-to-Speech Translation Task. The former includes three translation directions: English to German, English to Chinese, and English to Japanese, while the latter only includes the translation direction of English to Chinese. We attend all three tracks (Constraint training, Constrained with Large Language Models training, and Unconstrained training) of offline speech translation task, using the cascade model architecture. Under the constrained training track, we train an ASR model from scratch, and then employ R-Drop and domain data selection to train the NMT model. In the constrained with Large Language Models training track, we use Wav2vec 2.0 and mBART50 for ASR model training initialization, and then train the LLama2-7B-based MT model using continuous training with sentence-aligned parallel data, supervised fine-tuning, and contrastive preference optimization. In the unconstrained training track, we fine-tune the whisper model for speech recognition, and then ensemble the translation results of NMT models and LLMs to produce superior translation output. For the speech-to-speech translation Task, we initially employ the offline speech translation system described above to generate the translated text. Then, we utilize the VITS model to generate the corresponding speech and employ the OpenVoice model for timbre cloning.

1 Introduction

Recent advances in deep learning allow us to address traditional NLP tasks in a new and significantly different manner. One such task is speech translation, involving automatic speech recognition (ASR) (Gulati et al., 2020) system and machine translation (MT) (Vaswani et al., 2017) system. Another task is speech-to-speech translation (S2S), which involves ASR system, MT system, and text-to-speech (TTS) (Ren et al., 2020) system. Recent trends tend to utilize a single neural network to directly translate input speech from one language to text or speech in another language, bypassing intermediate symbolic representations. The results shows that the performance of end-to-end models is nearing that of cascade solutions, but the effectiveness comparison between the two technologies remains unclear. Both methods face specific challenges. The primary challenge with the end-to-end approach is the lack of training data, while the cascade method has to go through the ASR, MT and even TTS processes, leading to the errors accumulation. Due to the data insufficiency in end-to-end training, We ultimately chose the cascade approach on the IWSLT 2024 offline speech translation task and speech-to-speech translation task.

For the IWSLT offline speech translation task, we apply different training strategies across the three tracks, adapting to diverse data and model conditions. In the constrained training track, we initiate training with an ASR model from scratch, followed by the utilization of R-Drop (Wu et al., 2021) and domain data selection (Wang et al., 2019b) techniques to train the NMT model. Within the constrained with Large Language Models (LLMs) training track, we commence ASR model training initialization using Wav2vec 2.0 (Baevski et al., 2020) and mBART50 (Tang et al., 2020). Subsequently, we train the LLama2-7B-based (Touvron et al., 2023) MT model through continual pre-training with sentence-aligned parallel data (Guo et al., 2024), supervised fine-tuning (Xu et al., 2023), and contrastive preference optimization (CPO) (Xu et al., 2024). In the unconstrained training track, we fine-tune the whisper model (Radford et al., 2023) for speech recognition, and then ensemble (Farinhas et al., 2023) the translation outputs of NMT models and LLMs to generate superior translation result. For the IWSLT S2S translation task, we initially employ the offline speech translation system described above to

Proceedings of the 21st International Conference on Spoken Language Translation (IWSLT 2024), pages 94–100
August 15-16, 2024 ©2024 Association for Computational Linguistics

generate the translated text. Next, we utilize the VITS (Kim et al., 2021) model to generate the corresponding speech and employ the OpenVoice (Qin et al., 2023) model for timbre cloning.

In comparison to last year, our cascade offline speech translation system and S2S translation system is performing significantly better, particularly following translation hypothesis ensembling with NMT models and LLMs.

2 Datasets and Preprocessing

2.1 ASR Data

There are six different datasets used in the training of our ASR models, such as MuST-C V2 (Cattoni et al., 2021), LibriSpeech (Panayotov et al., 2015), TED-LIUM 3 (Hernandez et al., 2018), CoVoST 2(Wang et al., 2020), VoxPopuli (Wang et al., 2021), Europarl-ST (Iranzo-Sánchez et al., 2020), as described in Table 1. We use the exactly same data processing strategy to train our ASR models following the configuration of (Wang et al., 2022). We extend one data augmentation method (Zhang et al., 2022): adjacent voices are concatenated to generate longer training speeches. Tsiamas et al. (2022) propose Supervised Hybrid Audio Segmentation (SHAS), a method that can effectively learn the optimal segmentation from any manually segmented speech corpus. In the test phase, we use SHAS to split long audios into shorter segments.

Dataset	Duration(h)
LibriSpeech	960
MuST-C	590
CoVoST	1802
TEDLIUM3	453
Europarl	161
VoxPopuli	1270

Table 1: Data statistics of ASR corpus.

2.2 MT Data

We use the same data processing strategy following (Wu et al., 2023) to extract our MT data from the officially available text-parallel and speech-to-text-parallel data. Table 2 illustrates the bilingual data sizes after labse filtering (Feng et al., 2022) and domain selection (Wang et al., 2019b).

language pairs	en2de	en2ja	en2zh
Clean Data	5.8M	5.6M	2.2M
Domain Data	0.4M	0.4M	0.4M

Table 2: Bilingual data sizes of MT corpus.

3 ASR Model

3.1 Constrained training

In this track, we train the constrained ASR model using the Conformer (Gulati et al., 2020) and U2 (Zhang et al., 2020) model architectures. The first model is standard auto-regressive ASR models built upon the Transformer architecture. The last one is a unified model that can perform both streaming and non-streaming ASR, supported by the dynamic chunking training strategy. The model configurations are as follows:

1) **Conformer**: The encoder is composed of 2 layers of VGG and 16 layers of Conformer, and the decoder is composed of 6 layers of Transformer. The embedding size is 1024, and the hidden size of FFN is 4096, and the attention head is 16.

2) **U2**: Two convolution subsampling layers with kernel size 3*3 and stride 2 are used in the front of the encoder. We use 12 Conformer layers for the encoder and 6 Transformer layers for the decoder. The embedding size is 1024, and the hidden size of FFN is 4096, and the attention head is 16.

During the training of ASR models, we set the batch size to the maximum of 20,000 frames percard. Inverse sqrt is used for lr scheduling with warm-up steps set to 10,000 and peak lr set as 5e-4. Adam is used as the optimizer. All ASR models are trained on 8 NPUs for 100 epochs. Parameters for last 5 epochs are averaged. Audio features are normalized with utterance-level CMVN for Conformer, and with global CMVN for U2. All audio inputs are augmented with spectral augmentation (Park et al., 2019), and Connectionist Temporal Classification (CTC) is added to make the model converge better.

3.2 Constrained with LLMs training

LLM is currently the mainstream method in the field of artificial intelligence. In ASR, the pre-training model has been proved to be an effective means to improve the quality, especially the models such as wav2vec (Schneider et al., 2019) and Hubert (Hsu et al., 2021) have been proposed in recent years. Li et al. (2020) combine the encoder of wav2vec2 (Baevski et al., 2020) and the decoder of mBART50 (Tang et al., 2020) to fine-tune an end2end model. We also adopt a similar strategy, but combine the encoder of wav2vec2 and the decoder of mBART50 to fine-tune an ASR model (w2v2-mBART). Due to the modality mismatch between pre-training and fine-tuning, in order to better train cross-attention, we freeze the self-attention of the encoder and decoder. We first use all the constrained data for fine-tuning, and only use the MUST-C data after 30 epochs of training.

3.3 Unconstrained training

Whisper (Radford et al., 2023) is an automatic speech recognition (ASR) system trained on 680,000 hours of multilingual and multitask supervised data collected from the web. It show that the use of such a large and diverse dataset leads to improved robustness to accents, background noise and technical language. The Whisper architecture is a simple end-to-end approach, implemented as an encoder-decoder Transformer. Even though it enables transcription in multiple languages, we only use its speech recognition feature, transcribing audio files to English text. In this task, we use it as a pre-trained model, and use the MUST-C dataset for fine-tuning to improve its performance in specific domains. We trained for 2 epochs with a small learning rate of 10e-6.

4 MT Model

4.1 Constrained training

Transformer stands as the state-of-the-art model in recent machine translation evaluations. Research to enhance this model type is divided into two main avenues: one focuses on using wider networks (e.g., Transformer-Big) (Vaswani et al., 2017), while the other emphasizes deeper language representations (e.g., Deep Transformer (Wang et al., 2017, 2019a)). Under the constrained conditions, we combine these two improvements, adopt the Deep Transformer-Big model structure, and utilize the clean bilingual data filtered by the labse model (Feng et al., 2022) to train the NMT model from scratch. The primary features of Deep Transformer-Big include pre-layer normalization, a 25-layer encoder, a 6-layer decoder, 16-head self-attention, 1024-dimensional embedding, and 4096-dimensional FFN embedding.

To regularize the training of NMT and alleviate the inconsistency between training and inference caused by the randomness of dropout(Srivastava et al., 2014; Gao et al., 2022), we introduce R-Drop(Wu et al., 2021), which forces the output distributions of different sub-models generated by dropout to be consistent with each other.

Since the quality of the translation model is easily affected by the domain, we try to select domain-related data to incrementally train the model. We adopted the domain adaptation strategy by (Wang et al., 2019b). The strategy uses a small amount of in-domain data to tune the base model, and then leverages the differences between the tuned model and the base to score bilingual data. The score is calculated based on formula 1.

$$score = \frac{logP(y|x;\theta_{in}) - logP(y|x;\theta_{base})}{|y|} \quad (1)$$

Where θ_{base} denotes the base model; θ_{in} denotes the model after fine-tuning on a small amount of in-domain data, and |y| denotes the length of the sentence. Higher score means higher quality.

Specifically, we use TED and MUST-C data as in-domain data. We score all the training bilingual data through Equation 1, and filter out 80% - 90% of the data according to the score distribution. We use the remaining 0.4M in-domain data to continue training on the previous model.

In the training of NMT models, each model undergoes training utilizing 8 NPUs. The batch size remains fixed at 6144, the update frequency is 2, the dropout is 0.1, and the learning rate is maintained at 5e-4. A total of 4000 warmup steps are executed, and the model is saved every 2000 steps. Additionally, λ is set to 5 for R-Drop.

4.2 Constrained with LLMs training

Generative LLMs have made significant strides in various NLP tasks. However, these advancements have not fully translated to translation tasks, particularly for medium-sized models, which still trail behind traditional supervised encoder-decoder translation models. Previous studies have attempted to enhance the translation ability of these LLMs through prompt translation (Zhang et al., 2023; Moslem et al., 2023), but the improvements remain limited. Fortunately, recent research is making more progress through supervised fine-tuning (SFT) (Zeng et al., 2024), and showing that it is possible to break away from the reliance on massive amounts of parallel data that traditional translation models typically require.

Translate this from [source language] to [target language]:
[source language]: <source_sentence>
[target language]:

Figure 1: The translation prompt used for training and evaluation. [source language] and [target language] represent the full name of the language written in English format, e.g., Translate this from English to Chinese.

Among the officially designated LLMs, we opt to perform MT tasks based on the Llama2-7B base model. To enhance the cross-lingual capability of Llama2-7B, we first adopt the method of continual pre-training with sentence-aligned parallel data (Guo et al., 2024). We construct the data for this format from the clean data listed in Table 2.

Since Guo et al. discovered that constructing translation instruction written in the source language notably improves performance. We then use the domain data to construct a dataset of translation instructions in English format, and leverage this source-language consistent instruction for SFT. The translation prompt used for training and evaluation is shown in Figure 1.

Finally, we introduce CPO (Xu et al., 2024), which trains the model to avoid producing adequate but imperfect translations. To generate the triplet data, we additionally fine-tune a relatively small LM (BLOOM (Shoeybi et al., 2019)) and generate the output for each instance using a simple sampling strategy. With examples of correct and incorrect translations, the model is optimized to distinguish high-quality translations.

During the fine-tuning of LLMs, We adopt LoRA (Hu et al., 2021) method to fine-tune the LLM on 8 NPUs. The epoch size is 1, the batch size is 128, the maximum text length is 512, and the learning rate is 2e-3. Additionally, the weight decay is 0.01.

4.3 Unconstrained training

LLMs are becoming a one-fits-many solution, but they sometimes hallucinate or produce unreliable output. In the unconstrained track, we utilize translation hypothesis ensembling with NMT models and LLMs (Farinhas et al., 2023). First, we gather translation hypotheses from various NMTs and LLMs. Next, we utilize the external model COMET (Rei et al., 2022) to select the optimal result. This involves calculating the average COMET score between each translation hypothesis and the other hypotheses to determine its quality score. Subsequently, we choose the translation hypothesis with the highest quality score as the best result.

5 TTS Model

Several recent end-to-end TTS models enabling single-stage training and parallel sampling have been proposed, but their sample quality does not match that of two-stage TTS systems. VITS (Kim et al., 2021) is a parallel end-to-end TTS method that generates more natural sounding audio than current two-stage models. The method adopts variational inference augmented with normalizing flows and an adversarial training process, which improves the expressive power of generative modeling. In the S2S translation system, we first use the speech translation system to generate the translation text, and then use the VITS model to generate the corresponding speech.

To improve the similarity of synthesized audio's timbre to that of the source language audio, we also use OpenVoice (Qin et al., 2023) model for timbre cloning. It is a versatile voice cloning approach that requires only a short audio clip from the reference speaker to replicate their voice and generate speech in multiple languages.

6 Experiments and Results

The only difference between our S2S translation system and speech translation system is the addition of TTS and timbre cloning modules. Since we did not perform additional training on these two modules, we only present the experimental results of the speech translation system.

We utilize the open-source fairseq (Ott et al., 2019) for training the NMT model, the open-source ALMA (Xu et al., 2023) for fine-tuning LLM model. We assess the ASR models using the word error rate (WER) and evaluate the MT models using case-sensitive SacreBLEU (Post, 2018) and COMET scores. Our ASR system is evaluated on the test sets of tst-COM, while our MT system is evaluated on the test sets of tst-COM and tst2022.

Table 3 presents our final evaluation results for three language pairs across the constrained training, constrained with LLM training, and unconstrained training tracks. As the final evaluation result shows,

	en2de		en2ja		en2zh	
Cascade System	BLEU	COMET	BLEU	COMET	BLEU	COMET
Constrained	**33.64**	0.7762	**19.19**	0.7992	**34.77**	0.8046
Constrained with LLMs	22.55	0.7646	15.70	0.8253	32.66	0.8230
Unconstrained	33.18	**0.7925**	18.46	**0.8325**	33.76	**0.8358**

Table 3: BLEU and COMET of speech translation on tst-2022 test set.

the cascade system based on the NMT model perform better in the BLEU metric, while the cascade system based on the LLM model perform better in the COMET metric. When ensembling the translation results of both NMT and LLM, the cascade system is performing well in both BLEU and COMET.

6.1 ASR Results

We compare the results of different model architectures, the overall experimental results about ASR is described in Table 4. We evaluated our system on tst-COM test set. For long audio in the test set, we use SHAS for segmentation. We calculate the WER after the reference and hypothesis are lowercased and the punctuation is removed. In Table 4, all ASR systems achieve good performance, and the results are relatively close.

ASR System	tst-COM
Conformer	5.3
U2	6.1
w2v2-mBART	4.9
Whisper	4.5
Whisper fine-tuning	**4.3**

Table 4: WER of ASR on tst-COM test set.

6.2 MT Results

When evaluating the MT model, we use the Whisper fine-tuning model transcription results as the source text. Since the NMT model performs well on BLEU, we are using BLEU to evaluate the performance of the NMT model at each stage on the tst-COM test set. While the LLM model performs well on COMET, we are using COMET to evaluate the performance of the LLM model at each stage on the tst-2022 test set.

Table 5 is illustrating the BLEU of the NMT model being trained in each phase on the tst-COM test set. These results highlight the importance of employing the domain data selection method to carefully choose domain-specific data for further fine-tuning the model to facilitate domain adaptation. Following this, we utilize tst-dev as a more precise domain dataset for additional fine-tuning, resulting in even greater quality improvements.

NMT System	en2de	en2ja	en2zh
R-Drop baseline	32.65	13.88	27.14
+ Domain data selection	36.33	16.42	27.48
+ tst-dev fine-tuning	38.12	20.05	28.86

Table 5: BLEU of NMT model on tst-COM test set.

Table 6 shows the COMET of the LLM model fine-tuning at each stage on the tst-2022 test set. From the results, it becomes evident that the three methods of continuous training with Interlinear Text Format Documents, SFT, and CPO are orthogonal and can all improve the machine translation capabilities of LLM.

LLM System	en2de	en2ja	en2zh
Llama2-7B	0.5966	0.6925	0.6934
+ continual pre-training	0.7555	0.8016	0.8141
+ SFT	0.7641	0.8150	0.8220
+ CPO	0.7646	0.8253	0.8230

Table 6: COMET of LLM model on tst-2022 test set.

7 Conclusion

This paper presents our cascade speech translation system and S2S translation system in the IWSLT 2024 evaluation. We try several ASR model training strategies and achieve good performance. For the MT system, we explore two research directions based on NMT and LLM, and enhanced them through various technical means. Finally, we achieve further improvements by ensembling the translation results of NMT models and LLMs. For the TTS, we directly use open source models to generate speech and timbre clones. Our experimental results show that LLM-based ASR and MT are promising research directions.

References

Alexei Baevski, Yuhao Zhou, Abdelrahman Mohamed, and Michael Auli. 2020. wav2vec 2.0: A framework for self-supervised learning of speech representations. *Advances in neural information processing systems*, 33:12449–12460.

Roldano Cattoni, Mattia Antonino Di Gangi, Luisa Bentivogli, Matteo Negri, and Marco Turchi. 2021. Must-c: A multilingual corpus for end-to-end speech translation. *Computer Speech & Language*, 66:101155.

António Farinhas, José GC de Souza, and André FT Martins. 2023. An empirical study of translation hypothesis ensembling with large language models. *arXiv preprint arXiv:2310.11430*.

Fangxiaoyu Feng, Yinfei Yang, Daniel Cer, Naveen Arivazhagan, and Wei Wang. 2022. Language-agnostic bert sentence embedding. In *Proceedings of the 60th Annual Meeting of the Association for Computational Linguistics (Volume 1: Long Papers)*, pages 878–891.

Pengzhi Gao, Zhongjun He, Hua Wu, and Haifeng Wang. 2022. Bi-simcut: A simple strategy for boosting neural machine translation. *arXiv preprint arXiv:2206.02368*.

Anmol Gulati, James Qin, Chung-Cheng Chiu, Niki Parmar, Yu Zhang, Jiahui Yu, Wei Han, Shibo Wang, Zhengdong Zhang, Yonghui Wu, et al. 2020. Conformer: Convolution-augmented transformer for speech recognition. *arXiv preprint arXiv:2005.08100*.

Jiaxin Guo, Hao Yang, Zongyao Li, Daimeng Wei, Hengchao Shang, and Xiaoyu Chen. 2024. A novel paradigm boosting translation capabilities of large language models. *arXiv preprint arXiv:2403.11430*.

François Hernandez, Vincent Nguyen, Sahar Ghannay, Natalia Tomashenko, and Yannick Esteve. 2018. Tedlium 3: Twice as much data and corpus repartition for experiments on speaker adaptation. In *Speech and Computer: 20th International Conference, SPECOM 2018, Leipzig, Germany, September 18–22, 2018, Proceedings 20*, pages 198–208. Springer.

Wei-Ning Hsu, Benjamin Bolte, Yao-Hung Hubert Tsai, Kushal Lakhotia, Ruslan Salakhutdinov, and Abdelrahman Mohamed. 2021. Hubert: Self-supervised speech representation learning by masked prediction of hidden units. *IEEE/ACM Transactions on Audio, Speech, and Language Processing*, 29:3451–3460.

Edward J Hu, Yelong Shen, Phillip Wallis, Zeyuan Allen-Zhu, Yuanzhi Li, Shean Wang, Lu Wang, and Weizhu Chen. 2021. Lora: Low-rank adaptation of large language models. *arXiv preprint arXiv:2106.09685*.

Javier Iranzo-Sánchez, Joan Albert Silvestre-Cerda, Javier Jorge, Nahuel Roselló, Adria Giménez, Albert Sanchis, Jorge Civera, and Alfons Juan. 2020. Europarl-st: A multilingual corpus for speech translation of parliamentary debates. In *ICASSP 2020-2020 IEEE International Conference on Acoustics, Speech and Signal Processing (ICASSP)*, pages 8229–8233. IEEE.

Jaehyeon Kim, Jungil Kong, and Juhee Son. 2021. Conditional variational autoencoder with adversarial learning for end-to-end text-to-speech. In *International Conference on Machine Learning*, pages 5530–5540. PMLR.

Xian Li, Changhan Wang, Yun Tang, Chau Tran, Yuqing Tang, Juan Pino, Alexei Baevski, Alexis Conneau, and Michael Auli. 2020. Multilingual speech translation with efficient finetuning of pretrained models. *arXiv preprint arXiv:2010.12829*.

Yasmin Moslem, Rejwanul Haque, John D Kelleher, and Andy Way. 2023. Adaptive machine translation with large language models. In *24th Annual Conference of the European Association for Machine Translation*, page 227.

Myle Ott, Sergey Edunov, Alexei Baevski, Angela Fan, Sam Gross, Nathan Ng, David Grangier, and Michael Auli. 2019. fairseq: A fast, extensible toolkit for sequence modeling. *arXiv preprint arXiv:1904.01038*.

Vassil Panayotov, Guoguo Chen, Daniel Povey, and Sanjeev Khudanpur. 2015. Librispeech: an asr corpus based on public domain audio books. In *2015 IEEE international conference on acoustics, speech and signal processing (ICASSP)*, pages 5206–5210. IEEE.

Daniel S Park, William Chan, Yu Zhang, Chung-Cheng Chiu, Barret Zoph, Ekin D Cubuk, and Quoc V Le. 2019. Specaugment: A simple data augmentation method for automatic speech recognition. *arXiv preprint arXiv:1904.08779*.

Matt Post. 2018. A call for clarity in reporting bleu scores. *arXiv preprint arXiv:1804.08771*.

Zengyi Qin, Wenliang Zhao, Xumin Yu, and Xin Sun. 2023. Openvoice: Versatile instant voice cloning. *arXiv preprint arXiv:2312.01479*.

Alec Radford, Jong Wook Kim, Tao Xu, Greg Brockman, Christine McLeavey, and Ilya Sutskever. 2023. Robust speech recognition via large-scale weak supervision. In *International Conference on Machine Learning*, pages 28492–28518. PMLR.

Ricardo Rei, José GC De Souza, Duarte Alves, Chrysoula Zerva, Ana C Farinha, Taisiya Glushkova, Alon Lavie, Luisa Coheur, and André FT Martins. 2022. Comet-22: Unbabel-ist 2022 submission for the metrics shared task. In *Proceedings of the Seventh Conference on Machine Translation (WMT)*, pages 578–585.

Yi Ren, Chenxu Hu, Xu Tan, Tao Qin, Sheng Zhao, Zhou Zhao, and Tie-Yan Liu. 2020. Fastspeech 2: Fast and high-quality end-to-end text to speech. *arXiv preprint arXiv:2006.04558*.

Steffen Schneider, Alexei Baevski, Ronan Collobert, and Michael Auli. 2019. wav2vec: Unsupervised pre-training for speech recognition. *arXiv preprint arXiv:1904.05862*.

Mohammad Shoeybi, Mostofa Patwary, Raul Puri, Patrick LeGresley, Jared Casper, and Bryan Catanzaro. 2019. Megatron-lm: Training multi-billion parameter language models using model parallelism. *arXiv preprint arXiv:1909.08053*.

Nitish Srivastava, Geoffrey Hinton, Alex Krizhevsky, Ilya Sutskever, and Ruslan Salakhutdinov. 2014. Dropout: a simple way to prevent neural networks from overfitting. *The journal of machine learning research*, 15(1):1929–1958.

Yuqing Tang, Chau Tran, Xian Li, Peng-Jen Chen, Naman Goyal, Vishrav Chaudhary, Jiatao Gu, and Angela Fan. 2020. Multilingual translation with extensible multilingual pretraining and finetuning. *arXiv preprint arXiv:2008.00401*.

Hugo Touvron, Louis Martin, Kevin Stone, Peter Albert, Amjad Almahairi, Yasmine Babaei, Nikolay Bashlykov, Soumya Batra, Prajjwal Bhargava, Shruti Bhosale, et al. 2023. Llama 2: Open foundation and fine-tuned chat models. *arXiv preprint arXiv:2307.09288*.

Ioannis Tsiamas, Gerard I Gállego, José AR Fonollosa, and Marta R Costa-jussà. 2022. Shas: Approaching optimal segmentation for end-to-end speech translation. *arXiv preprint arXiv:2202.04774*.

Ashish Vaswani, Noam Shazeer, Niki Parmar, Jakob Uszkoreit, Llion Jones, Aidan N Gomez, Łukasz Kaiser, and Illia Polosukhin. 2017. Attention is all you need. *Advances in neural information processing systems*, 30.

Changhan Wang, Morgane Riviere, Ann Lee, Anne Wu, Chaitanya Talnikar, Daniel Haziza, Mary Williamson, Juan Pino, and Emmanuel Dupoux. 2021. Voxpopuli: A large-scale multilingual speech corpus for representation learning, semi-supervised learning and interpretation. *arXiv preprint arXiv:2101.00390*.

Changhan Wang, Anne Wu, and Juan Pino. 2020. Covost 2 and massively multilingual speech-to-text translation. *arXiv preprint arXiv:2007.10310*.

Minghan Wang, Jiaxin Guo, Yinglu Li, Xiaosong Qiao, Yuxia Wang, Zongyao Li, Chang Su, Yimeng Chen, Min Zhang, Shimin Tao, et al. 2022. The hw-tsc's simultaneous speech translation system for iwslt 2022 evaluation. In *Proceedings of the 19th International Conference on Spoken Language Translation (IWSLT 2022)*, pages 247–254.

Mingxuan Wang, Zhengdong Lu, Jie Zhou, and Qun Liu. 2017. Deep neural machine translation with linear associative unit. *arXiv preprint arXiv:1705.00861*.

Qiang Wang, Bei Li, Tong Xiao, Jingbo Zhu, Changliang Li, Derek F Wong, and Lidia S Chao. 2019a. Learning deep transformer models for machine translation. *arXiv preprint arXiv:1906.01787*.

Wei Wang, Isaac Caswell, and Ciprian Chelba. 2019b. Dynamically composing domain-data selection with clean-data selection by" co-curricular learning" for neural machine translation. *arXiv preprint arXiv:1906.01130*.

Lijun Wu, Juntao Li, Yue Wang, Qi Meng, Tao Qin, Wei Chen, Min Zhang, Tie-Yan Liu, et al. 2021. R-drop: Regularized dropout for neural networks. *Advances in Neural Information Processing Systems*, 34:10890–10905.

Zhanglin Wu, Daimeng Wei, Zongyao Li, Zhengzhe Yu, Shaojun Li, Xiaoyu Chen, Hengchao Shang, Jiaxin Guo, Yuhao Xie, Lizhi Lei, et al. 2023. Treating general mt shared task as a multi-domain adaptation problem: Hw-tsc's submission to the wmt23 general mt shared task. In *Proceedings of the Eighth Conference on Machine Translation*, pages 170–174.

Haoran Xu, Young Jin Kim, Amr Sharaf, and Hany Hassan Awadalla. 2023. A paradigm shift in machine translation: Boosting translation performance of large language models. *arXiv preprint arXiv:2309.11674*.

Haoran Xu, Amr Sharaf, Yunmo Chen, Weiting Tan, Lingfeng Shen, Benjamin Van Durme, Kenton Murray, and Young Jin Kim. 2024. Contrastive preference optimization: Pushing the boundaries of llm performance in machine translation. *arXiv preprint arXiv:2401.08417*.

Jiali Zeng, Fandong Meng, Yongjing Yin, and Jie Zhou. 2024. Teaching large language models to translate with comparison. In *Proceedings of the AAAI Conference on Artificial Intelligence*, 17, pages 19488–19496.

Biao Zhang, Barry Haddow, and Alexandra Birch. 2023. Prompting large language model for machine translation: A case study. In *International Conference on Machine Learning*, pages 41092–41110. PMLR.

Binbin Zhang, Di Wu, Zhuoyuan Yao, Xiong Wang, Fan Yu, Chao Yang, Liyong Guo, Yaguang Hu, Lei Xie, and Xin Lei. 2020. Unified streaming and non-streaming two-pass end-to-end model for speech recognition. *arXiv preprint arXiv:2012.05481*.

Weitai Zhang, Zhongyi Ye, Haitao Tang, Xiaoxi Li, Xinyuan Zhou, Jing Yang, Jianwei Cui, Pan Deng, Mohan Shi, Yifan Song, et al. 2022. The ustc-nelslip offline speech translation systems for iwslt 2022. In *Proceedings of the 19th International Conference on Spoken Language Translation (IWSLT 2022)*, pages 198–207.

HW-TSC's Speech to Text Translation System for IWSLT 2024 in Indic track

Bin Wei, Zongyao Li, Jiaxin Guo, Daimeng Wei, Zhanglin Wu, Xiaoyu Chen, Zhiqiang Rao, Shaojun Li, Yuanchang Luo, Hengchao Shang, Hao Yang, Yanfei Jiang
Huawei Translation Service Center, Beijing, China
{weibin29,lizongyao, guojiaxin1, weidaimeng, wuzhanglin2, chenxiaoyu35, raozhiqiang, lishaojun18, luoyuanchang1, shanghengchao,yanghao30,jiangyanfei}@huawei.com

Abstract

This article introduces the process of HW-TSC and the results of IWSLT 2024 Indic Track Speech to Text Translation. We designed a cascade system consisting of an ASR model and a machine translation model to translate speech from one language to another. For the ASR part, we directly use whisper large v3 as our ASR model. Our main task is to optimize the machine translation model (en2ta, en2hi, en2bn). In the process of optimizing the translation model, we first use bilingual corpus to train the baseline model. Then we use monolingual data to construct pseudo-corpus data to further enhance the baseline model. Finally, we filter the parallel corpus data through the labse(Feng et al., 2022) filtering method and finetune the model again, which can further improve the BLEU score. We also selected domain data from bilingual corpus to finetune previous model to achieve the best results.

1 Introduction

This article describes the Indic track speech-to-text translation task submitted by HW-TSC at IWSLT 2024.

From a system architecture perspective, current research on speech-to-text translation can be divided into two forms: end-to-end and cascade systems. Cascade systems usually consist of a speech recognition (ASR) module and a text-to-text machine translation (MT) module. Although integrating these modules may be complex, the results are still very satisfactory as long as there are sufficient data resources to train each module. Additionally, the end-to-end approach can generate translation results directly from the unified model with speech input. However, what we need to know is that the parallel data required to train an end-to-end speech translation model is extremely scarce.

2 Methods

Our approach ultimately adopts a cascade approach.

2.1 ASR

In our cascaded system we have whisper-large-v3 as our ASR module. The researchers of Whisper(Radford et al., 2023) has scaled up the supervised speech recognition dataset from thousands to 680,000 hours. Pretraining on such a large-scale weakly supervised dataset enables the model to be applicable to various data types or domains. Furthermore, Whisper has expanded the scope of weakly supervised pretraining to include multilingual and multitask scenarios. Therefore, we ultimately chose the powerful recognition-capable Whisper-large-v3 model as our ASR module.

2.2 MT

Our cascade system includes the Transformer (Vaswani et al., 2017) as the MT module, which has become a prevalent method for machine translation in recent years. The Transformer has achieved impressive results, even with a primitive architecture that requires minimal modification. To improve the offline MT model performance, we utilize multiple training strategies.

2.2.1 labse

Language-agnostic BERT Sentence Embedding (Feng et al., 2022) is an effective parallel corpus filtering method, which can effectively filter out high-quality bilingual data. We can use the filtered high-quality bilinguals and then finetune our model. Finally, we applied this method to this competition, which greatly improved the results in the three directions. In this experiment, we get 37 million filtered high-quality bilinguals in the en2ta direction, 55 million filtered high-quality bilinguals in the en2hi direction, and 43 million filtered high-quality

Proceedings of the 21st International Conference on Spoken Language Translation (IWSLT 2024), pages 101–104
August 15-16, 2024 ©2024 Association for Computational Linguistics

bilinguals in the en2bn direction from bilingual data.

2.2.2 Data Diversification

Data Diversification (DD) (Nguyen et al., 2020) is a simple but effective strategy to boost neural machine translation (NMT) (Bahdanau et al., 2015) performance. It diversifies the training data by using the predictions of multiple forward and backward models and then merging them with the original dataset on which the final NMT model is trained. This method is more effective than knowledge distillation and dual learning. Finally,

2.2.3 Forward Translation

Forward translation (FT) (Abdulmumin, 2021) uses source-side monolingual data to improve model performance. The general procedure of FT involves three steps: (1) randomly sampling a subset from large-scale source monolingual data; (2) using a "teacher" NMT model to translate the subset into the target language, thereby constructing synthetic parallel data; and (3) combining the synthetic and authentic parallel data to train a "student" NMT model.

2.2.4 Back Translation

Augmenting parallel training data with back-translation (BT) (Sennrich et al., 2016; Wei et al., 2023) has been shown effective for improving NMT using target monolingual data. Numerous works have expanded the understanding of BT and investigated various approaches to generate synthetic source sentences. Edunov et al. found that back-translations obtained via sampling or noised beam outputs tend to be more effective than those via beam or greedy search in most scenarios. For optimal joint use with FT, we employ sampling back-translation (ST) (Edunov et al., 2018).

2.2.5 Domain Fine-tuning

Previous studies have shown that fine-tuning a model with in-domain data can significantly enhance its performance. We use the model scoring method to select data from the bilingual training data that are close to the dev set in domain, and then use these domain data to finetune the model, which can further improve the result. Finally, we select 12 million domain data in the en2ta direction, 15 million domain data in the en2hi direction, and 10 million domain data in the en2bn direction from the bilingual training data.

2.2.6 Regularized Dropout

Regularized Dropout (R-Drop) (Wu et al., 2021) improves performance over standard dropout, especially for recurrent neural networks on tasks with long input sequences. It ensures more consistent regularization while maintaining model uncertainty estimates. The consistent masking also improves training efficiency compared to standard dropout. Overall, Regularized Dropout is an enhanced dropout technique that often outperforms standard dropout.

3 Experiments Setup

3.1 ASR

In our cascade system, we use whisper-large-v3 as our ASR module, which we will not introduce here.

3.2 MT

3.2.1 Model

For our experiments using the MT model, we utilize the Transformer deep model architecture. The configuration of the MT model is as follows:n_encoder layers = 35, n_decoder layers = 3, n_heads = 8, d_hidden = 512, d_FFN = 2048.

3.2.2 Dataset

To train the MT model, we collected all available parallel corpora from the official website and selected paralla data similar to the dev domain. The amount of data is shown in Table 1. We first trained respective baseline models in the three directions using bilingual data. Then, we construct pseudo-corpus based on existing monolingual data in each language direction to gradually enhance the baseline model.

	Bilingual	Source	Target
en-ta	57M	200M	70M
en-hi	80M	200M	230M
en-bn	82M	200M	190M

Table 1: Bilingual and monolingual data used for training.

3.2.3 Training

We utilize the open-source Fairseq (Ott et al., 2019) for training, with the following main parameters: each model is trained using 8 GPUs, with a batch size of 2048, a parameter update frequency of 32, and a learning rate of 5e-4. Additionally, a label smoothing value of 0.1 was used, with 4000 warmup steps and a dropout of 0.1. The Adam optimizer is also employed, with ß1 = 0.9 and ß2 = 0.98. During the inference phase, a beam size of 4 is used. The length penalties are set to 1.0.

3.3 Results

We can see results From Table 2, In the field of machine translation, Domain Finetuning, Forward Translation, and labse filter method are frequently employed methods to enhance translation quality. It is evident from Table 4 that these training strategies can effectively improve the overall quality of the system.

Language-pair	Training strategies	Bleu
en-hi	Bilingual baseline	51.9
	+ FT+BT	53.8
	+ labse Bilingual Finetune	54.7
	+ Domain Finetune	64.8
en-ta	Bilingual baseline	41.9
	+ FT+BT	42.2
	+ labse Bilingual Finetune	43.1
	+ Domain Finetune	45.2
en-bn	Bilingual baseline	38
	+ FT+BT	40.4
	+ labse Bilingual Finetune	42.1
	+ Domain Finetune	44.8

Table 2: All the results for dev testsets in three directions(EN-HI,EN-TA,EN-BN).FT means Forward Translation. BT means Back Translation.

At the same time, we also calculated the blue of NLLB-200-3.3B (Costa-jussà et al., 2022) in three directions, as shown in Table 3, for comparison with our results. As can be seen from Table 2 and Table 3, our model is far better than the NLLB model.

Language-pair	NLLB baseline
en-hi	40.9
en-ta	20.4
en-bn	25.7

Table 3: NLLB-200-3.3B results for dev testsets in three directions(EN-HI,EN-TA,EN-BN).

4 Conclusion

In this paper, we report on our work on IWSLT2024 speech-to-text translation evaluation in Indic Track. We mainly introduce our cascade system and the main optimization processes and methods of the MT model. We improve the final results by focusing on optimizing the MT model. For cascade systems, the impact of the MT model on the results is crucial. For the future we plan to further explore the direction of end-to-end systems.

References

Idris Abdulmumin. 2021. Enhanced back-translation for low resource neural machine translation using self-training. In *Information and Communication Technology and Applications: Third International Conference, ICTA 2020, Minna, Nigeria, November 24–27, 2020, Revised Selected Papers*, volume 1350, page 355. Springer Nature.

Dzmitry Bahdanau, Kyunghyun Cho, and Yoshua Bengio. 2015. Neural machine translation by jointly learning to align and translate. In *3rd International Conference on Learning Representations, ICLR 2015, San Diego, CA, USA, May 7-9, 2015, Conference Track Proceedings*.

Marta R Costa-jussà, James Cross, Onur Çelebi, Maha Elbayad, Kenneth Heafield, Kevin Heffernan, Elahe Kalbassi, Janice Lam, Daniel Licht, Jean Maillard, et al. 2022. No language left behind: Scaling human-centered machine translation. *arXiv preprint arXiv:2207.04672*.

Sergey Edunov, Myle Ott, Michael Auli, and David Grangier. 2018. Understanding back-translation at scale. In *Proceedings of the 2018 Conference on Empirical Methods in Natural Language Processing*, page 489. Association for Computational Linguistics.

Fangxiaoyu Feng, Yinfei Yang, Daniel Cer, Naveen Arivazhagan, and Wei Wang. 2022. Language-agnostic BERT sentence embedding. In *Proceedings of the 60th Annual Meeting of the Association for Computational Linguistics (Volume 1: Long Papers)*, pages 878–891, Dublin, Ireland. Association for Computational Linguistics.

Xuan-Phi Nguyen, Shafiq Joty, Wu Kui, and Ai Ti Aw. 2020. Data diversification: a simple strategy for neural machine translation. In *Proceedings of the 34th International Conference on Neural Information Processing Systems*, pages 10018–10029.

Myle Ott, Sergey Edunov, Alexei Baevski, Angela Fan, Sam Gross, Nathan Ng, David Grangier, and Michael Auli. 2019. fairseq: A fast, extensible toolkit for sequence modeling. In *Proceedings of the 2019 Conference of the North American Chapter of the Association for Computational Linguistics (Demonstrations)*, pages 48–53, Minneapolis, Minnesota. Association for Computational Linguistics.

Alec Radford, Jong Wook Kim, Tao Xu, Greg Brockman, Christine McLeavey, and Ilya Sutskever. 2023. Robust speech recognition via large-scale weak supervision. In *International Conference on Machine Learning*, pages 28492–28518. PMLR.

Rico Sennrich, Barry Haddow, and Alexandra Birch. 2016. Improving neural machine translation models with monolingual data. In *54th Annual Meeting of the Association for Computational Linguistics*, pages 86–96. Association for Computational Linguistics (ACL).

Ashish Vaswani, Noam Shazeer, Niki Parmar, Jakob Uszkoreit, Llion Jones, Aidan N Gomez, Łukasz Kaiser, and Illia Polosukhin. 2017. Attention is all you need. *Advances in neural information processing systems*, 30.

Daimeng Wei, Zhanglin Wu, Hengchao Shang, Zongyao Li, Minghan Wang, Jiaxin Guo, Xiaoyu Chen, Zhengzhe Yu, and Hao Yang. 2023. Text style transfer back-translation. In *Proceedings of the 61st Annual Meeting of the Association for Computational Linguistics*, pages 7944–7959, Toronto, Canada.

Lijun Wu, Juntao Li, Yue Wang, Qi Meng, Tao Qin, Wei Chen, Min Zhang, Tie-Yan Liu, et al. 2021. R-drop: Regularized dropout for neural networks. *Advances in Neural Information Processing Systems*, 34:10890–10905.

Multi-Model System for Effective Subtitling Compression

Carol-Luca Gasan and **Vasile Păiș**
Research Institute for Artificial Intelligence "Mihai Drăgănescu", Romanian Academy
Bucharest, Romania

Abstract

This paper presents RACAI's system used for the shared task of "Subtitling track: Subtitle Compression" (the English to Spanish language direction), organized as part of "the 21st edition of The International Conference on Spoken Language Translation (IWSLT 2024)". The proposed system consists of multiple models whose outputs are then ensembled using an algorithm, which has the purpose of maximizing the similarity of the initial and resulting text. We present the introduced datasets and the models' training strategy, along with the reported results on the proposed test set.

1 Introduction

Subtitles play a vital role in ensuring accessibility and comprehension of audiovisual (AV) content for viewers with diverse needs, including those with hearing impairments or language barriers. However, traditional subtitling methods often generate text exceeding recommended reading speed constraints, hindering comprehension and viewer engagement. This problem becomes particularly pronounced for audiences with slower reading speeds or limited language proficiency.

In the context of the 21st edition of The International Conference on Spoken Language Translation (IWSLT 2024), the Subtitle Compression task, part of the Subtitling track, required participants to propose systems that rephrase subtitles that are non-compliant with the reading speed constraint without limitations on the training data conditions. This paper describes the possibility of using large language models (LLMs) to achieve this while trying to benefit from the initial content in the source language. Sometimes, sentences have formats that make them hard to compress, especially when a translation step has been made. The most fundamental example of such inconvenience is regarding idioms. They might not have perfect equivalents in the target language, and thus, their compression becomes even more challenging to process. Problems of this kind can be partially solved by initially compressing the sentence in the source language and then translating it. Our contribution is twofold: a) we introduce a new method that is able to combine the predictions of multiple models; b) we explore different parameters for the proposed algorithm and present the results on the shared task dataset.

The rest of the paper is structured as follows: Section 2 presents related work, Section 3 describes the method proposed, including dataset description (in Section 3.3), model training (in Section 3.4) and ensemble process (in Section 3.5); results are given in Section 4 and we conclude in Section 5.

2 Related work

In this section, we explore the various methodologies and research efforts that have contributed to the development of compression tasks. Although the compression task is inherently monolingual, we consider not only the works focused on text summarization but also those addressing automatic subtitling, machine translation (MT), and automatic speech recognition (ASR). This is because these domains often employ similar techniques and face comparable challenges in reducing and transforming textual data while maintaining its essential information and coherence.

2.1 Automatic subtitling

Recent advancements in speech translation (ST) have focused on developing systems that can translate spoken language directly into another language, bypassing the need for separate automatic speech recognition and machine translation (MT) steps. This approach, known as end-to-end ST, has shown promising results. Papi et al. (2023a) build on this progress by exploring the use of direct architectures for both simultaneous translation (SimulST) and

Proceedings of the 21st International Conference on Spoken Language Translation (IWSLT 2024), pages 105–112
August 15-16, 2024 ©2024 Association for Computational Linguistics

automatic subtitling tasks. Their work contributes to the growing body of research on efficient and effective methods for real-time speech translation applications. Bahar et al. (2023) tackle the same task, by proposing En-Ru and En-Pt production models, which support formality control via prefix tokens.

2.2 Text summarization models

Sentence compression has been extensively explored using various transformer-based architectures. The T5 model (Raffel et al., 2023) employs a text-to-text transformer architecture, leveraging its encoder-decoder structure to identify and eliminate redundant information through a process of denoising and reconstruction. Specifically, T5 uses a unified framework that converts all NLP tasks into a text-to-text format, allowing it to adapt to sentence compression tasks through task-specific prompting and fine-tuning.

BART (Lewis et al., 2020) utilizes a novel denoising autoencoder approach, where the input sentence is corrupted through token masking and deletion, and the model is trained to reconstruct the original sentence. During pre-training, BART learns to predict the original tokens from their corrupted versions, developing a robust understanding of sentence structure and semantics. This pre-training objective enables the model to develop a strong ability to recognize and remove redundant information.

The Llama2 model (Touvron et al., 2023) relies on a combination of masked language modelling and denoising objectives to learn a robust representation of language. Specifically, it uses a multi-task learning framework that jointly optimizes masked language modelling, sentiment analysis, and next-sentence prediction tasks. This multi-task learning approach enables Llama2 to develop a comprehensive understanding of language syntax, semantics, and pragmatics.

2.3 Automatic speech recognition

Automatic speech recognition (ASR) has witnessed significant advancements with the emergence of transformer-based architectures. The Whisper model (Radford et al., 2023) employs a conditional waveform-to-text model that leverages a combination of self-supervised learning and supervised finetuning to achieve state-of-the-art performance on various ASR benchmarks. It uses a multi-task learning framework that jointly optimizes masked acoustic modelling, phoneme recognition, and sentence transcription tasks, enabling it to learn robust representations of spoken language that can generalize across different accents, languages, and recording conditions.

2.4 Translation models

Machine translation has seen significant advancements with the development of large-scale transformer-based models. NLLB (No Language Left Behind) (Team et al., 2022) is a family of translation models that aim to bridge the gap between high-resource and low-resource languages. NLLB uses a multilingual masked language modelling objective to pre-train a single model on a massive dataset of 50 languages, enabling it to learn shared representations across languages and achieve state-of-the-art performance on various translation benchmarks. NLLB employs a novel "language-agnostic" approach that treats all languages equally, without relying on language-specific adapters or fine-tuning, making it particularly effective for low-resource languages.

2.5 Summarization Datasets

The development of effective text summarization models relies heavily on the availability of high-quality, linguistically diverse datasets. In this regard, the Google Sentence Compression (Filippova and Altun, 2013) dataset is a prominent resource, comprising approximately 200,000 sentence pairs extracted from news articles. Each pair consists of an original sentence and its corresponding compressed version, with an average compression ratio of 35%. Notably, this dataset is primarily composed of English sentences, with a focus on formal, written language.

TaPaCo (Scherrer, 2020) is a freely available paraphrase corpus that offers a unique resource for natural language processing (NLP) research. Extracted from the Tatoeba database, a crowdsourced platform primarily designed for language learners, TaPaCo provides a vast collection of paraphrases in 73 languages.

The PAWS-X (PAWS eXtended) (Yang et al., 2019) dataset takes a multilingual approach to text summarization, featuring a diverse range of texts from the web in four languages: English, French, German, and Spanish. With over 1 million pairs of original texts and their corresponding summaries, PAWS-X provides a comprehensive benchmark for evaluating cross-lingual summarization performance. The dataset's structure is noteworthy, with each instance comprising a source text, a target summary, and corresponding metadata such as language labels and genre information.

3 Method

3.1 Overview

Our proposed method analyzes both the original text in English and the translated text in Spanish in order to have an alternative approach in case the latter is not being compressed within the established limits. Therefore, we had to obtain the initial subtitles in the language of the video through an automatic speech recognition model. With that in mind, we can compress and translate the English text in this exact order such that we obtain a new set of Spanish sentences to be fitted within the time intervals presented in the given SRT file. We define a sentence based on the presence of strong punctuation; a sentence may span over multiple time intervals in the SRT file. Having a series of alternatives for each sentence that has to be processed, we run an algorithm to determine the assignment of the compressed sentences that maximizes the similarity between the reference and the prediction texts. A general representation of the method is presented in Figure 1.

3.2 Performance identifiers and metrics

We focused on multiple metrics to define the performance of our models and to determine a relation of order between sentences with the same meaning.

ROUGE (Recall-Oriented Understudy for Gisting Evaluation) (Lin, 2004) is a set of metrics used to evaluate the quality of summarization models. It measures the overlap between the generated summary and the reference summary, focusing on recall (i.e., how much of the reference summary is covered by the generated summary). There are several variants of ROUGE, including:

a) ROUGE-1: measures the overlap of unigrams (single words) between the generated and reference summaries;

b) ROUGE-2: measures the overlap of bigrams (pairs of adjacent words) between the generated and reference summaries;

c) ROUGE-L: measures the longest common subsequence between the generated and reference summaries.

ROUGE scores range from 0 to 1, with higher scores indicating better summarization quality.

BLEU (Bilingual Evaluation Understudy) (Papineni et al., 2002) is a metric used to evaluate the quality of machine translation models, but it can also be applied to summarization tasks. It measures the similarity between the generated summary and the reference summary based on n-gram overlap. BLEU calculates the precision of n-grams (sequences of n items) in the generated summary compared to the reference summary. BLEU scores range from 0 to 1, with higher scores indicating better summarization quality.

MPNet (Quyen and Kim, 2023) is a type of neural network architecture that uses word embeddings to represent words as vectors in a high-dimensional space. In this context, MPNet is used to calculate the distance between words or phrases in the generated summary and the reference summary. The distance calculation can be done using various metrics, such as cosine similarity (in this case), Euclidean distance, or Manhattan distance. The resulting distance score can be used to evaluate the semantic similarity between the generated and reference summaries.

BLEURT (BERT-based Learned Utility for Ranking Translation Outputs) (Sellam et al., 2020) is a metric that evaluates the quality of summarization models using a BERT-based approach. It learns to predict a utility score for each generated summary based on its similarity to the reference summary. BLEURT analyzes different factors, including:

a) Fluency: measures the grammatical correctness and coherence of the generated summary;

b) Relevance: measures the degree to which the generated summary covers the main points and ideas of the original text;

c) Informativeness: measures the amount of new information presented in the generated summary;

d) Coherence: measures the degree to which the generated summary is well-organized and easy to follow.

The BLEURT score is a weighted sum of these individual metrics, providing a comprehensive evaluation of the generated summary's quality.

3.3 Dataset Choice and Creation

As part of the gathered Spanish corpora, PAWS-X and TaPaCo were used as they are, while Google's Sentence Compression dataset was filtered to eliminate pairs of sentences with very low compression rate. In addition to these resources, we created a new one (Sent-Comp-ES) by translating Google's

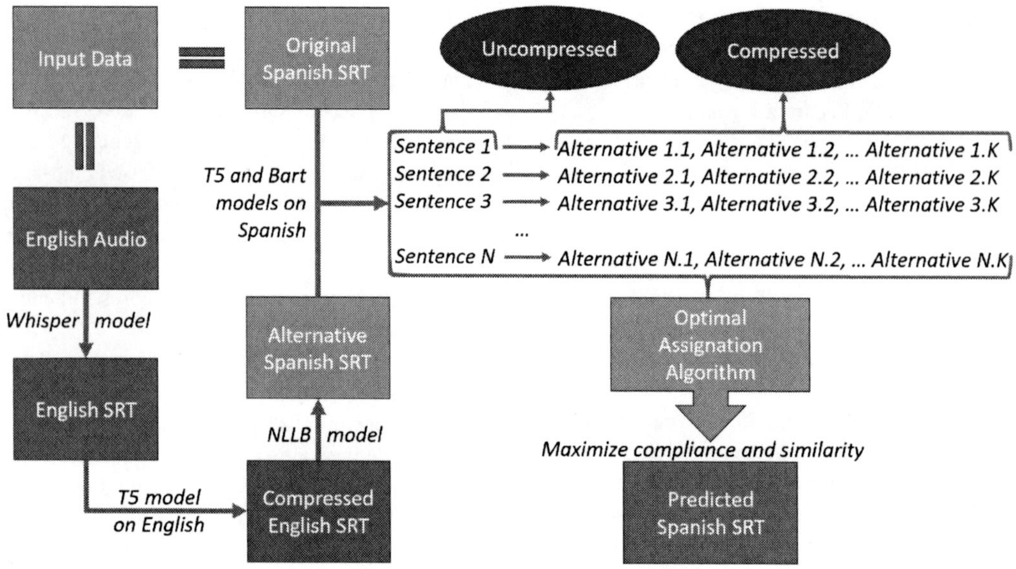

Figure 1: Scheme of the overall transformation.

Dataset	Language	Dimension
Sent. Comp.	English	200k
Sent-Comp-Es	Spanish	53k
TaPaCo	Spanish	85k
PAWS-X (filtered)	Spanish	9k

Table 1: Datasets used for extractive summarization.

Sentence Compression dataset (referred as Sent. Comp. later in the paper) for extractive summarization (i.e., the task of selecting a subset of words from a sentence to form a summary). In the transformation process, multiple rules have been established such that the quality of the data is preserved, with the downside of obtaining less data than the initial resource. The conducted steps are in exact order:

a) Eliminate the English pairs with an associated compression rate smaller than 10% for sentences with at least 10 characters;

b) Eliminate the English pairs with an associated ROUGE score smaller than 0.8;

c) Translate the remaining sentences to Spanish using Facebook's NLLB model;

d) Eliminate the Spanish pairs not respecting the extractive summarization pattern (i.e., eliminate those pairs for which the compressed sentence is not a subsequence of words from the initial sentence);

e) Check again for the associated compression rate and ROUGE score while keeping the same constraints as aforementioned;

In the end, from 200k pairs of English sentences, we formed 53k pairs of Spanish sentences that can be used for extractive summarization training. Furthermore, all processed data can be as well used for abstractive summarization.

3.4 Model Choice and Training

Since this paper focuses on an ensemble selection system, we had to define the models we want to use and train. Regarding the Spanish text models, we finetuned the base checkpoints of T5 and Bart, while for Llama2, we chose the 13B parameters checkpoint. Through the previous models, we propose to tackle both extractive and abstractive summarization. On the other hand, for the audio processing, since it can be assumed that for generating the given Spanish text, a variant of the original English text is already composed, we decided to go with a pre-trained large checkpoint of the Whisper v2 model. Wee feed the model pre-segmented audio by taking timestamps of the original Spanish SRT, without activating the internal VAD. For the English text summarization, a pre-trained large checkpoint of T5 was used.

T5 and Bart were trained on a joint dataset containing TaPaCo, PAWS-X and Sent-Comp-ES, totaling at 147k pairs of sentences, with a simple prompt, namely *"comprimir: "* (en: *"compress: "*).

Model	Learning Rate	Epoch	Avg. Compression	ROUGE	BLEU	MPNET
T5-base	1e-4	4	48%	0.60	0.23	0.81
T5-base	2e-5	4	47%	0.61	0.20	0.74
T5-base	1e-4	15	46%	0.61	0.24	0.81
Bart-base	2e-5	4	46%	0.60	0.24	0.82
Bart-base	2e-5	15	47%	0.62	0.25	0.84
Llama2-13B	1e-4	1	18%	0.57	0.23	0.80
Llama2-13B	1e-4	4	33%	0.60	0.24	0.85

Table 2: Metrics obtained on the gathered corpora while training for Spanish sentence compression.

We also finetuned Llama2 on all the data available (200k pairs) using QLoRA (Dettmers et al., 2023), with a more complex prompt trying to settle the context and the general task:

```
### TAREA: Parafrasee la frase de entrada para hacerla lo más corta posible en términos de número de caracteres, conservando el significado inicial y teniendo una gramática y puntuación correctas. Si no es posible o no está seguro, mantenga la frase sin cambios.
### SENTENCIA SIN COMPRIMIR: <UNCOMP>
### SENTENCIA COMPRIMIDA: <COMP>

(Note: the <UNCOMP> and <COMP> tokens are replacing the uncompressed and compressed sentences respectively.)
```

Table 2 contains the results acquired during training. According to the reported performance and considering Llama2's inference time, we decided to exclude it from the prediction system. Another important reason is that Llama2 was trained for abstractive summarization, which makes the reconstruction of the SRT file from sentences really difficult.

3.5 Algorithm Development

In order to present the proposed algorithm, let us standardize the problem to be solved. We have N sentences distributed among M time intervals, where a sentence might be covering multiple intervals. Each sentence can be written as a set of word sequences, representing its splits among the time intervals it overlaps. Using the summarization models, we obtain for each given sentence a set of at most K other sentences split in the same manner (possible because the extractive summarization preserves the order of the words), along with some metrics defining the resemblance to the uncompressed text. Considering known the time intervals' lengths, we can determine if a split is compliant by taking into account the dimension of the newly formed word sequence. We define the following notion as well: the score of an assignment is the weighted sum of similarity scores where the weights are length-based. The score is between 0 and 1, a score of one being obtained for the initial sentences. The length of a sentence is defined as the number of characters.

A baseline approach is to go through all the possible combinations of assigned sentences and choose the one with a maximal score that is also compliant. The complexity of this algorithm is in terms of $O((M+N)*K^N)$. Our proposed algorithm achieves a complexity of $O((M+N)*K*\alpha)$, where α is the maximum length of a split. The main idea of the algorithm is to denote critical points as the time intervals that contain words from more than one sentence. Then, we just have to analyze the best obtainable score until a certain checkpoint, while consuming a certain number of characters from the maximum allowed within that time interval. This is achievable using dynamic programming and it reduces the complexity to the one previously mentioned. The pseudo code for obtaining the maximum score can be seen in Figure 2. The optimal solution can be easily reconstructed by maintaining a backward array during the update of the *dp* array, which allows backtracking from the final state to the initial state to retrieve the sequence of selected sentences.

4 Results

The dev set proposed within the shared task consists of 7 SRT files, part of the EuroParl Interviews (EPI) en-es test set, whereas the test set concerns AV docs from the ITV entertainment series, all generated by the non-participating (Papi et al., 2023b). The reported results of our submission can be seen in Table 3, where ChrF is a metric introduced by

Algorithm 1 Compute Maximum Score

```
Input:
capacity - array of size M + 1 (stores time interval capacities)
interval - array of pairs (stores start and end times for each sentence)
quality - matrix of size (N + 1) × (K + 1) (stores similarity scores)
quantity - 3D matrix of size (N + 1) × (K + 1) × (interval[i].right − interval[i].left) (stores word sequence lengths)
dp - matrix of size (N + 1) × (maximum capacity across intervals) (stores maximum score achievable)
Initialize dp
dp[0][0] = 0                                        ▷ base case, no sentences processed
for i = 1 to N do
    dp[i] ← array filled with −∞                    ▷ initialize scores for current sentence
end for
Loop through sentences
for i = 1 to N do
    if interval[i].left ≠ interval[i - 1].right then
        Get maximum score from previous sentence    ▷ no addition possible
        for j = 1 to K do                           ▷ loop through candidate sentences for current
            Update dp with score from previous + current sentence similarity
        end for
    else if interval[i].left < interval[i].right then
        for j = 1 to K do                           ▷ loop through candidate sentences for current
            for last = 0 to capacity[i.left] − quantity[i][j][0] do   ▷ check if candidate fits
                Update dp with score from previous + current sentence similarity
            end for
        end for
    else
        for curr = capacity[i.left] down to 0 do    ▷ loop through capacities
            for j = 1 to K do                       ▷ loop through candidate sentences for current
                if candidate fits current capacity then
                    Update dp with score from previous + current sentence similarity
                end if
            end for
        end for
    end if
end for
Find maximum score across all capacities for the last sentence
max_score ← −∞
for i = 0 to capacity[M] do
    max_score ← max(max_score, dp[N][i])
end for
Output: max_score
```

Figure 2: Pseudo code for obtaining the maximum score.

Method	BLEU	ChrF	TER	BLEURT	CPS
ref	-	-	-	-	89.98
ori test-set	8.71	29.18	81.08	0.213571	69.97
baseline	7.70	27.52	81.27	0.18917	100.00
RACAI	7.51	26.60	80.33	0.194613	94.29

Table 3: Reported results on the proposed test set.

(Popović, 2015) , and TER (Translation Edit Rate) represents the minimum number of edits needed to change a hypothesis so that it exactly matches one of the references, normalized by the average length of the references. In addition, the methods' acronyms in Table 3 respect the following notations:

a) ref: reference subtitles used to compute BLEU/ChrF/TER/BLEURT scores;

b) ori test-set: original subtitles to be compressed;

c) ori test-set-1line: original subtitles where those segmented in more lines are unsegmented in 1-line;

d) baseline: hard cut at max number of charsq compatible with subtitle duration;

e) RACAI: subtitles generated with the system described in this paper.

5 Conclusion

This paper presents RACAI's system for the "Subtitling track: Subtitle Compression" shared task, focusing on compressing subtitles from English to Spanish while maintaining readability within reading speed constraints. Our system leverages multiple large language models (LLMs) to generate alternative compressed sentences for the original text. An ensemble selection algorithm then chooses the most suitable compressed options based on similarity metrics. This approach allows us to benefit from the strengths of various models and address potential shortcomings of individual models.

Future work could explore the incorporation of additional metrics or quality estimation techniques within the ensemble selection algorithm. Additionally, investigating the effectiveness of the system on different language pairs or domains could be valuable, such as including the Romanian language. We previously had an interest for processing Romanian language speech using Whisper (Gasan and Păiș, 2023). Overall, this work contributes to the development of automatic subtitling systems that ensure accessibility and comprehension for diverse audiences.

References

Parnia Bahar, Patrick Wilken, Javier Iranzo-Sánchez, Mattia Di Gangi, Evgeny Matusov, and Zoltán Tüske. 2023. Speech translation with style: AppTek's submissions to the IWSLT subtitling and formality tracks in 2023. In *Proceedings of the 20th International Conference on Spoken Language Translation (IWSLT 2023)*, pages 251–260, Toronto, Canada (in-person and online). Association for Computational Linguistics.

Tim Dettmers, Artidoro Pagnoni, Ari Holtzman, and Luke Zettlemoyer. 2023. Qlora: Efficient finetuning of quantized llms. *Preprint*, arXiv:2305.14314.

Katja Filippova and Yasemin Altun. 2013. Overcoming the lack of parallel data in sentence compression. In *Proceedings of the 2013 Conference on Empirical Methods in Natural Language Processing*, pages 1481–1491, Seattle, Washington, USA. Association for Computational Linguistics.

Carol-Luca Gasan and Vasile Păiș. 2023. Investigation of Romanian speech recognition improvement by incorporating Italian speech data. In *The 18th International Conference on Linguistic Resources and Tools for Natural Language Processing (ConsILR-2023)*.

Mike Lewis, Yinhan Liu, Naman Goyal, Marjan Ghazvininejad, Abdelrahman Mohamed, Omer Levy, Veselin Stoyanov, and Luke Zettlemoyer. 2020. BART: Denoising sequence-to-sequence pre-training for natural language generation, translation, and comprehension. In *Proceedings of the 58th Annual Meeting of the Association for Computational Linguistics*, pages 7871–7880, Online. Association for Computational Linguistics.

Chin-Yew Lin. 2004. ROUGE: A package for automatic evaluation of summaries. In *Text Summarization Branches Out*, pages 74–81, Barcelona, Spain. Association for Computational Linguistics.

Sara Papi, Marco Gaido, Alina Karakanta, Mauro Cettolo, Matteo Negri, and Marco Turchi. 2023a. Direct Speech Translation for Automatic Subtitling. *Transactions of the Association for Computational Linguistics*, 11:1355–1376.

Sara Papi, Marco Gaido, and Matteo Negri. 2023b. Direct models for simultaneous translation and automatic subtitling: FBK@IWSLT2023. In *Proceedings of the 20th International Conference on Spoken Language Translation (IWSLT 2023)*, pages 159–168, Toronto, Canada (in-person and online). Association for Computational Linguistics.

Kishore Papineni, Salim Roukos, Todd Ward, and Wei-Jing Zhu. 2002. Bleu: a method for automatic evaluation of machine translation. In *Proceedings of the 40th Annual Meeting of the Association for Computational Linguistics*, pages 311–318, Philadelphia, Pennsylvania, USA. Association for Computational Linguistics.

Maja Popović. 2015. chrF: character n-gram F-score for automatic MT evaluation. In *Proceedings of the Tenth Workshop on Statistical Machine Translation*, pages 392–395, Lisbon, Portugal. Association for Computational Linguistics.

Van Toan Quyen and Min Young Kim. 2023. Mpnet: Multiscale predictions based on feature pyramid network for semantic segmentation. In *2023 Fourteenth International Conference on Ubiquitous and Future Networks (ICUFN)*, pages 114–119.

Alec Radford, Jong Wook Kim, Tao Xu, Greg Brockman, Christine Mcleavey, and Ilya Sutskever. 2023. Robust speech recognition via large-scale weak supervision. In *Proceedings of the 40th International Conference on Machine Learning*, volume 202 of *Proceedings of Machine Learning Research*, pages 28492–28518. PMLR.

Colin Raffel, Noam Shazeer, Adam Roberts, Katherine Lee, Sharan Narang, Michael Matena, Yanqi Zhou, Wei Li, and Peter J. Liu. 2023. Exploring the limits of transfer learning with a unified text-to-text transformer. *Preprint*, arXiv:1910.10683.

Yves Scherrer. 2020. Tapaco: A corpus of sentential paraphrases for 73 languages.

Thibault Sellam, Dipanjan Das, and Ankur Parikh. 2020. BLEURT: Learning robust metrics for text generation. In *Proceedings of the 58th Annual Meeting of the Association for Computational Linguistics*, pages 7881–7892, Online. Association for Computational Linguistics.

NLLB Team, Marta R. Costa-jussà, James Cross, Onur Çelebi, Maha Elbayad, Kenneth Heafield, Kevin Heffernan, Elahe Kalbassi, Janice Lam, Daniel Licht, Jean Maillard, Anna Sun, Skyler Wang, Guillaume Wenzek, Al Youngblood, Bapi Akula, Loic Barrault, Gabriel Mejia Gonzalez, Prangthip Hansanti, John Hoffman, Semarley Jarrett, Kaushik Ram Sadagopan, Dirk Rowe, Shannon Spruit, Chau Tran, Pierre Andrews, Necip Fazil Ayan, Shruti Bhosale, Sergey Edunov, Angela Fan, Cynthia Gao, Vedanuj Goswami, Francisco Guzmán, Philipp Koehn, Alexandre Mourachko, Christophe Ropers, Safiyyah Saleem, Holger Schwenk, and Jeff Wang. 2022. No language left behind: Scaling human-centered machine translation. *Preprint*, arXiv:2207.04672.

Hugo Touvron, Louis Martin, Kevin Stone, Peter Albert, Amjad Almahairi, Yasmine Babaei, Nikolay Bashlykov, Soumya Batra, Prajjwal Bhargava, Shruti Bhosale, Dan Bikel, Lukas Blecher, Cristian Canton Ferrer, Moya Chen, Guillem Cucurull, David Esiobu, Jude Fernandes, Jeremy Fu, Wenyin Fu, Brian Fuller, Cynthia Gao, Vedanuj Goswami, Naman Goyal, Anthony Hartshorn, Saghar Hosseini, Rui Hou, Hakan Inan, Marcin Kardas, Viktor Kerkez, Madian Khabsa, Isabel Kloumann, Artem Korenev, Punit Singh Koura, Marie-Anne Lachaux, Thibaut Lavril, Jenya Lee, Diana Liskovich, Yinghai Lu, Yuning Mao, Xavier Martinet, Todor Mihaylov, Pushkar Mishra, Igor Molybog, Yixin Nie, Andrew Poulton, Jeremy Reizenstein, Rashi Rungta, Kalyan Saladi, Alan Schelten, Ruan Silva, Eric Michael Smith, Ranjan Subramanian, Xiaoqing Ellen Tan, Binh Tang, Ross Taylor, Adina Williams, Jian Xiang Kuan, Puxin Xu, Zheng Yan, Iliyan Zarov, Yuchen Zhang, Angela Fan, Melanie Kambadur, Sharan Narang, Aurelien Rodriguez, Robert Stojnic, Sergey Edunov, and Thomas Scialom. 2023. Llama 2: Open foundation and fine-tuned chat models. *Preprint*, arXiv:2307.09288.

Yinfei Yang, Yuan Zhang, Chris Tar, and Jason Baldridge. 2019. PAWS-X: A cross-lingual adversarial dataset for paraphrase identification. In *Proceedings of the 2019 Conference on Empirical Methods in Natural Language Processing and the 9th International Joint Conference on Natural Language Processing (EMNLP-IJCNLP)*, pages 3687–3692, Hong Kong, China. Association for Computational Linguistics.

FBK@IWSLT Test Suites Task: Gender Bias evaluation with MuST-SHE

Beatrice Savoldi, Marco Gaido, Matteo Negri, Luisa Bentivogli
Fondazione Bruno Kessler
{bsavoldi,mgaido,negri,bentivo}@fbk.eu

Abstract

This paper presents the FBK contribution to the IWSLT-2024 "Test suites" shared subtask, part of the Offline Speech Translation Task. Our contribution consists of the MuST-SHE^{IWSLT24} benchmark evaluation, designed to assess gender bias in speech translation. By focusing on the en-de language pair, we rely on a newly created test suite to investigate systems' ability to correctly translate feminine and masculine gender. Our results indicate that – under realistic conditions – current ST systems achieve reasonable and comparable performance in correctly translating both feminine and masculine forms when contextual gender information is available. For ambiguous references to the speaker, however, we attest a consistent preference towards masculine gender, thus calling for future endeavours on the topic. Towards this goal we make MuST-SHE^{IWSLT24} freely available at: https://mt.fbk.eu/must-she/

1 Introduction

In today's interconnected world, speech translation technology stands as a cornerstone of global communication, facilitating seamless interactions across linguistic barriers. Indeed, the last few years have seen notable advancements for the task of speech-to-text translation (ST), which has made strides in generic performance (Bentivogli et al., 2021; Anastasopoulos et al., 2021, 2022; Agarwal et al., 2023). Also, the emergence massively multilingual solutions has greatly expanded the language coverage of competitive "one-model-fits-all" speech models (Radford et al., 2022; Communication et al., 2023; Peng et al., 2024; Pratap et al., 2024).

Amid such advancements, there arise the increasing need to pair traditional overall quality assessments of ST with more fine-grained analyses by accounting for relevant aspects of translations. It is within this context that the IWSLT Test Suites shared task emerges, aiming to provide a dedicated evaluation framework for specific dimensions of the ST output, which are otherwise overlooked with generic test sets and holistic metrics.

In light of the above, our contribution is dedicated to the critical themes of gender bias in automatic translation (Costa-jussà, 2019; Savoldi, 2023; Vanmassenhove, 2024).[1] Given the large-scale deployment of ST, biased translations are not only relevant from a technical perspective, where gender-related errors negatively impact the accuracy of automatic translation. Rather, biased and non-inclusive systems can pose the concrete risk of under/misrepresenting gender minorities by over-producing masculine forms and reinforcing gendered stereotypes (Blodgett et al., 2020; Sun et al., 2019). Indeed, gendered linguistic expressions affect the representation and perception of individuals (Stahlberg et al., 2007; Corbett, 2013; Gygax et al., 2019), and are actively used as a tool to negotiate the social, personal, and political reality of gender (Hellinger and Motschenbacher, 2015). A such, models that systematically favor masculine over feminine forms fail to properly recognize women, can reduce feminine visibility, and offer an unequal service quality (Crawford, 2017).

This paper presents the FBK participation in the Test Suites shared task by conducting evaluations on the **MuST-SHE**^{IWSLT24} en-de dataset. It represents the newly created *speech-to-text* extension of the English→German *textual-only* portion of MuST-SHE (Savoldi et al., 2023), a multilingual gender bias benchmark (Bentivogli et al., 2020).

In the hereby presented evaluations, we obtained translations of our test suites by systems that are part of the Offline Speech Translation Task of the 21st International Conference on Spoken Language

[1] Its relevance is also attested by the creation of dedicated workshops on theme of gender bias and inclusivity, such as GeBNLP (Hardmeier et al., 2022) and GITT (Vanmassenhove et al., 2023).

Proceedings of the 21st International Conference on Spoken Language Translation (IWSLT 2024), pages 113–119
August 15-16, 2024 ©2024 Association for Computational Linguistics

Form		Category 1: *Ambiguous first-person references*	Speaker
Fem.	src	The other hat that I've worn in my work is as **an activist**...	She
	Ref$_{De}$	Der andere Hut, den ich bei meiner Arbeit getragen habe, ist **der**<den> **Aktivistin**<Aktivist>...	
Masc.	src	I mean, I'm a **journalist**.	He
	Ref$_{De}$	Ich meine, ich bin **Journalist** <Journalistin>.	
		Category 2: *Unambiguous references with gender cue in context*	
Fem.	src	A college classmate wrote me a couple weeks ago and she said ...	He
	Ref$_{De}$	**Eine**<Ein> **Kommilitonin**<Kommiliton> hat mir vor ein paar Wochen geschrieben und gesagt...	
Masc.	src	I decided to pay a visit to **the manager** [...] and he pointed ...	She
	Ref$_{De}$	Also entschied ich mich **den**<die>**Filialleiter**<Filialleiterin> zu besuchen [...]	

Table 1: Textual portion of MuST-SHE (Savoldi et al., 2023), with annotated segments organized per category. For each gender-neutral word referring to a human entity in the English source sentence (SRC), the reference translation (REF) shows the corresponding gender-marked (Fem/Masc) forms, annotated with their wrong <gender-swapped> forms. The last column provides information about the speaker's gender.

Translation (IWSLT 2024). Specifically, we evaluated 13 systems for MuST-SHE^{IWSLT24} en-de.

2 MuST-SHE^{IWSLT24}

MuST-SHE^{IWSLT24} is a test suite designed to evaluate the ability of ST systems to correctly translate gender. It is composed of 200 segments that require the translation of – at least – one English gender-neutral word into the corresponding masculine or feminine target word(s) in German.[2] The test suite is created as an extension of MuST-SHE, a multilingual, natural benchmark built on TED talks data (Bentivogli et al., 2020). The original corpus comprises ∼3,000 (*audio, transcript, translation*) triplets annotated with qualitatively differentiated gender-related phenomena for thee language pairs: English→ French/Italian/Spanish. Recently, MuST-SHE was also extended to English→ German for the MT task – i.e. MuST-SHE^{WMT23} (Savoldi et al., 2023). However, since it only consists of a textual portion (*transcript, translation*), it does not allow for the evaluation of ST models.

Here, we introduce the expansion of **MuST-SHE English→ German for the ST task**, by incorporating the additional speech input portion so as to obtain (*audio, transcript, translation*) triplets.

2.1 Audio Portion Creation

To ensure conformity, the dataset audio portion was obtained by following the same automatic procedures used for MuST-SHE and other TED-based resources, as reported in (Cattoni et al., 2021). Accordingly, from the official TED website we downloaded the videos of the talks included in the textual portion of MuST-SHE English→ German. On this basis, *i)* audio tracks were extracted from the videos, and *ii)* an alignment procedure was applied to split talks into segments and generate aligned (*audio, transcript, translation*) triplets. Since this automatic procedure generates 90% of properly aligned triples on average (Cattoni et al., 2021), we performed qualitative checks. Two evaluators – both students proficient in the German language and with a background in Applied Linguistics[3] – reviewed all the extracted audios and corrected any audio-text misalignment.[4] Hence, we ensured the quality of all audio segments included in MuST-SHE^{IWSLT24}, and the exact alignment of each (*audio, transcript, translation*) triplet.

2.2 Dataset Features

MuST-SHE is designed to evaluate the translation of a source English neutral word into its corresponding target gender-marked one(s) in the context of human referents, e.g. en: ***the good friend***, de: ***der/die*** *gute* ***Freund/in***. To allow for fine-grained analyses, each segment in MuST-SHE is enriched with the following annotations:

· GENDER, which allows to distinguish results for Feminine (Fem) and Masculine (Masc) forms, thus revealing a potential gender gap.

· CATEGORY, which differentiates between **CAT1**

[2]See §5 for a discussion on the use of (binary) gender as a variable.

[3]Their work was carried out during an internship at FBK.

[4]We relied on the ELAN annotation tool: https://archive.mpi.nl/tla/elan.

– first-person references to be translated according to the speakers' linguistic expression of gender[5] (e.g. *I am a teacher*) – and **CAT2** – references to any participant, to be translated in agreement with gender information available in the sentence (e.g. *He/she* is a *teacher*). These categories allow analysing models' behaviour across unambiguous and ambiguous gender translation instances.[6]

· GENDER-SWAPPED WORDS, providing, for each target gender-marked word annotated in MuST-SHE reference translations, a corresponding wrong form swapped in the opposite gender (e.g. en: *she is **a friend***; de: *Sie ist* ***eine<ein> Freundin<Freund>***). As described in §3.2, such pairs of annotated target gender-marked words are a key feature of MuST-SHE, which enables gender-focused evaluations.

All above-mentioned dimensions are already provided with the textual portion of MuST-SHE English→ German, and are consequently also included in MuST-SHE^{IWSLT24}. In Table 1, we show examples of annotated (*transcript, translation*) segments from the corpus. Overall dataset statistics are provided in Table 2.

	CAT1	CAT2
Fem.	23 *(35)*	77 *(121)*
Masc.	23 *(38)*	77 *(155)*
Tot.	200 *(349)*	

Table 2: MuST-SHE^{IWSLT24} statistics: number of sentences and (*gender-marked target words*).

3 Experimental Settings

3.1 Models

The test suite evaluation is carried out on the systems that were submitted to the IWSLT Offline Speech Translation tasks. Overall, four different participants – i.e. HW-TSC, CMU, NYA, and KIT – submitted a total of 13 models. Of those, six models were presented as primary system submission, while the other 7 models are additional, contrastive models. All systems contributions are built upon *cascade* architectures, which resolve the ST task as pipelined ASR+MT solutions.

Since the participants (with the only exception of NYA) segmented the sentences before generating the outputs, we isolated the predicted translation for each reference sentence by means of the mWERSegmenter tool (Matusov et al., 2005). This procedure mirrors what is done in the standard evaluation of the offline task (Agarwal et al., 2023).

3.2 Evaluation

Following the original MuST-SHE evaluation protocol described in Gaido et al. (2020), MuST-SHE^{IWSLT24} evaluation allows to focus on the gender realization of the target gender-marked forms, which are annotated in the reference translations together with their *wrong*, gender-swapped form (see Table 1). The evaluation is carried out in two steps, and by matching the annotated (*correct/wrong*) gender-marked words against the ST output. Accordingly, we first calculate the **Term Coverage** as the proportion of gender-marked words annotated in the MuST-SHE references (either in the correct or wrong form) that are actually generated by the system, on which the accuracy of gender realization is therefore *measurable*. Then, we define **Gender Accuracy** as the proportion of correct gender realizations among the words on which it is *measurable*. This evaluation method[7] has several advantages. On one side, *term coverage* unveils the precise amount of words on which systems' gender realization is measurable. On the other, *gender accuracy* directly informs about systems' performance on gender translation and related gender bias: scores below 50% indicate that the system produces the wrong gender more often than the correct one, thus signalling a particularly strong biased behaviour.

4 Results

In Table 3 we present the MuST-SHE^{IWSLT24} results of the 13 IWSLT Offline ST cascade models. Starting from **coverage scores** (All-Cov), all models achieve overall positive results, which range from ~70% (`HW-TSC_CONSTRAINED-wLLM.primary`) to 74.79% (`HW-TSC_CONSTRAINED.primary`). Hence, these models produce a good amount of

[5]Speaker's gender information is provided for each segment. Note that gender has been labeled based on the personal pronouns the speakers used to describe themselves in their publicly available personal TED section.

[6]For *direct* ST solutions that directly translate from the audio input without intermediate textual representations, CAT1 can also reveal whether such models leverage speakers' voice as an unwanted cue to translate gender. See Gaido et al. (2020).

[7]The evaluation script is publicly available at: `https://github.com/hlt-mt/FBK-fairseq/blob/master/examples/speech_to_text/scripts/gender/mustshe_gender_accuracy.py`.

Model	All-Cov	All-Acc	F-Acc	M-Acc	1F-Acc	1M-Acc	2F-Acc	2M-Acc
HW-TSC_CONSTRAINED.primary	**74.79**	**82.99**	**84.44**	81.70	**68.18**	85.71	**87.61**	80.80
HW-TSC_UNCONSTRAINED.primary	73.93	82.52	82.96	82.12	65.22	85.71	86.61	81.30
HW-TSC_UNCONSTRAINED.contrastive	75.07	81.72	81.16	82.24	56.52	85.71	86.09	81.45
CMU_mbr_ensemble_all_50+50+50.primary	73.07	81.36	80.00	**82.73**	50.00	80.00	87.50	**83.33**
CMU_beam_5.contrastive	74.21	80.56	79.58	81.51	52.00	76.00	85.47	82.64
CMU_mbr_50.contrastive	73.93	80.21	80.14	80.28	55.17	70.83	86.61	82.20
NYA.contrastive3	72.21	79.72	77.37	81.94	39.13	**86.96**	85.09	80.99
HW-TSC_CONSTRAINED-wLLM.primary	70.49	79.70	78.63	80.71	45.45	79.17	85.32	81.03
NYA.contrastive1	72.49	79.64	77.54	81.69	39.13	**86.96**	85.22	80.67
NYA.primary	72.49	79.64	77.54	81.69	39.13	**86.96**	85.22	80.67
NYA.contrastive2	73.35	79.51	78.99	80.00	45.83	76.00	85.96	80.83
KIT.primary	71.92	77.70	78.03	77.40	43.48	65.38	85.32	80.00
KIT.contrastive1	71.92	77.42	78.20	76.71	40.91	65.38	85.59	79.17
standard dev.	±.1.3	±.1.6	±.2.1	±.1.8	±.9.4	±.7.8	±.0.8	±.1.0

Table 3: MuST-SHE^{IWSLT24} results for en-de. Systems are ranked based on overall Gender Accuracy (All-Acc). Primary model submissions in violet color.

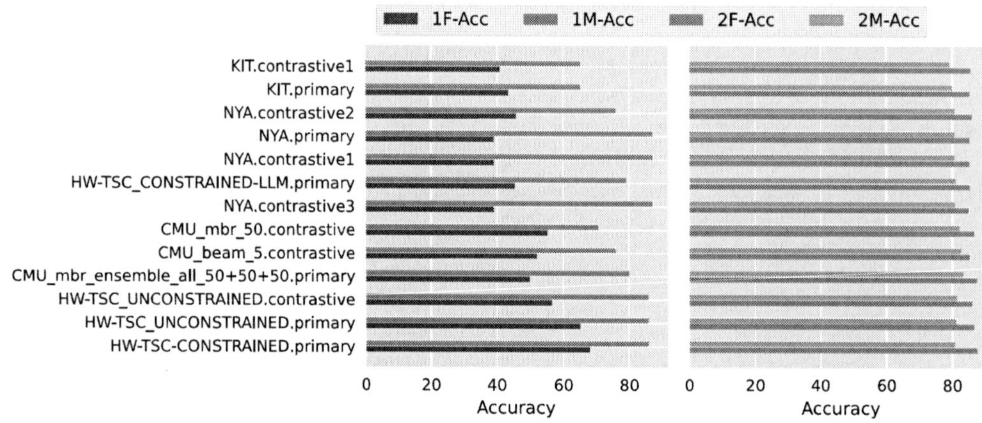

Figure 1: MuST-SHE^{IWSLT24} accuracy results across categories 1 and 2 per each gender (F/M).

gender-marked words that can be evaluated with regards to the accuracy of their gender realization.

Moving onto the **overall accuracy scores** (All-Acc), we can see that – while there is still room for improvement – all of the evaluated ST systems achieve reasonable results, by being able to correctly translate gender with an accuracy of at least 77.42% (`KIT.contrastive1`) up to 84.44% for `HW-TSC_CONSTRAINED.primary`. Similar accuracy ranges are attested also by disaggregating results across feminine (F-ACC) and masculine (M-Acc) genders. Interestingly, such results show that none of the models exhibit perfectly equal performance across both genders. Still, the divide is fairly limited, with *i)* a comparable number of ST systems achieving slightly higher results on either the feminine or masculine set of MuST-SHE, and *ii)* little variation in scores across the 13 models, as attested in terms of standard deviation. If we go more fine-grained into disaggregated results, however, we unveil a higher degree of variation.

In Figure 1, we report results across categories for masculine (1M and 2M) and feminine gender realizations (1F and 2F). On the one hand, for unambiguous gender translation from CAT2, systems are slightly better in performing feminine gender translation. Instead, results on CAT1 unveil a wide gender gap, where feminine accuracy is consistently lower compared to its masculine counterpart. In fact, most models tend to generate the correct feminine form in less than 50% of the cases, namely below random chance. The ST model `HW-TSC_CONSTRAINED-wLLM.primary`, which overall emerges as the best system for gender translation, still remains at 68.18%.

To conclude, our results show that – when confronted with ambiguous source sentences – current ST models tend to favour the generation of masculine forms in the German target language. We acknowledge that the phenomena subject to our analysis (gender bias) are not currently accounted for in the design of ST systems, which are rather designed with the goal of optimizing overall translation quality. Towards the creation of fairer ST technology, however, we hope that our evaluation will raise awareness in the community, and encourage the development of capable models, which can equally accommodate feminine and masculine language.

5 Conclusion

This paper summarizes the results of our IWSLT-2024 Test Suites evaluation, which focused on gender bias in translation. To this aim, we have introduced the *speech* expansion of the en-de MuST-SHE test set. Overall, results on MuST-SHE^{IWSLT24} show that the evaluated ST systems are reasonably good at translating gender under realistic conditions, achieving comparable results across feminine and masculine gender translation. Also, all models are quite robust, and show a similar behaviour for translation of unambiguous gender phenomena, where they can rely on contextual gender information. However, for ambiguous cases where the input sentence does not inform about the gender form to be used in translation, we confirm a strong skew where all systems favour masculine generation almost by default. This finding calls for further research endeavours and evaluation initiatives to counter gender bias in ST and measure future advances.

Limitations

The main limitation of this work concerns the limited size of data points (i.e. gender-marked words) available for evaluation. As such, even in the case of gender performance parity, the dataset does not allow to make conclusive statements about the *absence* of bias in the assessed models. Despite its restricted size, however, MuST-SHE^{IWSLT24} provides a first glimpse into understanding and monitoring en-de systems' behaviour with respect to gender bias and translation.

Ethics Statement

The use of gender as a variable in this paper warrants some reflections. Namely, when working on the evaluation of speaker-related gender translation for MuST-SHE (i.e. Category 1) we solely focus on the rendering of their reported linguistic gender expressions. No assumptions about speakers' self determined identity (GLAAD, 2007) – which cannot be directly mapped from pronoun usage (Cao and Daumé III, 2020; Ackerman, 2019) – has been made.

Also, in our diagnosis of gender bias we only account for feminine and masculine linguistic forms, which are those traditionally in use and the only represented in the used data. However, we stress that – by working on binary forms – we do not imply or impose a binary vision on the extra-linguistic reality of gender, which is rather a spectrum (D'Ignazio and Klein, 2020). Also, we acknowledge the current challenges faced for grammatical gender languages like German in fully implementing neutral language (Paolucci et al., 2023), and support the rise of both non-binary language (Shroy, 2016; Gabriel et al., 2018; Conrod, 2020) and translation technologies (Lauscher et al., 2023; Gromann et al., 2023).

Acknowledgements

The work presented in this paper is funded by the European Union's Horizon research and innovation programme under grant agreement No 101135798, project Meetween (My Personal AI Mediator for Virtual MEETtings BetWEEN People) and the PNRR project FAIR - Future AI Research (PE00000013), under the NRRP MUR program funded by the NextGenerationEU. Also, we would like to thank the 2022 FBK internship students Sabrina Raus and Abess Benissmail from the University of Bolzano: the creation of MuST-SHE^{IWSLT24} was made possible by their work.

References

Lauren Ackerman. 2019. Syntactic and cognitive issues in investigating gendered coreference. *Glossa: a Journal of General linguistics*, 4(1).

Milind Agarwal, Sweta Agrawal, Antonios Anastasopoulos, Luisa Bentivogli, Ondřej Bojar, Claudia Borg, Marine Carpuat, Roldano Cattoni, Mauro Cettolo, Mingda Chen, William Chen, Khalid Choukri, Alexandra Chronopoulou, Anna Currey, Thierry Declerck, Qianqian Dong, Kevin Duh, Yannick Estève, Marcello Federico, Souhir Gahbiche, Barry Haddow, Benjamin Hsu, Phu Mon Htut, Hirofumi Inaguma, Dávid Javorský, John Judge, Yasumasa Kano, Tom Ko, Rishu Kumar, Pengwei Li, Xutai Ma, Prashant Mathur, Evgeny Matusov, Paul McNamee, John P. McCrae, Kenton Murray, Maria Nadejde,

Satoshi Nakamura, Matteo Negri, Ha Nguyen, Jan Niehues, Xing Niu, Atul Kr. Ojha, John E. Ortega, Proyag Pal, Juan Pino, Lonneke van der Plas, Peter Polák, Elijah Rippeth, Elizabeth Salesky, Jiatong Shi, Matthias Sperber, Sebastian Stüker, Katsuhito Sudoh, Yun Tang, Brian Thompson, Kevin Tran, Marco Turchi, Alex Waibel, Mingxuan Wang, Shinji Watanabe, and Rodolfo Zevallos. 2023. FINDINGS OF THE IWSLT 2023 EVALUATION CAMPAIGN. In *Proceedings of the 20th International Conference on Spoken Language Translation (IWSLT 2023)*, pages 1–61, Toronto, Canada (in-person and online). Association for Computational Linguistics.

Antonios Anastasopoulos, Loïc Barrault, Luisa Bentivogli, Marcely Zanon Boito, Ondřej Bojar, Roldano Cattoni, Anna Currey, Georgiana Dinu, Kevin Duh, Maha Elbayad, Clara Emmanuel, Yannick Estève, Marcello Federico, Christian Federmann, Souhir Gahbiche, Hongyu Gong, Roman Grundkiewicz, Barry Haddow, Benjamin Hsu, Dávid Javorský, Věra Kloudová, Surafel Lakew, Xutai Ma, Prashant Mathur, Paul McNamee, Kenton Murray, Maria Nădejde, Satoshi Nakamura, Matteo Negri, Jan Niehues, Xing Niu, John Ortega, Juan Pino, Elizabeth Salesky, Jiatong Shi, Matthias Sperber, Sebastian Stüker, Katsuhito Sudoh, Marco Turchi, Yogesh Virkar, Alexander Waibel, Changhan Wang, and Shinji Watanabe. 2022. Findings of the IWSLT 2022 evaluation campaign. In *Proceedings of the 19th International Conference on Spoken Language Translation (IWSLT 2022)*, pages 98–157, Dublin, Ireland (in-person and online). Association for Computational Linguistics.

Antonios Anastasopoulos, Ondřej Bojar, Jacob Bremerman, Roldano Cattoni, Maha Elbayad, Marcello Federico, Xutai Ma, Satoshi Nakamura, Matteo Negri, Jan Niehues, Juan Pino, Elizabeth Salesky, Sebastian Stüker, Katsuhito Sudoh, Marco Turchi, Alexander Waibel, Changhan Wang, and Matthew Wiesner. 2021. FINDINGS OF THE IWSLT 2021 EVALUATION CAMPAIGN. In *Proceedings of the 18th International Conference on Spoken Language Translation (IWSLT 2021)*, pages 1–29, Bangkok, Thailand (online). Association for Computational Linguistics.

Luisa Bentivogli, Mauro Cettolo, Marco Gaido, Alina Karakanta, Alberto Martinelli, Matteo Negri, and Marco Turchi. 2021. Cascade versus direct speech translation: Do the differences still make a difference? In *Proceedings of the 59th Annual Meeting of the Association for Computational Linguistics and the 11th International Joint Conference on Natural Language Processing (Volume 1: Long Papers)*, pages 2873–2887, Online. Association for Computational Linguistics.

Luisa Bentivogli, Beatrice Savoldi, Matteo Negri, Mattia A. Di Gangi, Roldano Cattoni, and Marco Turchi. 2020. Gender in danger? evaluating speech translation technology on the MuST-SHE corpus. In *Proceedings of the 58th Annual Meeting of the Association for Computational Linguistics*, pages 6923–6933, Online. Association for Computational Linguistics.

Su Lin Blodgett, Solon Barocas, Hal Daumé III, and Hanna Wallach. 2020. Language (technology) is power: A critical survey of "bias" in NLP. In *Proceedings of the 58th Annual Meeting of the Association for Computational Linguistics*, pages 5454–5476, Online. Association for Computational Linguistics.

Yang Trista Cao and Hal Daumé III. 2020. Toward gender-inclusive coreference resolution. In *Proceedings of the 58th Annual Meeting of the Association for Computational Linguistics*, pages 4568–4595, Online. Association for Computational Linguistics.

Roldano Cattoni, Mattia A. Di Gangi, Luisa Bentivogli, Matteo Negri, and Marco Turchi. 2021. MuST-C: A multilingual corpus for end-to-end speech translation. *Computer Speech & Language*, 66:101155.

Seamless Communication, Loïc Barrault, Yu-An Chung, Mariano Coria Meglioli, David Dale, Ning Dong, Mark Duppenthaler, Paul-Ambroise Duquenne, Brian Ellis, Hady Elsahar, Justin Haaheim, John Hoffman, Min-Jae Hwang, Hirofumi Inaguma, Christopher Klaiber, Ilia Kulikov, Pengwei Li, Daniel Licht, Jean Maillard, Ruslan Mavlyutov, Alice Rakotoarison, Kaushik Ram Sadagopan, Abinesh Ramakrishnan, Tuan Tran, Guillaume Wenzek, Yilin Yang, Ethan Ye, Ivan Evtimov, Pierre Fernandez, Cynthia Gao, Prangthip Hansanti, Elahe Kalbassi, Amanda Kallet, Artyom Kozhevnikov, Gabriel Mejia Gonzalez, Robin San Roman, Christophe Touret, Corinne Wong, Carleigh Wood, Bokai Yu, Pierre Andrews, Can Balioglu, Peng-Jen Chen, Marta R. Costa-jussà, Maha Elbayad, Hongyu Gong, Francisco Guzmán, Kevin Heffernan, Somya Jain, Justine Kao, Ann Lee, Xutai Ma, Alex Mourachko, Benjamin Peloquin, Juan Pino, Sravya Popuri, Christophe Ropers, Safiyyah Saleem, Holger Schwenk, Anna Sun, Paden Tomasello, Changhan Wang, Jeff Wang, Skyler Wang, and Mary Williamson. 2023. Seamless: Multilingual Expressive and Streaming Speech Translation.

Kirby Conrod. 2020. Pronouns and gender in language. *The Oxford Handbook of Language and Sexuality*.

Greville G. Corbett. 2013. *The Expression of Gender*. De Gruyter.

Marta R. Costa-jussà. 2019. An analysis of Gender Bias studies in Natural Language Processing. *Nature Machine Intelligence*, 1:495–496.

Kate Crawford. 2017. The Trouble with Bias. In *Conference on Neural Information Processing Systems (NIPS) – Keynote*, Long Beach, California.

Catherine D'Ignazio and Lauren F Klein. 2020. *Data feminism*. MIT Press, London, UK.

Ute Gabriel, Pascal M. Gygax, and Elisabeth A. Kuhn. 2018. Neutralising linguistic sexism: Promising but cumbersome? *Group Processes & Intergroup Relations*, 21(5):844–858.

Marco Gaido, Beatrice Savoldi, Luisa Bentivogli, Matteo Negri, and Marco Turchi. 2020. Breeding gender-aware direct speech translation systems. In *Proceedings of the 28th International Conference on Computational Linguistics*, pages 3951–3964, Barcelona, Spain (Online). International Committee on Computational Linguistics.

GLAAD. 2007. Media Reference Guide - Transgender.

Dagmar Gromann, Manuel Lardelli, Katta Spiel, Sabrina Burtscher, Lukas Daniel Klausner, Arthur Mettinger, Igor Miladinovic, Sigrid Schefer-Wenzl, Daniela Duh, and Katharina Bühn. 2023. Participatory research as a path to community-informed, gender-fair machine translation. In *Proceedings of the First Workshop on Gender-Inclusive Translation Technologies*, pages 49–59, Tampere, Finland. European Association for Machine Translation.

Pascal M. Gygax, Daniel Elmiger, Sandrine Zufferey, Alan Garnham, Sabine Sczesny, Lisa von Stockhausen, Friederike Braun, and Jane Oakhill. 2019. A Language Index of Grammatical Gender Dimensions to Study the Impact of Grammatical Gender on the Way We Perceive Women and Men. *Frontiers in Psychology*, 10:1604.

Christian Hardmeier, Christine Basta, Marta R. Costa-jussà, Gabriel Stanovsky, and Hila Gonen, editors. 2022. *Proceedings of the 4th Workshop on Gender Bias in Natural Language Processing (GeBNLP)*. Association for Computational Linguistics, Seattle, Washington.

Marlis Hellinger and Heiko Motschenbacher. 2015. *Gender Across Languages. The Linguistic Representation of Women and Men*, volume IV. John Benjamins, Amsterdam, the Netherlands.

Anne Lauscher, Debora Nozza, Ehm Miltersen, Archie Crowley, and Dirk Hovy. 2023. What about "em"? how commercial machine translation fails to handle (neo-)pronouns. In *Proceedings of the 61st Annual Meeting of the Association for Computational Linguistics (Volume 1: Long Papers)*, pages 377–392, Toronto, Canada. Association for Computational Linguistics.

Evgeny Matusov, Gregor Leusch, Oliver Bender, and Hermann Ney. 2005. Evaluating machine translation output with automatic sentence segmentation. In *Proceedings of the Second International Workshop on Spoken Language Translation*, Pittsburgh, Pennsylvania, USA.

Angela Balducci Paolucci, Manuel Lardelli, and Dagmar Gromann. 2023. Gender-fair language in translation: A case study. In *Proceedings of the First Workshop on Gender-Inclusive Translation Technologies*, pages 13–23, Tampere, Finland. European Association for Machine Translation.

Yifan Peng, Jinchuan Tian, William Chen, Siddhant Arora, Brian Yan, Yui Sudo, Muhammad Shakeel, Kwanghee Choi, Jiatong Shi, Xuankai Chang, Jee weon Jung, and Shinji Watanabe. 2024. Owsm v3.1: Better and faster open whisper-style speech models based on e-branchformer.

Vineel Pratap, Andros Tjandra, Bowen Shi, Paden Tomasello, Arun Babu, Sayani Kundu, Ali Elkahky, Zhaoheng Ni, Apoorv Vyas, Maryam Fazel-Zarandi, et al. 2024. Scaling speech technology to 1,000+ languages. *Journal of Machine Learning Research*, 25(97):1–52.

Alec Radford, Jong Wook Kim, Tao Xu, Greg Brockman, Christine McLeavey, and Ilya Sutskever. 2022. Robust Speech Recognition via Large-Scale Weak Supervision. ArXiv:2212.04356 [cs, eess].

Beatrice Savoldi. 2023. Gender bias in automatic translation. *Università degli studi di Trento*.

Beatrice Savoldi, Marco Gaido, Matteo Negri, and Luisa Bentivogli. 2023. Test suites task: Evaluation of gender fairness in MT with MuST-SHE and INES. In *Proceedings of the Eighth Conference on Machine Translation*, pages 252–262, Singapore. Association for Computational Linguistics.

Alyx J. Shroy. 2016. Innovations in gender-neutral French: Language practices of nonbinary French speakers on Twitter. *Ms., University of California, Davis*.

Dagmar Stahlberg, Friederike Braun, Lisa Irmen, and Sabine Sczesny. 2007. Representation of the Sexes in Language. *Social communication*, pages 163–187.

Tony Sun, Andrew Gaut, Shirlyn Tang, Yuxin Huang, Mai ElSherief, Jieyu Zhao, Diba Mirza, Elizabeth Belding, Kai-Wei Chang, and William Yang Wang. 2019. Mitigating gender bias in natural language processing: Literature review. In *Proceedings of the 57th Annual Meeting of the Association for Computational Linguistics*, pages 1630–1640, Florence, Italy. Association for Computational Linguistics.

Eva Vanmassenhove. 2024. Gender bias in machine translation and the era of large language models. *arXiv preprint arXiv:2401.10016*.

Eva Vanmassenhove, Beatrice Savoldi, Luisa Bentivogli, Joke Daems, and Janiça Hackenbuchner, editors. 2023. *Proceedings of the First Workshop on Gender-Inclusive Translation Technologies*. European Association for Machine Translation, Tampere, Finland.

SimulSeamless: FBK at IWSLT 2024 Simultaneous Speech Translation

Sara Papi and **Marco Gaido** and **Matteo Negri** and **Luisa Bentivogli**
Fondazione Bruno Kessler, Italy
{mgaido,spapi,negri,bentivo}@fbk.eu

Abstract

This paper describes the FBK's participation in the Simultaneous Translation Evaluation Campaign at IWSLT 2024. For this year's submission in the speech-to-text translation (ST) sub-track, we propose **SimulSeamless**, which is realized by combining AlignAtt and SeamlessM4T in its medium configuration. The SeamlessM4T model is used "off-the-shelf" and its simultaneous inference is enabled through the adoption of AlignAtt, a SimulST policy based on cross-attention that can be applied without any retraining or adaptation of the underlying model for the simultaneous task. We participated in all the Shared Task languages (English→ {German, Japanese, Chinese}, and Czech→English), achieving acceptable or even better results compared to last year's submissions. SimulSeamless, covering more than 143 source languages and 200 target languages, is released at https://github.com/hlt-mt/FBK-fairseq/.

1 Introduction

Simultaneous speech-to-text translation (SimulST) is the task in which a model has to provide a textual translation into the target language while continuously receiving an incremental speech input in the source language.

SimulST poses additional difficulties to standard offline ST, as it has to find the optimal balance between translation quality and output latency, which is the time delay between an utterance being spoken and the corresponding translation being emitted. This balance – often referred to as "quality-latency tradeoff" – depends on the application scenario (Fantinuoli and Prandi, 2021), which can span many domains such as online meetings, lectures, conference talks, and live shows.

Due to the growing interest in SimulST technologies, this task has been included in the IWSLT Evaluation Campaigns[1] since 2020. The increasing interest has led to numerous direct and cascade models participating in the challenge every year (Ansari et al., 2020; Anastasopoulos et al., 2021, 2022; Agarwal et al., 2023), all vying for the title of the best approach to realize a SimulST system from scratch. More recently, the practice of using models without ad-hoc training for the simultaneous scenario has become widespread (Polák et al., 2022; Gaido et al., 2022; Papi et al., 2023a; Polák et al., 2023; Yan et al., 2023; Huang et al., 2023), demonstrating that competitive or even superior results can be achieved compared to systems specifically tailored for SimulST (Papi et al., 2022a). Among the strategies used to repurpose standard (offline) ST models for SimulST (Liu et al., 2020; Papi et al., 2022a, 2023c), AlignAtt (Papi et al., 2023b) emerged as the best one, achieving new state-of-the-art results. AlignAtt exploits speech-translations alignments based on cross-attention scores to guide the simultaneous inference, overcoming the limitations of the previous approach relying on attention (Papi et al., 2023c).

Alongside the increased interest in the SimulST task, especially during the last year, we have witnessed an explosion in the use of large models (Latif et al., 2023), including speech foundation models (Radford et al., 2023; Pratap et al., 2023; Barrault et al., 2023a; Zhang et al., 2023). These models are now commonly used alone or in combination with large language models (Gaido et al., 2024) for generic ST tasks. Among these, SeamlessM4T (Barrault et al., 2023a) has emerged as one of the most promising multimodal and multilingual models, covering more than 143 source languages and 200 target languages.

For this year's submission to the IWSLT Evaluation Campaign on Simultaneous Translation, we, therefore, propose to combine the best of both

[1] https://iwslt.org/

Proceedings of the 21st International Conference on Spoken Language Translation (IWSLT 2024), pages 120–127
August 15-16, 2024 ©2024 Association for Computational Linguistics

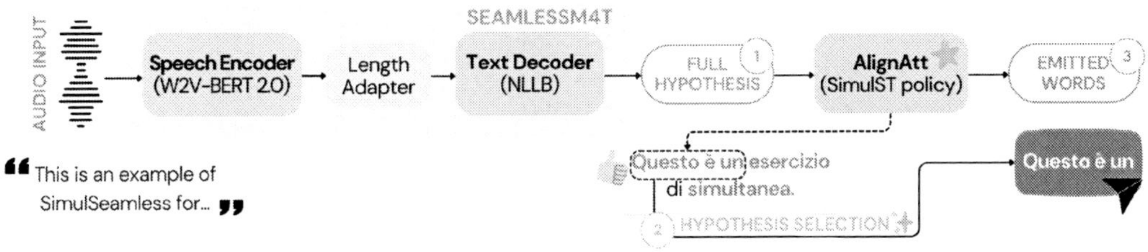

Figure 1: Representation of the SeamlessM4T model combined with AlignAtt: SimulSeamless.

worlds to obtain a multilingual model without any training or adaptation for the SimulST task. This results in **SimulSeamless**, consisting of the SeamlessM4T model used "off-the-shelf" repurposed for simultaneous inference using AlignAtt.

From empirical results on the task, we show that SimulSeamless can achieve acceptable or even better results compared to last year's participants, despite not being retrained or fine-tuned either for the simultaneous task or on paired data in the evaluated languages. Moreover, SimulSeamless is a generic multilingual model that can be used for any allowed translation direction supported by the underlying SeamlessM4T model, covering more than 143 source languages and 200 target languages. The code is released under the Apache 2.0 Licence at `https://github.com/hlt-mt/FBK-fairseq/blob/master/fbk_works/SIMULSEAMLESS.md`.

2 SimulSeamless

Similarly to previous years (Gaido et al., 2022; Papi et al., 2023a), we participated in the Simultaneous Translation evaluation campaign, focusing on the speech-to-text translation sub-track. For this year's submission, we opted for the use of the new SeamlessM4T model, which is allowed for the task,[2] as the underlying model of the SimulST policy AlignAtt. This policy can be applied to any standard (i.e., offline-trained) model without the need for retraining or adaptation.

In the following, both these elements and their combination are explained in detail.

SeamlessM4T. SeamlessM4T (Barrault et al., 2023a) (or Massively Multilingual & Multimodal Machine Translation) is a family of models based on pre-trained models including W2V BERT 2.0, and NLLB (Costa-jussà et al., 2022), whose encoder and decoder respectively are used for the speech-to-text modality. W2V-BERT is a Conformer-based model (Gulati et al., 2020) composed of 24 layers, with a total of ~600M parameters, and trained on 1 million hours of open speech audio data to learn self-supervised speech representations. It processes the audio features obtained by applying 80-dimensional Mel filterbanks to the audio waveform. The W2V-BERT encoder is followed by a Length Adapter based on a modified version of the M-adaptor (Zhao et al., 2022), which is a Transformer-based model (Vaswani et al., 2017) that is in charge of compressing the speech representation (by a factor of 8) through attention pooling. The compressed input representations are then fed to the NLLB decoder, in its 1.3B parameters configuration, to produce the translations. The final model was obtained after training on both manual and automatically aligned speech translation data with a total of 406,000 hours.

AlignAtt. AlignAtt (Papi et al., 2023b) is a SimulST policy that relies on cross-attention to make decisions about whether to emit translated words or wait for additional information in the simultaneous scenario. At each time step, the cross-attention scores are exploited to obtain audio-translation alignments by uniquely assigning the predicted words to the audio frames (encoder states) having the maximum attention score. Then, it is checked, for each word, if it has been aligned with one of the last f frames, which is the parameter handling the latency of the model. If this is true, the emission is stopped, otherwise, the next word is evaluated. The idea behind AlignAtt is that, if a word is aligned with one of the last received audio frames, the encoded information could be unstable and/or not sufficient to reliably predict that word. Conversely, if a word mostly attends to a more stable and earliest-received encoded information, it can be safely predicted. With this formulation, AlignAtt simplifies the previous EDAtt policy (Papi et al., 2023c) by eliminating the dependency on additional hyper-parameters while achieving com-

[2] `https://iwslt.org/2024/simultaneous`

petitive or even better results.

SeamlessM4T + AlignAtt = SimulSeamless. Since AlignAtt is applicable to any standard ST models without the need for re-training or adaptation, we chose to apply it directly to the SeamlessM4T model in its medium configuration, realizing **SimulSeamless**. This solution is completely different from SeamlessStreaming (Barrault et al., 2023b), which is obtained through an expensive ad-hoc finetuning of the Seamless model for the simultaneous task based on EMMA – efficient monotonic multi-head attention (Ma et al., 2023). Since SeamlessM4T already covers all the languages evaluated in the Simultaneous track, the model is used completely "off-the-shelf". The SimulSeamless model is shown in Figure 1.

3 Experimental Settings

We used the available checkpoint of the SeamlessM4T model provided on HuggingFace in its "medium" configuration,[3] with a total of 1.2B parameters.

The results are reported on the benchmarks used for the submission, which is MuST-C (Cattoni et al., 2021) v2.0 tst-COMMON for en-{de, ja, zh}, and the dev set provided for the task for cs-en. The scores are computed using the SimulEval toolkit (Ma et al., 2020).[4] Translation quality is evaluated using BLEU score with sacreBLEU (Post, 2018)[5]. Latency is reported using Average Lagging (AL) (Ma et al., 2019) since it is the metric used for the final scoring. Length Adaptive Average Lagging (LAAL) (Papi et al., 2022b) and Average Token Delay (ATD) (Kano et al., 2022) are also evaluated and included in the final results since they are official metrics reported for the task.[6] Both latency and BLEU scores are computed at the character level for Chinese and Japanese while the standard `13a` tokenizer is used for sacreBLEU, and word-level latency is computed for the other languages. Additionally, computationally aware metrics are presented to account for the real elapsed time, which also considers the computational cost of running the underlying model. The inference was run using a single GPU NVIDIA V100 with 16GB of RAM.

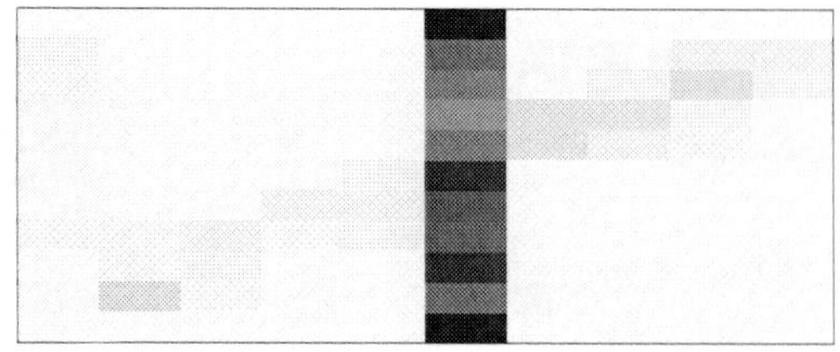

Figure 2: Example of skewed cross-attention scores representation towards some frames.

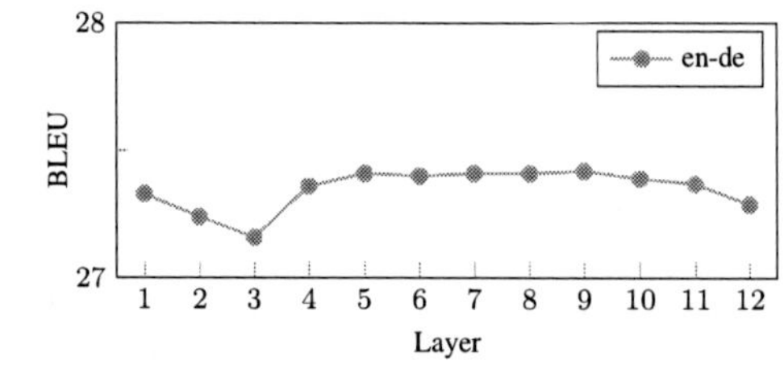

(a) English to German

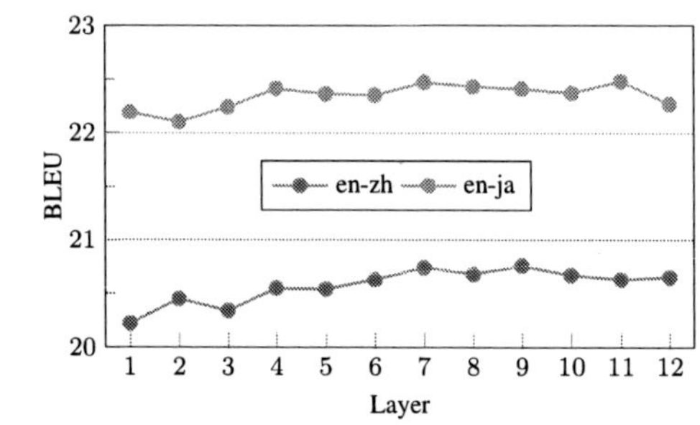

(b) English to Chinese and Japanese

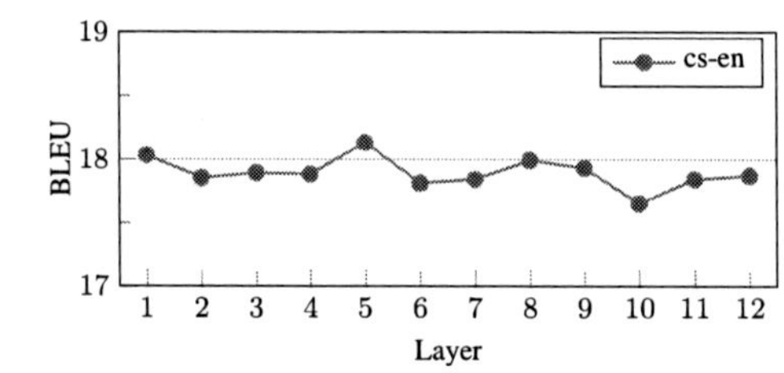

(c) Czech to English

Figure 3: Translation quality (BLEU↑) scores of SimulSeamless on MuST-C v2.0 tst-COMMON for English (en) to German (de), Japanese (ja), and Chinese (zh), and on the IWSLT 2024 dev set for Czech (cs) to English by varying the decoder layer from which cross-attention scores are extracted from.

For the AlignAtt policy, we set the size of the speech chunk processed by the model at each time step to 1s for English to German and Czech to English, 800ms for English to Chinese, and 400ms for English to Japanese. To achieve latency close to an AL of 2s required for the submission, we set

[3]`https://huggingface.co/facebook/seamless-m4t-medium`

[4]We used the `f1f5b9a` commit that is the last version with the remove evaluation working, which is needed to run SimulEval using Docker containers.

[5]Version 2.4.0.

[6]`https://iwslt.org/2024/simultaneous`

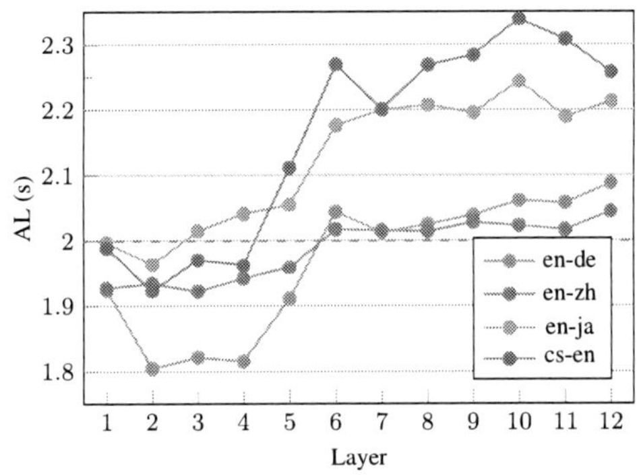

Figure 4: Latency (AL↓) scores of SimulSeamless on MuST-C v2.0 tst-COMMON for English (en) to German (de), Japanese (ja), and Chinese (zh), and on the IWSLT 2024 dev set for Czech (cs) to English by varying the decoder layer from which cross-attention scores are extracted from.

the hyper-parameter handling the latency f to 1 for en-ja and en-zh, 6 for en-de, and 9 for cs-en. The cross-attention scores are normalized frame-wise before applying AlignAtt to avoid the cross-attention weights being skewed to some frame representation, as shown in Figure 2.

4 Results

4.1 Submission Selection

For selecting the best setting, we analyzed the performance by varying the layer from which cross-attention scores are extracted since simply averaging them across layers led to worse results, as also already found in (Papi et al., 2023c). The layer-wise quality results are shown in Figure 3 while layer-wise latency results close to AL=2s are shown in Figure 4.

It can be seen from the Layer-AL(s) curves (Figure 4) that Layer 5 represents a threshold layer starting from which the latency increases significantly without, however, similar significant quality improvements in terms of BLEU (Figure 3). The only acceptable layers to achieve an AL$\leq$2s for en-ja are layers 1 and 2 while this set is extended to layer 4 for cs-en, and up to layer 5 for en-de and en-zh. Among the two admissible layers for en-ja, we chose for the final submission the one maximizing the quality, which is Layer 1. For en-zh, we followed a similar approach by choosing Layer 4, which achieves the highest BLEU score with an admissible latency. The choice of Layer 4 is also maintained for en-de and cs-en since we found that is the layer achieving the best quality-latency tradeoff between BLEU and AL.

4.2 Comparison with Last Year's Participants

In Table 1, we report the scores for the final submission for each language pair, including LAAL and ATD latency metrics and their corresponding computationally aware scores. SimulSeamless is compared with all the participants of last year: CMU (Yan et al., 2023), CUNI-KIT (Polák et al., 2023), FBK (Papi et al., 2023a), HW-TSC (Guo et al., 2023), NAIST (Fukuda et al., 2023), and XIAOMI (Huang et al., 2023). Comparisons are not reported for cs-en since it is a new language direction for the task.

First, it can be noticed that SimulSeamless achieves the best translation quality and, in general, the best quality-latency trade-off for en-ja. Conversely, it struggles to achieve very competitive results in en-de and, especially, in en-zh. However, it is important to notice that SimulSeamless is the only model that has not been fine-tuned on the IWSLT-allowed data for the task, which include the MuST-C v2.0 training set. Therefore, it is a more generic and multilingual system covering more than 143 source languages and 200 target languages.[7]

Furthermore, an overlap has been identified between the MuST-C tst-COMMON and the ST-TED dataset (Zhang and Ao, 2022), which was allowed for last year's task. Some participants, unaware of this issue, employed the ST-TED dataset (e.g., CUNI-KIT and XIAOMI). Therefore, the results achieved by last year's submissions on the MuST-C tst-COMMON may not be entirely reliable. In addition, it has been recently found another possible overlap with TED2020, which may invalidate other scores.[8]

In conclusion, SimulSeamless allows for acceptable or even better results compared to last year's participants in the SimulST Evaluation Campaign while being generic and potentially applicable to all translation directions supported by the underlying SeamlessM4T model without any retraining or adaptation.

[7]We are not able to exclude that MuST-C has been used for training the "off-the-shelf" SeamlessM4T but no ad-hoc fine-tuning on the data and/or language pairs has been performed for our participation.

[8]Unaware of this overlap, participations from CMU and HW-TSC used this dataset.

Lang. Pair	Model	BLEU ↑	AL ↓	LAAL ↓	ATD ↓
en-de	CMU†	30.4	1.92	1.99	-
	CUNI-KIT†	31.4	1.955 (3.072)	-	-
	FBK†	30.70	1.888 (2.939)	2.069 (3.052)	1.797 (2.364)
	HW-TSC‡	33.54	1.88	-	-
	NAIST	29.98	1.964	2.173	1.894
	SimulSeamless†	27.37	1.815 (3.012)	1.993 (3.137)	1.778 (2.353)
en-ja	NAIST	15.32	1.974	2.291	0.548
	CUNI-KIT†	15.3	1.982 (3.489)	-	-
	HW-TSC‡	17.89	1.98	-	-
	SimulSeamless†	22.19	1.997 (4.018)	2.137 (4.272)	0.580 (2.728)
en-zh	NAIST	22.11	1.471	1.907	0.668
	CUNI-KIT†	26.6	1.987 (3.508)	-	-
	HW-TSC‡	27.23	1.98	-	-
	XIAOMI†	26.59	1.966	-	-
	SimulSeamless†	20.56	1.942 (3.388)	2.080 (3.465)	0.765 (1.933)
cs-en	**SimulSeamless**†	18.03	1.988 (3.755)	2368 (3.999)	2.778 (3.399)

Table 1: Results on the MuST-C v2.0 tst-COMMON (for en-{de, ja, zh}) and IWSLT 2024 dev (for cs-en) considering BLEU and all the latency metrics (in seconds) reported for the task. Results in brackets are computationally aware but computed with different environments between systems. † indicates systems trained offline and tested in simultaneous. ‡ indicates cascade systems.

5 Conclusions

We introduced FBK's system designed for participation in the IWSLT 2024 Evaluation Campaigns in Simultaneous Translation and, specifically, the speech-to-text sub-track (SimulST). Our submission is characterized by the "off-the-self" use of the SeamlessM4T model for direct speech translation, repurposed for the simultaneous scenario by means of AlignAtt. AlignAtt is a SimulST policy that leverages cross-attention scores to guide simultaneous inference without any further modification or adaptation of the underlying model. The combination of SeamlessM4T and AlignAtt results in SimulSeamless, which supports all translation pairs of the Evaluation Campaign (English to German, Japanese, and Chinese, and Czech to English). SimulSeamless, to be released upon paper acceptance, achieves acceptable or even superior results compared to last year's participants. Moreover, it can be used for any language pairs enabled by the underlying SeamlessM4T model, potentially covering more than 143 source languages and 200 target languages.

Acknowledgments

The work presented in this paper is funded by the European Union's Horizon research and innovation programme under grant agreement No 101135798, project Meetween (My Personal AI Mediator for Virtual MEETtings BetWEEN People), and the PNRR project FAIR - Future AI Research (PE00000013), under the NRRP MUR program funded by the NextGenerationEU.

References

Milind Agarwal, Sweta Agrawal, Antonios Anastasopoulos, Luisa Bentivogli, Ondřej Bojar, Claudia Borg, Marine Carpuat, Roldano Cattoni, Mauro Cettolo, Mingda Chen, William Chen, Khalid Choukri, Alexandra Chronopoulou, Anna Currey, Thierry Declerck, Qianqian Dong, Kevin Duh, Yannick Estève, Marcello Federico, Souhir Gahbiche, Barry Haddow, Benjamin Hsu, Phu Mon Htut, Hirofumi Inaguma, Dávid Javorský, John Judge, Yasumasa Kano, Tom Ko, Rishu Kumar, Pengwei Li, Xutai Ma, Prashant Mathur, Evgeny Matusov, Paul McNamee, John P. McCrae, Kenton Murray, Maria Nadejde, Satoshi Nakamura, Matteo Negri, Ha Nguyen, Jan Niehues, Xing Niu, Atul Kr. Ojha, John E. Ortega, Proyag Pal, Juan Pino, Lonneke van der Plas, Peter Polák, Elijah Rippeth, Elizabeth Salesky, Jiatong Shi, Matthias Sperber, Sebastian Stüker, Katsuhito Sudoh, Yun Tang, Brian Thompson, Kevin Tran, Marco Turchi, Alex Waibel, Mingxuan Wang, Shinji Watanabe, and Rodolfo Zevallos. 2023. FINDINGS OF THE IWSLT 2023 EVALUATION CAMPAIGN. In *Proceedings of the 20th International Conference on Spoken Language Translation (IWSLT 2023)*, pages 1–61, Toronto, Canada (in-person and online). Association for Computational Linguistics.

Antonios Anastasopoulos, Loïc Barrault, Luisa Bentivogli, Marcely Zanon Boito, Ondřej Bojar, Roldano Cattoni, Anna Currey, Georgiana Dinu, Kevin Duh, Maha Elbayad, Clara Emmanuel, Yannick Estève, Marcello Federico, Christian Federmann, Souhir Gahbiche, Hongyu Gong, Roman Grundkiewicz, Barry Haddow, Benjamin Hsu, Dávid Javorský, Věra Kloudová, Surafel Lakew, Xutai Ma, Prashant Mathur, Paul McNamee, Kenton Murray, Maria Nădejde, Satoshi Nakamura, Matteo Negri, Jan Niehues, Xing Niu, John Ortega, Juan Pino, Elizabeth Salesky, Jiatong Shi, Matthias Sperber, Sebastian Stüker, Katsuhito Sudoh, Marco Turchi, Yogesh Virkar, Alexander Waibel, Changhan Wang, and Shinji Watanabe. 2022. Findings of the IWSLT 2022 evaluation campaign. In *Proceedings of the 19th International Conference on Spoken Language Translation (IWSLT 2022)*, pages 98–157, Dublin, Ireland (in-person and online).

Antonios Anastasopoulos, Ondřej Bojar, Jacob Bremerman, Roldano Cattoni, Maha Elbayad, Marcello Federico, Xutai Ma, Satoshi Nakamura, Matteo Negri, Jan Niehues, Juan Pino, Elizabeth Salesky, Sebastian Stüker, Katsuhito Sudoh, Marco Turchi, Alexander Waibel, Changhan Wang, and Matthew Wiesner. 2021. FINDINGS OF THE IWSLT 2021 EVALUATION CAMPAIGN. In *Proceedings of the 18th International Conference on Spoken Language Translation (IWSLT 2021)*, pages 1–29, Bangkok, Thailand (online).

Ebrahim Ansari, Amittai Axelrod, Nguyen Bach, Ondřej Bojar, Roldano Cattoni, Fahim Dalvi, Nadir Durrani, Marcello Federico, Christian Federmann, Jiatao Gu, Fei Huang, Kevin Knight, Xutai Ma, Ajay Nagesh, Matteo Negri, Jan Niehues, Juan Pino, Elizabeth Salesky, Xing Shi, Sebastian Stüker, Marco Turchi, Alexander Waibel, and Changhan Wang. 2020. FINDINGS OF THE IWSLT 2020 EVALUATION CAMPAIGN. In *Proceedings of the 17th International Conference on Spoken Language Translation*, pages 1–34, Online.

Loïc Barrault, Yu-An Chung, Mariano Cora Meglioli, David Dale, Ning Dong, Paul-Ambroise Duquenne, Hady Elsahar, Hongyu Gong, Kevin Heffernan, John Hoffman, et al. 2023a. Seamlessm4t-massively multilingual & multimodal machine translation. *arXiv preprint arXiv:2308.11596*.

Loïc Barrault, Yu-An Chung, Mariano Coria Meglioli, David Dale, Ning Dong, Mark Duppenthaler, Paul-Ambroise Duquenne, Brian Ellis, Hady Elsahar, Justin Haaheim, et al. 2023b. Seamless: Multilingual expressive and streaming speech translation. *arXiv preprint arXiv:2312.05187*.

Roldano Cattoni, Mattia Antonino Di Gangi, Luisa Bentivogli, Matteo Negri, and Marco Turchi. 2021. Must-c: A multilingual corpus for end-to-end speech translation. *Computer Speech & Language*, 66:101155.

Marta R Costa-jussà, James Cross, Onur Çelebi, Maha Elbayad, Kenneth Heafield, Kevin Heffernan, Elahe Kalbassi, Janice Lam, Daniel Licht, Jean Maillard, et al. 2022. No language left behind: Scaling human-centered machine translation. *arXiv preprint arXiv:2207.04672*.

Claudio Fantinuoli and Bianca Prandi. 2021. Towards the evaluation of automatic simultaneous speech translation from a communicative perspective. In *Proceedings of the 18th International Conference on Spoken Language Translation (IWSLT 2021)*, pages 245–254, Bangkok, Thailand (online). Association for Computational Linguistics.

Ryo Fukuda, Yuta Nishikawa, Yasumasa Kano, Yuka Ko, Tomoya Yanagita, Kosuke Doi, Mana Makinae, Sakriani Sakti, Katsuhito Sudoh, and Satoshi Nakamura. 2023. NAIST simultaneous speech-to-speech translation system for IWSLT 2023. In *Proceedings of the 20th International Conference on Spoken Language Translation (IWSLT 2023)*, pages 330–340, Toronto, Canada (in-person and online). Association for Computational Linguistics.

Marco Gaido, Sara Papi, Dennis Fucci, Giuseppe Fiameni, Matteo Negri, and Marco Turchi. 2022. Efficient yet competitive speech translation: FBK@IWSLT2022. In *Proceedings of the 19th International Conference on Spoken Language Translation (IWSLT 2022)*, pages 177–189, Dublin, Ireland (in-person and online). Association for Computational Linguistics.

Marco Gaido, Sara Papi, Matteo Negri, and Luisa Bentivogli. 2024. Speech translation with speech foundation models and large language models: What is there and what is missing? *arXiv preprint arXiv:2402.12025*.

Anmol Gulati, James Qin, Chung-Cheng Chiu, Niki Parmar, Yu Zhang, Jiahui Yu, Wei Han, Shibo Wang, Zhengdong Zhang, Yonghui Wu, and Ruoming Pang. 2020. Conformer: Convolution-augmented Transformer for Speech Recognition. In *Proc. Interspeech 2020*, pages 5036–5040.

Jiaxin Guo, Daimeng Wei, Zhanglin Wu, Zongyao Li, Zhiqiang Rao, Minghan Wang, Hengchao Shang, Xiaoyu Chen, Zhengzhe Yu, Shaojun Li, Yuhao Xie, Lizhi Lei, and Hao Yang. 2023. The HW-TSC's simultaneous speech-to-text translation system for IWSLT 2023 evaluation. In *Proceedings of the 20th International Conference on Spoken Language Translation (IWSLT 2023)*, pages 376–382, Toronto, Canada (in-person and online). Association for Computational Linguistics.

Wuwei Huang, Mengge Liu, Xiang Li, Yanzhi Tian, Fengyu Yang, Wen Zhang, Jian Luan, Bin Wang, Yuhang Guo, and Jinsong Su. 2023. The xiaomi AI lab's speech translation systems for IWSLT 2023 offline task, simultaneous task and speech-to-speech task. In *Proceedings of the 20th International Conference on Spoken Language Translation (IWSLT 2023)*, pages 411–419, Toronto, Canada (in-person and online). Association for Computational Linguistics.

Yasumasa Kano, Katsuhito Sudoh, and Satoshi Nakamura. 2022. Average token delay: A latency metric for simultaneous translation. *arXiv preprint arXiv:2211.13173*.

Siddique Latif, Moazzam Shoukat, Fahad Shamshad, Muhammad Usama, Heriberto Cuayáhuitl, and Björn W Schuller. 2023. Sparks of Large Audio Models: A Survey and Outlook. *arXiv preprint arXiv:2308.12792*.

Danni Liu, Gerasimos Spanakis, and Jan Niehues. 2020. Low-Latency Sequence-to-Sequence Speech Recognition and Translation by Partial Hypothesis Selection. In *Proc. Interspeech 2020*, pages 3620–3624.

Mingbo Ma, Liang Huang, Hao Xiong, Renjie Zheng, Kaibo Liu, Baigong Zheng, Chuanqiang Zhang, Zhongjun He, Hairong Liu, Xing Li, Hua Wu, and Haifeng Wang. 2019. STACL: Simultaneous translation with implicit anticipation and controllable latency using prefix-to-prefix framework. In *Proceedings of the 57th Annual Meeting of the Association for Computational Linguistics*, pages 3025–3036, Florence, Italy.

Xutai Ma, Mohammad Javad Dousti, Changhan Wang, Jiatao Gu, and Juan Pino. 2020. SIMULEVAL: An evaluation toolkit for simultaneous translation. In *Proceedings of the 2020 Conference on Empirical Methods in Natural Language Processing: System Demonstrations*, pages 144–150, Online.

Xutai Ma, Anna Sun, Siqi Ouyang, Hirofumi Inaguma, and Paden Tomasello. 2023. Efficient monotonic multihead attention. *arXiv preprint arXiv:2312.04515*.

Sara Papi, Marco Gaido, and Matteo Negri. 2023a. Direct models for simultaneous translation and automatic subtitling: FBK@IWSLT2023. In *Proceedings of the 20th International Conference on Spoken Language Translation (IWSLT 2023)*, pages 159–168, Toronto, Canada (in-person and online). Association for Computational Linguistics.

Sara Papi, Marco Gaido, Matteo Negri, and Marco Turchi. 2022a. Does simultaneous speech translation need simultaneous models? In *Findings of the Association for Computational Linguistics: EMNLP 2022*, pages 141–153, Abu Dhabi, United Arab Emirates.

Sara Papi, Marco Gaido, Matteo Negri, and Marco Turchi. 2022b. Over-generation cannot be rewarded: Length-adaptive average lagging for simultaneous speech translation. In *Proceedings of the Third Workshop on Automatic Simultaneous Translation*, pages 12–17, Online.

Sara Papi, Matteo Negri, and Marco Turchi. 2023b. Alignatt: Using attention-based audio-translation alignments as a guide for simultaneous speech translation. In *Proc. of Interspeech 2023*, Dublin, Ireland.

Sara Papi, Matteo Negri, and Marco Turchi. 2023c. Attention as a guide for simultaneous speech translation. In *Proceedings of the 61st Annual Meeting of the Association for Computational Linguistics (Volume 1: Long Papers)*, pages 13340–13356, Toronto, Canada. Association for Computational Linguistics.

Peter Polák, Danni Liu, Ngoc-Quan Pham, Jan Niehues, Alexander Waibel, and Ondřej Bojar. 2023. Towards efficient simultaneous speech translation: CUNI-KIT system for simultaneous track at IWSLT 2023. In *Proceedings of the 20th International Conference on Spoken Language Translation (IWSLT 2023)*, pages 389–396, Toronto, Canada (in-person and online). Association for Computational Linguistics.

Peter Polák, Ngoc-Quan Pham, Tuan Nam Nguyen, Danni Liu, Carlos Mullov, Jan Niehues, Ondřej Bojar, and Alexander Waibel. 2022. CUNI-KIT system for simultaneous speech translation task at IWSLT 2022. In *Proceedings of the 19th International Conference on Spoken Language Translation (IWSLT 2022)*, pages 277–285, Dublin, Ireland (in-person and online). Association for Computational Linguistics.

Matt Post. 2018. A call for clarity in reporting BLEU scores. In *Proceedings of the Third Conference on Machine Translation: Research Papers*, pages 186–191, Brussels, Belgium.

Vineel Pratap, Andros Tjandra, Bowen Shi, Paden Tomasello, Arun Babu, Sayani Kundu, Ali Elkahky, Zhaoheng Ni, Apoorv Vyas, Maryam Fazel-Zarandi, Alexei Baevski, Yossi Adi, Xiaohui Zhang, Wei-Ning Hsu, Alexis Conneau, and Michael Auli. 2023. Scaling Speech Technology to 1,000+ Languages. *arXiv*.

Alec Radford, Jong Wook Kim, Tao Xu, Greg Brockman, Christine Mcleavey, and Ilya Sutskever. 2023. Robust speech recognition via large-scale weak supervision. In *Proceedings of the 40th International Conference on Machine Learning*, volume 202 of *Proceedings of Machine Learning Research*, pages 28492–28518.

Ashish Vaswani, Noam Shazeer, Niki Parmar, Jakob Uszkoreit, Llion Jones, Aidan N Gomez, Ł ukasz Kaiser, and Illia Polosukhin. 2017. Attention is all you need. In *Advances in Neural Information Processing Systems*, volume 30. Curran Associates, Inc.

Brian Yan, Jiatong Shi, Soumi Maiti, William Chen, Xinjian Li, Yifan Peng, Siddhant Arora, and Shinji Watanabe. 2023. CMU's IWSLT 2023 simultaneous speech translation system. In *Proceedings of the 20th International Conference on Spoken Language Translation (IWSLT 2023)*, pages 235–240, Toronto, Canada (in-person and online). Association for Computational Linguistics.

Yu Zhang, Wei Han, James Qin, Yongqiang Wang, Ankur Bapna, Zhehuai Chen, Nanxin Chen, Bo Li, Vera Axelrod, Gary Wang, et al. 2023. Google usm: Scaling automatic speech recognition beyond 100 languages. *arXiv preprint arXiv:2303.01037*.

Ziqiang Zhang and Junyi Ao. 2022. The YiTrans speech translation system for IWSLT 2022 offline shared task. In *Proceedings of the 19th International Conference on Spoken Language Translation (IWSLT 2022)*, pages 158–168, Dublin, Ireland (in-person and online). Association for Computational Linguistics.

Jinming Zhao, Hao Yang, Gholamreza Haffari, and Ehsan Shareghi. 2022. M-Adapter: Modality Adaptation for End-to-End Speech-to-Text Translation. In *Proc. Interspeech 2022*, pages 111–115.

The SETU-DCU Submissions to IWSLT 2024 Low-Resource Speech-to-Text Translation Tasks

Maria Zafar[†], **Antonio Castaldo**[δ], **Neha Gajakos, Prashanth Nayak, Rejwanul Haque**[†], **Andy Way**

[†]South East Technological University, Carlow, Ireland

[δ]Università di Pisa, Italy

ADAPT Centre, Dublin City University, Ireland

C00304029@setu.ie,antonio.castaldo@phd.unipi.it,neha.gajakos@adaptcentre.ie
prashanth.nayak@adaptcentre.ie,rejwanul.haque@setu.ie,andy.way@adaptcentre.ie

Abstract

Natural Language Processing (NLP) research and development has experienced rapid progression in the recent times due to advances in deep learning. The introduction of pre-trained large language models (LLMs) is at the core of this transformation, significantly enhancing the performance of machine translation (MT) and speech technologies. This development has also led to fundamental changes in modern translation and speech tools and their methodologies. However, there remain challenges when extending this progress to underrepresented dialects and low-resource languages, primarily due to the need for more data.

This paper details our submissions to the IWSLT speech translation (ST) tasks. We used the Whisper model for the automatic speech recognition (ASR) component. We then used mBART and NLLB as cascaded systems for utilising their MT capabilities. Our research primarily focused on exploring various dialects of low-resource languages and harnessing existing resources from linguistically related languages. We conducted our experiments for two morphologically diverse language pairs: Irish-to-English and Maltese-to-English. We used BLEU, chrF and COMET for evaluating our MT models.

1 Introduction

The introduction of the Transformer architecture (Vaswani et al., 2017) is considered to be a groundbreaking development in NLP. This innovation has led to the rise of LLMs, which have become the catalyst for the AI revolution we are presently witnessing. LLMs have consistently pushed the boundaries of research by improving upon the state-of-the-art across various NLP tasks. The variants of Transformer such as the Transducer (Chen et al., 2021), Conformer (Nguyen et al., 2021), and ESPnet (Watanabe et al., 2018) have become essential to the success observed in a range of speech tasks, including both text-to-speech and speech-to-text MT.

This study explores low-resource speech-to-text translation, focusing on Irish-to-English and Maltese-to-English language pairs. We focused on developing our ST systems following two standard approaches:

- End-to-End (E2E) system: An E2E system in ST performs translation from one language to another without any intermediate steps. This process uses a single model to manage the entire translation process.

- Cascaded System: A cascaded system in ST uses a two-step process. First, it converts speech into text using ASR, and then it translates that text into another language. This process uses separate models in each step.

The rest of the paper is organised as follows: Section 2 describes our related work. Our datasets are explained in Section 3. Section 4 describes the models we used. In Section 5, we discuss our experiments and results. We conclude with avenues for future work in Section 6.

2 Related Work

This section discusses some foremost papers related to our work. Hussein et al. (2023) recently utilise LLMs for MT, such as mBART (Liu et al., 2020) and NLLB-200 (Team et al., 2022), which they used within both E2E and cascaded ST frameworks. Furthermore, enhancements in ASR were achieved by employing pseudo-labeling for data augmentation and adjusting for channel variations in telephone speech data. Additionally, they employed Minimum Bayes-Risk decoding to optimise the integration of their E2E and cascaded ST systems. The proposed framework led to impressive results.

Proceedings of the 21st International Conference on Spoken Language Translation (IWSLT 2024), pages 128–133
August 15-16, 2024 ©2024 Association for Computational Linguistics

Ortega et al. (2023) utilised the Fairseq S2T framework[1], where they used *log mel-scale filter bank* (Ortega et al., 2023) features for audio representation and Transformer for translation. Their systems integrated ASR and MT into the framework sequentially. The system's ASR component was powered by a pre-trained XLS-R model (Babu et al., 2021), enhanced with a fine-tuning step. At the same time, translations were performed using an MT system developed from a fine-tuned LLM. They found that in low-resource settings, like Quechua-to-Spanish, direct ST methods (combining ASR and MT) tended to outperform standalone LLM applications.

Mbuya and Anastasopoulos (2023) used self-supervised pre-trained speech models to improve translation performance in specific applications. Their study utilised self-supervised models such as Wav2vec 2.0 (Baevski et al., 2020), XLSR-53, and Hubert (Hsu et al., 2021). Their findings indicated that the Wav2vec 2.0 and Hubert models achieved similar performance levels in tasks involving low-resource languages and dialects. Moreover, they found that the Wav2vec 2.0 model performed better after removing its top three layers, a modification that the Hubert model did not require. In contrast, the XLSR-53 model showed weaker results in low-resource contexts but excelled in translating dialects, outperforming both Wav2vec 2.0 and Hubert in those scenarios.

Vakharia et al. (2023) investigated a novel approach termed "style embedding intervention" for low-resource formality control in spoken language translation. By assigning distinct style vectors to individual input tokens their proposed method comprehended and managed the subtleties of translating between formal and informal styles. They found that their approach surpasses previous "additive style intervention" techniques, particularly for the English-to-Korean translation task, enhancing average matched accuracy. After analysing their "style embedding intervention" model, they found that most of the style information was acquired in the <bos> (beginning of the sentence) token, further improving the average matched accuracy.

In their study, Radhakrishnan et al. (2023) employed a basic E2E framework based on Transformers and explored various techniques such as replacing encoder blocks with Conformer and pre-training the encoder. Their approach resulted in a substantial improvement in translation quality.

Williams et al. (2023) utilised a cascaded approach for their ST systems. For the ASR component, they used the XLS-R model. The MT component was based on mBART-50. They conducted experiments for English-to-Maltese language pairs, with the approach showing significant improvement over their baseline systems.

Experiments by Kesiraju et al. (2023) used E2E translation framework based on a bilingual ASR system. The model was jointly trained using Connectionist Temporal Classification and attention mechanisms. Furthermore, they employed techniques such as speed perturbation for data augmentation and re-scoring the top hypotheses using an external language model. They also introduced a cascaded system that utilised the same bilingual ASR and MT systems. Their experiments demonstrated significant improvements over the baseline for the Hindi-to-Marathi language pair.

The systems submitted to the previous year's IWLST offline and low-resource speech translation tracks employed various strategies for improving the performance of E2E or cascaded systems. As for ASR, several submissions adopted a mix of Transformer and conformer models (Zhang et al., 2022; Nguyen et al., 2021) or fine-tuned existing models (Zhang and Ao, 2022; Zanon Boito et al., 2022; Denisov et al., 2021). These efforts resulted in improved ASR performance through techniques such as training ASR on synthetic data with added punctuation, noise-filtering, and domain-specific fine-tuning (Zhang and Ao, 2022; Zhang et al., 2022), or integrating an intermediate model to refine the ASR output concerning casing and punctuation (Nguyen et al., 2021). As for MT, they predominantly relied on Transformer-based architectures (Zhang et al., 2022; Nguyen et al., 2021) or fine-tuning on preexisting LLMs (Zhang and Ao, 2022). Additionally, methods employed to improve MT performance included multi-task learning (Denisov et al., 2021), training the MT component robustly on noisy ASR output data (Nguyen et al., 2021), and re-ranking and de-noising techniques (Ding and Tao, 2021).

While there have been extensive and rapid developments in ST, the field of low-resource and dialect ST still needs to be explored. In this paper, we discuss our submissions to the IWSLT ST task. We conducted our experiments for two low-resource language pairs: Maltese-to-English and

[1]Fairseq: `https://github.com/facebookresearch/fairseq/tree/main`

Irish-to-English.

3 Datasets

We utilised the data provided by IWSLT for our experiments. The data statistics are detailed in Table 1.

Irish-to-English		
	Audios	Sentences
Train	7,478	7,478
Dev	1,120	1,120
Test	347	347
Maltese-to-English		
Train + Dev	7,542	7,542
Test	1,864	1,864

Table 1: Statistics of the datasets used.

4 Cascaded System

This section describes the architecture of our cascaded system. Like standard cascaded ST systems, our ASR and MT models are interconnected, i.e. the output from the ASR model serves as the input to the MT system. For this experiment, we selected the OpenAI Whisper model[2] (Radford et al., 2022) as our ASR system. We fine-tuned the OpenAI Whisper small model on Maltese speech to optimise its ASR capabilities. As for the MT component, we used two different pre-trained models, mBART-50[3] (Liu et al., 2020) and NLLB-200-distilled-600M[4] (Team et al., 2022). Both models were fine-tuned on the Maltese-to-English bilingual data.

As pointed out above, we used the OpenAI Whisper model as our ASR system. We aligned the data format with the model's input requirements to prepare our data. This involved removing unnecessary data chunks from the dataset, eliminating special characters, and converting the sentences to lowercase. Since our input audio was sampled at 48kHz, we downsampled it to 16kHz before passing it to the OpenAI Whisper feature extractor, as 16kHz is the sampling rate expected by the model. Additionally, we adjusted the audio inputs to the correct sampling rate using the "cast column" method. This operation does not alter the audio files directly but instead instructs the dataset to resample the audio samples on-the-fly the first time they are loaded.

We empirically identified that the following hyperparameter settings provided us the best results: batch size of 16, learning rate of 1e-5, 500 warmup steps, 30,000 max steps, per-device eval batch size of 8, generation max length of 225, and intervals of 1,000 steps for saving and evaluating, and 25 steps for logging.

4.1 The MT systems

As previously discussed, we choose mBART-50 and NLLB-200-distilled-600M as the choice of our MT models. We fine-tuned these models on the Maltese-to-English bilingual data (cf. Table 1). For the purpose of our evaluation, we used the BLEU (Papineni et al., 2002), COMET (Rei et al., 2020), and ChrF (Popović, 2015) metrics.

5 End-to-end System

Our submission for the English-Irish language pair comprises a fine-tuned version of OpenAI Whisper Small[5] to perform direct ST. Note that in this experiment, the audio files are resampled at 16kHz. This experiments were carried out for Irish-to-English only. In terms of hyperparameters selection, for our E2E experimentation, we identified that the following settings provided us the best results: batch size of 16, learning rate of 1e-5, 500 warmup steps, 1 gradient accumulation steps, generation max length of 225, and intervals of 500 steps for saving and evaluating. The model was fine-tuned over three epochs. We also integrated early stopping with `Patience = 2`. The data preprocessing pipeline was the same as the one used for the cascaded system (see Section 4).

6 Results

This section discusses the results that we obtained from our experiments. Table 2 shows the results obtained by evaluating our models on the evaluation test set while Table 3 shows the results obtained on blind test set provided by IWSLT. We can see from Table 2 that our models are reasonably good in the Maltese-to-English translation task. Our primary submission for Maltese-to-English was based on cascaded setup (Whisper + NLLB fine-tuning). For this setup, we obtained 52.60 BLEU, 72.12 chrF and 0.831 COMET points on the IWSLT 2023 evaluation test set. Our contrastive system is also

[2]Whisper: https://openai.com/research/whisper

[3]mBART-50: https://huggingface.co/facebook/mbart-large-50

[4]NLLB-200: https://ai.meta.com/research/no-language-left-behind/

[5]Whisper: https://openai.com/research/whisper

Model	BLEU	ChrF	COMET
Maltese-English			
Whisper-small	56.67	81.92	0.84
NLLB-200-600M	52.6	72.12	0.83
mBART-50	44.7	65.53	0.79
Irish-English			
Whisper-small (E2E)	0.14	33.05	-

Table 2: Results for our translation systems on evaluation test set.

a cascaded system; however, this time, we used mBART-50 as the decoder. This setup provided us 44.70 BLEU, 65.53 chrF, 0.796 COMET points on the evaluation test set. Fine-tuning OpenAI's Whisper model for the English-to-Irish language pair has led to a performance improvement, despite the fact that the language is unsupported and unavailable in the model's training data. Unfortunately, the BLEU score remains low, probably due to instances of overgeneration and undergeneration. The ChrF score, which measures character-based similarity, is higher but still indicates room for improvement as far as translation quality is concerned.

The results obtained on the blind test set are shown in Table 3. For our primary submission for Maltese-to-English we obtained 56.67 BLEU and 81.92 chrF2 points on the IWSLT 2024 blind test sets. Like above, our contrastive systems were cascaded systems; the first and second contrastive systems provided us 52.6 BLEU and 72.12 chrF2 and 44.70 BLEU and 65.53 chrF2 points, respectively. For our primary submission for English-to-Irish language pair we obtained 0.6 BLEU and 15.4 ChrF2 points on the test set.

As shown in Table 2 and Table 3, our best performing system is cascaded system with whisper-small and NLLB-200-600M. However, E2E are better than cascaded system due to the fact that in cascaded systems errors from the ASR can severely impact the performance of the subsequent component (MT). In contarst, E2E models can learn to directly map source language speech to the target language text. Their ability to process input in a single pass can significantly reduce latency compared to cascaded systems that involve multiple stages of processing, thereby avoiding intermediate errors. Our team secured second position for the Maltese-to-English translation task in this competition.

	BLEU	ChrF2
Maltese-English		
Primary	56.67	81.92
Constrastive1-Data1	52.6	72.12
Constrastive1-Data2	44.7	65.53
Irish-English		
Primary	0.6	15.4

Table 3: Official results for our translation systems on blind set.

7 Conclusion

In this study, we discussed our ST models for the IWSLT 2024 Low-Resource Task for both Irish-English and Maltese-English language pairs. Our proposed architecture offers numerous benefits: it is both computationally and data-efficient, supports both speech-to-text and text-to-text translations (including transcription), enhances knowledge transfer which boosts performance in low-resource languages, and exhibits robust translation capabilities.

Future investigations will focus on a detailed assessment of our architecture's ASR functionality and explore the use of adapters within the speech representation model. Additionally, a thorough examination of the optimal layers will be necessary when the speech representation model is not updated.

References

Arun Babu, Changhan Wang, Andros Tjandra, Kushal Lakhotia, Qiantong Xu, Naman Goyal, Kritika Singh, Patrick von Platen, Yatharth Saraf, Juan Pino, Alexei Baevski, Alexis Conneau, and Michael Auli. 2021. Xls-r: Self-supervised cross-lingual speech representation learning at scale. *Preprint*, arXiv:2111.09296.

Alexei Baevski, Henry Zhou, Abdelrahman Mohamed, and Michael Auli. 2020. wav2vec 2.0: A framework for self-supervised learning of speech representations. *Preprint*, arXiv:2006.11477.

Xie Chen, Yu Wu, Zhenghao Wang, Shujie Liu, and Jinyu Li. 2021. Developing real-time streaming transformer transducer for speech recognition on large-scale dataset. *Preprint*, arXiv:2010.11395.

Pavel Denisov, Manuel Mager, and Ngoc Thang Vu. 2021. IMS' systems for the IWSLT 2021 low-resource speech translation task. In *Proceedings of the 18th International Conference on Spoken Language Translation (IWSLT 2021)*, pages 175–181, Bangkok, Thailand (online). Association for Computational Linguistics.

Liang Ding and Dacheng Tao. 2021. The USYD-JD speech translation system for IWSLT2021. In *Proceedings of the 18th International Conference on Spoken Language Translation (IWSLT 2021)*, pages 182–191, Bangkok, Thailand (online). Association for Computational Linguistics.

Wei-Ning Hsu, Benjamin Bolte, Yao-Hung Hubert Tsai, Kushal Lakhotia, Ruslan Salakhutdinov, and Abdelrahman Mohamed. 2021. Hubert: Self-supervised speech representation learning by masked prediction of hidden units. *Preprint*, arXiv:2106.07447.

Amir Hussein, Cihan Xiao, Neha Verma, Thomas Thebaud, Matthew Wiesner, and Sanjeev Khudanpur. 2023. JHU IWSLT 2023 dialect speech translation system description. In *Proceedings of the 20th International Conference on Spoken Language Translation (IWSLT 2023)*, pages 283–290, Toronto, Canada (in-person and online). Association for Computational Linguistics.

Santosh Kesiraju, Karel Beneš, Maksim Tikhonov, and Jan Černocký. 2023. BUT systems for IWSLT 2023 Marathi - Hindi low resource speech translation task. In *Proceedings of the 20th International Conference on Spoken Language Translation (IWSLT 2023)*, pages 227–234, Toronto, Canada (in-person and online). Association for Computational Linguistics.

Yinhan Liu, Jiatao Gu, Naman Goyal, Xian Li, Sergey Edunov, Marjan Ghazvininejad, Mike Lewis, and Luke Zettlemoyer. 2020. Multilingual Denoising Pre-training for Neural Machine Translation. *Transactions of the Association for Computational Linguistics*, 8:726–742.

Jonathan Mbuya and Antonios Anastasopoulos. 2023. Gmu systems for the iwslt 2023 dialect and low-resource speech translation tasks. In *Proceedings of the 20th International Conference on Spoken Language Translation (IWSLT 2023)*, pages 269–276.

Tuan Nam Nguyen, Thai Son Nguyen, Christian Huber, Ngoc-Quan Pham, Thanh-Le Ha, Felix Schneider, and Sebastian Stüker. 2021. KIT's IWSLT 2021 offline speech translation system. In *Proceedings of the 18th International Conference on Spoken Language Translation (IWSLT 2021)*, pages 125–130, Bangkok, Thailand (online). Association for Computational Linguistics.

John Ortega, Rodolfo Zevallos, and William Chen. 2023. QUESPA submission for the IWSLT 2023 dialect and low-resource speech translation tasks. In *Proceedings of the 20th International Conference on Spoken Language Translation (IWSLT 2023)*, pages 261–268, Toronto, Canada (in-person and online). Association for Computational Linguistics.

Kishore Papineni, Salim Roukos, Todd Ward, and Wei-Jing Zhu. 2002. Bleu: a method for automatic evaluation of machine translation. In *Proceedings of the 40th Annual Meeting of the Association for Computational Linguistics*, pages 311–318, Philadelphia, Pennsylvania, USA. Association for Computational Linguistics.

Maja Popović. 2015. chrF: character n-gram F-score for automatic MT evaluation. In *Proceedings of the Tenth Workshop on Statistical Machine Translation*, pages 392–395, Lisbon, Portugal. Association for Computational Linguistics.

Alec Radford, Jong Wook Kim, Tao Xu, Greg Brockman, Christine McLeavey, and Ilya Sutskever. 2022. Robust speech recognition via large-scale weak supervision. *Preprint*, arXiv:2212.04356.

Balaji Radhakrishnan, Saurabh Agrawal, Raj Prakash Gohil, Kiran Praveen, Advait Vinay Dhopeshwarkar, and Abhishek Pandey. 2023. Sri-b's systems for iwslt 2023 dialectal and low-resource track: Marathi-hindi speech translation. In *Proceedings of the 20th International Conference on Spoken Language Translation (IWSLT 2023)*, pages 449–454.

Ricardo Rei, Craig Stewart, Ana C Farinha, and Alon Lavie. 2020. COMET: A neural framework for MT evaluation. In *Proceedings of the 2020 Conference on Empirical Methods in Natural Language Processing (EMNLP)*, pages 2685–2702, Online. Association for Computational Linguistics.

NLLB Team, Marta R. Costa-jussà, James Cross, Onur Çelebi, Maha Elbayad, Kenneth Heafield, Kevin Heffernan, Elahe Kalbassi, Janice Lam, Daniel Licht, Jean Maillard, Anna Sun, Skyler Wang, Guillaume Wenzek, Al Youngblood, Bapi Akula, Loic Barrault, Gabriel Mejia Gonzalez, Prangthip Hansanti, John Hoffman, Semarley Jarrett, Kaushik Ram Sadagopan, Dirk Rowe, Shannon Spruit, Chau Tran, Pierre Andrews, Necip Fazil Ayan, Shruti Bhosale, Sergey Edunov, Angela Fan, Cynthia Gao, Vedanuj Goswami, Francisco Guzmán, Philipp Koehn, Alexandre Mourachko, Christophe Ropers, Safiyyah Saleem, Holger Schwenk, and Jeff Wang. 2022. No language left behind: Scaling human-centered machine translation. *Preprint*, arXiv:2207.04672.

Priyesh Vakharia, Pranjali Basmatkar, et al. 2023. Low-resource formality controlled nmt using pre-trained lm. In *Proceedings of the 20th International Conference on Spoken Language Translation (IWSLT 2023)*, pages 321–329.

Ashish Vaswani, Noam Shazeer, Niki Parmar, Jakob Uszkoreit, Llion Jones, Aidan N Gomez, Łukasz Kaiser, and Illia Polosukhin. 2017. Attention is all you need. *Advances in neural information processing systems*, 30.

Shinji Watanabe, Takaaki Hori, Shigeki Karita, Tomoki Hayashi, Jiro Nishitoba, Yuya Unno, Nelson Enrique Yalta Soplin, Jahn Heymann, Matthew Wiesner, Nanxin Chen, Adithya Renduchintala, and Tsubasa Ochiai. 2018. Espnet: End-to-end speech processing toolkit. *Preprint*, arXiv:1804.00015.

Aiden Williams, Kurt Abela, Rishu Kumar, Martin Bär, Hannah Billinghurst, Kurt Micallef, Ahnaf Mozib Samin, Andrea DeMarco, Lonneke van der Plas, and Claudia Borg. 2023. Um-dfki maltese speech translation. In *Proceedings of the 20th International Conference on Spoken Language Translation (IWSLT 2023)*, pages 433–441.

Marcely Zanon Boito, John Ortega, Hugo Riguidel, Antoine Laurent, Loïc Barrault, Fethi Bougares, Firas Chaabani, Ha Nguyen, Florentin Barbier, Souhir Gahbiche, and Yannick Estève. 2022. ON-TRAC consortium systems for the IWSLT 2022 dialect and low-resource speech translation tasks. In *Proceedings of the 19th International Conference on Spoken Language Translation (IWSLT 2022)*, pages 308–318, Dublin, Ireland (in-person and online). Association for Computational Linguistics.

Weitai Zhang, Zhongyi Ye, Haitao Tang, Xiaoxi Li, Xinyuan Zhou, Jing Yang, Jianwei Cui, Pan Deng, Mohan Shi, Yifan Song, Dan Liu, Junhua Liu, and Lirong Dai. 2022. The USTC-NELSLIP offline speech translation systems for IWSLT 2022. In *Proceedings of the 19th International Conference on Spoken Language Translation (IWSLT 2022)*, pages 198–207, Dublin, Ireland (in-person and online). Association for Computational Linguistics.

Ziqiang Zhang and Junyi Ao. 2022. The YiTrans speech translation system for IWSLT 2022 offline shared task. In *Proceedings of the 19th International Conference on Spoken Language Translation (IWSLT 2022)*, pages 158–168, Dublin, Ireland (in-person and online). Association for Computational Linguistics.

Automatic Subtitling and Subtitle Compression: FBK at the IWSLT 2024 Subtitling track

Marco Gaido, Sara Papi, Mauro Cettolo, Roldano Cattoni, Andrea Piergentili, Matteo Negri, Luisa Bentivogli
Fondazione Bruno Kessler, Trento, Italy
{mgaido,spapi,cettolo,cattoni,apiergentili,negri,bentivo}@fbk.eu

Abstract

The paper describes the FBK submissions to the Subtitling track of the 2024 IWSLT Evaluation Campaign, which covers both the Automatic Subtitling and the Subtitle Compression task for two language pairs: English to German and English to Spanish. For the *Automatic Subtitling* task, we submitted two systems each covering one of the two proposed training conditions, namely constrained and unconstrained: *i)* a direct model, trained in constrained conditions, that produces the SRT files from the audio without intermediate outputs (e.g., transcripts), and *ii)* a cascade solution that integrates only free-to-use and freely trained components, either taken off-the-shelf or developed in-house. Results show that, on both language pairs, our direct model outperforms both cascade and direct systems trained in constrained conditions in last year's edition of the campaign, while our solution assemblying pre-trained models is competitive with the best 2023 systems, although they were fine-tuned on task specific training data. For the *Subtitle Compression* task, our primary submission involved prompting a Large Language Model in zero-shot mode to shorten subtitles that exceed the reading speed limit of 21 characters per second. Our results highlight the challenges inherent in shrinking out-of-context sentence fragments that are automatically generated and potentially error-prone, underscoring the need for future studies to develop targeted solutions.

1 Introduction

In response to the growing amount of audiovisual content produced every day, the task of automatically generating subtitles has seen increasing attention (Álvarez et al., 2015; Vitikainen and Koponen, 2021), with the goal of fostering the accessibility of the material by overcoming language barriers. In light of this, starting from the 2023 edition, the IWSLT Evaluation Campaign includes the Automatic Subtitling task, in which participants had to generate well-formed subtitles in German and Spanish starting from the corresponding English audio (Agarwal et al., 2023). In addition to requiring high-quality translations of the audio content, correct subtitles also need the translated text to be split into blocks (each of them possibly split into 2 lines) in a way that minimizes the users' cognitive effort (Bogucki, 2004; Khalaf, 2016; Cintas and Remael, 2021), and these blocks have to be presented on-screen with the correct timing, i.e. in sync with the original audio.

Although there is no absolute rule to determine the cognitive effort required to read a subtitle, typical constraints to keep it low include: *i)* not having more than 2 lines per block (LPB); *ii)* keeping the number of characters per line (CPL) below a given threshold, which was set to 42 in the IWSLT 2023 campaign; and *iii)* avoiding excessive reading speed expressed in the number of characters per second (CPS) to be read by the user, which was set to 21. Good subtitles should hence be displayed in text blocks that conform to these rules, and their adherence to the constraints can be measured as the percentage of blocks compliant with them. Since automatic subtitling systems can fail in fully matching all the above constraints, the IWSLT 2024 campaign introduced an additional Subtitle Compression sub-task,[1] which requires to reduce the number of characters in each block of pre-generated subtitles to an extent that satisfies the reading speed constraint, without compromising its semantic content.

This paper describes FBK's submissions to both tasks (Automatic Subtitling and Subtitle Compression) of the IWSLT 2024 Subtitling track. Our submitted systems cover both language directions under evaluation, namely English-German (en-de) and English-Spanish (en-es).

Regarding Automatic Subtitling, we explored

[1] https://iwslt.org/2024/subtitling

Proceedings of the 21st International Conference on Spoken Language Translation (IWSLT 2024), pages 134–144
August 15-16, 2024 ©2024 Association for Computational Linguistics

two approaches that led to two submissions, one for each training condition, constrained and unconstrained. On the one hand, following the promising results obtained by the first direct models for automatic subtitling (Papi et al., 2023a), we trained a direct subtitling model (§2.1) in constrained conditions, i.e. using only the data allowed by the organizers for this setting. We call this model *direct* as it generates the subtitles in the target languages (including block and line delimiters) as well as timestamps without any intermediate discrete content representation, such as textual transcripts of the audio. In this respect, it is different from the two *direct* models submitted in the 2023 edition as both required the generation of intermediate transcripts for the timestamps estimation, either by using an auxiliary automatic speech recognition (ASR) system (Bahar et al., 2023) or by using auxiliary modules of the direct speech translation (ST) system (Papi et al., 2023b). On the other hand, we created a pipeline system (§2.2) within the AI4Culture[2] EU project, which binds us to use only code and models released under licenses as permissive as possible. Lastly, our primary submission to the newly proposed Subtitle Compression task (§2.3) tackled the problem with an LLM-based approach. To this aim, we explored a first basic solution by prompting the model in zero-shot mode to shorten candidate hypotheses exceeding the 21 CPS limit, and compared it with simpler, word/character deletion strategies.

2 Systems Description

In this section, we first describe the direct (§2.1) and cascade (§2.2) Automatic Subtitling systems, and then our Subtitle Compression submissions (§2.3).

2.1 Direct Subtitling with SBAAM

Our direct subtitling system is based on an encoder-decoder architecture, made of a 12-layer Conformer[3] encoder (Gulati et al., 2020) and a 6-layer Transformer decoder (Vaswani et al., 2017). It is trained to predict the translation in the target language with end of line (<eol>) and end of block (<eob>) delimiters to learn both to translate and segment into subtitle units. Moreover, we add a Connectionist Temporal Classification (CTC) on target module (Yan et al., 2023) on top of the encoder that is trained with the same target as the autoregressive Transformer decoder. In addition, to reduce the computational cost of our model, we include a CTC compression module in the 8th encoder layer (Gaido et al., 2021). This module is trained to predict the transcription of the audio, but no transcript is generated at inference time and the module only averages similar vectors without producing any textual representation of the source.

The end-to-end training is realized with a composite loss ($\mathcal{L}$) that sums the label smoothing cross-entropy (CE) loss (Szegedy et al., 2016) on the decoder outputs with the CTC loss of the CTC on target module, and the CTC loss of the CTC compression module. By defining t as the transcript of an audio sample, and x and y as the target translation augmented with <eob> and <eol> delimiters, we can formalize the loss as:

$$\mathcal{L} = \lambda_1 \, \mathrm{CTC}(h_8, t) + \lambda_2 \, \mathrm{CTC}(h, y) + \lambda_3 \, \mathrm{CE}(\mathcal{D}(h, y), y)$$

where $\lambda_{1,2,3}$ control the relative weight of the losses, h_8 is the output of the 8th encoder layer, h is the encoder output, and D is the Transformer decoder. In our experiments, we follow the indication of (Yan et al., 2023) and set $(\lambda_1, \lambda_2, \lambda_3)$ to (1.0, 2.0, 5.0).

The inference phase, instead, combines only the probabilities predicted by the CTC on target module and by the decoder, following the joint CTC/attention framework with CTC rescoring (Watanabe et al., 2017; Yan et al., 2023). This method involves rescoring the next-token probabilities produced by the decoder using the probabilities of the candidate prefixes obtained from the CTC on target module (TgtCTC):

$$p = p_{\mathcal{D}}(y_i | h, y_{0,\dots,i-1}) + \alpha \, p_{\mathrm{TgtCTC}}(y_{0,\dots,i} | h)$$

where α is a hyperparameter that controls the weight of the CTC rescoring.

The output of this inference is the translated text with subtitle boundaries. As such, we still miss a key element for subtitles: the start and end timestamps of each block, which control how long and when they have to be displayed on the screen. To estimate them, we rely on the Speech Block Attention Area Maximization (SBAAM) method (Gaido et al., 2024). SBAAM leverages the encoder-decoder attention to create alignments

[2] https://pro.europeana.eu/project/ai4culture-an-ai-platform-for-the-cultural-heritage-data-space

[3] We use the padding-safe implementation tested with `pangolinn` by Papi et al. (2024).

between the generated subtitles and the source audio, as done in many works both in text-to-text scenarios (Tang et al., 2018; Zenkel et al., 2019; Garg et al., 2019; Chen et al., 2020) and, more recently, speech-to-text ones (Papi et al., 2023c; Alastruey et al., 2023). In fact, SBAAM first applies a mean-standard deviation normalization to the attention matrix on the text axis (clipping all negative values to a small $-\epsilon$ quantity to avoid penalizing in different ways unnecessary areas). Then, for each block boundary (<eob>) in the generated text, it iteratively determines the timing of the <eob> by selecting the splitting point that maximizes the area of the current block with the audio up to that point and the remaining blocks with the rest of the audio.

Once all the <eob>s in the output have been processed, all blocks will have start and end timings.

Experimental Details. The input of our models is represented by 80 Mel-filterbank features extracted every 10 ms with a window of 25 ms. The input features are then processed with two 1D convolutional layers with stride 2 that reduce the input length by a factor of 4. We use 512 for the encoder and the decoder embedding dimensions and 2048 hidden features in the feed-forward layers. The vocabularies are based on unigram SentencePiece (Kudo, 2018), with size 8,000 for the English source and 16,000 for the target (either German or Spanish). The total number of parameters of our models is 133M. The final models are obtained by averaging the last 7 checkpoints obtained from the trainings, which are performed on 4 NVIDIA Ampere GPU A100 (64GB VRAM). At inference time, when long unsegmented audios have to be subtitled, the audio is first segmented into smaller audio chunks with SHAS[4] (Tsiamas et al., 2022). The code used to create the models is available at: `https://github.com/hlt-mt/FBK-fairseq`.

Training Data. The models are trained on most of the datasets admitted for the "constrained" submission type. These include all the available ST corpora, namely MuST-Cinema (Karakanta et al., 2020), EuroParl-ST (Iranzo-Sánchez et al., 2020), and CoVoST v2 (Wang et al., 2020). Also, we leverage most of the available ASR datasets (CommonVoice (Ardila et al., 2020), LibriSpeech (Panayotov et al., 2015), TEDLIUM v3 (Hernandez et al., 2018), and VoxPopuli (Wang et al., 2021)), by automatically translating the transcripts into the two target languages using the NeMo MT models.[5] <eol> and <eob> tags are added to both transcripts and translations of all datasets, except for MuST-Cinema that already include them, using the multimodal segmenter by Papi et al. (2022).

2.2 Cascade Subtitling

As stated in the introduction, within the EU AI4Culture project, we developed a cascade subtitling system combining free-to-use components only. Most of them are taken off-the-shelf, while others were developed in-house. The entire system is publicly available at `https://github.com/hlt-mt/FBK-subtitler`.

The pipeline is shown in Figure 1 and concatenates the following modules:

Audio segmenter: Speech recognition and speech translation models are unable to process long audios, which then have to be split into shorter segments. As in the direct architecture, here too SHAS is used to carry out this task. It is worth noting that, in general, each audio segment contains multiple subtitles. SHAS code and models are released under the very permissive MIT license.

Speech recognition system: To transcribe the input speech, we opted for Whisper[6] (`large-v3`) to date one of the best ASR systems covering English, licensed under the MIT license. Whisper generates transcripts already split in subtitles, each supplied with start and end timestamps. However, two main issues can affect Whisper's outputs: hallucinations and lack of segmentation in lines, both handled by specific modules of the pipeline.

Hallucination removal filter: It removes hallucinations, a well-known concern of LLMs, which refers to the generation of text that is erroneous, nonsensical, or detached from reality. Here, only *shallow* hallucinations are considered, i.e. those involving the syntax of subtitles but not their semantics. We observed two types of shallow hallucinations, *within* and *across* subtitles. The first type refers to the repetition of single words or short n-grams many consecutive times within a subtitle. The second type refers to instances where the same transcript is repeated an anomalous number of times across consecutive subtitles. We implemented a script which heuristically detects and

[4]`https://github.com/mt-upc/SHAS`

[5]Publicly available at: `https://docs.nvidia.com/deeplearning/nemo/user-guide/docs/en/main/nlp/machine_translation/machine_translation.html`

[6]`https://github.com/openai/whisper`

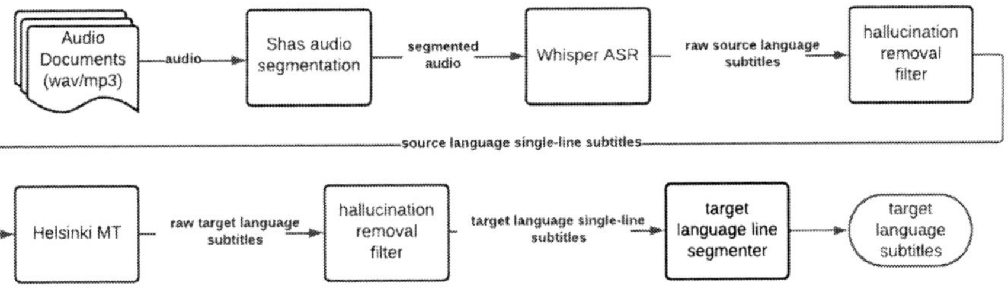

Figure 1: The cascade subtitling system based on pre-trained LLMs.

removes such phenomena from subtitles; in the pipeline, it is used downstream of both the ASR and the MT models.

Machine translation system: It performs the translation of a text (here: the text in each subtitle generated by Whisper, amended by hallucinations) from a source language into the target language. Various freely usable pre-trained LLMs have been tested in a preliminary investigation, namely NLLB,[7] mBART-50,[8] Helsinki Opus-MT.[9] The outcomes indicated the Helsinki Opus-MT as the best performer. Code and models are released under the MIT license.

Text segmenter: In general, its goal would be splitting the input text into fragments suitable, in terms of both quality and compliance to spatio-temporal constraints, to be displayed on the screen. However, since here the goal is solely to split too long, single line subtitles generated from the previous stages of the pipeline into two lines, we implemented a script that splits subtitles longer than 42 characters into two lines rewarding: the compliance of both lines with the 42-character limit, a similar length of the two lines, and the presence of a punctuation mark at the end of the first line.

2.3 Subtitle Compression

The newly introduced Subtitle Compression task required participants to rephrase subtitles provided by the task organizers that did not comply with the reading speed constraint of 21 CPS.

The material to be automatically processed was presented to participants as standard SRT (SubRip File Format) files that include: i) the text of sequentially numbered subtitles, which can be either one or two lines, and ii) timing information for each subtitle (i.e. timestamps in the format `hours:minutes:seconds,milliseconds`), indicating how long the subtitle should stay on the screen. As per the task guidelines, the goal was to exclusively work at the text level, compressing subtitles' text when necessary and without modifying the time boundaries. To achieve this, given the lack of indications on which automatic subtitles needed correction, we relied on the subtitle compliance script also provided by the task organizers. This allowed us to reliably identify the subtitle candidates requiring text compression and focus exclusively on rephrasing them.

The identified subtitles (39.8% and 30.0% of the total for en-de and en-es, respectively) underwent the compression phase, for which we devised two strategies. The first one, selected for our primary submission, is *user-oriented*: its goal is to target the CPS constraint with an LLM-based, fluency-driven approach aimed at preserving the readability of the compressed subtitles and, in turn, user experience. The second strategy, selected for our contrastive submissions, is more *metric-oriented*. Its goal is to shorten non-CPS-compliant subtitles by removing function words with varying levels of aggressiveness.

User-oriented approach (GPT – primary). Our LLM-based compression approach exploits GPT-4 (OpenAI, 2024) (model `gpt-4-0613`, with default parameters except for the temperature, which we set to 0), which was prompted in zero-shot mode with the instruction: "`Shorten this [LANGUAGE] text to a maximum of [TARGET_NUMCHARS] characters while preserving the original words as much as possible: [TEXT]`", where:

- `LANGUAGE` indicates the language of the subtitle, either "German" or "Spanish";
- `TARGET_NUMCHARS` specifies the maximum al-

[7]https://github.com/facebookresearch/fairseq/tree/nllb/

[8]https://huggingface.co/facebook/mbart-large-50

[9]https://huggingface.co/models?sort=trending&search=Helsinki-NLP

lowed length for the compressed subtitle, measured in characters including spaces. The target value is calculated based on the total on-screen time of the subtitle, which is determined by subtracting its start time from its end time and then multiplying this duration by 21 (e.g., with 3.2 seconds of on-screen time, TARGET_NUMCHARS is 67.2, truncated to 67);

- TEXT is the original subtitle that needs to be compressed.

The choice of the overall approach was driven by the aim to preserve the user experience by leveraging the generation capabilities of large language models. In fact, simpler and more aggressive methods, such as the metric-oriented ones presented in the next paragraph, can easily improve the rate of subtitles compliant with the CPS limit but at the cost of losing important information and detracting their readability. In an opposite direction, our LLM-based approach aims to strike a balance between improving CPS values and retaining the original information through targeted and meaning-preserving rephrasing.

Our zero-shot prompting strategy was primarily driven by fast-development reasons. In fact, we expect significant improvements by feeding the model with exemplars, i.e., via in-context learning (Brown et al., 2020). We opted for a simpler, cheaper, and more conservative approach to establish a starting point and a reference baseline for future in-depth comparative experiments. For similar reasons, we opted for a solution that concentrates on individual subtitles instead of operating on full sentences. Though likely more effective, letting the LLM reformulate *full* sentences in a shorter way would have introduced the additional burden of rearranging the resulting content into timed subtitles afterward. This is certainly a promising direction for future improvements.

Metric-oriented approach (`Del_*` – contrastive). For our contrastive submissions, we designed "metric-oriented" solutions that aim to improve CPS by aggressively reducing the length of subtitles through simple character or word deletions. The goal was to measure the extent to which this baseline approach affects the readability of subtitles. Along this direction, we explored a range of options which share the common trait of removing from the non-CPS-compliant subtitles specific categories of function words identified from pre-compiled lists downloaded from the web.[10] Word removal is carried out with varying levels of aggressiveness, ranging from *i)* the deletion of articles (`Del_articles`) to *ii)* the deletion of articles, prepositions, and adverbs (`Del_art/prep/adv`), and *iii)* the deletion of all function words (`Del_all-func-wrds`). On the one side, these strategies avoid the loss of important content in the original subtitles and the presence of incomplete words in the output, as it happens in the Baseline approach proposed by the task organizers. On the other side, they intervene in the syntactic structure of the subtitles, altering them in a way that improves CPS but penalizes both readability and automatic evaluation with reference-based metrics.

3 Results

As a recap, FBK submitted the following runs:

Automatic Subtitling task

- Primary run in Constrained condition: FBK_{24}^{drct} (§2.1)
- Primary run in Unconstrained condition: FBK_{24}^{cscd} (§2.2)

Subtitle Compression task

- Primary run: GPT (§2.3, paragraph "User-oriented approach")
- Contrastive1 run: `del all func wrds` (§2.3, "Metric-oriented approach")
- Contrastive2 run: `del art/prep/adv` (§2.3, "Metric-oriented approach")

3.1 Automatic Subtitling

Results on subtitling task are provided in Tables 1, 2, and 3. Table 1 compares the *SubER* (Wilken et al., 2022) scores,[11] the primary metric of the task, computed on the subtitles of the development set generated by our systems and by the best systems at IWSLT 2023 in constrained and unconstrained conditions. Table 2 shows global results, i.e., on subtitles of all domains, on test23 of our runs as provided to us by organizers, and of the best primary runs at IWSLT 2023, as published in (Agarwal et al., 2023). Table 3 gathers results, global and on each domain, on test24 of our runs

[10] `https://github.com/Yoast/javascript/tree/develop/packages/yoastseo/src/researches`

[11] When we do state otherwise, we compute SubER without casing and punctuation, as done in the previous evaluation campaign for the sake of fair comparison with previous scores.

		en-de							
		TED		*ITV*		*PELOTON*		*AVG*	
system	**cnd**	SubER		SubER		SubER		SubER	
		cased	uncased	cased	uncased	cased	uncased	cased	uncased
AppTek$_{23}^{cscd}$	C	-	63.0	-	83.6	-	87.6	-	78.1
FBK$_{23}^{drct}$	C	69.4	-	83.7	-	79.1	-	77.4	-
AppTek$_{23}^{cscd}$	U	-	64.3	-	71.4	-	71.9	-	69.2
FBK$_{24}^{drct}$	C	61.6	62.1	80.0	80.7	75.6	78.2	72.4	73.7
FBK$_{24}^{cscd}$	U	69.0	69.0	79.3	78.9	73.4	76.1	73.9	74.7

		en-es							
		TED		*ITV*		*PELOTON*		*AVG*	
system	**cnd**	SubER		SubER		SubER		SubER	
		cased	uncased	cased	uncased	cased	uncased	cased	uncased
AppTek$_{23}^{cscd}$	C	-	48.8	-	82.1	-	79.0	-	70.0
FBK$_{23}^{drct}$	C	52.5	-	82.2	-	80.3	-	71.7	-
TLT$_{23}$	U	-	45.9	-	71.3	-	74.9	-	64.0
FBK$_{24}^{drct}$	C	49.5	47.5	79.1	79.5	79.3	80.8	70.3	70.3
FBK$_{24}^{cscd}$	U	49.2	48.0	72.2	73.5	73.9	76.9	65.1	66.1

Table 1: SubER (↓) comparison with the best cascade (AppTek$_{23}^{cscd}$ – Bahar et al. 2023 – and TLT$_{23}$ – Perone 2023 – for en-es) and direct (FBK$_{23}^{drct}$) models trained on constrained/unconstrained (C/U of column cnd) conditions from the IWSLT 2023 Evaluation Campaign on automatic subtitling for en-de and en-es validation sets. The results of our systems are reported in bold.

			Subtitle quality	**Translation quality**			**Subtitle compliance**		
en-	**system**	**cnd**	**SubER↓**	**BLEU↑**	**ChrF↑**	**BLEURT↑**	**CPS↑**	**CPL↑**	**LPB↑**
-de	FBK$_{24}^{drct}$	C	74.26	13.08	34.77	.3742	72.75	89.35	99.96
	AppTek$_{23}^{cscd}$	C	77.14	12.40	33.17	.3300	93.01	100.00	100.00
	FBK$_{24}^{cscd}$	U	73.78	16.46	39.07	.4454	61.44	93.04	100.00
	AppTek$_{23}^{cscd}$	U	70.23	15.10	37.39	.4291	87.87	100.00	100.00
-es	FBK$_{24}^{drct}$	C	70.09	19.16	41.58	.3972	73.08	91.64	99.97
	AppTek$_{23}^{cscd}$	C	72.33	17.72	38.49	.3467	95.30	100.00	100.00
	FBK$_{24}^{cscd}$	U	66.02	23.87	46.53	.4811	67.56	94.25	100.00
	TLT$_{23}$	U	67.29	22.54	46.40	.4993	85.51	99.53	100.00

Table 2: Global subtitling results (ALL) of 2024 FBK submissions and of 2023 best primary runs on test2023.

			Subtitle quality	**Translation quality**			**Subtitle compliance**		
en-	**system**	**dmn**	**SubER↓**	**BLEU↑**	**ChrF↑**	**BLEURT↑**	**CPS↑**	**CPL↑**	**LPB↑**
-de	FBK$_{24}^{drct}$	TED	57.50	25.79	54.78	.6114	83.10	83.69	100.00
		ITV	78.90	9.67	28.43,	.2911	70.45	90.04	99.97
		PLT	80.68	7.71	30.45	.3542	82.16	92.77	100.00
		ALL	73.99	13.48	36.12	.3775	76.19	88.86	99.99
	FBK$_{24}^{cscd}$	TED	63.26	22.94	53.70	.5872	79.99	89.52	100.00
		ITV	79.92	14.86	35.16	.4048	54.20	91.12	100.00
		PLT	78.34	11.30	34.13	.4202	76.52	96.99	100.00
		ALL	75.56	16.23	40.10	.4503	64.64	91.79	100.00
-es	FBK$_{24}^{drct}$	TED	39.86	45.63	69.63	.7441	82.43	86.59	100.00
		ITV	77.00	11.91	31.95	.2986	70.61	92.60	100.00
		PLT	79.70	11.88	40.05	.4329	82.26	89.58	100.00
		ALL	67.13	22.03	44.69	.4277	76.00	90.35	100.00
	FBK$_{24}^{cscd}$	TED	40.75	45.69	69.20	.7500	83.42	90.31	100.00
		ITV	70.82	18.92	40.17	.4262	60.85	93.46	100.00
		PLT	74.17	16.18	44.42	.5108	80.24	97.03	100.00
		ALL	63.01	26.60	49.64	.5174	69.97	93.28	100.00

Table 3: Detailed subtitling results of FBK submissions on test2024.

as provided to us by organizers. Besides SubER that measures overall subtitle quality, Table 2 and Table 3 include BLEU (Papineni et al., 2002), ChrF (Popović, 2015) and TER (Snover et al., 2006) for translation quality and CPS, CPL and LPB conformity[12] for subtitling guideline compliance.

By looking at SubER scores of Table 1 and Table 2, we notice that our direct system outperforms not only the best direct system submitted last year but also the best cascade in constrained conditions. This superiority is consistent over all domains and language pairs. Also, focusing on Table 2, this is confirmed by all the translation quality metrics on test2023. In the unconstrained setting, instead, the results are less clear. Our cascade system achieves a lower (hence, better) SubER than the unconstrained submissions from last year on the en-es section of test2023 while, on the en-de section, it has a higher SubER than $AppTek_{23}^{cscd}$, in contrast with the definitely higher translation quality scores.

Back to the comparison between our direct constrained system and our cascade unconstrained solution, we notice consistent trends over all the evaluation sets (validation, test2023, test2024). The direct system achieves better scores on the TED domain, which is the only one covered by the training data allowed for the constrained setting, but falls behind by a large margin on the other two (ITV and PELOTON), especially on en-es. This result is not surprising as the unconstrained system has been trained on a wide range of domains and is therefore more robust to domain shifts. Regarding subtitle compliance, interesting trends emerge: the cascade system has higher CPL compliance (~+3% across all settings), while the direct system outperforms it in terms of CPS compliance (+6-12%). The latter aspect may be motivated by the direct access to the source audio of the direct system (which is also guided by the CTC module that directly maps the audio sequence to the textual output).

3.2 Subtitle Compression

The results for the subtitle compression task are reported in Table 4 in terms of BLEURT and CPS (as a measure of reading speed compliance). BLEURT results are computed in two ways, either considering the provided subtitles as references or by using the actual subtitle references. The former results serve as a proxy of translation quality, as well as a way to measure the distance between the original subtitles to be modified and the resulting modified ones (i.e. as an indicator of how radical the applied changes are). The latter ones, instead, provide real translation quality measurements. For the sake of discussion, the table includes the results of the `Baseline` as provided by the task organizers and those of an unsubmitted metric-oriented solution (`Del_articles`), besides those of our official primary (GPT) and contrastive submissions (`Del_all-func-wrds` and `Del_art/prep/adv`).

Overall, the scores for the two languages indicate different levels of difficulty but exhibit similar trends. Specifically, en-es appears to be an easier direction, as indicated by higher translation quality (BLEURT) and reading speed compliance scores (CPS) compared to en-de. Unsurprisingly, the **BLEURT scores computed against the provided original subtitles (i.e., vs. [1])** are significantly higher than those computed against the actual references (vs. [0]). This indicates the tendency of the proposed methods to apply rather conservative changes. This holds particularly for the metric-oriented approaches (`Del_*`), which are actually designed to do so. Still, the relatively high BLEURT results of the user-oriented approach (`GPT`) are a symptom of local and rather moderate changes, which likely do not suffer from major issues related to hallucinations and/or under-generation into too short subtitles. Regarding the **BLEURT scores computed against the actual subtitle references (i.e., vs. [0])**, the results drop significantly, attesting that a large quality gap between all methods and human subtitles still exists. Interestingly, however, the gap between metric and user-oriented approaches shrinks on en-es and even disappears on en-de, where `GPT` achieves results that are substantially equivalent to those of `Del_art/prep/adv`.

For both languages and evaluation conditions the higher conservativeness of metric-oriented approaches is not sufficient to yield acceptable CPS results. First, the least aggressive one (the unsubmitted `Del_articles`), which consistently achieves the highest BLEURT computed on the provided references, is definitely the worst one in terms of CPS. Second, also the other ones (our contrastive submissions `Del_art/prep/adv` and `Del_all-func-wrds`) attain lower reading speed conformity compared to the LLM-based user-oriented approach. Aimed to strike a balance between translation quality and CPS conformity, our

[12]Computed with the script provided by Papi et al. (2023a): `https://github.com/hlt-mt/FBK-fairseq/blob/master/examples/speech_to_text/scripts/subtitle_compliance.py`

id	Subtitles		de BLEURT↑ vs. [0]	de BLEURT↑ vs. [1]	de CPS↑	es BLEURT↑ vs. [0]	es BLEURT↑ vs. [1]	es CPS↑
0	`Reference`		-	-	86.47	-	-	89.98
1	`Provided`		.1946	-	60.25	.2136	-	69.97
2	`Baseline`		.1720	.7871	100.00	.1892	.8766	100.00
	method	submission						
3	`Del_articles`	`not submitted`	-	.9230	65.92	-	.9700	73.80
4	`Del_art/prep/adv`	`FBK contrastive2`	.1890	.9071	67.94	.2113	.9572	75.74
5	`Del_all-func-wrds`	`FBK contrastive1`	.1811	.8365	83.36	.2033	.9123	87.48
6	`GPT`	`FBK primary`	.1895	.8370	84.81	.2063	.9062	90.66

Table 4: Subtitle Compression results. For both languages, BLEURT scores are computed both against the reference subtitles ([0]) and the provided original subtitles ([1]).

primary submission (`GPT`) consistently achieves the best CPS scores (84.81 for en-de, 90.66 for en-es). Paired with the above observations about translation quality, these results suggest that LLM-based approaches to subtitle compression are a promising direction for future explorations.

The trade-off between BLEURT and CPS is further highlighted by the plot in Figure 2 where, between the two extremes represented by `Provided` ([1]) and `Baseline` ([2]) subtitles, the subtitles generated through metric-oriented strategies ([4] and [5]) are placed according to a nearly linear relationship. The exception are `GPT`'results which slightly deviate from this linear trend, as a confirmation of our intuition: generative, user-oriented strategies are capable to perform pinpointed text reductions to pursue CPS compliance without a catastrophic loss of the original subtitles' meaning.

Overall, our results indicate that, even though it is a sub-task of a very complex problem such as automatic subtitling, subtitle compression has its own difficulties. On the one hand, the generative approach based on LLMs is intuitively promising because, unlike rough trimming strategies that are incompatible with the user experience, it targets a compression that is respectful of the subtitles' semantic content. On the other hand, however, this approach faces the challenge of reformulating text material that is potentially error-prone and often does not come in the form of well-formed sentences but rather as text spans representing sentence portions or words spanning contiguous phrases. At least in the zero-shot prompting modality, the combination of these two aspects makes the task extremely challenging for LLMs. As a matter of fact, upon preliminary analysis of the generated compressions, LLMs often reveal a tendency to generate sentence-like outputs, attempting to "complete" their generations with hallucinated content, a behavior that can only be exacerbated in the presence of errors in the subtitle to be compressed. The opposite potential issue, represented by "over-compressing" the subtitle beyond the allowed number of characters, is rarely observed.

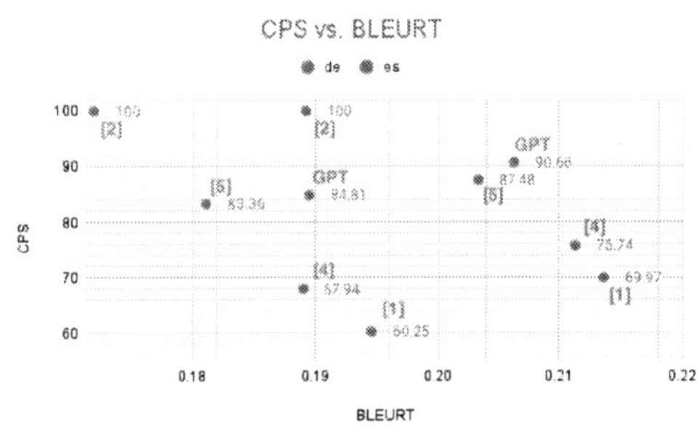

Figure 2: Scatter plot of compression results from Table 4 (BLEURT against the reference subtitles).

4 Conclusions

We presented the FBK's submissions to the Automatic Subtitling and Subtitle Compression tasks of the IWSLT 2024 Evaluation Campaign. For Automatic Subtitling, we proposed two systems: a direct model trained under constrained conditions and a cascade architecture integrating free-to-use components. Our direct model showcased superior performance compared to constrained direct and cascade submissions of the last year. The cascade solution proved competitive with top-performing unconstrained and fine-tuned 2023 runs. For Subtitle Compression, our primary submission exploits GPT in zero-shot prompting mode to shorten subtitles exceeding the reading speed limit of 21 CPS. While promising, this approach revealed the complexities of compressing out-of-context automatically generated sentence fragments, underscoring the necessity for further research in this area.

Acknowledgments

The work presented in this paper is co-funded by the European Union under the project *AI4Culture: An AI platform for the cultural heritage data space* (Action number 101100683). Marco Gaido is supported by the PNRR project FAIR - Future AI Research (PE00000013), under the NRRP MUR program funded by the NextGenerationEU. We acknowledge the CINECA award (MAGIS) under the ISCRA initiative, for the availability of high-performance computing resources and support.

References

Milind Agarwal, Sweta Agrawal, Antonios Anastasopoulos, Luisa Bentivogli, Ondřej Bojar, Claudia Borg, Marine Carpuat, Roldano Cattoni, Mauro Cettolo, Mingda Chen, William Chen, Khalid Choukri, Alexandra Chronopoulou, Anna Currey, Thierry Declerck, Qianqian Dong, Kevin Duh, Yannick Estève, Marcello Federico, Souhir Gahbiche, Barry Haddow, Benjamin Hsu, Phu Mon Htut, Hirofumi Inaguma, Dávid Javorský, John Judge, Yasumasa Kano, Tom Ko, Rishu Kumar, Pengwei Li, Xutai Ma, Prashant Mathur, Evgeny Matusov, Paul McNamee, John P. McCrae, Kenton Murray, Maria Nadejde, Satoshi Nakamura, Matteo Negri, Ha Nguyen, Jan Niehues, Xing Niu, Atul Kr. Ojha, John E. Ortega, Proyag Pal, Juan Pino, Lonneke van der Plas, Peter Polák, Elijah Rippeth, Elizabeth Salesky, Jiatong Shi, Matthias Sperber, Sebastian Stüker, Katsuhito Sudoh, Yun Tang, Brian Thompson, Kevin Tran, Marco Turchi, Alex Waibel, Mingxuan Wang, Shinji Watanabe, and Rodolfo Zevallos. 2023. FINDINGS OF THE IWSLT 2023 EVALUATION CAMPAIGN. In *Proceedings of the 20th International Conference on Spoken Language Translation (IWSLT 2023)*, pages 1–61, Toronto, Canada (in-person and online). Association for Computational Linguistics.

Belen Alastruey, Aleix Sant, Gerard I. Gállego, David Dale, and Marta R. Costa-jussà. 2023. Speechalign: a framework for speech translation alignment evaluation. *Preprint*, arXiv:2309.11585.

Aitor Álvarez, Carlos Mendes, Matteo Raffaelli, Tiago Luís, Sérgio Paulo, Nicola Piccinini, Haritz Arzelus, João Neto, Carlo Aliprandi, and Arantza Pozo. 2015. Automating live and batch subtitling of multimedia contents for several european languages. *Multimedia Tools and Applications*, 75:1–31.

Rosana Ardila, Megan Branson, Kelly Davis, Michael Kohler, Josh Meyer, Michael Henretty, Reuben Morais, Lindsay Saunders, Francis Tyers, and Gregor Weber. 2020. Common voice: A massively-multilingual speech corpus. In *Proceedings of the 12th Language Resources and Evaluation Conference*, pages 4218–4222, Marseille, France.

Parnia Bahar, Patrick Wilken, Javier Iranzo-Sánchez, Mattia Di Gangi, Evgeny Matusov, and Zoltán Tüske. 2023. Speech translation with style: AppTek's submissions to the IWSLT subtitling and formality tracks in 2023. In *Proceedings of the 20th International Conference on Spoken Language Translation (IWSLT 2023)*, pages 251–260, Toronto, Canada (in-person and online). Association for Computational Linguistics.

Łukasz Bogucki. 2004. The constraint of relevance in subtitling. *The Journal of Specialised Translation*.

Tom Brown, Benjamin Mann, Nick Ryder, Melanie Subbiah, Jared D Kaplan, Prafulla Dhariwal, Arvind Neelakantan, Pranav Shyam, Girish Sastry, Amanda Askell, et al. 2020. Language models are few-shot learners. *Advances in neural information processing systems*, 33:1877–1901.

Yun Chen, Yang Liu, Guanhua Chen, Xin Jiang, and Qun Liu. 2020. Accurate word alignment induction from neural machine translation. In *Proceedings of the 2020 Conference on Empirical Methods in Natural Language Processing (EMNLP)*, pages 566–576, Online.

Jorge Díaz Cintas and Aline Remael. 2021. *Subtitling: Concepts and Practices*. Translation practices explained. Routledge.

Marco Gaido, Mauro Cettolo, Matteo Negri, and Marco Turchi. 2021. CTC-based compression for direct speech translation. In *Proceedings of the 16th Conference of the European Chapter of the Association for Computational Linguistics: Main Volume*, pages 690–696, Online.

Marco Gaido, Sara Papi, Matteo Negri, Mauro Cettolo, and Luisa Bentivogli. 2024. SBAAM! Eliminating Transcript Dependency in Automatic Subtitling. In *Proceedings of the 62nd Annual Meeting of the Association for Computational Linguistics (Volume 1: Long Papers)*, Bangkok, Thailand.

Sarthak Garg, Stephan Peitz, Udhyakumar Nallasamy, and Matthias Paulik. 2019. Jointly learning to align and translate with transformer models. In *Proceedings of the 2019 Conference on Empirical Methods in Natural Language Processing and the 9th International Joint Conference on Natural Language Processing (EMNLP-IJCNLP)*, pages 4453–4462, Hong Kong, China.

Anmol Gulati, James Qin, Chung-Cheng Chiu, Niki Parmar, Yu Zhang, Jiahui Yu, Wei Han, Shibo Wang, Zhengdong Zhang, Yonghui Wu, and Ruoming Pang. 2020. Conformer: Convolution-augmented Transformer for Speech Recognition. In *Proc. Interspeech 2020*, pages 5036–5040.

François Hernandez, Vincent Nguyen, Sahar Ghannay, Natalia Tomashenko, and Yannick Estève. 2018. Tedlium 3: Twice as much data and corpus repartition for experiments on speaker adaptation. In *Speech and Computer*, pages 198–208, Cham.

Javier Iranzo-Sánchez, Joan Albert Silvestre-Cerdà, Javier Jorge, Nahuel Roselló, Adrià Giménez, Albert Sanchis, Jorge Civera, and Alfons Juan. 2020. Europarl-st: A multilingual corpus for speech translation of parliamentary debates. In *ICASSP 2020 - 2020 IEEE International Conference on Acoustics, Speech and Signal Processing (ICASSP)*, pages 8229–8233.

Alina Karakanta, Matteo Negri, and Marco Turchi. 2020. MuST-cinema: a speech-to-subtitles corpus. In *Proc. of the 12th Language Resources and Evaluation Conference*, pages 3727–3734, Marseille, France.

Bilal Khalaf. 2016. An introduction to subtitling: Challenges and strategies. *International Journal of Comparative Literature and Translation Studies*, 3.

Taku Kudo. 2018. Subword regularization: Improving neural network translation models with multiple subword candidates. In *Proceedings of the 56th Annual Meeting of the Association for Computational Linguistics (Volume 1: Long Papers)*, pages 66–75, Melbourne, Australia. Association for Computational Linguistics.

OpenAI. 2024. Gpt-4 technical report. *Preprint*, arXiv:2303.08774.

Vassil Panayotov, Guoguo Chen, Daniel Povey, and Sanjeev Khudanpur. 2015. Librispeech: An asr corpus based on public domain audio books. In *2015 IEEE International Conference on Acoustics, Speech and Signal Processing (ICASSP)*, pages 5206–5210.

Sara Papi, Marco Gaido, Alina Karakanta, Mauro Cettolo, Matteo Negri, and Marco Turchi. 2023a. Direct Speech Translation for Automatic Subtitling. *Transactions of the Association for Computational Linguistics*, 11:1355–1376.

Sara Papi, Marco Gaido, and Matteo Negri. 2023b. Direct models for simultaneous translation and automatic subtitling: FBK@IWSLT2023. In *Proceedings of the 20th International Conference on Spoken Language Translation (IWSLT 2023)*, pages 159–168, Toronto, Canada (in-person and online). Association for Computational Linguistics.

Sara Papi, Marco Gaido, Andrea Pilzer, and Matteo Negri. 2024. When Good and Reproducible Results are a Giant with Feet of Clay: The Importance of Software Quality in NLP. In *Proceedings of the 62nd Annual Meeting of the Association for Computational Linguistics (Volume 1: Long Papers)*, Bangkok, Thailand.

Sara Papi, Alina Karakanta, Matteo Negri, and Marco Turchi. 2022. Dodging the data bottleneck: Automatic subtitling with automatically segmented ST corpora. In *Proceedings of the 2nd Conference of the Asia-Pacific Chapter of the Association for Computational Linguistics and the 12th International Joint Conference on Natural Language Processing (Volume 2: Short Papers)*, pages 480–487, Online only.

Sara Papi, Matteo Negri, and Marco Turchi. 2023c. Attention as a guide for simultaneous speech translation. In *Proceedings of the 61st Annual Meeting of the Association for Computational Linguistics (Volume 1: Long Papers)*, pages 13340–13356, Toronto, Canada. Association for Computational Linguistics.

Kishore Papineni, Salim Roukos, Todd Ward, and Wei-Jing Zhu. 2002. Bleu: a method for automatic evaluation of machine translation. In *Proceedings of the 40th Annual Meeting of the Association for Computational Linguistics*, pages 311–318, Philadelphia, Pennsylvania, USA. Association for Computational Linguistics.

Simone Perone. 2023. Matesub: The translated subtitling tool at the IWSLT2023 subtitling task. In *Proceedings of the 20th International Conference on Spoken Language Translation (IWSLT 2023)*, pages 461–464, Toronto, Canada (in-person and online). Association for Computational Linguistics.

Maja Popović. 2015. chrF: character n-gram F-score for automatic MT evaluation. In *Proceedings of the Tenth Workshop on Statistical Machine Translation*, pages 392–395, Lisbon, Portugal. Association for Computational Linguistics.

Matthew Snover, Bonnie Dorr, Rich Schwartz, Linnea Micciulla, and John Makhoul. 2006. A study of translation edit rate with targeted human annotation. In *Proceedings of the 7th Conference of the Association for Machine Translation in the Americas: Technical Papers*, pages 223–231, Cambridge, Massachusetts, USA. Association for Machine Translation in the Americas.

Christian Szegedy, Vincent Vanhoucke, Sergey Ioffe, Jon Shlens, and Zbigniew Wojna. 2016. Rethinking the inception architecture for computer vision. In *Proceedings of the IEEE conference on computer vision and pattern recognition*, pages 2818–2826.

Gongbo Tang, Rico Sennrich, and Joakim Nivre. 2018. An analysis of attention mechanisms: The case of word sense disambiguation in neural machine translation. In *Proceedings of the Third Conference on Machine Translation: Research Papers*, pages 26–35, Brussels, Belgium.

Ioannis Tsiamas, Gerard I. Gállego, José A. R. Fonollosa, and Marta R. Costa-jussà. 2022. SHAS: Approaching optimal Segmentation for End-to-End Speech Translation. *Preprint*, arXiv:2202.04774.

Ashish Vaswani, Noam Shazeer, Niki Parmar, Jakob Uszkoreit, Llion Jones, Aidan N Gomez, Ł ukasz Kaiser, and Illia Polosukhin. 2017. Attention is all you need. In *Advances in Neural Information Processing Systems*, volume 30.

Kaisa Vitikainen and Maarit Koponen. 2021. Automation in the intralingual subtitling process: Exploring productivity and user experience. *Journal of Audiovisual Translation*, 4(3):44–65.

Changhan Wang, Morgane Riviere, Ann Lee, Anne Wu, Chaitanya Talnikar, Daniel Haziza, Mary Williamson, Juan Pino, and Emmanuel Dupoux. 2021. VoxPopuli: A large-scale multilingual speech corpus for representation learning, semi-supervised learning and interpretation. In *Proceedings of the 59th Annual Meeting of the Association for Computational Linguistics and the 11th International Joint Conference on Natural Language Processing (Volume 1: Long Papers)*, pages 993–1003, Online.

Changhan Wang, Anne Wu, and Juan Pino. 2020. Covost 2: A massively multilingual speech-to-text translation corpus. *Preprint*, arXiv:2007.10310.

Shinji Watanabe, Takaaki Hori, Suyoun Kim, John R. Hershey, and Tomoki Hayashi. 2017. Hybrid ctc/attention architecture for end-to-end speech recognition. *IEEE Journal of Selected Topics in Signal Processing*, 11(8):1240–1253.

Patrick Wilken, Panayota Georgakopoulou, and Evgeny Matusov. 2022. SubER - a metric for automatic evaluation of subtitle quality. In *Proceedings of the 19th International Conference on Spoken Language Translation (IWSLT 2022)*, pages 1–10, Dublin, Ireland (in-person and online).

Brian Yan, Siddharth Dalmia, Yosuke Higuchi, Graham Neubig, Florian Metze, Alan W Black, and Shinji Watanabe. 2023. CTC alignments improve autoregressive translation. In *Proceedings of the 17th Conference of the European Chapter of the Association for Computational Linguistics*, pages 1623–1639, Dubrovnik, Croatia.

Thomas Zenkel, Joern Wuebker, and John DeNero. 2019. Adding interpretable attention to neural translation models improves word alignment. *arXiv preprint arXiv:1901.11359*.

UM IWSLT 2024 Low-Resource Speech Translation: Combining Maltese and North Levantine Arabic

Sara Nabhani **Aiden Williams** **Miftahul Jannat**

Kate Rebecca Belcher **Melanie Galea** **Anna Taylor**

Kurt Micallef **Claudia Borg**

Department of Artificial Intelligence, University of Malta
{sara.nabhani.23, aiden.williams.19, miftahul.jannat.23, kate.belcher.23, melanie.galea.20, anna.taylor.23, kurt.micallef, claudia.borg}@um.edu.mt

Abstract

The IWSLT low-resource track encourages innovation in the field of speech translation, particularly in data-scarce conditions. This paper details our submission for the IWSLT 2024 low-resource track shared task for Maltese-English and North Levantine Arabic-English spoken language translation using an unconstrained pipeline approach. Using language models, we improve ASR performance by correcting the produced output. We present a 2 step approach for MT using data from external sources showing improvements over baseline systems. We also explore transliteration as a means to further augment MT data and exploit the cross-lingual similarities between Maltese and Arabic.

1 Introduction

There are a variety of challenges inherent in spoken language translation for low-resource languages. By definition, these languages have very limited data available to use for natural language processing (NLP) tasks. The majority of current work on NLP targets just 20 out of the approximately 7,000 languages used worldwide, leading to a significant gap in research and negative impacts on excluded speech communities (Joshi et al., 2020; Magueresse et al., 2020). While most machine learning tasks are performed using vast amounts of data, models for low-resource languages must be adapted to work with less data or other strategies must be employed to augment the existing data.

In this paper, we present our submission for the 2024 IWSLT low-resource shared task. Concretely, we submit two systems for speech translation to English, from Maltese and North Levantine Arabic. The main motivation for focusing on these two languages is their similarity to one another which we aim to exploit to improve the performance of our pipeline speech translation system.

As a well-known case of diglossia, the Arabic language has a notable distinction between the formal variety used in written communication, political speech, and the educational system – known as Modern Standard Arabic (MSA) – and the informal varieties primarily used in spoken communication – collectively referred to as Dialectal Arabic (DA). These dialects exhibit considerable diversity influenced by geographical and socio-economic factors, diverging significantly from MSA in phonology, morphology, lexicon, and syntax (Zbib et al., 2012). On the other hand, Maltese is a Semitic language derived from Siculo-Arabic (Borg and Azzopardi-Alexander, 1997), with a notable mutual intelligibility with Tunisian DA (Čéplö et al., 2016). Its evolution independently from the Arab world – particularly its substantial influence from Italian and English and its use of a modified Latin alphabet – makes it a distinct language and not an Arabic dialect.

We split the task of spoken language translation into two sequential tasks consisting of automatic speech recognition (ASR) and machine translation (MT). This process transforms speech in a low-resource language into text in a high-resource language, namely English for this shared task. At the same time, splitting the task into ASR and MT allows us to exploit existing multilingual models and source larger corpora for each sub-task to improve their performance in the target language. All of our code is made publicly available.[1]

2 Related Work

In order to examine past approaches to low-resource spoken language translation, this literature review includes an overview of previous IWSLT low-resource track submissions and our ASR and

[1] https://github.com/saranabhani/iwslt-2024-um-pipeline

Proceedings of the 21st International Conference on Spoken Language Translation (IWSLT 2024), pages 145–155
August 15-16, 2024 ©2024 Association for Computational Linguistics

MT systems as well as our innovative approach to data augmentation through transliteration.

2.1 Previous IWSLT Low-Resource Track Approaches

For the 2023 IWSLT Shared Task (Agarwal et al., 2023), Williams et al. (2023a) submitted five systems for Maltese-English spoken language translation as part of the low-resource track in the unconstrained setting. This marked the first time that Maltese was included in the IWSLT low-resource track campaign, with this submission being the sole entry in its category, making it a unique approach in this context. All of the systems employed a pipeline approach, making use of XLS-R (Conneau et al., 2020) for ASR and mBART-50 (Tang et al., 2020) for MT, fine-tuned using various training data. In their primary approach, their model was exclusively fine-tuned on Maltese data resulting in a BLEU score of 0.6. Contrasting with the Maltese-only model, they explored four alternative approaches by incorporating corpora from Arabic, French, Italian, or a combination of all three in conjunction with the Maltese data. The most successful configuration, with a BLEU score of 0.7, was achieved by fine-tuning the ASR system on a combination of Maltese data with 50 hours each of Arabic, French, and Italian data from the CommonVoice speech corpus (Williams et al., 2023a).

While our submission utilizes a pipeline approach, the alternative is an end-to-end system where a single neural network is trained to jointly perform both ASR and MT (Sethiya and Maurya, 2023). This approach offers several advantages by significantly reducing training time, allowing for quicker development of models, and necessitating lower memory resources compared to other methods, which can be particularly beneficial for environments with constraints on computational processing power. Additionally, by integrating ASR and MT into an end-to-end system, it mitigates the risk of errors propagating from the ASR output to the MT input, which is a common problem in pipeline systems (Sethiya and Maurya, 2023). However, speech translation systems that operate end-to-end require parallel data containing both speech audio signals on the source side and translated transcriptions on the target side. Acquiring such parallel data can pose challenges, even for languages with readily available components for pipeline-based systems. Consequently, the pipeline approach is often deemed more feasible and realistic (Alves et al., 2020).

For the 2023 IWSLT Quechua-Spanish speech translation task in the low-resource track, E. Ortega et al. (2023) utilized a variety of systems both constrained and unconstrained, with one of the few pipeline-based methods submitted for this task. The primary constrained system employed a direct speech translation model based on the Fairseq speech-to-text (S2T) framework (Wang et al., 2020). To create audio representations, this system made use of log mel-scale filter banks for features and a transformer for translations. With a BLEU score of 1.25, their primary system surpassed the performance of the pipeline alternatives in the constrained setting. On the other hand, the primary unconstrained system employed a pipeline approach on the additional 60 hours of speech data made available, where speech transcriptions were generated using a pretrained XLS-R based multilingual model augmented by a fine-tuned language model (Park et al., 2019), and translations were generated using the fine-tuned Flores-101 model from Guzmán et al. (2019). The unconstrained pipeline approach performed much better with a BLEU score of 15.36 for the primary model. Their findings reveal that the use of a pretrained language model with fine-tuning is necessary for cascaded spoken language translation (ASR and MT combined in a pipeline) in low-resource scenarios for Quechua to Spanish translation. This work further demonstrates the immense value of access to additional data, which yielded nearly 14 BLEU points improvement for the unconstrained task when applied to both ASR and MT systems compared to the limited data used in the constrained setting (E. Ortega et al., 2023). Accordingly, our approach also utilizes an unconstrained pipeline of an XLS-R-based ASR model and a fine-tuned pretrained MT model considering it was found to have the best results for this submission.

2.2 Automatic Speech Recognition

Due to their extensive multilingual pretraining, Wav2Vec 2.0 models (Baevski et al., 2020) are able to acquire and utilize cross-lingual speech representations to improve accuracy for ASR. The XLS-R model presented by Babu et al. (2022) underwent pretraining of Wav2Vec 2.0 models for as many as 128 distinct languages including Maltese, using 436,000 hours of unannotated speech data from diverse sources including the Mozilla Common Voice (Ardila et al., 2020), BABEL (Gales et al., 2014), and Multilingual LibriSpeech (Pratap et al., 2020) speech corpora. Specifically, this system incorporates 9,000 hours of unannotated Maltese speech sourced from the Voxpopuli corpus (Wang et al., 2021). Notably, the largest model is pretrained using a cumulative total of 56 thousand hours of speech data (Conneau et al., 2020). This represents an increase in both the amount of data and the languages covered.

A common practice in the field of ASR is to use a language model to reduce errors in the generated transcription. This technique was used in the development of Wav2Vec 2.0 (Baevski et al., 2020) and Deepspeech 2 (Amodei et al., 2016). Leveraging an external language model trained on domain-specific textual data has the potential to increase the accuracy of ASR systems by minimizing errors in content.

Moreover, due to the scarcity of high-quality labelled data in DA, the models based on XLS-R emerge as optimal solutions for leveraging available datasets and adapting ASR to distinct Arabic variants through fine-tuning, as highlighted by Waheed et al. (2023) in their work on VoxArabica. These models not only capitalize on existing resources but also offer the adaptability to accommodate the nuances of various Arabic dialects, thus addressing the challenges associated with the limited availability of labelled data for DA.

2.3 Machine Translation

Past approaches to multilingual neural machine translation treat it as a sequence-to-sequence task, where an encoder is utilized to process an input sequence in the source language and a decoder is used to generate the corresponding output sequence in the target language. With massively multilingual translation, a model undergoes training on multiple translation directions simultaneously. While this approach can facilitate advantageous cross-lingual transfer among related languages, it also carries the risk of amplifying interference between unrelated languages.

In this work we make use of the NLLB model (NLLB Team et al., 2022) for MT. It uses a single SentencePiece model to tokenize the text sequences by training it across all languages using a total of 100M sentences sampled from primary bitext data. For equitable representation of low-resource languages, high-resource ones are downsampled and low-resource ones are upsampled, using a sampling temperature of five. The resulting vocabulary size of the trained SentencePiece model is 256,000, ensuring comprehensive representation across the diverse range of supported languages. The choice of this model is highly motivated by its inclusion of a large number of languages, notably Maltese and North Levantine Arabic (NLLB Team et al., 2022).

2.4 Transliteration

From a simplified linguistic perspective, Maltese can be regarded as a variant of Arabic with a significant level of code-switching to Italian and a modified Latin alphabet. Past work suggests that transliterating Maltese could serve as a viable strategy for benefiting from cross-lingual similarities with Arabic (Micallef et al., 2023). In the approach taken by Micallef et al. (2023), the transliteration process involves two main steps: mapping and ranking. Initially, Maltese text tokens and characters in Latin script are mapped to one or more corresponding alternatives in Arabic script. Subsequently, a separate component either ranks these alternatives or employs a deterministic hard-coded baseline.

This approach is further developed in Micallef et al. (2024) by taking a mixed pipeline and integrating a combination of transliteration and translation based on the etymology of Maltese words. This is motivated by the results of Micallef et al. (2023), where the advantages of transliterating Arabic-origin words were limited by the corresponding disadvantages of distancing Italian and English-origin words from their etymological source through transliteration. A mixed pipeline gave promising results on downstream tasks, establishing the technique as a competitive approach for Maltese NLP tasks.

3 Automatic Speech Recognition

3.1 Data Sources

For Maltese, we use the training sets provided by the shared task namely Common Voice 7.0 (Ardila et al., 2020) and MASRI (Hernandez Mena et al., 2020). The speech corpus is made up of around 50 hours of Maltese speech data.

To train our Arabic ASR system, we opted to use a 50-hour subset from the Common Voice project (Ardila et al., 2020), as this would contain roughly the same data that we used for Maltese ASR. While a training set for North Levantine Arabic would have been preferred, there was no data provided for the shared task, nor were we able to find ASR data for North Levantine Arabic. Furthermore, even though a Tunisian Arabic training set could be used, we did not make use of this to train, since North Levantine Arabic is more closely related to MSA than Tunisian Arabic (Kwaik et al., 2018).

3.2 Approach

For the ASR component of the pipeline, we continue to build off of previous work done for both DA and Maltese ASR. As concluded in Williams et al. (2023b), fine-tuning the Wav2Vec 2.0 XLS-R model (Babu et al., 2022) with around 50 hours of Maltese speech data produces the best Maltese ASR model to date and was used in the IWSLT 2023 submission by Williams et al. (2023a). A similar XLS-R based ASR model is employed for DA by leveraging data for MSA.

In addition, for Maltese, we incorporate language models with the ASR system to get more accurate speech transcriptions. For this we use n-gram models built using the KenLM language modelling toolkit (Heafield, 2011), which assign scores to sequences of words. This aids in selecting the best candidates through beam search for improved ASR output. We use KenLM mainly as it has been used for other state-of-the-art ASR publications as well as in previous work on Maltese in particular. We make use of the 6-gram word-level LM produced by Hernandez Mena et al. (2020) as a baseline to compare our own KenLM n-gram models which was trained on Korpus Malti v3.0 (Gatt and Čéplö, 2013). We produce 2 additional word-level n-gram language models for Maltese: a 3-gram and a 4-gram, both trained on the Korpus Malti v4.1 Shuffled train dataset[2] (Micallef et al., 2022). We note that Korpus Malti v4 used here is substantially larger than the v3 used for the 6-gram baseline.

3.3 Results and Discussion

Table 1 shows the WER score for all languages considered on the shared task development set. For both Maltese and North Levantine Arabic, a single model is trained, but for Maltese we show the models' performance without adding a language model as well as incorporating each language model.

For Maltese, we see that all models perform comparably, but models using a language model give better results. In addition, when using the 3-gram and 4-gram models, these give better results than the 6-gram model, which we attribute to the larger data used to train the former models.

[2] https://huggingface.co/datasets/MLRS/korpus_malti/tree/4.1.0/data/shuffled

Data	Language Model	Dev Set
		WER ↓
CV+MASRI	-	0.12
CV+MASRI	3-gram	**0.10**
CV+MASRI	4-gram	**0.10**
CV+MASRI	6-gram	0.11

(a) Maltese

Data	Language Model	Dev Set
		WER ↓
Common Voice	-	**1.08**

(b) North Levantine Arabic

Table 1: Speech Recognition Results

The overall performance of our Arabic approach was limited by the lack of North Levantine Arabic speech data, which severely impacted the accuracy of the ASR system when tested on Levantine data. We provide a brief qualitative error analysis of the Arabic ASR outputs to highlight this.

We looked at a sample of the ASR output generated from North Levantine Arabic audio data using our model trained on MSA. The analysis of specific examples reveals various errors that significantly impact the usability of the ASR system for Levantine speech recognition. Table 2 shows a few examples of the output, highlighting various inconsistencies with the reference text.

Phonetic errors were a common issue across the examples. For instance, in Sample 2c, the system outputted “سأدمت” for “فقدمت” (I applied) likely due to the similar pronunciation of “س” and “ف” at the start of word, and the dialect-specific pronunciation of “ق” (qaf) as a glottal stop [ʔ] in Levantine Arabic, which is similar to “ء” (hamza). Additionally, in Sample 2a, segmentation errors featured prominently, as seen where “هييكان” should have been segmented into “هي كان” (she was). In Sample 2d, “تأريبالنامبل شتشويالأمور” exemplifies improper segmentation, where “شوي” (a little) and “الامور” (matters) were incorrectly merged as “شتشويالأمور".

Lexical errors were evident, particularly in Sample 2b, where “التشيكيين” (the Czechs) was incorrectly outputted as “ تشكيم", missing both the prefix “ال” (the) and misinterpreting the main noun due to a phonetic mix-up of “م” and “ن”, which are both nasal consonants. Phonetic confusion also occurred

Reference	تشغيل	مسابقة	اسمها	كان	هي
Transcription	[tʃaɣi:l]	[musa:baʔat]	[ʔisme:ha]	[ka:n]	[hiyye]
ASR Output	تشغيل	مثمة	اسما	هييكان	
Transcription	[tʃaɣi:l]	[maθmat]	[ʔisma]	[hiyyeka:n]	

(a)

Reference	التشيكيين	عن	احكي	راح	مش
Transcription	[ittʃi:kijji:n]	[ʕan]	[ʔaħki]	[ra:ħ]	[miʃ]
ASR Output	تشكيم	عن	مرحك		
Transcription	[tʃaki:m]	[ʕan]	[marħak]		

(b)

Reference	عليها	فقدمت
Transcription	[ʕalejha]	[faqaddamat]
ASR Output	علي	سأدمت
Transcription	[ʕali]	[saʔaddamat]

(c)

Reference	سوريـا	في	الأمور	شوي	بلشت	تقريبا	ما
Transcription	[su:rja]	[fi:]	[ilʔumu:r]	[ʃwayy]	[ballaʃat]	[taqri:ban]	[ma]
ASR Output	سوريـة	بي	تأريبالنمبل	شتشويالأمور			ما
Transcription	[su:rja]	[bi:]	[taʔri:ba:lnmbal]	[ʃatʃwa:ilʔumu:r]			[ma]

(d)

Table 2: Reference transcription samples compared to the system output produced by our ASR system

in Sample 2d, where "في [fi:]" (in) was replaced with "بي [bi:]". In the case of "سوريا" (Syria), the ASR output was "سورية", only differing by the final character. These two characters have the same pronunciation in word-final position, so the difference is just orthographic.

The analysis revealed that the Character Error Rate (CER) was consistently better than the Word Error Rate (WER), highlighting that while individual characters are often recognized correctly, the system struggles to assemble these into correct word forms. This indicates foundational competence at the character level but significant challenges in managing the complexity of word formation, especially considering the morphological and contextual nuances of North Levantine Arabic.

Whilst some character-level errors seem to be due to similar phonetic characteristics of different characters, it is clear that multiple errors can be attributed to Levantine-specific dialectal differences, most prominently the "ق" (qaf) and "ء" (hamza) distinction. These character-level errors impact word-level recognition and subsequent performance on the downstream machine translation task.

The prevalence of errors due to dialectal differences underscores the need to integrate Levantine-specific training data and develop a dedicated language model to handle the nuances brought by dialectal variations.

4 Machine Translation

4.1 Data Sources

To train our translation models we make use of a variety of sources for parallel data including those provided for the shared task as well as others which we could find. The datasets used are summarized in Table 3.

To train our Maltese translation model, we used a combined dataset of Common Voice (CV) (Ardila et al., 2020) and MASRI project (Hernandez Mena et al., 2020) (henceforth referred to as CV+MASRI), both of which were the datasets provided officially for the shared task. In addition, we also used OPUS-100, which is a comprehensive English-focused dataset (Zhang et al., 2020; Tiedemann, 2012). The dataset consists of 100 languages and English is common in every 99 translated language pairs. We chose this dataset because of its vastness, especially considering it offered 1M parallel sentences for the English and Maltese pair. We preprocessed the data to drop any data points that were empty as well as duplicate instances.

For our Arabic translation systems, we utilized a range of datasets. Specifically, we used the North Levantine (APC)-MSA-English textual data provided for the task (Sellat et al., 2023), along with the IWSLT 2022 Tunisian Arabic (AEB) speech translation data (Anastasopoulos et al., 2022). Additionally, the MSA data, which was included with both the Tunisian and Levantine datasets, was also used. However, since the size of this data was miniscule, we also incorporated the Arab-Acquis MSA-English parallel data (Habash et al., 2017). To further augment the Arabic data, we also incorporated the CV+MASRI Maltese dataset, which was transliterated to match the script of our primary data as detailed in Section 4.2 (referred to as MLT_{ARA}). We merged datasets from the same dialect or language obtained from multiple sources and shuffled them to ensure diversity and randomness in our training process.

Since the speech transcriptions do not produce casing and punctuation information, and the evaluation for the shared task also ignores these features, we preprocess all translation data as such. For both

Dataset	Train Size	Validation Size
CV	3,773	1,235
MASRI	4,811	648
CV+MASRI	8,584	1,883
OPUS-100	672,196	-

(a) Maltese Model

Language/Dialect	Train Size	Validation Size
APC	99,519	21,081
AEB	173,612	-
MSA	133,074	-
MLT$_{\text{ARA}}$	8,886	1,883

(b) Arabic Model

Table 3: Data used to train the MT models and size in number of sentences

languages, preprocessing included text normalization such as converting to lowercase and removing punctuation, while retaining hyphens and apostrophes for Maltese datasets, as these characters hold linguistic significance in Maltese. In addition, for Arabic we also remove diacritics.

4.2 Transliteration

Following Micallef et al. (2023, 2024), we explored integrating transliteration of Maltese into Arabic script, due to the close relationship between Maltese and Arabic as Semitic languages. We took inspiration from this approach to supplement the data used for training the Arabic Machine Translation system. Since Micallef et al. (2024) saw more promising results when using a mixed pipeline of transliteration, that involved transliterating Maltese words of Arabic origin and translating the other words, we continue with this mixed approach. We utilize the etymology model and mapping systems from Micallef et al. (2024). Specifically, we follow the $\texttt{X}_{\texttt{ara}}$/$\texttt{T}_{\texttt{ara}}$ pipeline, which transliterates tokens of Arabic-origin and symbols, translating everything else to Arabic.

However, we make certain modifications to this to better suit our approach. Firstly, we modify the translation component by swapping out the precomputed word translations from Google Translate with a pretrained NLLB model (NLLB Team et al., 2022), as extracting translations using Google Translate was too expensive, especially considering the different outputs produced by the ASR while experimenting. Translation is performed into Tunisian Arabic (AEB) instead of MSA, using English as a pivot language. The reason for doing this is that translating through English generally yields better results rather than going directly to Arabic, due to the larger availability of parallel data, and this is also observed empirically in Micallef et al. (2024).

Secondly, we merge tokens to more closely reflect the way in which Arabic is written, reducing the signals from Maltese tokenization. For example, "u il-kelma" (English 'and the word'), are written together in Arabic script as one word, "والكلمة", where "و" is the conjunction corresponding to "u" (and), "ال" is the definite article corresponding to "il-" (the), and the rest of the word corresponds to "kelma" (word). The annotation for such token mappings from Micallef et al. (2023), includes special markers indicating that such words would be merged in Arabic, so given the 3 tokens *u*, *il-*, and *kelma*, the system would initially output و+, ال+, and كلمة, which we merge into a single word. While Micallef et al. (2023, 2024) ignore this signal as they mostly deal with token tagging tasks, we use this signal to merge words. Note that using this method, punctuation symbols are still space separated, but since the data is preprocessed to remove such symbols, this is not an issue in our case.

We applied the transliteration pipeline to the Maltese datasets provided for the shared task (CV+MASRI). The training dataset provided additional data for training the Arabic MT model. In addition to the data augmentation benefit of integrating transliterated Maltese (henceforth referred to as MLT$_{\text{ARA}}$) for Arabic-English MT, this also increases the cross-lingual capacities of our Arabic MT model, allowing for the evaluation of MLT$_{\text{ARA}}$ ASR outputs using the Arabic MT model.

4.3 Approach

We explored various machine translation (MT) systems for translating North Levantine Arabic and Maltese into English. Initially, we established a baseline by fine-tuning the NLLB 1.3B model[3] (NLLB Team et al., 2022) on the shared task data, specifically on the CV+MASRI dataset for Maltese and the AEB dataset for Arabic.

Subsequently, we experimented with different fine-tuning strategies. We first attempted a two-

[3]`https://huggingface.co/facebook/nllb-200-1.3B`

Fine-Tuning Data		Dev Set
Stage 1	Stage 2	BLEU ↑
-	CV+MASRI	60.3
OPUS-100	-	37.6
OPUS-100	CV+MASRI	**60.6**
MSA	APC+AEB+MLT$_{ARA}$	37.0

(a) Maltese

Fine-Tuning Data		Dev Set
Stage 1	Stage 2	BLEU ↑
-	APC	34.3
MSA	APC	**39.5**
MSA	APC+AEB	37.6
MSA	APC+AEB+MLT$_{ARA}$	37.4

(b) Levantine Arabic

Table 4: Machine Translations Results

stage fine-tuning process where we fine-tune with a large dataset from a different domain or dialect. For the first stage, we considered the OPUS-100 data for the Maltese model and the MSA data for the Arabic model, while the second stage included the same data used for the baseline for both languages. Additionally, for the Arabic we tested fine-tuning with a mix of Levantine (APC) and Tunisian (AEB) data, as well as a combination of Levantine (APC), Tunisian (AEB), and transliterated Maltese (MLT$_{ARA}$) data. The training on MLT$_{ARA}$, allows us to evaluate this system on both the Maltese and North Levantine development sets.

The same hyperparameters were applied across both MT systems: a learning rate of 2e-5, and a weight decay of 0.01. The training was conducted over three epochs.

4.4 Results and Discussion

Table 4 reports the BLEU scores of the Maltese and Arabic models on the transcriptions having reference translations from the respective development sets for Maltese and North Levantine Arabic.

The results for Maltese are reported in Table 4a. We see that fine-tuning using OPUS-100 only, is detrimental compared to the baseline system trained only on CV+MASRI. However, including both OPUS-100 and CV+MASRI yields the best performance. Furthermore, when evaluating the Arabic model trained on transliterated Maltese, in addition to other Arabic data, we observe that it is the worst-performing model. However, the performance is quite comparable to that obtained for the model fine-tuned only on OPUS-100.

Table 4b shows the performance of each of the experimented machine translation systems on the APC validation set. Among the experimented methods, the best performance on the North Levantine Arabic development set was achieved using the two-stage fine-tuning process that started with MSA data followed by Levantine data.

An important observation that arose from our experimentation was the impact of adding MLT$_{ARA}$ data to the training of the Arabic MT system. We can see that the system fine-tuned firstly on MSA data and subsequently on APC, AEB, and MLT$_{ARA}$ gave very competitive results for Arabic MT, with a difference in dev performance of just 0.2 BLEU compared to the same system without MLT$_{ARA}$ data. By comparison, the same system performed comparably to Arabic on the Maltese dev set (after being transliterated) with a BLEU of 37.0. Whilst the machine translation systems fine-tuned specifically for Maltese still significantly outperformed the Arabic system fine-tuned with MLT$_{ARA}$ data, we note that adding MLT$_{ARA}$ data in the fine-tuning of Arabic MT systems can vastly improve the cross-lingual capacity of the model, with substantial benefits to the performance on Maltese, and very little impact on the MT performance for Arabic.

5 Speech Translation Pipeline

Following our evaluation on individual tasks in Sections 3 and 4, we now combine both systems by first getting the transcription using an ASR system and then passing this transcription through the MT system to get the translation. The best-performing ASR and MT systems on our validation sets were selected for the pipelines.

For Maltese, we only choose the MT system trained with the 2 stage training, OPUS-100+CV+MASRI (which we refer to as MLT$_{LAT}$) and combine it with the ASR systems with the 3-gram, 4-gram, and 6-gram models, to compose our Primary, Contrastive 1, and Contrastive 2 systems, respectively. For North Levantine Arabic, we use the only trained model for ASR, paired with all 3 MT systems which made use of 2 stage training, namely MSA+APC+AEB, MSA+APC+AEB+MLT$_{ARA}$, and MSA+APC, to compose our Primary, Contrastive 1, and Contrastive 2 systems, respectively. Table 5 summarises the results obtained with these pipelines on the development and testing sets, on ASR only and Speech Translation (ASR+MT). For the Arabic test

Pipeline	ASR System	MT System	Dataset	Dev Set		Test Set	
				WER ↓	BLEU ↑	WER ↓	BLEU ↑
Primary	3-gram	MLT_{LAT}	CV	0.098	**58.4**	0.094	**60.9**
			MASRI	0.239	**42.9**	**0.233**	**43.9**
			CV+MASRI	**0.10**	**52.1**	**0.143**	**52.4**
Contrastive 1	4-gram	MLT_{LAT}	CV	0.097	**58.4**	0.094	**60.9**
			MASRI	0.239	**42.9**	**0.233**	**43.9**
			CV+MASRI	**0.10**	**52.1**	**0.143**	**52.4**
Contrastive 2	6-gram	MLT_{LAT}	CV	**0.096**	58.3	**0.093**	**60.9**
			MASRI	**0.238**	42.7	0.234	43.7
			CV+MASRI	0.11	51.9	**0.143**	52.3

(a) Maltese

Pipeline	ASR System	MT System	Dev Set		Test Set		
			WER ↓	BLEU ↑	BLEU ↑	COMET ↑	ChrF ↑
Primary	Common Voice	MSA+APC+AEB	**1.08**	**5.0**	4.74	53.69	24.10
Contrastive 1	Common Voice	MSA+APC+AEB+MLT_{ARA}	**1.08**	4.8	**5.09**	**53.78**	**24.50**
Contrastive 2	Common Voice	MSA+APC	**1.08**	3.7	3.53	51.96	21.56

(b) North Levantine Arabic

Table 5: Speech Translation Pipeline Results

set, only Speech Translation results were provided.

As seen in Table 5a, all Maltese systems perform competitively with each other. Similar to the findings for the ASR system reported in Section 3, the Primary and Contrastive 1 systems get the best results with the 3-gram and 4-gram models, and the Contrastive 2 system is slightly behind with the 6-gram model. The best systems obtain 52.4 BLEU on the test set.

The results on the North Levantine Arabic data are shown in Table 5b. The systems all achieve low overall BLEU scores, due to the poor performance on ASR as outlined in Section 3. With a pipeline, we observe that using APC data only in addition to MSA performs the worst (Contrastive 2), and that adding data from other languages and dialects we achieve better BLEU scores with the Primary and Contrastive 1 systems.

6 Conclusion

Overall, this paper presented our findings for Maltese and North Levantine Arabic spoken language translation into English with a pipeline system in the unconstrained setting for the 2024 IWSLT low-resource track shared task. For our approach we fine-tune a Wav2Vec 2.0 XLS-R model for ASR, and an NLLB model for MT. We enhance the ASR model by correcting the outputs with a language model. Moreover, we augment the MT data from additional sources and employ a two-stage fine-tuning process to improve performance. Additionally, we exploit the cross-lingual similarities between Maltese and Arabic by transliterating Maltese to Arabic script, observing interesting performance boosts.

In terms of limitations, the lack of training data for North Levantine Arabic impeded the progress of our ASR system. By using MSA to train our Arabic ASR models, the resulting system struggled with non-standard pronunciation and dialect-specific variation. Furthermore, the absence of testing data for Tunisian Arabic hindered our models considering its close similarity with Maltese.

More general improvements could be undertaken in future work such as hyper-parameter tuning and supplementing currently available data with back-translation. Rather than relying solely on parallel data, implementing backtranslation with larger monolingual corpora holds promise for improving the MT systems discussed in this paper.

Acknowledgments

We acknowledge the assistance of the LT-Bridge Project (GA 952194) and DFKI for the use of their Virtual Laboratory.

References

Milind Agarwal, Sweta Agrawal, Antonios Anastasopoulos, Luisa Bentivogli, Ondřej Bojar, Claudia Borg, Marine Carpuat, Roldano Cattoni, Mauro Cettolo, Mingda Chen, William Chen, Khalid Choukri, Alexandra Chronopoulou, Anna Currey, Thierry Declerck, Qianqian Dong, Kevin Duh, Yannick Estève, Marcello Federico, Souhir Gahbiche, Barry Haddow, Benjamin Hsu, Phu Mon Htut, Hirofumi Inaguma, Dávid Javorský, John Judge, Yasumasa Kano, Tom Ko, Rishu Kumar, Pengwei Li, Xutai Ma, Prashant Mathur, Evgeny Matusov, Paul McNamee, John P. McCrae, Kenton Murray, Maria Nadejde, Satoshi Nakamura, Matteo Negri, Ha Nguyen, Jan Niehues, Xing Niu, Atul Kr. Ojha, John E. Ortega, Proyag Pal, Juan Pino, Lonneke van der Plas, Peter Polák, Elijah Rippeth, Elizabeth Salesky, Jiatong Shi, Matthias Sperber, Sebastian Stüker, Katsuhito Sudoh, Yun Tang, Brian Thompson, Kevin Tran, Marco Turchi, Alex Waibel, Mingxuan Wang, Shinji Watanabe, and Rodolfo Zevallos. 2023. FINDINGS OF THE IWSLT 2023 EVALUATION CAMPAIGN. In *Proceedings of the 20th International Conference on Spoken Language Translation (IWSLT 2023)*, pages 1–61, Toronto, Canada (in-person and online). Association for Computational Linguistics.

Diego Alves, Askars Salimbajevs, and Mārcis Pinnis. 2020. *Data Augmentation for Pipeline-Based Speech Translation.*

Dario Amodei, Sundaram Ananthanarayanan, Rishita Anubhai, Jingliang Bai, Eric Battenberg, Carl Case, Jared Casper, Bryan Catanzaro, Qiang Cheng, Guoliang Chen, Jie Chen, Jingdong Chen, Zhijie Chen, Mike Chrzanowski, Adam Coates, Greg Diamos, Ke Ding, Niandong Du, Erich Elsen, Jesse Engel, Weiwei Fang, Linxi Fan, Christopher Fougner, Liang Gao, Caixia Gong, Awni Hannun, Tony Han, Lappi Vaino Johannes, Bing Jiang, Cai Ju, Billy Jun, Patrick LeGresley, Libby Lin, Junjie Liu, Yang Liu, Weigao Li, Xiangang Li, Dongpeng Ma, Sharan Narang, Andrew Ng, Sherjil Ozair, Yiping Peng, Ryan Prenger, Sheng Qian, Zongfeng Quan, Jonathan Raiman, Vinay Rao, Sanjeev Satheesh, David Seetapun, Shubho Sengupta, Kavya Srinet, Anuroop Sriram, Haiyuan Tang, Liliang Tang, Chong Wang, Jidong Wang, Kaifu Wang, Yi Wang, Zhijian Wang, Zhiqian Wang, Shuang Wu, Likai Wei, Bo Xiao, Wen Xie, Yan Xie, Dani Yogatama, Bin Yuan, Jun Zhan, and Zhenyao Zhu. 2016. Deep speech 2: end-to-end speech recognition in english and mandarin. In *Proceedings of the 33rd International Conference on International Conference on Machine Learning - Volume 48*, ICML'16, page 173–182. JMLR.org.

Antonios Anastasopoulos, Loïc Barrault, Luisa Bentivogli, Marcely Zanon Boito, Ondřej Bojar, Roldano Cattoni, Anna Currey, Georgiana Dinu, Kevin Duh, Maha Elbayad, Clara Emmanuel, Yannick Estève, Marcello Federico, Christian Federmann, Souhir Gahbiche, Hongyu Gong, Roman Grundkiewicz, Barry Haddow, Benjamin Hsu, Dávid Javorský, Věra Kloudová, Surafel Lakew, Xutai Ma, Prashant Mathur, Paul McNamee, Kenton Murray, Maria Nădejde, Satoshi Nakamura, Matteo Negri, Jan Niehues, Xing Niu, John Ortega, Juan Pino, Elizabeth Salesky, Jiatong Shi, Matthias Sperber, Sebastian Stüker, Katsuhito Sudoh, Marco Turchi, Yogesh Virkar, Alexander Waibel, Changhan Wang, and Shinji Watanabe. 2022. Findings of the IWSLT 2022 evaluation campaign. In *Proceedings of the 19th International Conference on Spoken Language Translation (IWSLT 2022)*, pages 98–157, Dublin, Ireland (in-person and online). Association for Computational Linguistics.

Rosana Ardila, Megan Branson, Kelly Davis, Michael Kohler, Josh Meyer, Michael Henretty, Reuben Morais, Lindsay Saunders, Francis Tyers, and Gregor Weber. 2020. Common voice: A massively-multilingual speech corpus. In *Proceedings of the Twelfth Language Resources and Evaluation Conference*, pages 4218–4222, Marseille, France. European Language Resources Association.

Arun Babu, Changhan Wang, Andros Tjandra, Kushal Lakhotia, Qiantong Xu, Naman Goyal, Kritika Singh, Patrick von Platen, Yatharth Saraf, Juan Pino, et al. 2022. Xls-r: Self-supervised cross-lingual speech representation learning at scale.

Alexei Baevski, Yuhao Zhou, Abdelrahman Mohamed, and Michael Auli. 2020. wav2vec 2.0: A framework for self-supervised learning of speech representations. In *Advances in Neural Information Processing Systems*, volume 33, pages 12449–12460. Curran Associates, Inc.

Albert Borg and Marie Azzopardi-Alexander. 1997. *Maltese: Descriptive Grammars.* Routledge, London and New York.

Alexis Conneau, Alexei Baevski, Ronan Collobert, Abdelrahman Mohamed, and Michael Auli. 2020. Unsupervised cross-lingual representation learning for speech recognition. *CoRR*, abs/2006.13979.

John E. Ortega, Rodolfo Zevallos, and William Chen. 2023. QUESPA submission for the IWSLT 2023 dialect and low-resource speech translation tasks. In *Proceedings of the 20th International Conference on Spoken Language Translation (IWSLT 2023)*, pages 261–268, Toronto, Canada (in-person and online). Association for Computational Linguistics.

Mark JF Gales, Kate M Knill, Anton Ragni, and Shakti P Rath. 2014. Speech recognition and keyword spotting for low-resource languages: Babel project research at CUED. In *Fourth International workshop on spoken language technologies for under-resourced languages (SLTU-2014)*, pages 16–23. International Speech Communication Association (ISCA).

Albert Gatt and Slavomír Čéplö. 2013. Digital Corpora and Other Electronic Resources for Maltese. In *Proceedings of the International Conference on Corpus Linguistics*, pages 96–97. UCREL, Lancaster, UK.

Francisco Guzmán, Peng-Jen Chen, Myle Ott, Juan Pino, Guillaume Lample, Philipp Koehn, Vishrav Chaudhary, and Marc'Aurelio Ranzato. 2019. The FLORES evaluation datasets for low-resource machine translation: Nepali–English and Sinhala–English. In *Proceedings of the 2019 Conference on Empirical Methods in Natural Language Processing and the 9th International Joint Conference on Natural Language Processing (EMNLP-IJCNLP)*, pages 6098–6111, Hong Kong, China. Association for Computational Linguistics.

Nizar Habash, Nasser Zalmout, Dima Taji, Hieu Hoang, and Maverick Alzate. 2017. A parallel corpus for evaluating machine translation between Arabic and European languages. In *Proceedings of the 15th Conference of the European Chapter of the Association for Computational Linguistics: Volume 2, Short Papers*, pages 235–241, Valencia, Spain. Association for Computational Linguistics.

Kenneth Heafield. 2011. KenLM: Faster and smaller language model queries. In *Proceedings of the Sixth Workshop on Statistical Machine Translation*, pages 187–197, Edinburgh, Scotland. Association for Computational Linguistics.

Carlos Daniel Hernandez Mena, Albert Gatt, Andrea DeMarco, Claudia Borg, Lonneke van der Plas, Amanda Muscat, and Ian Padovani. 2020. MASRI-HEADSET: A Maltese corpus for speech recognition. In *Proceedings of the Twelfth Language Resources and Evaluation Conference*, pages 6381–6388, Marseille, France. European Language Resources Association.

Pratik Joshi, Sebastin Santy, Amar Budhiraja, Kalika Bali, and Monojit Choudhury. 2020. The state and fate of linguistic diversity and inclusion in the NLP world. In *Proceedings of the 58th Annual Meeting of the Association for Computational Linguistics*, pages 6282–6293, Online. Association for Computational Linguistics.

Kathrein Abu Kwaik, Motaz Saad, Stergios Chatzikyriakidis, and Simon Dobnik. 2018. A lexical distance study of Arabic dialects. *Procedia Computer Science*, 142:2–13. Arabic Computational Linguistics.

Alexandre Magueresse, Vincent Carles, and Evan Heetderks. 2020. Low-resource languages: A review of past work and future challenges. *Preprint*, arXiv:2006.07264.

Kurt Micallef, Fadhl Eryani, Nizar Habash, Houda Bouamor, and Claudia Borg. 2023. Exploring the impact of transliteration on NLP performance: Treating Maltese as an Arabic dialect. In *Proceedings of the Workshop on Computation and Written Language (CAWL 2023)*, pages 22–32, Toronto, Canada. Association for Computational Linguistics.

Kurt Micallef, Albert Gatt, Marc Tanti, Lonneke van der Plas, and Claudia Borg. 2022. Pre-training data quality and quantity for a low-resource language: New corpus and BERT models for Maltese. In *Proceedings of the Third Workshop on Deep Learning for Low-Resource Natural Language Processing*, pages 90–101, Hybrid. Association for Computational Linguistics.

Kurt Micallef, Nizar Habash, Claudia Borg, Fadhl Eryani, and Houda Bouamor. 2024. Cross-lingual transfer from related languages: Treating low-resource Maltese as multilingual code-switching. In *Proceedings of the 18th Conference of the European Chapter of the Association for Computational Linguistics (Volume 1: Long Papers)*, pages 1014–1025, St. Julian's, Malta. Association for Computational Linguistics.

NLLB Team, Marta R. Costa-jussà, James Cross, Onur Çelebi, Maha Elbayad, Kenneth Heafield, Kevin Heffernan, Elahe Kalbassi, Janice Lam, Daniel Licht, Jean Maillard, Anna Sun, Skyler Wang, Guillaume Wenzek, Al Youngblood, Bapi Akula, Loic Barrault, Gabriel Mejia Gonzalez, Prangthip Hansanti, John Hoffman, Semarley Jarrett, Kaushik Ram Sadagopan, Dirk Rowe, Shannon Spruit, Chau Tran, Pierre Andrews, Necip Fazil Ayan, Shruti Bhosale, Sergey Edunov, Angela Fan, Cynthia Gao, Vedanuj Goswami, Francisco Guzmán, Philipp Koehn, Alexandre Mourachko, Christophe Ropers, Safiyyah Saleem, Holger Schwenk, and Jeff Wang. 2022. No language left behind: Scaling human-centered machine translation. *Preprint*, arXiv:2207.04672.

Daniel Park, William Chan, Yu Zhang, Chung-Cheng Chiu, Barret Zoph, Ekin Cubuk, and Quoc Le. 2019. Specaugment: A simple data augmentation method for automatic speech recognition.

Vineel Pratap, Qiantong Xu, Anuroop Sriram, Gabriel Synnaeve, and Ronan Collobert. 2020. MLS: A large-scale multilingual dataset for speech research. In *Interspeech 2020*. ISCA.

Hashem Sellat, Shadi Saleh, Mateusz Krubiński, Adam Pospíšil, Petr Zemánek, and Pavel Pecina. 2023. UFAL parallel corpus of north levantine 1.0. LINDAT/CLARIAH-CZ digital library at the Institute of Formal and Applied Linguistics (ÚFAL), Faculty of Mathematics and Physics, Charles University.

Nivedita Sethiya and Chandresh Kumar Maurya. 2023. End-to-end speech-to-text translation: A survey. *Preprint*, arXiv:2312.01053.

Yuqing Tang, Chau Tran, Xian Li, Peng-Jen Chen, Naman Goyal, Vishrav Chaudhary, Jiatao Gu, and Angela Fan. 2020. Multilingual translation with extensible multilingual pretraining and finetuning. *CoRR*, abs/2008.00401.

Jörg Tiedemann. 2012. Parallel data, tools and interfaces in OPUS. In *Proceedings of the Eighth International Conference on Language Resources and Evaluation (LREC'12)*, pages 2214–2218, Istanbul, Turkey. European Language Resources Association (ELRA).

Abdul Waheed, Bashar Talafha, Peter Sullivan, AbdelRahim Elmadany, and Muhammad Abdul-Mageed. 2023. Voxarabica: A robust dialect-aware arabic speech recognition system. *Preprint*, arXiv:2310.11069.

Changhan Wang, Morgane Riviere, Ann Lee, Anne Wu, Chaitanya Talnikar, Daniel Haziza, Mary Williamson, Juan Pino, and Emmanuel Dupoux. 2021. VoxPopuli: A large-scale multilingual speech corpus for representation learning, semi-supervised learning and interpretation. In *Proceedings of the 59th Annual Meeting of the Association for Computational Linguistics and the 11th International Joint Conference on Natural Language Processing (Volume 1: Long Papers)*, pages 993–1003, Online. Association for Computational Linguistics.

Changhan Wang, Yun Tang, Xutai Ma, Anne Wu, Dmytro Okhonko, and Juan Pino. 2020. Fairseq S2T: Fast speech-to-text modeling with fairseq. In *Proceedings of the 1st Conference of the Asia-Pacific Chapter of the Association for Computational Linguistics and the 10th International Joint Conference on Natural Language Processing: System Demonstrations*, pages 33–39, Suzhou, China. Association for Computational Linguistics.

Aiden Williams, Kurt Abela, Rishu Kumar, Martin Bär, Hannah Billinghurst, Kurt Micallef, Ahnaf Mozib Samin, Andrea DeMarco, Lonneke van der Plas, and Claudia Borg. 2023a. UM-DFKI Maltese speech translation. In *Proceedings of the 20th International Conference on Spoken Language Translation (IWSLT 2023)*, pages 433–441, Toronto, Canada (in-person and online). Association for Computational Linguistics.

Aiden Williams, Andrea Demarco, and Claudia Borg. 2023b. The applicability of Wav2Vec2 and Whisper for low-resource Maltese ASR. In *Proc. 2nd Annual Meeting of the ELRA/ISCA SIG on Under-resourced Languages (SIGUL 2023)*, pages 39–43.

Rabih Zbib, Erika Malchiodi, Jacob Devlin, David Stallard, Spyros Matsoukas, Richard Schwartz, John Makhoul, Omar F. Zaidan, and Chris Callison-Burch. 2012. Machine translation of Arabic dialects. In *Proceedings of the 2012 Conference of the North American Chapter of the Association for Computational Linguistics: Human Language Technologies*, pages 49–59, Montréal, Canada. Association for Computational Linguistics.

Biao Zhang, Philip Williams, Ivan Titov, and Rico Sennrich. 2020. Improving massively multilingual neural machine translation and zero-shot translation. In *Proceedings of the 58th Annual Meeting of the Association for Computational Linguistics*, pages 1628–1639, Online. Association for Computational Linguistics.

Slavomír Čéplö, Ján Bátora, Adam Benkato, Jiří Milička, Christophe Pereira, and Petr Zemánek. 2016. Mutual intelligibility of spoken Maltese, Libyan Arabic, and Tunisian Arabic functionally tested: A pilot study. *Folia Linguistica*, 50(2):583–628.

UOM-Constrained IWSLT 2024 Shared Task Submission - Maltese Speech Translation

Kurt Abela **Md Abdur Razzaq Riyadh** **Melanie Galea** **Alana Busuttil**

Roman Kovalev **Aiden Williams** **Claudia Borg**

kurt.abela@um.edu.mt, md.riyadh.23@um.edu.mt, melanie.galea.20@um.edu.mt, alana.busuttil.20@um.edu.mt, roman.a.kovalev.23@um.edu.mt, aiden.williams.19@um.edu.mt, claudia.borg@um.edu.mt,

Abstract

This paper presents our IWSLT-2024 shared task submission on the low-resource track. This submission forms part of the constrained setup; implying limited data for training. Following the introduction, this paper consists of a literature review defining previous approaches to speech translation, as well as their application to Maltese, followed by the defined methodology, evaluation and results, and the conclusion. A cascaded submission on the Maltese to English language pair is presented; consisting of a pipeline containing: a DeepSpeech 1 Automatic Speech Recognition (ASR) system, a KenLM model to optimise the transcriptions, and finally an LSTM machine translation model. The submission achieves a 0.5 BLEU score on the overall test set, and the ASR system achieves a word error rate of 97.15%. Our code is made publicly available[1].

1 Introduction

Speech Translation (ST) may be defined as the task of transforming audio in a source language to its transcription in a target language. ST is generally tackled through two main approaches: the first being an end-to-end approach; with the source language audio serving as input to the model, which in turn produces a transcription in the target language as output, the second being a pipeline or cascading approach; suggesting multiple systems with varying responsibilities, primarily generating ASR transcription and machine translation. A Meta-Net White Paper series confirms the Maltese language as low-resourced; meaning it has little support for speech technology, including translation tasks (Rosner and Joachimsen, 2012).

This paper introduces a cascading system that utilises an ASR system to generate transcriptions in the source language, a language model to improve the transcriptions and finally, a machine translation system to produce the transcription in the target language. The following sections define the current state of research into low-resource speech translation, followed by a methodology and discussion.

2 Literature Review

The literature review focuses on previous attempts at Automated Speech Recognition (ASR) and Machine Translation (MT), in particular, when applied to the Maltese language. Furthermore, the main models attempted for this task are defined, these being: HMM, DeepSpeech 1 for ASR, LSTM and Transformers for MT.

2.1 Previous IWSLT Low-Resource Track Attempts

In 2023, the shared task set by IWSLT consisted of "benchmarking and promoting speech translation technology for a diverse range of dialects and low-resource language".

Among other attempts, QUESPA (E. Ortega et al., 2023a) submitted two cascade systems to the constrained setting, where ASR and MT were combined together in a pipeline. One of these cascade systems used wav2letter+ (Pratap et al., 2019) - a fast open-source speech recognition system; the other one was an implementation of a conformer architecture along with OpenNMT translation system (Klein et al., 2017), which was trained on constrained ST and MT data. Both of these models demonstrated relatively poor performance compared to the other submissions, with a BLEU score of less than 1.

Previous attempts in both constrained and unconstrained settings, proved that this task is still a major challenge. Using powerful massively pre-trained ASR models; such as Wav2Vec 2.0, in combination with multilingual decoders has been an emerging trend, and oftentimes produces excellent

[1] https://github.com/melanie-galea/uom_constrained

Proceedings of the 21st International Conference on Spoken Language Translation (IWSLT 2024), pages 156–161
August 15-16, 2024 ©2024 Association for Computational Linguistics

results. Training a self-supervised model and producing artificial supervision has proven to be an effective approach (Zanon Boito et al., 2022). Additionally, several methods were employed to improve the performance of cascade systems, such as voice activity detection for segmentation (Zhang et al., 2022; Ding and Tao, 2021), as well as training the ASR on synthetic data with noise filtering and domain-specific fine-tuning (Zhang et al., 2022).

2.2 HMM and DeepSpeech for Maltese ASR

Our work attempts two instruments for ASR: Hidden Markov Model and DeepSpeech 1. The former used to be a preferred method since the 1970s (Rabiner, 1989). As demonstrated by Ellis and Morgan (1999), the size of a model plays a significant role, especially when it comes to the quantity of training data and the trainable parameters. The latter was made difficult due to hardware and design limitations. A survey conducted by Nagpal et al. (2019) showed that deep learning approaches could still deliver effective results for ASR.

This led to the development of end-to-end supervised neural network models such as DeepSpeech 1 (Hannun et al., 2014) and then DeepSpeech 2 (Amodei et al., 2015), which had successfully outperformed Hidden Markov Models for English ASR. In speech-related fields, labelled data is usually referred to as annotated data. Although the use of large amounts of annotated data proved beneficial for these models, access to data at these scales became a limitation for development, especially in the case of low-resource languages. This led to the use of unannotated data in unsupervised training, with cases described in Lee et al. (2009)'s and Radford et al. (2016)'s work, or self-supervised learning, namely the work done on the Wav2Vec system (Schneider et al., 2019).

These acoustic models have the capacity to generate understandable transcriptions at the character level. Yet, these transcriptions often harbour inaccuracies, such as substituting phonetically similar words or misspelling due to language orthography idiosyncrasies. Consequently, enhancing ASR systems by incorporating an external language model trained on domain-specific text can boost their performance. A common strategy employed is the use of a simple n-gram model. The KenLM language modelling tool (Heafield, 2011) is able to achieve high processing efficiency and language modelling quality by assigning a score to a sequence of n words. This is particularly useful in ASR to be able to select between multiple possible candidates through beam search. Deepspeech supports the integration of KenLM language models to enhance the quality of the ASR output.

2.3 Machine Translation

While some systems have reached human parity in certain domains in machine translation, this is yet to be achieved for low-resource languages (Hassan et al., 2018). The primary challenge lies in parallel data scarcity. The efforts in solving this issue focus on various other aspects such as exploiting shared language features between a high and low resource language as well as techniques for data augmentation.

Her and Kruschwitz (2024) used German-Bavarian parallel data to train a transformer model and then used that to back-translate and augment the training set. They then used that data to fine-tune a German-French neural translation model given its similarity to the source language. Nzeyimana (2024) focused on improving the performance of machine translation models by improving predictions of the morphological features. Their method was based on the fact that sub-word tokenizers split the words on a surface level and are prone to losing morphological features. Encoding morphological features as input to the model improves performance. E. Ortega et al. (2023b) used the Transformer architecture (Vaswani et al., 2017) to develop a machine translation system as part of their pipeline for an automatic speech recognition system for Quechua to Spanish.

Before Transformers (Vaswani et al., 2017), RNN (Rumelhart et al., 1986) was widely used for natural language processing. RNN with self-attention proved quite effective for machine translation, achieving state-of-the-art performance (Sutskever et al., 2014), (Bahdanau et al., 2014).

Research on machine translation for Maltese is quite limited. One of the earliest works was on statistical machine translation where the authors focused their attention on phrase extraction for proper phrase alignment (Rosner and Bajada, 2007). In their work on Maltese automatic speech recognition (ASR), Williams et al. (2023) leveraged the pre-trained mBART model. However, their system was evaluated as a whole (ASR - MT) and does not represent the model's true capability for machine translation on Maltese as the input is the ASR output.

3 Methodology

3.1 Automatic Speech Recognition

3.1.1 Hidden Markov Models

Hidden Markov Models (HMMs) were trained for ASR (Rabiner, 1989) on the MASRI dataset, totaling to 6 hours and 39 minutes. The model was trained using Mel Frequency Cepstral Coefficient (MFCC) features derived from the WAV files and their corresponding verbatim transcription.

3.1.2 DeepSpeech

A DeepSpeech v1 (Hannun et al., 2014) model was trained on both MASRI and CV datasets, containing 6 hours 39 minutes and 5 hours 11 minutes respectively, totalling nearly 12 hours. The model was trained using Maltese WAV files and their corresponding verbatim transcription. Development, Testing and Training csv files therefore contain the WAV file dataset root, its corresponding transcription, and file size in bytes. The text was pre-processed; characters cases were converted to lower-case, non-alphabetic characters removed except for the hyphen and apostrophe. Accented letters were included in order to better support the model's understanding of pronunciation. An alphabet was created including special Maltese characters.

The training code was cloned through the git DeepSpeech branch, and all required dependencies were installed. Finally, the training, development and testing files, along with a layer size of 64 units wide, rather than the default 2048. The dropout was set to 0.4, and a batch size of 100 was used to train the model. The model was trained for 250 epochs. The hyper-parameters were set with the limited data-set size in mind. The relatively smaller size of the model parameters was beneficial for our experiment; it is usually the case that a larger parameter size causes the model to over-fit when trained on a small training set such as ours.

The DeepSpeech model was selected over the HMM due to higher performance. The HMM scored a WER of 112.33%, whilst DeepSpeech model scored a WER of 97.15%.

3.2 KenLM

Initial experimentation involved investigating the impact of both word-level and character-level n-grams on a set of erroneous test data. Upon examining the alterations made by KenLM on this sample dataset, it was deduced that a word-level KenLM model was more apt for the task.

The KenLM toolkit (Heafield, 2011) was used to train a probabilistic 3-gram model on the Korpus Malti v4.0 Shuffled training subset (Micallef et al., 2022) [2], which is resource referred to by the shared task organizers. Before training said model, the corpus was pre-processed to not include punctuation, apart from the hyphen and apostrophe, with all text lowercased. The KenLM model, once trained, served as a tool to decode the ASR output, employing a beam search algorithm. This process converted probabilities into textual transcripts, which were subsequently delivered by the system.

3.3 Machine Translation

All models are built using the Fairseq (Ott et al., 2019) library. The Fairseq library allows for easy implementation of a MT system through CLI commands, meaning minimal code is needed to create a fully working MT system.

Three different architectures were experimented with, namely Transformer (base), Transformer (large) and an LSTM. The base transformer version (Vaswani et al. (2017)) has six encoder and decoder layers with 512 dimensions each. There are eight attention heads for both the encoders and decoders, with 2048 dimensions for each. The large version of the transformer architecture has 1024 dimensions for each layer and 4096 dimensions for each attention head. There are also 16 attention heads in total. Thirdly, an LSTM architecture (Hochreiter and Schmidhuber, 1997) was used, which consists of a single-layer bidirectional encoder-decoder model with a hidden size of 512 for both the encoder and decoder.

LSTMs have generally fallen out of favour recently due to Transformers achieving better results. However, it was hypothesised that given the lack of data, LSTMs may still prove to be just as effective in this scenario. This is due to the fact that Transformers require a lot of data to be effective, and in low-resource settings such as this one, older techniques such as LSTM may perform better (Przystupa and Abdul-Mageed, 2019).

The data was pre-processed by training a SentencePiece tokenizer from scratch on the given training set. The training set was then pre-processed using this tokenizer.

[2] https://huggingface.co/datasets/MLRS/korpus_malti/viewer/shuffled

The 3 defined models (LSTM, base Transformer and large Transformer) were trained with the same hyperparameters. We performed an evaluation of all three models on the dev set and achieved the results in Table 1. It was ultimately concluded that LSTMs performed best. The LSTM model was therefore selected, and further hyperparameter tuning was performed for improved results.

Table 1: Results of the different architectures on the development set

Architecture	BLEU	CHRF-2
LSTM	**25.76**	**44.57**
Transformer (Base)	24.54	44.15
Transformer (Large)	25.20	43.57

For hyperparameter tuning, Akiba et al. (2019) was used to find optimal values for learning rate, dropout, warm-up duration and weight decay. The optimal learning rate was found to be 0.003 and dropout at 0.04. The learning rate scheduler was set with warm-up updates of 8522. Each model was trained for a maximum of 1,000,000 steps but all of them converged much sooner. The final LSTM model was trained for 4 minutes with early stopping. The training was stopped early when the validation BLEU did not improve for 10 steps.

4 Evaluation and Results

This section presents and discusses the models' results. The official results for our constrained task submission are presented in Tables 2 and 3. The final pipeline result was significantly influenced by the ASR performance. It can be extrapolated that the high Word Error Rate (WER) of the ASR is a result of the limited training data, which was not adequate to train a capable ASR system. Incoherent speech recognition outputs were considered 'out of domain' by the machine translation system since it was trained on meaningful data.

Table 2: Official results for the constrained task - BLEU score

Test Set	BLEU score
CV	0.6
Masri	0.2
Overall	0.5

To further evaluate and understand the results, specific outputs of both the ASR as well as the MT system were analysed.

Table 3: Official results for the constrained task - Word Error Rate

Test Set	Word Error Rate
CV	97.0%
Masri	97.43%
Overall	97.15%

Table 4: Results of the pipeline system with and without the use of a KenLM.

Test Set		BLEU	CHRF-2
Without KenLM	CV	0.48	15.79
	Masri	**0.23**	14.50
With KenLM	CV	**0.52**	**15.97**
	Masri	0.21	**14.73**

It may be noted that the ASR output is relatively poor; with most outputs consisting of invalid Maltese words. In addition to using Deepspeech 1, we made use of a KenLM trained specifically for this task, but whilst some improvements were seen, as illustrated in Table 4, it was not enough to compensate for the model's inability to accurately transcribe the Maltese language.

To further illustrate the ASR issues, the first audio file of the CV test set was transcribed by the model as: *"dan ma sarqat"*. The first two words were predicted correctly, however, the last word was invalid. The correct transcription should have been: *"dan ma sar qatt"*, meaning *"this was never done"*.

Since this is a pipeline setup, the resulting transcription was passed to the MT system. The translated output was *"this doesn't happen to him"*. The output here was not surprising, since the two words that the ASR got correct (*dan ma*) roughly mean *he has never [...]*. Since the word that the ASR got incorrect does not exist in the Maltese language (*sarqat*), it is likely that the MT system treated it as an unknown token.

Admittedly, this was one of the few examples that the ASR system performed well in. Results were exceptionally poor when a named entity was included. For example, the name *Simon Busuttil* was outputted as *sajminbużutiel*. This is expected due to the small size of the training data. Apart from this, the ASR model struggled to understand when a word starts and ends. In most cases, the output sounds phonetically similar to what the actual transcription should be, however, the spelling is incorrect. For example, the word *mhux* was transcribed as *mux*, which is understandable as the 'h' is silent. Overall, the ASR model performed poorly, with most resulting sentences not resembling the actual transcription, highlighted by the 97.15% WER.

These errors naturally propogated to the MT system. Since the dataset of the MT system is also constrained and very limited in nature, it did not have the implicit understanding of the language to identify the typos written by the ASR system (such as *mux* instead of *mhux*). This is even harder with phonetic misspellings. Generally, the MT system output a (seemingly) random response since the input given by the ASR system is equally poor.

Overall, it is evident that an increase in training data would have yielded better results. The ASR set-up makes it difficult to evaluate the MT system alone, given the model pipelining and overall poor performance.

5 Conclusion and Future Work

This paper presents the different approaches to ST for low-resource languages under constrained settings. A short overview of previous research into challenges associated with speech translation was presented, as well as specific attempts and pipelines used for the task. The final pipeline consisted of a DeepSpeech 1 model, KenLM model and LSTM model, each fine-tuned for the task at hand. The final results show that the constrained setting has an extreme impact on the models performance, with a final WER of 97.15%. The very poor ASR performance highlights the challenges present in low-resource settings. Future work on ASR includes the use of higher-quality training data, as well as dealing with named entities in the data itself. It is also suspected that pre-trained models would likely yield better results in low-resourced environments, helping to compensate for data scarcity.

References

Takuya Akiba, Shotaro Sano, Toshihiko Yanase, Takeru Ohta, and Masanori Koyama. 2019. Optuna: A next-generation hyperparameter optimization framework. *Preprint*, arXiv:1907.10902.

Dario Amodei, Rishita Anubhai, Eric Battenberg, Carl Case, Jared Casper, Bryan Catanzaro, Jingdong Chen, Mike Chrzanowski, Adam Coates, Greg Diamos, Erich Elsen, Jesse Engel, Linxi Fan, Christopher Fougner, Tony Han, Awni Hannun, Billy Jun, Patrick LeGresley, Libby Lin, Sharan Narang, Andrew Ng, Sherjil Ozair, Ryan Prenger, Jonathan Raiman, Sanjeev Satheesh, David Seetapun, Shubho Sengupta, Yi Wang, Zhiqian Wang, Chong Wang, Bo Xiao, Dani Yogatama, Jun Zhan, and Zhenyao Zhu. 2015. Deep speech 2: End-to-end speech recognition in english and mandarin. *Preprint*, arXiv:1512.02595.

Dzmitry Bahdanau, Kyunghyun Cho, and Yoshua Bengio. 2014. Neural machine translation by jointly learning to align and translate. *arXiv preprint arXiv:1409.0473*.

Liang Ding and Dacheng Tao. 2021. The USYD-JD speech translation system for IWSLT2021. In *Proceedings of the 18th International Conference on Spoken Language Translation (IWSLT 2021)*, pages 182–191, Bangkok, Thailand (online). Association for Computational Linguistics.

John E. Ortega, Rodolfo Zevallos, and William Chen. 2023a. QUESPA submission for the IWSLT 2023 dialect and low-resource speech translation tasks. In *Proceedings of the 20th International Conference on Spoken Language Translation (IWSLT 2023)*, pages 261–268, Toronto, Canada (in-person and online). Association for Computational Linguistics.

John E. Ortega, Rodolfo Zevallos, and William Chen. 2023b. QUESPA Submission for the IWSLT 2023 Dialect and Low-resource Speech Translation Tasks. In *Proceedings of the 20th International Conference on Spoken Language Translation (IWSLT 2023)*, pages 261–268, Toronto, Canada (in-person and online). Association for Computational Linguistics.

D. Ellis and N. Morgan. 1999. Size matters: an empirical study of neural network training for large vocabulary continuous speech recognition. In *1999 IEEE International Conference on Acoustics, Speech, and Signal Processing. Proceedings. ICASSP99 (Cat. No.99CH36258)*, volume 2, pages 1013–1016 vol.2.

Awni Hannun, Carl Case, Jared Casper, Bryan Catanzaro, Greg Diamos, Erich Elsen, Ryan Prenger, Sanjeev Satheesh, Shubho Sengupta, Adam Coates, and Andrew Y. Ng. 2014. Deep speech: Scaling up end-to-end speech recognition. *Preprint*, arXiv:1412.5567.

Hany Hassan, Anthony Aue, Chang Chen, Vishal Chowdhary, Jonathan Clark, Christian Federmann, Xuedong Huang, Marcin Junczys-Dowmunt, William Lewis, Mu Li, et al. 2018. Achieving human parity on automatic chinese to english news translation. *arXiv preprint arXiv:1803.05567*.

Kenneth Heafield. 2011. KenLM: Faster and smaller language model queries. In *Proceedings of the Sixth Workshop on Statistical Machine Translation*, pages 187–197, Edinburgh, Scotland. Association for Computational Linguistics.

Wan-Hua Her and Udo Kruschwitz. 2024. Investigating Neural Machine Translation for Low-Resource Languages: Using Bavarian as a Case Study. *arXiv preprint*. ArXiv:2404.08259 [cs].

Sepp Hochreiter and Jürgen Schmidhuber. 1997. Long short-term memory. *Neural computation*, 9(8):1735–1780.

Guillaume Klein, Yoon Kim, Yuntian Deng, Jean Senellart, and Alexander Rush. 2017. OpenNMT: Open-source toolkit for neural machine translation. In *Proceedings of ACL 2017, System Demonstrations*, pages 67–72, Vancouver, Canada. Association for Computational Linguistics.

Honglak Lee, Yan Largman, Peter Pham, and Andrew Y. Ng. 2009. Unsupervised feature learning for audio classification using convolutional deep belief networks. In *Proceedings of the 22nd International Conference on Neural Information Processing Systems*, NIPS'09, page 1096–1104, Red Hook, NY, USA. Curran Associates Inc.

Kurt Micallef, Albert Gatt, Marc Tanti, Lonneke van der Plas, and Claudia Borg. 2022. Pre-training data quality and quantity for a low-resource language: New corpus and BERT models for Maltese. In *Proceedings of the Third Workshop on Deep Learning for Low-Resource Natural Language Processing*, pages 90–101, Hybrid. Association for Computational Linguistics.

Shaveta Nagpal, Munish Kumar, · Maruthi, Rohit Ayyagari, and · Kumar. 2019. A survey of deep learning and its applications: A new paradigm to machine learning. *Archives of Computational Methods in Engineering*.

Antoine Nzeyimana. 2024. Low-resource neural machine translation with morphological modeling. *arXiv preprint*. ArXiv:2404.02392 [cs].

Myle Ott, Sergey Edunov, Alexei Baevski, Angela Fan, Sam Gross, Nathan Ng, David Grangier, and Michael Auli. 2019. fairseq: A fast, extensible toolkit for sequence modeling. In *Proceedings of NAACL-HLT 2019: Demonstrations*.

Vineel Pratap, Awni Hannun, Qiantong Xu, Jeff Cai, Jacob Kahn, Gabriel Synnaeve, Vitaliy Liptchinsky, and Ronan Collobert. 2019. Wav2letter++: A fast open-source speech recognition system. In *ICASSP 2019 - 2019 IEEE International Conference on Acoustics, Speech and Signal Processing (ICASSP)*, pages 6460–6464.

Michael Przystupa and Muhammad Abdul-Mageed. 2019. Neural machine translation of low-resource and similar languages with backtranslation. In *Proceedings of the Fourth Conference on Machine Translation (Volume 3: Shared Task Papers, Day 2)*, pages 224–235.

L.R. Rabiner. 1989. A tutorial on hidden markov models and selected applications in speech recognition. *Proceedings of the IEEE*, 77(2):257–286.

Alec Radford, Luke Metz, and Soumith Chintala. 2016. Unsupervised representation learning with deep convolutional generative adversarial networks. *Preprint*, arXiv:1511.06434.

Michael Rosner and Jo-Ann Bajada. 2007. Phrase extraction for machine translation. Accepted: 2017-10-17T13:30:37Z Publisher: University of Malta. Faculty of ICT.

Mike Rosner and Jan Joachimsen. 2012. *Il-Lingwa Maltija Fl-Era Diġitali – The Maltese Language in the Digital Age*. META-NET White Paper Series. Georg Rehm and Hans Uszkoreit (Series Editors). Springer.

David E Rumelhart, Geoffrey E Hinton, and Ronald J Williams. 1986. Learning internal representations by error propagation, parallel distributed processing, explorations in the microstructure of cognition, ed. de rumelhart and j. mcclelland. vol. 1. 1986. *Biometrika*, 71:599–607.

Steffen Schneider, Alexei Baevski, Ronan Collobert, and Michael Auli. 2019. wav2vec: Unsupervised Pre-Training for Speech Recognition. In *Proc. Interspeech 2019*, pages 3465–3469.

Ilya Sutskever, Oriol Vinyals, and Quoc V Le. 2014. Sequence to sequence learning with neural networks. *Advances in neural information processing systems*, 27.

Ashish Vaswani, Noam Shazeer, Niki Parmar, Jakob Uszkoreit, Llion Jones, Aidan N Gomez, Łukasz Kaiser, and Illia Polosukhin. 2017. Attention is all you need. *Advances in neural information processing systems*, 30.

Aiden Williams, Kurt Abela, Rishu Kumar, Martin Bär, Hannah Billinghurst, Kurt Micallef, Ahnaf Mozib Samin, Andrea DeMarco, Lonneke Van Der Plas, and Claudia Borg. 2023. UM-DFKI Maltese Speech Translation. In *Proceedings of the 20th International Conference on Spoken Language Translation (IWSLT 2023)*, pages 433–441, Toronto, Canada (in-person and online). Association for Computational Linguistics.

Marcely Zanon Boito, John Ortega, Hugo Riguidel, Antoine Laurent, Loïc Barrault, Fethi Bougares, Firas Chaabani, Ha Nguyen, Florentin Barbier, Souhir Gahbiche, and Yannick Estève. 2022. ON-TRAC consortium systems for the IWSLT 2022 dialect and low-resource speech translation tasks. In *Proceedings of the 19th International Conference on Spoken Language Translation (IWSLT 2022)*, pages 308–318, Dublin, Ireland (in-person and online). Association for Computational Linguistics.

Weitai Zhang, Zhongyi Ye, Haitao Tang, Xiaoxi Li, Xinyuan Zhou, Jing Yang, Jianwei Cui, Pan Deng, Mohan Shi, Yifan Song, Dan Liu, Junhua Liu, and Lirong Dai. 2022. The USTC-NELSLIP offline speech translation systems for IWSLT 2022. In *Proceedings of the 19th International Conference on Spoken Language Translation (IWSLT 2022)*, pages 198–207, Dublin, Ireland (in-person and online). Association for Computational Linguistics.

Compact Speech Translation Models via Discrete Speech Units Pretraining

Tsz Kin Lam and **Alexandra Birch** and **Barry Haddow**
School of Informatics, University of Edinburgh
{tlam, a.birch, bhaddow}@ed.ac.uk

Abstract

We propose a pretraining method to use Self-Supervised Speech (SSS) model to creating more compact Speech-to-text Translation. In contrast to using the SSS model for initialization, our method is more suitable to memory constrained scenario such as on-device deployment. Our method is based on Discrete Speech Units (DSU) extracted from the SSS model. In the first step, our method pretrains two smaller encoder-decoder models on 1) Filterbank-to-DSU (Fbk-to-DSU) and 2) DSU-to-Translation (DSU-to-Trl) data respectively. The DSU thus become the distillation inputs of the smaller models. Subsequently, the encoder from the Fbk-to-DSU model and the decoder from the DSU-to-Trl model are taken to initialise the compact model. Finally, the compact model is finetuned on the paired Fbk-Trl data. In addition to being compact, our method requires no transcripts, making it applicable to low-resource settings. It also avoids speech discretization in inference and is more robust to the DSU tokenization. Evaluation on CoVoST-2 (X-En) shows that our method has consistent improvement over the baseline in three metrics while being compact i.e., only half the SSS model size.

1 Introduction

In Speech-to-text Translation (ST), using Self-Supervised Speech (SSS) models, such as wav2vec 2.0 and HuBERT (Baevski et al., 2020; Hsu et al., 2021), as model initialization is now common to obtain the SOTA result (Agarwal et al., 2023). Nevertheless, such model initialisation makes the ST model less memory-adaptive and could impose a large memory footprint. These factors hinders on-device deployment that is crucial for privacy and useful in the absence of internet connection.

How can we use the SSS model(s) to create a more compact ST model? When using the SSS model for initialization, the corresponding ST model uses the dense representations of the SSS model for its task. Alternatively, an informative proxy, which requires less memory to obtain, for the dense representation may make the ST model more compact.

Discrete Speech Units (DSU) extracted from the SSS model can be such a good proxy. DSU are K-Means clusters of speech representations from selected layers of the SSS model. It represents sequence of discrete tokens, which are easier to model within a text processing architecture (Polyak et al., 2021; Chou et al., 2023). DSU sequences[1] are far smaller than the sequences of dense representations. Therefore, a straightforward method to distill the SSS models is to use DSU as speech inputs, aka the DSU-to-Translation (DSU-to-Trl) model. Although using DSU as inputs allows for transfer learning and a memory-adaptive model, using them at inference still requires storing and calling the quantization modules, i.e, the SSS model and the K-Means model.

We thus propose to use DSU for pretraining (PT) rather than as model input to make ST models more compact. Our method distils the SSS model by pretraining smaller models on the corresponding DSU. More specifically, our method firstly pretrains two smaller encoder-decoder models on 1) Filterbank-to-DSU (Fbk-to-DSU) and 2) DSU-to-Trl data respectively. The DSU thus become the distillation inputs of the smaller models. Subsequently, the encoder from the Fbk-to-DSU model and the decoder from the DSU-to-Trl model are taken to initialise the compact model. Finally, the compact model is finetuned on the paired Fbk-Trl data. Under this formulation, (1) we can use the SSS model to create a ST model that is adaptive to the memory footprint. (2) Our method requires no transcripts, unlike ASR-pretraining, making it applicable to low-resource

[1] In this paper, DSU and DSU sequences are used interchangeably. When we need to focus on a few units of the sequence, we call them DSU tokens.

Proceedings of the 21st International Conference on Spoken Language Translation (IWSLT 2024), pages 162–172
August 15-16, 2024 ©2024 Association for Computational Linguistics

settings. (3) Our method avoids using the quantization modules in inference. (4) Extensive results also show that our method is more robust to DSU tokenization than the DSU-to-Trl method.

We evaluate our method on CoVoST-2 (Wang et al., 2021) X-En language directions (21 in total) using multilingual ST. By using a HuBERT-Base model to extract the DSU, our method shows strong and consistent improvements in three evaluation metrics with respect to a ST model that is trained from scratch. Our main contributions are:

- We propose a pretraining method to distil the SSS model to creating a more compact ST model. Rather than competing with the SOTA ST models, adaptability to the memory footprint is our key focus.
- Our method uses DSU for pretraining rather than as model inputs. This lowers the inference cost, especially for on-device purpose, by avoiding the quantization modules (storage and running).
- We conduct extensive analysis to study the effect of DSU tokenization to both using DSU as model inputs and as pretraining. Our pretraining method is found to be more robust to different tokenizations.

2 Related Work

There are a number of related works that use DSU to enhance ST. Fang and Feng (2023) and Zhang et al. (2023b) use DSU to create more training data in a back-translation fashion. Chang et al. (2023) and Zhang et al. (2023b) explore the replacement of Filterbank by DSU as speech input. Furthermore, Yan et al. (2024) proposes a multi-tasking learning framework with hard parameter sharing, i.e., using a joint vocabulary for text tokens and DSU, to improve the speech-text modality gap. In contrast, we use DSU and its translation model for pretraining, resulting in a better Fbk-to-Trl model that has a shorter inference pipeline.

In the case of pretraining, Wu et al. (2023) use a single Speech-to-DSU model in pretraining for general speech-to-text purposes whereas we tailor the use for ST by using a pair of encoder-decoder models. Zhang et al. (2022b) also decompose ST into speech-to-unit and unit-to-text tasks. Their training is based on masked unit prediction, and it requires an extra unit-encoder module in inference. In contrast, we resort to supervised training on the DSU in acoustic pretraining and require no extra module in inference. More importantly, our goal is to make (multilingual) ST more compact, aiming also at low-resource settings where transcripts are not easily available, rather than learning a joint semantic space for both transcripts and audios.

3 Method

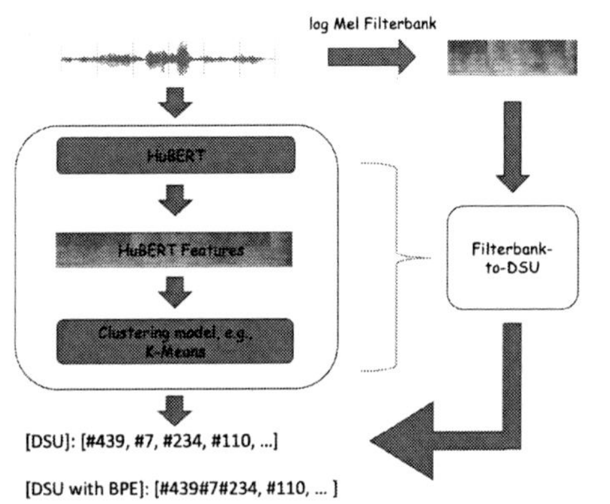

Figure 1: Illustration of the Fbk-to-DSU model. It is like an auto-encoding training process, but between a continuous format (log Mel Filterbank) and its discrete format (DSU) that is extracted from a HuBERT model.

Our method uses DSU in the form of pretraining to distil knowledge from the SSS (dense) representations to creating a more compact ST model.

In the first step, our method pretrains two smaller encoder-decoder models on 1) Fbk-to-DSU and 2) DSU-to-Trl data respectively. The Fbk-to-DSU model takes the log Mel Fbk as the encoder input and predicts the DSU sequence. The model is trained by an interpolation of Connectionist Temporal Classification (CTC, Graves et al. (2006)) loss that is applied to the last encoder layer and label-smoothed Cross-Entropy (CE) loss:

$$\mathcal{L}^{\text{Fbk-to-DSU}} = (1-\lambda_\alpha)\mathcal{L}_{\text{CE}}(\mathbf{U}|\mathbf{F})+\lambda_\alpha\mathcal{L}_{\text{CTC}}(\tilde{\mathbf{U}}|\mathbf{F}) \quad (1)$$

where $\mathbf{F} \in \mathbb{R}^{TxD}$, $\mathbf{U} \in \mathcal{U}$ and $\tilde{\mathbf{U}} \in \tilde{\mathcal{U}} = \{\mathcal{U}, blank\}$ are the Fbk, DSU and the CTC label sequences respectively. The CTC vocabulary correspond to an union of the same vocabulary used in the CE loss and a *blank* label. The idea is similar to an autoencoder, but the Fbk-to-DSU model is trained to map the Fbk inputs to its discrete form from the SSS model in a multi-task learning fashion (Figure 1). The DSU-to-Trl model learns via CE to predict the translations $\mathbf{Y}$ given $\mathbf{U}$: $\mathcal{L}^{\text{DSU-to-Trl}} = \mathcal{L}_{\text{CE}}(\mathbf{Y}|\mathbf{U})$. In essence, we use the DSU to bridge the speech and text modalities.

Next, we use the encoder of the Fbk-to-DSU model and the decoder (and its output layer) of the DSU-to-Trl model to initialise the compact model, followed by finetuning on the paired Fbk-Trl data using both CE and CTC loss (Gaido et al., 2021; Zhang et al., 2023a) on the translations:

$$\mathcal{L}^{\text{FT}} = (1 - \lambda_\beta)\mathcal{L}_{\text{CE}}(\mathbf{Y}|\mathbf{F}) + \lambda_\beta \mathcal{L}_{\text{CTC}}(\tilde{\mathbf{Y}}|\mathbf{F}) \quad (2)$$

where $\tilde{\mathbf{Y}} \in \tilde{\mathcal{Y}} = \{\mathcal{Y}, \mathit{blank}\}$.

3.1 Tokenization of DSU in different models

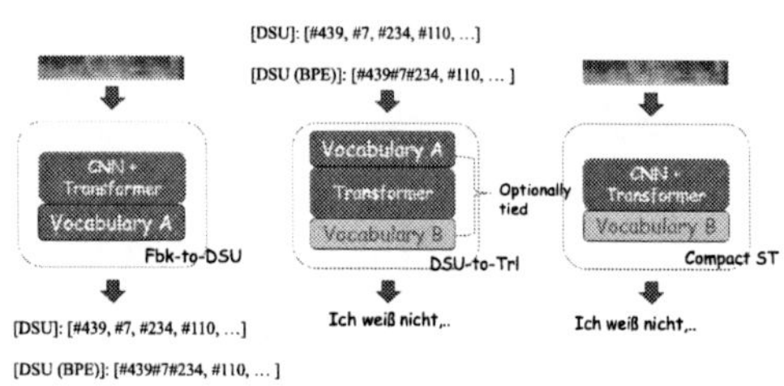

Figure 2: Aligning the DSU tokenization of the Fbk-to-DSU, DSU-to-Trl and compact ST model.

The discrete nature of DSU makes the above training process similar to the transcripts-based pretraining. However, DSU is self-supervised, whereas transcripts require human annotations. DSU are also much longer and can be represented with various sets of symbols.

The length issue could be relieved by merging sequential repetitions (Ao et al., 2022), e.g., '#1 #1 #1 #456 #456 #23' becomes '#1 #456 #23', where each DSU token is denoted by a #{integer}. Byte Pair Encoding (BPE) (Sennrich et al., 2016) could be applied to reduce the DSU sequence length further, e.g., '#1 #456 #23' could be split into a single subword unit: '#1#456#23'.

Since both Fbk-to-DSU and DSU-to-Trl models map to different targets, and DSU can be represented with various set of symbols, we align the tokenizations (or called vocabularies[2]) of the two models. Figure 2 provides an illustration. The vocabulary of the Fbk-to-DSU model (Vocabulary A) is identical to the source vocabulary of the DSU-to-Trl model (their weights are not shared since these two models are trained independently), whereas the target vocabulary (Vocabulary B) of the DSU-to-Trl model is identical to the target vocabulary of the final compact model (their weights are shared during initialisation). The DSU-to-Trl model is similar to a text translation model, so we also experiment of using separate vocabularies or a joint vocabulary. If a joint vocabulary of English subword units and DSU (BPE or not) is used, all the three models would have the same vocabulary, and the weights of the source and target vocabularies of the DSU-to-Trl model are also tied.

4 Experiments

4.1 Data Preprocessing

We follow standard practices to preprocess the CoVoST-2 X-En data. For speech inputs using 80-D log Mel Fbk, we computed the features for every 10ms with a 25ms window and then normalized them using its mean and variance computed over each channel. We use the BPE implementation from SENTENCEPIECE (Kudo and Richardson, 2018) and obtain vocabulary of size 8K on the English target, 16K on the (non-English) transcripts and 32K on the DSU, unless otherwise specified.

We use HuBERT-Base[3] model to extract the DSU by first downsampling the CoVoST-2 audio to 16KHz. Each audio data utterance is then converted into the DSU, i.e., the clustering indexes, by applying K-Means clustering (K=1,000; `MiniBatchKMeans` from SKLEARN) on its HuBERT representation from the 6th layer (Lakhotia et al., 2021). To train the K-Means model, we divide the 21 language pairs into three groups: 1) {ar, cy, et, id, ja, lv, mn, sl, sv, ta, tr}, 2) {nl, pt, ru, zh} and 3) {ca, de, es, fa, fr, it}. We then sample 1K instances for each language pair in group 1), which becomes 3K in group 2) and 12.5K in group 3), to create a multilingual training dataset of 98K instances for the K-Means model.

4.1.1 On the choice of using HuBERT-Base

Given the rapid advance in the SSS models, there are many alternatives, such as XLS-R (Babu et al., 2021) and Wavlm (Chen et al., 2022), for extracting the DSU for our method. These models are larger in scale and could be multilingual, thus providing DSU of higher qualities. The improvement of our method by using DSU from the HuBERT-Base would probably be a lower-bound, considering its

[2]We use vocabulary and tokenization interchangeably, since we did not apply subword regularisation.

[3]https://github.com/facebookresearch/fairseq/tree/main/examples/textless_nlp/gslm/speech2unit

relatively poor qualities to the bigger models. Since our goal is about compactness via DSU pretraining rather than comparing the DSU qualities across the SSS models, we took a simple HuBERT-Base model to illustrate the idea. Pretraining only on English audio data could also suggest hints on whether the DSU and our method could be generalised to languages that are unseen to the SSS models.

4.2 Model Configuration

All models are based on Transformer (Vaswani et al., 2017) with implementations from FAIRSEQ (Ott et al., 2019; Wang et al., 2020). In the Fbk-to-Token (i.e. transcriptions, DSU, or translations) models, the encoder has convolutional layers to downsample the Fbk by a factor of 4. There are 12-6 layers in the transformer encoder-decoder, whereas the embedding and feed-forward network (FFN) dimensions are 256 and 4,096 respectively, unless otherwise specified. It is worth noting that: (1) The Fbk-to-DSU model is not trained on the translations, so it is not directly comparable to the ST models. Its effect on ST lies on its pretrained encoder (Table 2). (2) The DSU-to-Trl model is a ST model which decoder can be used for initialization.

Scratch is a ST model trained on the paired speech-translation data without pretraining.

ASR Pretraining refers to a ST model whose encoder is initialized by a speech recognition task with CTC regularisation on the transcripts.

DSU-to-Trl follows the Transformer used in text translation. We use 6-6 layers in the encoder-decoder which the dimension of embedding and FFN is 256 and 2,048 respectively. In addition, we use "pre" layer-normalization (Nguyen and Salazar, 2019). Despite its smaller model size, its inference requires the quantization modules.

Hu-Transformer uses the entire HuBERT as the speech encoder initialization (Fang and Feng, 2023). For comparison to our DSU-Adapter, its subsequent encoder-decoder also has 1-6 layers.

DSU-Adapter is our proposed method. To better align the two pre-trained components, we also experiment with adding an extra encoder layer as a simple adapter layer after the pre-trained encoder. Because of the small model size, all model parameters are trainable. Since its decoder is initialized by the DSU-to-Trl method, its decoder FFN dimension is 2,048.

Enc-Init is a ST model that has its encoder initialized by the Fbk-to-DSU encoder. **EncDec-Init** is a DSU-Adapter model without the adapter layer.

4.3 Training and Inference

It is worth noting that we do not use extra audio data, e.g., Libri-Light (Kahn et al., 2020) in our (pretraining) experiments. Furthermore, we apply the following conditions in (pre-)training:

- We skip training data that are longer than 30 seconds (audio) or 1,024 target tokens.
- We apply SpecAugment (Park et al., 2019) with parameters: $\{F = 30, T = 40, m_F = 2, m_T = 2\}$ on Filterbank inputs.
- We share the embedding weights when using a joint vocabulary in the DSU-to-Trl model.
- We set λ_α and λ_β in CTC to 0.3 and the smoothing parameter to 0.1
- We initialize the encoder (decoder) with the last (best) checkpoint from the PT model.
- We use Adam optimizer with inverse square root scheduler for all model training.
- In all Fbk-to-Token models, the *effective mini-batch size*, *warm-up steps*, *peak learning rate* and *training steps* are 32K frames, 25K, 2e−3 and 60K steps respectively.
- Similarly, in all DSU-to-Trl models, we use 80K tokens, 10K, 5e−4 and 50K steps.
- Similarly, in Hu-Transformer, we use 4M frames, 4K, 1e−4 and 300K steps.

In inference, we average the last 5 checkpoints and use beam size of 5 in generation. All experiments are run on Nvidia A100 GPUs. It takes about 1 day for 2 A100 (40GB) GPUs to complete an experiment that uses Filterbank as speech inputs.

5 Results and Analysis

Before discussing the results, it is worth noting that (1) *Hu-Transformer is not memory-adaptive*, and (2) *ASR-Pretraining requires transcripts, unlike DSU which is self-supervised.* Both methods are introduced for reference purposes of if such resources are available.

AST model (#Params)	BLEU				chrF				COMET-22-DA			
	High	Mid	Low	All	High	Mid	Low	All	High	Mid	Low	All
Scratch (52M)	19.4	7.91	0.73	5.99	43.6	27.2	14.6	23.1	0.605	0.498	0.433	0.481
ASR-Pretraining (52M)	26.5	12.2	1.82	9.00	51.9	32.8	16.4	27.1	0.680	0.537	0.443	0.511
Hu-Transformer (113M)	24.3	11.4	2.18	8.60	49.9	31.9	17.0	26.8	0.650	0.522	0.439	0.499
DSU-Adapter (48M)	26.5	12.9	1.76	9.13	52.1	33.9	16.5	27.4	0.681	0.548	0.442	0.513

Table 1: Results in BLEU, chrF and COMET-22-DA on the test set of CoVoST-2 (X-En) by resource group. In all metrics, DSU-Adapter is much better than Hu-Transformer, which is 2.3 times larger, in both "High" and "Mid" groups. DSU-Adapter, which does not requires transcripts in training, is also on a par with ASR-Pretraining. The best result in each group is denoted by '_'.

5.1 Improvement brought by DSU-Adapter

We divide the 21 language pairs by resource level into: 1) "High": {ca, de, es, fr}, 2) "Mid": {fa, it, pt, ru and zh}, 3) "Low": {ar, cy, et, id, ja, lv, mn, nl, sl, sv, ta, tr} and 4) "All": the 21 languages pairs. We report the average BLEU[4] and chrF[5] over the test sets of each group using SACREBLEU (Post, 2018). In addition, we also provide the result in WMT22-COMET-DA (Rei et al., 2022), which the source inputs are the gold-reference transcripts.

Table 1 compares our DSU-Adapter and the baselines. Our DSU-Adapter is 3 BLEU (in the group "All") higher than the Scratch model. This shows that our proposed method of using DSU-pretraining can strengthen direct end-to-end ST without requiring transcripts and remain flexible in memory footprint (smaller in size than the HuBERT model). Furthermore, it is better than Hu-Transformer in spite of having half the parameters. For "Mid" and "High", the improvement in BLEU is 1.49 and 2.23 points respectively, but it falls short by 0.42 points for "Low". We also compare to ASR pretraining, which is not always applicable, e.g., in low-resource setting or perhaps even in an unwritten language (Zhang et al., 2022a). Surprisingly, our adapter is on a par with it, and its BLEU is 0.13 points better. The result remains consistent when it is measured in chrF and COMET.

5.1.1 Language-specific performance

Figure 3 shows the performance on each language pair in BLEU, chrF and COMET-22-DA. Our DSU-Adapter (in green triangles) show consistent improvement over the Scratch model (in blue circles) in all language pairs. Such improvement is rather surprising since HuBERT-Base was trained solely on English audio data. We hypothesized that the cross-lingual improvement is related to HuBERT's ability to capture language independent features, e.g. phonetic properties (Pasad et al., 2023).

Compared with Hu-Transformer, DSU-Adapter maintains an evident improvement over most language pairs in both "High" and "Mid" groups. Exceptions are in "fa" and "pt", but the lags are almost negligible. In group "Low", Hu-Transformer is slightly better, especially in "nl" and "sv" pairs. However, most translation in this group is barely around 2 BLEU, and the lags are small.

In most language pairs, DSU-Adapter performs similarly to ASR-pretraining (in red diamonds), except translating from "ru" audios. The improvement in this "ru-en" pair makes DSU-Adapter to have an evident advantage of 0.7 BLEU in the group "Mid".

5.2 Tokenization effect to the DSU-to-Trl method and the DSU-Adapter method

In this section, we investigate how tokenization, including BPE, affects the DSU-to-Trl method and the DSU-Adapter method. We are particularly interested in their robustness toward the tokenization, especially using BPE on the DSU, since tuning the quantization process and retraining the subsequent models is computationally expensive.

In Table 2, the 1st column "Has BPE on DSU?" indicates if BPE is applied on the DSU. If "Yes", multiple DSU could be merged into one subword unit, e.g., '#1 #456 #23 #999' could be merged into '#1#456#23#999'. The 2nd column "$|\mathcal{V}|$" shows the vocabulary configuration: its size, and if the model has a joint vocabulary. For example, "1K-8K" means that we use a vocabulary of size 1K for DSU and a second vocabulary of size 8K for English so that the DSU-to-Trl model would have separate vocabularies for the source (DSU) and target (English) sides. All results are in BLEU averaged over all language pairs, i.e., group "All".

[4] nrefs:1|case:mixed|eff:no|tok:13a|smooth:exp|version:2.3.1

[5] nrefs:1|case:mixed|eff:yes|nc:6|nw:0|space:no|version:2.3.1

Has BPE on DSU?	$\|\mathcal{V}\|$	DSU Length	Length Ratio	DSU-to-Trl (20M to 27M)	Enc-Init (52M to 70M)	EncDec-Init (46M to 64M)	DSU-Adapter (48M to 67M)
No	1K-8K	176	12.9	6.73	7.70	7.87	8.54
	1K-16K	"	14.1	6.36	7.50	8.00	8.43
	1K-32K	"	14.9	6.30	7.23	7.65	7.94
	8K	"	12.7	6.88	7.64	8.05	8.26
	16K	"	14.0	6.33	7.41	7.91	8.17
	32K	"	14.9	6.26	6.66	7.41	7.68
Yes	1K-8K	221	16.3	4.52	8.23	8.44	8.61
	16K-8K	129	9.5	5.06	8.51	8.76	8.95
	32K-8K	115	8.5	4.43	8.67	9.02	9.13
	8K	150	7.6	7.02	8.33	8.51	8.82
	16K	133	7.7	6.50	8.57	8.61	8.93
	32K	118	7.8	5.07	8.30	8.44	8.70

Table 2: (DSU) tokenization effect on 4 ST methods. Each ST model's performance on the CoVoST-2 test set is measured by BLEU on group "All". All 4 methods could perform better than the Scratch model of 5.99 BLEU as shown on Table 1. In general, darker (brighter) cells refer to weaker (stronger) models. The best two models apply both BPE on the DSU and separate vocabularies in PT (cells in yellow).

5.2.1 DSU-to-Trl: robust to tokenization?

When BPE is not applied on the DSU, those 6 DSU-to-Trl models have 6.48 ± 0.26 BLEU. Despite having smaller model size (<30M), they are better than the Scratch model of 5.99 BLEU.

When BPE is applied, the sequence length of DSU (DSU Length) could be shortened, which could in turn improve the performance, e.g. the best DSU-to-Trl model happens at configuration "8K" with 7.02 BLEU. However, the DSU-to-Trl method is quite unstable to the use of BPE, as reflected by the 5.12 ± 0.83 BLEU in the other 5 configurations. The correlation between the DSU sequence length, the source-target length ratio, and the ST performance is also not straightforward. For an example, the "32K" model (DSU length of 118) is about 2 BLEU behind to the "8K" model (DSU length of 150). Therefore, applying BPE on the DSU for length reduction should remain cautious.

5.2.2 The DSU-Adapter is more robust

Unlike DSU-to-Trl method, DSU-Adapter benefits more when BPE is applied to the DSU. Our proposed method has 8.86 ± 0.19 BLEU (over the 6 corresponding configurations), as opposed to 8.17 ± 0.32 BLEU when BPE is not applied. This observation is opposed to the DSU-to-Trl method which only scores 5.54 ± 1.07 BLEU (with also larger variance) when BPE is applied on the DSU but 6.48 ± 0.26 when BPE is not used. The improved mean score and its smaller variance suggests that the DSU-Adapter method is more (DSU) tokenization robust. We see this as a benefit of introducing the DSU, i.e., the SSS model knowledge, via PT rather than as model inputs.

On top of applying BPE on the DSU, using separate vocabularies in PT is preferred (the two yellow cells on Table 2) since it performs slightly better, and the DSU, which are not needed in the ST output, would not occupy the target vocabulary.

5.2.3 Ablation: initialisation in DSU-Adapter

Having similar model sizes, e.g. about 50M parameters (Table 2), DSU-Adapter is better than both EncDec-Init and Enc-Init methods. The translation performance in BLEU (averaged over the 12 vocabularies) is 8.51 ± 0.44, 8.22 ± 0.51, and 7.99 ± 0.61 respectively. Encoder-initialization seems more crucial than decoder-initialization, as reflected by the fact that the best DSU-Adapter model comes from a combination with the weakest DSU-to-Trl model of 4.43 BLEU.

5.3 Is CTC applicable also to DSU?

Similar to ST methods that use pretrained components, our method could be limited by the *pretraining modality gap* (Liu et al., 2020; Le et al., 2023). Motivated by prior works, we investigate mitigating it with CTC. A crucial difference to the prior works is that our method uses DSU for pre-training rather than transcripts.

We thus study applying CTC in our method at

Has CTC in DSU PT?	Has CTC in ST FT?	High	Mid	Low	All
No	No	25.81	9.91	1.46	8.14
No	Yes	26.10	11.35	1.69	8.71
Yes	No	25.94	10.82	1.51	8.44
Yes	Yes	26.12	11.53	1.73	8.74

Table 3: Effect of CTC on Fbk-to-DSU PT and/or ST FT to the DSU-Adapter method. All results are in BLEU and the best in each group is denoted by '_'.

different training stages. Owing to the large number of vocabulary configurations on Table 2, we only experiment with: 1) "No-BPE 1K-8K", 2) "BPE 8K", 3) "BPE 32K" and 4) "BPE 32K-8K". In each training stage, we report the effect of CTC to the ST performance (per resource group) by averaging the BLEU of these 4 configurations.

Table 3 presents the analysis of applying CTC on our DSU-Adapter method. The training condition "Has CTC in DSU PT" refers to the case of applying CTC on the *discrete speech units* in Fbk-to-DSU pretraining, whereas "Has CTC in ST FT" refers to the case of applying CTC on the *translations* in ST finetuning, i.e., on the paired Fbk-Trl data. Our result shows that CTC helps on either stage, but the gain is 0.27 BLEU more in ST finetuning. Using them jointly still helps, but the marginal gain is barely 0.03 BLEU.

6 Limitations and future works

In the previous sections, we discuss the noticeable benefits of our DSU-pretraining method in creating a more compact ST model. In spite of this, there are several factors that are not thoroughly explored and could improve the model performance further:

K-Means clustering We did not inspect the clustering size (fixed to $1,000$) and the number of training instances (only fixed to $98,000$) used in training the K-Means clustering model. Apart from tuning its hyper-parameters, using other techniques, such as residual vector quantisation (Zeghidour et al., 2021; Défossez et al., 2022) and multiple codebooks (Guo et al., 2023), might bring better improvement.

Other acoustic encoders We did not experiment other acoustic encoders, such as conformer (Gulati et al., 2020; Papi et al., 2023) and E-Branchformer (Peng et al., 2023). This stronger encoders should provide further gains for our method since they also enjoy the benefit of pretraining.

A stronger pretrained decoder Apart from strengthening the encoder, the DSU-to-Trl model and hence its decoder (used in initialisation) could also be improved, e.g. via back-translation, upsampling the textual sequence (Yan et al., 2024) and pretraining with more text data, while maintaining the small decoder size.

Further analyses In addition to improving our pretraining method for better model compactness, there are other related research directions worth further analyzing. One direction would be how, in terms of acoustic pretraining, DSU compared with transcripts (if available in that language) over different data scales. Another interesting research direction would be the comparison and analysis of using DSU or dense features in a large pretrained model setting, such as Whisper (Radford et al., 2023) and Large Language Models.

7 Conclusion

In this paper, we consider a memory-constrained setting for ST. Our proposed method uses DSU in the form of pretraining to distil the knowledge from the Self-Supervised Speech model to creating more compact Speech-to-text Translation. Our compact model, i.e., the DSU-Adapter, shows strong and consistent improvements in three evaluation metrics over the baselines. In contrast to using DSU as model inputs, our method does not require quantization modules in inference and shows stronger robustness to the DSU tokenization. Finally, our method requires no transcripts, making it also suitable for low-resource setting.

Acknowledgements

This work was funded by UK Research and Innovation (UKRI) under the UK government's Horizon Europe funding guarantee (grant number 10039436: UTTER). The computations described in this research were performed using the Baskerville Tier 2 HPC service (https://www.baskerville.ac.uk/). Baskerville was funded by the EPSRC and UKRI through the World Class Labs scheme (EP/T022221/1) and the Digital Research Infrastructure programme (EP/W032244/1) and is operated by Advanced Research Computing at the University of Birmingham.

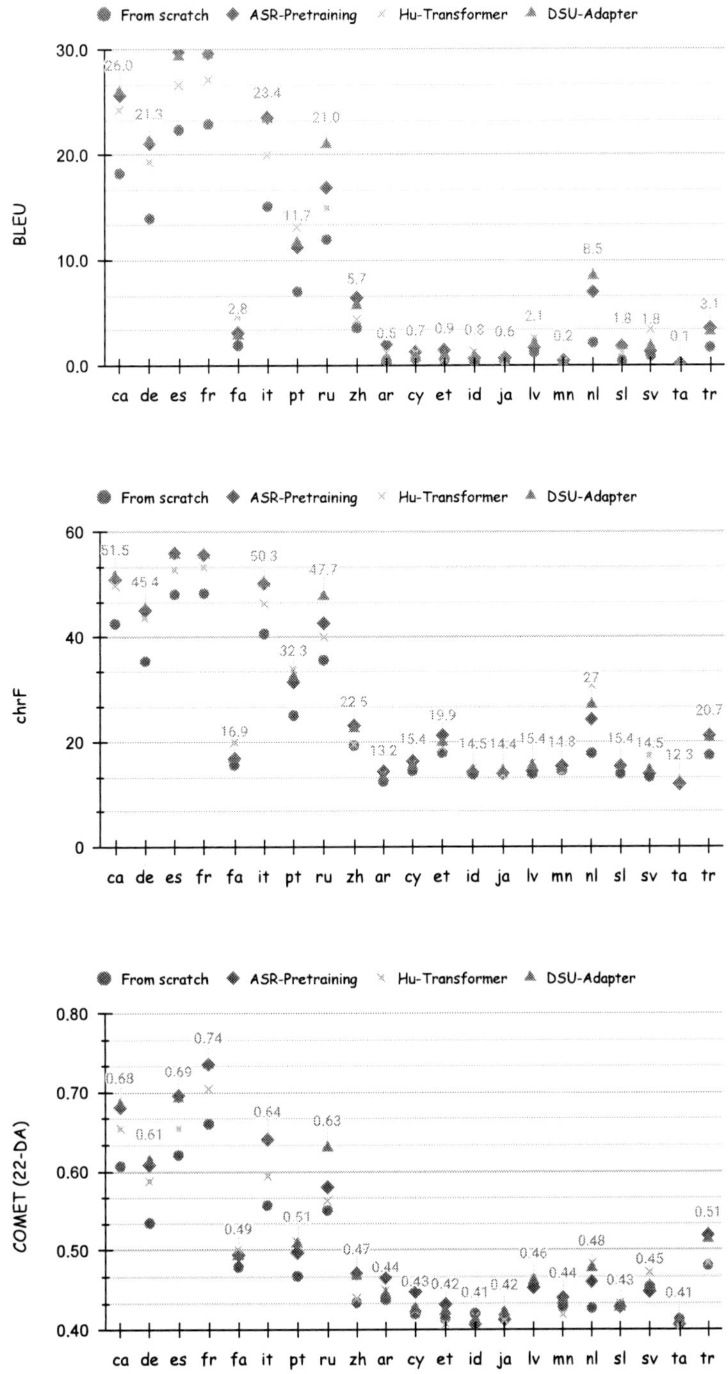

Figure 3: Results in BLEU, chrF and COMET-22-DA on each language pair of CoVoST-2 (X-En).

References

Milind Agarwal, Sweta Agrawal, Antonios Anastasopoulos, Luisa Bentivogli, Ondřej Bojar, Claudia Borg, Marine Carpuat, Roldano Cattoni, Mauro Cettolo, Mingda Chen, William Chen, Khalid Choukri, Alexandra Chronopoulou, Anna Currey, Thierry Declerck, Qianqian Dong, Kevin Duh, Yannick Estève, Marcello Federico, Souhir Gahbiche, Barry Haddow, Benjamin Hsu, Phu Mon Htut, Hirofumi Inaguma, Dávid Javorský, John Judge, Yasumasa Kano, Tom Ko, Rishu Kumar, Pengwei Li, Xutai Ma, Prashant Mathur, Evgeny Matusov, Paul McNamee, John P. McCrae, Kenton Murray, Maria Nadejde, Satoshi Nakamura, Matteo Negri, Ha Nguyen, Jan Niehues, Xing Niu, Atul Kr. Ojha, John E. Ortega, Proyag Pal, Juan Pino, Lonneke van der Plas, Peter Polák, Elijah Rippeth, Elizabeth Salesky, Jiatong Shi, Matthias Sperber, Sebastian Stüker, Katsuhito Sudoh, Yun Tang, Brian Thompson, Kevin Tran, Marco Turchi, Alex Waibel, Mingxuan Wang, Shinji Watanabe, and Rodolfo Zevallos. 2023. FINDINGS OF THE IWSLT 2023 EVALUATION CAMPAIGN. In *Proceedings of the 20th International Conference on Spoken Language Translation (IWSLT 2023)*, pages 1–61, Toronto, Canada (in-person and online). Association for Computational Linguistics.

Junyi Ao, Ziqiang Zhang, Long Zhou, Shujie Liu, Haizhou Li, Tom Ko, Lirong Dai, Jinyu Li, Yao Qian, and Furu Wei. 2022. Pre-Training Transformer Decoder for End-to-End ASR Model with Unpaired Speech Data. In *Proc. Interspeech 2022*, pages 2658–2662.

Arun Babu, Changhan Wang, Andros Tjandra, Kushal Lakhotia, Qiantong Xu, Naman Goyal, Kritika Singh, Patrick von Platen, Yatharth Saraf, Juan Pino, et al. 2021. Xls-r: Self-supervised cross-lingual speech representation learning at scale. *arXiv preprint arXiv:2111.09296*.

Alexei Baevski, Yuhao Zhou, Abdelrahman Mohamed, and Michael Auli. 2020. wav2vec 2.0: A framework for self-supervised learning of speech representations. *Advances in neural information processing systems*, 33:12449–12460.

Xuankai Chang, Brian Yan, Kwanghee Choi, Jeeweon Jung, Yichen Lu, Soumi Maiti, Roshan Sharma, Jiatong Shi, Jinchuan Tian, Shinji Watanabe, et al. 2023. Exploring speech recognition, translation, and understanding with discrete speech units: A comparative study. *arXiv preprint arXiv:2309.15800*.

Sanyuan Chen, Chengyi Wang, Zhengyang Chen, Yu Wu, Shujie Liu, Zhuo Chen, Jinyu Li, Naoyuki Kanda, Takuya Yoshioka, Xiong Xiao, et al. 2022. Wavlm: Large-scale self-supervised pre-training for full stack speech processing. *IEEE Journal of Selected Topics in Signal Processing*, 16(6):1505–1518.

Ju-Chieh Chou, Chung-Ming Chien, Wei-Ning Hsu, Karen Livescu, Arun Babu, Alexis Conneau, Alexei Baevski, and Michael Auli. 2023. Toward joint language modeling for speech units and text. In *Findings of the Association for Computational Linguistics: EMNLP 2023*, pages 6582–6593, Singapore. Association for Computational Linguistics.

Alexandre Défossez, Jade Copet, Gabriel Synnaeve, and Yossi Adi. 2022. High fidelity neural audio compression. *arXiv preprint arXiv:2210.13438*.

Qingkai Fang and Yang Feng. 2023. Back translation for speech-to-text translation without transcripts. In *Proceedings of the 61st Annual Meeting of the Association for Computational Linguistics (Volume 1: Long Papers)*, pages 4567–4587, Toronto, Canada. Association for Computational Linguistics.

Marco Gaido, Mauro Cettolo, Matteo Negri, and Marco Turchi. 2021. CTC-based compression for direct speech translation. In *Proceedings of the 16th Conference of the European Chapter of the Association for Computational Linguistics: Main Volume*, pages 690–696, Online. Association for Computational Linguistics.

Alex Graves, Santiago Fernández, Faustino J. Gomez, and Jürgen Schmidhuber. 2006. Connectionist temporal classification: labelling unsegmented sequence data with recurrent neural networks. In *Machine Learning, Proceedings of the Twenty-Third International Conference (ICML 2006), Pittsburgh, Pennsylvania, USA, June 25-29, 2006*, volume 148 of *ACM International Conference Proceeding Series*, pages 369–376. ACM.

Anmol Gulati, James Qin, Chung-Cheng Chiu, Niki Parmar, Yu Zhang, Jiahui Yu, Wei Han, Shibo Wang, Zhengdong Zhang, Yonghui Wu, and Ruoming Pang. 2020. Conformer: Convolution-augmented Transformer for Speech Recognition. In *Proc. Interspeech 2020*, pages 5036–5040.

Liyong Guo, Xiaoyu Yang, Quandong Wang, Yuxiang Kong, Zengwei Yao, Fan Cui, Fangjun Kuang, Wei Kang, Long Lin, Mingshuang Luo, et al. 2023. Predicting multi-codebook vector quantization indexes for knowledge distillation. In *ICASSP 2023-2023 IEEE International Conference on Acoustics, Speech and Signal Processing (ICASSP)*, pages 1–5. IEEE.

Wei-Ning Hsu, Benjamin Bolte, Yao-Hung Hubert Tsai, Kushal Lakhotia, Ruslan Salakhutdinov, and Abdelrahman Mohamed. 2021. Hubert: Self-supervised speech representation learning by masked prediction of hidden units. *IEEE/ACM Transactions on Audio, Speech, and Language Processing*, 29:3451–3460.

Jacob Kahn, Morgane Rivière, Weiyi Zheng, Evgeny Kharitonov, Qiantong Xu, Pierre-Emmanuel Mazaré, Julien Karadayi, Vitaliy Liptchinsky, Ronan Collobert, Christian Fuegen, Tatiana Likhomanenko, Gabriel Synnaeve, Armand Joulin, Abdelrahman Mohamed, and Emmanuel Dupoux. 2020. Libri-light: A benchmark for ASR with limited or no supervision. In *2020 IEEE International Conference on Acoustics, Speech and Signal Processing, ICASSP 2020,*

Barcelona, Spain, May 4-8, 2020, pages 7669–7673. IEEE.

Taku Kudo and John Richardson. 2018. SentencePiece: A simple and language independent subword tokenizer and detokenizer for neural text processing. In *Proceedings of the 2018 Conference on Empirical Methods in Natural Language Processing: System Demonstrations*, pages 66–71, Brussels, Belgium. Association for Computational Linguistics.

Kushal Lakhotia, Eugene Kharitonov, Wei-Ning Hsu, Yossi Adi, Adam Polyak, Benjamin Bolte, Tu-Anh Nguyen, Jade Copet, Alexei Baevski, Abdelrahman Mohamed, and Emmanuel Dupoux. 2021. On generative spoken language modeling from raw audio. *Transactions of the Association for Computational Linguistics*, 9:1336–1354.

Phuong-Hang Le, Hongyu Gong, Changhan Wang, Juan Pino, Benjamin Lecouteux, and Didier Schwab. 2023. Pre-training for speech translation: CTC meets optimal transport. In *Proceedings of the 40th International Conference on Machine Learning*, volume 202 of *Proceedings of Machine Learning Research*, pages 18667–18685. PMLR.

Yuchen Liu, Junnan Zhu, Jiajun Zhang, and Chengqing Zong. 2020. Bridging the modality gap for speech-to-text translation. *arXiv preprint arXiv:2010.14920*.

Toan Q. Nguyen and Julian Salazar. 2019. Transformers without tears: Improving the normalization of self-attention. In *Proceedings of the 16th International Conference on Spoken Language Translation*, Hong Kong. Association for Computational Linguistics.

Myle Ott, Sergey Edunov, Alexei Baevski, Angela Fan, Sam Gross, Nathan Ng, David Grangier, and Michael Auli. 2019. fairseq: A fast, extensible toolkit for sequence modeling. In *Proceedings of the 2019 Conference of the North American Chapter of the Association for Computational Linguistics (Demonstrations)*, pages 48–53, Minneapolis, Minnesota. Association for Computational Linguistics.

Sara Papi, Marco Gaido, Andrea Pilzer, and Matteo Negri. 2023. When good and reproducible results are a giant with feet of clay: The importance of software quality in nlp. *arXiv preprint arXiv:2303.16166*.

Daniel S. Park, William Chan, Yu Zhang, Chung-Cheng Chiu, Barret Zoph, Ekin D. Cubuk, and Quoc V. Le. 2019. SpecAugment: A Simple Data Augmentation Method for Automatic Speech Recognition. In *Proc. Interspeech 2019*, pages 2613–2617.

Ankita Pasad, Bowen Shi, and Karen Livescu. 2023. Comparative layer-wise analysis of self-supervised speech models. In *ICASSP 2023-2023 IEEE International Conference on Acoustics, Speech and Signal Processing (ICASSP)*, pages 1–5. IEEE.

Yifan Peng, Kwangyoun Kim, Felix Wu, Brian Yan, Siddhant Arora, William Chen, Jiyang Tang, Suwon Shon, Prashant Sridhar, and Shinji Watanabe. 2023. A Comparative Study on E-Branchformer vs Conformer in Speech Recognition, Translation, and Understanding Tasks. In *Proc. INTERSPEECH 2023*, pages 2208–2212.

Adam Polyak, Yossi Adi, Jade Copet, Eugene Kharitonov, Kushal Lakhotia, Wei-Ning Hsu, Abdelrahman Mohamed, and Emmanuel Dupoux. 2021. Speech Resynthesis from Discrete Disentangled Self-Supervised Representations. In *Proc. Interspeech 2021*, pages 3615–3619.

Matt Post. 2018. A call for clarity in reporting BLEU scores. In *Proceedings of the Third Conference on Machine Translation: Research Papers*, pages 186–191, Brussels, Belgium. Association for Computational Linguistics.

Alec Radford, Jong Wook Kim, Tao Xu, Greg Brockman, Christine McLeavey, and Ilya Sutskever. 2023. Robust speech recognition via large-scale weak supervision. In *International Conference on Machine Learning*, pages 28492–28518. PMLR.

Ricardo Rei, José G. C. de Souza, Duarte Alves, Chrysoula Zerva, Ana C Farinha, Taisiya Glushkova, Alon Lavie, Luisa Coheur, and André F. T. Martins. 2022. COMET-22: Unbabel-IST 2022 submission for the metrics shared task. In *Proceedings of the Seventh Conference on Machine Translation (WMT)*, pages 578–585, Abu Dhabi, United Arab Emirates (Hybrid). Association for Computational Linguistics.

Rico Sennrich, Barry Haddow, and Alexandra Birch. 2016. Neural machine translation of rare words with subword units. In *Proceedings of the 54th Annual Meeting of the Association for Computational Linguistics (Volume 1: Long Papers)*, pages 1715–1725, Berlin, Germany. Association for Computational Linguistics.

Ashish Vaswani, Noam Shazeer, Niki Parmar, Jakob Uszkoreit, Llion Jones, Aidan N Gomez, Łukasz Kaiser, and Illia Polosukhin. 2017. Attention is all you need. *Advances in neural information processing systems*, 30.

Changhan Wang, Yun Tang, Xutai Ma, Anne Wu, Dmytro Okhonko, and Juan Pino. 2020. Fairseq S2T: Fast speech-to-text modeling with fairseq. In *Proceedings of the 1st Conference of the Asia-Pacific Chapter of the Association for Computational Linguistics and the 10th International Joint Conference on Natural Language Processing: System Demonstrations*, pages 33–39, Suzhou, China. Association for Computational Linguistics.

Changhan Wang, Anne Wu, Jiatao Gu, and Juan Pino. 2021. CoVoST 2 and Massively Multilingual Speech Translation. In *Proc. Interspeech 2021*, pages 2247–2251.

Felix Wu, Kwangyoun Kim, Shinji Watanabe, Kyu Jeong Han, Ryan McDonald, Kilian Q. Weinberger, and Yoav Artzi. 2023. Wav2seq: Pre-training speech-to-text encoder-decoder models using pseudo languages. In *IEEE International Conference on Acoustics, Speech and Signal Processing ICASSP 2023, Rhodes Island, Greece, June 4-10, 2023*, pages 1–5. IEEE.

Brian Yan, Xuankai Chang, Antonios Anastasopoulos, Yuya Fujita, and Shinji Watanabe. 2024. Cross-modal multi-tasking for speech-to-text translation via hard parameter sharing. In *ICASSP 2024 - 2024 IEEE International Conference on Acoustics, Speech and Signal Processing (ICASSP)*, pages 11941–11945.

Neil Zeghidour, Alejandro Luebs, Ahmed Omran, Jan Skoglund, and Marco Tagliasacchi. 2021. Soundstream: An end-to-end neural audio codec. *IEEE/ACM Transactions on Audio, Speech, and Language Processing*, 30:495–507.

Biao Zhang, Barry Haddow, and Rico Sennrich. 2022a. Revisiting end-to-end speech-to-text translation from scratch. In *International Conference on Machine Learning*, pages 26193–26205. PMLR.

Biao Zhang, Barry Haddow, and Rico Sennrich. 2023a. Efficient CTC regularization via coarse labels for end-to-end speech translation. In *Proceedings of the 17th Conference of the European Chapter of the Association for Computational Linguistics*, pages 2264–2276, Dubrovnik, Croatia. Association for Computational Linguistics.

Dong Zhang, Rong Ye, Tom Ko, Mingxuan Wang, and Yaqian Zhou. 2023b. DUB: Discrete unit back-translation for speech translation. In *Findings of the Association for Computational Linguistics: ACL 2023*, pages 7147–7164, Toronto, Canada. Association for Computational Linguistics.

Ziqiang Zhang, Long Zhou, Junyi Ao, Shujie Liu, Lirong Dai, Jinyu Li, and Furu Wei. 2022b. SpeechUT: Bridging speech and text with hidden-unit for encoder-decoder based speech-text pre-training. In *Proceedings of the 2022 Conference on Empirical Methods in Natural Language Processing*, pages 1663–1676, Abu Dhabi, United Arab Emirates. Association for Computational Linguistics.

QUESPA Submission for the IWSLT 2024 Dialectal and Low-resource Speech Translation Task

John E. Ortega[1], **Rodolfo Zevallos**[2], **William Chen**[3], **Ibrahim Said Ahmad**[1]
[1]Northeastern University, USA, [2]Universitat Pompeu Fabra, Spain
[3]Carnegie Mellon University, USA
contact email: j.ortega@northeastern.edu

Abstract

This article describes the **QUESPA** team speech translation (ST) submissions for the Quechua to Spanish (QUE–SPA) track featured in the Evaluation Campaign of IWSLT 2024: dialectal and low-resource speech translation. Two main submission types were supported in the campaign: *constrained* and *unconstrained*. This is our second year submitting our ST systems to the IWSLT shared task and we feel that we have achieved novel performance, surpassing last year's submissions. Again, we were able to submit six total systems of which our best (primary) *constrained* system consisted of an ST model based on the Fairseq S2T framework where the audio representations were created using log mel-scale filter banks as features and the translations were performed using a transformer. The system was similar to last year's submission with slight configuration changes, allowing us to achieve slightly higher performance (2 BLEU). Contrastingly, we were able to achieve much better performance than last year on the *unconstrained* task using a larger pre-trained language (PLM) model for ST (without cascading) and the inclusion of parallel QUE–SPA data found on the internet. The fine-tuning of Microsoft's SpeechT5 model in a ST setting along with the addition of new data and a data augmentation technique allowed us to achieve 19.7 BLEU. Additionally, we present the other four submissions (2 constrained and 2 unconstrained) which are part of additional efforts of hyper-parameter and configuration tuning on existent models and the inclusion of Whisper for speech recognition.

1 Introduction

Speech Translation (ST) has historically been a difficult task due to the lack of parallel data required to train neural end-to-end systems. As such, the traditional approach to this task has been to use a cascade of distinct modules, separating ST into the subtasks of Automatic Speech Recognition (ASR) and Machine Translation (MT). While this allows ST systems to benefit from the advances in Pretrained Language Models (PLMs) for ASR and MT, creating usable models for low-resource languages has remained a challenge due to the lack of support for these languages in PLMs. Findings from previous iterations of IWSLT (Antonios et al., 2022; Agarwal et al., 2023a) clearly show this phenomena: large-scale ensembling and multilingual supervised pre-training are required to even reach 15 BLEU (Papineni et al., 2002) in low-resource pairs such as Quechua–Spanish.

This year, the IWSLT 2024 (Agarwal et al., 2023b) evaluation campaign for low-resource and dialect speech translation has included several language pairs for which many teams have submitted to the *unconstrained* task. Some language pairs such as Bemba–English have recorded BLEU scores as low as 0.5. We feel that as second-time entries we are able to rely on previously built ST systems to leverage our work on the Quechua to Spanish (QUE–SPA) language pair.

Quechua is an indigenous language spoken by more than 8 million people in South America. It is mainly spoken in Peru, Ecuador, and Bolivia where the official high-resource language is Spanish. It is a highly inflective language based on its suffixes which agglutinate and found to be similar to other languages like Finnish. It is worthwhile to note that previous work (Ortega and Pillaipakkamnatt, 2018; Ortega et al., 2020) has been somewhat successful in identifying the inflectional properties of Quechua such as agglutination where another high-resource language, namely Finnish, can aid for translation purposes achieving nearly 20 BLEU on religious-based (text-only) tasks. The average number of morphemes per word (synthesis) is about two times larger than English. English typically has around 1.5 morphemes per word and Quechua has about 3 morphemes per word. There are two main region divisions of Quechua known

Proceedings of the 21st International Conference on Spoken Language Translation (IWSLT 2024), pages 173–181
August 15-16, 2024 ©2024 Association for Computational Linguistics

as Quechua I and Quechua II. This data set consists of two main types of Quechua spoken in Ayacucho, Peru (Quechua Chanka ISO:quy) and Cusco, Peru (Quechua Collao ISO:quz) which are both part of Quechua II and, thus, considered a "southern" languages. We label the data set with que - the ISO norm for Quechua II mixtures.

The **QUESPA** team this year consists of four organizers from three different institutions: Northeastern University, Carnegie Melon University, and Pompeu Fabra University. A new organizer has been introduced this year who has expertise in African languages. All of the IWSLT 2023 organizers have continued to work on the project; all of the previous organizers have had experience with the QUE–SPA language pair in the past. In this article, we report the QUESPA consortium submission for the IWSLT 2024 and once again focus on the low-resource task at hand by combining *all* the two dialects *Quechua I and II* into one.

The rest of this article is organized as follows. Section 2 presents the related work. The experiments for QUE–SPA low-resource track are presented in Section 3. Section 4 provides results from the six submitted systems and concludes this work.

2 Related Work

In this section, we first cover the different approaches used in previous speech processing shared tasks for Quechua (Section 2.1). We then discuss prior work that used a similar strategy to our primary submission to the unconstrained track (Section 2.2).

2.1 Quechua Speech Processing

The previous iteration of IWSLT (Agarwal et al., 2023a) was the first time that Quechua–Spanish was featured in the low-resource ST track. Due to the small amount of available paired data, the participants focused on exploiting PLMs for speech and/or text in the unconstrained track. The teams all converged on using XLS-R 128 (Babu et al., 2021) as the pre-trained speech encoder, while NLLB 200 (NLLB Team et al., 2022) was the most popular text PLM. However, the teams used the PLMs in very different manners. QUESPA (E. Ortega et al., 2023) separated the PLMs into distinct systems for an ASR+MT cascade, GMU (Mbuya and Anastasopoulos, 2023) performed full finetuning on XLS-R for direct ST, and NLE (Gow-Smith et al., 2023) combined the two PLMs via adapter fine-tuning. By using PLMs for both the input and output modalities, NLE and QUESPA obtained the best performances at 15.7 and 15.4 BLEU respectively. For the constrained track, developing a usable system was far more difficult to achieve. In this setup, the best performing model was a direct ST system by GMU that achieved 1.46 BLEU. The QUESPA team adopted a near-identical strategy to achieve 1.25 BLEU.

Quechua–Spanish ST was also featured as part of a similar competition in the 2022 edition of AmericasNLP (Ebrahimi et al., 2022). Similar to IWSLT 2023, participants experimented with different ways of leveraging PLMs. XLS-R and NLLB were popular choices, but some teams also experimented with DeltaLM (Ma et al., 2021) and Whisper (Radford et al., 2023).

Quechua was most recently part of the 2023 ML-SUPERB Challenge (Shi et al., 2023), which tasked participants on evaluating different self-supervised (SSL) speech encoders on long-tail languages. Chen et al. (2023a) found that XLS-R 128 outperformed all other SSL encoders on Quechua, further validating its popularity in the other competitions.

2.2 Multilingual Speech Processing

Multilingual training is a common strategy to facilitate cross-lingual transfer learning, with the goal of boosting performance on low-resource languages. While this is generally done by pairing high-resource languages with low-resource ones, it can also be beneficial in settings where only low-resource languages are available. Chen et al. (2023b) trained multilingual ASR systems on 102 languages, each in a low-resource setting, and obtained state-of-the-art (SOTA) results on the FLEURS benchmark (Conneau et al., 2023). Radford et al. (2023) and Peng et al. (2023) then combined multilingual ASR and ST at scale, developing SOTA models through supervised training on hundreds of thousands of audio. Our strategy for the unconstrained track can be viewed as a combination of these two methods, enhancing performance on Quechua–Spanish using multilingual ST training with other low-resource languages.

3 Quechua-Spanish

In this section we present our experiments for the QUE–SPA dataset provided in the low-resource ST track at IWSLT 2024, identical to the dataset from

IWSLT 2023. As a reminder, the audio consists of contains 1 hour and 40 minutes of *constrained* speech along with its corresponding translations and nearly 48 hours of ASR data (with transcriptions) from the Siminichik (Cardenas et al., 2018) corpus. As an additional constrained setting, the dataset offers the QUE–SPA MT corpus from previous neural MT work (Ortega et al., 2020). The audio and corresponding transcriptions along with their translations are mostly made of radio broadcasting from the mountainous region in the Andes, Peru. This dataset has been used in other tasks but not in its entirety (Ebrahimi et al., 2023, 2022).

We present the six submissions for both the *constrained* and *unconstrained* as follows:

1. a primary constrained system that uses a direct ST approach with a extra small transformer (Vaswani et al., 2017; Wang et al., 2020);
2. a contrastive 1 constrained system that uses a direct ST approach with a medium (default) transformer (Vaswani et al., 2017; Wang et al., 2020) along with several data augmentation techniques;
3. a contrastive 2 constrained system that uses a direct ST approach with a medium (default) transformer (Vaswani et al., 2017; Wang et al., 2020) without data augmentation techniques;
4. a primary unconstrained system consisting of a SpeechT5 model fine-tuned for speech translation with one data augmentation technique;
5. a contrastive 1 unconstrained system consisting of a SpeechT5 model fine-tuned for speech translation with two data augmentation techniques;
6. a contrastive 2 unconstrained system consisting of a Whisper (Radford et al., 2023) ASR model fine-tuned for speech translation and cascaded with the NLLB MT system.

We present the experimental settings and results for all systems starting off with constrained systems in Section 3.1 and continuing with the unconstrained systems in Section 3.2. Finally, we offer results and discussion in Section 4.

3.1 Constrained Setting

Identical to last year, the IWSLT 2024 constrained setting for QUE–SPA consists of two main datasets.

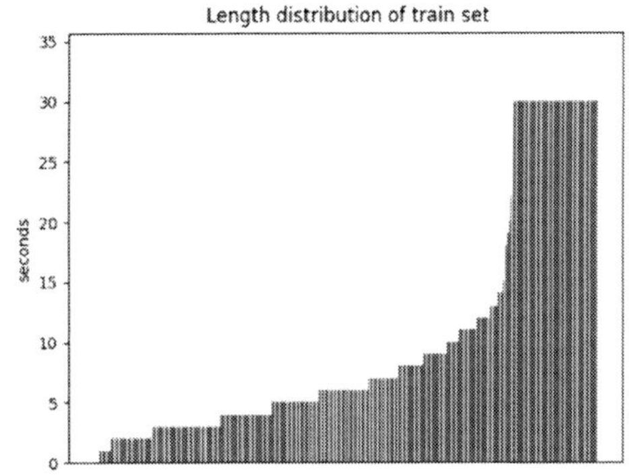

Figure 1: Training set audio lengths vary from 1 to 30 seconds while validation and test set are 30 seconds long.

First, the speech translation dataset consists of 1 hour and 40 minutes divided into 573 training files, 125 validation files, and 125 test files where each file is a .wav file with a corresponding transcription and human-validated translation from Siminchik (Cardenas et al., 2018). Secondly, there is a MT data set combined by previous work (Ortega et al., 2020) which consists of 100 daily magazine article sentences and 51140 sentences which are of religious context in nature.

This year, one of the findings we observed is that the dataset has uneven distributions between training and validation/test. The training set largely consisted of utterances shorter than 20 seconds (Figure 1), while the validation and test set was almost exclusively 30 seconds long inputs. This is something that the organizers plan to rearrange for next year's challenged, but this type of mismatch can be considered a hurdle due to the difference (smaller utterances result in unbalance). For this submission, we found it somewhat difficult to train direct ST systems under the constrained settings. However, we present the following systems that mitigate the concern considering that our results outperform the best performing *constrained* systems.

Development of the *Primary*, *Contrastive 1*, and *Contrastive 2* systems consisted of an extension of the original ST systems built in IWSLT 2023. During development, several experiments led us to the best performing systems (Primary and Contrastive 2). The developmental process is documented in Table 1 for a historical way of showing our path to the final systems.

Model Type	Optimization	Learning Rate	Checkpoint	BLEU
s2t_transformer	Adam	0.002	best of the last 10 on 500 epochs	0.9
s2t_transformer_xs	Adamax	0.0001	best of the last 10 on 500 epochs	0.6
2t_transformer_xs	Adamax	0.0001	best of the last 10 on 500 epochs	0.6
s2t_transformer_xs	Adam	0.0001	best of the last 10 on 500 epochs	0.7
s2t_transformer_large	Adam	0.001	best of the last 10 on 500 epochs	0.0
s2t_transformer	Adamax	0.001	best of the last 10 on 500 epochs	1.0
s2t_transformer	Adamax	0.001	best of the last 10 on 400 epochs	1.0
s2t_transformer	Adamax	0.001	best of the last 10 on 300 epochs	1.0
s2t_transformer	Adamax	0.001	best of the last 10 on 200 epochs	1.0
s2t_transformer	Adamax	0.001	best of the last 10 on 100 epochs	1.0
s2t_transformer	Adamax	0.001	avg of the last 10 on 400 epochs	1.4

Table 1: BLEU scores on developmental models for the *contrained* settings using beam size of five.

3.1.1 Primary System

The **Primary** System is similar to previous work (Ortega et al., 2023). The dataset has not changed since their work and our system consists of the use of a direct ST approach.

Again, we use the Fairseq (Ott et al., 2019) toolkit to perform direct ST using the 573 training files, a total of 1.6 hours of audio. The use of feature extraction through log mel-filter bank (MFB) features and is still based on the S2T approach by (Wang et al., 2020). Identically, we generate a 1k unigram vocabulary for the Spanish text using SentencePiece (Kudo and Richardson, 2018), with no pre-tokenization. This year's model consists of a convolutional feature extractor and transformer encoder-decoder (Vaswani et al., 2017), also known as the "extra-small transformer", (s2t_transformer_xs) with 6 encoder layers and 3 decoder layers. Error is measured using cross entropy and optimization is done using Adam. Our model was run for 500 epochs with a learning rate of .0002. For this submission, the main difference is that we use a device that allows us to **average** the 10 last checkpoints through PyTorch[1]. We compared the average to the best of the last 10 checkpoints and found that the average performed better.

3.1.2 Contrastive 1 System

The **Contrastive 1** system is based on a transformer much like the Primary system. However, Contrastive 1 uses two novel techniques introduced that were not present in the IWSLT 2023 QUESPA submission (Ortega et al., 2023): (1) a new model size which contains more layers and (2) five new data augmentation techniques based on the data at hand.

As was done in the Primary system, the Fairseq (Ott et al., 2019) toolkit is used to perform direct ST on the training data of 1.6 hours of audio. Identical feature extraction techniques are used via the log mel-filter bank (MFB) features from the S2T approach in previous work (Wang et al., 2020). Also, we generate a 1k unigram vocabulary for the Spanish text using SentencePiece (Kudo and Richardson, 2018), with no pre-tokenization.

The first main difference is the model. The Contrastive 1 model consists of a convolutional feature extractor and transformer encoder-decoder (Vaswani et al., 2017); but it uses the medium-sized transformer, also known as the "transformer", (s2t_transformer) with 12 encoder layers and 6 decoder layers. Additionally, Contrastive 1 has 8 decoder attention heads as opposed to 4 in the Primary system.

The second difference we consider a *major* difference – the use of data augmentation to increase the input size. Augmentation techniques were used from previous work using LibRosa[2]. More specifically, code can be found online[3] to reproduce our experiments. The increase in the input training dataset increased four fold using the following four techniques for augmentation: *Noise*, *Roll*, *Time*, and *Pitch*. The noise addition (augmentation) is done using an aggregation of 0.009. The Roll adjustment is of $sr/10$. Time is through a stretch factor of 0.4 and Pitch is of -5. With the increase of input size, experiments ran slower yet were not of significant impact. We save further iterations of data augmentation as future work as we believe that is has had an impact here.

Error is measured using cross entropy and optimization is done using Adam. Other hyperparameter choices that were not the same as the Primary submission include the exclusion of **SpecAugment** (Park et al., 2019) as an audio aug-

[1] https://pytorch.org/

[2] https://librosa.org/

[3] https://colab.research.google.com/gist/keyurparalkar/5a

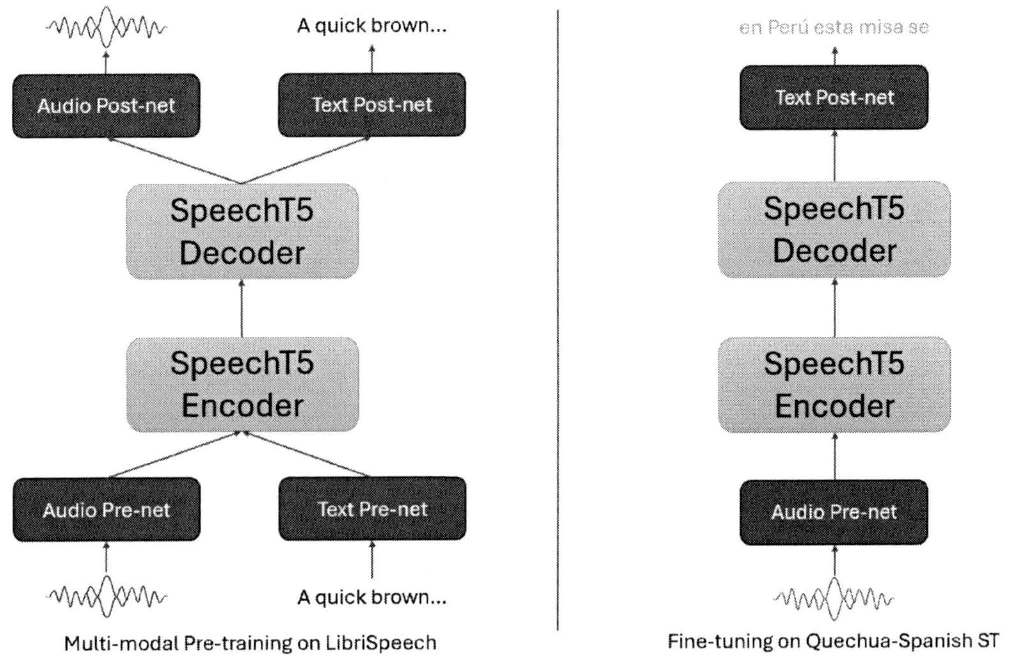

Figure 2: The best-performing *unconstrained* speech translation pipeline. We use a pre-trained SpeechT5 (Ao et al., 2022) on English, and fine-tune it on direct Quechua-to-Spanish ST.

mentation technique and the choice of 200 epochs as opposed to 500 used in the Primary submission. An average checkpoint method was used identical to the one in the Primary system (average of the last 10 checkpoints using Pytorch).

3.1.3 Contrastive 2 System

The **Contrastive 2** System is identical to the constrained Primary system in Section 3.1.1 with one main difference – model size. The model size of this Contrastive 2 system uses a medium-sized transformer known as the "transformer", (s2t_transformer) with 12 encoder layers and 6 decoder layers identical to the Contrastive 1 system defined in Section 3.1.2. All other hyperparameters were identical to the Primary system with the exception of the number of epochs which was 400 as opposed to 500.

3.2 Unconstrained Setting

Just like in IWSLT 2023, the organizers provided a total of 48 hours of audio along with their corresponding transcriptions. In addition, we translated the 48 hours of audio provided by the organizers into Spanish. Furthermore, we utilized a portion of the AmericasNLP[4] (ANLP) 2022 speech translation competition corpus, which consists of 19 minutes of Guarani and 29 minutes of Bribri, fully translated into Spanish. Although it is not a Quechua corpus, these languages have morphological similarities with Quechua, so we decided to experiment to see if that improves our models. Finally, all the datasets described in this section allowed for further fine-tuning of the previously trained end-to-end speech translation model.

3.2.1 Primary System

The Primary System for the unconstrained setting consists of a pre-trained model called SpeechT5 (Ao et al., 2022) , which was trained on 960 hours of audio from LibriSpeech. SpeechT5 consists of 12 Transformer encoder blocks and 6 Transformer decoder blocks, with a model dimension of 768, an internal dimension (FFN) of 3,072, and 12 attention heads. Additionally, the voice encoder's pre-net includes 7 blocks of temporal convolutions. Both the pre-net and post-net of the voice decoder used the same configuration as in Shen et al. (2018), except that the number of channels in the post-net is 256. For the text encoder/decoder's pre/post-

[4] https://turing.iimas.unam.mx/americasnlp/2022_st.html

Team **QUESPA** BLEU and CHRF Scores			
Constrained			
System	**Description**	**BLEU**	**CHRF**
primary	mfb + s2t-extrasmall + avg	2.0	30.0
contrastive 1	mfb + s2t-med + aug + avg	1.3	30.9
contrastive 2	mfb + s2t-med + avg	1.4	30.3
Unconstrained			
System	**Description**	**BLEU**	**CHRF**
primary	speechT5 + aug	16.0	52.2
contrastive 1	speechT5 + anlp + da-tts + nlpaug*	19.7	43.1
contrastive 2	whisper asr + nllb mt	11.1	44.6

Table 2: Team QUESPA results for the Quechua to Spanish low-resource task at IWSLT 2024.

net, a shared embedding layer with a dimension of 768 is utilized. For vector quantization, two codebooks with 100 entries each are used for the shared codebook module. The model was trained using the normalized training text from the LibriSpeech language model as unlabeled data, which contains 400 million sentences. Training was optimized using Adam (Kingma and Ba, 2015), with a learning rate that linearly increases during the first 8% of updates up to a maximum of 0.0002.

We fine-tuned SpeechT5[5] for Speech Translation using the SpeechT5 fine-tuning recipe[6] for Speech-Translation with the same hyperparameter settings. We used the 48 hours of audio provided by the organizers. We applied nlpaug a data augmentation technique (noise, distortion, duplication)[7] (Ma, 2019), resulting in a total of 96h: 48h original + 48h synthetic data.

3.2.2 Contrastive 1 System

The Contrastive 1 system is nearly identical to the Primary System for the unconstrained setting. However, we used the 48 hours described in 3.2, totally translate to Spanish. Moreover, we added 19 minutes of Guarani and 29 minutes of Bribi, along with their translations as described 3.2. Additionally, we applied two data augmentation techniques: (1) nlpaug (Ma, 2019) and (2) DA-TTS (Zevallos et al., 2022), which involves generating synthetic text and audio using a delexicalization algorithm and a TTS system for the source language (Quechua). These two data augmentation techniques generated 48 hours and 48 hours respectively. We used in total 151h and 48 min: 55h (new dataset) + 48 min (ANLP dataset) + 48h nlpaug + 48h DA-TTS.

[5]https://github.com/microsoft/SpeechT5

[6]https://github.com/microsoft/SpeechT5/tree/main/SpeechT5

[7]https://github.com/makcedward/nlpaug

3.2.3 Contrastive 2 System

The Constrastive 2 system is a new introduction this year for our team. We felt that the Whisper (Radford et al., 2023) ASR model would outperform QUESPA's 2023 cascaded system (Section 4 Table 1, *called fleurs+lm+floresmt*) (Ortega et al., 2023). However, despite the use of the same machine translation system (floresmt) (NLLB Team et al., 2022), we were unable to achieve better performance.

We use a Whisper ASR model that has been pre-trained on multiple languages (multi-lingual). In total, the Whisper model is trained on 680,000 hours of which 117,000 is multilingual, including nearly 96 languages. We use the medium variant of Whisper, which has 770M parameters. In our experiments, we fine-tune the Whisper model on the ASR training data, as the first part of an ASR+MT cascade. The output from Whisper (Quecha text) is then used as input to the same MT system from last year (called floresmt) that translates that Quechua text to Spanish.

4 Results and Discussion

Results are presented in Table 2. The constrained systems continue to be a difficult problem to solve with our best-performing system scoring a maximum of 2 BLEU (1.96 when measured with two decimal points). It is clear that a constrained system of this nature could not be deployed in the wild at this point. Nonetheless, it is a promising increase of nearly 1 BLEU point when compared to IWSLT 2023 results. Additionaly, the novel addition of data augmentation has proven to be a good first step to solving the constrained problem. In past

IWSLT tasks and in the current one, constrained systems are not realistically able to achieve much more than 5 BLEU points when the audio data is less than 5 hours in length.

For the unconstrained setting, our findings have shown that in the past year several novel PLMs have been created that surpass previous models. It is clear that Speech Translation as a task is becoming more solvable with pre-trained techniques that perform transfer learning. The combination of the Microsoft Speech T5 model with data augmentation as shown in Figure 2 is a new approach that has not been applied to the QUE–SPA language pair in the past and can be considered the best performing system as of this date to our knowledge. Previous systems based on w2vletter (Pratap et al., 2019) performed well but did not surpass the Microsoft Speech T5 Model in our experiments.

5 Conclusion and Future Work

Our submission to the IWSLT 2024 (Agarwal et al., 2023b) evaluation campaign for low-resource and dialect speech translation has included novelties based on the most state-of-the-art techniques for ASR and ST. More specifically, we have been successful by changing the sizes of the models in the *constrained* setting and changing the type of models in the *unconstrained* setting. Additionally, we have shown that different data augmentation techniques can be used for increased performance on both tasks.

We save for future work the experimentation of data augmentation techniques which seem to be the most advantageous novelty in this year's submission. In our opinion, data augmentation can be used for benefits in both the unconstrained and constrained tasks. Our plan for future IWSLT tasks is to experiment with and without features like SpecAugment, roll addition, and more.

References

Milind Agarwal, Sweta Agrawal, Antonios Anastasopoulos, Ondřej Bojar, Claudia Borg, Marine Carpuat, Roldano Cattoni, Mauro Cettolo, Mingda Chen, William Chen, Khalid Choukri, Alexandra Chronopoulou, Anna Currey, Thierry Declerck, Qianqian Dong, Yannick Estève, Kevin Duh, Marcello Federico, Souhir Gahbiche, Barry Haddow, Benjamin Hsu, Phu Mon Htut, Hirofumi Inaguma, Dávid Javorský, John Judge, Yasumasa Kano, Tom Ko, Rishu Kumar, Pengwei Li, Xutail Ma, Prashant Mathur, Evgeny Matusov, Paul McNamee, John P. McCrae, Kenton Murray, Maria Nadejde, Satoshi Nakamura, Matteo Negri, Ha Nguyen, Jan Niehues, Xing Niu, Atul Ojha Kr., John E. Ortega, Proyag Pal, Juan Pino, Lonneke van der Plas, Peter Polák, Elijah Rippeth, Elizabeth Salesky, Jiatong Shi, Matthias Sperber, Sebastian Stüker, Katsuhito Sudoh, Yun Tang, Brian Thompson, Kevin Tran, Marco Turchi, Alex Waibel, Mingxuan Wang, Shinji Watanabe, and Rodolfo Zevallos. 2023a. Findings of the IWSLT 2023 Evaluation Campaign. In *Proceedings of the 20th International Conference on Spoken Language Translation (IWSLT 2023)*. Association for Computational Linguistics.

Milind Agarwal, Sweta Agrawal, Antonios Anastasopoulos, Ondřej Bojar, Claudia Borg, Marine Carpuat, Roldano Cattoni, Mauro Cettolo, Mingda Chen, William Chen, Khalid Choukri, Alexandra Chronopoulou, Anna Currey, Thierry Declerck, Qianqian Dong, Yannick Estève, Kevin Duh, Marcello Federico, Souhir Gahbiche, Barry Haddow, Benjamin Hsu, Phu Mon Htut, Hirofumi Inaguma, Dávid Javorský, John Judge, Yasumasa Kano, Tom Ko, Rishu Kumar, Pengwei Li, Xutail Ma, Prashant Mathur, Evgeny Matusov, Paul McNamee, John P. McCrae, Kenton Murray, Maria Nadejde, Satoshi Nakamura, Matteo Negri, Ha Nguyen, Jan Niehues, Xing Niu, Atul Ojha Kr., John E. Ortega, Proyag Pal, Juan Pino, Lonneke van der Plas, Peter Polák, Elijah Rippeth, Elizabeth Salesky, Jiatong Shi, Matthias Sperber, Sebastian Stüker, Katsuhito Sudoh, Yun Tang, Brian Thompson, Kevin Tran, Marco Turchi, Alex Waibel, Mingxuan Wang, Shinji Watanabe, and Rodolfo Zevallos. 2023b. Findings of the IWSLT 2024 Evaluation Campaign. In *Proceedings of the 21st International Conference on Spoken Language Translation (IWSLT 2024)*. Association for Computational Linguistics.

Anastasopoulos Antonios, Barrault Loc, Luisa Bentivogli, Marcely Zanon Boito, Bojar Ondřej, Roldano Cattoni, Currey Anna, Dinu Georgiana, Duh Kevin, Elbayad Maha, et al. 2022. Findings of the iwslt 2022 evaluation campaign. In *Proceedings of the 19th International Conference on Spoken Language Translation (IWSLT 2022)*, pages 98–157. Association for Computational Linguistics.

Junyi Ao, Rui Wang, Long Zhou, Chengyi Wang, Shuo Ren, Yu Wu, Shujie Liu, Tom Ko, Qing Li, Yu Zhang, Zhihua Wei, Yao Qian, Jinyu Li, and Furu Wei. 2022. SpeechT5: Unified-modal encoder-decoder pre-training for spoken language processing. In *Proceedings of the 60th Annual Meeting of the Association for Computational Linguistics (Volume 1: Long Papers)*, pages 5723–5738, Dublin, Ireland. Association for Computational Linguistics.

Arun Babu, Changhan Wang, Andros Tjandra, Kushal Lakhotia, Qiantong Xu, Naman Goyal, Kritika Singh, Patrick von Platen, Yatharth Saraf, Juan Pino, et al. 2021. Xls-r: Self-supervised cross-lingual speech representation learning at scale. *arXiv preprint arXiv:2111.09296*.

Ronald Cardenas, Rodolfo Zevallos, Reynaldo Baquerizo, and Luis Camacho. 2018. Siminchik: A speech corpus for preservation of southern quechua. *ISI-NLP 2*, page 21.

Chih-Chen Chen, William Chen, Rodolfo Zevallos, and John Ortega. 2023a. Evaluating self-supervised speech representations for indigenous american languages. *arXiv preprint arXiv:2310.03639*.

William Chen, Brian Yan, Jiatong Shi, Yifan Peng, Soumi Maiti, and Shinji Watanabe. 2023b. Improving massively multilingual asr with auxiliary CTC objectives. *arXiv preprint arXiv:2302.12829*.

Alexis Conneau, Min Ma, Simran Khanuja, Yu Zhang, Vera Axelrod, Siddharth Dalmia, Jason Riesa, Clara Rivera, and Ankur Bapna. 2023. Fleurs: Few-shot learning evaluation of universal representations of speech. In *2022 IEEE Spoken Language Technology Workshop (SLT)*, pages 798–805.

John E. Ortega, Rodolfo Zevallos, and William Chen. 2023. QUESPA submission for the IWSLT 2023 dialect and low-resource speech translation tasks. In *Proceedings of the 20th International Conference on Spoken Language Translation (IWSLT 2023)*, pages 261–268, Toronto, Canada (in-person and online). Association for Computational Linguistics.

Abteen Ebrahimi, Manuel Mager, Shruti Rijhwani, Enora Rice, Arturo Oncevay, Claudia Baltazar, María Cortés, Cynthia Montaño, John E Ortega, Rolando Coto-Solano, et al. 2023. Findings of the americasnlp 2023 shared task on machine translation into indigenous languages. In *Proceedings of the Workshop on Natural Language Processing for Indigenous Languages of the Americas (AmericasNLP)*, pages 206–219.

Abteen Ebrahimi, Manuel Mager, Adam Wiemerslage, Pavel Denisov, Arturo Oncevay, Danni Liu, Sai Koneru, Enes Yavuz Ugan, Zhaolin Li, Jan Niehues, Monica Romero, Ivan G Torre, Tanel Alumäe, Jiaming Kong, Sergey Polezhaev, Yury Belousov, Wei-Rui Chen, Peter Sullivan, Ife Adebara, Bashar Talafha, Alcides Alcoba Inciarte, Muhammad Abdul-Mageed, Luis Chiruzzo, Rolando Coto-Solano, Hilaria Cruz, Sofía Flores-Solórzano, Aldo Andrés Alvarez López, Ivan Meza-Ruiz, John E. Ortega, Alexis Palmer, Rodolfo Joel Zevallos Salazar, Kristine Stenzel, Thang Vu, and Katharina Kann. 2022. Findings of the second americasnlp competition on speech-to-text translation. In *Proceedings of the NeurIPS 2022 Competitions Track*, volume 220 of *Proceedings of Machine Learning Research*, pages 217–232. PMLR.

Edward Gow-Smith, Alexandre Berard, Marcely Zanon Boito, and Ioan Calapodescu. 2023. NAVER LABS Europe's multilingual speech translation systems for the IWSLT 2023 low-resource track. In *Proceedings of the 20th International Conference on Spoken Language Translation (IWSLT 2023)*, pages 144–158, Toronto, Canada (in-person and online). Association for Computational Linguistics.

Diederik P. Kingma and Jimmy Ba. 2015. Adam: A method for stochastic optimization. In *ICLR 2015, Conference Track Proceedings*.

Taku Kudo and John Richardson. 2018. Sentencepiece: A simple and language independent subword tokenizer and detokenizer for neural text processing. *arXiv preprint arXiv:1808.06226*.

Edward Ma. 2019. Nlp augmentation. https://github.com/makcedward/nlpaug.

Shuming Ma, Li Dong, Shaohan Huang, Dongdong Zhang, Alexandre Muzio, Saksham Singhal, Hany Hassan Awadalla, Xia Song, and Furu Wei. 2021. Deltalm: Encoder-decoder pre-training for language generation and translation by augmenting pretrained multilingual encoders. *arXiv preprint arXiv:2106.13736*.

Jonathan Mbuya and Antonios Anastasopoulos. 2023. GMU systems for the IWSLT 2023 dialect and low-resource speech translation tasks. In *Proceedings of the 20th International Conference on Spoken Language Translation (IWSLT 2023)*, pages 269–276, Toronto, Canada (in-person and online). Association for Computational Linguistics.

NLLB Team, Marta R. Costa-jussà, James Cross, Onur Çelebi, Maha Elbayad, Kenneth Heafield, Kevin Heffernan, Elahe Kalbassi, Janice Lam, Daniel Licht, Jean Maillard, Anna Sun, Skyler Wang, Guillaume Wenzek, Al Youngblood, Bapi Akula, Loic Barrault, Gabriel Mejia-Gonzalez, Prangthip Hansanti, John Hoffman, Semarley Jarrett, Kaushik Ram Sadagopan, Dirk Rowe, Shannon Spruit, Chau Tran, Pierre Andrews, Necip Fazil Ayan, Shruti Bhosale, Sergey Edunov, Angela Fan, Cynthia Gao, Vedanuj Goswami, Francisco Guzmán, Philipp Koehn, Alexandre Mourachko, Christophe Ropers, Safiyyah Saleem, Holger Schwenk, and Jeff Wang. 2022. No language left behind: Scaling human-centered machine translation.

John E Ortega, Richard Castro Mamani, and Kyunghyun Cho. 2020. Neural machine translation with a polysynthetic low resource language. *Machine Translation*, 34(4):325–346.

John E Ortega and Krishnan Pillaipakkamnatt. 2018. Using morphemes from agglutinative languages like quechua and finnish to aid in low-resource translation. *Technologies for MT of Low Resource Languages (LoResMT 2018)*, page 1.

John E Ortega, Rodolfo Zevallos, and William Chen. 2023. Quespa submission for the iwslt 2023 dialect and low-resource speech translation tasks. In *Proceedings of the 20th International Conference on Spoken Language Translation (IWSLT 2023)*, pages 261–268.

Myle Ott, Sergey Edunov, Alexei Baevski, Angela Fan, Sam Gross, Nathan Ng, David Grangier, and Michael Auli. 2019. fairseq: A fast, extensible toolkit for sequence modeling. In *NAACL (Demonstrations)*, pages 48–53, Minneapolis, Minnesota. Association for Computational Linguistics.

Kishore Papineni, Salim Roukos, Todd Ward, and Wei-Jing Zhu. 2002. Bleu: a method for automatic evaluation of machine translation. In *Proceedings of the 40th annual meeting of the Association for Computational Linguistics*, pages 311–318.

Daniel S Park, William Chan, Yu Zhang, Chung-Cheng Chiu, Barret Zoph, Ekin D Cubuk, and Quoc V Le. 2019. Specaugment: A simple data augmentation method for automatic speech recognition. *arXiv preprint arXiv:1904.08779*.

Yifan Peng, Jinchuan Tian, Brian Yan, Dan Berrebbi, Xuankai Chang, Xinjian Li, Jiatong Shi, Siddhant Arora, William Chen, Roshan Sharma, Wangyou Zhang, Yui Sudo, Muhammad Shakeel, Jee-Weon Jung, Soumi Maiti, and Shinji Watanabe. 2023. Reproducing whisper-style training using an open-source toolkit and publicly available data. In *2023 IEEE Automatic Speech Recognition and Understanding Workshop (ASRU)*, pages 1–8.

Vineel Pratap, Awni Y. Hannun, Qiantong Xu, Jeff Cai, Jacob Kahn, Gabriel Synnaeve, Vitaliy Liptchinsky, and Ronan Collobert. 2019. Wav2letter++: A fast open-source speech recognition system. *IEEE International Conference on Acoustics, Speech and Signal Processing (ICASSP)*, pages 6460–6464.

Alec Radford, Jong Wook Kim, Tao Xu, Greg Brockman, Christine Mcleavey, and Ilya Sutskever. 2023. Robust speech recognition via large-scale weak supervision. In *Proceedings of the 40th International Conference on Machine Learning*, volume 202 of *Proceedings of Machine Learning Research*, pages 28492–28518. PMLR.

Jonathan Shen, Ruoming Pang, Ron J Weiss, Mike Schuster, Navdeep Jaitly, Zongheng Yang, Zhifeng Chen, Yu Zhang, Yuxuan Wang, Rj Skerrv-Ryan, et al. 2018. Natural tts synthesis by conditioning wavenet on mel spectrogram predictions. In *2018 IEEE international conference on acoustics, speech and signal processing (ICASSP)*, pages 4779–4783. IEEE.

Jiatong Shi, William Chen, Dan Berrebbi, Hsiu-Hsuan Wang, Wei-Ping Huang, En-Pei Hu, Ho-Lam Chuang, Xuankai Chang, Yuxun Tang, Shang-Wen Li, Abdelrahman Mohamed, Hung-Yi Lee, and Shinji Watanabe. 2023. Findings of the 2023 ml-superb challenge: Pre-training and evaluation over more languages and beyond. In *2023 IEEE Automatic Speech Recognition and Understanding Workshop (ASRU)*, pages 1–8.

Ashish Vaswani, Noam Shazeer, Niki Parmar, Jakob Uszkoreit, Llion Jones, Aidan N Gomez, Łukasz Kaiser, and Illia Polosukhin. 2017. Attention is all you need. *Advances in neural information processing systems*, 30.

Changhan Wang, Yun Tang, Xutai Ma, Anne Wu, Dmytro Okhonko, and Juan Pino. 2020. fairseq s2t: Fast speech-to-text modeling with fairseq. *arXiv preprint arXiv:2010.05171*.

Rodolfo Zevallos, Nuria Bel, Guillermo Cámbara, Mireia Farrús, and Jordi Luque. 2022. Data augmentation for low-resource quechua asr improvement. *arXiv preprint arXiv:2207.06872*.

Speech Data from Radio Broadcasts for Low Resource Languages

Bismarck Bamfo Odoom
Johns Hopkins University
bodoom1@jhu.edu

Paola Leibny Garcia
Johns Hopkins University
lgarci27@jhu.edu

Prangthip Hansanti
Meta AI
prangthiphansanti@meta.com

Loïc Barrault
Meta AI
loicbarrault@meta.com

Christophe Ropers
Meta AI
chrisropers@meta.com

Matthew Wiesner
Johns Hopkins University
wiesner@jhu.edu

Kenton Murray
Johns Hopkins University
kenton@jhu.edu

Alex Mourachko
Meta AI
alexmourachko@meta.com

Philipp Koehn
Johns Hopkins University
phi@jhu.edu

Abstract

We created a collection of speech data for 48 low resource languages. The corpus is extracted from radio broadcasts and processed with novel speech detection and language identification models based on a manually vetted subset of the audio for 10 languages. The data is made publicly available. [1]

1 Introduction

While automatic speech recognition systems have seen great gains in recognition accuracy, even under challenging acoustic conditions, this success is highly uneven across the languages in the world. For many languages in the world, even reliable audio training data is not easily available.

Motivated by this, we set out to collect and make publicly available speech data for languages that fall below the top one hundred languages, broadly measured by number of speakers and commercial relevance. We present a novel audio data set for 48 low resource languages. We report on manual efforts to vet collected audio data as well as automatic methods to extract speech from mixed audio data (especially discarding music) and language identification.

We collected this data mostly from radio broadcasts by recording audio streams available at Radio Garden[2]. These audio broadcasts are identified by location which gives us some guidance to which broadcasts are likely to contain audio in a desired language. We record audio snippets of 10–60 seconds in length. Since much of the audio data contains music, we developed a speech detection model to automatically identify audio files that consist of speech data and not music or other non-speech data.

Since there are no reliable speech language identification models or even identified speech data for a subset of these languages, we manually vetted audio data for 10 languages to create a corpus of about 5 hours of audio per language that has been verified by native speakers to be speech in each of the targeted languages.

With these tools in place (speech crawling, speech detection, speech language identification), we scaled up the effort to 48 languages. The resulting corpus of speech data consists of about 3000 hours of clean raw speech suspected to be in these low-resourced languages. Upon further filtering with language identification (LID) systems, this results in about 450 hours of clean speech.

2 Related Work

Foley et al. (2024) use audio data from Radio Garden to learn a mapping from speech to a geographic location. Conneau et al. (2022) create a dataset of 101 languages by recording audio from native speakers. The audio recorded stems from the Flores-101 dataset which consists of English sentences from Wikipedia translated into 101 languages. Pratap et al. (2023) introduce a massively multilingual dataset for over 1000+ languages based on recordings of publicly available religious texts. They further train self-supervised, automatic speech recognition, text-to-speech synthesis, and language identification models on this dataset. Radford et al. (2022) introduce a large-scale multilingual weakly supervised dataset consisting of about 680k hours of audio for speech

[1] https://huggingface.co/datasets/jhu-clsp/radio-broadcast

[2] https://radio.garden/

Proceedings of the 21st International Conference on Spoken Language Translation (IWSLT 2024), pages 182–187
August 15-16, 2024 ©2024 Association for Computational Linguistics

recognition. They showed that scaling the amount of data greatly improves the performance and robustness of speech recognition systems.

Unlabeled speech data has many uses in building speech applications. Representation learning methods like HuBERT (Hsu et al., 2021) and w2v-BERT (Chung et al., 2021) use raw speech data to distill semantic speech tokens from audio. Large-scale models such as Whisper (Radford et al., 2022), MMS (Pratap et al., 2023), or Seamless (Communication et al., 2023) rely partly on raw speech data to scale to hundreds of languages.

3 Corpus Collection

The sources of our data are radio broadcasts that are transmitted freely over the Internet. We use Radio Garden to discover and identify stations that broadcast in languages we target. Radio Garden identifies radio stations with the location from which they broadcast — which provides a pool of candidate stations for each language, based on the region where the language is spoken. The broadcasts are accessible through an API call.

We filter this pool of candidate stations by checking manually if they likely broadcast in the targeted language (opposed to, say, English) or exclusively broadcast music. Since this effort often relies on researchers that are not familiar with the languages, the process is necessarily imperfect. Another obstacle is that some radio station broadcasts are not reliably delivered over the Radio Garden platform, leading to gaps in the data collection.

We break up the audio signal into segments of different lengths, ranging from 10 to 60 seconds. The raw audio is also converted to the FLAC files and re-sampled to 16kHz. We collected this data throughout 2023 and early 2024.

4 Speech Detection

To filter out audio files containing music, we use a convolutional recurrent neural network (CRNN) (Hung et al., 2022) which was trained on a high-quality dataset (Hung et al., 2022) of speech and music activity labels. The CRNN model predicts the probability of music and speech for each audio frame.

We also use a feature-based model that calculates the average energy in each chunk of the audio spectrogram. This energy level indicates the intensity of the audio within that chunk. Chunks with energy levels higher than 0.5 are classified as music.

We set the detection threshold of the CRNN model to 0.9 and that of the feature-based model to 0.5. Audio files classified as not having music in them by both models are kept and the rest are discarded.

5 Manual Vetting

We are addressing several languages for which we do not have reliable language identification methods, or even any speech data that is verified to be in the presumed language. Hence, we engaged speakers of these languages to verify that speech audio that we presumed to be in their language was indeed in their language.

We carried out this manual vetting for Igbo, Luo (a.k.a. Dholuo), Ganda (a.k.a. Luganda), Nyanja, Maithili, Marwari, Santali, Meitei (a.k.a. Manipuri), Yue Chinese, and Central Kurdish. We recruited native speakers of these languages through language service providers. We carried out this vetting process through three phases, with increasingly larger quantities and more detailed questions.

Phase 1 Since we collected audio from only a few radio stations, our first question was to know which of them are reliable sources of speech data in the targeted languages. We sampled about a hundred 30-second speech segments per language and asked the language experts to assess whether those were indeed in their language. We also encouraged them to identify other language(s) that may be present in utterances, as well as the presence of non-speech or incomprehensible audio. For several languages, the experts also reported code-mixing with other languages, especially for Maithili, Marwari, Meitei, and Santali. Table 1(a) shows the results of the study. We considered as *good* those samples that have at least 90% audio in the targeted language. For 3 languages, we repeated the exercise since the first phase did not yield sufficient positively identified audio segments.

Phase 2 In the second phase, we scaled up the experiment to more audio samples. Here, the audio samples were of different lengths (10s, 20s, 30s, and 60 seconds). We also asked detailed questions about music being present in the background, speech being spontaneous or scripted, and about the presence of multiple speakers. Table 1(b) shows the results of the study. For most of the languages,

(a) Phase 1: Language identification

Language	Good	Total	Other languages detected
Central Kurdish	1+45	67+119	Arabic, Kurdish Bahdini, Kurdish Kurmanji, English
Ganda	47	95	English, Swahili
Igbo	12	90	Nigerian Pidgin English, Latin American Spanish, English-Spanish (Spanglish), Yoruba, US English, Pidgin, Nigerian English, British English
Luo	73	94	Swahili, English
Maithili	80	104	Nepali, Hindi, English
Marwari	55+92	120+120	-
Meitei	94	99	Hindi
Nyanja	58	91	English
Santali	0+45	107+120	Bengali, Hindi, English
Yue	59	91	Mandarin

(c) Phase 2: Larger sample, more detailed questions

Language	Total	Good	Music (yes/no)		Scripted/Spontaneous		Speakers (1/more)	
Central Kurdish	640	407	44	363	71	336	190	217
Ganda	645	577	296	281	262	315	306	271
Igbo	636	235	185	50	157	78	96	139
Luo	645	473	463	10	441	32	396	77
Maithili	480	352	31	321	195	157	245	107
Marwari	640	208	176	32	173	35	139	69
Meitei	624	516	89	427	175	341	263	253
Nyanja	644	435	282	153	267	169	256	180
Santali	640	309	105	204	248	61	125	184
Yue	646	354	58	296	24	272	51	248

(c) Phase 3: Scaling up data sizes for some languages with cleaner sources

Language	Total	Good	Music (yes/no)		Scripted/Spontaneous		Speakers (1/more)	
Central Kurdish	240	237	4	213	41	196	131	106
Ganda	105	102	17	85	55	47	60	42
Igbo	216	195	11	184	0	195	145	50
Maithili	337	331	21	263	47	284	72	191
Meitei	222	222	8	213	164	57	172	49
Nyanja	222	216	15	201	138	78	115	101
Santali	640	640	57	573	42	598	380	260
Yue	285	284	4	280	17	267	41	243

Table 1: Manual vetting of speech data by language experts: The goal of this study was to identify 5 hours of vetted audio in the targeted language to be able to train language identification models.

	FLEURS									
	C.Kurdish	Ganda	Igbo	Luo	Marwari	Maithili	Meitei	Nyanja	Santali	Yue
MMS	98.3	99.8	98.3	99.6	-	-	-	95.1	-	99.9
Ours	87.7	88.9	10.6	0.4	-	-	-	46.3	-	88.5
	RADIO BROADCAST									
	C. Kurdish	Ganda	Igbo	Luo	Marwari	Maithili	Meitei	Nyanja	Santali	Yue
MMS	99.2	62.8	85.1	61.6	-	54.5	43.4	98.1	86.1	99.9
Ours	**99.9**	**92.4**	64.7	**93.2**	-	**97.1**	**99.9**	88.7	**95.2**	99.3

Table 2: Comparing the accuracy of our LID model to the MMS LID model (Pratap et al., 2023) on the FLEURS and radio broadcasts test sets

Language	Hours
Central Kurdish	3.30
Ganda	4.96
Igbo	1.14
Luo	4.00
Maithili	1.95
Manipuri	4.38
Marwari	1.65
Nyanja	3.56
Santali	2.63
Sorani	3.39
Yue	2.96

Table 3: Amount of data per language used to train our LID models.

there is often some music in the background. The amount of scripted vs. spontaneous speech as well the number of speakers in the audio varies by language.

Phase 3 Since our goal was to collect at least 5 hours of vetted audio, we repeated the Phase 2 study on additional audio samples using the same vetting protocol. Table 1(c) shows the results. Given the feedback from the second phase, we were able to identify generally cleaner audio sources to be vetted, resulting in a much larger ratio of them assessed to be good and without background music. For logistical reasons, we were not able to do this for Luo and Marwari.

We will release the audio with meta data from the annotation effort publicly.

6 Language Identification

The LID system follows Villalba et al. (2023). Essentially, our LID uses log-Mel-filter banks with 64 filters as feature extractor. The features were short-time mean normalized with a 3-second window. Silence portions (frames) were removed using an energy voice activity detector (VAD) based on Kaldi. This VAD classifies each frame as speech or non-speech based on the average log-energy in a window.

The language embedding architecture follows the x-vector process (Snyder et al., 2017, 2018) as described by Villalba et al. (2023). It consists of an encoder that extracts frame-level discriminant embeddings, a pooling mechanism, and a classification head. We used the Res2Net architecture as the encoder. The system uses the datasets in the *Training Open* condition for training the language embedding. For the backend, the system employs a linear Gaussian classifier with a single Gaussian per target language, and a shared-covariance across languages. The system is trained on about 30 hours of audio in 10 languages. Table 3 shows the distribution of data per language.

As shown in Table 2, we compare the performance of our LID model to the MMS LID model (Pratap et al., 2023) on the FLEURS (Conneau et al., 2022) benchmark and a carefully selected test set comprising radio broadcast recordings. FLEURS is in a similar domain to the data used to train the MMS model, and the test set of radio broadcasts is in the same domain as the data used to train our model. The MMS LID model was trained on 1000 times more data as compared to ours.

Luo's severe performance drop on FLEURS is due to the difference in the dialects in FLEURS and radio broadcast test sets. The poor performance of Igbo on both test sets is due to the small amount of data in Igbo used in training the LID system. For most languages, our LID model outperforms the

MMS model on the radio broadcast data.

7 Corpus

With all the tools in place, we scaled up the effort to collect audio speech data for all the targeted 48 languages. Table 4 gives details about the number of hours of audio data we handled at various processing stages: (1) the number of hours of crawled audio expected to be in the targeted language, (2) the number of hours after speech detected, and (3) what remained after a language ID filter.

For the 10 targeted languages (bold in the table), we collected substantial amounts of data, ranging from 12.43 hours (Marwari) to 178.55 hours (Maithili) after music detection and language ID filtering.

Scaling up to 48 language was challenging as we could not repeat the expensive first stage of annotations to identify radio stations which broadcast in the languages of interest. We randomly pick radio stations within locations we believe speak the languages of interest and collect data from them. Since we did not run annotations for the new languages we did not have ground-truth data to train LID models for those languages. We rely on the MMS LID model for these languages. Specifically, we use the variant trained on 4017 languages.

The amount of data collected per language varies due to the number of radio stations we collected data from at each time. For some languages, we identified many radio stations that broadcast in the language of interest, enabling us to collect hundreds of hours of data. Also, we aggressively filtered the corpus for music, which greatly affected the amount of data we collected for some languages. We could not report on the amount of data after LID for Egyptian, Morrocan, and Pashto as the MMS model does not support them. Other languages with no data after LID had none of the top predictions of the audio files to be in the language. This data was collected from early 2023 to early 2024.

8 Conclusion

We collected a large corpus of speech audio for 48 languages from audio sources. We focused special attention to 10 languages for which we built language identification models based on manually vetted audio data. We will release all audio data (manually vetted and automatically filtered) open source with a liberal license for research and commercial use. We hope that this data fosters research

Languages	**Crawled**	**Clean**	**LID**
Amharic	83.74	20.44	7.94
Armenian	82.35	9.03	2.13
Assamese	85.03	16.77	0.13
Azerbaijani	96.71	4.45	1.79
Belarusian	101.53	0.84	0.10
Bosnian	63.48	3.67	1.29
Cebuano	64.53	1.00	0.02
C. Kurdish	**75.53**	**46.74**	**23.51**
Egyptian	108.19	10.32	-
Galician	75.35	31.60	0.69
Ganda	**293.65**	**125.97**	**24.25**
Georgian	65.25	1.42	0.05
Gujarati	95.99	0.13	0.02
Icelandic	134.99	11.22	5.47
Igbo	**137.95**	**12.12**	**4.21**
Irish	200.41	15.62	0.06
Javanese	25.37	5.97	0.14
Kannada	40.53	1.94	0.96
Kazakh	83.67	4.07	1.58
Khmer	21.99	2.59	2.07
Konkani	72.93	4.01	-
Kyrgyz	51.05	6.75	1.26
Lao	108.27	10.19	1.91
Luo	**409.3**	**243.38**	**48.46**
Macedonian	62.66	0.51	0.24
Maithili	**2860.84**	**1722.91**	**178.55**
Maltese	89.75	14.68	4.51
Meitei	**299.50**	**129.97**	**18.13**
Marathi	139.25	25.06	9.24
Marwari	**155.46**	**118.05**	**12.43**
Mongolian	33.25	2.91	0.66
Moroccan	184.80	11.73	-
Nepali	53.15	3.61	0.81
Nyanja	**251.11**	**79.20**	**22.41**
Odia	106.61	1.20	-
Oromo	117.52	14.77	0.18
Panjabi	45.63	0.57	-
Pashto	40.81	6.58	-
Santali	**272.65**	**120.06**	**20.45**
Shona	70.19	15.71	3.17
Sindhi	33.22	10.38	0.19
Swiss German	584.60	86.86	-
Tajik	26.34	1.21	0.49
Telugu	28.98	0.51	0.10
Uzbek	49.71	5.88	2.44
Welsh	67.29	2.14	0.12
Yue	**117.28**	**101.21**	**64.70**
Zulu	49.51	24.03	0.04

Table 4: Statistics of the collected audio data (in hours). The focus languages for which we performed manual vetting and more thorough radio station selection are in bold.

in low resource speech technology.

Limitations

The legal status of web crawled data is currently in a gray area. We argue that the released data set falls under fair use since we are releasing disconnected snippets and do not interfere with the commercial use of the original broadcasts.

References

Yu-An Chung, Yu Zhang, Wei Han, Chung-Cheng Chiu, James Qin, Ruoming Pang, and Yonghui Wu. 2021. W2v-bert: Combining contrastive learning and masked language modeling for self-supervised speech pre-training. *CoRR*, abs/2108.06209.

Seamless Communication, Loïc Barrault, Yu-An Chung, Mariano Coria Meglioli, David Dale, Ning Dong, Mark Duppenthaler, Paul-Ambroise Duquenne, Brian Ellis, Hady Elsahar, Justin Haaheim, John Hoffman, Min-Jae Hwang, Hirofumi Inaguma, Christopher Klaiber, Ilia Kulikov, Pengwei Li, Daniel Licht, Jean Maillard, Ruslan Mavlyutov, Alice Rakotoarison, Kaushik Ram Sadagopan, Abinesh Ramakrishnan, Tuan Tran, Guillaume Wenzek, Yilin Yang, Ethan Ye, Ivan Evtimov, Pierre Fernandez, Cynthia Gao, Prangthip Hansanti, Elahe Kalbassi, Amanda Kallet, Artyom Kozhevnikov, Gabriel Mejia Gonzalez, Robin San Roman, Christophe Touret, Corinne Wong, Carleigh Wood, Bokai Yu, Pierre Andrews, Can Balioglu, Peng-Jen Chen, Marta R. Costa-jussá, Maha Elbayad, Hongyu Gong, Francisco Guzmán, Kevin Heffernan, Somya Jain, Justine Kao, Ann Lee, Xutai Ma, Alex Mourachko, Benjamin Peloquin, Juan Pino, Sravya Popuri, Christophe Ropers, Safiyyah Saleem, Holger Schwenk, Anna Sun, Paden Tomasello, Changhan Wang, Jeff Wang, Skyler Wang, and Mary Williamson. 2023. Seamless: Multilingual expressive and streaming speech translation. Technical report, Meta FAIR.

Alexis Conneau, Min Ma, Simran Khanuja, Yu Zhang, Vera Axelrod, Siddharth Dalmia, Jason Riesa, Clara Rivera, and Ankur Bapna. 2022. Fleurs: Few-shot learning evaluation of universal representations of speech.

Patrick Foley, Matthew Wiesner, Bismarck Bamfo Odoom, Leibny Paola Garcia, Kenton Murray, and Philipp Koehn. 2024. Where are you from? geolocating speech and applications to language identification. In *Proceedings of the Annual Meeting of the North American Chapter of the Association for Computational Linguistcs (NAACL)*.

Wei-Ning Hsu, Benjamin Bolte, Yao-Hung Hubert Tsai, Kushal Lakhotia, Ruslan Salakhutdinov, and Abdelrahman Mohamed. 2021. Hubert: Self-supervised speech representation learning by masked prediction of hidden units. *CoRR*, abs/2106.07447.

Yun-Ning Hung, Chih-Wei Wu, Iroro Orife, Aaron Hipple, William Wolcott, and Alexander Lerch. 2022. A large TV dataset for speech and music activity detection. In *J AUDIO SPEECH MUSIC PROC*.

Vineel Pratap, Andros Tjandra, Bowen Shi, Paden Tomasello, Arun Babu, Sayani Kundu, Ali Elkahky, Zhaoheng Ni, Apoorv Vyas, Maryam Fazel-Zarandi, Alexei Baevski, Yossi Adi, Xiaohui Zhang, Wei-Ning Hsu, Alexis Conneau, and Michael Auli. 2023. Scaling speech technology to 1,000+ languages.

Alec Radford, Jong Wook Kim, Tao Xu, Greg Brockman, Christine McLeavey, and Ilya Sutskever. 2022. Robust speech recognition via large-scale weak supervision.

David Snyder, Daniel Garcia-Romero, Daniel Povey, and Sanjeev Khudanpur. 2017. Deep Neural Network Embeddings for Text-Independent Speaker Verification. In *Proceedings of the 18th Annual Conference of the International Speech Communication Association, INTERSPEECH 2017*, pages 999–1003, Stockholm, Sweden. ISCA.

David Snyder, Daniel Garcia-Romero, Gregory Sell, Daniel Povey, and Sanjeev Khudanpur. 2018. X-Vectors : Robust DNN Embeddings for Speaker Recognition. In *Proceedings of the IEEE International Conference on Acoustics, Speech and Signal Processing, ICASSP 2018*, pages 5329–5333, Alberta, Canada. IEEE.

Jesús Villalba, Jonas Borgstrom, Maliha Jahan, Saurabh Kataria, Leibny Paola Garcia, Pedro Torres-Carrasquillo, and Najim Dehak. 2023. Advances in Language Recognition in Low Resource African Languages: The JHU-MIT Submission for NIST LRE22. In *Proc. INTERSPEECH 2023*, pages 521–525.

JHU IWSLT 2024 Dialectal and Low-resource System Description

Nathaniel R. Robinson[1] **Kaiser Sun**[1] **Cihan Xiao**[1] **Niyati Bafna**[1] **Weiting Tan**[1]
Haoran Xu[1] **Henry Li Xinyuan**[1] **Ankur Kejriwal**[1] **Sanjeev Khudanpur**[1,2]
Kenton Murray[1,2] **Paul McNamee**[2]
[1]Johns Hopkins University Center for Language and Speech Processing
[2]Human Language Technology Center of Excellence
Baltimore, USA
{nrobin38,hsun74,cxiao7,nbafna1,wtan12,hxu64,xli257,khudanpur,kenton,
mcnamee}@jhu.edu; akejriw2@alumni.jh.edu

Abstract

Johns Hopkins University (JHU) submitted systems for all eight language pairs in the 2024 Low-Resource Language Track. The main effort of this work revolves around fine-tuning large and publicly available models in three proposed systems: i) end-to-end speech translation (ST) fine-tuning of SEAMLESSM4T v2; ii) ST fine-tuning of Whisper; iii) a cascaded system involving automatic speech recognition with fine-tuned Whisper and machine translation with NLLB. On top of systems above, we conduct a comparative analysis of different training paradigms, such as intra-distillation of NLLB, joint training and curriculum learning of SEAMLESSM4T v2, and multi-task learning and pseudo-translation with Whisper. Our results show that the best-performing approach differs by language pairs, but that i) fine-tuned SEAMLESSM4T v2 tends to perform best for source languages on which it was pre-trained, ii) multi-task training helps Whisper fine-tuning, iii) cascaded systems with Whisper and NLLB tend to outperform Whisper alone, and iv) intra-distillation helps NLLB fine-tuning.

1 Introduction

With recent developments in data-driven machine learning and Transformer-based models (Vaswani et al., 2017), speech translation (ST) systems (which accept spoken input in one language and automatically output corresponding text in another) have undergone major strides in performance (Radford et al., 2023; Barrault et al., 2023; Sperber and Paulik, 2020). While these works demonstrate the effectiveness of using large pretrained models for speech translation between high-resource language pairs and establish new state-of-the-art (SOTA) performance in these setups, less attention has been devoted to whether these advances also benefit low-resource language pairs, and how they compare with SOTA systems for these languages.

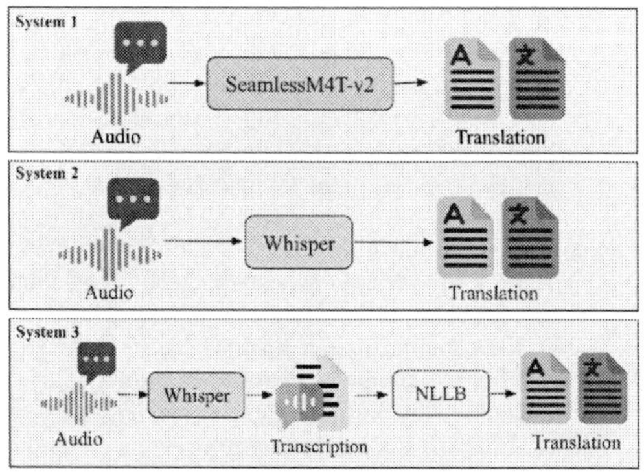

Figure 1: Proposed frameworks for fine-tuning.

Some of the populations with the greatest need for ST tools are those speaking low-resource languages, which typically have less institutional support and funding for the development for NLP and speech tools (He et al., 2024; Kesiraju et al., 2023b; Karakasidis et al., 2023): some speak minority languages in the areas where they live and need translation tools to communicate across a language barrier, or to consume or search for information more effectively online (Neto et al., 2020). Certain populations speaking low-resource languages may also have low literacy rates or limited writing traditions in their native languages, increasing the imperative for speech-based, rather than text-based, translation systems (Besacier et al., 2006).

In this work, we developed ST systems for eight language pairs, as organized in the IWSLT 2024 Dialectal and Low-resource Speech Translation Shared Task. We approached this problem by leveraging systems pre-trained on a large amount of multilingual data and subsequently fine-tuning them for specific tasks: both end-to-end speech ST and cascaded ST (i.e. transcription followed by text-based translation). We compared different approaches and pre-trained models for each language pair, and we experimented with combining data from multi-

Proceedings of the 21st International Conference on Spoken Language Translation (IWSLT 2024), pages 188–201
August 15-16, 2024 ©2024 Association for Computational Linguistics

ple related languages into the same train set.

Among the systems introduced, the approaches based on SEAMLESSM4T v2 (Barrault et al., 2023) outperform others for language pairs that it has seen during pretraining and for which supervised ST data are available (e.g. mar-hin, gle-eng, bho-hin, and mlt-eng). In other cases, a cascaded system is the most successful of the proposed approaches, namely, for apc-eng, bem-eng, que-spa, and tmh-fra.

2 Prior Work

A number of prior studies introduce methods aiming to address low-resource ST. In IWSLT's evaluation for low-resource and dialectal ST 2023, Agarwal et al. (2023) note three practices that consistently help performance: (1) use of pre-trained models, (2) systems combining both end-to-end and cascaded models, and (3) synthetic data augmentation. These recommendations inform our decisions to fine-tune pre-trained models and experiment with both cascaded and end-to-end approaches.

Williams et al. (2023) used cascaded ST systems for Quechua-to-Spanish ST in IWSLT challenge 2023. Shanbhogue et al. (2023) fine-tuned pre-trained speech models, and E. Ortega et al. (2023); Laurent et al. (2023) leveraged both pre-trained speech and text models in cascaded systems. Deng et al. (2023); Hussein et al. (2023) explored both end-to-end and cascaded ST. The most comparable submission to ours from the 2023 challenge was that of Mbuya and Anastasopoulos (2023), who used pre-trained models and applied them to several language pairs. With the findings and recommendations from prior work, we adapt a similar approach, but fine-tuning SEAMLESSM4T v2 (Barrault et al., 2023), Whisper (Radford et al., 2023), and NLLB (NLLB Team et al., 2022) instead of self-supervised learning representations (SSLR). Our approach differs from works described above, primarily in that we fine-tune models trained for automatic speech recognition (ASR), machine translation (MT), and ST, rather than fine-tuning representations obtained from language modeling objectives, such as wav2vec2 (Baevski et al., 2020), HuBERT (Hsu et al., 2021), XLS-R (Babu et al., 2022), or mBART (Liu et al., 2020a), for the tasks of ASR, MT, and ST. The findings from our systems shed light on the potential benefits provided by the pretrained multilingual models.

3 Task Description

On the challenge website this year,[1] the organizers stated, "The goal of this shared task is to benchmark and promote speech translation technology for a diverse range of dialects and low-resource languages." To forward this aim, this year's task focuses on ST for eight language pairs: Levantine Arabic to English (apc-eng), Bemba to English (bem-eng), Bhojpuri to Hindi (bho-hin), Irish to English (gle-eng), Maltese to English (mlt-eng), Marathi to Hindi (mar-eng), Quechua to Spanish (que-spa), and Tamasheq to French (tmh-fra). Levantine is one of the most spoken Arabic dialects, with the majority native-speaking populations in Syria, Lebanon, Palestine, and Jordan. Both Levantine Arabic and Maltese are Semitic languages of the Afroasiatic family. Bemba is a Bantu language of the Niger-Congo family, spoken by over 30% of Zambia's population (Sikasote and Anastasopoulos, 2022). Bhojpuri, Hindi, and Marathi are Indo-Aryan languages; Hindi and Marathi are Scheduled languages in India and have government backing for their support, whereas Bhojpuri, like many other languages on the so-called Hindi Belt, lacks official status, has a much smaller writing tradition, and is only recently gaining attention in NLP (Kumar et al., 2022; Mundotiya et al., 2021; Bafna et al., 2023). Each of the source languages is low-resource, with Tamasheq, Bemba, and Levantine Arabic having the fewest Wikipedia articles overall (Robinson et al., 2023). Despite their low digital support, these languages have a large native speaker base, including Marathi's 83 million, according to Ethnologue.[2]

The organizers provide different varieties of data for each of these language pairs. We used predominantly provided datasets, along with some external data, all of which are outlined in Table 1. We differentiate datasets of four types: **ASR**, indicating source language speech with corresponding transcriptions; **E2E**, indicating source language speech with corresponding target language translations that could supervise end-to-end ST; **MT**, indicating source language text with corresponding target language translations; and **ST**, indicating source language speech with both corresponding transcriptions and target language translations.

Though this year's task accepts both *unconstrained* submissions, allowing the use of external

[1] https://iwslt.org/2024/low-resource

[2] https://www.ethnologue.com/

datasets and pre-trained models, and *constrained* submissions, our submission is limited to the *unconstrained* track, since all of our methods involved fine-tuning pre-trained models.

4 Proposed Methods

We introduce three primary frameworks, which are applied to different language pairs according to the availability of the data: (1) we fine-tune SEAMLESSM4T v2 for end-to-end ST using **E2E** data; (2) we fine-tune Whisper (Radford et al., 2023) for end-to-end ST using **E2E** (and optionally **ASR**) data; (3) to form a cascaded ST system, we fine-tune Whisper for ASR using **ASR** data, then fine-tune NLLB for machine translation (MT) using **MT** data. The fine-tuning approaches are illustrated in Figure 1. Note that each **ST** dataset contains exactly one **E2E**, **ASR**, and **MT** dataset implicitly.

We explore various methodological additions to these methods. We look at joint fine-tuning and curriculum learning with the SEAMLESSM4T v2-based approaches. We investigate several fine-tuning setups for the Whisper-based systems, including pseudo-translation fine-tuning, multitask training with ASR and MT as well as ASR-only and ST-only fine-tuning. We also looked at intra-distillation as a method of enhancing NLLB in MT. These ideas are further detailed below.

4.1 SEAMLESSM4T v2-based systems

Barrault et al. (2023) introduce SEAMLESSM4T v2, a model capable of end-to-end expressive and multilingual translations in a streaming fashion. SEAMLESSM4T v2 supports multilingual input and output in both speech and text modalities, with a dedicated sub-model handling each modality combination. It has 2.3B parameters and is pretrained on 1M hours of unlabeled audio in 143 languages, using the `w2v-BERT XL` architecture (Chung et al., 2021). It is then fine-tuned on text MT into English (`x-eng`) for 95 languages, ASR for 96 languages, ST into English for 89 languages, and speech-to-speech translation into English for 95 languages, and out of English `eng-x` for 35 languages. The pretraining languages of SEAMLESSM4T v2 include English, Irish, Maltese, Hindi, Marathi, and Arabic,[3] but not Quechua, Tamasheq, or Bemba.

[3]We assume that the pretraining corpus also contains some Levantine and Tunisian Arabic, but these languages are not labeled distinctly from each other.

Our Systems We fine-tune SEAMLESSM4T v2 on **E2E** ST data, aiming to leverage the vast pretraining and ASR and ST capabilities of SEAMLESSM4T v2, which we expect to be beneficial in data-scarce scenarios. Although the SEAMLESSM4T v2 models are evaluated mostly on X-Eng/Eng-X directions in Barrault et al., 2023, we hypothesize that they will succeed in X-X directions post-finetuning, due to ASR pretraining in source and target languages. Note that this approach is only applicable to language pairs where **E2E** data are available (`gle-eng`, `mlt-eng`, `aeb-eng`, `bem-eng`, `que-spa`, `tmh-fre`, `mar-hin`, `bho-hin`). We also evaluate the zero-shot performance of SEAMLESSM4T v2 on these language pairs.

Experimental Setup For each language pair, we fine-tune SEAMLESSM4T `v2-large` for four epochs, with a learning rate of 1×10^{-6} and batch size of 32. For `que-spa` translation, we use learning rate 1×10^{-8} for 15 epochs due to its small dataset size. For `bem-eng` and `tmh-fra`, a learning rate of 1×10^{-7} is used for training. The full hyperparameter list and details of hyperparameter tuning are included in Appendix A.1.

4.1.1 Multilingual training

Mixed Data Training For pairs with the same target language (`gle-eng+mlt-eng`, `bho-hin+mar-hin`), we fine-tune SEAMLESSM4T v2 on the combined dataset created by concatenating and shuffling the data, using the same hyperparameter settings as in Section A.1.

Curriculum Training Tunisian Arabic (`aeb`) and Maltese are both Semitic languages and share close linguistic relationships. We use a 12.6-hour subset of the Tunisian Arabic-to-English (`aeb-eng`) **ST** data used by Hussein et al. (2023) to conduct a curriculum training attempt using Tunisian as an augmentation for Maltese. The model undergoes initial fine-tuning on `aeb-eng` ST for two epochs with a learning rate of 1×10^{-6}, followed by a 5-epoch-fine-tuning on `mlt-eng` at a learning rate of 1×10^{-7}.

4.2 Whisper-based systems

Whisper (Radford et al., 2023) is an end-to-end multi-task speech model based on a transformer-like encoder-decoder architecture. For this study, we focus primarily on its LARGE-V2 variant, which is pre-trained on 680k hours of multilingual ASR

Lang.	Type	Amount	Size	Genre(s)	Sources
apc-eng	ASR	28h	3.2GB	Spontaneous speech	Makhoul et al. (2005)
	MT	120k lines	84MB	Subtitles	Sellat et al. (2023)
bem-eng	ST	180h	21GB	Dialogue description	Sikasote et al. (2023)
	ASR	24h	3.0GB	Read speech	Sikasote and Anastasopoulos (2022)
bho-hin	E2E	25h	2.6GB	News audio	Agarwal et al. (2023)
gle-eng	E2E	11h	2.2GB	Read speech	Agarwal et al. (2023)
mlt-eng	ST	14h	1.6GB	Telephone speech	CV; Hernandez Mena et al. (2020)
	MT	2.1M lines	710MB	Web-crawled	Bañón et al. (2023, 2020)
mar-hin	E2E	30h	3.5GB	News audio	Agarwal et al. (2023)
	ASR	1100h	150GB	Read speech; News	CV; He et al. (2020); Bhogale et al. (2022)
que-spa	ST	1.7h	300MB	Radio	Ortega et al. (2020)
	ASR	48h	5.2GB	Radio	Cardenas et al. (2018)
	MT	26k lines	3.7MB	Mixed; Magazine	Tiedemann (2012); Ortega et al. (2020)
tmh-fra	E2E	19h	2.2GB	Radio	Zanon Boito et al. (2022)

Table 1: Data information. "CV" refers to Common Voice (https://commonvoice.mozilla.org/).

and X-to-Eng speech translation data. During pre-training, the model is exposed to over 90 languages, including English, Marathi, Hindi, Maltese, and modern standard Arabic. However, Bemba, Bhojpuri, Quechua, Levantine Arabic, and Tamasheq, are absent from the pre-training data.

To address the gaps in language coverage and enhance model performance across diverse linguistic settings, we fine-tune the model in various ways tailored to specific scenarios. As the original model's pre-training setup, we manipulate the prompt and supervision of the utterances at fine-tuning time to guide the model to perform different tasks, as detailed in the subsequent sections. In addition, for languages previously unseen by the model, we expand its vocabulary and embedding layer to create new language tags for the model to take condition on.

4.2.1 Fine-tuning paradigms

ASR-only Fine-tuning For language pairs with only **ASR** data or a limited amount of **E2E** or **ST** data, such as apc-eng and que-spa, Whisper is trained with only the ASR objective to serve as an ASR module in a cascaded system. The training and decoding prompt used is the conventional <|src-lang|><|transcribe|>. The resulting cascaded system's MT module is an NLLB model described in § 4.3.

E2E-only Fine-tuning We train with Whisper's ST-only objective for the tmh-fra pair. However, because Whisper is pre-trained for X-Eng ST only, instead of directly translating into French, we fine-tune the system to translate Tamasheq speech into English text. Specifically, we translate the French labels of the **E2E** data into English using NLLB out of the box to formulate a tmh-eng **E2E** dataset. We then fine-tune Whisper with this dataset and utilize the trained model as the ASR module for a cascaded system, whose MT module is also NLLB. Similarly, English-to-French translation is conducted out-of-the-box.

Pseudo-translation For bho-hin and mar-hin language pairs, due to the absence of 3-way parallel **ST** data, the phylogenetic proximity between the languages, and the non-English-centric translation directions, we explore a novel adaptation of the model which we call *pseudo-translation*. Specifically, to enable Whisper to translate into non-English languages, we prompt the model to "transcribe" the source language speech signals with the target language transcription prompt, i.e. <|tgt-lang|><|transcribe|>. Conceptually, this is equivalent to treating Bhojpuri and Marathi as pseudo-Hindi speech and conducting ASR (an approach that is especially linguistically motivated in the case of Bhojpuri, as it is closely related to Hindi). Such design is motivated by the fact that Whisper is pre-trained with weakly supervised data, which implicitly empowers the model's audio-conditioned language model to perform some extent of de-noising. Consequently, we may model the non-English translation process as a noisy transcription task with the proposed prompts.

Multi-task Learning Previous yet unpublished experiments suggest that multi-task learning (MTL) tends to improve the model's performance across downstream metrics. Hence, for bem-eng and mlt-eng, as the 3-way parallel **ST** data is sufficient, we fine-tune Whisper on both the ASR and E2E ST tasks with E2E X-Eng ST being the end goal. In particular, we create the ASR and E2E ST dataset objectives respectively with their corresponding prompts, i.e. <|src-lang|><|transcribe|> and <|src-lang|><|translate|>, and concatenate them to form a multi-task dataset for fine-tuning, allowing the sampler to draw samples with different supervisions stochastically. Kesiraju et al.'s (2023a) use a large amount of Marathi ASR data (He et al., 2020; Bhogale et al., 2022) for Marathi-to-Hindi ST. Therefore, we further extend the idea of constructing data to mar-hin, which has abundant non-parallel ASR and E2E ST data yet no 3-way parallel data. We combine the pseudo-translation technique to perform non-parallel ASR and E2E pseudo-ST multi-task training.[4]

4.2.2 Whisper training details

We employ a range of techniques to expedite the training of Whisper and optimize the utilization of our hardware resources. Specifically, we adopt Low-Rank Adapters (LoRA) (Hu et al., 2021), gradient checkpointing (Chen et al., 2016), and Zero Redundancy Optimizer (ZeRO) (Rajbhandari et al., 2020) to fine-tune all Whisper models. We allow trainable decomposed weight matrices with a rank of 200 for the embedding layer, all the attention layers, and the first feed-forward layer in the transformer blocks, resulting in a total of 289,157,200 trainable parameters, approximately 16% of the original model's parameter count.

We apply conventional speech data augmentation in the fine-tuning process, including SpecAug (Park et al., 2019) and speed perturbation (Ko et al., 2015) with parameters 0.9, 1.0, 1.1.

4.3 NLLB fine-tuning

NLLB Team et al.'s (2022) NLLB is an encoder-decoder framework designed for extensive multilingual translation across more than 200 languages. It incorporates the sparsely gated mixture of experts (Du et al., 2022) to balance enhanced modeling capacity with efficient training and inference. Training of the NLLB model involves three objectives—translation loss, denoising loss, and language modeling loss—all calculated using the negative log-likelihood (NLL) loss function but with distinct datasets. Translation loss utilizes clean parallel texts, while denoising loss employs techniques from denoising auto-encoders (Liu et al., 2020b) that introduce noise into the source text. The language modeling objective of NLLB uses monolingual data to train the decoder.

Vanilla Fine-tuning We fine-tune the open-source NLLB model[5] with the released MT corpora for apc-eng, bem-eng, and que-spa. Specifically, we use the distilled 600M-parameter NLLB model as the base model and fine-tune the model with NLL loss. Following NLLB Team et al. (2022), we append language tokens on both source and target sequences during training and force decode the target language token during inference. We use a learning rate of 1×10^{-4} and set the maximum number of target tokens per batch to 1600. We train all translation models on a single V100 machine and accumulate gradient updates every 4 steps.

Fine-tuning with Intra-distillation We also fine-tune with intra-distillation (ID), which is an effective task-agnostic training method, aiming to encourage all parameters to contribute equally (Xu et al., 2022, 2023). Given an input batch, ID needs to forward pass the model K times to obtain K outputs and each time a random subset of parameters is zeroed out. The core idea of ID is to minimize the difference of these K outputs to approximately minimizing the contribution gap of the parameters that are zeroed-out, because the K outputs are forced to be the same with different zeroed parameters. Let $\{p_1, \cdots, p_i, \cdots, p_K\}$ denote the K outputs. The ID loss is then formulated by the X-divergence (Xu et al., 2022) to minimize the difference of K outputs as

$$\mathcal{L}_{id} = \frac{1}{K}\sum_{i=1}^{K} \mathbb{KL}(p_i \parallel \bar{p}) + \mathbb{KL}(\bar{p} \parallel p_i)$$
$$\text{where } \bar{p} = \frac{1}{K}\sum_{i=1}^{K} p_i$$

Let the original task loss be $\mathcal{L}_i$ for the ith pass. Then, the total loss is a combination of the original task loss and ID loss, given as

$$\min \frac{1}{K}\sum_{i=1}^{K} \mathcal{L}_i + \alpha\mathcal{L}_{id}$$

[4]Note that in this case, since the ST data is used for pseudo-translation, only <|translate|> tags are used.

[5]Available at: https://huggingface.co/docs/transformers/en/model_doc/nllb

where α is a hyper-parameter to control the strength of ID.

5 Results and Discussion

Table 2 displays the results for all of our MT systems. We calculate scores using the same BLEU (Papineni et al., 2002) configuration as the task organizers.[6] We include scores from internal **Dev** and **Test** sets when available, as well as the official **Eval** scores. Details of data splitting are in Appendix A.2. The results show that SEAMLESSM4T v2 systems perform best for half of the language pairs: bho-hin, gle-eng, mar-hin, and mlt-eng. Cascaded systems employing Whisper and NLLB for MT performed best for the others: apc-eng, bem-eng, que-spa, and tmh-fra. (Note these first three language pairs employed Whisper for ASR and a fine-tuned NLLB model for MT, while tmh-fra employed Whisper for X-Eng ST and NLLB out of the box for MT into French.)

5.1 End-to-end ST

The SEAMLESSM4T v2 models' poor performance on bem-eng, que-spa, and tmh-fra is likely due to the absence of Bemba, Quechua, or Tamasheq in its pre-training corpus. We include zero-shot results for SEAMLESSM4T v2 out of the box in Table 3, which illustrate that the pre-trained model already performs well on mlt-eng and gle-eng,[7] but poorly on unseen language pairs.

We remark that our fine-tuning process brings notable improvements for bho-hin, mar-hin, and mlt-eng. In particular, SEAMLESSM4T v2 is successful for bho-hin despite not being pre-trained explicitly on Bhojpuri data, possibly because the Hindi pretraining data contains some Bhojpuri, or because SEAMLESSM4T v2 is capable of extrapolating fairly well to Bhojpuri given its high linguistic similarity to Hindi. Interestingly, the mixed data training (comb.) for language pairs sharing a target language does not significantly improve performance for either source language, though we expected it to benefit the lower-resource pair. In the case of gle,mlt-eng, there are domain differences (read speech vs. telephonic speech) between the fine-tuning corpora, possibly resulting in unhelpful or negative interference; Irish and Maltese are also not linguistically related, limiting cross-lingual transfer. On the other hand, with bho,mar-hin, Marathi and Bhojpuri both belong to the Indic subfamily of languages, and the speech translation data for both respective language pairs is from the news domain, averaging about 7 seconds each. The lack of success of joint fine-tuning for both these setups resonates with the findings of Sun et al. (2023), which presents several experiments showing that multilingual training for speech translation may not always benefit low-resource languages. We also note that curriculum training likewise did not improve performance for mlt-eng.

In our evaluation of Whisper systems, we emphasize two significant observations. Firstly, as anticipated, the BLEU scores for the mar-hin and bho-hin language pairs validate the efficacy of the proposed pseudo-translation method. This finding not only demonstrates that the model is capable of handling non-English translations with minimal fine-tuning, but also underscores its adaptability to linguistically similar language pairs. Secondly, the consistent performance gain observed with Whisper MTL over Whisper E2E as illustrated by the mar-hin results underscores the advantages of multi-task learning. This method treats fine-tuning on multiple tasks as involving one primary task and several auxiliary tasks, which collectively contribute to enhanced outcomes on all tasks involved.

5.2 Cascaded ST

Cascaded ST via fine-tuned Whisper for ASR and fine-tuned NLLB for MT is our best-performing approach for apc-eng, bem-eng, and que-spa, though it is much better for apc-eng and bem-eng than for que-spa. The relatively low performance of que-spa can be possibly attributed to it being a non-English-centric translation direction.

Table 4 presents the ASR performance of the fine-tuned Whisper models on 5 language pairs with different objectives. Those trained with the ASR-only objective are used solely as the ASR module in cascaded systems, while the systems trained with the multi-task learning objective are used for both direct translation and ASR for cascaded systems. Interestingly, we observe that for Bemba, the CERs (25.1 for **dev** and 17.9 for the **test1** set) are significantly lower than the WERs. We find through manual inspection that the model

[6]With sacrebleu signature nrefs:1 | case:lc | eff:no | tok:13a | smooth:exp | version:2.0.0.

[7]There is a considerable discrepancy between the gle-eng dev and test scores from IWSLT 2023, with the latter being suspiciously high. Mbuya and Anastasopoulos (2023) suggest that the inflated test scores may be due to overlap between train and test sets.

Lang.	System	Submisson	Dev	Test	Eval	Lang.	System	Submisson	Dev	Test	Eval
apc-eng	Whisper+NLLB+ID	primary	-	**32.0**	**16.0**	tmh-fra	Whisper+NLLB	primary	**8.0**	**7.0**	**6.1**
	Whisper+NLLB	contrastive1	-	30.2	14.7		Seamless	contrastive1	0.3	1.3	0.5
bem-eng	Whisper+NLLB+ID	primary	**26.3**	**30.4**	**32.6**	mar-hin	Seamless	primary	**32.1**	**40.9**	**37.7**
	Whisper+NLLB	contrastive1	22.6	29.0	27.0		Seamless comb.	contrastive1	31.0	39.4	37.3
	Whisper MTL	contrastive2	23.5	27.8	26.7		Whisper MTL	contrastive2	26.3	34.9	28.5
	Seamless	-	6.6	15.4	-		Whisper E2E	-	24.4	32.8	-
bho-hin	Seamless	primary	**34.9**	-	**24.4**	que-spa	Whisper+NLLB+ID	primary	**15.7**	**11.7**	**12.5**
	Seamless comb.	contrastive1	34.5	-	23.9		Whisper+NLLB	contrastive1	6.9	6.1	6.4
	Whisper E2E	contrastive2	28.6	-	12.2		Seamless	contrastive2	1.8	0.9	0.9
mlt-eng	Seamless	primary	**52.9**	**54.2**	-	gle-eng	Seamless	primary	25.2	**52.7**	15.3
	Seamless curr.	contrastive1	47.3	47.1	-		Seamless comb.	contrastive1	**27.6**	51.6	**16.0**
	Whisper MTL	contrastive2	34.5	35.1	-						
	Seamless comb.	-	51.6	53.1	-						

Table 2: BLEU scores for each system. **Dev** and **Test** denote our internal tuning and test sets, when available. **Eval** denotes the official evaluation. apc-eng **Test** scores are from text-only MT, since our data had no source speech-to-translation alignments for ST evaluation. "ID" indicates use of intra-distillation with NLLB fine-tuning. "Comb." refers to mixed data training, and "curr." refers to curriculum training.

Lang.	Dev_{zero}	Dev_{ft}
bem-eng	0.9	**6.6**
gle-eng	**27.7**	25.2
mar-hin	0.0	**32.1**
mlt-eng	47.8	**52.9**
que-spa	**1.9**	1.8
tmh-fra	0.4	**8.0**

Table 3: Zero-shot and fine-tuned performance of SEAMLESSM4T v2 on dev set. Model generally improves after fine-tuning, except for que-spa and gle-eng.

Lang.	Objective	Dev	Test
apc-eng	ASR-only	11.5	10.4
que-eng	ASR-only	34.4	34.5
bem-eng	MTL	57.3	47.3
mar-hin	MTL	37.2	37.3
mlt-eng	MTL	23.8	-

Table 4: WER of the Whisper model fine-tuned on each language. *ASR-only* suggests that the model is trained to perform ASR-only to serve as an ASR module for a cascaded system, whereas *MTL* suggests that the model is trained to perform E2E ST and ASR.

tends to make minor spelling errors, presumably due to its unfamiliarity with the language's writing system, as suggested by the decent proficiency in its translation performance. This may cause error propagation in cascaded ST.

In our MT module, we implemented intra-distillation to enhance ST results by balancing the contributions of the model parameters. Consistent with prior studies Xu et al. (2022, 2023), intra-distillation consistently improves performance across all evaluated translation directions, with the most significant enhancement observed for que-spa. MT performance was reasonably high for the three language pairs for which we employed cascaded ST. The cascaded approach for mlt-eng performs poorly, likely because our Maltese bitexts were noisy. Additionaly, NLLB has already been pre-trained on Maltese and may not benefit further from the noisy post-training.

6 Conclusion and Future Work

In this work, we describe our submitted systems for all eight language pairs in the IWSLT 2024 Low-Resource Language Track. We explore various fine-tuning approaches for large publicly available pre-trained models, compare end-to-end and cascaded systems, as well as investigate the benefits of joint and curriculum training, multitask learning, as well as intra-distillation. We find that the best-performing strategy is language-pair dependent, with fine-tuned SEAMLESSM4T v2 generally performing best on languages that are included in its pretraining corpus. Fine-tuned Whisper generally performed better with multi-task fine-tuning than standard fine-tuning, and better still when employed in a cascaded system with fine-tuned NLLB (with best results employing intra-distillation).

For future improvements, augmenting MT fine-tuning data with ASR hypotheses, as in Gow-Smith et al. (2023), could equip NLLB better for cascaded ST. Future work could also employ data augmentation of text and speech data, as in Shanbhogue et al. (2023), via textual back-translation (Sennrich et al., 2016), speech synthesis for augmentation (Rossenbach et al., 2020; Robinson et al., 2022), or other methods. Lastly, future research could employ the use of SSLR, or employ the large amounts of raw audio available—particularly for Tamasheq—to train SSLR systems, following Gow-Smith et al. (2023).

References

Milind Agarwal, Sweta Agrawal, Antonios Anastasopoulos, Luisa Bentivogli, Ondřej Bojar, Claudia Borg, Marine Carpuat, Roldano Cattoni, Mauro Cettolo, Mingda Chen, William Chen, Khalid Choukri, Alexandra Chronopoulou, Anna Currey, Thierry Declerck, Qianqian Dong, Kevin Duh, Yannick Estève, Marcello Federico, Souhir Gahbiche, Barry Haddow, Benjamin Hsu, Phu Mon Htut, Hirofumi Inaguma, Dávid Javorský, John Judge, Yasumasa Kano, Tom Ko, Rishu Kumar, Pengwei Li, Xutai Ma, Prashant Mathur, Evgeny Matusov, Paul McNamee, John P. McCrae, Kenton Murray, Maria Nadejde, Satoshi Nakamura, Matteo Negri, Ha Nguyen, Jan Niehues, Xing Niu, Atul Kr. Ojha, John E. Ortega, Proyag Pal, Juan Pino, Lonneke van der Plas, Peter Polák, Elijah Rippeth, Elizabeth Salesky, Jiatong Shi, Matthias Sperber, Sebastian Stüker, Katsuhito Sudoh, Yun Tang, Brian Thompson, Kevin Tran, Marco Turchi, Alex Waibel, Mingxuan Wang, Shinji Watanabe, and Rodolfo Zevallos. 2023. FINDINGS OF THE IWSLT 2023 EVALUATION CAMPAIGN. In *Proceedings of the 20th International Conference on Spoken Language Translation (IWSLT 2023)*, pages 1–61, Toronto, Canada (in-person and online). Association for Computational Linguistics.

Arun Babu, Changhan Wang, Andros Tjandra, Kushal Lakhotia, Qiantong Xu, Naman Goyal, Kritika Singh, Patrick von Platen, Yatharth Saraf, Juan Pino, et al. 2022. Xls-r: Self-supervised cross-lingual speech representation learning at scale.

Alexei Baevski, Yuhao Zhou, Abdelrahman Mohamed, and Michael Auli. 2020. wav2vec 2.0: A framework for self-supervised learning of speech representations. *Advances in neural information processing systems*, 33:12449–12460.

Niyati Bafna, Cristina España-Bonet, Josef Van Genabith, Benoît Sagot, and Rachel Bawden. 2023. Cross-lingual strategies for low-resource language modeling: A study on five Indic dialects. In *Actes de CORIA-TALN 2023. Actes de la 30e Conférence sur le Traitement Automatique des Langues Naturelles (TALN), volume 1 : travaux de recherche originaux – articles longs*, pages 28–42, Paris, France. ATALA.

Marta Bañón, Pinzhen Chen, Barry Haddow, Kenneth Heafield, Hieu Hoang, Miquel Esplà-Gomis, Mikel L. Forcada, Amir Kamran, Faheem Kirefu, Philipp Koehn, Sergio Ortiz Rojas, Leopoldo Pla Sempere, Gema Ramírez-Sánchez, Elsa Sarrías, Marek Strelec, Brian Thompson, William Waites, Dion Wiggins, and Jaume Zaragoza. 2020. ParaCrawl: Web-scale acquisition of parallel corpora. In *Proceedings of the 58th Annual Meeting of the Association for Computational Linguistics*, pages 4555–4567, Online. Association for Computational Linguistics.

Marta Bañón, Malina Chichirau, Miquel Esplà-Gomis, Mikel L. Forcada, Aarón Galiano-Jiménez, Cristian García-Romero, Taja Kuzman, Nikola Ljubešić, Rik van Noord, Leopoldo Pla Sempere, Gema Ramírez-Sánchez, Peter Rupnik, Vít Suchomel, Antonio Toral, and Jaume Zaragoza-Bernabeu. 2023. Maltese-english parallel corpus MaCoCu-mt-en 2.0. Slovenian language resource repository CLARIN.SI.

Loïc Barrault, Yu-An Chung, Mariano Coria Meglioli, David Dale, Ning Dong, Mark Duppenthaler, Paul-Ambroise Duquenne, Brian Ellis, Hady Elsahar, Justin Haaheim, et al. 2023. Seamless: Multilingual expressive and streaming speech translation. *arXiv preprint arXiv:2312.05187*.

Laurent Besacier, Bowen Zhou, and Yuqing Gao. 2006. Towards speech translation of non written languages. In *2006 IEEE Spoken Language Technology Workshop*, pages 222–225. IEEE.

Kaushal Santosh Bhogale, Abhigyan Raman, Tahir Javed, Sumanth Doddapaneni, Anoop Kunchukuttan, Pratyush Kumar, and Mitesh M. Khapra. 2022. Effectiveness of mining audio and text pairs from public data for improving asr systems for low-resource languages. *arXiv preprint*.

Ronald Cardenas, Rodolfo Zevallos, Reynaldo Baquerizo, and Luis Camacho. 2018. Siminchik: A speech corpus for preservation of southern quechua.

Tianqi Chen, Bing Xu, Chiyuan Zhang, and Carlos Guestrin. 2016. Training deep nets with sublinear memory cost. *Preprint*, arXiv:1604.06174.

Yu-An Chung, Yu Zhang, Wei Han, Chung-Cheng Chiu, James Qin, Ruoming Pang, and Yonghui Wu. 2021. W2v-bert: Combining contrastive learning and masked language modeling for self-supervised speech pre-training. In *2021 IEEE Automatic Speech Recognition and Understanding Workshop (ASRU)*, pages 244–250. IEEE.

Pan Deng, Shihao Chen, Weitai Zhang, Jie Zhang, and Lirong Dai. 2023. The USTC's dialect speech translation system for IWSLT 2023. In *Proceedings of the 20th International Conference on Spoken Language Translation (IWSLT 2023)*, pages 102–112, Toronto, Canada (in-person and online). Association for Computational Linguistics.

Nan Du, Yanping Huang, Andrew M. Dai, Simon Tong, Dmitry Lepikhin, Yuanzhong Xu, Maxim Krikun, Yanqi Zhou, Adams Wei Yu, Orhan Firat, Barret Zoph, Liam Fedus, Maarten Bosma, Zongwei Zhou, Tao Wang, Yu Emma Wang, Kellie Webster, Marie Pellat, Kevin Robinson, Kathleen Meier-Hellstern, Toju Duke, Lucas Dixon, Kun Zhang, Quoc V Le, Yonghui Wu, Zhifeng Chen, and Claire Cui. 2022. Glam: Efficient scaling of language models with mixture-of-experts. *Preprint*, arXiv:2112.06905.

John E. Ortega, Rodolfo Zevallos, and William Chen. 2023. QUESPA submission for the IWSLT 2023 dialect and low-resource speech translation tasks. In

Proceedings of the 20th International Conference on Spoken Language Translation (IWSLT 2023), pages 261–268, Toronto, Canada (in-person and online). Association for Computational Linguistics.

Edward Gow-Smith, Alexandre Berard, Marcely Zanon Boito, and Ioan Calapodescu. 2023. NAVER LABS Europe's multilingual speech translation systems for the IWSLT 2023 low-resource track. In *Proceedings of the 20th International Conference on Spoken Language Translation (IWSLT 2023)*, pages 144–158, Toronto, Canada (in-person and online). Association for Computational Linguistics.

Fei He, Shan-Hui Cathy Chu, Oddur Kjartansson, Clara Rivera, Anna Katanova, Alexander Gutkin, Isin Demirsahin, Cibu Johny, Martin Jansche, Supheakmungkol Sarin, and Knot Pipatsrisawat. 2020. Open-source multi-speaker speech corpora for building Gujarati, Kannada, Malayalam, Marathi, Tamil and Telugu speech synthesis systems. In *Proceedings of the Twelfth Language Resources and Evaluation Conference*, pages 6494–6503, Marseille, France. European Language Resources Association.

Taiqi He, Kwanghee Choi, Lindia Tjuatja, Nathaniel R. Robinson, Jiatong Shi, Shinji Watanabe, Graham Neubig, David R. Mortensen, and Lori Levin. 2024. Wav2gloss: Generating interlinear glossed text from speech. *Preprint*, arXiv:2403.13169.

Carlos Daniel Hernandez Mena, Albert Gatt, Andrea DeMarco, Claudia Borg, Lonneke van der Plas, Amanda Muscat, and Ian Padovani. 2020. MASRI-HEADSET: A Maltese corpus for speech recognition. In *Proceedings of the Twelfth Language Resources and Evaluation Conference*, pages 6381–6388, Marseille, France. European Language Resources Association.

Wei-Ning Hsu, Benjamin Bolte, Yao-Hung Hubert Tsai, Kushal Lakhotia, Ruslan Salakhutdinov, and Abdelrahman Mohamed. 2021. Hubert: Self-supervised speech representation learning by masked prediction of hidden units. *IEEE/ACM Transactions on Audio, Speech, and Language Processing*, 29:3451–3460.

Edward J. Hu, Yelong Shen, Phillip Wallis, Zeyuan Allen-Zhu, Yuanzhi Li, Shean Wang, Lu Wang, and Weizhu Chen. 2021. Lora: Low-rank adaptation of large language models. *Preprint*, arXiv:2106.09685.

Amir Hussein, Cihan Xiao, Neha Verma, Thomas Thebaud, Matthew Wiesner, and Sanjeev Khudanpur. 2023. JHU IWSLT 2023 dialect speech translation system description. In *Proceedings of the 20th International Conference on Spoken Language Translation (IWSLT 2023)*, pages 283–290, Toronto, Canada (in-person and online). Association for Computational Linguistics.

Georgios Karakasidis, Nathaniel Robinson, Yaroslav Getman, Atieno Ogayo, Ragheb Al-Ghezi, Ananya Ayasi, Shinji Watanabe, David R. Mortensen, and Mikko Kurimo. 2023. Multilingual tts accent impressions for accented asr. In *Text, Speech, and Dialogue*, pages 317–327, Cham. Springer Nature Switzerland.

Santosh Kesiraju, Karel Beneš, Maksim Tikhonov, and Jan Černocký. 2023a. BUT systems for IWSLT 2023 Marathi - Hindi low resource speech translation task. In *Proceedings of the 20th International Conference on Spoken Language Translation (IWSLT 2023)*, pages 227–234, Toronto, Canada (in-person and online). Association for Computational Linguistics.

Santosh Kesiraju, Marek Sarvaš, Tomáš Pavlíček, Cécile Macaire, and Alejandro Ciuba. 2023b. Strategies for improving low resource speech to text translation relying on pre-trained asr models. In *INTERSPEECH 2023*. ISCA.

Tom Ko, Vijayaditya Peddinti, Daniel Povey, and Sanjeev Khudanpur. 2015. Audio augmentation for speech recognition. In *Proc. Interspeech 2015*, pages 3586–3589.

Ritesh Kumar, Siddharth Singh, Shyam Ratan, Mohit Raj, Sonal Sinha, Bornini Lahiri, Vivek Seshadri, Kalika Bali, and Atul Kr Ojha. 2022. Annotated speech corpus for low resource indian languages: Awadhi, bhojpuri, braj and magahi. *arXiv preprint arXiv:2206.12931*.

Antoine Laurent, Souhir Gahbiche, Ha Nguyen, Haroun Elleuch, Fethi Bougares, Antoine Thiol, Hugo Riguidel, Salima Mdhaffar, Gaëlle Laperrière, Lucas Maison, Sameer Khurana, and Yannick Estève. 2023. ON-TRAC consortium systems for the IWSLT 2023 dialectal and low-resource speech translation tasks. In *Proceedings of the 20th International Conference on Spoken Language Translation (IWSLT 2023)*, pages 219–226, Toronto, Canada (in-person and online). Association for Computational Linguistics.

Yinhan Liu, Jiatao Gu, Naman Goyal, Xian Li, Sergey Edunov, Marjan Ghazvininejad, Mike Lewis, and Luke Zettlemoyer. 2020a. Multilingual denoising pre-training for neural machine translation. *Transactions of the Association for Computational Linguistics*, 8:726–742.

Yinhan Liu, Jiatao Gu, Naman Goyal, Xian Li, Sergey Edunov, Marjan Ghazvininejad, Mike Lewis, and Luke Zettlemoyer. 2020b. Multilingual denoising pre-training for neural machine translation. *Transactions of the Association for Computational Linguistics*, 8:726–742.

John Makhoul, Bushra Zawaydeh, Frederick Choi, and David Stallard. 2005. Bbn/aub darpa babylon levantine arabic speech and transcripts. *Linguistic Data Consortium (LDC), LDC Catalog No.: LDC2005S08*.

Jonathan Mbuya and Antonios Anastasopoulos. 2023. GMU systems for the IWSLT 2023 dialect and low-resource speech translation tasks. In *Proceedings of the 20th International Conference on Spoken Language Translation (IWSLT 2023)*, pages 269–276,

Toronto, Canada (in-person and online). Association for Computational Linguistics.

Rajesh Kumar Mundotiya, Manish Kumar Singh, Rahul Kapur, Swasti Mishra, and Anil Kumar Singh. 2021. Linguistic resources for bhojpuri, magahi, and maithili: statistics about them, their similarity estimates, and baselines for three applications. *Transactions on Asian and Low-Resource Language Information Processing*, 20(6):1–37.

Antonio Carvalho Neto, Fernanda Versiani, Kelly Pellizari, Carolina Mota-Santos, and Gustavo Abreu. 2020. Latin american, african and asian immigrants working in brazilian organizations: facing the language barrier. *Revista Economia & Gestão*, 20(55).

NLLB Team, Marta R. Costa-jussà, James Cross, Onur Çelebi, Maha Elbayad, Kenneth Heafield, Kevin Heffernan, Elahe Kalbassi, Janice Lam, Daniel Licht, Jean Maillard, Anna Sun, Skyler Wang, Guillaume Wenzek, Al Youngblood, Bapi Akula, Loic Barrault, Gabriel Mejia-Gonzalez, Prangthip Hansanti, John Hoffman, Semarley Jarrett, Kaushik Ram Sadagopan, Dirk Rowe, Shannon Spruit, Chau Tran, Pierre Andrews, Necip Fazil Ayan, Shruti Bhosale, Sergey Edunov, Angela Fan, Cynthia Gao, Vedanuj Goswami, Francisco Guzmán, Philipp Koehn, Alexandre Mourachko, Christophe Ropers, Safiyyah Saleem, Holger Schwenk, and Jeff Wang. 2022. No language left behind: Scaling human-centered machine translation.

John E Ortega, Richard Castro Mamani, and Kyunghyun Cho. 2020. Neural machine translation with a polysynthetic low resource language. *Machine Translation*, 34(4):325–346.

Kishore Papineni, Salim Roukos, Todd Ward, and Wei-Jing Zhu. 2002. Bleu: a method for automatic evaluation of machine translation. In *Proceedings of the 40th Annual Meeting of the Association for Computational Linguistics*, pages 311–318, Philadelphia, Pennsylvania, USA. Association for Computational Linguistics.

Daniel S. Park, William Chan, Yu Zhang, Chung-Cheng Chiu, Barret Zoph, Ekin D. Cubuk, and Quoc V. Le. 2019. Specaugment: A simple data augmentation method for automatic speech recognition. In *Interspeech 2019*. ISCA.

Alec Radford, Jong Wook Kim, Tao Xu, Greg Brockman, Christine Mcleavey, and Ilya Sutskever. 2023. Robust speech recognition via large-scale weak supervision. In *Proceedings of the 40th International Conference on Machine Learning*, volume 202 of *Proceedings of Machine Learning Research*, pages 28492–28518. PMLR.

Samyam Rajbhandari, Jeff Rasley, Olatunji Ruwase, and Yuxiong He. 2020. Zero: Memory optimizations toward training trillion parameter models. *Preprint*, arXiv:1910.02054.

Nathaniel Robinson, Perez Ogayo, Swetha Gangu, David R Mortensen, and Shinji Watanabe. 2022. When is tts augmentation through a pivot language useful? In *Proceedings of the Annual Conference of the International Speech Communication Association, INTERSPEECH*, volume 2022, pages 3538–3542.

Nathaniel Robinson, Perez Ogayo, David R. Mortensen, and Graham Neubig. 2023. ChatGPT MT: Competitive for high- (but not low-) resource languages. In *Proceedings of the Eighth Conference on Machine Translation*, pages 392–418, Singapore. Association for Computational Linguistics.

Nick Rossenbach, Albert Zeyer, Ralf Schlüter, and Hermann Ney. 2020. Generating synthetic audio data for attention-based speech recognition systems. In *ICASSP 2020 - 2020 IEEE International Conference on Acoustics, Speech and Signal Processing (ICASSP)*, pages 7069–7073.

Hashem Sellat, Shadi Saleh, Mateusz Krubiński, Adam Pospíšil, Petr Zemánek, and Pavel Pecina. 2023. UFAL parallel corpus of north levantine 1.0. LINDAT/CLARIAH-CZ digital library at the Institute of Formal and Applied Linguistics (ÚFAL), Faculty of Mathematics and Physics, Charles University.

Rico Sennrich, Barry Haddow, and Alexandra Birch. 2016. Improving neural machine translation models with monolingual data. In *Proceedings of the 54th Annual Meeting of the Association for Computational Linguistics (Volume 1: Long Papers)*, pages 86–96, Berlin, Germany. Association for Computational Linguistics.

Akshaya Vishnu Kudlu Shanbhogue, Ran Xue, Soumya Saha, Daniel Zhang, and Ashwinkumar Ganesan. 2023. Improving low resource speech translation with data augmentation and ensemble strategies. In *Proceedings of the 20th International Conference on Spoken Language Translation (IWSLT 2023)*, pages 241–250, Toronto, Canada (in-person and online). Association for Computational Linguistics.

Claytone Sikasote and Antonios Anastasopoulos. 2022. BembaSpeech: A speech recognition corpus for the Bemba language. In *Proceedings of the Thirteenth Language Resources and Evaluation Conference*, pages 7277–7283, Marseille, France. European Language Resources Association.

Claytone Sikasote, Eunice Mukonde, Md Mahfuz Ibn Alam, and Antonios Anastasopoulos. 2023. BIG-C: a multimodal multi-purpose dataset for Bemba. In *Proceedings of the 61st Annual Meeting of the Association for Computational Linguistics (Volume 1: Long Papers)*, pages 2062–2078, Toronto, Canada. Association for Computational Linguistics.

Matthias Sperber and Matthias Paulik. 2020. Speech translation and the end-to-end promise: Taking stock of where we are. In *Proceedings of the 58th Annual Meeting of the Association for Computational Linguistics*, pages 7409–7421, Online. Association for Computational Linguistics.

Haoran Sun, Xiaohu Zhao, Yikun Lei, Shaolin Zhu, and Deyi Xiong. 2023. Towards a deep understanding of multilingual end-to-end speech translation. In *Findings of the Association for Computational Linguistics: EMNLP 2023*, pages 14332–14348, Singapore. Association for Computational Linguistics.

Jörg Tiedemann. 2012. Parallel data, tools and interfaces in OPUS. In *Proceedings of the Eighth International Conference on Language Resources and Evaluation (LREC'12)*, pages 2214–2218, Istanbul, Turkey. European Language Resources Association (ELRA).

Ashish Vaswani, Noam Shazeer, Niki Parmar, Jakob Uszkoreit, Llion Jones, Aidan N Gomez, Łukasz Kaiser, and Illia Polosukhin. 2017. Attention is all you need. *Advances in neural information processing systems*, 30.

Aiden Williams, Kurt Abela, Rishu Kumar, Martin Bär, Hannah Billinghurst, Kurt Micallef, Ahnaf Mozib Samin, Andrea DeMarco, Lonneke van der Plas, and Claudia Borg. 2023. UM-DFKI Maltese speech translation. In *Proceedings of the 20th International Conference on Spoken Language Translation (IWSLT 2023)*, pages 433–441, Toronto, Canada (in-person and online). Association for Computational Linguistics.

Haoran Xu, Philipp Koehn, and Kenton Murray. 2022. The importance of being parameters: An intra-distillation method for serious gains. In *Proceedings of the 2022 Conference on Empirical Methods in Natural Language Processing*, pages 170–183, Abu Dhabi, United Arab Emirates. Association for Computational Linguistics.

Haoran Xu, Jean Maillard, and Vedanuj Goswami. 2023. Language-aware multilingual machine translation with self-supervised learning. In *Findings of the Association for Computational Linguistics: EACL 2023*, pages 526–539, Dubrovnik, Croatia. Association for Computational Linguistics.

Marcely Zanon Boito, Fethi Bougares, Florentin Barbier, Souhir Gahbiche, Loïc Barrault, Mickael Rouvier, and Yannick Estève. 2022. Speech resources in the Tamasheq language. In *Proceedings of the Thirteenth Language Resources and Evaluation Conference*, pages 2066–2071, Marseille, France. European Language Resources Association.

A Additional Experimental Details

A.1 SEAMLESSM4T v2 hyperparameters

For SEAMLESSM4T v2 models, the longest audio length is truncated at 30 seconds. To ensure full reproducibility of the result, a random seed of 42 is deployed. We perform a minimum hyperparameter search for each language pair between the learning rate of $\{10^{-5}, 10^{-6}, 10^{-7}\}$. For each language pair, we fine-tune a SEAMLESSM4T `v2-large` for four epochs, with a learning rate of 1×10^{-6} and batch size of 32. For Quecha-to-Spanish (`que-spa`) translation, a learning rate of 1×10^{-8} is used for training 15 epochs due to its small dataset size. For all the training trials, a constant learning rate scheduler and a warm-up step of 50 is used. During inference, the maximum generation length is constrained to 256 tokens with greedy decoding.

A.2 Split details

We split data into train, dev, and test when possible, for tuning and internal evaluation. We split Makhoul et al.'s (2005) Levantine Arabic **ASR** data, Sikasote et al.'s (2023) Bemba **ST** data, He et al.'s (2020) Marathi **ASR** data, Cardenas et al.'s (2018) Quechua **ASR** data, and Tiedemann's (2012) `que-spa` **MT** bitext ourselves using a 90-5-5 split. We split Sellat et al.'s (2023) `apc-eng` **MT** bitext ourselves with a 90-5-5 split but then performed our internal test on a 1000-line subset of the held out data. For the large `mlt-eng` **MT** bitexts from Bañón et al. (2023, 2020), we split the data ourselves with a 99-0.5-0.5 and a 98-1-1 split, respectively. We also split Bhogale et al.'s (2022) large Marathi **ASR** dataset ourselves with a 99-0.5-0.5 split. We used the creator's own splits for Sikasote and Anastasopoulos's (2022) Bemba **ASR** data, Agarwal et al.'s (2023) `mar-hin` **E2E** data, Tiedemann's (2012) `que-spa` **MT** bitext, Zanon Boito et al.'s (2022) `tmh-fra` **E2E** data, and the Hindi **ASR** data from Common Voice. We did the same with Agarwal et al.'s (2023) `gle-eng` **E2E** data, using the test set from the 2023 challenge as our internal test set. For the `mlt-eng` **ST** data from Common Voice and Hernandez Mena et al. (2020) and the `que-spa` **ST** data from Ortega et al. (2020), we used their own train and dev splits and then split the dev set in half to create an internal test set. We used Agarwal et al.'s (2023) own train and dev splits without creating an internal test set.

B Instance Length Distribution

We show the length distribution in Figure 2 and Figure 3. Overall, most datasets show a normal distribution with a slightly skewed tail except for `que-spa`, the amount of instances for which is the smallest. However, we identify some extraordinarily long instances in `bem-eng` training set. These outlier instances can lead to out-of-memory instances if left untreated. Therefore, we truncate the instances that are over 30 seconds when training SEAMLESSM4T v2 and limit the generation length to 256 new tokens.

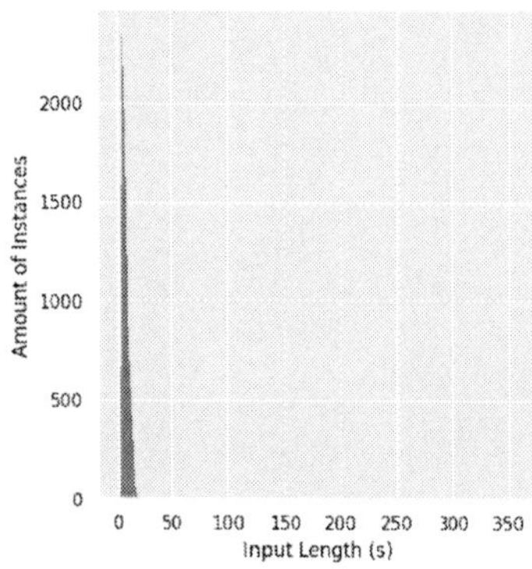

(a) bem-eng TRAINING SET

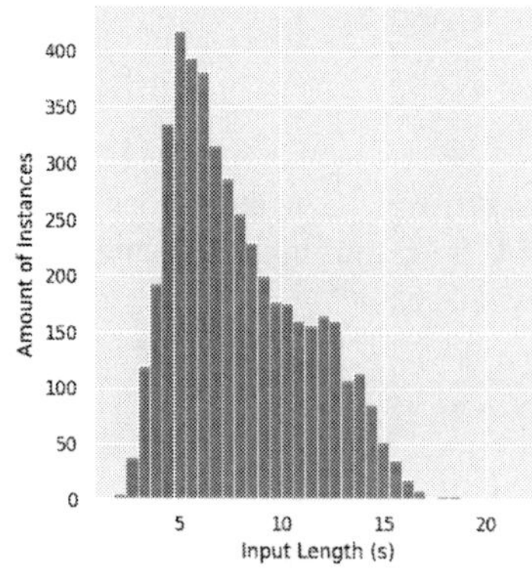

(b) bem-eng DEVELOPMENT SET

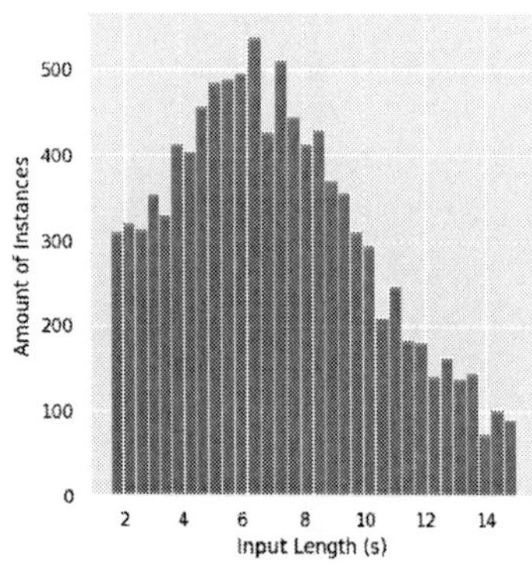

(c) bho-hin TRAINING SET

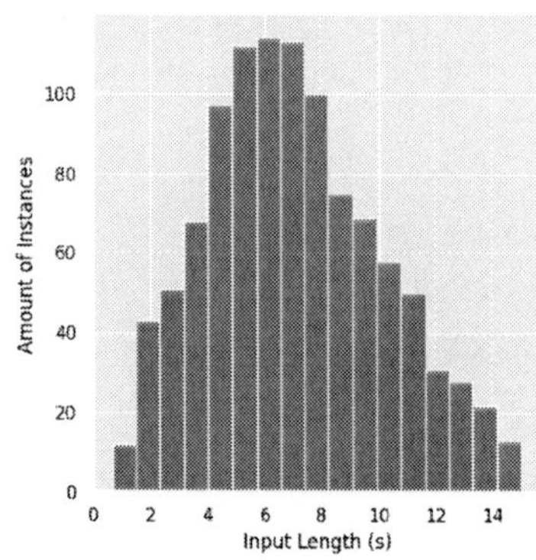

(d) bho-hin DEVELOPMENT SET

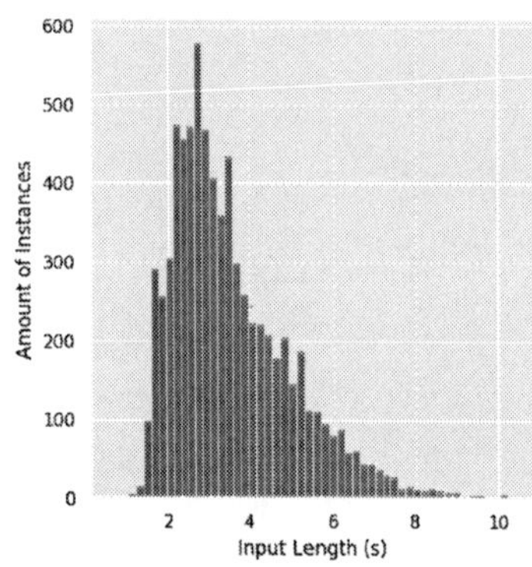

(e) gle-eng TRAINING SET

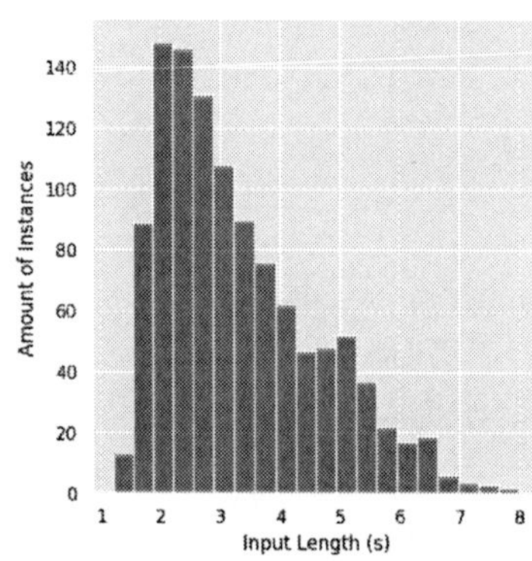

(f) gle-eng DEVELOPMENT SET

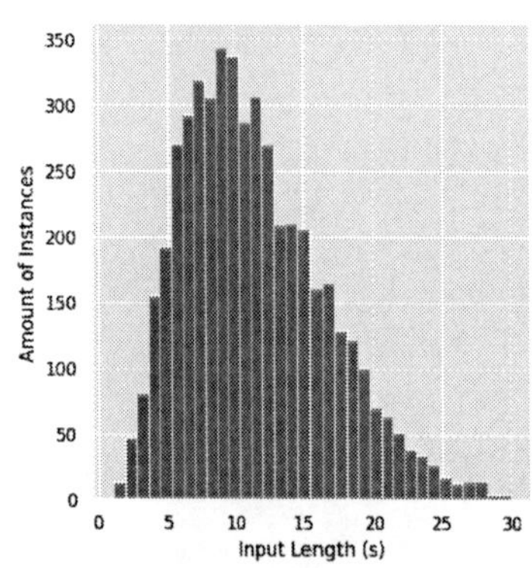

(g) tmh-fra TRAINING SET

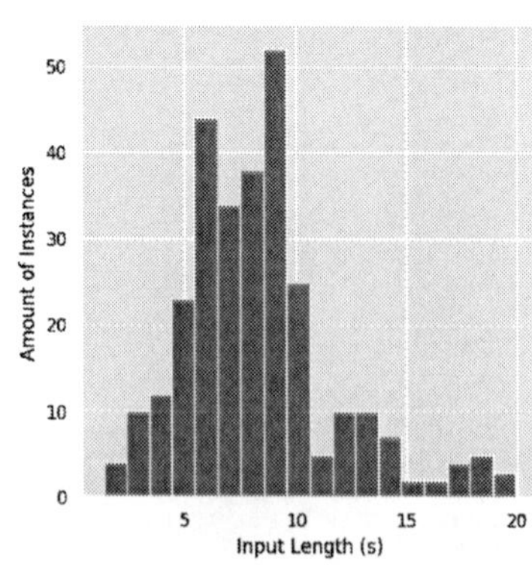

(h) tmh-fra DEVELOPMENT SET

Figure 2: Length distribution (seconds) for each language pair.

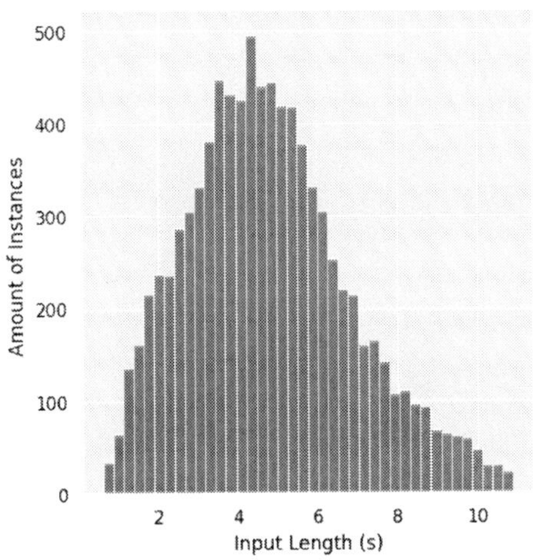

(a) mlt-eng TRAINING SET

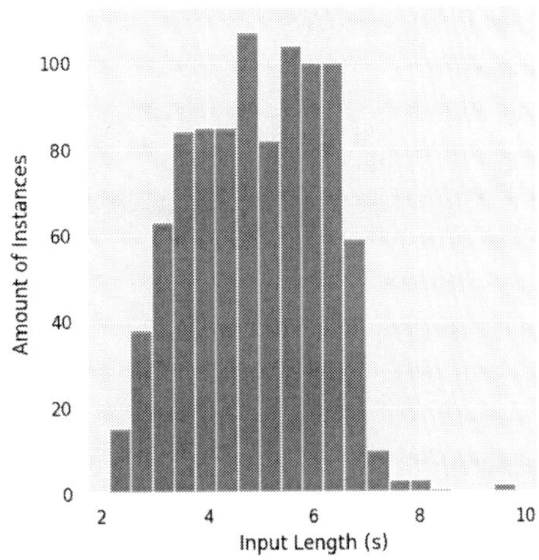

(b) mlt-eng DEVELOPMENT SET

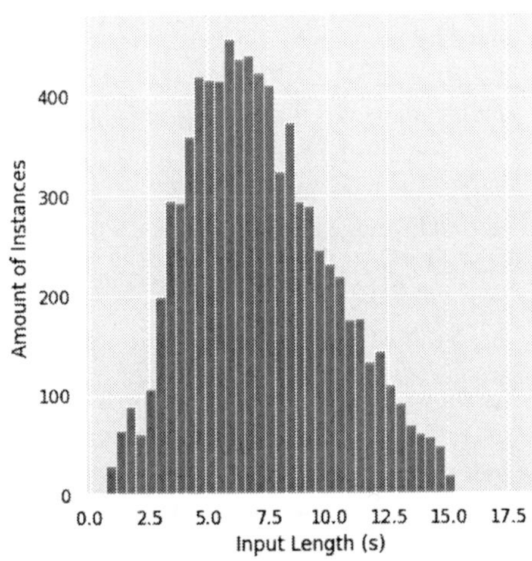

(c) mar-hin TRAINING SET

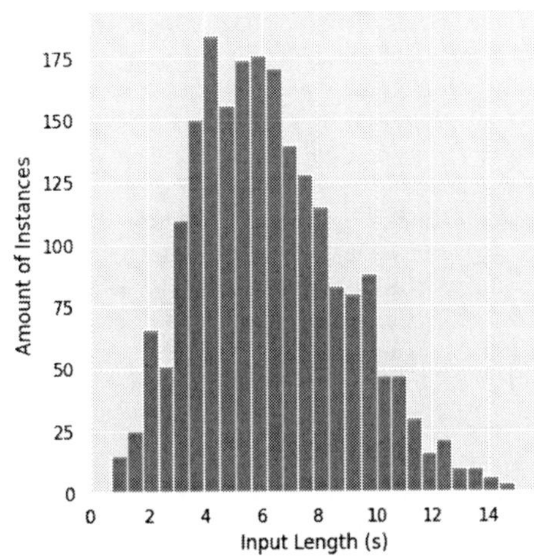

(d) mar-hin DEVELOPMENT SET

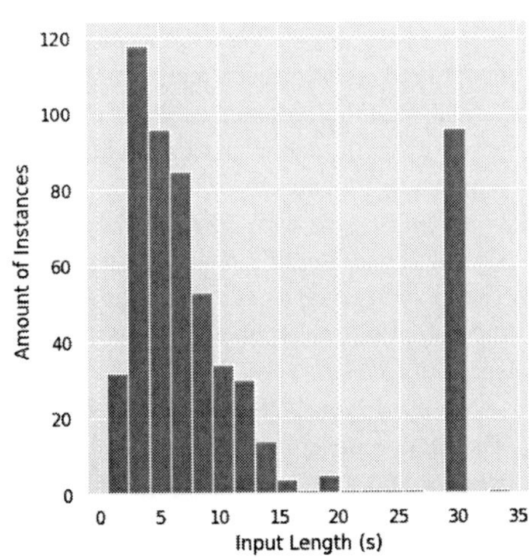

(e) que-spa TRAINING SET

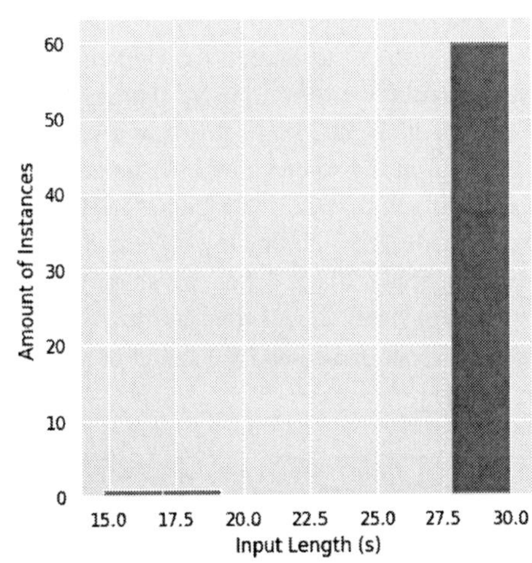

(f) que-spa DEVELOPMENT SET

Figure 3: Length distribution (seconds) for each language pair (continued).

CMU's IWSLT 2024 Simultaneous Speech Translation System

Xi Xu* **Siqi Ouyang*** **Lei Li**
Language Technologies Institute, Carnegie Mellon University, USA
{xixu, siqiouya, leili}@cs.cmu.edu

Abstract

This paper describes CMU's submission to the IWSLT 2024 Simultaneous Speech Translation (SST) task for translating English speech to German text in a streaming manner. Our end-to-end speech-to-text (ST) system integrates the WavLM speech encoder, a modality adapter, and the Llama2-7B-Base model as the decoder. We employ a two-stage training approach: initially, we align the representations of speech and text, followed by full fine-tuning. Both stages are trained on MuST-c v2 data with cross-entropy loss. We adapt our offline ST model for SST using a simple fixed hold-n policy. Experiments show that our model obtains an offline BLEU score of 31.1 and a BLEU score of 29.5 under 2 seconds latency on the MuST-C-v2 tst-COMMON.

1 Introduction

This paper presents CMU's submission to the IWSLT 2024 (Carpuat et al., 2024) Simultaneous Speech Translation (SST) task, focusing on streaming English speech to German text translation. Recent advancements in large language models (LLMs) have demonstrated their potential to be a strong backbone for offline ST (Huang et al., 2023; Zhang et al., 2023). In this year's submission, we build an end-to-end offline ST model with WavLM (Chen et al., 2022) and Llama2-7B-Base (Touvron et al., 2023) following the practice of LST (Zhang et al., 2023). Then we adapt the offline model for simultaneous translation.

We prepare our end-to-end ST model in the following steps:

1. Offline ST with WavLM and Llama2-7B-base.
2. Online adaptation of offline model via hold-n policy and incremental beam search.

*Equal contribution.

2 Task Description

The IWSLT 2024 SST track[1] English-German direction is a shared task for streaming speech-to-text translation of English TED talks. The task requires the system to generate the translation without modifying its previous outputs. The average lagging (AL) (Ma et al., 2019) of SST systems must be below 2 seconds on MuST-C v2.0 tst-COMMON set (Di Gangi et al., 2019). Note that AL has been modified from its original definition (Ma et al., 2020a).

Following the constraint of data and pretrained weights, we use MuST-C v2.0 as the only training set and leverage pretrained models of WavLM and Llama2-7B-Base.

3 System Description

As shown in Figure 1, our offline ST models consists of three primary components: a speech encoder, an adapter, and a LLM decoder.

For the speech encoder, we employ the WavLM model [2], which has been pre-trained on 94,000 hours data including LibriLight (Kahn et al., 2020), VoxPopuli (Wang et al., 2021) and GigaSpeech (Chen et al., 2021). We use the output of last encoder layer as the speech representation.

The modality adapter consists of two components: a length adapter and a modality adapter. The length adapter consists of two 1-dimensional convolutional layers with a kernel size of 5, a stride size of 2, padding of 2, and a hidden size of 1024. The modality adapter is a linear layer that projects the output of the length adapter to the embedding space of LLM.

We use Llama2-7B-Base as the LLM decoder. The LLM decoder takes the output of the modality adapter and autoregressively generate the target text translation.

[1] https://iwslt.org/2024/simultaneous

[2] https://huggingface.co/microsoft/wavlm-large

Proceedings of the 21st International Conference on Spoken Language Translation (IWSLT 2024), pages 202–207
August 15-16, 2024 ©2024 Association for Computational Linguistics

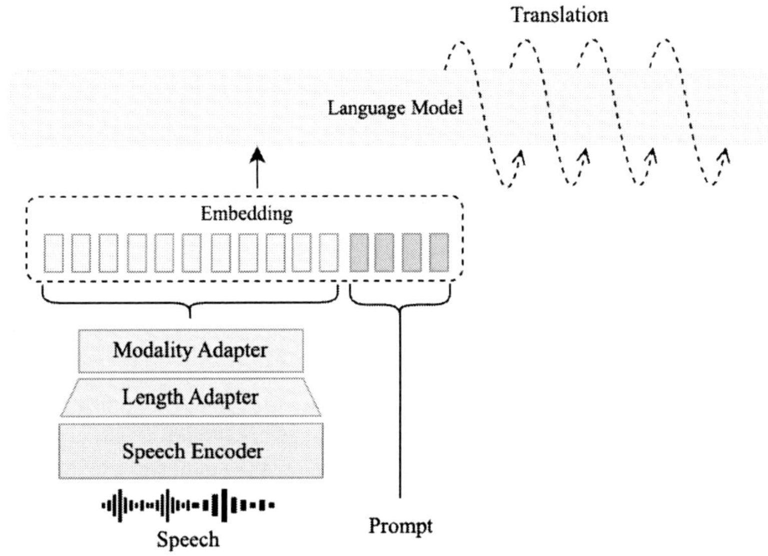

Figure 1: Offline ST model architecture based on WavLM encoder and Llama2 7B decoder.

3.1 Offline Speech Translation (ST)

For each sample, given speech X^S, the reference translation X^T, and the prompt X^P, we initially transform the speech signal into a feature representation via the speech encoder:

$$H^S = \text{Encoder}(X^S), \quad (1)$$

where $H^S = [h_1^S, \ldots, h_T^S]$ with T denoting the sequence length of the feature representation. To reconcile the length difference between the speech feature sequence H^S and its corresponding text, we downsample the speech with a length adapter.

To clarify further, the length adapter transforms H^S using a pair of 1-dimensional convolutional layers, which can be represented as:

$$Z^S = \text{Length adapter}(H^S; k, s, p, h), \quad (2)$$

where k is the kernel size, s is the stride, p is the padding, and h denotes the number of convolutional filters. The reduced temporal dimension is $Z^S = [z_1^S, \ldots, z_N^S]$, where

$$N = \left\lfloor \frac{T - k + 2p}{s} \right\rfloor + 1, \quad (3)$$

Next, a projector is applied to transform the speech features Z^S into E^S with the same dimension as the LLM input embedding. We use a single hidden layer as the projector,

$$E^S = \text{Linear}(Z^S). \quad (4)$$

Finally, we feed the speech embedding E^S, translation embedding E^T, and prompt embedding E^P into the template to compose the final input E of LLM,

$$E^T = \text{Emb}(\text{Tokenizer}(X^T)), \quad (5)$$

$$E^P = \text{Emb}(\text{Tokenizer}(X^P)), \quad (6)$$

$$E = \begin{cases} \text{Template}(E^S, E^P, E^T) & \text{if training,} \\ \text{Template}(E^S, E^P, \tilde{E}^T) & \text{if inference,} \end{cases} \quad (7)$$

where Emb is the LLM embedding layer, $\tilde{E}^T$ is the embedding of model's previously generated tokens.

The template is formatted as:

<P> USER: <S> ASSISTANT:<T>

where *<P>* represents the system prompt[3], *<S>* denotes the speech embedding, and *<T>* is the target reference or generated translation.

We finetune our offline ST model following a 2-stage strategy. In the first stage, we finetune the speech encoder together with the adapters, while keeping the LLM frozen. In the second stage, we finetune the entire model. We employ cross entropy loss in both stages. In addition, we apply rule-based filtering (Ouyang et al., 2022) of the dataset

[3]We use the following system prompt: "You are a large language and speech assistant. You are able to understand the speech content that the user provides, and assist the user with a variety of tasks using natural language. Follow the instructions carefully and explain your answers in detail."

MODEL	QUALITY	LATENCY		
OFFLINE SPEECH TRANSLATION (ST)	SACREBLEU ↑	AL ↓	LAAL ↓	LAAL_CA ↓
WavLM-LLaMA2 (Ours)	31.1	5.85	5.85	7.09
SIMUL SPEECH TRANSLATION (SST)	SACREBLEU ↑	AL ↓	LAAL ↓	LAAL_CA ↓
WavLM-LLaMA2-AlignAtt (Papi et al., 2023)	27.8	2.00	2.21	2.93
WavLM-LLaMA2 (Ours)	29.5	1.96	2.22	3.16

Table 1: Results of our English to German ST/SST models on MuST-C-v2 tst-COMMON. Latency for offline ST is calculated using a wait-k policy with k set to infinity.

Algorithm 1 Selective Output of Speech Chunk Hypotheses

procedure SELECTIVEOUTPUT(hyps, n)
  prunedHyps = {}
  for $c \in \{1, \ldots, C\}$ **do**
    $W^{(c)} = \text{hyps}[c]$
    $l = |W^{(c)}|$
    if source_finished **then**
      $\text{prunedHyps}[c] = W^{(c)}$
    else
      $n' = \min(n, l)$
      $W^{(c)}_{\text{prefix}} = W^{(c)}_{0:l-n'}$
      if $W^{(c)}_{\text{prefix}}$ is not empty **then**
        $\text{prunedHyps}[c] = W^{(c)}_{\text{prefix}}$
      else
        action = Read
        break
      end if
    end if
  end for
  return prunedHyps
end procedure

to clean the unnecessary speaker names from the training set.

3.2 Simultaneous Speech Translation (SST)

We adapt our offline ST model for streaming inference using hold-n policy. Our scheme uses a fixed duration (e.g. 2 seconds) to compute the encoder representations on chunks of input speech. With each new chunk, we re-compute the encoder representations using the entire given input speech.

As shown in Algorithm 1, for each chunk c, we obtain the corresponding hypotheses $W^{(c)}$ using beam search given partial speech input. We then determine the number of tokens n' to withhold based on the minimum of the predefined value n and the length of the current chunk's hypotheses l. The prefix $W^{(c)}_{\text{prefix}}$ is obtained by selecting the tokens from index 0 to $l - n'$.

4 Experimental Setup

We use the AdamW optimizer with a cosine learning rate decay and a warmup ratio of 0.2. The learning rate commences at 2e-4 for the first training stage and is reduced to 2e-5 for the second stage. We train the first stage for 6 epochs and train the second stage for 1 epoch.

We employ an early stopping strategy with a patience of 6 epochs, evaluating every 1000 steps in Stage 1 and every 200 steps in Stage 2. The batch size is set to 128 for both stages. All models are trained on 4 Nividia A6000 GPUs with Deepspeed's ZeRO training strategy. The training times for the first and second stages are approximately 29 hours and 9 hours, respectively. We select the checkpoints with the lowest dev loss for testing.

For offline testing, we use a beam size of 4 to generate translations. In the simultaneous testing scenario, we set the start seconds to 2, indicating the initial wait time before processing speech chunks. We employ a hold-n strategy with n set to 7, meaning that the last 7 tokens of each chunk are withheld until more context is available. The beam size is set to 4, and the chunk size is set to 2500ms.

We evaluate translation quality using SacreBLEU (Post, 2018). We evaluate translation latency for SST with average lagging (AL) (Ma et al., 2020b) and length-adaptive average lagging (LAAL) (Papi et al., 2022) using SimulEval toolkit (Ma et al., 2020b).

5 Results

Table 1 shows the quality and latency of our SST system as measured on En-De tst-COMMON. We also include the offline ST performance of our model for reference. We implement the Alignatt policy (Papi et al., 2023) as a baseline for our model, we set start seconds to 2, speech segment size to 1000ms. We set number of frames to 20 and

LLM	Wav2vec Stage1	Wav2vec Stage2	WavLM Stage1	WavLM Stage2
TowerInstruct	-	-	29.64	-
Tower	29.35	30.53	30.11	31.64
LLaMA2	-	30.02	25.50	30.31

Table 2: SacreBLEU score of different Speech Encoder and LLMs, all models are trained on the original MuST-C 2.0 data without data cleaning.

use attention from all layers of the LLM decoder with greedy decoding.

From ST to SST, we observe a 5% quality degradation (31.1 to 29.5 SacreBLEU). However, this comes with significant latency improvements. The Average Lagging (AL) decreases from 5.85 to 1.96 seconds, a 66.5% reduction. The Length Adaptive Average Lagging (LAAL) improves from 5.85 to 2.22 seconds, a 62.1% decrease.

We also investigate the impacts of different LLMs and speech encoders, as shown in Table 2. We compare WavLM with a CTC fine-tuned Wav2vec 2.0 large model[4]. This Wav2vec model was pre-trained on 53.2k hours of untranscribed speech from LibriVox and fine-tuned on 960 hours of transcribed speech from Librispeech, as well as on pseudo-labels. Our results show that replacing Wav2vec with WavLM yields a significant improvement: a 1.1 BLEU score increase when using the Tower LLM (Alves et al., 2024) as the decoder, and a 0.3 BLEU score increase with LLaMA2 as the decoder. This suggests that the performance gains from a well-pretrained speech encoder are more pronounced when coupled with LLMs of higher translation capability.

Our analysis of the performance between different LLMs used as decoders shows that the Tower LLM[5], subjected to continued pre-training on a curated multilingual dataset of 20 billion high-quality tokens, exhibits a marked performance advantage over LLaMA2 in the initial stage of training. However, during the second stage, when the LLM backend is trainable, Tower quickly overfits, implying potential overlap between the MuST-C corpus and the data involved in Tower's pretraining. Tower Instruct[6], which undergoes supervised fine-tuning (SFT) on instruction dataset for various translation-related tasks, achieves a slightly lower BLEU score compared to the base model. To mitigate overfitting during the second stage of training with Tower, a reduced learning rate of 7e-6 is used, compared to the 2e-5 learning rate applied to LLaMA2 training.

6 Conclusion

In this paper, we describe the submission of CMU's English to German simultaneous speech-to-text translation systems for the IWSLT 2024 Simultaneous track. We start by building a offline speech-to-text system which leverages self-supervised speech and text foundation models. We then adapt this offline model for streaming inference, enabling simultaneous speech-to-text translation.

Acknowledgements

We would like to thank Shinji Watanabe and Brian Yan for their suggestions on system development. Siqi Ouyang is supported by an Amazon Research Award. This work used the Extreme Science and Engineering Discovery Environment (XSEDE) (Towns et al., 2014), which is supported by National Science Foundation grant number ACI-1548562; specifically, the Bridges system (Nystrom et al., 2015), as part of project cis230075p, which is supported by NSF award number ACI-1445606, at the Pittsburgh Supercomputing Center.

References

Duarte M. Alves, José Pombal, Nuno M. Guerreiro, Pedro H. Martins, João Alves, Amin Farajian, Ben Peters, Ricardo Rei, Patrick Fernandes, Sweta Agrawal, Pierre Colombo, José G. C. de Souza, and André F. T. Martins. 2024. Tower: An open multilingual large language model for translation-related tasks.

Marine Carpuat, Marcello Federico, Alex Waibel, Jan Niehues, Sebastian Stüker, Elizabeth Salesky, and Atul Kr. Ojha. 2024. Findings of the IWSLT 2024 Evaluation Campaign. In *Proceedings of the 21st International Conference on Spoken Language Translation (IWSLT 2024)*. Association for Computational Linguistics.

Guoguo Chen, Shuzhou Chai, Guan-Bo Wang, Jiayu Du, Wei-Qiang Zhang, Chao Weng, Dan Su, Daniel Povey, Jan Trmal, Junbo Zhang, Mingjie Jin, Sanjeev Khudanpur, Shinji Watanabe, Shuaijiang Zhao, Wei Zou, Xiangang Li, Xuchen Yao, Yongqing Wang,

[4]https://dl.fbaipublicfiles.com/fairseq/wav2vec/wav2vec_vox_960h_pl.pt

[5]https://huggingface.co/Unbabel/TowerBase-7B-v0.1

[6]https://huggingface.co/Unbabel/TowerInstruct-7B-v0.1

Zhao You, and Zhiyong Yan. 2021. GigaSpeech: An Evolving, Multi-Domain ASR Corpus with 10,000 Hours of Transcribed Audio. In *Proc. Interspeech 2021*, pages 3670–3674.

Sanyuan Chen, Chengyi Wang, Zhengyang Chen, Yu Wu, Shujie Liu, Zhuo Chen, Jinyu Li, Naoyuki Kanda, Takuya Yoshioka, Xiong Xiao, Jian Wu, Long Zhou, Shuo Ren, Yanmin Qian, Yao Qian, Jian Wu, Michael Zeng, Xiangzhan Yu, and Furu Wei. 2022. Wavlm: Large-scale self-supervised pre-training for full stack speech processing. *IEEE Journal of Selected Topics in Signal Processing*, 16(6):1505–1518.

Mattia A. Di Gangi, Roldano Cattoni, Luisa Bentivogli, Matteo Negri, and Marco Turchi. 2019. MuST-C: a Multilingual Speech Translation Corpus. In *Proceedings of the 2019 Conference of the North American Chapter of the Association for Computational Linguistics: Human Language Technologies, Volume 1 (Long and Short Papers)*, pages 2012–2017, Minneapolis, Minnesota. Association for Computational Linguistics.

Zhichao Huang, Rong Ye, Tom Ko, Qianqian Dong, Shanbo Cheng, Mingxuan Wang, and Hang Li. 2023. Speech translation with large language models: An industrial practice.

J. Kahn, M. Rivière, W. Zheng, E. Kharitonov, Q. Xu, P. E. Mazaré, J. Karadayi, V. Liptchinsky, R. Collobert, C. Fuegen, T. Likhomanenko, G. Synnaeve, A. Joulin, A. Mohamed, and E. Dupoux. 2020. Libri-light: A benchmark for asr with limited or no supervision. In *ICASSP 2020 - 2020 IEEE International Conference on Acoustics, Speech and Signal Processing (ICASSP)*, pages 7669–7673. `https://github.com/facebookresearch/libri-light`.

Mingbo Ma, Liang Huang, Hao Xiong, Renjie Zheng, Kaibo Liu, Baigong Zheng, Chuanqiang Zhang, Zhongjun He, Hairong Liu, Xing Li, Hua Wu, and Haifeng Wang. 2019. STACL: Simultaneous translation with implicit anticipation and controllable latency using prefix-to-prefix framework. In *Proceedings of the 57th Annual Meeting of the Association for Computational Linguistics*, pages 3025–3036, Florence, Italy. Association for Computational Linguistics.

Xutai Ma, Mohammad Javad Dousti, Changhan Wang, Jiatao Gu, and Juan Pino. 2020a. SIMULEVAL: An evaluation toolkit for simultaneous translation. In *Proceedings of the 2020 Conference on Empirical Methods in Natural Language Processing: System Demonstrations*, pages 144–150, Online. Association for Computational Linguistics.

Xutai Ma, Mohammad Javad Dousti, Changhan Wang, Jiatao Gu, and Juan Pino. 2020b. Simuleval: An evaluation toolkit for simultaneous translation. In *Proceedings of the EMNLP*.

Nicholas A Nystrom, Michael J Levine, Ralph Z Roskies, and J Ray Scott. 2015. Bridges: a uniquely flexible hpc resource for new communities and data analytics. In *Proceedings of the 2015 XSEDE Conference: Scientific Advancements Enabled by Enhanced Cyberinfrastructure*, pages 1–8.

Siqi Ouyang, Rong Ye, and Lei Li. 2022. On the impact of noises in crowd-sourced data for speech translation. In *Proceedings of the 19th International Conference on Spoken Language Translation (IWSLT 2022)*, pages 92–97, Dublin, Ireland (in-person and online). Association for Computational Linguistics.

Sara Papi, Marco Gaido, Matteo Negri, and Marco Turchi. 2022. Over-generation cannot be rewarded: Length-adaptive average lagging for simultaneous speech translation. In *Proceedings of the Third Workshop on Automatic Simultaneous Translation*, pages 12–17.

Sara Papi, Marco Turchi, and Matteo Negri. 2023. Alignatt: Using attention-based audio-translation alignments as a guide for simultaneous speech translation. In *INTERSPEECH 2023*, interspeech_2023. ISCA.

Matt Post. 2018. A call for clarity in reporting BLEU scores. In *Proceedings of the Third Conference on Machine Translation: Research Papers*, pages 186–191, Brussels, Belgium. Association for Computational Linguistics.

Hugo Touvron, Louis Martin, Kevin Stone, Peter Albert, Amjad Almahairi, Yasmine Babaei, Nikolay Bashlykov, Soumya Batra, Prajjwal Bhargava, Shruti Bhosale, Dan Bikel, Lukas Blecher, Cristian Canton Ferrer, Moya Chen, Guillem Cucurull, David Esiobu, Jude Fernandes, Jeremy Fu, Wenyin Fu, Brian Fuller, Cynthia Gao, Vedanuj Goswami, Naman Goyal, Anthony Hartshorn, Saghar Hosseini, Rui Hou, Hakan Inan, Marcin Kardas, Viktor Kerkez, Madian Khabsa, Isabel Kloumann, Artem Korenev, Punit Singh Koura, Marie-Anne Lachaux, Thibaut Lavril, Jenya Lee, Diana Liskovich, Yinghai Lu, Yuning Mao, Xavier Martinet, Todor Mihaylov, Pushkar Mishra, Igor Molybog, Yixin Nie, Andrew Poulton, Jeremy Reizenstein, Rashi Rungta, Kalyan Saladi, Alan Schelten, Ruan Silva, Eric Michael Smith, Ranjan Subramanian, Xiaoqing Ellen Tan, Binh Tang, Ross Taylor, Adina Williams, Jian Xiang Kuan, Puxin Xu, Zheng Yan, Iliyan Zarov, Yuchen Zhang, Angela Fan, Melanie Kambadur, Sharan Narang, Aurelien Rodriguez, Robert Stojnic, Sergey Edunov, and Thomas Scialom. 2023. Llama 2: Open foundation and fine-tuned chat models.

J. Towns, T. Cockerill, M. Dahan, I. Foster, K. Gaither, A. Grimshaw, V. Hazlewood, S. Lathrop, D. Lifka, G. D. Peterson, R. Roskies, J. R. Scott, and N. Wilkins-Diehr. 2014. Xsede: Accelerating scientific discovery. *Computing in Science & Engineering*, 16(5):62–74.

Changhan Wang, Morgane Riviere, Ann Lee, Anne Wu, Chaitanya Talnikar, Daniel Haziza, Mary Williamson, Juan Pino, and Emmanuel Dupoux. 2021. VoxPopuli: A large-scale multilingual speech corpus for representation learning, semi-supervised learning and interpretation. In *Proceedings of the 59th Annual Meeting of the Association for Computational Linguistics and the 11th International Joint Conference on Natural Language Processing (Volume 1: Long Papers)*, pages 993–1003, Online. Association for Computational Linguistics.

Hao Zhang, Nianwen Si, Yaqi Chen, Wenlin Zhang, Xukui Yang, Dan Qu, and Xiaolin Jiao. 2023. Tuning large language model for end-to-end speech translation.

HW-TSC's Submissions To the IWSLT2024 Low-resource Speech Translation Tasks

Jiawei Zheng, Hengchao Shang, Zongyao Li, Zhanglin Wu, Daimeng Wei, Zhiqiang Rao, Shaojun Li,Jiaxin Guo,Bin wei,Yuhao Xie,Yuanchang Luo, Hao Yang
Huawei Translation Service Center, Beijing, China
{zhengjiawei15,shanghengchao,lizongyao,wuzhanglin2, weidaimeng, raozhiqiang,lishaojun18, guojiaxin1,weibin29,xieyuhao2,luoyuanchang1,yanghao30}@huawei.com

Abstract

In this work, we submitted our systems to the low-resource track of the IWSLT 2024 Speech Translation Campaign. Our systems tackled the unconstrained condition of the Dialectal Arabic North Levantine (ISO-3 code: apc) to English language pair. We proposed a cascaded solution consisting of an automatic speech recognition (ASR) model and a machine translation (MT) model. It was noted that the ASR model employed the pre-trained Whisper-large-v3 model to process the speech data, while the MT model adopted the Transformer architecture. To improve the quality of the MT model, it was stated that our system utilized not only the data provided by the competition but also an additional 54 million parallel sentences. Ultimately, we reported that our final system achieved a BLEU score of 24.7 for apc-to-English translation.

1 Introduction

The IWSLT 2024 Speech Translation Campaign featured a low-resource track that posed a challenging task: translating dialectal Arabic speech to English text. This language pair is particularly demanding due to the scarcity of available training data and the complexity of handling dialectal Arabic variations. To tackle this problem, we propose a cascaded approach that leverages state-of-the-art models for automatic speech recognition (ASR) and machine translation (MT).

End-to-end models, which directly map audio inputs to translated text outputs, heavily rely on the availability of paired audio and transcription data. For low-resource tasks, acquiring such data can be exceptionally challenging. Consequently, we adopted a cascaded model architecture, which decouples the speech recognition and translation components. This approach allows us to leverage additional parallel text data to enhance the MT module's performance, ultimately benefiting the overall speech translation task.

Our ASR model is built upon the whisper-large-v3 architecture, a powerful pre-trained model that has demonstrated impressive performance in transcribing diverse speech data.By employing this model, we aim to accurately transcribe the dialectal Arabic speech inputs, to capture the nuances and variations present in the spoken language.

For the MT component, we adopt the Transformer architecture(Vaswani et al., 2017), which has become the de facto standard for modern neural machine translation systems. The Transformer model is known for its ability to effectively capture long-range dependencies and produce high-quality translations, making it well-suited for the task at hand.

To further enhance the performance of our MT system, we augment the provided training data with a substantial amount of additional parallel data, totaling 54 million sentence pairs. This data augmentation strategy aims to improve the model's robustness and generalization capabilities, enabling it to better handle the complexities of translating between dialectal Arabic and English.

By combining the strengths of these two powerful models in a cascaded fashion, we aim to deliver a robust and accurate speech-to-text translation system for the IWSLT 2024 low-resource track, pushing the boundaries of what is achievable in this challenging language pair.

2 Data

2.1 Data Source

We used two sets of data to train our machine translation (MT) model. Firstly, we utilized a dataset provided by the IWSLT 2024 competition, comprising approximately 42 million lines of MSA-English bilingual data. This data is sourced from various platforms including Opensubtitles[1], UN[2],QED[3]

[1] https://opus.nlpl.eu/OpenSubtitles-v2018.php
[2] https://conferences.unite.un.org/UNCorpus
[3] https://opus.nlpl.eu/QED-v2.0a.php

Proceedings of the 21st International Conference on Spoken Language Translation (IWSLT 2024), pages 208–211
August 15-16, 2024 ©2024 Association for Computational Linguistics

,TED[4],GlobalVoices[5],News-Commentary[6]. These datasets are of high quality and provide a solid foundation for our MT model to learn the correspondences and translation patterns between the two languages.

However, due to the inherent differences between dialectal Arabic and MSA, relying solely on the official dataset may not cover all linguistic phenomena of the target language pair. Therefore, to enhance the generalization capability of our MT model, we additionally utilized approximately 73 million lines of Arabic-English bilingual data. These datasets cover a wider range of dialectal language phenomena, enabling our MT model to better understand dialectal Arabic and produce more accurate and fluent translations into English. The data size is shown in Table 1.

Data Source	Volume
IWSLT 2024 Official Dataset	42M
Additional Arabic-English Bilingual Data	73M

Table 1: Uncleaned Bilingual used for training.

2.2 Data Pre-processing

The data preprocessing pipeline follows our previous work (Wei et al., 2021). We employed various strategies, including deduplication, XML content processing, language identification based on langid (Lui and Baldwin, 2012), and filtering using fast-align (Dyer et al., 2013). These preprocessing steps help improve the quality of the corpus and ensure consistency in the training data.

For the sake of conciseness, we will not elaborate on the specific details of the preprocessing steps. Interested readers can refer to the relevant papers for more information. Overall, this established set of data preprocessing strategies provides high-quality training data for our machine translation system, laying the foundation for achieving excellent translation performance. The size of the preprocessed data is shown in Table 2.

3 Methods

We employed a cascade approach for the Spoken Language Translation (ST) task, leveraging both Automatic Speech Recognition (ASR) and Machine Translation (MT) models. The cascade model consists of two stages: the ASR stage and the MT stage.

[4]https://opus.nlpl.eu/TED2020-v1.php

[5]https://opus.nlpl.eu/GlobalVoices-v2017q3.php

[6]https://opus.nlpl.eu/News-Commentary-v16.php

Data Source	Volume
IWSLT 2024 Official Dataset	27M
Additional Arabic-English Bilingual Data	54M
Total	81M

Table 2: Cleaned Bilingual used for training.

3.1 ASR

The automatic speech recognition (ASR) module plays a crucial role in speech-to-text translation systems. To obtain high-quality speech transcriptions, we chose to employ the whisper-large-v3 model proposed by OpenAI as our system's ASR module.

Whisper(Radford et al., 2023) is a powerful speech recognition model that has learned to map raw audio to speech units through self-supervised pretraining. It not only excels in high-resource languages like English but also demonstrates outstanding performance in various low-resource languages. The latest large-v3 version further scales up the model size and leverages larger datasets for pretraining, thereby enhancing its recognition accuracy.

One of the primary motivations for adopting the whisper-large-v3 model, is its robust ability to handle diverse language variations and accents. Dialectal Arabic exhibits a rich variety of speech variations, necessitating the ASR system to possess sufficient robustness to accommodate these differences. Whisper, with its powerful modeling capabilities, can effectively adapt to such speech diversity, laying the foundation for subsequent machine translation processes.

3.2 MT

Our cascaded system utilizes the Transformer architecture as the MT module, which has become the predominant approach for machine translation in recent years. Remarkably, the Transformer achieves impressive results even with its original architecture requiring minimal modifications. To further boost the performance of our offline MT model, we employed a variety of training strategies.

3.2.1 LaBSE

LaBSE (Feng et al., 2020) acts as a natural filter for parallel corpora, efficiently extracting high-quality bilingual data. We can utilize this filtered high-quality bilingual data to fine-tune our models, thereby acting as a natural denoising process. We applied this method to the current competition, resulting in a subtle improvement in BLEU scores.

3.2.2 Curriculum Learning

A practical curriculum learning (CL) approach for NMT should address two key issues: ranking training examples by difficulty and modifying the sampling procedure based on ranking (Zhang et al., 2019). For ranking, we estimate example difficulty using domain features (Wang et al., 2020). The domain feature is calculated as:

$$q(x, y) = \frac{\log P(y|x; \theta_{in}) - \log P(y|x; \theta_{out})}{|y|} \quad (1)$$

Where θ_{in} is an in-domain NMT model, while θ_{out} is an out-of-domain model. The novel domain is treated as in-domain.

We fine-tune the model on the valid set to get the teacher model and select top 40% of the highest scoring data for finetuning.

3.2.3 Regularized Dropout

Regularized Dropout (R-Drop) (Wu et al., 2021) improves performance over standard dropout, especially for recurrent neural networks on tasks with long input sequences. It ensures more consistent regularization while maintaining model uncertainty estimates. The consistent masking also improves training efficiency compared to standard dropout. Overall, Regularized Dropout is an enhanced dropout technique that often outperforms standard dropout.

4 Experiments

4.1 ASR

Whisper is a powerful speech recognition model based on self-supervised pretraining, exhibiting exceptional performance across multiple languages, particularly in handling diverse speech variations and accents. Given the rich variety of dialects in Arabic, the robustness of the ASR model is paramount. With its outstanding modeling capabilities, Whisper can effectively adapt to such speech diversity. Considering Whisper's remarkable performance in multilingual ASR tasks, we directly employed its latest large-v3 version without any modifications to the model itself. Our objective is to fully leverage this powerful pretrained model as the core ASR component within our cascaded system, providing high-quality speech transcription inputs for the entire speech translation pipeline.

4.2 MT

Model For our experiments using the MT model,we utilize the Transformer deep model architecture.The configuration of the MT model is as follows:nencoder layers = 35, ndecoder layers = 3, nheads =8, dhidden = 512, dF F N = 2048.

Training We use SacreBLEU (Post, 2018) to measure system performances. We utilize the open-source Fairseq (Ott et al., 2019) for training, with the following main parameters: each model is trained using 8 GPUs,with a batch size of 2048, a parameter update frequency of 4, and a learning rate of 5e-4. Additionally, a label smoothing value of 0.1 was used,with 4000 warmup steps and a dropout of 0.1,The Adam optimizer is also employed, with 1 = 0.9 and 2 = 0.98. During the inference phase, a beam size of 4 is used. The length penalties are set to 1.0.

5 Results

The multi-step fine-tuning method first pretrains a base model on large-scale general-domain corpora, and then conducts multiple rounds of fine-tuning on the task-specific data, with each round optimizing the model based on the previous round. This approach leverages general knowledge, addresses data distribution mismatch issues, and avoids overfitting. After each round of fine-tuning, the BLEU metric is used to evaluate the translation quality, serving as the basis for determining whether to proceed with the next round of fine-tuning. Through this gradual fine-tuning process, the model's performance can be progressively enhanced.Table 3 shows our baseline results and the fine-tuning results at each step.

Traing Stategies	BLEU
All Bilingual baseline	17.6
+ LaBSE bitext Finetune	17.7
+ Curriculum Learning +R-Drop	24.7

Table 3: BLEU scores of apc→en NMT system on IWSLT low-resource test set.

5.1 Ablation study of different bilingual data

According to the experimental results shown in Table 4, we conducted an ablation study to determine whether the additional bilingual data contributes to improving the performance of the machine translation model. We can clearly see that by adding Arabic-to-English bilingual data, the model can better capture dialectal Arabic knowledge.

Traing Stategies	BLEU
IWSLT 2024 Official Bilingual baseline	15.7
All Bilingual baseline	17.6

Table 4: BLEU Scores for Different Bilingual Data

6 Conclusion

Our research has led to the following key conclusions: Firstly, for the Arabic-to-English translation task, incorporating additional bilingual corpus data significantly enhanced model performance. These corpora contained rich knowledge of Arabic dialects, enabling the model to better learn and translate these special language variants, thereby improving the overall translation quality. Secondly, we adopted advanced training strategies such as Curriculum Learning and R-drop, which also brought substantial performance gains to the machine translation model. Curriculum Learning facilitated gradual learning from easy to difficult scenarios, while R-drop effectively mitigated overfitting issues and improved the model's generalization capability. These strategies were the core methods employed in our submission, yielding outstanding practical results.

References

Chris Dyer, Victor Chahuneau, and Noah A Smith. 2013. A simple, fast, and effective reparameterization of ibm model 2. In *Proceedings of the 2013 Conference of the North American Chapter of the Association for Computational Linguistics: Human Language Technologies*, pages 644–648.

Fangxiaoyu Feng, Yinfei Yang, Daniel Cer, Naveen Arivazhagan, and Wei Wang. 2020. Language-agnostic bert sentence embedding. *arXiv preprint arXiv:2007.01852*.

Marco Lui and Timothy Baldwin. 2012. langid. py: An off-the-shelf language identification tool. In *Proceedings of the ACL 2012 system demonstrations*, pages 25–30.

Myle Ott, Sergey Edunov, Alexei Baevski, Angela Fan, Sam Gross, Nathan Ng, David Grangier, and Michael Auli. 2019. fairseq: A fast, extensible toolkit for sequence modeling. In *Proceedings of the 2019 Conference of the North American Chapter of the Association for Computational Linguistics (Demonstrations)*, pages 48–53.

Matt Post. 2018. A call for clarity in reporting bleu scores. In *Proceedings of the Third Conference on Machine Translation: Research Papers*, page 186. Association for Computational Linguistics.

Alec Radford, Jong Wook Kim, Tao Xu, Greg Brockman, Christine McLeavey, and Ilya Sutskever. 2023. Robust speech recognition via large-scale weak supervision. In *International Conference on Machine Learning*, pages 28492–28518. PMLR.

Ashish Vaswani, Noam Shazeer, Niki Parmar, Jakob Uszkoreit, Llion Jones, Aidan N Gomez, Łukasz Kaiser, and Illia Polosukhin. 2017. Attention is all you need. *Advances in neural information processing systems*, 30.

Wei Wang, Ye Tian, Jiquan Ngiam, Yinfei Yang, Isaac Caswell, and Zarana Parekh. 2020. Learning a multi-domain curriculum for neural machine translation. In *Proceedings of the 58th Annual Meeting of the Association for Computational Linguistics*, pages 7711–7723.

Daimeng Wei, Zongyao Li, Zhanglin Wu, Zhengzhe Yu, Xiaoyu Chen, Hengchao Shang, Jiaxin Guo, Minghan Wang, Lizhi Lei, Min Zhang, et al. 2021. Hw-tsc's participation in the wmt 2021 news translation shared task. In *Proceedings of the Sixth Conference on Machine Translation*, pages 225–231.

Lijun Wu, Juntao Li, Yue Wang, Qi Meng, Tao Qin, Wei Chen, Min Zhang, Tie-Yan Liu, et al. 2021. R-drop: Regularized dropout for neural networks. *Advances in Neural Information Processing Systems*, 34:10890–10905.

Xuan Zhang, Pamela Shapiro, Gaurav Kumar, Paul McNamee, Marine Carpuat, and Kevin Duh. 2019. Curriculum learning for domain adaptation in neural machine translation. In *Proceedings of NAACL-HLT*, pages 1903–1915.

CMU's IWSLT 2024 Offline Speech Translation System: A Cascaded Approach For Long-Form Robustness

Brian Yan*[1] Patrick Fernandes*[1] Jinchuan Tian[1] Siqi Ouyang[1]
William Chen[1] Karen Livescu[1,2] Lei Li[1] Graham Neubig[1] Shinji Watanabe[1,3]
[1]Language Technologies Institute, Carnegie Mellon University, USA
[2]Toyota Technological Institute at Chicago, University of Chicago, USA
[3]Human Language Technology Center of Excellence, Johns Hopkins University, USA
{byan, pfernand}@cs.cmu.edu

Abstract

This work describes CMU's submission to the IWSLT 2024 Offline Speech Translation (ST) Shared Task for translating English speech to German, Chinese, and Japanese text. We are the first participants to employ a *long-form* strategy which directly processes unsegmented recordings without the need for a separate voice-activity detection stage (VAD). We show that the Whisper automatic speech recognition (ASR) model has a hallucination problem when applied out-of-the-box to recordings containing non-speech noises, but a simple noisy fine-tuning approach can greatly enhance Whisper's long-form robustness across multiple domains. Then, we feed English ASR outputs into fine-tuned NLLB machine translation (MT) models which are decoded using COMET-based Minimum Bayes Risk. Our VAD-free ASR+MT cascade is tested on TED talks, TV series, and workout videos and shown to outperform prior winning IWSLT submissions and large open-source models.

1 Introduction

CMU's submission to the IWSLT 2024 Offline Speech Translation shared task is a cascaded automatic speech recognition (ASR) and machine translation (MT) system designed to effectively translate English speech from long unsegmented recordings, such as TED talks, TV series, and workout videos, into German, Chinese, and Japanese text.

Typically systems are *short-form*, meaning they are dependent on some voice-activity detection to first convert long recordings which contain speech and non-speech noises into short segments of speech. This makes it relatively easy to train a short-form model and test it on similar clean speech segments. However, these systems exhibit alarming brittleness in the wild; results from recent iterations of the Offline ST track have shown large fluctuations in performance between different segmentations of the same test set (Anastasopoulos et al., 2021, 2022; Agarwal et al., 2023).

Why are these short-form systems brittle in-the-wild (or in IWSLT by proxy)? Our view is that these systems are plagued by train/test mismatch. Common training sets, e.g. MuST-C (Di Gangi et al., 2019), are produced using sentence-level forced alignment. In other words, this training segmentation can only be obtained given a reference. For a blind test set however, forced alignment is not possible. Instead, practitioners have resorted to using VAD with additional tricks to reduce the train/test mismatch, such as heuristically replicating segment characteristics (Inaguma et al., 2021) or modeling the segmentation pattern of training data (Tsiamas et al., 2022). These methods of approximating the training data segmentation may work within a single domain but are complex to configure for multi-domain scenarios.

In this work, we explore *long-form* processing of unsegmented recordings via a 30 second sliding window as an alternative to segment-dependent speech processing. Our system consists of:

1. Whisper-based ASR (Radford et al., 2023) applied in long-form inference §3.1.1, after a simple noisy fine-tuning procedure which greatly enhances robustness to non-speech noises §3.1.2
2. NLLB-based MT (Costa-jussà et al., 2022), fine-tuned and decoded via Minimum Bayes-Risk §3.2

Our experiments first show that Whisper out-of-the-box has a hallucination problem caused by non-speech noises during long-form inference. We then show that our noisy fine-tuning broadly addresses these hallucinations. Finally, we show the ultimate cascaded ST performance across multiple domains: TED talks, TV series, and workout videos.

2 Task Description

The IWSLT 2024 Offline Speech Translation shared task consists of three language

Proceedings of the 21st International Conference on Spoken Language Translation (IWSLT 2024), pages 212–217
August 15-16, 2024 ©2024 Association for Computational Linguistics

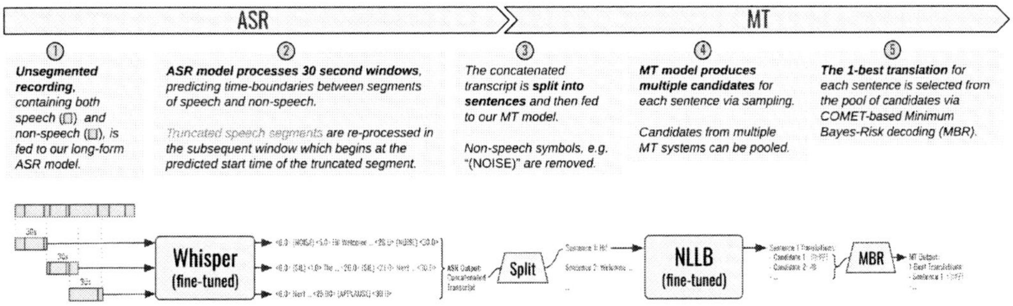

Figure 1: Summary of our cascaded system. ASR: long-form processing of unsegmented recordings. MT: sentence-based translation with Minimum Bayes-Risk decoding.

pairs: English-to-German, English-to-Chinese, and English-to-Japanese. For all three language pairs, unsegmented TED talks (5-20 min) are given as shared task evaluation data. As a dev set, we use the provided tst2020 (TED'20), tst2021 (TED'21), and tst2022 (TED'22) for English-to-German and tst2022 (TED'22) for English-to-Chinese and English-to-Japanese.

For English-to-German, systems are also tested on additional domains: TV series (45-60 min), workout videos (10-20 min), and accented speech (5-20 min). We therefore use two additional dev sets obtained from the IWSLT 2024 Subtitling shared task: ITV and Peloton.

We evaluate ASR using case-sensitive punctuated word error-rate (WER ↓) against recording-level references. We evaluate MT systems using COMET ↑ (Rei et al., 2020) against sentence-level references. We evaluate ST systems using COMET after first performing minimum WER alignment of our hypothesis to sentence-level references. Note that for Chinese and Japanese, this alignment is done at the character level.

We use MuST-C v3 (Di Gangi et al., 2019) for fine-tuning ASR models on the TED domain. We use TED2020 for fine-tuning English-to-German MT and MuST-C for English-to-Chinese and English-to-Japanese. For multi-domain fine-tuning we also add Bazinga TV series ASR data (Lerner et al., 2022) and a 500k subset of OpenSubtitles MT data (Creutz, 2018). Note that our use of Bazinga (as well as the use of Whisper) puts our system under the "Unconstrained" designation.

3 System Description

Figure 1 summarizes the components in our ASR+MT cascade. The following section describes the system in greater detail, referring at times to the summary figure.

3.1 ASR

3.1.1 Long-Form Inference

As illustrated in Steps 1 and 2 of Figure 1, we deploy Whisper in a long-form mode. Under this scheme, the window size is always 30 seconds (or the remainder of the recording). Although the window size is fixed, the hop size is dynamic and based on the predicted time-boundaries of speech segments. As shown in Step 2, the final speech segment in a window is considered to be truncated if the predicted end-time is within 1 second of the end of the window. To avoid transcribing with a truncated utterance, the next window starts from the start-time of the truncated utterance.

For non-speech noises, the expected behavior is that the model produces a special symbol, e.g. (NOISE), along with time-boundaries. **However, we found that Whisper Large-v2 frequently hallucinates on non-speech such as music and applause.**[1] These errors can be categorized as oscillations in which the auto-regressive decoder enters a bad state causing long repeated garbage outputs.

Whisper applies an inference time patch to address these oscillations, somewhat obscuring the lack of long-form robustness in the model out-of-the-box. This patch detects oscillations via a heuristic repetition factor, then if high repetitions are detected then it falls back to sampling. If the sampling output is still high in repetitions, then it falls back to sampling with greater and greater temperature. Eventually, the model either escapes from the oscillations (typically by producing EOS) or exhausts

[1]We also tested Large-v3 and found that hallucinations to be more severe than Large-v2, perhaps due to error compounding from the semi-supervision used in Large-v3.

Model	TED'20	TED'21	TED'22	ITV	Peloton
Whisper	54.9	8.3	5.8	38.9	47.9
+ Fallback on Oscillation	1.6	2.4	2.1	6.5	4.2
Whisper ft on TED + Baz	**0.9**	**1.2**	1.9	6.9	5.9
+ Fallback on Oscillation	**0.9**	**1.2**	**1.1**	**3.5**	**3.4**

Table 1: Insertion error-rates of Whisper out-of-the-box vs Whisper after Noisy Fine-tuning. High insertions indicates frequent oscillation.

the allotted number of fallback decodings.

3.1.2 Noisy Fine-tuning

Motivated by the apparent lack of long-form robustness described in the previous section, we propose a simple fine-tuning strategy to improve the Whisper's ability to predict the special non-speech token: ⟨NOISE⟩. We prepare fine-tuning data by taking consecutive 30 second segments from the unsegmented recordings. Using given sentence-level forced alignments, we obtain references containing transcribed speech and noises. Critically, the 30 second segments also include untranscribed noises; these non-speech portions were originally cut out via forced alignment (they represent the durations between speech segments). If these untranscribed non-speech portions exceed 1 second in duration, we add a new ⟨NOISE⟩ token in the target.

In practice (see §4.1), this noisy fine-tuning encompasses non-speech noises that Whisper out-of-the-box struggles with. After fine-tuning, the model does not produce oscillations and rather produces the ⟨NOISE⟩ token which is cleaned before scoring ASR and feeding into MT.

3.2 MT

ASR outputs, which are cased and punctuated, are concatenated at a recording-level (Step 3). This recording-level ASR output is then split into sentences and subsequently fed into our MT model.

For each language-pair, we fine-tune NLLB 1B and NLLB 3B on TED data. For English-German we also fine-tune a separate NLLB 1B model on TED + OpenSubtitles data.

During inference, we generate a set of candidate translations via epsilon-sampling (Step 4). We then (optionally) pool the candidate translations across multiple MT systems. Finally, the 1-best translation is chosen using COMET-based Minimum Bayes-Risk decoding (Yan et al., 2022).

4 Results

4.1 Noisy Fine-Tuning Improves Whisper's Long-Form Robustness

Table 1 shows ASR insertion error-rates for Whisper out-of-the-box versus Whisper with noisy fine-tuning. As can be seen from the high insertion error-rates in row 1, Whisper without fine-tuning and without relying on the fallback-based inference-time patch (described in §3.1.1) has a major oscillation problem. Noisy fine-tuning greatly reduces this problem, as can be seen from row 3. Our results show that noisy fine-tuning improved performance on all domains, so we have reason to believe that the improved long-form robustness generalizes to some extent. The fallback method still improves the fine-tuned model, indicating that some oscillations still remain, but this inference-time patch is not critical as it was out-of-the-box.

Note that fallback is applied in all subsequent ASR results unless otherwise indicated.

4.2 ST Results

Table 2 shows the ASR, MT, and ST performances of our fine-tuned models versus their out-of-the-box counterparts for English-German. For ASR, fine-tuning on TED + Bazinga versus fine-tuning on TED-only improved the TV series performance (ITV) while maintaining the performance on TED.

For MT, the NLLB 3B fine-tuned model was the best across all sets. The NLLB 1B models fine-tuned on TED versus on TED + OpenSubtitles performed similarly. We use all three MT models in our final ensemble.

Table 3 shows a single-domain version of the same story for English-Chinese and English-Japanese. For these pairs, we use the TED-only fine-tuned ASR model and we do not use any TED + OpenSubtitles fine-tuned MT models.

4.3 COMET-Based Minimum Bayes-Risk

Table 4 shows the impact of COMET-based MBR compared to beam search. We observed improvements up to 50 samples per system. Further, ensembling slightly improves results.

4.4 Benchmarking vs. Prior Works

Finally, Table 5 compares our VAD-free cascaded approach to prior works. Note we're showing BLEU score (Post, 2018) in this table for compatibility with prior studies.

Model	TED'20	TED'21	TED'22	ITV	Peloton	TED Avg	Non-TED Avg
ASR	WER ↓						
Whisper (Large-v2)	10.8	10.1	9.3	30.9	24.2	10.1	27.6
Whisper ft on TED	8.8	**7.5**	**7.8**	27.5	**22.3**	**8.0**	24.9
Whisper ft on TED + Bazinga (Baz)	**8.7**	7.7	**7.8**	**25.0**	22.4	8.1	**23.7**
MT	COMET ↑						
NLLB 1B	0.8093	0.7825	0.7845	0.6322	0.6162	0.7921	0.6242
NLLB 1B ft on TED	0.8229	0.8006	0.7977	0.6638	0.6348	0.8071	0.6493
NLLB 1B ft on TED + OpenSubtitles (OS)	0.8219	0.7991	0.7943	0.6598	0.6396	0.8051	0.6497
NLLB 3B	0.8171	0.7892	0.7892	0.6472	0.6200	0.7985	0.6336
NLLB 3B ft on TED	**0.8242**	**0.8053**	**0.8010**	**0.6697**	**0.6548**	**0.8102**	**0.6623**
ST (ASR→MT)	COMET ↑						
Whisper → NLLB 1B	0.7891	0.7622	0.7691	0.5920	0.6119	0.7735	0.6020
Whisper → NLLB 3B	0.7954	0.7705	0.7779	0.6012	0.6152	0.7813	0.6082
Whisper ft on TED → NLLB 1B ft on TED	0.8050	0.7872	0.7844	0.6311	0.6111	0.7922	0.6211
Whisper ft on TED + Baz → NLLB 1B ft on TED (①)	0.8053	0.7856	0.7855	0.6501	0.6087	0.7921	0.6294
Whisper ft on TED + Baz → NLLB 1B ft on TED + OS (②)	0.8018	0.7872	0.7827	0.6537	0.6086	0.7906	0.6312
Whisper ft on TED + Baz → NLLB 3B ft on TED (③)	**0.8059**	**0.7911**	**0.7875**	**0.6562**	**0.6183**	**0.7948**	**0.6373**
MBR Ensemble (① + ② + ③)	-	-	**0.8104**	**0.6647**	**0.6293**	-	**0.6470**

Table 2: ASR/MT/ST results for English-German across TED and non-TED domains.

Lang	Model	MT	ST
En-Zh	NLLB 1B	0.7864	0.7309
En-Zh	NLLB 1B ft on TED (①)	**0.8362**	**0.8082**
En-Zh	NLLB 3B	0.7464	0.7279
En-Zh	NLLB 3B ft on TED (②)	**0.8362**	0.8078
En-Zh	MBR Ensemble (① + ②)	-	**0.8295**
En-Ja	NLLB 1B	0.8300	0.7568
En-Ja	NLLB 1B ft on TED (①)	0.8625	**0.8086**
En-Ja	NLLB 3B	0.7854	0.7715
En-Ja	NLLB 3B ft on TED (②)	**0.8639**	0.8046
En-Ja	MBR Ensemble (① + ②)	-	**0.8363**

Table 3: MT/ST results for English-Chinese and English-Japanese.

Model	Decoding	TED'22	ITV	Peloton
NLLB 1B ft on TED	Beam (5)	0.7855	0.6501	0.6087
NLLB 1B ft on TED (①)	MBR (50)	**0.8038**	**0.6570**	**0.6180**
NLLB 1B ft on TED + OS	Beam (5)	0.7827	0.6537	0.6086
NLLB 1B ft on TED + OS (②)	MBR (50)	**0.8009**	**0.6628**	**0.6207**
NLLB 3B ft on TED	Beam (5)	0.7875	0.6562	0.6183
NLLB 3B ft on TED (③)	MBR (50)	**0.8076**	**0.6632**	**0.6286**
Ensemble (① + ② + ③)	MBR (50 ea.)	**0.8104**	**0.6647**	**0.6293**

Table 4: Beam search vs. MBR decoding.

5 Conclusion

We describe our IWSLT 2024 Offline Speech Translation system which is based on long-form processing of unsegmented recordings. Our system consists of fine-tuned Whisper and NLLB components of a cascade. We evaluate our system on TED talks, TV series, and workout videos.

Type	Model	Uses VAD	TED'22
Cascade	IWSLT 2022 Top (Zhang et al., 2022)	✓	23.9
Cascade	Our Single Best Model	✗	**24.5**
Direct	SeamlessM4T (Barrault et al., 2023)	✓	16.2
Direct	WavLM+mBART (Yan et al., 2023)	✓	19.2
Direct	OWSM 3.1 (Peng et al., 2024b)	✗	18.4
Direct	OWSM-CTC (Peng et al., 2024a)	✗	**19.6**

Table 5: BLEU score comparison with prior works.

Acknowledgements

Brian Yan and Shinji Watanabe are supported by the Human Language Technology Center of Excellence. This work used the Extreme Science and Engineering Discovery Environment (XSEDE) (Towns et al., 2014), which is supported by National Science Foundation grant number ACI-1548562; specifically, the Bridges system (Nystrom et al., 2015), as part of project cis210027p, which is supported by NSF award number ACI-1445606, at the Pittsburgh Supercomputing Center. This work also used GPUs donated by the NVIDIA Corporation.

References

Milind Agarwal, Sweta Agrawal, Antonios Anastasopoulos, Ondřej Bojar, Claudia Borg, Marine Carpuat, Roldano Cattoni, Mauro Cettolo, Mingda Chen, William Chen, Khalid Choukri, Alexandra Chronopoulou, Anna Currey, Thierry Declerck, Qianqian Dong, Yannick Estève, Kevin Duh, Marcello Federico, Souhir Gahbiche, Barry Haddow, Benjamin Hsu, Phu Mon Htut, Hirofumi Inaguma, Dávid Javorský, John Judge, Yasumasa Kano, Tom Ko, Rishu

Kumar, Pengwei Li, Xutail Ma, Prashant Mathur, Evgeny Matusov, Paul McNamee, John P. McCrae, Kenton Murray, Maria Nadejde, Satoshi Nakamura, Matteo Negri, Ha Nguyen, Jan Niehues, Xing Niu, Atul Ojha Kr., John E. Ortega, Proyag Pal, Juan Pino, Lonneke van der Plas, Peter Polák, Elijah Rippeth, Elizabeth Salesky, Jiatong Shi, Matthias Sperber, Sebastian Stüker, Katsuhito Sudoh, Yun Tang, Brian Thompson, Kevin Tran, Marco Turchi, Alex Waibel, Mingxuan Wang, Shinji Watanabe, and Rodolfo Zevallos. 2023. Findings of the IWSLT 2023 Evaluation Campaign. In *Proceedings of the 20th International Conference on Spoken Language Translation (IWSLT 2023)*. Association for Computational Linguistics.

Antonios Anastasopoulos, Loc Barrault, Luisa Bentivogli, Marcely Zanon Boito, Ondřej Bojar, Roldano Cattoni, Anna Currey, Georgiana Dinu, Kevin Duh, Maha Elbayad, et al. 2022. Findings of the iwslt 2022 evaluation campaign. In *Proceedings of the 19th International Conference on Spoken Language Translation (IWSLT 2022)*, pages 98–157. Association for Computational Linguistics.

Antonios Anastasopoulos, Ondřej Bojar, Jacob Bremerman, Roldano Cattoni, Maha Elbayad, Marcello Federico, Xutai Ma, Satoshi Nakamura, Matteo Negri, Jan Niehues, Juan Pino, Elizabeth Salesky, Sebastian Stüker, Katsuhito Sudoh, Marco Turchi, Alexander Waibel, Changhan Wang, and Matthew Wiesner. 2021. FINDINGS OF THE IWSLT 2021 EVALUATION CAMPAIGN. In *Proceedings of the 18th International Conference on Spoken Language Translation (IWSLT 2021)*, pages 1–29, Bangkok, Thailand (online). Association for Computational Linguistics.

Loïc Barrault, Yu-An Chung, Mariano Cora Meglioli, David Dale, Ning Dong, Paul-Ambroise Duquenne, Hady Elsahar, Hongyu Gong, Kevin Heffernan, John Hoffman, et al. 2023. Seamlessm4t-massively multilingual & multimodal machine translation. *arXiv preprint arXiv:2308.11596*.

Marta R Costa-jussà, James Cross, Onur Çelebi, Maha Elbayad, Kenneth Heafield, Kevin Heffernan, Elahe Kalbassi, Janice Lam, Daniel Licht, Jean Maillard, et al. 2022. No language left behind: Scaling human-centered machine translation. *arXiv preprint arXiv:2207.04672*.

Mathias Creutz. 2018. Open subtitles paraphrase corpus for six languages. *arXiv preprint arXiv:1809.06142*.

Mattia A. Di Gangi, Roldano Cattoni, Luisa Bentivogli, Matteo Negri, and Marco Turchi. 2019. MuST-C: a Multilingual Speech Translation Corpus. In *Proceedings of the 2019 Conference of the North American Chapter of the Association for Computational Linguistics: Human Language Technologies, Volume 1 (Long and Short Papers)*, pages 2012–2017, Minneapolis, Minnesota. Association for Computational Linguistics.

Hirofumi Inaguma, Brian Yan, Siddharth Dalmia, Pengcheng Guo, Jiatong Shi, Kevin Duh, and Shinji Watanabe. 2021. Espnet-st iwslt 2021 offline speech translation system. *IWSLT 2021*, page 100.

Paul Lerner, Juliette Bergoënd, Camille Guinaudeau, Hervé Bredin, Benjamin Maurice, Sharleyne Lefevre, Martin Bouteiller, Aman Berhe, Léo Galmant, Ruiqing Yin, et al. 2022. Bazinga! a dataset for multi-party dialogues structuring. In *13th Conference on Language Resources and Evaluation (LREC 2022)*, pages 3434–3441.

Nicholas A Nystrom, Michael J Levine, Ralph Z Roskies, and J Ray Scott. 2015. Bridges: a uniquely flexible hpc resource for new communities and data analytics. In *Proceedings of the 2015 XSEDE Conference: Scientific Advancements Enabled by Enhanced Cyberinfrastructure*, pages 1–8.

Yifan Peng, Yui Sudo, Muhammad Shakeel, and Shinji Watanabe. 2024a. Owsm-ctc: An open encoder-only speech foundation model for speech recognition, translation, and language identification. *arXiv preprint arXiv:2402.12654*.

Yifan Peng, Jinchuan Tian, William Chen, Siddhant Arora, Brian Yan, Yui Sudo, Muhammad Shakeel, Kwanghee Choi, Jiatong Shi, Xuankai Chang, et al. 2024b. Owsm v3. 1: Better and faster open whisper-style speech models based on e-branchformer. *arXiv preprint arXiv:2401.16658*.

Matt Post. 2018. A call for clarity in reporting bleu scores. *WMT 2018*, page 186.

Alec Radford, Jong Wook Kim, Tao Xu, Greg Brockman, Christine McLeavey, and Ilya Sutskever. 2023. Robust speech recognition via large-scale weak supervision. In *International Conference on Machine Learning*, pages 28492–28518. PMLR.

Ricardo Rei, Craig Stewart, Ana C Farinha, and Alon Lavie. 2020. Comet: A neural framework for mt evaluation. *arXiv preprint arXiv:2009.09025*.

J. Towns, T. Cockerill, M. Dahan, I. Foster, K. Gaither, A. Grimshaw, V. Hazlewood, S. Lathrop, D. Lifka, G. D. Peterson, R. Roskies, J. R. Scott, and N. Wilkins-Diehr. 2014. Xsede: Accelerating scientific discovery. *Computing in Science & Engineering*, 16(5):62–74.

Ioannis Tsiamas, Gerard I Gállego, José AR Fonollosa, et al. 2022. Shas: Approaching optimal segmentation for end-to-end speech translation.

Brian Yan, Patrick Fernandes, Siddharth Dalmia, Jiatong Shi, Yifan Peng, Dan Berrebbi, Xinyi Wang, Graham Neubig, and Shinji Watanabe. 2022. Cmu's iwslt 2022 dialect speech translation system. In *Proceedings of the 19th International Conference on Spoken Language Translation (IWSLT 2022)*, pages 298–307.

Brian Yan, Jiatong Shi, Soumi Maiti, William Chen, Xinjian Li, Yifan Peng, Siddhant Arora, and Shinji Watanabe. 2023. Cmu's iwslt 2023 simultaneous speech translation system. In *Proceedings of the 20th International Conference on Spoken Language Translation (IWSLT 2023)*, pages 235–240.

Weitai Zhang, Zhongyi Ye, Haitao Tang, Xiaoxi Li, Xinyuan Zhou, Jing Yang, Jianwei Cui, Pan Deng, Mohan Shi, Yifan Song, Dan Liu, Junhua Liu, and Lirong Dai. 2022. The USTC-NELSLIP offline speech translation systems for IWSLT 2022. In *Proceedings of the 19th International Conference on Spoken Language Translation (IWSLT 2022)*, pages 198–207, Dublin, Ireland (in-person and online). Association for Computational Linguistics.

NAIST Simultaneous Speech Translation System for IWSLT 2024

Yuka Ko Ryo Fukuda Yuta Nishikawa Yasumasa Kano Tomoya Yanagita
Kosuke Doi Mana Makinae Haotian Tan Makoto Sakai
Sakriani Sakti Katsuhito Sudoh Satoshi Nakamura
Nara Institute of Science and Technology, Japan
ko.yuka.kp2@is.naist.jp

Abstract

This paper describes NAIST's submission to the simultaneous track of the IWSLT 2024 Evaluation Campaign: English-to-{German, Japanese, Chinese} speech-to-text translation and English-to-Japanese speech-to-speech translation. We develop a multilingual end-to-end speech-to-text translation model combining two pre-trained language models, HuBERT and mBART. We trained this model with two decoding policies, Local Agreement (LA) and AlignAtt. The submitted models employ the LA policy because it outperformed the AlignAtt policy in previous models. Our speech-to-speech translation method is a cascade of the above speech-to-text model and an incremental text-to-speech (TTS) module that incorporates a phoneme estimation model, a parallel acoustic model, and a parallel WaveGAN vocoder. We improved our incremental TTS by applying the Transformer architecture with the AlignAtt policy for the estimation model. The results show that our upgraded TTS module contributed to improving the system performance.

1 Introduction

This paper presents NAIST's simultaneous speech translation (SimulST) systems for the English-to-{German, Japanese, Chinese} speech-to-text track and the English-to-Japanese speech-to-speech track within the simultaneous track of the IWSLT 2024 Evaluation Campaign.

Simultaneous translation involves generating translations incrementally based on partial input, and it requires interpreters who can provide accurate and fluent translations while minimizing delay.

Early SimulST systems are based on a cascade of automatic speech recognition (ASR) and machine translation modules (*e.g.,* Fügen et al., 2007; Bangalore et al., 2012; Yarmohammadi et al., 2013; Oda et al., 2014; Arivazhagan et al., 2020), but they suffer from error propagation and added latency imposed by the ASR module. Recently, an end-to-end approach has become popular (Agarwal et al., 2023), and this approach has been demonstrated to achieve a better quality-latency trade-off.

Conventional end-to-end SimulST models have employed training strategies and architectures designed for a simultaneous setting. However, that approach not only requires additional effort in system development but also results in high computational costs. To alleviate such problems, Papi et al. (2022a) proposed a single model trained on offline translation data for the simultaneous scenario. Applying a simultaneous decoding policy to an offline speech translation (ST) model in SimulST inference enables the model to generate outputs similar to simultaneous translation. Furthermore, a decoding policy determines whether to generate partial output or wait for more input.

Using an offline ST model with a simultaneous decoding policy has become popular because no specific task adaptation is required for a SimulST task. Among several simultaneous decoding policies (Cho and Esipova, 2016; Dalvi et al., 2018; Ma et al., 2019, 2020b; Nguyen et al., 2021), Local Agreement (LA) (Liu et al., 2020) is widely used and won the SimulST task at the IWSLT 2022 Evaluation Campaign (Anastasopoulos et al., 2022). The LA policy extracts the longest common prefixes from the n consecutive chunks as stable hypotheses. However, it requires a long computation time to obtain the longest common prefix.

Since simultaneous translation requires *real-time* translation, a policy that runs fast is desirable. Papi et al. (2023) proposed a decoding policy called AlignAtt, which takes the alignments of the source and target tokens using cross attention information. Under computation-aware settings, Papi et al. (2023) have shown that AlignAtt can generate translations with lower latency compared to the LA policy, and it is capable of reaching a latency of 2 sec or less.

For the IWSLT 2024 Evaluation Campaign, we

Proceedings of the 21st International Conference on Spoken Language Translation (IWSLT 2024), pages 218–230
August 15-16, 2024 ©2024 Association for Computational Linguistics

developed two types of speech-to-text translation models with different decoding policies and compared them. One is based on LA and the other on AlignAtt. The LA-based model demonstrates better quality than the AlignAtt-based one within the given latency constraints, while the AlignAtt policy works better in a low-latency region in computation-aware settings.

For the English-to-Japanese speech-to-speech track, we developed a cascade of the above SimulST model and an incremental text-to-speech module using a phoneme and prosodic symbol estimation model, a parallel acoustic model, and a parallel WaveGAN vocoder. In last year's submission, our speech-to-speech translation method suffered from the quality of the synthesized speech and possible ASR errors (Fukuda et al., 2023). The authors reported that the character error rate of the NAIST 2023 speech-to-speech translation output exceeded that of the SimulST text output by over 28%. Therefore, we upgraded our TTS module by incorporating Transformer architecture and AlignAtt in the estimation model.

2 System Architecture

This section describes the architecture of our SimulST systems. First, we explain the decoding policies used for our translation modules. Then, we present the details of our simultaneous speech-to-text and speech-to-speech translation methods.

2.1 Decoding Policies

2.1.1 Local Agreement

Liu et al. (2020) introduced the concept of Local Agreement to find a stable prefix translation hypothesis in simultaneous translation scenarios where inputs are processed in fixed-length chunks. This method assesses the stability of a hypothesis at step t by comparing it with the hypothesis at step t 1, thus determining the agreeing prefix (i.e., the longest common prefix) between them. The underlying principle is that the translation outputs with consistent agreeing prefixes, as the input prefixes increase, are likely to be reliable. Building upon this idea, Polák et al. (2022) extended it to encompass agreement among prefixes over n consecutive steps (LA-n), with their experiments showing that $n = 2$ performs effectively in the context of SimulST. Based on these findings, we employed LA-2 as a SimulST policy and adjusted the input chunk length (in milliseconds) to manage the trade-off between quality and latency.

2.1.2 AlignAtt

Papi et al. (Papi et al., 2023) proposed AlignAtt, a method that leverages encoder-decoder attention information in Transformer to establish alignment between source and target tokens during inference. According to the AlignAtt policy, if a target token aligns with tokens beyond the last f tokens of the source speech, it implies that adequate information has been provided to generate that token. Consequently, if a target token aligns solely with the last f tokens from the source, generation is paused to await additional speech input. In our implementation, we use cross attention from the decoder to the length adapter for AlignAtt.

2.2 Simultaneous Speech-to-Text Translation

Our speech-to-text SimulST system uses multilingual offline speech translation models for the prefix-to-prefix translation required for SimulST. These models are based on large-scale pre-trained speech and text models adopting Hidden-Unit BERT (HuBERT) (Hsu et al., 2021) and mBART50 (Tang et al., 2020), following Polák et al. (2022). We initialized our ST models with the HuBERT speech encoder and the mBART50 text decoder, which were fine-tuned using English ASR data and multilingual MT data, respectively. In addition, we applied Inter-connection (Nishikawa and Nakamura, 2023) for the concatenated ST model. Inter-connection is a method that aggregates the information from each layer of a pre-trained speech model with weighted sums and then passes it into the decoder by connecting the intermediate layer of the speech encoder and the text decoder. We also fine-tuned the multilingual ST model using bilingual prefix pairs in English-to-{German, Japanese, Chinese} extracted using *Bilingual Prefix Alignment* (Kano et al., 2022). Bilingual Prefix Alignment is a method used to generate augmented prefix-to-prefix data based on a pre-trained offline model, and the SimulST model fine-tuned on those data will generate high quality output in a low-latency range compared to a model trained solely on offline data. After training these models, we applied the decoding policies in Section 2.1 to the ST model for controlling latency ranges.

2.3 Simultaneous Speech-to-Speech Translation

Our English-to-Japanese speech-to-speech simultaneous translation is a cascade of the speech-to-text translation model (Section 2.2) and the incremental TTS module. In decoding steps, prefixes generated from the translation model are passed to the TTS module incrementally. Then, the TTS module judges whether to wait for more inputs or generate a partial hypothesis.

2.3.1 Incremental Text-to-Speech Synthesis

Incremental TTS consists of three modules: a phoneme estimator with a prosodic symbol for the Japanese language, an acoustic feature predictor, and a neural vocoder.

The phoneme estimator predicts the phonemes of SimulST outputs and prosodic symbols in the Japanese language in parallel using a Transformer model. This module uses three prosodic symbols to represent rising and falling pitches, and phrase boundary. It works simultaneously with the input based on the AlignAtt policy using models trained in full-sentence conditions. In TTS, it is assumed that there is monotonicity between input and output sequences, so there is little need to make delayed decisions and reorder, as is the case in LA. Therefore, we applied AlignAtt to TTS in this study. We modified the original Transformer architecture by adding two embedding input layers and two linear output layers to its decoder. The self-attention mask was applied to both the encoder and the decoder sides because the subsequent sequences should not be used in the inference time in the incremental condition.

The acoustic feature predictor predicts acoustic features from the phonemes and prosodic symbols mentioned above, and then the neural vocoder synthesizes speech in parallel. Its acoustic model is based on FastPitch (Łańcucki, 2021) with an additional adapter as an average phoneme power predictor. Its encoder uses two independent embedding layers for phoneme and prosodic sequences and concatenates their embedding vectors into a single sequence as the input to the Transformer model. Fastpitch estimates an acoustic feature sequence with predicted duration, pitch, and power in parallel. Parallel WaveGAN synthesizes a speech waveform for the given acoustic features and noise sequences.

3 Experimental Setting

3.1 Data

3.1.1 Simultaneous Speech-to-Text Translation

We trained our multilingual ST model on MuST-C v2.0 (Di Gangi et al., 2019) and CoVoST-2 (Wang et al., 2020) for all language pairs: English-to-German (En-De), English-to-Japanese (En-Ja), and English-to-Chinese (En-Zh). For the En-De setting, we also used MuST-C v1.0, Europarl-ST (Iranzo-Sánchez et al., 2020), and TED-LIUM (Rousseau et al., 2012). In our training data, the development and test portions of CoVoST-2 and Europarl-ST were also included. We used the MuST-C v2.0 tst-COMMON data as the evaluation data. We tokenized all of the text data in the corpora using a multilingual SentencePiece tokenizer with 250,000 subword units, distributed with the mBART50 model.

For the En-Ja setting, we trained a model that applied a data filtering approach on the prefix translation pairs for the Bilingual Prefix Alignment data. We empirically set the ratio of the number of samples in the input speech to the number of tokens in the output at 4000. Any utterance exceeding the maximum ratio was excluded from the training data. In order to prevent discrepancies in sentence structure and word order between the source and target languages in fine-tuned models and thus avoid favoring shorter output.

3.1.2 Incremental Text-to-Speech Synthesis

We used the JSUT corpus (Sonobe et al., 2017) for training our FastPitch and Parallel WaveGAN. The numbers of sentences in the training, development, and test data were 7196, 250, and 250, respectively. For JSUT labels, we used the open-source repository . We used the Balanced Corpus of Contemporary Written Japanese (Maekawa et al., 2014) for training the phoneme and prosodic symbol estimation model. These symbols were obtained from the text using Open Jtalk for training the estimation system. The same algorithm converted these symbols (Kurihara et al., 2021), and symbols were separated into two sequences by adding blank tokens in prosodic symbols. The training, development, and test data were approximately 1.4 M, 10 K, and 10 K sentences, respectively. We also used the training portion of MuST-C as additional training data.

---

https://github.com/r9y9/jsut-lab
https://open-jtalk.sourceforge.net

3.2 Simultaneous Speech-to-Text Translation

We developed an end-to-end speech-to-text model by initializing it with two pre-trained models: HuBERT for the speech encoder and mBART50 for the text decoder. Furthermore, the encoder and decoder are interconnected via Inter-connection (Nishikawa and Nakamura, 2023) and a length adapter (Tsiamas et al., 2022). Speech input is provided as waveforms sampled at a rate of 16 kHz, which are then normalized to have zero mean and unit variance.

We applied checkpoint averaging to the offline SimulST model. During checkpoint averaging, model checkpoints were saved every 1000 training steps, and the averaged parameter values from the five best models, based on loss in the development data, were selected for the final model.

Subsequently, one epoch of fine-tuning was conducted on the training data, focusing solely on prefix alignment pairs in MuST-C v2. For this fine-tuning stage, the learning rate was reduced to 2.5×10^{-5}, using translation pairs obtained via Bilingual Prefix Alignment.

For our SimulST strategies, we implemented both Local Agreement and AlignAtt policies. Specifically, we used Local Agreement with $n = 2$ (LA-2). To adaptively control the quality-latency trade-off, we varied the chunk size from 200 to 1000 ms. During hypothesis generation for input chunks, a beam search with a beam size of five was employed. For the AlignAtt policy, we set the chunk size to 800 ms. In AlignAtt, the parameter f directly governs the model's latency: smaller values of f imply that fewer frames are considered inaccessible by the model, thereby reducing the likelihood of the stopping condition being met and the resulting lower latency occurring. To adjust the quality-latency trade-off, we varied the parameter f from 1 to 12. See Appendix A for the detailed parameters of the speech-to-text model.

3.3 Simulaneous Speech-to-Speech Translation

Our simultaneous speech-to-speech system was a cascade of the speech-to-text translation module and the incremental TTS module. The parameter settings for the translation module were the same as those for the speech-to-text model, as described in Section 3.2

3.3.1 Incremental Text-to-Speech Synthesis

The incremental TTS is composed of three modules: a phoneme estimator with a prosodic symbol for the Japanese language, an acoustic feature predictor, and a neural vocoder.

For the phoneme estimator, the input vocabulary size was set to 21001. The output vocabulary was set to 40 for phoneme and 4 for prosodic symbols. The parameter of the AlignAtt policy f was set to 1 in the phoneme and prosodic symbol estimation modules. See Appendix B for the detailed parameters of the TTS model.

Speech was downsampled from 48 kHz to 22.05 kHz, and an 80-dimensional Mel spectrum was used for the acoustic features. The size of the Fourier transform, frameshift length, window length, and window function were 2048, 10 ms, 50 ms, and Hann window, respectively.

Our acoustic feature predictor mostly followed FastPitch structures, and the power predictor was added behind the pitch predictor.

For the neural vocoder, experimental conditions for Parallel WaveGAN were the same as in the original paper, except for the parameters related to acoustic features and speech.

3.4 Evaluation

We assessed our systems using the SimulEval (Ma et al., 2020a) toolkit and evaluated the translation quality of the SimulST systems using BLEU with sacreBLEU . We also measured translation latency by the following metrics:

- Average Lagging (AL) (Ma et al., 2019)
- Length Adaptive Average Lagging (LAAL) (Papi et al., 2022b)
- Average Token Delay (ATD) (Kano et al., 2024)
- Average Proportion (AP) (Cho and Esipova, 2016)
- Differentiable Average Lagging (DAL) (Cherry and Foster, 2019)

For the SimulS2S system, translation quality was evaluated using BLEU scores obtained after transcribing the output speech with Whisper (Radford et al., 2022) (ASR_BLEU). Translation latency was evaluated using ATD along with Start_Offset and End_Offset (Agarwal et al., 2023).

AL is a widely used latency metric for both text-to-text and speech-to-text simultaneous translation. However, while AL focuses on the time translation

https://github.com/facebookresearch/SimulEval

https://github.com/mjpost/sacrebleu

Table 1: Results of submitted speech-to-text systems on MuST-C v2 tst-COMMON

Language pair	Chunk size	BLEU	LAAL	AL	AP	DAL	ATD
En-De	960 ms	29.978	2193.352	1973.799	0.846	2863.481	1887.436
En-Ja	835 ms	15.329	2269.591	1868.759	0.893	2878.447	541.729
En-Zh	910 ms	22.300	2245.997	1959.588	0.839	2811.262	897.994

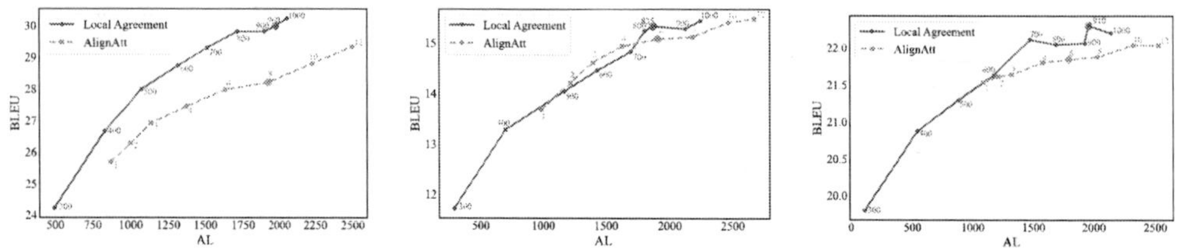

(a) BLEU and AL in En-De (b) BLEU and AL in En-Ja (c) BLEU and AL in En-Zh

Figure 1: Results of **Local Agreement** and **AlignAtt** policies with AL on the speech-to-text systems. Circled dot in LA graph indicates our submitted system. Circled dot in AlignAtt graph indicates the best model satisfying the task requirement of IWSLT 2024 Shared Task.

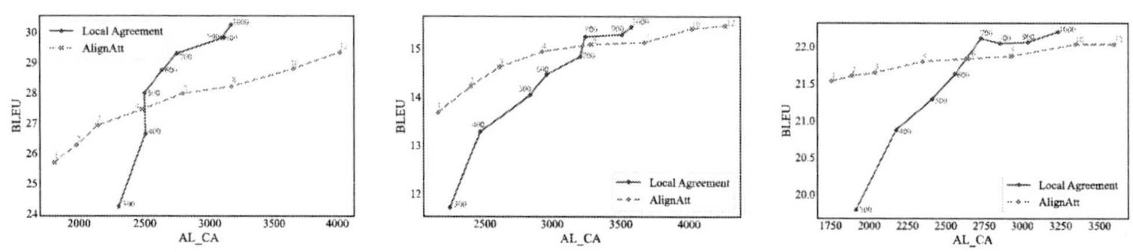

(a) BLEU and AL_CA in En-De (b) BLEU and AL_CA in En-Ja (c) BLEU and AL_CA in En-Zh

Figure 2: Results of **Local Agreement** and **AlignAtt** policies with AL_CA on the the speech-to-text systems

Table 2: Results of offline ST in submitted speech-to-text systems on MuST-C v2 tst-COMMON

Language pair	BLEU
En-De	31.00
En-Ja	15.98
En-Zh	24.98

begins, it does not adequately consider the time each input chunk's translation ends. In scenarios where speech segments are generated sequentially, as in speech-to-speech translation, the translation output may be delayed if the preceding outputs occupy the speech output channel. Consequently, AL may not be suitable for evaluating the latency of speech-to-speech simultaneous translation. Instead, we employ ATD, which includes delays caused by output in the latency calculation. ATD computes delays by calculating the average time difference between each source token and its corresponding target token. In the SimulEval setup, assuming each word requires 300 ms to be spoken, both the input and output speech are segmented into 300-ms intervals, treating these segments as tokens for ATD calculations.

4 Experiment Results

4.1 Simultaneous Speech-to-Text System

We chose one submission for each language direction, ensuring that the settings met the task requirement of $AL \leq 2$ sec. The submission model is based on the LA policy, since it outperformed the AlignAtt policy used in earlier models.

4.1.1 NAIST 2023 model vs. 2024 model

Table 1 shows the results of the submitted speech-to-text systems evaluated on MuST-C v2 tst-COMMON. Although the system architecture of our submitted models was the same as that of last year's models, the chunk size settings were different in every language pair. Using different chunk size settings slightly improved the BLEU scores in every language pair (see Appendix C for the scores for our 2023 submission). We also show the results of the offline ST in submitted speech-to-text systems on MuST-C v2 tst-COMMON in Table 2.

4.1.2 Local Agreement vs. AlignAtt Policies

Figure 1 shows BLEU and AL trade-offs in non-computation-aware conditions. When comparing the results of the LA and AlignAtt policies, there was little difference observed in En-Ja (Figure 1 (b)), while there were relatively large gaps in BLEU in En-De and En-Zh, especially in the high latency region (Figures 1 (a) and (c)).

Figure 2 shows the BLEU and AL trade-offs in computation-aware conditions. In all language pairs, the AlignAtt policy was better in the low-latency region, while the LA policy was better in the high-latency regions.

4.1.3 Non-Computation-Aware vs. Computation-Aware Latency

The quality-latency trade-off results differed significantly between the non-computation-aware and the computation-aware conditions. The LA policy requires a relatively long computation time to obtain the longest common prefixes. This is especially true when the source speech is divided into many small segments. Therefore, the latency increases significantly when a small chunk size is set (see Figure 2).

The main constraint of the IWSLT 2024 Shared Task (*i.e.*, latency is measured in a non-computation-aware setting) may have been advantageous for the LA policy. In fact our LA-based system outperformed our AlignAtt-based one. However, in reality, the LA policy is time-consuming, and thus the AlignAtt policy may be better suited to practical applications.

4.2 Simultaneous Speech-to-Speech System

We submitted a model with the LA policy for the En-Ja speech-to-speech track. We selected a model configured with a chunk size of 950 ms, which satisfies the task requirement Start_Offset $\leq$ 2.5 sec. Table 3 shows the results of our speech-to-speech model (LA (NAIST 2024)). We also developed a model with the AlignAtt policy, but the LA model achieved higher ASR_BLEU than the AlignAtt model. The quality-latency trade-offs in non-computation-aware and computation-aware conditions are shown in Figures 3 and 4.

4.2.1 NAIST 2023 model vs. 2024 model

Our submitted model outperformed our last year's submission (LA (NAIST 2023)). We compared our 2024 submission with the 2023 one to clarify what contributed to improving the score. The significant difference between the two systems lies in the upgraded TTS, which has an estimation model based on Transformer architecture with the AlignAtt policy (see Section 3.3).

When comparing the output from the speech translation modules, there was little difference in BLEU scores between the two systems (2023 system: 14.93; 2024 system: 15.44) . However, the performance of our 2024 system, which was measured by ASR_BLEU, was more than 2 points higher than that of our 2023 system. The results suggest that our new TTS contributed to the improved score. We listened to samples of synthesized speech and observed that the outputs from the 2024 system tended to be more natural in accent and intonation compared to those from the 2023 system.

4.2.2 Local Agreement vs. AlignAtt Policies

We further compared the model with the LA policy (our 2024 submission) with the model with the AlignAtt policy. Comparing the translation modules of the two systems, the difference in translation quality measured by BLEU was about 0.4 points (15.44 and 15.09 for the LA and the AlignAtt models, respectively). This gap is almost the same as the gap in the evaluation scores of the speech-to-speech systems (ASR_BLEU, see Table 3).

Although no difference was observed in BLEU scores, a comparison between the output from the speech-to-speech system (*i.e.*, transcribed speech) with the output from the translation module suggests that the policy difference affects the TTS performance. We extracted sentences that satisfy the following criteria: (1) translations from the translation modules were identical between the two policies, but (2) transcribed speeches were different between the two systems.

The chunk size setting for the 2024 speech-to-speech system was different from that for the 2024 speech-to-text system.

Table 3: Results of submitted SimulS2S system on the MuST-C v2 tst-COMMON

System	Chunk size	ASR_BLEU	Start_Offset	End_Offset	ATD
LA (NAIST 2023)	650 ms	9.873	2495.010	4134.752	3278.809
LA (NAIST 2024)	950 ms	12.082	2425.485	3745.743	3792.405
AlignAtt	800 ms (f=6)	11.650	2493.908	3505.377	3682.920

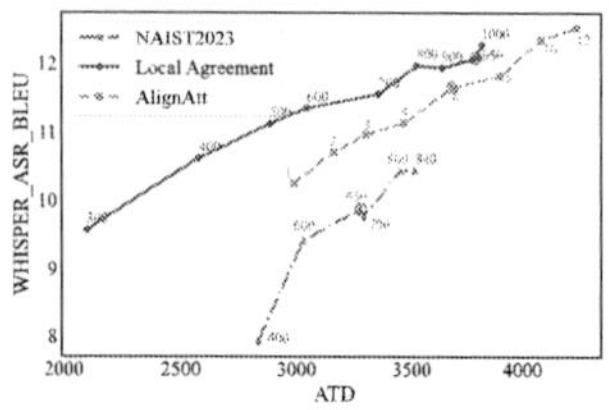

(a) BLEU and ATD

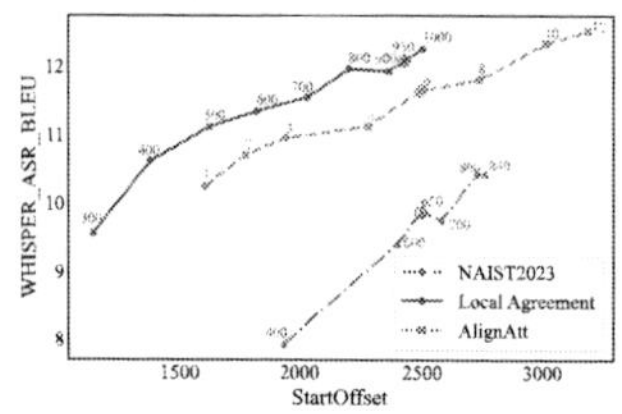

(b) BLEU and Start_Offset

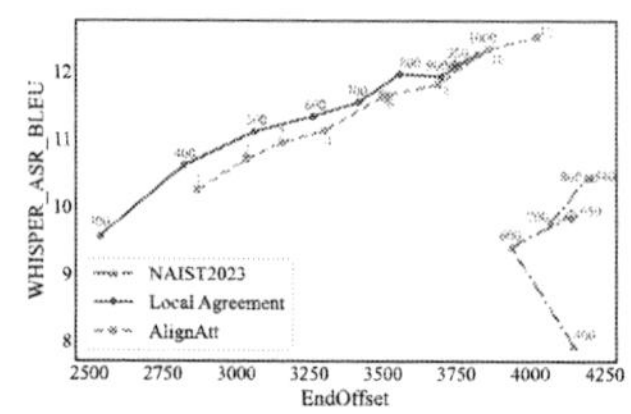

(c) BLEU and End_Offset

Figure 3: Results of **Local Agreement** and **AlignAtt** policies with ATD, Start_Offset, and End_Offset on speech-to-speech systems. Circled dot in LA graph indicates submitted system. Circled dot in AlignAtt graph indicates the best model satisfying the task requirement of IWSLT 2024 Shared Task.

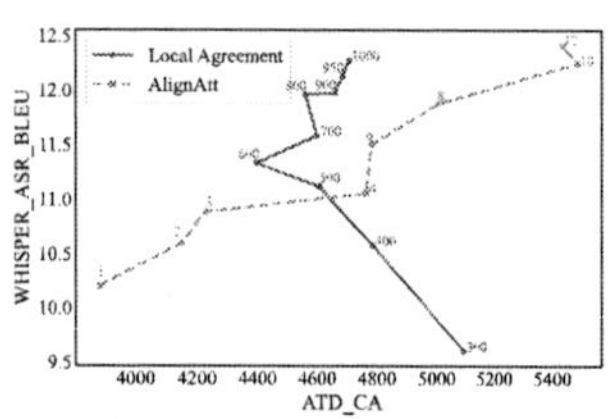

(a) BLEU and ATD_CA

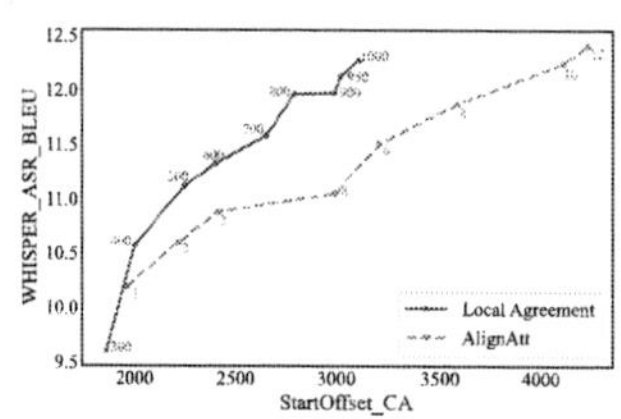

(b) BLEU and Start_Offset_CA

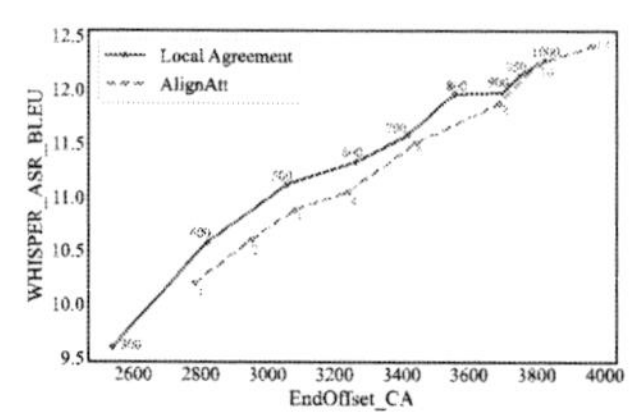

(c) BLEU and End_Offset_CA

Figure 4: Results of **Local Agreement** and **AlignAtt** policies with ATD_CA, Start_Offset_CA and End_Offset_CA on speech-to-speech translation systems.

We computed BLEU scores using extracted sentences (N=414) while regarding the outputs from the translation modules as references. The score for the LA policy was more than 2 points higher than that for the AlignAtt policy (67.79 and 65.46, respectively). In addition, the transcribed speech for AlignAtt was shorter than that for LA (sys_len: 6364 and 6464, respectively). These results suggest that the manner of passing the translations to the TTS was different between the two decoding policies (*e.g.*, timing) and affected the TTS performance.

Our analysis suggests that the output from the LA policy was more suitable for our TTS than that from the AlignAtt policy because the LA policy generated longer partial output with more confident agreement. On the other hand, the AlignAtt policy tended to generate prefixes whose boundaries did not correspond to meaningful units and sometimes divided a word in the middle of it. Figure 5 shows an example of the timing difference in passing the translations to the TTS. This figure compares the output prefixes generated from the translation modules with different decoding policies and the output prefixes generated from the TTS module along with the timing information. In this example, the translations generated from the translation modules are identical between the LA and AlignAtt policies. However, the prefixes (see Tgt text in Figure 5) and the timing when they were passed to the TTS module were different between the two decoding policies. In this example, the LA policy tended to generate semantically coherent prefixes, which resulted in more successful output from the TTS module (see Tgt speech). On the other hand, the AlignAtt policy divided the word "フォーミュ

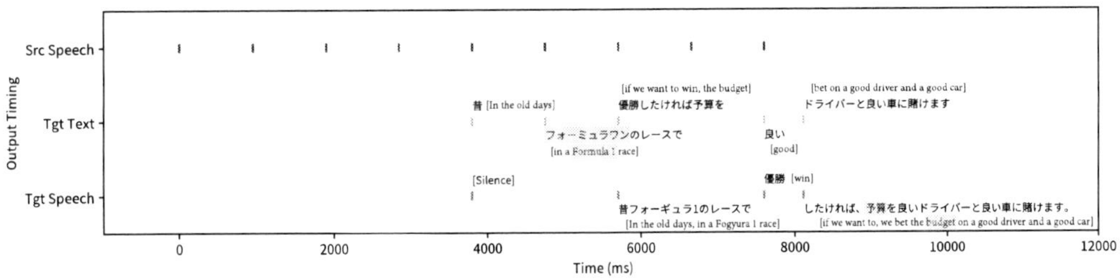

(a) LA (chunk size = 950 ms)

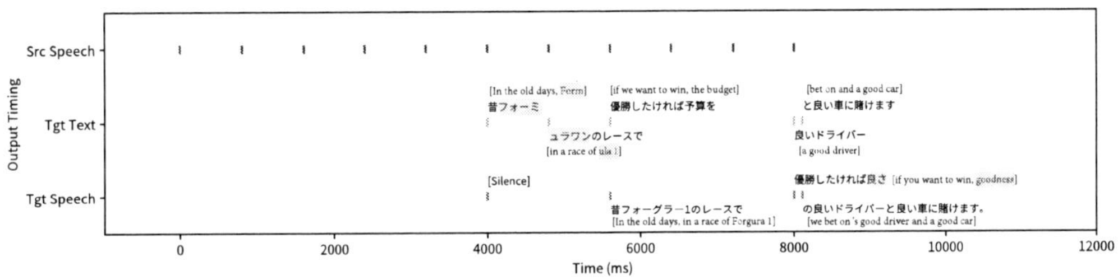

(b) AlignAtt (chunk size = 800 ms, f = 6)

Figure 5: Example of timing difference in passing translations to the TTS between the LA and AlignAtt policies. Translations generated by speech-to-text models were identical between the two policies, but outputs from the TTS module were different.

ラワン [Formula 1]" into two prefixes, "フォーミ [Form]" and "ユラワン [ula 1]." When the boundaries of the prefixes do not correspond to the meaning units or words are divided into prefixes, it might be difficult to capture the context of a sentence, which results in poor performance of the TTS module. In this example, the word "予算 [budget]" (pronounced as *yosan*) was wrongly recognized as "良さ [goodness]" (pronounced as *yosa*) in the system with the AlignAtt policy. The results suggest that feeding stable prefixes to the TTS module is important in our speech-to-speech system. Future study will involve making the AlignAtt policy generate more stable prefixes.

4.2.3 Non-Computation-Aware vs. Computation-Aware Latency

Figures 3 and 4 show the results in non-computation-aware and computation-aware settings, respectively. When the latency was measured by the Start_Offset and the End_Offset, there were no large differences between the results in non-computation-aware and computation-aware settings. However, when latency was measured by ATD, the quality-latency trade-offs exhibited different trends in non-computation-aware and computation-aware settings.

Start_Offset does not include computation time as a delay because Start_Offset is measured only at the start of translation. Therefore, Start_Offset is not appropriate as the latency metric in computation-aware settings. Moreover, Start_Offset and End_Offset measure the delay at a single point in the translation and does not consider the delays in the middle section of the translation.

In contrast, ATD measures the delay at multiple points and has a higher correlation with Ear-Voice Span, which is often used as a reference latency metric in human interpretation research (Kano et al., 2024). As the segments become smaller, the number of segments increases. This increases the number of comparison processes at the inference of LA. Therefore, the computation time becomes larger as the segment size becomes smaller and BLEU becomes lower in the low-latency range of LA, which is only shown in Figure 4a.

In a computation-aware setting, we observed that the AlignAtt policy outperformed the LA policy in the low-latency region (Figure 4). In practical situations, the LA policy might be time-consuming for a speech-to-speech system. One future direction would be improving the performance of a model with the AlignAtt policy.

5 Conclusions

In this paper, we described our SimulST systems for the IWSLT 2024 Simultaneous Speech Translation task. Experimental results demonstrated the effectiveness of AlignAtt by comparison to Local Agreement in terms of computation-aware latency, especially in the low-latency range. Our speech-to-speech translation system also showed the effectiveness of applying AlignAtt to the TTS model and resulted in better performance compared to our IWSLT 2023 system. This time, our speech-to-text method used HuBERT with the mBART model, while our TTS method only used the Parallel WaveGAN vocoder. In the future, we will investigate other methods such as WavLM (Chen et al., 2022) and Hi-Fi GAN (Kong et al., 2020).

Acknowledgements

Part of this work was supported by JSPS KAKENHI Grant Number JP21H05054.

References

Milind Agarwal, Sweta Agrawal, Antonios Anastasopoulos, Luisa Bentivogli, Ondřej Bojar, Claudia Borg, Marine Carpuat, Roldano Cattoni, Mauro Cettolo, Mingda Chen, William Chen, Khalid Choukri, Alexandra Chronopoulou, Anna Currey, Thierry Declerck, Qianqian Dong, Kevin Duh, Yannick Estève, Marcello Federico, Souhir Gahbiche, Barry Haddow, Benjamin Hsu, Phu Mon Htut, Hirofumi Inaguma, Dávid Javorský, John Judge, Yasumasa Kano, Tom Ko, Rishu Kumar, Pengwei Li, Xutai Ma, Prashant Mathur, Evgeny Matusov, Paul McNamee, John P. McCrae, Kenton Murray, Maria Nadejde, Satoshi Nakamura, Matteo Negri, Ha Nguyen, Jan Niehues, Xing Niu, Atul Kr. Ojha, John E. Ortega, Proyag Pal, Juan Pino, Lonneke van der Plas, Peter Polák, Elijah Rippeth, Elizabeth Salesky, Jiatong Shi, Matthias Sperber, Sebastian Stüker, Katsuhito Sudoh, Yun Tang, Brian Thompson, Kevin Tran, Marco Turchi, Alex Waibel, Mingxuan Wang, Shinji Watanabe, and Rodolfo Zevallos. 2023. FINDINGS OF THE IWSLT 2023 EVALUATION CAMPAIGN. In *Proceedings of the 20th International Conference on Spoken Language Translation (IWSLT 2023)*, pages 1–61, Toronto, Canada (in-person and online). Association for Computational Linguistics.

Antonios Anastasopoulos, Loïc Barrault, Luisa Bentivogli, Marcely Zanon Boito, Ondřej Bojar, Roldano Cattoni, Anna Currey, Georgiana Dinu, Kevin Duh, Maha Elbayad, Clara Emmanuel, Yannick Estève, Marcello Federico, Christian Federmann, Souhir Gahbiche, Hongyu Gong, Roman Grundkiewicz, Barry Haddow, Benjamin Hsu, Dávid Javorský, Věra Kloudová, Surafel Lakew, Xutai Ma, Prashant Mathur, Paul McNamee, Kenton Murray, Maria Nădejde, Satoshi Nakamura, Matteo Negri, Jan Niehues, Xing Niu, John Ortega, Juan Pino, Elizabeth Salesky, Jiatong Shi, Matthias Sperber, Sebastian Stüker, Katsuhito Sudoh, Marco Turchi, Yogesh Virkar, Alexander Waibel, Changhan Wang, and Shinji Watanabe. 2022. Findings of the IWSLT 2022 evaluation campaign. In *Proceedings of the 19th International Conference on Spoken Language Translation (IWSLT 2022)*, pages 98–157, Dublin, Ireland (in-person and online). Association for Computational Linguistics.

Naveen Arivazhagan, Colin Cherry, Isabelle Te, Wolfgang Macherey, Pallavi Baljekar, and George Foster. 2020. Re-translation strategies for long form, simultaneous, spoken language translation. In *ICASSP 2020-2020 IEEE International Conference on Acoustics, Speech and Signal Processing (ICASSP)*, pages 7919–7923. IEEE.

Srinivas Bangalore, Vivek Kumar Rangarajan Sridhar, Prakash Kolan, Ladan Golipour, and Aura Jimenez. 2012. Real-time incremental speech-to-speech translation of dialogs. In *Proceedings of the 2012 Conference of the North American Chapter of the Association for Computational Linguistics: Human Language Technologies*, pages 437–445, Montréal, Canada. Association for Computational Linguistics.

Sanyuan Chen, Chengyi Wang, Zhengyang Chen, Yu Wu, Shujie Liu, Zhuo Chen, Jinyu Li, Naoyuki Kanda, Takuya Yoshioka, Xiong Xiao, et al. 2022. Wavlm: Large-scale self-supervised pre-training for full stack speech processing. *IEEE Journal of Selected Topics in Signal Processing*, 16(6):1505–1518.

Colin Cherry and George Foster. 2019. Thinking slow about latency evaluation for simultaneous machine translation. *arXiv preprint arXiv:1906.00048*.

Kyunghyun Cho and Masha Esipova. 2016. Can neural machine translation do simultaneous translation? *CoRR*, abs/1606.02012.

Fahim Dalvi, Nadir Durrani, Hassan Sajjad, and Stephan Vogel. 2018. Incremental decoding and training methods for simultaneous translation in neural machine translation. In *Proceedings of the 2018 Conference of the North American Chapter of the Association for Computational Linguistics: Human Language Technologies, Volume 2 (Short Papers)*, pages 493–499, New Orleans, Louisiana. Association for Computational Linguistics.

Mattia A. Di Gangi, Roldano Cattoni, Luisa Bentivogli, Matteo Negri, and Marco Turchi. 2019. MuST-C: a Multilingual Speech Translation Corpus. In *Proceedings of the 2019 Conference of the North American Chapter of the Association for Computational Linguistics: Human Language Technologies, Volume 1 (Long and Short Papers)*, pages 2012–2017, Minneapolis, Minnesota. Association for Computational Linguistics.

Christian Fügen, Alex Waibel, and Muntsin Kolss. 2007. Simultaneous translation of lectures and speeches. *Machine translation*, 21:209–252.

Ryo Fukuda, Yuta Nishikawa, Yasumasa Kano, Yuka Ko, Tomoya Yanagita, Kosuke Doi, Mana Makinae, Sakriani Sakti, Katsuhito Sudoh, and Satoshi Nakamura. 2023. NAIST simultaneous speech-to-speech translation system for IWSLT 2023. In *Proceedings of the 20th International Conference on Spoken Language Translation (IWSLT 2023)*, pages 330–340, Toronto, Canada (in-person and online). Association for Computational Linguistics.

Wei-Ning Hsu, Benjamin Bolte, Yao-Hung Hubert Tsai, Kushal Lakhotia, Ruslan Salakhutdinov, and Abdelrahman Mohamed. 2021. Hubert: Self-supervised speech representation learning by masked prediction of hidden units.

Javier Iranzo-Sánchez, Joan Albert Silvestre-Cerdà, Javier Jorge, Nahuel Roselló, Adrià Giménez, Albert Sanchis, Jorge Civera, and Alfons Juan. 2020. Europarl-st: A multilingual corpus for speech translation of parliamentary debates. In *ICASSP 2020 - 2020 IEEE International Conference on Acoustics, Speech and Signal Processing (ICASSP)*, pages 8229–8233.

J. Kahn, M. Rivière, W. Zheng, E. Kharitonov, Q. Xu, P. E. Mazaré, J. Karadayi, V. Liptchinsky, R. Collobert, C. Fuegen, T. Likhomanenko, G. Synnaeve, A. Joulin, A. Mohamed, and E. Dupoux. 2020. Libri-light: A benchmark for asr with limited or no supervision. In *ICASSP 2020 - 2020 IEEE International Conference on Acoustics, Speech and Signal Processing (ICASSP)*, pages 7669–7673. `https://github.com/facebookresearch/libri-light`.

Yasumasa Kano, Katsuhito Sudoh, and Satoshi Nakamura. 2022. Simultaneous neural machine translation with prefix alignment. In *Proceedings of the 19th International Conference on Spoken Language Translation (IWSLT 2022)*, pages 22–31, Dublin, Ireland (in-person and online). Association for Computational Linguistics.

Yasumasa Kano, Katsuhito Sudoh, and Satoshi Nakamura. 2024. Average token delay: A duration-aware latency metric for simultaneous translation. *Journal of Natural Language Processing*, 31(3):To appear.

Eugene Kharitonov, Morgane Rivière, Gabriel Synnaeve, Lior Wolf, Pierre-Emmanuel Mazaré, Matthijs Douze, and Emmanuel Dupoux. 2020. Data augmenting contrastive learning of speech representations in the time domain. *arXiv preprint arXiv:2007.00991*.

Jungil Kong, Jaehyeon Kim, and Jaekyoung Bae. 2020. Hifi-gan: Generative adversarial networks for efficient and high fidelity speech synthesis. *Advances in neural information processing systems*, 33:17022–17033.

Kiyoshi Kurihara, Nobumasa Seiyama, and Tadashi Kumano. 2021. Prosodic features control by symbols as input of sequence-to-sequence acoustic modeling for neural tts. *IEICE Transactions on Information and Systems*, 104(2):302–311.

Danni Liu, Gerasimos Spanakis, and Jan Niehues. 2020. Low-Latency Sequence-to-Sequence Speech Recognition and Translation by Partial Hypothesis Selection. In *Proc. Interspeech 2020*, pages 3620–3624.

Mingbo Ma, Liang Huang, Hao Xiong, Renjie Zheng, Kaibo Liu, Baigong Zheng, Chuanqiang Zhang, Zhongjun He, Hairong Liu, Xing Li, Hua Wu, and Haifeng Wang. 2019. STACL: Simultaneous translation with implicit anticipation and controllable latency using prefix-to-prefix framework. In *Proceedings of the 57th Annual Meeting of the Association for Computational Linguistics*, pages 3025–3036, Florence, Italy. Association for Computational Linguistics.

Xutai Ma, Mohammad Javad Dousti, Changhan Wang, Jiatao Gu, and Juan Pino. 2020a. SIMULEVAL: An evaluation toolkit for simultaneous translation. In *Proceedings of the 2020 Conference on Empirical Methods in Natural Language Processing: System Demonstrations*, pages 144–150, Online. Association for Computational Linguistics.

Xutai Ma, Juan Pino, and Philipp Koehn. 2020b. SimulMT to SimulST: Adapting simultaneous text translation to end-to-end simultaneous speech translation. In *Proceedings of the 1st Conference of the Asia-Pacific Chapter of the Association for Computational Linguistics and the 10th International Joint Conference on Natural Language Processing*, pages 582–587, Suzhou, China. Association for Computational Linguistics.

Kikuo Maekawa, Makoto Yamazaki, Toshinobu Ogiso, Takehiko Maruyama, Hideki Ogura, Wakako Kashino, Hanae Koiso, Masaya Yamaguchi, Makiro Tanaka, and Yasuharu Den. 2014. Balanced corpus of contemporary written japanese. *Language resources and evaluation*, 48:345–371.

Ha Nguyen, Yannick Estève, and Laurent Besacier. 2021. An empirical study of end-to-end simultaneous speech translation decoding strategies. In *ICASSP 2021-2021 IEEE International Conference on Acoustics, Speech and Signal Processing (ICASSP)*, pages 7528–7532. IEEE.

Yuta Nishikawa and Satoshi Nakamura. 2023. Interconnection: Effective Connection between Pretrained Encoder and Decoder for Speech Translation. In *Proc. INTERSPEECH 2023*, pages 2193–2197.

Yusuke Oda, Graham Neubig, Sakriani Sakti, Tomoki Toda, and Satoshi Nakamura. 2014. Optimizing segmentation strategies for simultaneous speech translation. In *Proceedings of the 52nd Annual Meeting of the Association for Computational Linguistics (Volume 2: Short Papers)*, pages 551–556.

Sara Papi, Marco Gaido, Matteo Negri, and Marco Turchi. 2022a. Does simultaneous speech translation need simultaneous models? In *Findings of the Association for Computational Linguistics: EMNLP 2022*, pages 141–153, Abu Dhabi, United Arab Emirates. Association for Computational Linguistics.

Sara Papi, Marco Gaido, Matteo Negri, and Marco Turchi. 2022b. Over-generation cannot be rewarded: Length-adaptive average lagging for simultaneous speech translation. In *Proceedings of the Third Workshop on Automatic Simultaneous Translation*, pages 12–17, Online. Association for Computational Linguistics.

Sara Papi, Marco Turchi, and Matteo Negri. 2023. AlignAtt: Using Attention-based Audio-Translation Alignments as a Guide for Simultaneous Speech Translation. In *Proc. INTERSPEECH 2023*, pages 3974–3978.

Peter Polák, Ngoc-Quan Pham, Tuan Nam Nguyen, Danni Liu, Carlos Mullov, Jan Niehues, Ondřej Bojar, and Alexander Waibel. 2022. CUNI-KIT system for simultaneous speech translation task at IWSLT 2022. In *Proceedings of the 19th International Conference on Spoken Language Translation (IWSLT 2022)*, pages 277–285, Dublin, Ireland (in-person and online). Association for Computational Linguistics.

Alec Radford, Jong Wook Kim, Tao Xu, Greg Brockman, Christine McLeavey, and Ilya Sutskever. 2022. Robust speech recognition via large-scale weak supervision. *arXiv preprint arXiv:2212.04356*.

Anthony Rousseau, Paul Deléglise, and Y. Estève. 2012. Ted-lium: an automatic speech recognition dedicated corpus. In *International Conference on Language Resources and Evaluation*.

Ryosuke Sonobe, Shinnosuke Takamichi, and Hiroshi Saruwatari. 2017. Jsut corpus: free large-scale japanese speech corpus for end-to-end speech synthesis. *arXiv preprint arXiv:1711.00354*.

Yuqing Tang, Chau Tran, Xian Li, Peng-Jen Chen, Naman Goyal, Vishrav Chaudhary, Jiatao Gu, and Angela Fan. 2020. Multilingual translation with extensible multilingual pretraining and finetuning.

Ioannis Tsiamas, Gerard I. Gállego, Carlos Escolano, José Fonollosa, and Marta R. Costa-jussà. 2022. Pretrained speech encoders and efficient fine-tuning methods for speech translation: UPC at IWSLT 2022. In *Proceedings of the 19th International Conference on Spoken Language Translation (IWSLT 2022)*, pages 265–276, Dublin, Ireland (in-person and online). Association for Computational Linguistics.

Changhan Wang, Juan Pino, Anne Wu, and Jiatao Gu. 2020. CoVoST: A diverse multilingual speech-to-text translation corpus. In *Proceedings of the Twelfth Language Resources and Evaluation Conference*, pages 4197–4203, Marseille, France. European Language Resources Association.

Mahsa Yarmohammadi, Vivek Kumar Rangarajan Sridhar, Srinivas Bangalore, and Baskaran Sankaran. 2013. Incremental segmentation and decoding strategies for simultaneous translation. In *Proceedings of the Sixth International Joint Conference on Natural Language Processing*, pages 1032–1036, Nagoya, Japan. Asian Federation of Natural Language Processing.

Adrian Łańcucki. 2021. Fastpitch: Parallel text-to-speech with pitch prediction. In *ICASSP 2021 - 2021 IEEE International Conference on Acoustics, Speech and Signal Processing (ICASSP)*, pages 6588–6592.

A Speech-to-Text Parameter Settings

The speech encoder was initialized with HuBERT-Large, comprising a feature extractor trained on 60 K hours of unlabeled speech data from Libri-Light (Kahn et al., 2020), along with Transformer encoder layers. The feature extractor consists of seven convolutional layers with kernel sizes of (10, 3, 3, 3, 3, 2, 2), corresponding strides of (5, 2, 2, 2, 2, 2, 2), and 512 channels. The number of Transformer encoder layers is 24. The text decoder was initialized using the decoder component of mBART50. The decoder is composed of twelve Transformer layers, sharing an embedding layer and linear projection weights sized at 250,000. Each Transformer and feed-forward layer has dimensions of 1024 and 4096, respectively, with 16 attention heads. ReLU serves as the activation function, and layer normalization is applied before attention operations. The length adapter is implemented as a three-layer convolutional network featuring 1024 channels, a stride of 2, and a Gated Linear Unit (GLU) activation function. During training, each source audio was augmented (Kharitonov et al., 2020) prior to normalization, with a probability of 0.8. Multilingual models were trained using all of the data with a maximum source length of 400,000 frames and a target length of 1024 tokens. To achieve a batch size of approximately 32 million tokens, we employ gradient accumulation and data-parallel computations. We utilize the Adam optimizer with $\beta_1 = 0.99$, $\beta_2 = 0.98$, and a base learning rate of 2.5×10^{-4}. A tri-stage scheduler controls the learning rate, with warm-up, hold, and decay phases set to 0.15, 0.15, and 0.70, respectively. The initial and final learning rates are scaled to 0.01 compared to the base rate. Sentence averaging and gradient clipping of 20 are applied, along with a dropout probability of 0.1. Time masking is used for 10-length spans with a probability of 0.2, while channel masking is applied to 20-length spans with a probability of 0.1 in the output of the encoder's feature extractor. The loss function employed is cross-entropy with label smoothing of 20% probability mass.

B Incremental Text-to-Speech Parameter Settings

For the phoneme estimator, each Transformer layer, head, dimension of head, or dimension of Transformer model was 2, 8, 64, or 512, respectively. The embedded size of the encoder was the same as the dimension of the Transformer, and the embedding sizes of the decoder were 128 dimensions for the prosodic symbols and 512 dimensions for the phonemes. The batch size for training was 256. We used Adam optimizer with a learning rate of 0.1, $\beta_1 = 0.99$, $\beta_2 = 0.99$, and $\epsilon = 1e - 8$. The warmup scheduler is the same as that of the original Transformer. The size of the Fourier transform, frameshift length, window length, and window function were 2048, 10 ms, 50 ms, and Hann window, respectively. The changed settings were as follows: We used two embedding layers with a hidden size of 256, the hidden size in Transformer was 256, the number of heads was 2, the encoder and decoder had 4 layers, the first convolution layer in each FFT block in FastPitch had a kernel size of 3 and 256/1024 input/output channels, the second convolution layer in an FFT block had 1024/256 input/output channels with the same kernel size, the first convolution layer in each predictor had a kernel size of 3 and 256/256 input/output channels, and the second convolution layer in each predictor had 256/256 input/output channels with the same kernel size. We used Adam optimizer with a learning rate of 0.1, $\beta_1 = 0.99$, $\beta_2 = 0.99$, and $\epsilon = 1e - 9$. The batch size was 48. The schedule for the warmup followed FastPitch.

C NAIST 2023 Submission for Speech-to-Text

Table 4 shows the results for all chunk size settings for the En-De, En-Ja, and En-Zh models, respectively, used in our 2023 submission (Fukuda et al., 2023).

Table 4: Results of submitted speech-to-text systems on MuST-C v2 tst-COMMON in IWSLT 2023

Language pair	Chunk size	BLEU	LAAL	AL	AP	DAL	ATD
En-De	950 ms	29.975	2172.927	1964.329	0.846	2856.738	1893.749
En-Ja	840 ms	15.316	2290.716	1973.586	0.892	2889.950	547.752
En-Zh	700 ms	22.105	1906.995	1471.287	0.821	2436.948	667.780

Blending LLMs into Cascaded Speech Translation: KIT's Offline Speech Translation System for IWSLT 2024

Sai Koneru, Thai-Binh Nguyen, Ngoc-Quan Pham, Danni Liu, Zhaolin Li, Alexander Waibel, Jan Niehues

Karlsruhe Institute of Technology

firstname.lastname@kit.edu

Abstract

Large Language Models (LLMs) are currently under exploration for various tasks, including Automatic Speech Recognition (ASR), Machine Translation (MT), and even End-to-End Speech Translation (ST). In this paper, we present KIT's offline submission in the constrained + LLM track by incorporating recently proposed techniques that can be added to any cascaded speech translation. Specifically, we integrate Mistral-7B[1] into our system to enhance it in two ways. Firstly, we refine the ASR outputs by utilizing the N-best lists generated by our system and fine-tuning the LLM to predict the transcript accurately. Secondly, we refine the MT outputs at the document level by fine-tuning the LLM, leveraging both ASR and MT predictions to improve translation quality. We find that integrating the LLM into the ASR and MT systems results in an absolute improvement of 0.3% in Word Error Rate and 0.65% in COMET for tst2019 test set. In challenging test sets with overlapping speakers and background noise, we find that integrating LLM is not beneficial due to poor ASR performance. Here, we use ASR with chunked long-form decoding to improve context usage that may be unavailable when transcribing with Voice Activity Detection segmentation alone.

1 Introduction

This paper provides an overview of Karlsruhe Institute of Technology's speech translation (ST) system developed for the offline track of IWSLT 2024. We participated in the constrained plus large language models (LLMs) condition, focusing on the translation direction from English to German. Under this condition, LLMs with parameters of around 7 billion are allowed, and they have proven effective in many NLP tasks. One of the interesting aspects of this condition is how one can effectively integrate them into ST systems.

In recent years, there has been a significant interest in developing several open-sourced and medium-scale LLMs (Touvron et al., 2023; Jiang et al., 2023). The adaptability of LLMs to diverse tasks, using techniques such as In-Context-Learning (Brown et al., 2020) or Parameter-efficient fine-tuning with 4-bit quantization (Hu et al., 2021; Dettmers et al., 2024), enables their exploitation even with limited resources.

With these recent advancements, exploiting LLMs for ST shows great promise and offers several potential benefits. For instance, one common challenge in Automatic Speech Recognition (ASR) is dealing with input noise, which can often render it difficult to comprehend the speaker's words. However, LLMs, trained on vast amounts of data, may excel at predicting words compared to decoders trained solely during ASR. Moreover, LLMs possess a richer vocabulary and understanding of complex terminology that task-specific ASR systems may lack. Motivated by these advantages, various studies have explored the integration of LLMs into ASR (Chen et al., 2024; Pu et al., 2023), Machine Translation (MT) (Koneru et al., 2023), and ST (Hu et al., 2024).

Chen et al. (2024) employ the LLM to generate a new hypothesis based on the N-best list of the ASR model. This strategy relies on the observation that N-best lists tend to exhibit enough diversity, especially during uncertain conditions, allowing accurate transcript prediction by examining the list. On the other hand, for MT, Koneru et al. (2023) proposes leveraging the LLM to automatically postedit translations by analyzing the source and hypothesis documents to rectify contextual errors. Both approaches are system-agnostic and have demonstrated successful enhancement of system quality. Furthermore, it is also the case that cascaded systems are shown to be superior than end to end systems in previous IWSLT findings and submissions making the leveraging of LLMs

[1] mistralai/Mistral-7B-Instruct-v0.1

Proceedings of the 21st International Conference on Spoken Language Translation (IWSLT 2024), pages 231–239
August 15-16, 2024 ©2024 Association for Computational Linguistics

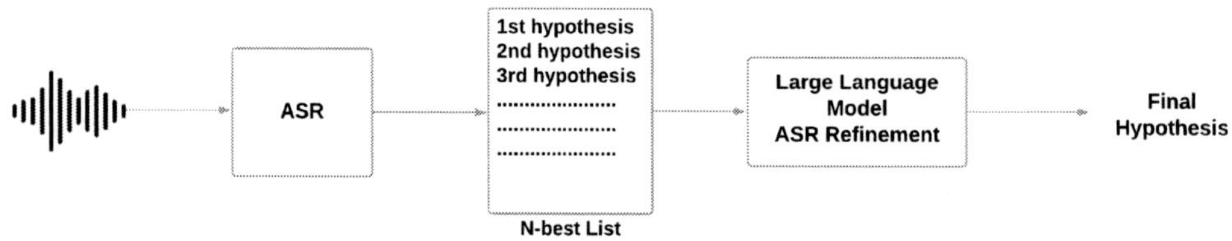

Figure 1: **ASR Refinement**: The ASR system generates a few candidate hypotheses with beam search, and the LLM generates a new hypothesis based on all the candidates as proposed in Chen et al. (2024). We use the top 5 candidates in all our experiments.

easily compatible. (Agarwal et al., 2023; Liu et al., 2023).

Our system builds on these two approaches to effectively use the LLMs to improve the cascaded ST pipeline by refining the intermediate outputs at both ASR and MT while maintaining its modular structure. We utilize pre-trained models to create the individual components and fine-tune them with the allowed data. Specifically, we employ WavLM (Chen et al., 2022) and MBART50 (Liu et al., 2020) to initialize the ASR, and NLLB-200 (3.3B) (Costa-jussà et al., 2022) for the MT module. As for the LLM, we opt for Mistral 7B Instruction-Tuned (Jiang et al., 2023), considering it to be the most recent model within the allowable options.

We present our main findings below:

- We demonstrate that LLMs can be tailored to enhance both ASR (Section 4.1) and MT systems (Section 4.2), resulting in an absolute improvement of 0.3% in Word Error Rate and 0.65% in COMET, respectively, on the tst2019 test set.

- While we observe significant enhancements in in-domain scenarios, we find that these techniques are not applicable in challenging scenarios (such as Overlapping Speakers, Background noise, etc.) due to poor ASR performance.

- We demonstrate that employing chunked long-form decoding[2] significantly improves ASR performance in challenging scenarios, such as the case of the ITV dev set. Specifically, we observe a decrease in the word error rate from 37.83% to 30.98%

2 Data

This section describes the evaluation and training data we use in our experiments. For evaluation, we report results on the tst2019 and ACLdev (Salesky et al., 2023) test sets to compare with findings from previous works (Anastasopoulos et al., 2021; Agarwal et al., 2023). We also use the EPTV (European Parlament activities), Itv (TV Series), and Peloton (Fitness TV) dev sets from the subtitling track consisting of overlapping speakers with different accents to evaluate the ASR performance in challenging scenarios.

As the data conditions did not change from IWSLT23 to this year, we rely on the data processed from last year's submission (KIT'23) (Liu et al., 2023). For the training data of ASR, we use the same system that used Common Voice (Ardila et al., 2020), LibriSpeech (Panayotov et al., 2015), MuST-C v2 (Di Gangi et al., 2019), TED-LIUM v3 (Hernandez et al., 2018), and VoxPopuli (Wang et al., 2021).

While for MT fine-tuning, we use the cleaned training data from last year created from the available parallel data. This includes Europarl v7 and v10 (Koehn, 2005), NewsCommentary v16, OpenSubtitles v2018 (Lison and Tiedemann, 2016), Tatoeba (Tiedemann, 2012), ELRC-CORDIS_News and TED2020 (Reimers and Gurevych, 2020) and consists in total of 23 million sentence pairs. For the rest of the paper, we refer to the full parallel data as *seed* and TED2020 as *in-domain*.

3 Overview

In this section, we provide an overview of our proposed cascaded system, detailing each individual component. First, the input audio is sent to the ASR system, which undergoes segmentation, and N-best lists are generated for each segmented utter-

[2] We derive the terminology from this blog post.

ance. Next, the top candidates in the N-best list are fed as input to the LLM, which is trained to refine the ASR output and generate a final ASR hypothesis. Following this, the final ASR hypotheses are passed on to the sentence-level MT system, which produces translations. Finally, the sentence-level automatic transcripts and translations are fed into another adapted LLM, which automatically post-edits and generates a coherent document translation of the talk.

3.1 Automatic Speech Recognition

We employed the ASR model from our previous year's submission (Liu et al., 2023), considering its effectiveness in transcribing the TED domain. For initialization, we utilized WavLM and mBART50 for the encoder and decoder, respectively, before fine-tuning on the ASR data described in Section 2. However, we encountered below-par ASR performance on the challenging sets EPTV, Itv, and Peloton.

We identified several issues that hindered the effectiveness of our ASR model with these sets. Firstly, the model itself was trained on single-talker datasets but inferred with multi-talker noisy datasets, leading to a mismatch in data distribution. Secondly, our typical use of the SHAS model for audio segmentation introduced challenges, as it sometimes missed segmentations and overlooked segments containing human speech.

Data shift is difficult to handle when the training dataset has not changed since last year. We focused more on handling the latter by incorporating long-form decoding. The key idea is to better use context (at the text or signal level) for decoding. The long audio file is chunked into smaller segments with a small overlap between adjacent segments. The model is run over each chunk, and the inferred text is joined at the strides by finding the longest common sequence between overlaps.

3.2 ASR refinement

Once we have generated the N-best list, we select the top 5 candidates and utilize an LLM to produce the final hypothesis as shown in Figure 1. In this step, we can adapt the LLM to the task using either few-shot prompting or LoRA fine-tuning techniques. We choose to fine-tune the LLM with adapters based on the findings from (Chen et al., 2024). However, it is crucial to train the LLM under conditions that simulate the test environment, where it should fix errors of our ASR output rather than on the whisper generated in Chen et al. (2024).

To generate the dataset for fine-tuning, we perform inference on our in-domain training data using the gold segmentation. We create pairs comprising the N-best list and the corresponding reference. It is worth noting that we utilized the same data to train the ASR system, which is not ideal. However, resource constraints prevented us from following the augmentation procedure that mitigates this, which we explain further in Section 3.4. Despite this limitation, manual analysis revealed that the ASR did not memorize the training data and produced similar N-best lists to those observed in the test conditions.

Following this, we fine-tuned the Mistral 7B Instruction-tuned LLM (Jiang et al., 2023) using QLoRA (Dettmers et al., 2024), to predict the gold reference based on the top candidates (see the prompt format below). Importantly, we chose not to shuffle the order of the top candidates when providing it in the prompt, as doing so would eliminate the ranking information provided to the LLM, which could be crucial for its performance.

```
Punctuate and Post-edit the hypothesis
based on the predictions:
Hyp 1 <SS> Hyp 2 <SS> Hyp 3 ..
Post-edited Hypothesis:
Gold Reference
```

3.3 Machine Translation

For building the MT system, we leverage the strong pre-trained model NLLB 200 3.3B (Costa-jussà et al., 2022) that is allowed in the constrained plus LLM track. We perform a two-step fine-tuning approach. Initially, we fine-tune the model on the *seed* data to adapt it to the spoken language domain. Subsequently, in the second step, we conduct in-domain fine-tuning on TED (in-domain) data, given its significance as one of the primary test sets in the offline track. Additionally, we implement checkpoint averaging to improve generalization with the last 3 checkpoints.

3.3.1 Restoring Punctuations

It is important to note that the ASR outputs lack punctuation. Therefore, we conducted experiments with two punctuators. First, we utilized the punctuations generated from the LLM ASR refinement process described in Section 3.2. Second, we employed a DeltaLM-based punctuation model, which was utilized in our previous year's submission (Liu

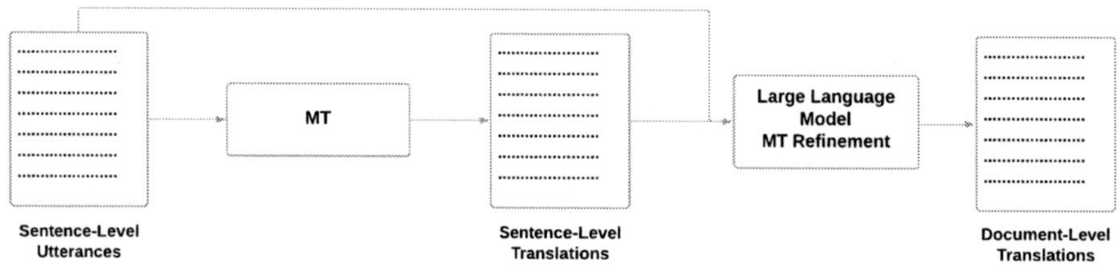

Figure 2: **Document Level MT Refinement**: The LLM trained to post-edit uses sentence-level transcripts and translations to generate a final document-level coherent and consistent translation.

et al., 2023). We observed that while the punctuations generated by the LLM were semantically correct, they often resulted in long sequences and led to a degradation in MT performance. As a result, we decided to opt for the second choice and segment the text into sentences using manually crafted rules.

3.4 Document-level Automatic Post-Editing

After translating the individual sentences with the fine-tuned NLLB, the outputs are not coherent as they are translated in isolation. Moreover, any ASR errors that might be fixed by observing the full document will be translated incorrectly. To mitigate this, we perform an additional step of document-level automatic post-editing using the source transcripts and sentence translations shown in Figure 2.

Similar to the situation outlined in Section 3.2, we encountered a lack of data for fine-tuning the LLM for document-level post-editing. Hence, we adopted the approach proposed by Koneru et al. (2023) to create the dataset. We divided the in-domain TED data into two halves, each containing English audio, English transcript, and German translation. Subsequently, we fine-tuned MT models on each half using the pre-trained models described in Sections 3.1 and 3.3. Following this, we conducted inference using the gold segmentation with our ASR and MT models trained on one half to the other half. This procedure generated a synthetic dataset with noisy ASR input, MT predictions, and corresponding gold references, leveraging the provided segmentation in the data.

We then use the synthetic dataset to create instances of document-level post-editing. We go through each talk and divide the transcripts into chunks, each chunk containing a maximum of 256 tokens corresponding to the LLM tokenizer. Then for each chunk, we use the transcript, hypothesis and reference to transform them into the format below and train the LLM to predict the gold reference given the noisy transcript and sentence-level hypothesis.

```
Noisy English Transcript:
ASR Hyp 1 <SS> ASR Hyp 2 <SS> ....
German Translations:
MT Hyp 1 <SS> MT Hyp 2 <SS> ....
Post-Edited German Translations:
Ref 1 <SS> Ref 2 <SS> ....
```

We use the delimiter "<SS>" to align with the input and perform sentence-level evaluation. Then, we again fine-tune the Mistral 7B Instruction-tuned LLM (Jiang et al., 2023) using QLoRA (Dettmers et al., 2024), training it to predict the gold reference given the noisy transcript and translations. We employ the sliding window with payload strategy during decoding as described in Koneru et al. (2023).

4 Results

4.1 Automatic Speech Recognition

To evaluate the benefit of the additional ASR refinement step described in Section 3.2, we compare the word error rate of our ASR system before and after post-editing, as shown in Table 1. The ASR performance improves in both cases, with a higher absolute improvement observed in the ACLdev set. The LLM is particularly beneficial in the ACLdev set, given that it contains terminology from the scientific domain where the LLM excels. We also observe a relative improvement of 10% in the TED talks, indicating that ASR refinement is beneficial.

	tst2019	ACLdev2023
KIT'23 (Liu et al., 2023) ASR	3.1	11.3
KIT'23 ASR + LLM Refine	2.8	10.6

Table 1: ASR word error rate scores on tst2019 and ACLdev2023 test sets. + LLM refine indicates that the N-best list was post-edited to generate the final hypothesis.

Model	*EPTV*	*ITV*	*Peloton*
KIT'23 ASR	26.43	37.83	**18.93**
KIT'23 ASR + Gold Seg	**16.84**	37.21	25.88
KIT'23 ASR + long-form	17.54	**30.98**	20.79
Seamless v2 (Barrault et al., 2023)	40.94	56.94	43.47

Table 2: ASR word error rate scores on the EPTV, Peloton and ITV dev set. Best scores for each set are highlighted in bold.

However, the performance of the same ASR system on the challenge set was below par. We conducted additional ablation studies and present the results in Table 2 for the challenge dev sets. We compared last year's ASR system with three conditions: providing gold segmentation, utilizing long-form decoding, and using the recently developed Seamless V2 (Barrault et al., 2023).

We observed that providing gold segmentation achieved a score of 16.84, demonstrating its crucial role in handling this challenging set for EPTV. Moreover, long-form decoding significantly narrowed the gap, decreasing the word error rate for both EPTV and ITV. Meanwhile, our ASR shows the best performance for Peloton without any modifications. Additionally, we evaluated Seamless to assess its robustness and found that its performance was severely lacking in comparison.

Based on these results, we use the ASR with standard segmentation for *TED* and *Peloton* test sets. For EPTV and ITV, we use the ASR system with long-form decoding. We found that the LLM cannot refine the N-best list given the poor WER of KIT'23 ASR for the latter test sets and generates long sequences with repetitions for most utterances. **Therefore, we do not perform any ASR or MT LLM refinements for *ITV* and *EPTV* sets and generate translations with a standard cascaded ST pipeline.**

4.2 Cascaded Speech Translation

In this section, we evaluate the final quality of our cascaded ST using the mwerSegmenter to realign the hypothesis with the reference segmentation. We report results with BLEU (Papineni et al., 2002) and Chrf2 (Popović, 2015) computed by Sacrebleu (Post, 2018). We also report the COMET (Rei et al., 2022) score using the default model[3].

Model	*tst2019*		
	BLEU	Chrf2	COMET
KIT'23 TED*	**28.4**	**58.8**	**78.87**
NLLB 3.3B	26.6	57.7	77.41
Seamless v2	25.5	57.0	76.65
NLLB 3.3B + Seed	26.9	57.9	77.87
NLLB 3.3B + Seed + TED	27.6	58.5	78.49

Table 3: MT scores using KIT'23 ASR as input calculated by resegmenting with mwerSegmenter. * indicates an unconstrained system that was trained on the same data sources but in more languages than what is allowed for IWSLT24. TED indicates the model adapted for TED and not ACLdev which was the official submission from KIT for IWSLT23

4.3 Two-step Fine-tuning

We presented a two-step fine-tuning approach to adapt our MT system in Section 3.3 to the target domain. We report the translation quality on tst2019 test set with this approach (last row) and other models for comparison in Table 3.

Firstly, we observe that Seamless performs inferiorly to NLLB across all translation metrics. Consequently, we proceeded with NLLB for further experiments.

Subsequently, fine-tuning the seed parallel data improved quality across all metrics, notably in-

[3]Unbabel/wmt22-comet-da

Model	*tst2019*			ACLdev2023		
	BLEU	Chrf2	COMET	BLEU	Chrf2	COMET
NLLB 3.3	26.6	57.7	77.41	35.0	63.9	74.83
NLLB 3.3 Seed	26.9	57.9	77.87	34.7	63.8	75.67
ASR Refine + NLLB 3.3 Seed	27.3	58.3	78.32	36.1	**65.0**	77.59
ASR Refine + NLLB 3.3 Seed + TED	28.3	58.8	78.98	34.8	63.7	77.25
ASR Refine + NLLB 3.3 Seed + TED + Doc APE	**28.7**	**59.1**	**79.63**	**36.4**	64.5	**78.64**

Table 4: MT scores using KIT'23 ASR as input calculated by resegmenting with mwerSegmenter. ASR Refine indicates an additional ASR refinement step with the LLM. Seed and TED indicate fine-tuning the NLLB 3.3 with seed alone or a two-step process with additional fine-tuning on TED. Doc APE indicates an LLM post-editing refinement to generate a coherent and consistent document. Best scores in each metric and test set are highlighted in bold.

creasing the score from 77.41 to 77.87 in COMET. Following this, with the assistance of second-step fine-tuning, we observed further improvements, resulting in scores reaching 78.49. However, it is important to note that this system still lags behind last year's submission, which was specifically adapted to the TED domain. Nevertheless, it's worth highlighting that this system was trained across multiple languages, placing it in the unconstrained condition for IWSLT24. Moreover, we could not replicate a similar adaptation process for NLLB due to resource and time constraints.

4.4 LLM Refinement

We proposed improving the ASR outputs and converting sentence-level to document-level translations using fine-tuned LLMs. We evaluate the benefits of the individual steps and report the results of our final cascaded ST system in Table 4 on tst2019 and ACLdev2023 test sets.

First, the benefits of two-step fine-tuning, ASR refinement, and document post-editing complement each other. Using KITs 23 ASR with NLLB 3.3 B as a baseline, we obtained 77.41 COMET in tst2019 test set. However, including all enhancements led to a total improvement of 2.23 COMET points. Furthermore, the improvements are consistent with both lexical and neural metrics.

Next, we observed that integrating LLMs provides significant benefits in the ACLdev set compared to the TED dev sets. This is plausible due to scientific terminology and accented speakers in the ACLdev set. Both of these challenges are well-suited for LLMs, as the quality of the initial systems is sufficient to utilize context and rectify mistakes reliably.

5 Conclusion

This system paper presented KIT's submission for the offline track in the constrained + LLMs condition, focusing on the English-to-German translation direction. Using modular techniques, we successfully integrated LLMs into any cascaded ST pipeline. Additionally, we highlighted the benefits of long-form decoding in scenarios involving noisy and overlapping speech.

For future work, we aim to explore robust techniques for integrating LLMs that can effectively handle challenging scenarios where ASR quality is sub-par. Furthermore, the translation's latency is quite high as it needs to call the LLM twice. However, integrating quality estimation techniques to decide when we need the LLM can limit the effects of the high latency problem.

Acknowledgments

This work is partly supported by the Helmholtz Programme-oriented Funding, with project number 46.24.01, named AI for Language Technologies, funding from the pilot program Core-Informatics of the Helmholtz Association (HGF). It also received partial support from the European Union's Horizon research and innovation programme under grant agreement No 101135798, project Meetween (My Personal AI Mediator for Virtual MEETtings BetWEEN People). The work was partly performed on the HoreKa supercomputer funded by the Ministry of Science, Research and the Arts Baden-Württemberg and by the Federal Ministry of Education and Research.

References

Milind Agarwal, Sweta Agarwal, Antonios Anastasopoulos, Luisa Bentivogli, Ondřej Bojar, Claudia Borg, Marine Carpuat, Roldano Cattoni, Mauro Cettolo, Mingda Chen, et al. 2023. Findings of the iwslt 2023 evaluation campaign. Association for Computational Linguistics.

Antonios Anastasopoulos, Ondřej Bojar, Jacob Bremerman, Roldano Cattoni, Maha Elbayad, Marcello Federico, Xutai Ma, Satoshi Nakamura, Matteo Negri, Jan Niehues, Juan Pino, Elizabeth Salesky, Sebastian Stüker, Katsuhito Sudoh, Marco Turchi, Alexander Waibel, Changhan Wang, and Matthew Wiesner. 2021. FINDINGS OF THE IWSLT 2021 EVALUATION CAMPAIGN. In *Proceedings of the 18th International Conference on Spoken Language Translation (IWSLT 2021)*, pages 1–29, Bangkok, Thailand (online). Association for Computational Linguistics.

Rosana Ardila, Megan Branson, Kelly Davis, Michael Kohler, Josh Meyer, Michael Henretty, Reuben Morais, Lindsay Saunders, Francis M. Tyers, and Gregor Weber. 2020. Common voice: A massively-multilingual speech corpus. In *Proceedings of The 12th Language Resources and Evaluation Conference, LREC 2020, Marseille, France, May 11-16, 2020*, pages 4218–4222. European Language Resources Association.

Loïc Barrault, Yu-An Chung, Mariano Cora Meglioli, David Dale, Ning Dong, Paul-Ambroise Duquenne, Hady Elsahar, Hongyu Gong, Kevin Heffernan, John Hoffman, et al. 2023. Seamlessm4t-massively multilingual & multimodal machine translation. *arXiv preprint arXiv:2308.11596*.

Tom Brown, Benjamin Mann, Nick Ryder, Melanie Subbiah, Jared D Kaplan, Prafulla Dhariwal, Arvind Neelakantan, Pranav Shyam, Girish Sastry, Amanda Askell, et al. 2020. Language models are few-shot learners. *Advances in neural information processing systems*, 33:1877–1901.

Chen Chen, Yuchen Hu, Chao-Han Huck Yang, Sabato Marco Siniscalchi, Pin-Yu Chen, and Eng-Siong Chng. 2024. Hyporadise: An open baseline for generative speech recognition with large language models. *Advances in Neural Information Processing Systems*, 36.

Sanyuan Chen, Chengyi Wang, Zhengyang Chen, Yu Wu, Shujie Liu, Zhuo Chen, Jinyu Li, Naoyuki Kanda, Takuya Yoshioka, Xiong Xiao, et al. 2022. Wavlm: Large-scale self-supervised pre-training for full stack speech processing. *IEEE Journal of Selected Topics in Signal Processing*, 16(6):1505–1518.

Marta R Costa-jussà, James Cross, Onur Çelebi, Maha Elbayad, Kenneth Heafield, Kevin Heffernan, Elahe Kalbassi, Janice Lam, Daniel Licht, Jean Maillard, et al. 2022. No language left behind: Scaling human-centered machine translation. *arXiv preprint arXiv:2207.04672*.

Tim Dettmers, Artidoro Pagnoni, Ari Holtzman, and Luke Zettlemoyer. 2024. Qlora: Efficient finetuning of quantized llms. *Advances in Neural Information Processing Systems*, 36.

Mattia A. Di Gangi, Roldano Cattoni, Luisa Bentivogli, Matteo Negri, and Marco Turchi. 2019. MuST-C: a Multilingual Speech Translation Corpus. In *Proceedings of the 2019 Conference of the North American Chapter of the Association for Computational Linguistics: Human Language Technologies, Volume 1 (Long and Short Papers)*, pages 2012–2017, Minneapolis, Minnesota. Association for Computational Linguistics.

François Hernandez, Vincent Nguyen, Sahar Ghannay, Natalia A. Tomashenko, and Yannick Estève. 2018. TED-LIUM 3: Twice as much data and corpus repartition for experiments on speaker adaptation. In *Speech and Computer - 20th International Conference, SPECOM 2018, Leipzig, Germany, September 18-22, 2018, Proceedings*, volume 11096 of *Lecture Notes in Computer Science*, pages 198–208. Springer.

Edward J Hu, Phillip Wallis, Zeyuan Allen-Zhu, Yuanzhi Li, Shean Wang, Lu Wang, Weizhu Chen, et al. 2021. Lora: Low-rank adaptation of large language models. In *International Conference on Learning Representations*.

Yuchen Hu, Chen Chen, Chao-Han Huck Yang, Ruizhe Li, Dong Zhang, Zhehuai Chen, and Eng Siong Chng. 2024. Gentranslate: Large language models are generative multilingual speech and machine translators. *arXiv preprint arXiv:2402.06894*.

Albert Q Jiang, Alexandre Sablayrolles, Arthur Mensch, Chris Bamford, Devendra Singh Chaplot, Diego de las Casas, Florian Bressand, Gianna Lengyel, Guillaume Lample, Lucile Saulnier, et al. 2023. Mistral 7b. *arXiv preprint arXiv:2310.06825*.

Philipp Koehn. 2005. Europarl: A parallel corpus for statistical machine translation. In *Proceedings of Machine Translation Summit X: Papers*, pages 79–86, Phuket, Thailand.

Sai Koneru, Miriam Exel, Matthias Huck, and Jan Niehues. 2023. Contextual refinement of translations: Large language models for sentence and document-level post-editing. *arXiv preprint arXiv:2310.14855*.

Pierre Lison and Jörg Tiedemann. 2016. OpenSubtitles2016: Extracting large parallel corpora from movie and TV subtitles. In *Proceedings of the Tenth International Conference on Language Resources and Evaluation (LREC'16)*, pages 923–929, Portorož, Slovenia. European Language Resources Association (ELRA).

Danni Liu, Thai Binh Nguyen, Sai Koneru, Enes Yavuz Ugan, Ngoc-Quan Pham, Tuan-Nam Nguyen, Tu Anh Dinh, Carlos Mullov, Alexander Waibel, and Jan Niehues. 2023. Kit's multilingual speech translation system for iwslt 2023. *arXiv preprint arXiv:2306.05320*.

Yinhan Liu, Jiatao Gu, Naman Goyal, Xian Li, Sergey Edunov, Marjan Ghazvininejad, Mike Lewis, and Luke Zettlemoyer. 2020. Multilingual denoising pre-training for neural machine translation. *Transactions of the Association for Computational Linguistics*, 8:726–742.

Sourab Mangrulkar, Sylvain Gugger, Lysandre Debut, Younes Belkada, Sayak Paul, and Benjamin Bossan. 2022. Peft: State-of-the-art parameter-efficient fine-tuning methods. `https://github.com/huggingface/peft`.

Myle Ott, Sergey Edunov, Alexei Baevski, Angela Fan, Sam Gross, Nathan Ng, David Grangier, and Michael Auli. 2019. fairseq: A fast, extensible toolkit for sequence modeling. In *Proceedings of the 2019 Conference of the North*. Association for Computational Linguistics.

Vassil Panayotov, Guoguo Chen, Daniel Povey, and Sanjeev Khudanpur. 2015. Librispeech: An ASR corpus based on public domain audio books. In *2015 IEEE International Conference on Acoustics, Speech and Signal Processing, ICASSP 2015, South Brisbane, Queensland, Australia, April 19-24, 2015*, pages 5206–5210. IEEE.

Kishore Papineni, Salim Roukos, Todd Ward, and Wei-Jing Zhu. 2002. Bleu: a method for automatic evaluation of machine translation. In *Proceedings of the 40th Annual Meeting of the Association for Computational Linguistics*, pages 311–318, Philadelphia, Pennsylvania, USA. Association for Computational Linguistics.

Maja Popović. 2015. chrF: character n-gram F-score for automatic MT evaluation. In *Proceedings of the Tenth Workshop on Statistical Machine Translation*, pages 392–395, Lisbon, Portugal. Association for Computational Linguistics.

Matt Post. 2018. A call for clarity in reporting BLEU scores. In *Proceedings of the Third Conference on Machine Translation: Research Papers*, pages 186–191, Brussels, Belgium. Association for Computational Linguistics.

Jie Pu, Thai-Son Nguyen, and Sebastian Stüker. 2023. Multi-stage large language model correction for speech recognition. *arXiv preprint arXiv:2310.11532*.

Ricardo Rei, José G. C. de Souza, Duarte Alves, Chrysoula Zerva, Ana C Farinha, Taisiya Glushkova, Alon Lavie, Luisa Coheur, and André F. T. Martins. 2022. COMET-22: Unbabel-IST 2022 submission for the metrics shared task. In *Proceedings of the Seventh Conference on Machine Translation (WMT)*, pages 578–585, Abu Dhabi, United Arab Emirates (Hybrid). Association for Computational Linguistics.

Nils Reimers and Iryna Gurevych. 2020. Making monolingual sentence embeddings multilingual using knowledge distillation. In *Proceedings of the 2020 Conference on Empirical Methods in Natural Language Processing (EMNLP)*, pages 4512–4525, Online. Association for Computational Linguistics.

Elizabeth Salesky, Kareem Darwish, Mohamed Al-Badrashiny, Mona Diab, and Jan Niehues. 2023. Evaluating Multilingual Speech Translation Under Realistic Conditions with Resegmentation and Terminology. In *Proceedings of the 20th International Conference on Spoken Language Translation (IWSLT 2023)*. Association for Computational Linguistics.

Jörg Tiedemann. 2012. Parallel data, tools and interfaces in OPUS. In *Proceedings of the Eighth International Conference on Language Resources and Evaluation (LREC'12)*, pages 2214–2218, Istanbul, Turkey. European Language Resources Association (ELRA).

Hugo Touvron, Louis Martin, Kevin Stone, Peter Albert, Amjad Almahairi, Yasmine Babaei, Nikolay Bashlykov, Soumya Batra, Prajjwal Bhargava, Shruti Bhosale, et al. 2023. Llama 2: Open foundation and fine-tuned chat models. *arXiv preprint arXiv:2307.09288*.

Changhan Wang, Morgane Riviere, Ann Lee, Anne Wu, Chaitanya Talnikar, Daniel Haziza, Mary Williamson, Juan Pino, and Emmanuel Dupoux. 2021. VoxPopuli: A large-scale multilingual speech corpus for representation learning, semi-supervised learning and interpretation. In *Proceedings of the 59th Annual Meeting of the Association for Computational Linguistics and the 11th International Joint Conference on Natural Language Processing (Volume 1: Long Papers)*, pages 993–1003, Online. Association for Computational Linguistics.

Thomas Wolf, Lysandre Debut, Victor Sanh, Julien Chaumond, Clement Delangue, Anthony Moi, Pierric Cistac, Tim Rault, Rémi Louf, Morgan Funtowicz, et al. 2019. Huggingface's transformers: State-of-the-art natural language processing. *arXiv preprint arXiv:1910.03771*.

A Appendix

We use the transformers library (Wolf et al., 2019) for fine-tuning our ASR and LLM and the fairseq toolkit (Ott et al., 2019) for fine-tuning NLLB 3.3B. For the ASR training, we set the *batch size* to 384, resulting in approximately 128 minutes per batch. We employ a *warmup strategy* over $2,000$ steps and a total of $100,000$ training steps. The *learning rate* is initialized to $1e-4$.

For the NLLB fine-tuning experiments, we use a *learning rate* set to $5e-5$, *label smoothing* to 0.1, *drop out* to 0.1, *attention drop-out* to 0.1. We use the *Adam optimizer* with *betas* to $(0,9,0.98)$ and the remaining optimizer parameters to default. We used a *batch size* of maximum 3096 making one step, *update-freq* to 16 and validating on the dev set after every epoch. We stopped the training after the dev loss did not increase after 10 epochs. For fine-tuning the LLM with QLoRA we use the peft (Mangrulkar et al., 2022) along with the transformers library. We add LoRA adapters to the target modules [*q_proj, k_proj, v_proj, o_proj, gate_proj, up_proj, down_proj*]. We set the *adapter rank* to 16, *alpha* to 32 and *lora dropout* to 0.1. We use a *batch size of* 8, *learning rate* of $5e-5$ with other parameters set to default. After every 200 steps, we validate and terminate the training if it does not improve 10 consecutive times.

During inference, we use beam search for all ASR, MT and LLM components. The ASR and MT decode with *beam size* of 5, whereas the LLM does it with *beam size* of 3.

ALADAN at IWSLT24 Low-resource Arabic Dialectal Speech Translation Task

Waad Ben Kheder[1], Josef Jon[2, 4], André Beyer[3], Abdel Messaoudi[1],
Rabea Affan[2], Claude Barras[1], Maxim Tychonov[2], and Jean-Luc Gauvain[1]

[1]Vocapia Research, France
[2]Lingea, Czechia
[3]Crowdee, Germany
[4]Charles University, Faculty of Mathematics and Physics, Institute of Formal and Applied Linguistics, Czechia

Abstract

This paper presents ALADAN's approach to the IWSLT 2024 Dialectal and Low-resource shared task, focusing on Levantine Arabic (apc) and Tunisian Arabic (aeb) to English speech translation (ST). Addressing challenges such as the lack of standardized orthography and limited training data, we propose a solution for data normalization in Dialectal Arabic, employing a modified Levenshtein distance and Word2vec models to find orthographic variants of the same word. Our system consists of a cascade ST system integrating two ASR systems (TDNN-F and Zipformer) and two NMT modules derived from pre-trained models (NLLB-200 1.3B distilled model and CohereAI's Command-R). Additionally, we explore the integration of unsupervised textual and audio data, highlighting the importance of multi-dialectal datasets for both ASR and NMT tasks. Our system achieves BLEU score of 31.5 for Levantine Arabic on the o□cial validation set.

1 Introduction

Speech translation (ST) systems play a crucial role in facilitating communication across languages and dialects, enabling access to information and services for diverse linguistic communities. However, developing accurate ST systems for dialectal Arabic poses significant challenges due to the scarcity of annotated data and the lack of standardized orthography. In particular, dialectal variants such as Levantine Arabic (apc) and Tunisian Arabic (aeb) are severely under-resourced in terms of Automatic Speech Recognition (ASR) and Neural Machine Translation (NMT) datasets.

These limitations present a major bottleneck in the development of high-quality ST systems and many works in previous IWSLT evaluations (Yan et al., 2022; Anastasopoulos et al., 2022; Agarwal et al., 2023; Hussein et al., 2023; Boito et al., 2022) explored various transfer techniques on the acoustic level by fine-tuning pre-trained speech encoders such as the Wav2vec 2.0 (Baevski et al., 2020) and HuBERT (Hsu et al., 2021) for ASR, or neural models such as NLLB-200 (Costa-jussà et al., 2022) and mBART (Liu et al., 2020) for NMT. The use of Modern Standard Arabic (MSA) datasets like MGB2 for dialect transfer (Costa-jussà et al., 2022; Tsiamas et al., 2022) has also been proven effective.

In recent years, more sophisticated ASR architectures such as the Zipformer (Yao et al., 2023) emerged as a more effective alternative to other transformer-based architectures like Conformers (Gulati et al., 2020) and Branchformer (Peng et al., 2022). In NLP, large language models (LLMs) (Achiam et al., 2023; Brown et al., 2020; Touvron et al., 2023; Le Scao et al., 2023; Jiang et al., 2023) have demonstrated strong performance across various tasks in mainstream languages, yet a notable constraint persists in their limited support for low-resource languages and dialects.

Building upon these novelties, we propose an approach that leverages pre-trained models and multi-dialectal resources for dialectal Arabic ST. We adopt a cascade ST system comprising two ASR systems (TDNN-F and Zipformer) and two NMT modules derived from pre-trained models (NLLB-200 and Command-R). Additionally, we develop a generic text normalization methodology for Dialectal Arabic and integrate crowd-sourced NMT data and multi-dialectal datasets like PADIC (Meftouh et al., 2015) to supplement the limited training data. The outcomes for Levantine Arabic (apc) are reported on the IWSLT2024 valid and test2024 sets, while the results for Tunisian Arabic (aeb) are provided for both validation and test set test1 and dev published in IWSLT2022.

Proceedings of the 21st International Conference on Spoken Language Translation (IWSLT 2024), pages 240–250
August 15-16, 2024 ©2024 Association for Computational Linguistics

2 Methods

2.1 Text normalization

Due to the lack of standardized conventions across various dialects, it is necessary to design text normalization procedures in order to mitigate ambiguity and facilitate dialectal data exploitation. In this section, we detail the approach used to normalize transcripts and texts written in Dialectal Arabic. While our research primarily targets Levantine Arabic (apc) and Tunisian Arabic (aeb), we opt for the term "Dialectal Arabic" to denote a broader range of dialects. Our text normalization process includes character-level and word-level normalization to ensure consistency and accuracy in representing linguistic content.

2.1.1 Character normalization

Multiple character-level normalizations were explored in previous work on the IWSLT22 speech translation task for Tunisian Arabic. Indeed, a good improvement in ASR and ST performance was reported in (Yan et al., 2022) after removing diacritics and single character words, and applying Alif/Ya/Ta-Marbuta normalization. Despite its reported efficiency, the Alif/Ya/Ta-Marbuta normalization can alter certain words, changing their meaning; eg. the words على ("on" in English) and علي ("Ali" in English) become one and the same once this normalization is applied. For this specific reason, this normalization will not be used in our work, and more effort is invested into word-level text normalization in order to fix the most frequent Alif/Ya/Ta-Marbuta -related problems. Moreover, it's important to note that using the "single character words" filtering strategy can be harmful in the case of Levantine Arabic, which has the proclitic ع, a very frequent word, corresponding to a reduced form of the على preposition (meaning "to" or "on"). Removing such words can result in the loss of valuable grammatical information and impact the performance of NMT models.

In our work, we start by applying a similar, but less aggressive normalization, which consists of converting all eastern Arabic numerals to western Arabic numerals and removing all diacritics. Then, we normalize rare characters like the non-Arabic letter ژ and other special characters representing loan sounds such as پ for /p/, ڤ or ڥ for /v/, and گ or ڨ for /g/. It is important to emphasize the fact that the character ڤ typically denotes the sound /g/ in Tunisian and Algerian dialects (usually normalized as ق) but often represents /v/ in other dialects (usually normalized as ف).

Table 1 summarizes the character normalization rules used in our experiments.

Dialect	Normalizations
All dialects	ژ => ر / پ => ب
Levantine Arabic	ڤ or ڥ => ف
Tunisian Arabic	ڤ => ق / ڥ => ف

Table 1: Characters normalization rules for different Arabic dialects.

2.1.2 Word normalization

The second step in text normalization operates at the word level and aims at fixing orthographic inconsistencies (words written in different forms) and limiting transcription errors (misspellings or typos).

Long words normalization: While analyzing the IWSLT "aeb" dataset, we noted a significant prevalence of lengthy words (more than 180 occurrences), often representing compound terms in Arabic or French. In most instances, these elongated words encapsulate entire French sentences and should be normalized to improve readability and reduce the amount of Out-of-Vocabulary (OOV) words. These words are segmented into constituent parts based on their semantic meaning in French as shown in Table 2.

A similar phenomenon can also be observed in Arabic words, corresponding, in most cases, to combined words. A simple method to identify such words is to search for final characters mid-word, namely the "Alif maksura" (ى) and "Ta marbouta" (ة). One example is the word "الجماعةهاذوكم", which is normalized as "الجماعة هاذوكم". This criterion can also reveal spelling mistakes in frequent words like the misspelled word صحح (meaning "correct" or "true") which should be normalized as صحيح.

Orthographic variant normalization:

In Dialectal Arabic transcripts, a single word may be written in various forms due to multiple factors. This variability often arises from the phonetic representation of words, where characters with similar pronunciations can be used interchangeably (such as "alif" and "alif maksura" at the end of a word). This phenomenon is also prevalent in foreign words where a word like "Google" can be written as قوقل, غوغل or جوجل depending on the country or the region, which reflects different interpretations of the loan sound /g/. French words containing nasal vowels (like /ɑ̃/, /ɔ̃/, /œ̃/ and /ɛ̃/)

	Example 1	Example 2
Original text	انترانمونيبليسنيموان	ألنابافيأتونسيون
Corresponding French	entraînement ni plus ni moins	elle n'a pas fait attention
Normalized text	انترانمون ني بليس ني موان	أل نا با في أتونسيون

Table 2: Two examples of elongated words corresponding to French phrases in the "aeb" IWSLT transcripts (before and after normalization).

can also be written in different ways; the most frequent ones being ـان /aːn/ or ـون /wn/.

To assist in our normalization efforts, we use a combination of orthographic and semantic similarities at the word level, by designing a weighted Levenshtein distance and using it in tandem with a Word2Vec model.

Weighted Levenshtein distance: In a recent work (Hajbi et al., 2024), a method for converting Moroccan Arabizi text to MSA based on a weighted Levenshtein distance was proposed. Inspired by this idea, we develop a weighted Levenshtein distance tailored specifically for Dialectal Arabic. This adjusted metric employs a higher cost when the insertion, removal, or substitution of a character is likely to result in the creation of a new word, particularly when consonants are altered in a word. Conversely, it assigns a lower cost when the insertion, removal, or substitution is attributable to an orthographic variant of the same word.

1. **Initialization:** All insertion, deletion and substitution costs ($\text{cost}_I(.)$, $\text{cost}_D(.)$ and $\text{cost}_S(.,.)$ respectively) are initialized to 1.
2. **Weights modification:**
   The costs are then modified as follows:

$$\begin{cases} \text{cost}_I(\text{v}_i) = \text{cost}_D(\text{v}_i) = 0.1,\ \forall \text{v}_i \in \mathbf{SV} \\ \text{cost}_I(\text{c}_i) = \text{cost}_D(\text{c}_i) = 1.5,\ \forall \text{c}_i \in \mathbf{C} \\ \text{cost}_S(\text{c}_i, \text{c}_j) = 1.5, \forall (\text{c}_i, \text{c}_j) \in \mathbf{C},\ i \neq j \\ \text{cost}_S(\text{c}_i, \text{c}_j) = 0.3, \forall (\text{c}_i, \text{c}_j) \in \mathbf{C}_1,\ i \neq j \\ \text{cost}_S(\text{a}_i, \text{a}_j) = 0.3, \forall (\text{a}_i, \text{a}_j) \in \mathbf{A},\ i \neq j \end{cases}$$

Where:

- **SV** = {و, ي, ا}; semi-vowels + Alif.
- **A** = {ا, أ, إ, آ, ٱ}; different variants of Alif.
- **C** = all Arabic letters, excluding semi-vowels (**SV**) and variants of Alif (**A**).
- $\mathbf{C}_1$ = {(ص, س), (ط, ت), (ذ, د), (ظ, ض)}; pairs of consonants used interchangeably in certain Arabic dialects (mainly emphatic consonants (Habash et al., 2012)).

It's important to mention that these cost values are determined empirically and can be further optimized to suit specific dialects.

By using this modified metric, the similarity between words such as بركينغ and باركنغ is diminished (two variants of the word "parking"), while the distance between باركينغ and ماركينغ is increased ("parking" vs. "marking").

In practice, relying solely on the weighted Levenshtein distance proves insufficient for effectively identifying orthographic variants of a word. This limitation arises primarily from the large size of the search space requiring the computation of distances between all pairs of words for each dialect, alongside the labor-intensive manual filtering requisite for determining the appropriate normalizations.

To address this challenge, we augment this string distance-based approach with a "semantic" proxy. This supplementary technique leverages a Word2Vec model to identify semantically similar words, thereby reducing the size of the search space prior to the application of string distance computation.

Word2vec model: Word2vec is a group of models which aim to represent words in a continuous vector space where words with similar meanings or contexts are closer to each other. This is achieved by learning representations of words based on the context in which they appear in a large corpus of text. Word2Vec identifies similar words by computing the cosine similarity (or other distance metrics) between their corresponding vectors. This model can either be implemented as a Continuous Bag of Words (CBOW) (Mikolov et al., 2013a) where a word is predicted given its context, or as a Skip-gram model (Mikolov et al., 2013b) where the context is predicted given a word. In our work, we use a CBOW model with a 100-dimensional word embeddings and a window size of 5. The similarity between the embeddings is computed as the cosine similarity (range = $[-1, 1]$).

The following algorithm is used to find the orthographic variants of each word:

For each word **w** in the vocabulary **V**:

1. Use the Word2vec model to find the 50 clos-

est words v_k to w using the cosine distance between their embeddings $emb_{\mathbf{v}_k}$: $\{\mathbf{v}_k \mid \cos(emb_{\mathbf{w}}, emb_{\mathbf{v}_k}) > 0.3,\ \forall \mathbf{v}_k \in \mathbf{V}\}$

2. Compute the weighted Levenshtein distance lev_W and keep the words $\mathbf{v}_k$ close to $\mathbf{w}$: $\{\mathbf{v}_k \mid \text{lev}_W(\mathbf{w}, \mathbf{v}_k) < 3\}$

Following this process, the largest clusters of words are identified and manually checked. These are some examples of apc/aeb clusters:

- The Tunisian word for "anyway": حاسيلو، حاصلو، حاسيول، حاصولو، حاصيله، حاصلو، حاصيلو.
- The Syrian word for "the computer": الكوبيوتير، الكمبيوتر.
- The French word "normalement": نرململن، نرمامون، نرمااللمون نورمومولون، نورمامون، نورماملن، نرململون، نورملومن، نورململان، نورماماملون، نورماملون.

2.2 ASR

Different architectures were tested in previous IWSLT evaluations for Dialectal Arabic and most of them opted for end-to-end architectures such as a Conformer encoder + CTC (Yan et al., 2022; Boito et al., 2022), a Branchformer encoder + a Transformer decoder (Hussein et al., 2023) showing the superiority of transformer-based architectures for this task. In recent years, the Zipformer architecture (Yao et al., 2023) was introduced as a more effective end-to-end model where, differently from Conformer that processes the sequence at a fixed frame rate of 25Hz, models use a U-Net-like structure and learn temporal representation at different resolutions in a more efficient way. The Zipformer architecture achieves state-of-the-art performance while capturing long-range dependencies and contextual information.

In crafting our ASR system, we prioritized compactness and speed in the selection of architectures. The ASR module developed in this work and used for the speech translation (ST) task comprises two distinct systems (TDNN-F and Zipformer), whose outputs are combined using the Recognizer Output Voting Error Reduction (ROVER) algorithm (Fiscus, 1997) for enhanced performance. Combining a TDNN-F model and an end-to-end model like Zipformer can be a powerful strategy to leverage the strengths of both approaches and achieve improved ASR performance. The TDNN-F model excels in its modular design, allowing for fine-tuning of each component independently while Zipformers streamline the ASR pipeline by implicitly learning relevant features from raw data and capturing long-range dependencies more effectively. Moreover, this system combination can mitigate some known limits of end-to-end architectures, such as high deletion errors, especially when dealing with long utterances (Chiu et al., 2021; Fox et al., 2024).

2.3 ST

We classify the systems we have experimented with based on their specificity into two categories: MT-only and prompt-driven LLMs.

2.3.1 MT-only

We experimented with multiple encoder-decoder Transformer models (see Section 3.3).

2.3.2 Prompt driven LLMs

Context Traditional MT models in the majority operate only on sentence level, without regard for a larger surrounding context. LLMs however are usually trained on longer chunks of text and can innately use the information in the context.

A simple way to translate a whole conversation using an LLM would be to use a prompt along the lines *``Translate the following conversation into English:* conversation"

One practical problem with this approach is that the task evaluation is still sentence-level, meaning we need to keep the same sentence boundaries across source and translated conversations. In our experience, this was difficult to achieve reliably with all the LLMs we have experimented with. There are multiple possible approaches to obtain the same segmentation as in the input:

- Sentence splitter -- Unreliable and introduces another tool into the pipeline
- Asking the model to keep the same number of lines: only works for documents with a small number of lines and even then, the model still moves the content across sentence boundaries
- Using separator token, e.g. [s] in the input to separate sentences and asking the model to keep it in the corresponding position in the translation -- similar issues as above
- Only translating one sentence at a time, but providing the whole context (source document and previously translated prefix) in the prompt

We have chosen to use the last option based on the experimental results. Our final prompt for context-aware NMT is shown in Listing 1.

2.4 Finetuning

We finetune some of the models on datasets described in Section 3.1. For traditional MT mod-

```
We need to translate a single line from conversation in Tunisian Arabic into English.
This is the conversation: {src_context}
The start of the conversation is already translated into English: {prev_context}
Translate the following line from {src_lang} to {tgt_lang}.
Be very literal, and only translate the content of the line, do not add any
explanations: {src_line}
```

Listing 1: The final context-aware prompt we used in our submission.

els, we finetune all the weights. For LLMs, we use QLoRA (Dettmers et al., 2023). The hyperparameters are described in Section 3.3.

2.5 Reranking

We rerank the outputs of multiple systems using Minimum Bayes Risk (MBR) decoding (Goel and Byrne, 2000; Kumar and Byrne, 2004; Freitag et al., 2021), with COMET22-DA (Rei et al., 2022) as the objective metric. MBR allows for the use of reference-based metrics for reranking even in cases where the reference is unavailable, by instead using the initial translation candidates as pseudo-references. For the final submission, we used a method introduced by Jon and Bojar (2023), which combines MBR decoding with a genetic algorithm to combine and mutate the translation candidates to create better quality translations.

3 Experiments

This section describes our experimental settings, used data and results.

3.1 Data

In this subsection, we list the datasets we used for training and evaluating our systems.

3.1.1 ASR data

Table 3 summarizes the audio data used to build our ASR models. To improve the robustness of our ASR system, these data are augmented using speed perturbation, additive noise and reverberation.

3.1.2 NMT data

Table 4 summarizes the textual data used to train the MT models and fine-tune the LLMs.

Constrained datasets: **IWSLT22** (LDC2022E01) consists of "aeb" speech, reference transcript and eng translations, containing 202k sentence pairs. The **UFAL parallel dataset** (Krubiński et al., 2023) contains multi-lingual parallel sentences (including "eng", "arb" and "apc").

Dataset	Dur.
Public supervised data	
GALE (BN/BC)	2800h
Tunisian Arabic (CTS) / IWSLT22	160h
Moroccan Arabic (CTS) / Appen [1]	30h
Levantine Arabic (CTS) / LDC [2]	250h
Internal supervised data	
Levantine Arabic (CTS)	365h
Egyptian Arabic (CTS)	135h
Algerian Arabic (CTS)	300h
Tunisian Arabic (Youtube)	20h
Moroccan Arabic (Youtube)	20h
Unsupervised data	
Tunisian Arabic (Radio)	150h
Total	4230h

Table 3: List of datasets used to train the ASR module.

Dataset	Dialect(s)	# sents.
UFAL	arb, apc	120k
LDC2012T09[3]	arz, apc	176.1k
IWSLT22[4]	aeb	202.4k
PADIC-ENG	arb, aeb, arq, apc, ary	44,8k
MADAR-ENG	25 cities	12k
Interviews	apc	4.8k
Global Voices	arb	63k
Crowd-sourced	apc	9.5k

Table 4: Datasets used for NMT finetuning.

Crowd-sourced data: We collaborate with our ALADAN partner, Crowdee[5], a micro-task crowdsourcing platform, to construct a parallel dataset for Levantine Arabic (apc) to English (eng) NMT. To ensure the high quality of the dataset, we design a linguistic assessment test consisting of 40 questions in Levantine Arabic. These questions cover various aspects, including Arabic grammar and multiple-choice translation exercises between "apc" and "eng".

In these tasks, transcripts from our internal Levantine Arabic CTS dataset (mentioned in Table 3) dataset are used as input, and the resulting dataset

[5]Crowdee—https://www.crowdee.de/

contains 9.5k parallel sentences.

PADIC-ENG: PADIC (Meftouh et al., 2015) is a multi-dialect dataset containing 6400 parallel sentences encompassing six distinct dialects: two Algerian variants, along with Palestinian, Syrian, Tunisian, and Moroccan Arabic, in addition to MSA. We translated the MSA side into English using the NLLB-1.3B model.

MADAR-ENG: MADAR (Bouamor et al., 2018) is a 25-way multiparallel dataset collected in 25 Arabic-speaking cities. We also translated the MSA side into English and paired the translation with source sides from cities located in Levantine or Tunisian Arabic-speaking regions.

Interviews: We scraped a website containing interviews in English with refugees and their experience with the integration in their new countries[6], resulting in 4.8k collected sentences. We translated the text into "apc" using the NLLB-1.3B model and used the resulting dataset as a backtranslation finetuning data. We have selected this website based on the domain similarity with the validation data.

LDC2012T09 contains dataset parallel sentences translated from Egyptian Arabic (arz), North Levantine Arabic (apc) and South Levantine Arabic (ajp) to English (eng). It was developed by Raytheon BBN, LDC, and Sakhr Software and provided to our project consortium for the purposes of the shared task free of charge by LDC.

Global Voices dataset was collected by the CASMACAT project. The Arabic-English part consists of 63k parallel sentences.

Apc-valid is provided by the organizers.[7]

3.2 ASR

3.2.1 ASR models

(A) TDNN-F: The first system, is based on the Factorized Time-Delay Neural Network (TDNN-F) architecture as outlined in (Povey et al., 2018). This model consists of 15 layers with approximately 28 million parameters. The ReLU layer dimension is set to 1920, with linear bottlenecks of dimensions $\{320, 240\}$. This acoustic model is coupled with an n-gram language model.

(B) Zipformer: The second system adopts an End-to-End architecture utilizing the Zipformer design, and more specifically the "Zipformer-M" configuration described in (Yao et al., 2023).

[6]https://socialscienceworks.org

[7]https://github.com/ufal/IWSLT2024_Levantine_Arabic_data

(C) Zipformer+TDNN-F: The output of the two developed ASR systems (A) and (B) are combined using the ROVER algorithm.

3.2.2 Training procedure

First, we train generic models (TDNN-F and Zipformer) using all available data to take advantage of the acoustic and linguistic similarities between different Arabic dialects. These pre-trained multi-dialect models are then fine-tuned using "apc" (or "aeb") -only data.

The TDNN-F model is pre-trained for 10 epochs (on all data) using lr=1e-3, then fine-tuned using LF-MMI-based transfer learning (Ghahremani et al., 2017) for 8 epochs using lr=2e-5, a primary lr-factor of 0.1 and a lr-factor of 1.0 for the last layer. The Zipformer model is pre-trained for 80 epochs (on all data) using the lr=4e-3 then ran 50 epochs for fine-tuning by using dialect-only data and lr=5e-3.

3.2.3 Results

Table 5 summarizes the WERs achieved by our ASR systems after applying the normalization procedure detailed in Section 2.1. This normalization significantly improved WERs for "apc" and "aeb" by 10% and 18%, respectively. The combined model achieved even greater improvements, demonstrating the complementarity of the two models and outperforming all WERs reported in (Agarwal et al., 2023) for "aeb".

	apc	**aeb**	
	apc-valid	**dev**	**test1**
(A) TDNN-F	26.5	39.9	40.8
(B) Zipformer	25.8	33.7	34.3
(C) Zipformer +TDNN-F	**23.6**	**32.7**	**33.1**

Table 5: WER (%) of ASR models on IWSLT24 Levantine Arabic (apc) validation and IWLST22 Tunisian Arabic (aeb) dev/test sets.

3.3 ST

We compare lower-cased BLEU (Papineni et al., 2002), ChrF (Popović, 2015) and COMET22-DA (Rei et al., 2022) scores of multiple systems on *apc-valid*, both on human transcriptions and in cascaded setting with our ASR systems.

3.3.1 Baselines

We have compared multiple open-source MT models (Costa-jussà et al., 2022; Kudugunta et al., 2023) and LLMs (Mesnard et al., 2024; Jiang

Type	Model	Human			ASR		
		BLEU	chrF	COMET	BLEU	chrF	COMET
MT	eTranslation	15.9	41	0.615	14.1	38.9	0.595
	GoogleTranslate	**29.9**	**55.7**	**0.780**	**26.3**	**51.6**	**0.747**
	MADLAD-10B	18.4	42.4	0.711	15.9	39.0	0.678
	NLLB200-1.3B	21.1	47.5	0.739	18.7	44.6	0.716
	NLLB200-600M	20.7	47.2	0.745	18.7	44.1	0.715
	NLLB200-3.3B	21.1	47.4	0.728	18.1	43.9	0.700
	Opus-MT	10.5	36.5	0.595	10.1	35.7	0.579
LLM	Jais-13B	21.9	45.5	0.755			
	Bloom-z	13.9	36.2	0.703			
	1-shot	15.1	37.5	0.716			
	Aya-101	16.1	42.3	0.711			
	1-shot	17.6	42.9	0.714			
	ALMA	7.1	32.0	0.587			
	1-shot	7.8	30.3	0.593			
	Mistral	8.5	35.4	0.620			
	1-shot	8.1	36.9	0.608			
	Gemma	6.7	31.8	0.563			
	1-shot	6.8	27.7	0.561			
	Command-R full+context	**29.5**	**54.1**	**0.805**			
	Command-R 4bit	24.3	49.8	0.778	20.7	46.2	0.737
	1-shot	25.6	50.4	0.785	21.7	46.6	0.749
	context	26.9	51.9	0.793	22.9	47.8	0.765
	1-shot + context	26.1	51.7	0.797	24.2	49.0	0.771

Table 6: Baseline models for ST. The first row displays the origin of the transcribed source file: *Human* are the transcriptions provided by the task organizers, *ASR* are the outputs of our Zipformer+TDNN-F ASR model. Missing values for *+context* in LLMs means that the given model was not able to provide the translation in the line-by-line format necessary for the evaluation. We did not evaluate most of the LLMs on the ASR transcriptions, since we already ruled these models out from the further experiments.

et al., 2023; Üstün et al., 2024; Sengupta et al., 2023; Muennighoff et al., 2022) in both sentence-to-sentence and context-aware translation. In the prompt-driven LLMs, we used a simple prompt in the form ``*Translate the following sentence from Levantine Arabic to English:* {source_sentence}" for sentence-to-sentence translation.

We evaluated the context-aware approach only with the LLMs and we used the prompt shown in Listing 1. We sample with temperature $t = 0.2$ based on preliminary experiments for the decoding. We compare 0-shot and 1-shot scenarios, with a short example taken directly from the valid set, so the model sees one short excerpt from the validation set with the correct translation.

The results are shown in Table 6. We see that the models vary greatly, with the best scores obtained by the commercial engine in the case of sentence-level, traditional MT models, and Command-R in the case of LLMs. The only LLM that responded well to our context-aware prompt was Command-R, for the other models, the output was not usable.

3.3.2 Finetuning

We selected one model from each category (MT, LLM): NLLB and Command-R, due to their best scores and good instruction-following capabilities in the case of the latter. We finetuned them on MT datasets listed in Section 3.1. The results on *apc-valid* are shown in Table 7.

For Command-R finetuning, we used the 4-bit quantized model (due to hardware limitations) and QLoRA with r values of 8, 16, 32 (at higher values we ran into memory issues), α equal to either $r/2$, r or $2r$ and learning rates set to either $1e-4$, $5e-5$ or $1e-5$. We did not see significant differences in metrics scores between these configurations. We ran the finetuning for 5000 updates with a batch size of 48, on a single A100 80GB GPU. Even though the number of updates only covers about 15% of the whole finetuning dataset, we did not see any improvements from continued training.

We also experimented with multiple decoding algorithms, namely sampling with temperature (Hinton et al., 2015; Ackley et al., 1985), contrastive search (Su and Collier, 2022; Su et al., 2022), locally typical sampling (Meister et al., 2023), and beam search (Graves, 2012). We did not find any significantly better configuration than sampling with $t = 0.2$.

#	Model	Human BLEU	Human chrF	Human COMET	ASR BLEU	ASR chrF	ASR COMET
1	**NLLB-1.3B**	21.1	47.5	0.739	18.7	44.6	0.716
2	+UFAL-APC	21.4	44.4	0.723	17.7	40.5	0.686
3	+IWSLT22	25.1	52.2	0.741	21.3	47.9	0.702
4	+3-transcribed	23.3	50.1	0.746	19.2	46.1	0.710
5	+LDC2012T09	27.8	53.6	0.764	23.8	49.8	0.725
6	+Interviews	21.8	49.9	0.740	19.2	46.8	0.707
7	+CrowdSourced	27.4	53.2	0.759	24	49.3	0.722
8	+GlobVoic	21.8	48.2	0.746	19.7	45.2	0.716
9	+MADAR-MT	19.5	44.1	0.734	17.3	41.2	0.701
10	+PADIC-ENG	26.6	52.7	0.757	23.3	49.1	0.718
11	*+2+3+4+5+10*	-	-	-	29.1	53.1	0.753
12	+3+4+5+6+10	30.1	56	0.777	26.4	52	0.737
13	+3+4+5+6+7+10*	30.6	56.2	0.780	27	52.2	0.742
14	**Command-R 4bit**	26.9	51.9	0.799	22.4	50.2	0.743
15	*+3+4+5+6+10*	34.4	58.1	0.805	30	53.4	0.771
16	+3+4+5+6+7+10*	33.8	57.9	0.806	30.1	53.4	0.768
17	15+MBR	34.5	58.4	0.812	31.1	54.6	0.781
18	*15+MBR-GA*	-	-	-	31.5	55	0.782

Table 7: Fintuning of NLLB-1.3B and Command-R-4bit models. Models marked with asterisk were trained after the end of the shared task and are not a part of the submission. The first row displays the origin of the transcribed source file: *Human* are the transcriptions provided by the task organizers, *ASR* are the outputs of our Zipformer+TDNN-F ASR model. Rows 18, 15, and 11 show our primary, first contrastive, and second contrastive submissions, respectively.

3.4 Final submission

Our primary submission consists of 26 best validation BLEU checkpoints from the finetuned Command-R model from row 15, combined using MBR decoding and a genetic algorithm (Jon and Bojar, 2023; Jon et al., 2023; row 18 in Table 7). We did not carry out the MBR-GA combining for the translations of the reference human transcriptions due to the computational requirements of the process. Our first contrastive submission is the translation from the single best LLM system we trained before the end of the competition (row 15). The second contrastive submission is the best NLLB model trained before the deadline, shown in row 11.

3.5 Conclusion

In this paper, we introduced a generic data normalization method for dialectal Arabic text using a modified Levenshtein distance metric and Word2vec word embeddings, improving ASR performance by up to 18%. We demonstrated the benefits of multi-dialectal modeling and combining models, achieving WERs of 23.6 on the "apc" validation set, 32.7 on the "aeb" dev set, and 33.1 on the "aeb" test1 set. In the MT part, we compared various MT models and LLMs, highlighting the superior performance of LLMs due to their larger context windows. By gathering additional training datasets, we demonstrated the effectiveness of traditional finetuning for NMT models and QLoRA finetuning for LLMs. Combining multiple finetuned models yielded a BLEU score of 31.5 on the "apc" validation set.

Acknowledgements

This work was funded by the the European Defence Fund (EDF) 2021 project ALADAN (Ai-based LAnguage technology development framework for Defence ApplicatioNs; Grant ID: 101102545). Views and opinions expressed are however those of the author(s) only and do not necessarily reflect those of the European Union or the European Commission. Neither the European Union nor the granting authority can be held responsible for them. We would like to express our gratitude to LDC for kindly providing the data used in this study.

References

Josh Achiam, Steven Adler, Sandhini Agarwal, Lama Ahmad, Ilge Akkaya, Florencia Leoni Aleman, Diogo Almeida, Janko Altenschmidt, Sam Altman, Shyamal Anadkat, et al. 2023. Gpt-4 technical report. *arXiv preprint arXiv:2303.08774*.

David H. Ackley, Geoffrey E. Hinton, and Terrence J.

Sejnowski. 1985. A learning algorithm for boltzmann machines. *Cogn. Sci.*, 9:147--169.

Milind Agarwal, Sweta Agarwal, Antonios Anastasopoulos, Luisa Bentivogli, Ondřej Bojar, Claudia Borg, Marine Carpuat, Roldano Cattoni, Mauro Cettolo, Mingda Chen, et al. 2023. Findings of the iwslt 2023 evaluation campaign. Association for Computational Linguistics.

Antonios Anastasopoulos, Loc Barrault, Luisa Bentivogli, Marcely Zanon Boito, Ondřej Bojar, Roldano Cattoni, Anna Currey, Georgiana Dinu, Kevin Duh, Maha Elbayad, et al. 2022. Findings of the iwslt 2022 evaluation campaign. In *Proceedings of the 19th International Conference on Spoken Language Translation (IWSLT 2022)*, pages 98--157. Association for Computational Linguistics.

Alexei Baevski, Yuhao Zhou, Abdelrahman Mohamed, and Michael Auli. 2020. wav2vec 2.0: A framework for self-supervised learning of speech representations. *Advances in neural information processing systems*, 33:12449--12460.

Marcely Zanon Boito, John Ortega, Hugo Riguidel, Antoine Laurent, Loïc Barrault, Fethi Bougares, Firas Chaabani, Ha Nguyen, Florentin Barbier, Souhir Gahbiche, et al. 2022. On-trac consortium systems for the iwslt 2022 dialect and low-resource speech translation tasks. *arXiv preprint arXiv:2205.01987.*

Houda Bouamor, Nizar Habash, Mohammad Salameh, Wajdi Zaghouani, Owen Rambow, Dana Abdulrahim, Ossama Obeid, Salam Khalifa, Fadhl Eryani, Alexander Erdmann, and Kemal Oflazer. 2018. The MADAR Arabic dialect corpus and lexicon. In *Proceedings of the Eleventh International Conference on Language Resources and Evaluation (LREC 2018)*, Miyazaki, Japan. European Language Resources Association (ELRA).

Tom Brown, Benjamin Mann, Nick Ryder, Melanie Subbiah, Jared D Kaplan, Prafulla Dhariwal, Arvind Neelakantan, Pranav Shyam, Girish Sastry, Amanda Askell, et al. 2020. Language models are few-shot learners. *Advances in neural information processing systems*, 33:1877--1901.

Chung-Cheng Chiu, Arun Narayanan, Wei Han, Rohit Prabhavalkar, Yu Zhang, Navdeep Jaitly, Ruoming Pang, Tara N Sainath, Patrick Nguyen, Liangliang Cao, et al. 2021. Rnn-t models fail to generalize to out-of-domain audio: Causes and solutions. In *2021 IEEE Spoken Language Technology Workshop (SLT)*, pages 873--880. IEEE.

Marta R Costa-jussà, James Cross, Onur Çelebi, Maha Elbayad, Kenneth Heafield, Kevin Heffernan, Elahe Kalbassi, Janice Lam, Daniel Licht, Jean Maillard, et al. 2022. No language left behind: Scaling human-centered machine translation. *arXiv preprint arXiv:2207.04672.*

Tim Dettmers, Artidoro Pagnoni, Ari Holtzman, and Luke Zettlemoyer. 2023. Qlora: Efficient finetuning of quantized llms. *Preprint*, arXiv:2305.14314.

Jonathan G Fiscus. 1997. A post-processing system to yield reduced word error rates: Recognizer output voting error reduction (rover). In *1997 IEEE Workshop on Automatic Speech Recognition and Understanding Proceedings*, pages 347--354. IEEE.

Jennifer Drexler Fox, Desh Raj, Natalie Delworth, Quinn McNamara, Corey Miller, and Migüel Jetté. 2024. Updated corpora and benchmarks for long-form speech recognition. In *ICASSP 2024-2024 IEEE International Conference on Acoustics, Speech and Signal Processing (ICASSP)*, pages 13246--13250. IEEE.

Markus Freitag, David Grangier, Qijun Tan, and Bowen Liang. 2021. Minimum bayes risk decoding with neural metrics of translation quality.

Pegah Ghahremani, Vimal Manohar, Hossein Hadian, Daniel Povey, and Sanjeev Khudanpur. 2017. Investigation of transfer learning for asr using lf-mmi trained neural networks. In *2017 IEEE Automatic Speech Recognition and Understanding Workshop (ASRU)*, pages 279--286. IEEE.

Vaibhava Goel and William J Byrne. 2000. Minimum bayes-risk automatic speech recognition. *Computer Speech & Language*, 14(2):115--135.

Alex Graves. 2012. Sequence transduction with recurrent neural networks. *Preprint*, arXiv:1211.3711.

Anmol Gulati, James Qin, Chung-Cheng Chiu, Niki Parmar, Yu Zhang, Jiahui Yu, Wei Han, Shibo Wang, Zhengdong Zhang, Yonghui Wu, et al. 2020. Conformer: Convolution-augmented transformer for speech recognition. *arXiv preprint arXiv:2005.08100.*

Nizar Habash, Mona T Diab, and Owen Rambow. 2012. Conventional orthography for dialectal arabic. In *LREC*, pages 711--718.

Soufiane Hajbi, Omayma Amezian, Nawfal El Moukhi, Redouan Korchiyne, and Younes Chihab. 2024. Moroccan arabizi-to-arabic conversion using rule-based transliteration and weighted levenshtein algorithm. *Scientific African*, 23:e02073.

Geoffrey Hinton, Oriol Vinyals, and Jeff Dean. 2015. Distilling the knowledge in a neural network. *Preprint*, arXiv:1503.02531.

Wei-Ning Hsu, Benjamin Bolte, Yao-Hung Hubert Tsai, Kushal Lakhotia, Ruslan Salakhutdinov, and Abdelrahman Mohamed. 2021. Hubert: Self-supervised speech representation learning by masked prediction of hidden units. *IEEE/ACM Transactions on Audio, Speech, and Language Processing*, 29:3451--3460.

Amir Hussein, Cihan Xiao, Neha Verma, Thomas Thebaud, Matthew Wiesner, and Sanjeev Khudanpur. 2023. Jhu iwslt 2023 dialect speech translation system description. In *Proceedings of the 20th International Conference on Spoken Language Translation (IWSLT 2023)*, pages 283--290.

Albert Q Jiang, Alexandre Sablayrolles, Arthur Mensch, Chris Bamford, Devendra Singh Chaplot, Diego de las Casas, Florian Bressand, Gianna Lengyel, Guillaume Lample, Lucile Saulnier, et al. 2023. Mistral 7b. *arXiv preprint arXiv:2310.06825*.

Josef Jon and Ondřej Bojar. 2023. Breeding machine translations: Evolutionary approach to survive and thrive in the world of automated evaluation. In *Proceedings of the 61st Annual Meeting of the Association for Computational Linguistics (Volume 1: Long Papers)*, pages 2191--2212, Toronto, Canada. Association for Computational Linguistics.

Josef Jon, Martin Popel, and Ondřej Bojar. 2023. CUNI at WMT23 general translation task: MT and a genetic algorithm. In *Proceedings of the Eighth Conference on Machine Translation*, pages 119--127, Singapore. Association for Computational Linguistics.

Mateusz Krubiński, Hashem Sellat, Shadi Saleh, Adam Pospíšil, Petr Zemánek, and Pavel Pecina. 2023. Multi-parallel corpus of north levantine arabic. In *Proceedings of ArabicNLP 2023*, pages 411--417.

Sneha Kudugunta, Isaac Caswell, Biao Zhang, Xavier Garcia, Christopher A. Choquette-Choo, Katherine Lee, Derrick Xin, Aditya Kusupati, Romi Stella, Ankur Bapna, and Orhan Firat. 2023. Madlad-400: A multilingual and document-level large audited dataset. *Preprint*, arXiv:2309.04662.

Shankar Kumar and William Byrne. 2004. Minimum Bayes-risk decoding for statistical machine translation. In *Proceedings of the Human Language Technology Conference of the North American Chapter of the Association for Computational Linguistics: HLT-NAACL 2004*, pages 169--176, Boston, Massachusetts, USA. Association for Computational Linguistics.

Teven Le Scao, Angela Fan, Christopher Akiki, Ellie Pavlick, Suzana Ilić, Daniel Hesslow, Roman Castagné, Alexandra Sasha Luccioni, François Yvon, Matthias Gallé, et al. 2023. Bloom: A 176b-parameter open-access multilingual language model.

Yinhan Liu, Jiatao Gu, Naman Goyal, Xian Li, Sergey Edunov, Marjan Ghazvininejad, Mike Lewis, and Luke Zettlemoyer. 2020. Multilingual denoising pre-training for neural machine translation. *Transactions of the Association for Computational Linguistics*, 8:726--742.

Karima Meftouh, Salima Harrat, Salma Jamoussi, Mourad Abbas, and Kamel Smaili. 2015. Machine translation experiments on padic: A parallel arabic dialect corpus. In *Proceedings of the 29th Pacific Asia conference on language, information and computation*, pages 26--34.

Clara Meister, Tiago Pimentel, Gian Wiher, and Ryan Cotterell. 2023. Locally typical sampling. *Transactions of the Association for Computational Linguistics*, 11:102--121.

Thomas Mesnard, Cassidy Hardin, Robert Dadashi, Surya Bhupatiraju, Shreya Pathak, Laurent Sifre, Morgane Rivière, Mihir Sanjay Kale, Juliette Love, et al. 2024. Gemma: Open models based on gemini research and technology. *arXiv preprint arXiv:2403.08295*.

Tomas Mikolov, Kai Chen, Greg Corrado, and Jeffrey Dean. 2013a. Efficient estimation of word representations in vector space. *arXiv preprint arXiv:1301.3781*.

Tomas Mikolov, Ilya Sutskever, Kai Chen, Greg S Corrado, and Jeff Dean. 2013b. Distributed representations of words and phrases and their compositionality. *Advances in neural information processing systems*, 26.

Niklas Muennighoff, Thomas Wang, Lintang Sutawika, Adam Roberts, Stella Biderman, Teven Le Scao, M Saiful Bari, Sheng Shen, Zheng-Xin Yong, Hailey Schoelkopf, et al. 2022. Crosslingual generalization through multitask finetuning. *arXiv preprint arXiv:2211.01786*.

Kishore Papineni, Salim Roukos, Todd Ward, and Wei-Jing Zhu. 2002. Bleu: a method for automatic evaluation of machine translation. In *Proceedings of the 40th Annual Meeting of the Association for Computational Linguistics*, pages 311--318, Philadelphia, Pennsylvania, USA. Association for Computational Linguistics.

Yifan Peng, Siddharth Dalmia, Ian Lane, and Shinji Watanabe. 2022. Branchformer: Parallel mlp-attention architectures to capture local and global context for speech recognition and understanding. In *International Conference on Machine Learning*, pages 17627--17643. PMLR.

Maja Popović. 2015. chrF: character n-gram F-score for automatic MT evaluation. In *Proceedings of the Tenth Workshop on Statistical Machine Translation*, pages 392--395, Lisbon, Portugal. Association for Computational Linguistics.

Daniel Povey, Gaofeng Cheng, Yiming Wang, Ke Li, Hainan Xu, Mahsa Yarmohammadi, and Sanjeev Khudanpur. 2018. Semi-orthogonal low-rank matrix factorization for deep neural networks. In *Interspeech*, pages 3743--3747.

Ricardo Rei, José G. C. de Souza, Duarte Alves, Chrysoula Zerva, Ana C Farinha, Taisiya Glushkova, Alon Lavie, Luisa Coheur, and André F. T. Martins. 2022. COMET-22: Unbabel-IST 2022 submission for the metrics shared task. In *Proceedings of the Seventh Conference on Machine Translation*

(WMT), pages 578--585, Abu Dhabi, United Arab Emirates (Hybrid). Association for Computational Linguistics.

Neha Sengupta, Sunil Kumar Sahu, Bokang Jia, Satheesh Katipomu, Haonan Li, Fajri Koto, Osama Mohammed Afzal, Samta Kamboj, Onkar Pandit, Rahul Pal, Lalit Pradhan, Zain Muhammad Mujahid, Massa Baali, Alham Fikri Aji, Zhengzhong Liu, Andy Hock, Andrew Feldman, Jonathan Lee, Andrew Jackson, Preslav Nakov, Timothy Baldwin, and Eric Xing. 2023. Jais and jais-chat: Arabic-centric foundation and instruction-tuned open generative large language models. *Preprint*, arXiv:2308.16149.

Yixuan Su and Nigel Collier. 2022. Contrastive search is what you need for neural text generation. *arXiv preprint arXiv:2210.14140*.

Yixuan Su, Tian Lan, Yan Wang, Dani Yogatama, Lingpeng Kong, and Nigel Collier. 2022. A contrastive framework for neural text generation. In *Advances in Neural Information Processing Systems*.

Hugo Touvron, Thibaut Lavril, Gautier Izacard, Xavier Martinet, Marie-Anne Lachaux, Timothée Lacroix, Baptiste Rozière, Naman Goyal, Eric Hambro, Faisal Azhar, et al. 2023. Llama: Open and efficient foundation language models. *arXiv preprint arXiv:2302.13971*.

Ioannis Tsiamas, Gerard I Gállego, Carlos Escolano, José Fonollosa, and Marta R Costa-jussà. 2022. Pretrained speech encoders and efficient fine-tuning methods for speech translation: Upc at iwslt 2022. In *Proceedings of the 19th International Conference on Spoken Language Translation (IWSLT 2022)*, pages 265--276.

Brian Yan, Patrick Fernandes, Siddharth Dalmia, Jiatong Shi, Yifan Peng, Dan Berrebbi, Xinyi Wang, Graham Neubig, and Shinji Watanabe. 2022. Cmu's iwslt 2022 dialect speech translation system. In *Proceedings of the 19th International Conference on Spoken Language Translation (IWSLT 2022)*, pages 298--307.

Zengwei Yao, Liyong Guo, Xiaoyu Yang, Wei Kang, Fangjun Kuang, Yifan Yang, Zengrui Jin, Long Lin, and Daniel Povey. 2023. Zipformer: A faster and better encoder for automatic speech recognition. *arXiv preprint arXiv:2310.11230*.

Ahmet Üstün, Viraat Aryabumi, Zheng-Xin Yong, Wei-Yin Ko, Daniel D'souza, Gbemileke Onilude, Neel Bhandari, Shivalika Singh, Hui-Lee Ooi, Amr Kayid, Freddie Vargus, Phil Blunsom, Shayne Longpre, Niklas Muennighoff, Marzieh Fadaee, Julia Kreutzer, and Sara Hooker. 2024. Aya model: An instruction finetuned open-access multilingual language model. *arXiv preprint arXiv:2402.07827*.

Enhancing Translation Accuracy of Large Language Models through Continual Pre-Training on Parallel Data

Minato Kondo[1] **Takehito Utsuro**[1] **Masaaki Nagata**[2]
[1]Deg. Prog. Sys.&Inf. Eng., Grad. Sch. Sci.&Tech., University of Tsukuba
[2]NTT Communication Science Laboratories, NTT Corporation, Japan
s2320743@_u.tsukuba.ac.jp, utsuro@_iit.tsukuba.ac.jp,
masaaki.nagata@_ntt.com

Abstract

In this paper, we propose a two-phase training approach where pre-trained large language models are continually pre-trained on parallel data and then supervised fine-tuned with a small amount of high-quality parallel data. To investigate the effectiveness of our proposed approach, we conducted continual pre-training with a 3.8B-parameter model and parallel data across eight different formats. We evaluate these methods on thirteen test sets for Japanese-to-English and English-to-Japanese translation. The results demonstrate that when utilizing parallel data in continual pre-training, it is essential to alternate between source and target sentences. Additionally, we demonstrated that the translation accuracy improves only for translation directions where the order of source and target sentences aligns between continual pre-training data and inference. In addition, we demonstrate that the LLM-based translation model is more robust in translating spoken language and achieves higher accuracy with less training data compared to supervised encoder-decoder models. We also show that the highest accuracy is achieved when the data for continual pre-training consists of interleaved source and target sentences and when tags are added to the source sentences.

1 Introduction

In machine translation, transformer encoder-decoder models (Vaswani et al., 2017), such as NLLB-200 (NLLB Team et al., 2022), mT5 (Xue et al., 2021), and mBART (Liu et al., 2020) predominate. The emergence of pre-trained Large Language Models (LLMs) composed solely of the transformer decoder, such as GPT series (Brown et al., 2020; OpenAI, 2023), has prompted the development of pre-trained LLMs, including, PaLM (Chowdhery et al., 2022), and LLaMA (Touvron et al., 2023). When translating with these LLMs, it is common to use in-context few-shot learning. According to Hendy et al. (2023), GPT-3 demonstrates comparable or superior accuracy to WMT-best for high-resource languages. Furthermore, as reported by Kocmi et al. (2023), GPT-4's 5-shot surpasses WMT-best's accuracy in most translation directions. However, Zhu et al. (2024) noted that in 8-shot scenarios, relatively small-scale LLMs (e.g., 7B parameters) exhibit lower accuracy than supervised encoder-decoder models. Therefore, it is necessary to investigate methods capable of achieving translation accuracy equivalent to existing translation models with relatively small-scale LLMs.

On the other hand, in models such as BERT (Devlin et al., 2019) and RoBERTa (Liu et al., 2019), which consist solely of transformer encoders, the effectiveness of continual pre-training, where pre-trained models are further trained on task-specific data such as classification to improve the accuracy of the task, has been reported (Jin et al., 2022; Ke et al., 2022). In the context of LLMs, continual pre-training has been reported to transfer models primarily pre-trained in English, such as LLaMA, to other languages (Cui et al., 2023). Additionally, when building LLM-based translation models, the effectiveness of conducting continual pre-training with either monolingual data, parallel data, or both, followed by supervised fine-tuning, has been reported, mainly when basing the model on primarily English pre-trained models such as LLaMA-2 (Xu et al., 2024a; Alves et al., 2024; Guo et al., 2024).

Although those recent publicaion in the context of LLMs are closely related to our study, this paper presents research conducted independently of those latest LLM-based translation studies such as Xu et al. (2024a); Alves et al. (2024); Guo et al. (2024). This paper proposes a two-phase training approach: continual pre-training on parallel data crawled from the web and supervised fine-tuning using a small amount of high-quality parallel data created by professional translators. To comprehen-

Proceedings of the 21st International Conference on Spoken Language Translation (IWSLT 2024), pages 251–268
August 15-16, 2024 ©2024 Association for Computational Linguistics

sively investigate methods for improving translation accuracy through continual pre-training, we conduct continual pre-training across eight data formats for Japanese-to-English (Ja ⇒ En) and English-to-Japanese (En ⇒ Ja) translations using a 3.8B-parameter LLM. We evaluate the translation accuracy on 13 test sets. Our paper's novelty compared to Xu et al. (2024a); Alves et al. (2024); Guo et al. (2024) lies in the following aspects.

- When conducting continual pre-training on data where source and target sentences appear alternately, the direction of language in which accuracy improves varies depending on the order of source and target sentences.
- LLM-based translation model is more robust in translating spoken language and achieves higher accuracy with less training data compared to supervised encoder-decoder models.
- When indicating the translation direction with tags ("<2en>" etc.) on data for continual pre-training, higher accuracy is achieved compared to simply concatenating source and target sentences.

2 Related Work

Parallel Data in Pre-Training from Scratch When pre-training LLMs from scratch, it is expected to use monolingual data. However, some reports incorporating bilingual data, such as parallel data, into the pre-training dataset can enhance the accuracy of downstream tasks. Briakou et al. (2023) show that incorporating parallel data into pre-training 1B and 8B parameter LLMs enhances translation accuracy in zero- and five-shot. Separate studies further show that including parallel data in the pre-training of the encoder-decoder model also improved performance in downstream multilingual and cross-lingual tasks (Kale et al., 2021; Schioppa et al., 2023).

LLMs-Based Translation Models Zhang et al. (2023) demonstrated that fine-tuning 15 multilingual LLMs using QLoRA for French-to-English translation surpasses the accuracy of both in-context few-shot learning and models trained from scratch. Conversely, Xu et al. (2024a) demonstrated that models predominantly pre-trained on English data, such as LLaMA-2, suffer reduced translation accuracy when translating into non-English target languages. Addressing this issue, they introduced ALMA, a method that employs fine-tuning monolingual data in the first stage, followed by supervised fine-tuning with a small quantity of high-quality parallel data in the second stage. Furthermore, there exists a report on improving translation accuracy by employing Contrastive Preference Optimization (CPO) for the second stage of supervised fine-tuning in ALMA (Xu et al., 2024b). In addition, the effectiveness of utilizing monolingual and parallel data in the first stage has been reported (Alves et al., 2024; Guo et al., 2024).

LLM-based translation models have only been evaluated on test data from the WMT General Machine Translation Task (Kocmi et al., 2022, 2023) and Flores-200 (NLLB Team et al., 2022). Therefore, their effectiveness compared to conventional supervised encoder-decoder models has not been sufficiently validated across various types of data. Additionally, the impact of continual pre-training data on translation accuracy remains unclear. Our study aims to address these two points.

3 Continual Pre-Training and Supervised Fine-Tuning with Parallel Data

We introduce a two-phase training to enhance the accuracy of translation of LLMs. In the first phase, we perform continual pre-training using parallel data crawled from the web, such as ParaCrawl (Bañón et al., 2020). Then, in the second phase, we conduct supervised fine-tuning with a small amount of high-quality parallel data. In LLM fine-tuning, the importance of data quality has been reported (Xu et al., 2024a; Zhou et al., 2023). However, it has also been reported that parallel data crawled from the web may have low data quality (Thompson et al., 2024). Therefore, we used data created by professional translators as high-quality parallel data.

3.1 Continual Pre-Training

Continual pre-training involves training on data where the source and target sentences appear alternately. Let the source sentences be denoted as $\{x_1, \ldots, x_n\}$ and the target sentences as $\{y_1, \ldots, y_n\}$, creating a dataset $\{x_1, y_1, \ldots, x_n, y_n\}$. With the tokens of the created dataset represented as $\mathbf{z} = \{z_1, z_2, \ldots, z_m\}$, we train the model parameters θ to minimize the following loss:

$$\mathcal{L}_1(\theta) = -\sum_t \log P(z_t | z_{t-c}, \ldots, z_{t-1}; \theta) \quad (1)$$

where c is the number of context lengths representing the maximum input length of LLMs. $\mathcal{L}_1(\theta)$ is a standard causal language modeling loss, which predicts the next word based on previous words (Radford et al., 2018). Therefore, we train by extracting $(z_{t-c}, \ldots, z_{t-1})$ from $\mathbf{z}$ in increments of c tokens, such that the source and target sentences alternate to predict the next word for each token. Extracting c tokens may result in the input's start and end being in the middle of the source or target sentence.

In pre-trained models such as LLaMA-2, primarily pre-trained in English, it has been reported that the effectiveness of utilizing monolingual data in continual pre-training, in addition to parallel data, is significant (Guo et al., 2024; Alves et al., 2024). The rationale behind continual pre-training with monolingual data is to acquire the generative ability in languages other than English. Therefore, in models where pre-training with monolingual data has been sufficiently conducted from scratch or where continual pre-training with monolingual data has been conducted, it is optional to conduct continual pre-training with monolingual data.

3.2 Supervised Fine-Tuning

After continual pre-training, we perform supervised fine-tuning with a small amount of high-quality parallel data. Let the source sentence be denoted by $\mathbf{x}$, the target sentence corresponding to $\mathbf{x}$ by $\mathbf{y}$, and the prompt by $I(\mathbf{x})$. We train the model parameters to minimize the following loss:

$$\mathcal{L}_2(\theta) = -\sum_{t=1}^{T} \log P\left(\mathbf{y}_t | \mathbf{y}_{<t}, I\left(\mathbf{x}\right); \theta\right) \quad (2)$$

where T represents the number of tokens in the target sentence, and $\mathbf{y}_t$ is the t-th token of the target sentence. While $\mathcal{L}_2(\theta)$ is also standard causal language modeling loss, it computes the loss only for the output of the target sentence (Xu et al., 2024a; Zhang et al., 2024). Therefore, we combine the prompt and target sentence (e.g., Translate "Good morning" into Japanese: おはよう) and input it into the model. The model predicts the next word for all input words, including the prompt portion. However, this portion is not used during inference and hence excluded from the loss.

4 Experiments

We conduct experiments on two NVIDIA RTX A6000 GPUs. Due to severely limited computational resources, we use a 3.8B parameters LLM, `rinna/bilingual-gpt-neox-4b` (rinna-4b)[1], which is already pre-trained on Japanese and English data, totaling 524B tokens, with 173B tokens in Japanese and 293B tokens in English. Since rinna-4b has undergone sufficient pre-training from scratch on monolingual data for both Japanese and English, as stated in Section 3, we believe that continual pre-training with monolingual data is unnecessary. Given that the model we employ is pre-trained on Japanese and English, we experiment with Japanese-to-English and English-to-Japanese translation tasks. All experiments utilizing rinna-4b are conducted using the open-source huggingface transformers library.[2]

4.1 Dataset

4.1.1 Continual Pre-Training

We utilize JParaCrawl v3.0 (Morishita et al., 2022) as the web-based parallel data comprising 21.8M parallel sentence pairs, the largest and newest dataset of English-Japanese parallel data available. From this dataset of 21.8M parallel sentence pairs, we sample 20.8M sentence pairs using LEALLA-large[3] (Mao and Nakagawa, 2023) for train data. Details on sampling are provided in Appendix A. For dev data, we use the dev and test data from WMT20 (Barrault et al., 2020) and the test data from WMT21 (Akhbardeh et al., 2021).

4.1.2 Supervised Fine-Tuning

We utilize the dev and test data of WMT20 and Flores-200 (NLLB Team et al., 2022), along with the train data from KFTT (Neubig, 2011) as train data, all created by professional translators. The train data for KFTT utilized in experiments consists of 10k instances randomly sampled from 440k samples. The resulting train data comprise 15k samples for both En $\Rightarrow$ Ja and Ja $\Rightarrow$ En. For dev data, we utilize the WMT21 test data. We use the prompts written in the following source language, based on the report by Xu et al. (2024a).[4]

En $\Rightarrow$ Ja

Translate this from English to Japanese:
English: {source sentence}
Japanese:

[1] `https://huggingface.co/rinna/bilingual-gpt-neox-4b`

[2] `https://github.com/huggingface/transformers`

[3] `https://huggingface.co/setu4993/LEALLA-large`

[4] The reason for writing prompts in the source sentence's language is that it is more natural to create translation prompts in the source sentence's language when translating.

Ja ⇒ En

これを日本語から英語に翻訳してください：
日本語：{source sentence}
英語：

4.1.3 Test Sets

We use the test sets employed by Morishita et al. (2022) to evaluate translation accuracy. Since we include the test data from WMT20 and WMT21 in the train and dev data for continual pre-training and supervised fine-tuning, we exclude these and add the test data from WMT22. As a result, there are 13 test sets: 5 for the En ⇒ Ja direction, 3 for the Ja ⇒ En direction, and 5 for both the En ⇒ Ja and En ⇒ Ja directions. For detailed information on the test sets, please refer to Table 6 of Appendix D.

4.2 Models

4.2.1 Baseline Models

We establish two baseline models as described below. The train data consists of the data described in Section 4.1.1 and Section 4.1.2, and the dev data is the WMT21 test data. Note that the data from JParaCrawl v3.0 is created by randomly sampling 10.4M parallel sentences, which is 50% of the total 20.8M parallel sentences, to be used respectively as the train data for En ⇒ Ja and Ja ⇒ En.

Transformer This model is a 1B-parameter transformer trained from scratch. The model architecture is based on mT5-large[5], with two modifications: reducing the vocab_size from 250,112 to 65,536, matching that of rinna-4b, and increasing the feed-forward network dimension from 2,816 to 4,096. As a result, the model has 24 layers each for the encoder and decoder, a model dimension of 1,024, 16 attention heads, a feed-forward network with GeGLU activation (Shazeer, 2020), and a dropout (Srivastava et al., 2014) of 0.1. The tokenizer is newly created using the sentencepiece library[6] (Kudo and Richardson, 2018) with the subword method set to unigram, character coverage to 0.9995, and byte-fallback enabled. Training is conducted with a total batch size of 4,096 for 15 epochs (38,160 steps), with validation every 1,000 steps, and it is terminated if the validation loss does not improve for three consecutive validations. We use AdamW optimizer (Loshchilov and Hutter, 2019), with $\beta_1 = 0.9, \beta_2 = 0.98, \epsilon = 1.0 \times 10^{-8}$. We set the weight decay and label smoothing (Szegedy et al., 2016) to 0.1, and gradient clipping (Pascanu et al., 2013) to 1.0. The peak learning rate is set to 1.0×10^{-3}, with a warmup ratio 0.1 and an inverse square root scheduler applied. Additionally, bfloat16, gradient checkpointing (Chen et al., 2016), and the deepspeed[7] (Rasley et al., 2020) ZeRO stage 2 are applied during training. Training is conducted on two NVIDIA RTX A6000 GPUs with these settings, taking 17 days.

Direct-SFT Direct-SFT consists of the rinna-4b directly supervised fine-tuning with parallel data, using LoRA tuning (Hu et al., 2022). We conduct supervised fine-tuning of this model using the prompts mentioned in Section 4.1.2. Furthermore, to approximate conditions for full-weight tuning, we apply LoRA to the linear layers of self-attention's query, key, value, and output, as well as the linear layers of the feed-forward network. We set the rank of LoRA to 16, resulting in 25.9M trainable parameters, which constitutes 0.68% of the parameters in rinna-4b.

4.2.2 Source and Target Sentences Ordering in Continual Pre-Training

We conduct continual pre-training with 4 patterns, varying the order in which source and target sentences. After continual pre-training with these 4 orders, we undergo supervised fine-tuning using the data and prompts described in Section 4.1.2 with full fine-tuning and LoRA tuning.

Mono As stated in Section 3.1, instead of alternating between source and target sentences, the approach involves sequences such as $(x_1, \ldots, x_n), (y_1, \ldots, y_n)$, where only the source or target sentences appear consecutively. Therefore, either Japanese-only or English-only sentences appear consecutively.

En-Ja Concatenating a Japanese translation immediately after each English sentence, making it parallel data only in the En ⇒ Ja.

Ja-En Concatenating an English translation immediately after each Japanese sentence, making it parallel data only in the Ja ⇒ En.

Mix Randomly sampling 10.4M, which is 50% from the total of 20.8M, from the En-Ja and Ja-En without duplication.

[5] https://huggingface.co/google/mt5-large

[6] https://github.com/google/sentencepiece

[7] https://github.com/microsoft/DeepSpeed

Metrics		Baseline models		Continual pre-training + Supervised fine-tuning							
				Mono		En-Ja		Ja-En		Mix	
		Transformer	Direct-SFT	full	LoRA	full	LoRA	full	LoRA	full	LoRA
BLEU	Avg.	13.9	12.2	6.3	5.9	15.4	**15.5**	7.3	7.2	14.7	14.9
	# Sig.	-	1	0	0	8	**9**	0	0	7	8
COMET	Avg.	79.0	79.6	75.6	74.8	**83.5**	83.3	76.9	76.8	82.9	82.9
	# Sig.	-	7	0	0	**8**	**8**	0	0	**8**	**8**

(a) En ⇒ Ja

Metrics		Baseline models		Continual pre-training + Supervised fine-tuning							
				Mono		En-Ja		Ja-En		Mix	
		Transformer	Direct-SFT	full	LoRA	full	LoRA	full	LoRA	full	LoRA
BLEU	Avg.	**17.3**	12.5	7.9	7.1	7.8	7.6	17.0	17.0	15.9	15.8
	# Sig.	-	0	0	0	0	0	0	0	0	0
COMET	Avg.	76.4	75.0	70.4	69.7	70.3	70.0	**77.8**	**77.7**	77.1	76.9
	# Sig.	-	0	0	0	0	0	**7**	6	5	5

(b) Ja ⇒ En

Table 1: Results of Baseline models and models continually pre-trained with four orders described in Section 4.2.2 then supervised fine-tuning. "Avg." represents the average result across 12 test sets, "# Sig." indicates the number of test sets showing significant differences from Transformer ($p < 0.05$), and full represents full fine-tuning. **Bold numbers** represent the highest scores in each line, and scores that surpass the Transformer are emphasized in green .

4.3 Hyperparameters

4.3.1 Continual Pre-Training

We use the AdamW optimizer, with $\beta_1 = 0.9, \beta_2 = 0.95, \epsilon = 1.0 \times 10^{-8}$. The context length is 2048, the same as when pre-training rinna-4b from scratch, and training is conducted for 1 epoch. We perform validation every 100 training steps. We use a cosine learning rate schedule with a warmup ratio of 1% and a peak learning rate of 1.5×10^{-4}. We use a weight decay of 0.1 and gradient clipping of 1.0. We utilize two NVIDIA RTX A6000 GPUs, processing 1 batch on each GPU with a gradient accumulation step of 128, achieving an adequate batch size 256. During training, bfloat16 precision, gradient checkpointing, and deepspeed ZeRO stage 2 are employed. With these configurations, it takes 10 days.

4.3.2 Supervised Fine-tuning

We perform supervised fine-tuning on the model that achieves the minimum validation loss in continual pre-training. We change the AdamW optimizer's parameter used in Section 4.3.1 only $\beta_2 = 0.95$ to $\beta_2 = 0.999$. Weight decay and gradient clipping are the same as Section 4.3.1. The peak learning rate is set to 3.0×10^{-5} for full fine-tuning and 2.0×10^{-4} for LoRA tuning, with a warmup ratio of 1% using an inverse square schedule. For LoRA, we set $r = 16, \alpha = 32$, and dropout to 0.05, applying to the linear layers of query, key, and value in the multi-head attention, resulting in approximately 6.4M trainable parameters corresponding to 0.17% of the rinna-4b's parameters. We conduct validation every 10% of the total training steps for Direct-SFT only, with 1 epoch and a batch size of 256. For all other cases, validation is performed every 100 training steps, with 5 epoch and the batch size of 64.

4.3.3 Inference

All models use the one with the minimum validation loss for inference, applying bfloat16. The Transformer, which has fewer parameters than the rinna-4b, employs beam search with a beam size of 4 due to its smaller number of parameters. At the same time, the rinna-4b-based models use greedy decoding with the prompt described in Section **??** for inference.

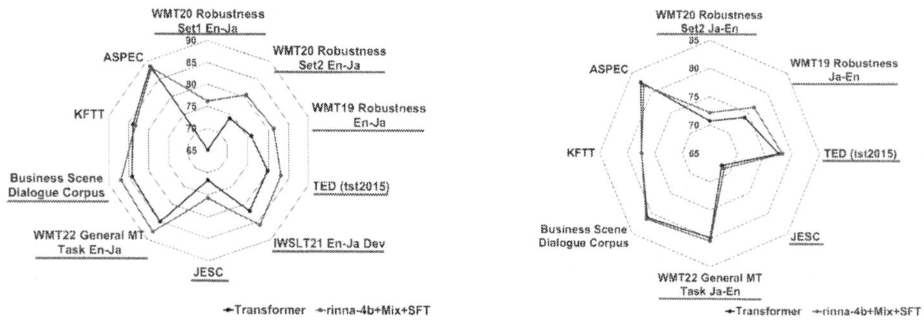

(a) En ⇒ Ja (b) Ja ⇒ En

Figure 1: Radar chart of COMET score. Blue line indicates the accuracy of the Transformer, while red line represents the accuracy of the model continually pre-trained with Mix format followed by supervised fine-tuning with full weight. Underlines indicate test sets with a significant difference compared to the Transformer ($p < 0.05$).

4.4 Metrics

We use BLEU[8] (Papineni et al., 2002) and COMET[9] (Rei et al., 2022) as evaluation metrics. We use `Unbabel/wmt22-comet-da` as COMET model.

5 Results

5.1 The Impact of Source and Target Sentences Order

Table 1 presents the results of baseline models compared to models continually pre-trained with three orders described in Section 4.2.2 and then supervised fine-tuning. All results of Table 1 can be found in Table 7 and Table 8 of Appendix D. Direct-SFT, which is directly fine-tuned, and Mono, which was pre-trained with parallel data treated as monolingual data, exhibit lower accuracy than the Transformer. On the other hand, continual pre-training improves accuracy only in the translation direction aligned with the parallel data. Therefore, continual pre-training with data where source and target sentences appear alternately is necessary to achieve high accuracy. Despite data in both the En ⇒ Ja and Ja ⇒ En translation directions, Mix exhibits improved accuracy, even though the input data's translation direction is inconsistent. This result suggests that LLMs can leverage the knowledge of the translation direction matching the order of the source and target sentences, and they can utilize the knowledge acquired from parallel sentences mixed in the training data.

[8] https://github.com/mjpost/sacrebleu
[9] https://github.com/Unbabel/COMET

5.2 Accuracy Comparison Across Test Sets

Figure 1 shows a radar chart of the COMET score of a model in which the Transformer and rinna-4b are continually pre-trained as a Mix, followed by supervised fine-tuning with full weight. In particular, the LLM-based translation model significantly outperforms the Transformer on the WMT19, 20 Robustness Task for the Reddit domain, and on the TED (tst2015), IWSLT21 En-Ja Dev, and JESC for the TED Talk and movie subtitles domains. This result suggests that the LLM-based translation model is more robust than the traditional encoder-decoder model regarding data containing spoken language.

6 Discussion

6.1 Data Format in Continual Pre-Training

Mixing data from two translation directions, as in the case of Mix, improves accuracy for both translation directions, allowing one model to be used for both. However, the accuracy is lower than continual pre-training with data from only one translation direction. Therefore, we investigate methods to enhance translation accuracy by explicitly indicating the translation direction for the data used in continual pre-training. Drawing inspiration from studies incorporating parallel data during pre-training from scratch, we conduct experiments on the following four formats.

Interleaved Translations This format directly concatenates the source and target sentences (Briakou et al., 2023), identical to the Mix described in Section 4.2.2.

Prefixed This format involves inserting the prefix written in the source sentence's language before the

Metrics		Transformer	Interleaved full	Interleaved LoRA	Prefix full	Prefix LoRA	Tagged full	Tagged LoRA	JSON full	JSON LoRA
BLEU	Avg.	13.9	14.7	14.9	15.1	**15.3**	15.0	15.1	14.2	14.9
	# Sig.	-	-	-	4	4	**6**	2	1	1
COMET	Avg.	79.0	82.9	82.9	83.0	**83.3**	83.2	**83.3**	82.1	82.9
	# Sig.	-	-	-	0	**5**	4	4	0	1

(a) En ⇒ Ja

Metrics		Transformer	Interleaved full	Interleaved LoRA	Prefix full	Prefix LoRA	Tagged full	Tagged LoRA	JSON full	JSON LoRA
BLEU	Avg.	16.8	15.9	15.8	16.3	16.1	16.2	**16.3**	15.5	15.8
	# Sig.	-	-	-	0	0	0	0	0	0
COMET	Avg.	76.4	77.1	76.9	**77.4**	77.2	77.3	77.2	76.9	76.9
	# Sig.	-	-	-	**3**	**3**	**3**	1	0	0

(b) Ja ⇒ En

Table 2: Results of Transformer and models continually pre-trained with four formats described in Section 6.1 then supervised fine-tuning. "# Sig." denotes the number of test sets showing significant differences for both Transformer and models continually pre-trained with Interleaved Translations (Interleaved), followed by supervised fine-tuning using the same fine-tuning method ($p < 0.05$). "Avg.", **bold numbers**, and green numbers follow the same conventions as Table 1.

Continual pre-training	Supervised fine-tuning	En ⇒ Ja (Average) BLEU	En ⇒ Ja (Average) COMET	Ja ⇒ En (Average) BLEU	Ja ⇒ En (Average) COMET
×	×	0.6	40.2	0.8	46.0
✓	×	8.2	69.9	9.9	69.3
×	✓	6.5	76.4	8.0	70.9
✓	✓	**15.0**	**83.2**	**16.2**	**77.3**

Table 3: Results of all combinations of continual pre-training and supervised fine-tuning. Continual pre-training is conducted in Tagged format mentioned in Section 6.1, and supervised fine-tuning is performed with full weight, utilizing the small amount of high-quality data and prompts described in Section 4.1.2. "✓" indicates whether continued pre-training or supervised fine-tuning is conducted. In contrast, "×" indicates the absence of either. **Bold numbers** indicate the maximum score in each column. When supervised fine-tuning is conducted, inference is undergone with zero-shot, while inference is performed with five-shot for other cases.

source sentence, followed by the concatenation of the target sentence (Kale et al., 2021). For En ⇒ Ja, the prefix "translate to Japanese: " is used, while for Ja ⇒ En, "英語に翻訳してください: " is employed.

Tagged This format involves inserting a tag before the source sentence that indicates the target sentence's language, such as "<2en>" and "<2ja>" (Schioppa et al., 2023).

JSON The JSON format is {"L1": {source}, "L2": {target}}, where "source" represents the source sentence, "target" represents the target sentence, and "L1", "L2" are the names of the source and target sentence's languages written in the source sentence's language.[10]

We conduct continual pre-training with these four formats and perform supervised fine-tuning under the same conditions as Section 4. All formats are conducted in the Mix format described in Section 4.2.2, with the continual pre-training data for En ⇒ Ja and Ja ⇒ En fixed to be the same. Table 2 presents the results of the Transformer and models continually pre-trained with the four formats. Among the four formats, Prefix and Tagged showed significant differences in BLEU and COMET metrics compared to the Transformer, and the models are continually pre-trained in the in-

[10]Given that the pre-training data for rinna-4b includes source code, this format aims to transfer the knowledge obtained from the source code to translation.

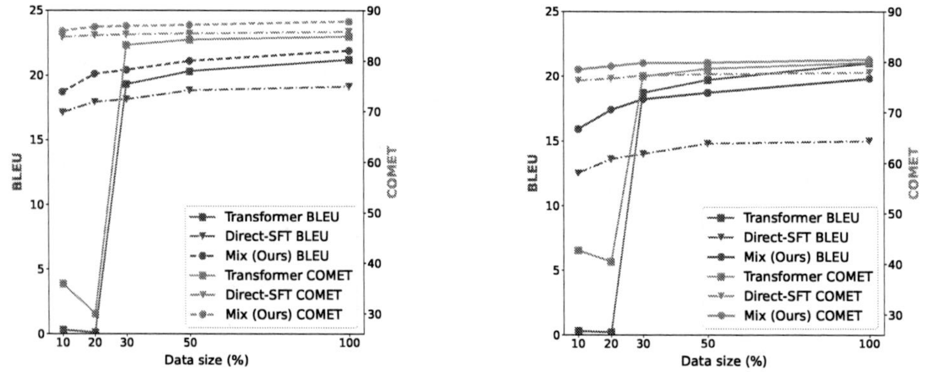

(a) En ⇒ Ja (b) Ja ⇒ En

Figure 2: Data curves for BLEU and COMET scores on WMT22 test data for Transformer, Direct-SFT, and Mix. Mix has been evaluated after completing supervised fine-tuning with LoRA tuning following continual pre-training. We experimented with data amounts of 10%, 20%, 30%, 50%, and 100% due to computational resource constraints. For the Transformer, we varied the proportion of data from JParaCrawl v3.0. At the same time, for Direct-SFT and Mix, since training was conducted for only one epoch, we consider the proportion of checkpoints equal to that of the training data and report the accuracy for each checkpoint.

terleaved translations format. This result suggests that the prefixed or tagged format demonstrates higher accuracy than interleaved translation, where source and target sentences are concatenated, indicating that from the convenience perspective, the Tagged format can achieve the highest accuracy most easily. Whether these formats can be applied to other translation directions and models remains a matter of our future work.

6.2 Effectiveness of Continual Pre-Training and Supervised Fine-Tuning

As an ablation study, we experiment with all combinations of continual pre-training and supervised fine-tuning. When supervised fine-tuning is conducted, the inference is made with a zero-shot, while for other cases, the inference is performed with a five-shot. We randomly sample five translation examples from the WMT21 test data for five-shot, and the same set of five samples is fixed for all inferences. Continual pre-training is conducted in the Tagged format as described in Section 6.1, and all inferences utilize the prompts described in Section 4.1.2 and employ bfloat16 precision and greedy decoding. Table 3 presents the results, while all results are shown in Table 10 of Appendix D. These results suggest that achieving high accuracy is most feasible when both continual pre-training and supervised fine-tuning are conducted while achieving high accuracy solely through continual pre-training or supervised fine-tuning alone is challenging.

6.3 How Much Parallel Data is Needed?

Figure 2 presents the data curves for these three models at 10%, 20%, 30%, 50%, and 100% data usage on the WMT22 test data. For the Transformer model, only the sampling rate from JParaCrawl v3.0 varies, while other settings remain the same as described in Section 4.2.1. As mentioned in Section 4.3, Direct-SFT performs supervised fine-tuning for one epoch, and Mix also performs continual pre-training for one epoch. Therefore, for these two models, the proportion of training data is equivalent to the proportion of checkpoints, and we report the accuracy for the checkpoints at 10%, 20%, 30%, 50%, and 100%. The Transformer shows very low accuracy, up to 10% and 20%, but there is a significant improvement in accuracy at 30%, after which the increase becomes gradual. When at 20%, the accuracy decreased compared to at 10%, possibly due to the instability in learning caused by the smaller data. On the other hand, Direct-SFT and Mix demonstrate significantly better accuracy at 10% and 20% compared to the Transformer, and like the Transformer, the accuracy increases gradually from 30% onwards. These results suggest that LLM-based translation models can achieve higher accuracy with less training data than supervised encoder-decoder models. Additionally, COMET scores for all three models show a gradual increase in accuracy from 30%, while BLEU scores con-

Source	So, what started as a bit of an inside joke with myself and a willful provocation, as become a thing.
Reference	ちょっとした自虐ネタで 気の利いた挑発をしたつもりが 社会現象にまで なってしまいました (What started as a bit of self-deprecating humor and a clever provocation has turned into a social phenomenon.)
Transformer 69.8	だから、私とのちょっとした内輪の冗談と意図的な挑発として始まったことは、ものになりました。 (So what started as a little inside joke and intentional provocation with me has become a thing.)
Mix (Ours) 77.8	それで、私と故意の挑発でちょっとした内輪の冗談から始まったものが、今では物議をかもすものになりました。 (So what started as a little inside joke between me and a deliberate provocation has now become a controversial thing.)

(a) IWSLT21 Simultaneous Translation En-Ja Dev

Source	It's a complex topic, so we're just going to dive right in at a complex place: New Jersey.
Reference	複雑なトピックですから 前置きはさておき 複雑な所から始めましょう ニュージャージー州です (It is a complex topic, so let us skip the introduction and start with the complicated place. New Jersey.)
Transformer 82.4	それは複雑なトピックなので、私たちは複雑な場所に飛び込むつもりです:ニュージャージー。 (It is a complex topic, so we are going to jump into a complex place:New Jersey.)
Mix (Ours) 88.4	複雑な話題なので、まずはニュージャージー州の複雑な場所から始めよう。 (It is a complex topic, so let us start with the complicated places in New Jersey.)

(b) TED (tst2015)

Table 4: Specific En ⇒ Ja translation results from the two test set comprising TED Talks domains. The numbers under the model names indicate the COMET scores, and the English text below the Japanese sentences shows the back-translations into English. The phrases requiring free translation and the corresponding reference and model output phrases are highlighted in red for source sentences. The results for Mix indicate that supervised fine-tuning with full weight is performed after continual pre-training.

tinue to improve even after 30%. This suggests that at least 3M sentence pairs are needed for the translation model to output sentences containing the same meaning as the reference, whereas more parallel data than the 10.4M sentence pairs is required to output sentences containing the exact words as the reference.

6.4 Specific Results of Spoken Language

To analyze the differences in translation between the LLM-based model and the encoder-decoder model for spoken language, Table 4 presents En ⇒ Ja translation examples from two test sets comprising TED Talks domain. In these two examples, the LLM-based translation model has achieved higher COMET scores than the Transformer. In Table 4a, the source sentence contains the phrase "a thing," which the reference translates as "社会現象" (a social phenomenon). In contrast, the Transformer translates "a thing" literally as "もの", and the LLM-based model translates it as "物議をかもすもの" (a controversial thing). Additionally, in Table 4b, the source sentence includes the word "dive," which the reference translates as "始めましょう" (let us start). The Transformer translates "dive" literally as "飛び込む" (jump into), whereas the LLM-based model correctly translates it as "始めよう" (let us start). These results suggest that the LLM-based translation model can perform free translation better than the traditional encoder-decoder model.

7 Conclusion

We propose a two-phase training approach comprising continual pre-training with interleaved source and target sentence data, followed by supervised fine-tuning using a small amount of high-quality parallel data. Our investigation comprehensively explores methods for enhancing translation accuracy through continual pre-training across eight data formats. Evaluation across 13 test sets reveals that models trained with continual pre-training followed by supervised fine-tuning outperform those supervised fine-tuned solely on parallel data. Furthermore, we observe variations in language direction accuracy improvement during continual pre-training based on the order of source and target sentences. We also demonstrate that LLM-based translation models are more robust in translating sentences containing spoken language, and achieve higher accuracy with less training data, compared to traditional encoder-decoder models. Additionally, augmenting source sentences with tags or using prefixes yields higher accuracy than simple concatenation. In larger LLMs than the rinna-4b model we utilized, such as LLaMA-2 7B and 13B, LoRA enables training with fewer computational resources. LoRA has been reported to be effective in translation tasks (Zhang et al., 2023; Guo et al., 2024). Therefore, it is essential to experiment with LoRA in the future to determine if similar results can be achieved and to investigate if similar results can be obtained with other LLMs.

8 Limitations

Our experiments and conclusions are based only on two translation directions (English-to-Japanese, Japanese-to-English) and `rinna/bilingual-gpt-neox-4b`, which is an LLM pre-trained in English and Japanese. Evaluation for other translation directions and LLMs has yet to be conducted. While in Section 6.3, we demonstrated that continual pre-training requires 3M parallel data, we anticipate that this may vary depending on the translation direction and model. Whether our approach applies to LLMs primarily pre-trained in English, such as XGLM and LLaMA, remains unverified, especially in low resource languages is challenging. Additionally, all the experiments are conducted using only the parameters described in Section 4.3, and an optimal hyperparameter search still needs to be performed. Especially in Direct-SFT, it should be noted that the importance of hyperparameters has been highlighted by Dettmers et al. (2023), and whether full fine-tuning and LoRA tuning demonstrate the same performance varies depending on the model, hyperparameters, and task.

9 Ethical statement

We have not conducted verification on significant risks associated with our research. While we propose a method that may enhance translation accuracy using LLMs, it is worth noting that Zhu et al. (2024) have reported GPT-4's 8-shot translation accuracy to be comparable to or below that of existing methods such as supervised encoder-decoder models. Therefore, even if the proposed method is applied to other LLMs, we do not think that there is a potential risk that the proposed method achieves too high translation accuracy so that it is to be abused.

This study uses a dataset from Morishita et al. (2022), available only for research and development purposes, inheriting potential biases from their datasets. We utilize open-source pre-trained LLM, and our experimental codes also leverage open-source libraries, as mentioned in Section 4. Therefore, this study's models, data, and tools adhere to the intended usages of those models, data, and tools.

References

Farhad Akhbardeh, Arkady Arkhangorodsky, Magdalena Biesialska, Ondřej Bojar, Rajen Chatterjee, Vishrav Chaudhary, Marta R. Costa-jussa, Cristina España-Bonet, Angela Fan, Christian Federmann, Markus Freitag, Yvette Graham, Roman Grundkiewicz, Barry Haddow, Leonie Harter, Kenneth Heafield, Christopher Homan, Matthias Huck, Kwabena Amponsah-Kaakyire, Jungo Kasai, Daniel Khashabi, Kevin Knight, Tom Kocmi, Philipp Koehn, Nicholas Lourie, Christof Monz, Makoto Morishita, Masaaki Nagata, Ajay Nagesh, Toshiaki Nakazawa, Matteo Negri, Santanu Pal, Allahsera Auguste Tapo, Marco Turchi, Valentin Vydrin, and Marcos Zampieri. 2021. Findings of the 2021 conference on machine translation (WMT21). In *Proceedings of the Sixth Conference on Machine Translation*, pages 1–88, Online. Association for Computational Linguistics.

Duarte M. Alves, José Pombal, Nuno M. Guerreiro, Pedro H. Martins, João Alves, Amin Farajian, Ben Peters, Ricardo Rei, Patrick Fernandes, Sweta Agrawal, Pierre Colombo, José G. C. de Souza, and André F. T. Martins. 2024. Tower: An open multilingual large language model for translation-related tasks. *arXiv:2402.17733*.

Antonios Anastasopoulos, Ondřej Bojar, Jacob Bremerman, Roldano Cattoni, Maha Elbayad, Marcello Federico, Xutai Ma, Satoshi Nakamura, Matteo Negri, Jan Niehues, Juan Pino, Elizabeth Salesky, Sebastian Stüker, Katsuhito Sudoh, Marco Turchi, Alexander Waibel, Changhan Wang, and Matthew Wiesner. 2021. FINDINGS OF THE IWSLT 2021 EVALUATION CAMPAIGN. In *Proceedings of the 18th International Conference on Spoken Language Translation (IWSLT 2021)*, pages 1–29, Bangkok, Thailand (online). Association for Computational Linguistics.

Marta Bañón, Pinzhen Chen, Barry Haddow, Kenneth Heafield, Hieu Hoang, Miquel Esplà-Gomis, Mikel L. Forcada, Amir Kamran, Faheem Kirefu, Philipp Koehn, Sergio Ortiz Rojas, Leopoldo Pla Sempere, Gema Ramírez-Sánchez, Elsa Sarrías, Marek Strelec, Brian Thompson, William Waites, Dion Wiggins, and Jaume Zaragoza. 2020. ParaCrawl: Web-scale acquisition of parallel corpora. In *Proceedings of the 58th Annual Meeting of the Association for Computational Linguistics*, pages 4555–4567, Online. Association for Computational Linguistics.

Loïc Barrault, Magdalena Biesialska, Ondřej Bojar, Marta R. Costa-jussà, Christian Federmann, Yvette Graham, Roman Grundkiewicz, Barry Haddow, Matthias Huck, Eric Joanis, Tom Kocmi, Philipp Koehn, Chi-kiu Lo, Nikola Ljubešić, Christof Monz, Makoto Morishita, Masaaki Nagata, Toshiaki Nakazawa, Santanu Pal, Matt Post, and Marcos Zampieri. 2020. Findings of the 2020 conference on machine translation (WMT20). In *Proceedings of the Fifth Conference on Machine Translation*, pages 1–55, Online. Association for Computational Linguistics.

Eleftheria Briakou, Colin Cherry, and George Foster. 2023. Searching for needles in a haystack: On the role of incidental bilingualism in PaLM's translation capability. In *Proceedings of the 61st Annual Meeting of the Association for Computational Linguistics (Volume 1: Long Papers)*, pages 9432–9452, Toronto, Canada. Association for Computational Linguistics.

Tom Brown, Benjamin Mann, Nick Ryder, Melanie Subbiah, Jared D Kaplan, Prafulla Dhariwal, Arvind Neelakantan, Pranav Shyam, Girish Sastry, Amanda Askell, Sandhini Agarwal, Ariel Herbert-Voss, Gretchen Krueger, Tom Henighan, Rewon Child, Aditya Ramesh, Daniel Ziegler, Jeffrey Wu, Clemens Winter, Chris Hesse, Mark Chen, Eric Sigler, Mateusz Litwin, Scott Gray, Benjamin Chess, Jack Clark, Christopher Berner, Sam McCandlish, Alec Radford, Ilya Sutskever, and Dario Amodei. 2020. Language models are few-shot learners. In *Advances in Neural Information Processing Systems*, volume 33, pages 1877–1901. Curran Associates, Inc.

Mauro Cettolo, Christian Girardi, and Marcello Federico. 2012. WIT3: Web inventory of transcribed and translated talks. In *Proceedings of the 16th Annual Conference of the European Association for Machine Translation*, pages 261–268, Trento, Italy. European Association for Machine Translation.

Tianqi Chen, Bing Xu, Chiyuan Zhang, and Carlos Guestrin. 2016. Training deep nets with sublinear memory cost. *arXiv:1604.06174*.

Aakanksha Chowdhery, Sharan Narang, Jacob Devlin, Maarten Bosma, Gaurav Mishra, Adam Roberts, Paul Barham, Hyung Won Chung, Charles Sutton, Sebastian Gehrmann, Parker Schuh, Kensen Shi, Sasha Tsvyashchenko, Joshua Maynez, Abhishek Rao, Parker Barnes, Yi Tay, Noam Shazeer, Vinodkumar Prabhakaran, Emily Reif, Nan Du, Ben Hutchinson, Reiner Pope, James Bradbury, Jacob Austin, Michael Isard, Guy Gur-Ari, Pengcheng Yin, Toju Duke, Anselm Levskaya, Sanjay Ghemawat, Sunipa Dev, Henryk Michalewski, Xavier Garcia, Vedant Misra, Kevin Robinson, Liam Fedus, Denny Zhou, Daphne Ippolito, David Luan, Hyeontaek Lim, Barret Zoph, Alexander Spiridonov, Ryan Sepassi, David Dohan, Shivani Agrawal, Mark Omernick, Andrew M. Dai, Thanumalayan Sankaranarayana Pillai, Marie Pellat, Aitor Lewkowycz, Erica Moreira, Rewon Child, Oleksandr Polozov, Katherine Lee, Zongwei Zhou, Xuezhi Wang, Brennan Saeta, Mark Diaz, Orhan Firat, Michele Catasta, Jason Wei, Kathy Meier-Hellstern, Douglas Eck, Jeff Dean, Slav Petrov, and Noah Fiedel. 2022. PaLM: Scaling language modeling with pathways. *arXiv:2204.02311*.

Yiming Cui, Ziqing Yang, and Xin Yao. 2023. Efficient and effective text encoding for chinese llama and alpaca. *arXiv:2304.08177*.

Tim Dettmers, Artidoro Pagnoni, Ari Holtzman, and Luke Zettlemoyer. 2023. QLoRA: Efficient finetuning of quantized llms. *arXiv:2305.14314*.

Jacob Devlin, Ming-Wei Chang, Kenton Lee, and Kristina Toutanova. 2019. BERT: Pre-training of deep bidirectional transformers for language understanding. In *Proceedings of the 2019 Conference of the North American Chapter of the Association for Computational Linguistics: Human Language Technologies, Volume 1 (Long and Short Papers)*, pages 4171–4186, Minneapolis, Minnesota. Association for Computational Linguistics.

Jiaxin Guo, Hao Yang, Zongyao Li, Daimeng Wei, Hengchao Shang, and Xiaoyu Chen. 2024. A novel paradigm boosting translation capabilities of large language models. In *Findings of the Association for Computational Linguistics: NAACL 2024*, pages 639–649, Mexico City, Mexico. Association for Computational Linguistics.

Amr Hendy, Mohamed Abdelrehim, Amr Sharaf, Vikas Raunak, Mohamed Gabr, Hitokazu Matsushita, Young Jin Kim, Mohamed Afify, and Hany Hassan Awadalla. 2023. How good are GPT models at machine translation? a comprehensive evaluation. *arXiv:2302.09210*.

Edward J Hu, yelong shen, Phillip Wallis, Zeyuan Allen-Zhu, Yuanzhi Li, Shean Wang, Lu Wang, and Weizhu Chen. 2022. LoRA: Low-rank adaptation of large language models. In *International Conference on Learning Representations*.

Xisen Jin, Dejiao Zhang, Henghui Zhu, Wei Xiao, Shang-Wen Li, Xiaokai Wei, Andrew Arnold, and Xiang Ren. 2022. Lifelong pretraining: Continually adapting language models to emerging corpora. In *Proceedings of BigScience Episode #5 – Workshop on Challenges & Perspectives in Creating Large Language Models*, pages 1–16, virtual+Dublin. Association for Computational Linguistics.

Mihir Kale, Aditya Siddhant, Rami Al-Rfou, Linting Xue, Noah Constant, and Melvin Johnson. 2021. nmT5 - is parallel data still relevant for pre-training massively multilingual language models? In *Proceedings of the 59th Annual Meeting of the Association for Computational Linguistics and the 11th International Joint Conference on Natural Language Processing (Volume 2: Short Papers)*, pages 683–691, Online. Association for Computational Linguistics.

Zixuan Ke, Haowei Lin, Yijia Shao, Hu Xu, Lei Shu, and Bing Liu. 2022. Continual training of language models for few-shot learning. In *Proceedings of the 2022 Conference on Empirical Methods in Natural Language Processing*, pages 10205–10216, Abu Dhabi, United Arab Emirates. Association for Computational Linguistics.

Tom Kocmi, Eleftherios Avramidis, Rachel Bawden, Ondřej Bojar, Anton Dvorkovich, Christian Federmann, Mark Fishel, Markus Freitag, Thamme Gowda, Roman Grundkiewicz, Barry Haddow, Philipp Koehn, Benjamin Marie, Christof Monz, Makoto Morishita, Kenton Murray, Makoto Nagata, Toshiaki Nakazawa, Martin Popel, Maja Popović, and Mariya Shmatova. 2023. Findings of the 2023 conference on machine translation (WMT23): LLMs are here but not quite there yet. In *Proceedings of the Eighth Conference on Machine Translation*, pages 1–42, Singapore. Association for Computational Linguistics.

Tom Kocmi, Rachel Bawden, Ondřej Bojar, Anton Dvorkovich, Christian Federmann, Mark Fishel, Thamme Gowda, Yvette Graham, Roman Grundkiewicz, Barry Haddow, Rebecca Knowles, Philipp Koehn, Christof Monz, Makoto Morishita, Masaaki Nagata, Toshiaki Nakazawa, Michal Novák, Martin Popel, and Maja Popović. 2022. Findings of the 2022 conference on machine translation (WMT22). In *Proceedings of the Seventh Conference on Machine Translation (WMT)*, pages 1–45, Abu Dhabi, United Arab Emirates (Hybrid). Association for Computational Linguistics.

Taku Kudo and John Richardson. 2018. SentencePiece: A simple and language independent subword tokenizer and detokenizer for neural text processing. In *Proceedings of the 2018 Conference on Empirical Methods in Natural Language Processing: System Demonstrations*, pages 66–71, Brussels, Belgium. Association for Computational Linguistics.

Xian Li, Paul Michel, Antonios Anastasopoulos, Yonatan Belinkov, Nadir Durrani, Orhan Firat, Philipp Koehn, Graham Neubig, Juan Pino, and Hassan Sajjad. 2019. Findings of the first shared task on machine translation robustness. In *Proceedings of the Fourth Conference on Machine Translation (Volume 2: Shared Task Papers, Day 1)*, pages 91–102, Florence, Italy. Association for Computational Linguistics.

Yinhan Liu, Jiatao Gu, Naman Goyal, Xian Li, Sergey Edunov, Marjan Ghazvininejad, Mike Lewis, and Luke Zettlemoyer. 2020. Multilingual denoising pretraining for neural machine translation. *Transactions of the Association for Computational Linguistics*, 8:726–742.

Yinhan Liu, Myle Ott, Naman Goyal, Jingfei Du, Mandar Joshi, Danqi Chen, Omer Levy, Mike Lewis, Luke Zettlemoyer, and Veselin Stoyanov. 2019. RoBERTa: A robustly optimized BERT pretraining approach. *arXiv:1907.11692*.

Ilya Loshchilov and Frank Hutter. 2019. Decoupled weight decay regularization. In *International Conference on Learning Representations*.

Zhuoyuan Mao and Tetsuji Nakagawa. 2023. LEALLA: Learning lightweight language-agnostic sentence embeddings with knowledge distillation. In *Proceedings of the 17th Conference of the European Chapter of the Association for Computational Linguistics*, pages 1886–1894, Dubrovnik, Croatia. Association for Computational Linguistics.

Makoto Morishita, Katsuki Chousa, Jun Suzuki, and Masaaki Nagata. 2022. JParaCrawl v3.0: A large-scale English-Japanese parallel corpus. In *Proceedings of the Thirteenth Language Resources and Evaluation Conference*, pages 6704–6710, Marseille, France. European Language Resources Association.

Toshiaki Nakazawa, Manabu Yaguchi, Kiyotaka Uchimoto, Masao Utiyama, Eiichiro Sumita, Sadao Kurohashi, and Hitoshi Isahara. 2016. ASPEC: Asian scientific paper excerpt corpus. In *Proceedings of the Tenth International Conference on Language Resources and Evaluation (LREC'16)*, pages 2204–2208, Portorož, Slovenia. European Language Resources Association (ELRA).

Graham Neubig. 2011. The Kyoto free translation task. `http://www.phontron.com/kftt`.

NLLB Team, Marta R. Costa-jussà, James Cross, Onur Çelebi, Maha Elbayad, Kenneth Heafield, Kevin Heffernan, Elahe Kalbassi, Janice Lam, Daniel Licht, Jean Maillard, Anna Sun, Skyler Wang, Guillaume Wenzek, Al Youngblood, Bapi Akula, Loic Barrault, Gabriel Mejia Gonzalez, Prangthip Hansanti, John Hoffman, Semarley Jarrett, Kaushik Ram Sadagopan, Dirk Rowe, Shannon Spruit, Chau Tran, Pierre Andrews, Necip Fazil Ayan, Shruti Bhosale, Sergey Edunov, Angela Fan, Cynthia Gao, Vedanuj Goswami, Francisco Guzmán, Philipp Koehn, Alexandre Mourachko, Christophe Ropers, Safiyyah Saleem, Holger Schwenk, and Jeff Wang. 2022. No language left behind: Scaling human-centered machine translation. *arXiv:2207.04672*.

OpenAI. 2023. GPT-4 technical report. *arXiv:2303.08774*.

Kishore Papineni, Salim Roukos, Todd Ward, and Wei-Jing Zhu. 2002. Bleu: a method for automatic evaluation of machine translation. In *Proceedings of the 40th Annual Meeting of the Association for Computational Linguistics*, pages 311–318, Philadelphia, Pennsylvania, USA. Association for Computational Linguistics.

Razvan Pascanu, Tomas Mikolov, and Yoshua Bengio. 2013. On the difficulty of training recurrent neural networks. In *Proceedings of the 30th International Conference on Machine Learning*, volume 28, pages 1310–1318, Atlanta, Georgia, USA. PMLR.

Reid Pryzant, Youngjoo Chung, Dan Jurafsky, and Denny Britz. 2018. JESC: Japanese-English subtitle corpus. In *Proceedings of the Eleventh International Conference on Language Resources and Evaluation (LREC 2018)*, Miyazaki, Japan. European Language Resources Association (ELRA).

Alec Radford, Karthik Narasimhan, Tim Salimans, and Ilya Sutskever. 2018. Improving language understanding by generative pre-training. *Technical report*.

Jeff Rasley, Samyam Rajbhandari, Olatunji Ruwase, and Yuxiong He. 2020. Deepspeed: System optimizations enable training deep learning models with over 100 billion parameters. In *Proceedings of the 26th*

ACM SIGKDD International Conference on Knowledge Discovery & Data Mining, page 3505–3506, New York, NY, USA. Association for Computing Machinery.

Ricardo Rei, José G. C. de Souza, Duarte Alves, Chrysoula Zerva, Ana C Farinha, Taisiya Glushkova, Alon Lavie, Luisa Coheur, and André F. T. Martins. 2022. COMET-22: Unbabel-IST 2022 submission for the metrics shared task. In *Proceedings of the Seventh Conference on Machine Translation (WMT)*, pages 578–585, Abu Dhabi, United Arab Emirates (Hybrid). Association for Computational Linguistics.

Matīss Rikters, Ryokan Ri, Tong Li, and Toshiaki Nakazawa. 2019. Designing the business conversation corpus. In *Proceedings of the 6th Workshop on Asian Translation*, pages 54–61, Hong Kong, China. Association for Computational Linguistics.

Andrea Schioppa, Xavier Garcia, and Orhan Firat. 2023. Cross-lingual supervision improves large language models pre-training. *arXiv:2305.11778*.

Thomas Scialom, Tuhin Chakrabarty, and Smaranda Muresan. 2022. Fine-tuned language models are continual learners. In *Proceedings of the 2022 Conference on Empirical Methods in Natural Language Processing*, pages 6107–6122, Abu Dhabi, United Arab Emirates. Association for Computational Linguistics.

Noam Shazeer. 2020. GLU variants improve transformer. *arXiv:2002.05202*.

Lucia Specia, Zhenhao Li, Juan Pino, Vishrav Chaudhary, Francisco Guzmán, Graham Neubig, Nadir Durrani, Yonatan Belinkov, Philipp Koehn, Hassan Sajjad, Paul Michel, and Xian Li. 2020. Findings of the WMT 2020 shared task on machine translation robustness. In *Proceedings of the Fifth Conference on Machine Translation*, pages 76–91, Online. Association for Computational Linguistics.

Nitish Srivastava, Geoffrey Hinton, Alex Krizhevsky, Ilya Sutskever, and Ruslan Salakhutdinov. 2014. Dropout: A simple way to prevent neural networks from overfitting. *Journal of Machine Learning Research*, 15(56):1929–1958.

Christian Szegedy, Vincent Vanhoucke, Sergey Ioffe, Jon Shlens, and Zbigniew Wojna. 2016. Rethinking the inception architecture for computer vision. In *2016 IEEE Conference on Computer Vision and Pattern Recognition (CVPR)*.

Brian Thompson, Mehak Preet Dhaliwal, Peter Frisch, Tobias Domhan, and Marcello Federico. 2024. A shocking amount of the web is machine translated: Insights from multi-way parallelism. *arXiv:2401.05749*.

Hugo Touvron, Louis Martin, Kevin Stone, Peter Albert, Amjad Almahairi, Yasmine Babaei, Nikolay Bashlykov, Soumya Batra, Prajjwal Bhargava, Shruti Bhosale, Dan Bikel, Lukas Blecher, Cristian Canton Ferrer, Moya Chen, Guillem Cucurull, David Esiobu, Jude Fernandes, Jeremy Fu, Wenyin Fu, Brian Fuller, Cynthia Gao, Vedanuj Goswami, Naman Goyal, Anthony Hartshorn, Saghar Hosseini, Rui Hou, Hakan Inan, Marcin Kardas, Viktor Kerkez, Madian Khabsa, Isabel Kloumann, Artem Korenev, Punit Singh Koura, Marie-Anne Lachaux, Thibaut Lavril, Jenya Lee, Diana Liskovich, Yinghai Lu, Yuning Mao, Xavier Martinet, Todor Mihaylov, Pushkar Mishra, Igor Molybog, Yixin Nie, Andrew Poulton, Jeremy Reizenstein, Rashi Rungta, Kalyan Saladi, Alan Schelten, Ruan Silva, Eric Michael Smith, Ranjan Subramanian, Xiaoqing Ellen Tan, Binh Tang, Ross Taylor, Adina Williams, Jian Xiang Kuan, Puxin Xu, Zheng Yan, Iliyan Zarov, Yuchen Zhang, Angela Fan, Melanie Kambadur, Sharan Narang, Aurelien Rodriguez, Robert Stojnic, Sergey Edunov, and Thomas Scialom. 2023. Llama 2: Open foundation and fine-tuned chat models. *arXiv:2307.09288*.

Ashish Vaswani, Noam Shazeer, Niki Parmar, Jakob Uszkoreit, Llion Jones, Aidan N Gomez, Ł ukasz Kaiser, and Illia Polosukhin. 2017. Attention is all you need. In *Advances in Neural Information Processing Systems*, volume 30. Curran Associates, Inc.

Haoran Xu, Young Jin Kim, Amr Sharaf, and Hany Hassan Awadalla. 2024a. A paradigm shift in machine translation: Boosting translation performance of large language models. In *The Twelfth International Conference on Learning Representations*.

Haoran Xu, Amr Sharaf, Yunmo Chen, Weiting Tan, Lingfeng Shen, Benjamin Van Durme, Kenton Murray, and Young Jin Kim. 2024b. Contrastive preference optimization: Pushing the boundaries of LLM performance in machine translation. In *Forty-first International Conference on Machine Learning*.

Linting Xue, Noah Constant, Adam Roberts, Mihir Kale, Rami Al-Rfou, Aditya Siddhant, Aditya Barua, and Colin Raffel. 2021. mT5: A massively multilingual pre-trained text-to-text transformer. In *Proceedings of the 2021 Conference of the North American Chapter of the Association for Computational Linguistics: Human Language Technologies*, pages 483–498, Online. Association for Computational Linguistics.

Renrui Zhang, Jiaming Han, Chris Liu, Aojun Zhou, Pan Lu, Yu Qiao, Hongsheng Li, and Peng Gao. 2024. LLaMA-adapter: Efficient fine-tuning of large language models with zero-initialized attention. In *The Twelfth International Conference on Learning Representations*.

Xuan Zhang, Navid Rajabi, Kevin Duh, and Philipp Koehn. 2023. Machine translation with large language models: Prompting, few-shot learning, and fine-tuning with QLoRA. In *Proceedings of the Eighth Conference on Machine Translation*, pages 468–481, Singapore. Association for Computational Linguistics.

Chunting Zhou, Pengfei Liu, Puxin Xu, Srini Iyer, Jiao Sun, Yuning Mao, Xuezhe Ma, Avia Efrat, Ping Yu,

LILI YU, Susan Zhang, Gargi Ghosh, Mike Lewis, Luke Zettlemoyer, and Omer Levy. 2023. LIMA: Less is more for alignment. In *Thirty-seventh Conference on Neural Information Processing Systems*.

Wenhao Zhu, Hongyi Liu, Qingxiu Dong, Jingjing Xu, Shujian Huang, Lingpeng Kong, Jiajun Chen, and Lei Li. 2024. Multilingual machine translation with large language models: Empirical results and analysis. In *Findings of the Association for Computational Linguistics: NAACL 2024*, pages 2765–2781, Mexico City, Mexico. Association for Computational Linguistics.

	En ⇒ Ja (Avg.)		Ja ⇒ En (Avg.)	
Model	BLEU	COMET	BLEU	COMET
ALMA-7B-Ja-V2	10.1	80.4	13.0	75.6
Tagged + SFT (full)	**15.0**	**83.2**	**16.2**	**77.3**

Table 5: Results of BLEU and COMET scores for ALMA-7B-Ja-V2 and the rinna-4b-based translation model. "Tagged + SFT (full)" represents the model continually pre-trained in the Tagged format as described in Section 6.1, followed by supervised fine-tuning with full weight.

A Sampling of JParaCrawl v3.0

We use 20.8M parallel sentences from JParaCrawl v3.0, initially consisting of 21.8M parallel sentences. We sample sentence pairs using cosine similarity scores between 0.4 and 0.95 based on sentence vector embeddings obtained from LEALLA-large. Parallel sentences with a similarity score below 0.4 are excluded, as a visual inspection revealed a significant presence of inappropriate samples, such as Japanese and English sentences with disproportionate lengths. Additionally, parallel sentences with similarity scores of 0.95 or higher are also excluded, as they consist of Japanese and English sentences that were nearly identical. This sampling results in 1.8B tokens when tokenized with the rinna-4b tokenizer.

B Comparison with ALMA

We compared with ALMA by using ALMA-7B-Ja-V2[11], which was trained similarly to ALMA with LLaMA-2 7B but with Russian replaced by Japanese among the languages experimented with ALMA. We compared against ALMA-Ja-V2 using the BLEU and COMET averages of 12 test sets, as shown in the Table 5. From these results, it is evident that the 3.8B LLM-based translation model outperforms the LLaMA-2-based ALMA-7B-Ja-V2. This result aligns with reports suggesting higher accuracy when using parallel data for continual pre-training (Alves et al., 2024; Guo et al., 2024) and the consistency with reports indicating that the influence of parallel data increases with fewer parameters (Kale et al., 2021; Briakou et al., 2023).

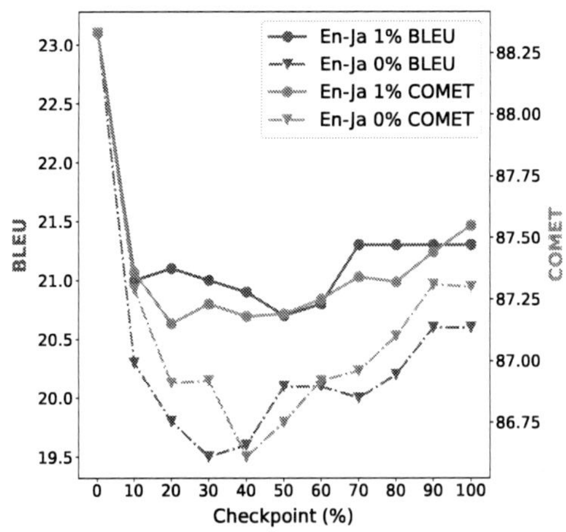

Figure 3: Data Curves for BLEU and COMET scores at each 10% checkpoint of En-Ja2Mix for En ⇒ Ja on WMT22 test data. All models at checkpoints have undergone supervised fine-tuning. The 0% on the x-axis represents the accuracy of En-Ja.

C Analyzing Catastrophic Forgetting

We conducted continual pre-training on En-Ja and then observed catastrophic forgetting by conducting continual pre-training on data, which was in the reverse direction. Based on reports suggesting preventing catastrophic forgetting by mixing data from tasks that should not be forgotten (Scialom et al., 2022), we mixed 1% of En-Ja data. This model is named En-Ja2Mix. Figure 3 shows the data curves for BLEU and COMET scores at each 10% checkpoint for En-Ja2Mix on the WMT22 test data, demonstrating En ⇒ Ja. As an ablation study, we also show the data curves for a scenario where the 1% of En-Ja data added to En-Ja2Mix is removed, and continual pre-training is conducted entirely with Ja-En data. From these data curves, it is observed that when conducting continual pre-training with En-Ja data and subsequently with data in the reverse direction, mixing 1% of the first continual pre-training data can mitigate the degradation in accuracy for En ⇒ Ja. Therefore, this suggests that in the continual pre-training of LLMs, incorporating a small proportion of data that one does not wish to be forgotten can suppress catastrophic forgetting.

D Detailed Tables

[11] https://huggingface.co/webbigdata/ALMA-7B-Ja-V2

Direction	Test set	Domain	# sentences
En ⇔ Ja	ASPEC (Nakazawa et al., 2016)	Scientific Papers	1,812
	JESC (Pryzant et al., 2018)	Movie Subtitles	2,000
	KFTT (Neubig, 2011)	Wikipedia Articles	1,160
	TED (tst2015) (Cettolo et al., 2012)	TED Talk	1,194
	Business Scene Dialogue Corpus (BSD) (Rikters et al., 2019)	Dialogues	2,120
En ⇒ Ja	WMT19 Robustness En-Ja (MTNT2019) (Li et al., 2019)	Reddit	1,392
	WMT20 Robustness Set1 En-Ja (Specia et al., 2020)	Wikipedia Comments	1,100
	WMT20 Robustness Set2 En-Ja (Specia et al., 2020)	Reddit	1,376
	IWSLT21 Simultaneous Translation En-Ja Dev (Anastasopoulos et al., 2021)	TED Talk	1,442
	WMT22 General Machine Translation Task En-Ja (Kocmi et al., 2022)	News, social, e-commerce, dialogue	2,037
Ja ⇒ En	WMT19 Robustness Ja-En (MTNT2019) (Li et al., 2019)	Reddit	1,111
	WMT20 Robustness Set2 Ja-En (Specia et al., 2020)	Reddit	997
	WMT22 General Machine Translation Task Ja-En (Kocmi et al., 2022)	News, social, e-commerce, dialogue	2,008

Table 6: Domain and Number of sentences in test sets. "# sentences" represents the number of sentences on the English side.

	Baseline Models		Continual pre-training + Supervised fine-tuning							
			Mono		En-Ja		Ja-En		Mix	
Test set	Transformer	Direct-SFT	full	LoRA	full	LoRA	full	LoRA	full	LoRA
ASPEC	**19.6**	15.4	5.1	4.6	19.1	19.0	6.6	6.4	18.4	18.5
JESC	5.8	5.0	3.6	3.4	**7.4***	7.3*	4.3	3.9	**7.4***	7.0*
KFTT	12.8	8.7	6.7	6.1	**15.5***	15.0*	7.1	6.3	14.1*	13.5
TED	12.2	10.9	5.4	5.1	12.7	12.8*	6.7	6.3	12.3	**12.9***
BSD	12.5	13.1*	7.5	7.5	14.4*	**15.5***	8.6	8.6	14.1*	15.2*
WMT19 R En-Ja	13.1	12.3	6.0	5.5	**15.2***	15.1*	6.7	6.7	14.4*	14.7*
WMT20 R Set1 En-Ja	16.9	15.3	7.1	6.5	18.4*	**19.5***	7.5	8.0	17.5	18.7*
WMT20 R Set2 En-Ja	12.9	12.1	5.5	4.9	**14.8***	**14.8***	6.8	6.8	13.9*	13.7*
IWSLT21 En-Ja Dev	12.2	9.8	5.3	5.2	**13.2***	**13.2***	6.6	7.0	12.8*	12.8*
WMT22 GMT En-Ja	21.2	19.1	11.0	9.8	**23.1***	**23.1***	11.9	11.7	22.0*	22.1*
Average	13.9	12.2	6.3	5.9	15.4	**15.5**	7.3	7.2	14.7	14.9
# Sig.	-	1	0	0	8	**9**	0	0	7	8

(a) BLEU

	Baseline Models		Continual pre-training + Supervised fine-tuning							
			Mono		En-Ja		Ja-En		Mix	
Test set	Transformer	Direct-SFT	full	LoRA	full	LoRA	full	LoRA	full	LoRA
ASPEC	88.5	87.0	78.7	77.1	88.6	**88.7**	80.5	80.7	88.1	88.2
JESC	71.7	72.8*	71.4	70.8	**76.0***	75.7*	72.4	72.4	75.7*	75.8*
KFTT	83.9	79.9	76.4	75.7	**84.4**	84.3	76.4	76.1	83.3	83.7
TED	79.7	80.6*	76.4	75.1	**83.6***	83.2*	78.1	77.7	83.0*	83.0*
BSD	84.2	85.7*	81.3	81.2	87.5*	**87.7***	82.9	83.1	87.0*	87.4*
WMT19 R En-Ja	75.8	77.0*	74.2	73.1	**81.7***	81.5*	75.3	75.1	81.2*	81.0*
WMT20 R Set1 En-Ja	65.2	68.2*	64.6	63.7	**76.8***	76.3*	65.6	66.3	76.2*	75.4*
WMT20 R Set2 En-Ja	74.0	76.1*	72.7	72.2	**81.6***	81.1*	74.8	74.6	80.6*	80.4*
IWSLT21 En-Ja Dev	81.8	82.2	79.4	78.8	**86.2***	85.9*	81.3	81.2	85.8*	85.8*
WMT22 GMT En-Ja	84.9	85.8*	80.8	79.8	**88.3***	**88.3***	82.1	81.0	87.8*	87.9*
Average	79.0	79.6	75.6	74.8	**83.5**	83.3	76.9	76.8	82.9	82.9
# Sig.	-	7	0	0	**8**	**8**	0	0	**8**	**8**

(b) COMET

Table 7: Results of En ⇒ Ja translation accuracy. Details of baseline models and models continually pre-trained with four orders described in Section 4.2.2 then supervised fine-tuning. **Bold numbers** represent the highest scores in each line, and scores that surpass the Transformer are emphasized in green. "*" indicates significant differences compared to Transformer," # Sig." indicates the number of test sets showing significant differences from Transformer ($p < 0.05$).

	Baseline Models		Continual pre-training + Supervised fine-tuning							
			Mono		En-Ja		Ja-En		Mix	
Test set	Transformer	Direct-SFT	full	LoRA	full	LoRA	full	LoRA	full	LoRA
ASPEC	**21.8**	16.0	8.8	7.9	9.4	8.5	20.3	20.4	19.1	19.4
JESC	**8.9**	6.3	4.6	4.0	4.1	4.3	8.5	8.8	7.9	7.7
KFTT	**21.0**	11.1	9.6	8.4	10.6	9.7	19.9	19.0	18.5	17.4
TED	14.7	10.6	7.4	6.3	6.9	6.6	14.7	**15.2**	14.3	14.4
BSD	**19.8**	16.0	9.4	8.8	8.5	9.2	20.1	20.4	18.7	18.6
WMT19 R Ja-En	17.2	14.2	8.3	6.9	8.3	7.1	**18.0**	17.1	16.4	16.5
WMT20 R Set2 Ja-En	**14.3**	10.8	5.6	5.4	5.4	5.4	13.9	14.1	13.0	13.0
WMT22 GMT Ja-En	21.0	15.0	9.5	9.4	9.3	9.9	20.8	**21.1**	19.1	19.3
Average	**17.3**	12.5	7.9	7.1	7.8	7.6	17.0	17.0	15.9	15.8
# Sig.	-	0	0	0	0	0	0	0	0	0

(a) BLEU

	Baseline Models		Continual pre-training + Supervised fine-tuning							
			Mono		En-Ja		Ja-En		Mix	
Test set	Transformer	Direct-SFT	full	LoRA	full	LoRA	full	LoRA	full	LoRA
ASPEC	**82.7**	80.4	74.8	74.2	75.3	74.8	82.5	82.5	81.9	82.1
JESC	68.0	67.2	64.3	63.2	64.3	63.5	69.2*	**69.3***	68.7*	68.6*
KFTT	77.4	73.5	70.1	69.4	70.5	70.3	**78.2***	77.8	77.4	76.6
TED	77.6	75.9	71.2	70.4	71.2	70.9	**78.7***	**78.7***	78.3*	78.1*
BSD	81.1	79.9	74.4	74.1	74.1	74.2	**82.9***	82.0*	81.4	81.1
WMT19 R Ja-En	74.0	74.2	69.6	68.6	69.0	68.4	**76.8***	76.3*	76.5*	76.2*
WMT20 R Set2 Ja-En	70.6	70.6	65.7	64.8	65.0	65.0	72.8*	**73.0***	72.2*	72.1*
WMT22 GMT Ja-En	79.9	77.9	73.4	72.6	72.7	72.9	81.0*	**82.0***	80.5*	80.4*
Average	76.4	73.8	70.4	69.7	70.3	70.0	**77.8**	77.7	77.1	76.9
# Sig.	-	0	0	0	0	0	**7**	6	5	5

(b) COMET

Table 8: Results of Ja ⇒ En translation accuracy. **Bold scores**, green numbers , "*", and "# Sig." are the same in Table 7.

Test set	Transformer	Interleaved full	Interleaved LoRA	Prefix full	Prefix LoRA	Tagged full	Tagged LoRA	JSON full	JSON LoRA
ASPEC	19.6 / 88.5	18.4 / 88.1	18.5 / 88.2	$18.8^{\dagger}$ / $88.5^{\dagger}$	18.6 / $88.5^{\dagger}$	$18.8^{\dagger}$ / $88.5^{\dagger}$	18.7 / $88.6^{\dagger}$	18.5 / $88.3^{\dagger}$	18.7 / $88.5^{\dagger}$
JESC	5.8 / 71.7	7.4* / 75.7*	7.0* / 75.8*	7.8* / 75.7*	6.9* / 75.8*	7.4* / 75.9*	6.8* / 75.8*	7.2* / 75.3*	6.6* / 75.7*
KFTT	12.8 / 83.9	14.1* / 83.3	13.5* / 83.7	$\mathbf{14.9}^{*\dagger}$ / 83.7	13.9* / 84.0	14.2* / 83.6	14.1* / 83.6	14.0* / 83.3	13.9* / 83.7
TED	12.2 / 79.7	12.3 / 83.0*	12.9* / 83.0*	12.6 / 83.0*	13.0* / 83.2*	$\mathbf{12.7}^{*\dagger}$ / $\mathbf{83.4}^{*\dagger}$	13.1* / 83.2*	$\mathbf{12.8}^{*\dagger}$ / 83.0*	13.0* / 83.2*
BSD	12.5 / 84.2	14.1* / 87.0*	15.2* / 87.4*	$\mathbf{14.7}^{*\dagger}$ / 87.2*	15.1* / 87.5*	$\mathbf{14.6}^{*\dagger}$ / 87.2*	14.9* / 87.5*	14.2* / 86.9*	14.9* / 87.4*
WMT19 R En-Ja	13.1 / 75.8	14.4* / 81.2*	14.7* / 81.0*	$\mathbf{15.3}^{*\dagger}$ / 81.3*	$\mathbf{15.4}^{*\dagger}$ / $\mathbf{81.7}^{*\dagger}$	$\mathbf{15.1}^{*\dagger}$ / $\mathbf{81.9}^{*\dagger}$	14.9* / $\mathbf{81.6}^{*\dagger}$	14.3* / 80.9*	14.5* / 81.3*
WMT20 R Set1 En-Ja	16.9 / 65.2	17.5 / 76.2*	18.7* / 75.4*	17.8* / 76.2*	$\mathbf{19.5}^{*\dagger}$ / $\mathbf{76.7}^{*\dagger}$	$\mathbf{18.0}^{*\dagger}$ / 76.6*	$\mathbf{19.2}^{*\dagger}$ / $\mathbf{76.8}^{*\dagger}$	12.1 / 69.6*	18.1* / 74.0*
WMT20 R Set2 En-Ja	12.9 / 74.0	13.9* / 80.6*	13.7 / 80.4*	14.0* / 80.7*	$\mathbf{14.8}^{*\dagger}$ / $\mathbf{80.9}^{*\dagger}$	$\mathbf{14.3}^{*\dagger}$ / $\mathbf{81.1}^{*\dagger}$	$\mathbf{14.5}^{*\dagger}$ / $\mathbf{81.1}^{*\dagger}$	13.6* / 80.0*	$\mathbf{14.3}^{*\dagger}$ / 80.6*
IWSLT21 En-Ja Dev	12.2 / 81.8	12.8* / 85.8*	12.8* / 85.8*	12.7* / 85.9*	13.0* / $\mathbf{86.0}^{*\dagger}$	12.7* / 86.0*	12.6 / 86.0*	12.6 / 85.7*	12.7* / $\mathbf{86.1}^{*\dagger}$
WMT22 GMT En-Ja	21.2 / 84.9	22.0* / 87.8*	22.1* / 87.9*	$\mathbf{22.7}^{*\dagger}$ / 88.0*	$\mathbf{22.7}^{*\dagger}$ / $\mathbf{88.2}^{*\dagger}$	$\mathbf{22.4}^{*\dagger}$ / $\mathbf{88.2}^{*\dagger}$	22.4* / $\mathbf{88.3}^{*\dagger}$	22.2* / 87.9*	22.4* / 88.1*
Average	13.9 / 79.0	14.7 / 82.9	14.9 / 82.9	15.1 / 83.0	15.3 / 83.3	15.0 / 83.2	15.1 / 83.3	14.2 / 82.1	14.9 / 82.9
# Sig.	-	-	-	4 / 0	4 / 5	6 / 4	2 / 4	1 / 0	1 / 1

(a) En ⇒ Ja

Test set	Transformer	Interleaved full	Interleaved LoRA	Prefix full	Prefix LoRA	Tagged full	Tagged LoRA	JSON full	JSON LoRA
ASPEC	21.8 / 82.7	19.1 / 81.9	19.4 / 82.1	$19.6^{\dagger}$ / $82.3^{\dagger}$	19.6 / 82.2	19.5 / 82.1	19.6 / 82.1	19.3 / 82.1	19.3 / 82.1
JESC	8.9 / 68.0	7.9 / 68.7*	7.7 / 68.6*	7.9 / $\mathbf{69.1}^{*\dagger}$	7.9 / $\mathbf{68.9}^{*\dagger}$	8.1 / 68.8*	8.0 / 68.7*	7.9 / 68.6*	7.8 / 68.7*
KFTT	21.0 / 77.4	18.5 / 77.4	17.4 / 76.6	18.9 / 77.6	$18.4^{\dagger}$ / $77.2^{\dagger}$	$19.0^{\dagger}$ / 77.4	$18.6^{\dagger}$ / $77.1^{\dagger}$	18.7 / 77.3	17.6 / 76.7
TED	14.7 / 77.4	14.3 / 78.3*	14.4 / 78.1*	14.1 / 78.4*	14.4 / 78.3*	14.6 / $\mathbf{78.8}^{*\dagger}$	14.2 / 78.3*	13.3 / 78.0*	14.1 / 78.3*
BSD	19.8 / 81.1	18.7 / 81.4	18.6 / 81.1	$19.5^{\dagger}$ / $\mathbf{81.6}^{*\dagger}$	$19.3^{\dagger}$ / $\mathbf{81.6}^{*\dagger}$	19.0 / 81.6*	18.9 / 81.6*	18.6 / 81.5*	18.8 / 81.3
WMT19 R Ja-En	17.2 / 74.0	16.4 / 76.5*	16.5 / 76.2*	$17.2^{\dagger}$ / 76.7*	16.8 / 76.2*	16.3 / 76.5*	16.9 / 76.5*	14.8 / 75.6*	15.9 / 75.6*
WMT20 R Set2 Ja-En	14.3 / 70.6	13.0 / 72.2*	13.0 / 72.1*	13.0 / 72.6*	13.4 / 72.6*	13.3 / $\mathbf{72.6}^{*\dagger}$	13.7 / 72.4*	12.1 / 71.7*	12.9 / 72.2*
WMT22 GMT Ja-En	21.0 / 79.9	19.1 / 80.5*	19.3 / 80.4*	$19.8^{\dagger}$ / $\mathbf{80.8}^{*\dagger}$	19.3 / $\mathbf{80.8}^{*\dagger}$	$20.0^{\dagger}$ / $\mathbf{80.8}^{*\dagger}$	$20.3^{\dagger}$ / $\mathbf{81.0}^{*\dagger}$	19.2 / 80.6*	19.8 / 80.6*
Average	17.3 / 76.4	15.9 / 77.1	15.8 / 76.9	16.3 / 77.4	16.1 / 77.2	16.2 / 77.3	16.3 / 77.2	15.5 / 76.9	15.8 / 76.9
# Sig.	-	-	-	0 / 3	0 / 3	0 / 3	0 / 1	0 / 0	0 / 0

(b) Ja ⇒ En

Table 9: Results of translation accuracy (BLEU / COMET). "*" indicates significant differences compared to Transformer, † indicates significant differences compared to the same fine-tuning method as Iterleaved Translations (Interleaved), **bold numbers** indicate significant differences in both Transformer and the same fine-tuning method as Interleaved Translations, and "# Sig." denotes the number of test sets where significant differences is observed in both Transformer and the same fine-tuning method as Interleaved Translations. ($p < 0.05$)

Test set	BLEU rinna-4b	BLEU rinna-4b + CPT	BLEU rinna-4b + SFT	BLEU rinna-4b + CPT + SFT	COMET rinna-4b	COMET rinna-4b + CPT	COMET rinna-4b + SFT	COMET rinna-4b + CPT + SFT
ASPEC	0.3	8.9	5.2	**18.8**	45.3	72.4	79.0	**88.5**
JESC	0.2	3.1	3.6	**7.4**	36.1	64.4	71.9	**75.9**
KFTT	0.3	4.2	6.8	**14.2**	41.4	66.8	76.4	**83.6**
TED	0.3	9.1	5.4	**12.7**	40.5	72.0	77.2	**83.4**
BSD	0.4	8.8	7.6	**14.6**	40.6	77.7	81.7	**87.2**
WMT19 R En-Ja	0.6	6.5	6.7	**15.1**	40.2	64.7	75.1	**81.9**
WMT20 R Set1 En-Ja	2.0	7.1	**7.7**	18.0	39.3	49.3	66.5	**76.6**
WMT20 R Set2 En-Ja	0.4	7.4	6.1	**14.3**	39.5	65.0	74.3	**81.1**
IWSLT21 En-Ja Dev	0.2	7.6	5.6	**12.7**	40.7	73.2	80.6	**86.0**
WMT22 GMT En-Ja	1.4	19.3	10.3	**22.4**	38.3	83.5	81.3	**88.2**
Average	0.6	8.2	6.5	**15.0**	40.2	69.9	76.4	**83.2**

(a) En ⇒ Ja

Test set	BLEU rinna-4b	BLEU rinna-4b + CPT	BLEU rinna-4b + SFT	BLEU rinna-4b + CPT + SFT	COMET rinna-4b	COMET rinna-4b + CPT	COMET rinna-4b + SFT	COMET rinna-4b + CPT + SFT
ASPEC	1.0	15.5	8.9	**19.5**	53.0	77.7	75.0	**82.1**
JESC	0.3	4.0	4.5	**8.1**	41.5	62.3	64.6	**68.8**
KFTT	0.2	9.6	10.0	**19.0**	44.0	66.7	71.1	**77.4**
TED	0.3	6.6	7.4	**14.6**	49.6	66.6	72.0	**78.8**
BSD	0.3	13.3	9.0	**19.0**	48.1	76.5	74.6	**81.6**
WMT19 R Ja-En	1.4	8.3	8.5	**16.3**	49.9	65.2	69.6	**76.5**
WMT20 R Set2 Ja-En	0.5	6.7	6.0	**13.3**	46.4	62.6	65.7	**72.6**
WMT22 GMT Ja-En	2.0	15.3	9.8	**20.0**	39.3	76.6	73.4	**80.8**
Average	0.8	9.9	8.0	**16.2**	46.0	69.3	70.9	**77.3**

(b) Ja ⇒ En

Table 10: Results of all combinations of continual pre-training and supervised fine-tuning (BLEU / COMET). **Bold numbers** indicate the highest scores in each line. "+ CPT" indicates continual pre-training in the Tagged format, described in Section 6.1. At the same time, "+ SFT" represents supervised fine-tuning with a small amount of high-quality parallel data, as described in Section 4.1.2. During supervised fine-tuning, zero-shot inference is performed, and five-shot inference is performed for others.

The KIT Speech Translation Systems for IWSLT 2024 Dialectal and Low-resource Track

Zhaolin Li, Enes Yavuz Ugan, Danni Liu, Carlos Mullov, Tu Anh Dinh, Sai Koneru, Alexander Waibel, Jan Niehues
Karlsruhe Institute of Technology
firstname.lastname@kit.edu

Abstract

This paper presents KIT's submissions to the IWSLT 2024 dialectal and low-resource track. In this work, we build systems for translating into English from speech in Maltese, Bemba, and two Arabic dialects Tunisian and North Levantine. Under the unconstrained condition, we leverage the pre-trained multilingual models by fine-tuning them for the target language pairs to address data scarcity problems in this track. We build cascaded and end-to-end speech translation systems for different language pairs and show the cascaded system brings slightly better overall performance. Besides, we find utilizing additional data resources boosts speech recognition performance but slightly harms machine translation performance in cascaded systems. Lastly, we show that Minimum Bayes Risk is effective in improving speech translation performance by combining the cascaded and end-to-end systems, bringing a consistent improvement of around 1 BLUE point.

1 Introduction

In this paper, we describe KIT's systems submitted to IWSLT 2024 Dialectal and Low-resource Track. We focus on three language pairs: Bemba (ISO code: bem) to English, Maltese (ISO code: mlt) to English, and Dialectal Arabic to English. The Dialectal Arabic language pair evaluates the performance of two Arabic vernaculars, namely Tunisian (ISO code: aeb) and North Levantine (ISO-3 code: apc). Maltese and Tunisian language pairs are available in IWSLT2023 (Agarwal et al., 2023), and the others are newly included this year. The submissions are under Unconstrained Conditions to leverage pre-trained models and additional data resources.

Recent advancements in dialectal and low-resource speech translation show the benefits of utilizing pre-trained models (Gow-Smith et al., 2022; Laurent et al., 2023; Hussein et al., 2023; Deng et al., 2023). Nowadays, the capacities of pre-trained models are expanded by incorporating more extensive data and expanding language coverage. This work leverages the state-of-the-art pre-trained models, including SeamelssM4T (Barrault et al., 2023), MMS (Pratap et al., 2023), and NLLB (NLLB Team et al., 2022).

Cascaded and End-to-End (E2E) are popular Speech Translation (ST) systems. The Cascaded system consists of Automatic Speech Recognition (ASR) and Machine Translation (MT) models, while the E2E systems integrate both functions into one model. Recent work shows the E2E system shows comparable performance to the cascaded system in speech translation(Liu et al., 2023; Zhou et al., 2023; Huang et al., 2023; Hrinchuk et al., 2023), while there needs research to show which system performs better on dialectal and low-resource scenarios (Deng et al., 2023; Laurent et al., 2023; Kesiraju et al., 2023; Shanbhogue et al., 2023; E. Ortega et al., 2023; Hussein et al., 2023).

Building ST systems for low-resource datasets always suffers from data limitations. Accordingly, we collect available training resources and investigate the training strategies for using them. Although datasets other than the development data might introduce domain differences that could potentially model performance, we explore the benefits of using extra-supervised data. Furthermore, we investigate adapter fine-tuning training to address data scarcity. By freezing the pre-trained parameters and only fine-tuning the adapter parameters, this approach decreases the number of trainable parameters.

In addition to building ST systems, this work explores the decoding approach Minimum Bayes Risk(MBR) to re-rank the candidate translation (Kumar and Byrne, 2004; Hussein et al., 2023) from the built systems. We explore the combination of individual systems and across systems, and our findings suggest combining translations from the

Proceedings of the 21st International Conference on Spoken Language Translation (IWSLT 2024), pages 269–276
August 15-16, 2024 ©2024 Association for Computational Linguistics

cascaded and the E2E systems is effective for all language pairs.

2 Data Description

2.1 Development and test data

The organizers provide the development data for each language pair, which is from the same dataset of the test data for evaluating systems. The development data was released at the beginning, and test data was released when the evaluation period started for the final comparison of submissions. As shown in Table 1, the development data of North Levantine has only a validation split, indicating the importance of transferring knowledge from other data resources, such as standard Arabic. We report the system performance on Tunisian development data, although we have no submission for it due to the unexpected unavailability of the test data at the end of the evaluation period. The Maltese language pair includes two datasets, and we report scores only on the Masri dataset because we use the train split of CV development for training. We evaluated the Bemba systems on the test split of development data, but we later found the test split was the same as the test data.

	Development			Test
Lang.	Train	Valid	Test	
apc	-	1126	-	974
aeb	202k	3833	4204	-
mlt_masri	4962	648	-	668
mlt_cv	3923	1235	-	1224
bem	82k	2782	2779	2779
bem_asr1	-	-	-	977
bem_asr2	-	-	-	3756

Table 1: Statistic on development and test data. Lang is the language code of the source language. The value indicates the number of sample. One sample of the datasets consists of the audio, transcript, and translation in English.

2.2 Additional data resource

Under the unconstrained condition, we collected additional datasets of the language pairs and explored leveraging these resources to improve model performance. The ASR data resources are publicly available except for the SyKIT and MINI dataset, which is the in-house dataset in the conversational domain. SyKIT is a dataset that consists of people from Syria conversing in dialogues on various topics via a Zoom setup. The MINI dataset is read speech and is based on an electronic version of the M.I.N.I. (International Neuropsychiatric Interview). The MT data resources are all from OPUS collection (Tiedemann, 2009).

Lang.	Corpus	Type	#Hour/#Sent.
apc	LDC2005S08	ASR	60h
	LDC2006S29	ASR	250h
	SyKIT	ASR	50h
	Tatoeba	MT	20
aeb	SRL46	ASR	12h
	GNOME	MT	646
ara	SLR148	ASR	111h
	MGB	ASR	1200h
	MINI	ASR	10h
	CCMatrix	MT	5M
	NLLB	MT	5M
	OpenSubtitles	MT	3M
bem	BembaSpech	ASR	24h
	NLLB	MT	427k
mlt	MASRI-Headset v2	ASR	7h
	MASRI-Farfield	ASR	10h
	MASRI-Booths	ASR	2h
	MASRI-MEP	ASR	1h
	MASRI-COMVO	ASR	7h
	MASRI-TUBE	ASR	13h
	NLLB	MT	14M
	DGT	MT	3.5M
	TildeMODEL	MT	2M

Table 2: Overview of the additional data resources.

2.3 Pre-processing

Due to computational limitations, the ASR and ST training data over 15 seconds is removed. Although the training scenario is low-resourced, statistics show only a very small portion of training samples are removed. Afterwards, we introduce data augmentation with Gaussian noise, time stretch, time mask, and frequency mask [1].

3 Method

We conduct preliminary evaluations on Tunisian dialects to assess systems performance and then apply the promising approaches to other languages for effective analysis. The motivation is that the Tunisian language pair has effective systems from IWSLT 2023 (Agarwal et al., 2023) for approach analysis.

3.1 Cascaded Systems

The cascaded system is composed of ASR and MT modules and allows each component to be optimized independently. We explore the ASR and MT modules individually to mitigate the requirement on the supervised ST data, aiming to leverage the supervised ASR and MT data individually.

[1]https://github.com/asteroid-team/torchaudiomentations

3.1.1 ASR

We build two ASR systems with MMS and SeamlessM4T to leverage pre-trained multilingual models. The MMS system is the encoder-only model with the CTC training loss, and the SeamelssM4T model is the encoder-decoder model with cross-entropy training loss. We build the MMS system because the MMS model is pre-trained with more than 1,400 languages, including Maltese and Bemba. The motivation for using SeamlessM4T is its capacity for multilingual generation as an encoder-decoder model.

Our initial findings indicated that the Seamlessm4t system exhibited superior performance on Tunisian and North Levantine data over the MMS system. Consequently, we directed our efforts toward enhancing this particular model.

Given the scarcity of supervised ASR data we explore training strategies of using only the development data or mixing all available training resources. Using all available data increases the amount of supervised data while bringing domain differences that might lead to performance degradation. Consequently, we explore the two-step fine-tuning serving as knowledge transfer. This entails initially fine-tuning the pre-trained model using all available ASR data, followed by training the fine-tuned model solely with the target data.

The amount of supervised data might be insufficient to fine-tune the parameters of the SeamlessM4T model fully. To address this, we explore the parameter-efficient fine-tuning approach Low-Rank Adapters (LORA) by adding and only fine-tuning the LORA adapter (Hu et al., 2021).

3.1.2 MT

The pre-trained SeamlessM4T is a multitask model that supports both audio and text inputs. Besides ASR, we also explore its capacity for MT. Note that Bemba and Maltest are covered in the pre-trained SeamelssM4T model while the Arabic dialects are not.

Apart from SeamlessM4T, we also fine-tune NLLB (NLLB Team et al., 2022) because the pre-trained model covers more language pairs, including all three language pairs of this paper. Given the large vocabulary size of 256K, we freeze the word embedding to save memory. We also follow the recommendations of Cooper Stickland et al. (2021) regarding fine-tuning pre-trained MT models on many-to-English directions and freezing the decoder apart from cross-attention.

Given the extremely limited MT data on the two Arabic dialects (apc and aeb; Table 2), we fine-tune SeamlessM4T or NLLB jointly on these languages along with modern standard Arabic (ara), resulting in a many-to-English system for {apc, aeb, ara}$\rightarrow$eng.

3.2 End-to-End Systems

The E2E system mitigates the error propagation issue in the cascaded system. We develop the E2E model with pre-trained SeamlessM4T consisting of a speech encoder and a text decoder. Since we don't have extra supervised data for ST, we focus on using the development data for our E2E exploration. In addition, we also investigate the effectiveness of fine-tuning with adapters using LORA.

3.3 System Combination

In addition to building ST systems, we explore combining the developed systems using Minimum Bayes Risk (MBR) decoding. MBR decoding is a method used to rerank the candidate translation output. Given a pool of hypothesis translations, MBR uses a utility metric to score each hypothesis against a set of pseudo-references. The hypothesis with the highest average score is then selected as the final translation.

Since the main evaluation metric is the BLEU score, we choose the utility metric as BLEU. For the end-to-end system, we generate 50 hypotheses using epsilon sampling (Hewitt et al., 2022) with temperature 1.0 and epsilon threshold 0.02. For the cascaded system, we generate 50 hypotheses using sampling with a temperature of 0.75. We then combine the hypotheses from both systems, resulting in a hypothesis pool of 100 samples. We use this same hypothesis pool as the pseudo-references to score each individual hypothesis.

4 Experiments and Results

4.1 Model Configuration

ASR We use the pre-trained MMS model with 300M parameters to build the CTC-based ASR system [2]. Compared with other configurations, it has fewer parameters to train and, therefore, fits better to this track. As for the encoder-decoder-based ASR system, we use the pre-trained SeamlessM4T model of the latest version with the large configuration [3]. To reduce the memory footprint, we

[2]https://huggingface.co/facebook/mms-300m

[3]https://huggingface.co/facebook/seamless-m4t-v2-large

use the dedicated model of SeamlessM4T for the speech-to-text task.

MT For the MT systems with SeamlessM4T, we use the same pre-trained model as for ASR but a dedicated model architecture for the text-to-text task [3]. Our finetuned NLLB models are based on the 1B distilled model (NLLB Team et al., 2022). Although the 3B variant gave better initial performance when used out-of-the-box, we could not directly finetune it due to memory constraints. When finetuning, we partially freeze the model as described in §3.1.2.

E2E ST For the ST systems, the pre-trained SeamlessM4T model is the same as for ASR and MT. Here, we use the dedicated SeamlessM4T model for the speech-to-text task[3].

Adapter This work investigates fine-tuning the adapters of LORA with SeamlessM4T models to reduce trainable parameters. We add adapters to all transformer layers of the encoder and decoder. The details regarding our implementation can be found in Appendix A

4.2 Evaluation

As the final evaluation uses lowercase and no punctuation, we follow the setup [4] to process the prediction and reference in the evaluation of this work. Specifically, we process the ASR predictions and references of Tunisian and North Levantine with *arabic_filter* and the other predictions and references with *english_fiter* in evaluation.

For the ASR task, we evaluate with Character Error Rate (CER) and Word Error Rate (WER) using package jiwer[5]. We evaluate MT and ST tasks with BLEU and chrF++ with package sacreBLEU[6].

4.3 ASR

As Table 3 shows, we explore two ASR systems: the encoder-only system with pre-trained MMS (A1) and the encoder-decoder system with pre-trained SeamlessM4T (A2). A2 outperforms A1 for Maltese and Tunisian and is comparable to A1 for Bemba. Considering the pre-trained languages of MMS cover Maltese and Bemba while those of SeamlessM4T only cover Maltese, we regard A2 with SeamlessM4T as a stronger ASR system for this track and explore enhancing this system

With training data in addition to the development data, we investigate training with all supervised ASR data, including the development data. We find using all data boosts Maltese with 5.1 WER points, and gains Bemba with 3.5 WER points. For Tunisian, we gain 3.8 WER points on the validation split but loss 5.2 WER points on the test split. The overfitting to the validation split indicates the importance of improving model robustness. We notice a clear decrease in comparing the scores between A2 and A3 for North Levantine, and we assume the dialect and domain differences are the main causes.

Building on A3, we investigate knowledge transfer from all training datasets to the target dataset with the second step of fine-tuning. Here, we explore full training (A4), which is the same as previous experiments, and adapter training with LORA (A5) as described in subsection 4.1. We find knowledge transfer is effective for North Levantine and Tunisian while not for Maltese and Bemba. The potential reason is the dialects have clear differences from other training datasets, and a second step of fine-tuning enables the model to be specialized on the target dataset. While all training datasets of Maltese or Bemba are from the same languages, the second step of fully fine-tuning (A4) fails to keep the knowledge learned in the first step of fine-tuning and causes performance degradation because of less supervised training data. On the contrary, we observe the knowledge transfer with adapter fine-tuning (A5) works on memorizing the knowledge in the first step but leads to no improvement over A3.

As described in subsection 2.1, the North Levantine has only the valid split in development data, so we implement different training strategies with details in Appendix C. Besides, the training for Tunisian A3 has modifications to other languages, and details are available in Appendix B.

In Table 3, we report the CER and WER scores with normalization for North Levantine and Tunisian, same as (Hussein et al., 2023), for comparison with systems of previous years. The normalization is performed on both the predictions and references and implemented with the camel_tools package [7]. The ASR results without normalization are in Appendix D. There are no scores for others

[4]https://github.com/kevinduh/iwslt22-dialect/blob/main/1_prepare_stm.py

[5]https://github.com/jitsi/jiwer

[6]https://github.com/mjpost/sacrebleu

[7]https://github.com/CAMeL-Lab/camel_tools

	Model	apc_valid	aeb_valid	aeb_test	mlt_masri_valid	bem_test
A1	wav2vec-mms	-	26.2/59.3	29.1/63.6	19.2/61.5	10.0/37.3
A2	SeamlessM4T development data	**39.1/55.3**	21.5/46.5	24.5/45.7	7.2/21.8	10.0/36.6
A3	SeamlessM4T all data	48.0/72.8	21.0/42.7	26.7/ 50.9	**5.7/16.7**	**9.3/33.1**
A4	A3 + transfer	44.6/68.7	**16.8/33.7**	**23.0/43.8**	8.6/24.0	9.6/33.6
A5	A3 + transfer LORA	-	20.9/42.1	25.7/49.1	5.9/17.6	9.3/33.1
	2023 best ASR	-	-/36.5	-/41.7		
B1	NLLB all MT data	**24.9/53.6**	**30.4/52.6**	**26.8/50.2**	31.2/53.7	**28.4/52.1**
B2	SeamlessM4T all MT data	17.9/44.8	16.9/37.9	13.2/34.9	41.6/63.8	28.0/52.9
B3	SeamelssM4T development data	-	5.3/24.3	4.7/23.8	**52.6/72.6**	**28.4/52.8**
	2023 best MT	-	30.5/-	26.4/-	-	-
C1	Best ASR + B1	16.1/40.3	24.7/47.7	20.2/43.9	-	27.5/51.6
C2	Best ASR + B3	-	-	-	47.1/69.1	27.0/52.0
D1	SeamlessM4T	-	22.3/44.9	19.3/42.7	47.2/69.2	27.7/51.3
D2	SeamelssM4T LORA	-	8.2/27.5	6.9/26.4	44.3/66.9	14.1/35.3
E1	Best Cascaded	-	24.4/47.1	20.6/43.6	47.3/69.3	27.6/51.6
E2	Best E2E	-	22.6/44.5	19.9/42.2	48.0/69.5	27.1/49.6
E3	Best Cascaded & E2E	-	**25.5/47.9**	**21.3/44.3**	**50.6/71.2**	**29.3/52.3**
	2023 Best ST	-	24.9/-	22.2/-	-	-

Table 3: Experimental results on development dataset. **A, B, C, D, and E** indicates the ASR, MT, cascaded ST, E2E ST, and MBR systems. The results for ASR are in the format of CER/WER, and those for MT and ST are in the format of BLEU/chrF++. The best ASR, MT and ST systems of 2023 IWSLT are both from (Hussein et al., 2023)

as they are new language pairs this year.

4.4 MT

As Table 3 shows, the system with pre-trained NLLB (B1) suppresses the system with SeamelessM4T (B2) models for North Levantine and Tunisian, and we assume the reason is that NLLB is pre-trained with datasets of North Levantine and Tunisian while SeamlessM4T not. In addition, we notice B1 gives inferior performance for Maltese and shows comparable performance for Bemba compared with B2, although both models cover these two languages in pre-training. We assume the difference in pre-training datasets leads to inconsistent findings for these language pairs because SeamlessM4t and NLLB have similar architectures and model sizes.

Rather than using all available training data, we explore training with only the development data to reduce the effects of domain differences (B3). We notice B3 brings a significant performance decline for Tunisian because its MT data is much less than that for B1 (see Table 2). On the contrary, we observe improvements for Maltese with 11.0 BLEU and 8.8 chrF points. We don't build an MT system (B3) for North Levantine as the supervised MT data is too little.

4.5 ST

We build the cascaded systems from the best ASR models, which are A2 for North Levantine, A4 for Tunisian, and A3 for Maltese and Bemba. The MT models for Arabic dialects are B1, and that for Maltese is B3. We investigate both B1 and B3 for Bemba as they show comparable performance as MT models, and we observe a slight improvement in using B3 on BLEU. We explore building a dedicated cascaded system with the normalized transcriptions for Tunisian, while it gives inferior results than the one without normalization.

Regarding E2E systems, we explore training SeamlessM4T with full fine-tuning and adapter fine-tuning. Full training shows clear advantages over adapter training for all languages in the low-resourced scenario, although more parameters need to be trained. Therefore, we assume only adapting the parameters of LORA is insufficient to fine-tune the SeamlessM4T models on the target language pairs.

4.6 Systems Combination

As can be seen from Table 3, when applying MBR decoding on the output of a single system (E1 and E2), the changes in BLEU and chrF scores are minor. However, when applying MBR decoding on the combined output of the best cascaded and the best end-to-end systems (Row E3), we observe consistent improvement of $\approx$ 1 BLEU point and $\approx$ 1 chrF point. This emphasizes the importance of output diversity when using ensembing methods like MBR decoding.

4.7 Submissions and Results

As for the final submission, we chose the MBR of combining the best cascaded and E2E systems as primary, and we chose cascaded as the contrastive1 system and E2E as the contrastive2 system. In addition, we submit the best ASR systems for evaluating the errors in acoustic recognition, which are described in subsection 4.5. The evaluation scores performed by the organizers are shown in Table 4. We notice the primary and contrastive 1 systems for North Levantine clearly outperform the contrastive 2 system, indicating the contributions of the multilingual MT model. We notice the ASR and ST systems achieve very high scores for Maltese, especially the CV partition. We guess one of the potential reasons is the pre-trained models touch the test data because the CommonVoice dataset is widely used in pre-training.

systems	apc	bem	mlt masri	mlt cv
ASR	-	33.2	19.3	2.4
ST primary	20.9	28.8	50.5	67.4
ST contrastive 1	19.7	27.0	46.3	64.2
ST contrastive 2	11.9	28.1	46.7	65.7

Table 4: Evaluation results on test data. The ASR system is evaluated with WER and the ST system is evaluated with BLEU

5 Conclusion

In this work, we develop the cascaded and E2E ST systems with pre-trained multilingual models. The cascaded system outperforms E2E systems for North Levantine and Tunisian and demonstrates comparable performance for Maltese and Bemba. While building the cascaded system, we find performance improvement by involving additional resources in ASR but observe performance degradation with that in MT. Furthermore, we demonstrate combining the cascaded and E2E system with MBR increases model performance for all language pairs. Comparing our system with previous systems for Tunisian, we note superior performance in the validation split but lagging results in the test split, suggesting the need for future investigations to enhance model robustness.

Acknowledgement This work is partly supported by the Helmholtz Programme-oriented Funding, with project number 46.24.01, named AI for Language Technologies, funding from the pilot program Core-Informatics of the Helmholtz Association (HGF). It also received partial support from the Federal Ministry of Education and Research (BMBF) of Germany under the number 01EF1803B (RELATER). The work was partly performed on the HoreKa supercomputer funded by the Ministry of Science, Research and the Arts Baden-Württemberg and by the Federal Ministry of Education and Research.

References

Milind Agarwal, Sweta Agrawal, Antonios Anastasopoulos, Luisa Bentivogli, Ondřej Bojar, Claudia Borg, Marine Carpuat, Roldano Cattoni, Mauro Cettolo, Mingda Chen, William Chen, Khalid Choukri, Alexandra Chronopoulou, Anna Currey, Thierry Declerck, Qianqian Dong, Kevin Duh, Yannick Estève, Marcello Federico, Souhir Gahbiche, Barry Haddow, Benjamin Hsu, Phu Mon Htut, Hirofumi Inaguma, Dávid Javorský, John Judge, Yasumasa Kano, Tom Ko, Rishu Kumar, Pengwei Li, Xutai Ma, Prashant Mathur, Evgeny Matusov, Paul McNamee, John P. McCrae, Kenton Murray, Maria Nadejde, Satoshi Nakamura, Matteo Negri, Ha Nguyen, Jan Niehues, Xing Niu, Atul Kr. Ojha, John E. Ortega, Proyag Pal, Juan Pino, Lonneke van der Plas, Peter Polák, Elijah Rippeth, Elizabeth Salesky, Jiatong Shi, Matthias Sperber, Sebastian Stüker, Katsuhito Sudoh, Yun Tang, Brian Thompson, Kevin Tran, Marco Turchi, Alex Waibel, Mingxuan Wang, Shinji Watanabe, and Rodolfo Zevallos. 2023. FINDINGS OF THE IWSLT 2023 EVALUATION CAMPAIGN. In *Proceedings of the 20th International Conference on Spoken Language Translation (IWSLT 2023)*, pages 1–61, Toronto, Canada (in-person and online). Association for Computational Linguistics.

Loïc Barrault, Yu-An Chung, Mariano Coria Meglioli, David Dale, Ning Dong, Mark Duppenthaler, Paul-Ambroise Duquenne, Brian Ellis, Hady Elsahar, Justin Haaheim, et al. 2023. Seamless: Multilingual expressive and streaming speech translation. *arXiv preprint arXiv:2312.05187*.

Asa Cooper Stickland, Xian Li, and Marjan Ghazvininejad. 2021. Recipes for adapting pre-trained monolingual and multilingual models to machine translation. In *Proceedings of the 16th Conference of the European Chapter of the Association for Computational Linguistics: Main Volume*, pages 3440–3453, Online. Association for Computational Linguistics.

Pan Deng, Shihao Chen, Weitai Zhang, Jie Zhang, and Lirong Dai. 2023. The USTC's dialect speech translation system for IWSLT 2023. In *Proceedings of the 20th International Conference on Spoken Language Translation (IWSLT 2023)*, pages 102–112, Toronto, Canada (in-person and online). Association for Computational Linguistics.

John E. Ortega, Rodolfo Zevallos, and William Chen. 2023. QUESPA submission for the IWSLT 2023 dialect and low-resource speech translation tasks. In *Proceedings of the 20th International Conference on Spoken Language Translation (IWSLT 2023)*, pages 261–268, Toronto, Canada (in-person and online). Association for Computational Linguistics.

Edward Gow-Smith, Mark McConville, William Gillies, Jade Scott, and Roibeard Ó Maolalaigh. 2022. Use of transformer-based models for word-level transliteration of the book of the dean of lismore. In *Proceedings of the 4th Celtic Language Technology Workshop within LREC2022*, pages 94–98, Marseille, France. European Language Resources Association.

John Hewitt, Christopher Manning, and Percy Liang. 2022. Truncation sampling as language model desmoothing. In *Findings of the Association for Computational Linguistics: EMNLP 2022*, pages 3414–3427, Abu Dhabi, United Arab Emirates. Association for Computational Linguistics.

Oleksii Hrinchuk, Vladimir Bataev, Evelina Bakhturina, and Boris Ginsburg. 2023. NVIDIA NeMo offline speech translation systems for IWSLT 2023. In *Proceedings of the 20th International Conference on Spoken Language Translation (IWSLT 2023)*, pages 442–448, Toronto, Canada (in-person and online). Association for Computational Linguistics.

Edward J. Hu, Yelong Shen, Phillip Wallis, Zeyuan Allen-Zhu, Yuanzhi Li, Shean Wang, Lu Wang, and Weizhu Chen. 2021. Lora: Low-rank adaptation of large language models.

Wuwei Huang, Mengge Liu, Xiang Li, Yanzhi Tian, Fengyu Yang, Wen Zhang, Jian Luan, Bin Wang, Yuhang Guo, and Jinsong Su. 2023. The xiaomi AI lab's speech translation systems for IWSLT 2023 offline task, simultaneous task and speech-to-speech task. In *Proceedings of the 20th International Conference on Spoken Language Translation (IWSLT 2023)*, pages 411–419, Toronto, Canada (in-person and online). Association for Computational Linguistics.

Amir Hussein, Cihan Xiao, Neha Verma, Thomas Thebaud, Matthew Wiesner, and Sanjeev Khudanpur. 2023. JHU IWSLT 2023 dialect speech translation system description. In *Proceedings of the 20th International Conference on Spoken Language Translation (IWSLT 2023)*, pages 283–290, Toronto, Canada (in-person and online). Association for Computational Linguistics.

Santosh Kesiraju, Karel Beneš, Maksim Tikhonov, and Jan Černocký. 2023. BUT systems for IWSLT 2023 Marathi - Hindi low resource speech translation task. In *Proceedings of the 20th International Conference on Spoken Language Translation (IWSLT 2023)*, pages 227–234, Toronto, Canada (in-person and online). Association for Computational Linguistics.

Shankar Kumar and William Byrne. 2004. Minimum Bayes-risk decoding for statistical machine translation. In *Proceedings of the Human Language Technology Conference of the North American Chapter of the Association for Computational Linguistics: HLT-NAACL 2004*, pages 169–176, Boston, Massachusetts, USA. Association for Computational Linguistics.

Antoine Laurent, Souhir Gahbiche, Ha Nguyen, Haroun Elleuch, Fethi Bougares, Antoine Thiol, Hugo Riguidel, Salima Mdhaffar, Gaëlle Laperrière, Lucas Maison, Sameer Khurana, and Yannick Estève. 2023. ON-TRAC consortium systems for the IWSLT 2023 dialectal and low-resource speech translation tasks. In *Proceedings of the 20th International Conference on Spoken Language Translation (IWSLT 2023)*, pages 219–226, Toronto, Canada (in-person and online). Association for Computational Linguistics.

Danni Liu, Thai Binh Nguyen, Sai Koneru, Enes Yavuz Ugan, Ngoc-Quan Pham, Tuan Nam Nguyen, Tu Anh Dinh, Carlos Mullov, Alexander Waibel, and Jan Niehues. 2023. KIT's multilingual speech translation system for IWSLT 2023. In *Proceedings of the 20th International Conference on Spoken Language Translation (IWSLT 2023)*, Toronto, Canada (in-person and online). Association for Computational Linguistics.

Sourab Mangrulkar, Sylvain Gugger, Lysandre Debut, Younes Belkada, Sayak Paul, and Benjamin Bossan. 2022. Peft: State-of-the-art parameter-efficient fine-tuning methods. `https://github.com/huggingface/peft`.

NLLB Team, Marta R. Costa-jussà, James Cross, Onur Çelebi, Maha Elbayad, Kenneth Heafield, Kevin Heffernan, Elahe Kalbassi, Janice Lam, Daniel Licht, Jean Maillard, Anna Y. Sun, Skyler Wang, Guillaume Wenzek, Al Youngblood, Bapi Akula, Loïc Barrault, Gabriel Mejia Gonzalez, Prangthip Hansanti, John Hoffman, Semarley Jarrett, Kaushik Ram Sadagopan, Dirk Rowe, Shannon Spruit, Chau Tran, Pierre Andrews, Necip Fazil Ayan, Shruti Bhosale, Sergey Edunov, Angela Fan, Cynthia Gao, Vedanuj Goswami, Francisco Guzmán, Philipp Koehn, Alexandre Mourachko, Christophe Ropers, Safiyyah Saleem, Holger Schwenk, and Jeff Wang. 2022. No language left behind: Scaling human-centered machine translation. *CoRR*, abs/2207.04672.

Vineel Pratap, Andros Tjandra, Bowen Shi, Paden Tomasello, Arun Babu, Sayani Kundu, Ali Elkahky, Zhaoheng Ni, Apoorv Vyas, Maryam Fazel-Zarandi, Alexei Baevski, Yossi Adi, Xiaohui Zhang, Wei-Ning Hsu, Alexis Conneau, and Michael Auli. 2023. Scaling speech technology to 1,000+ languages.

Akshaya Vishnu Kudlu Shanbhogue, Ran Xue, Soumya Saha, Daniel Zhang, and Ashwinkumar Ganesan. 2023. Improving low resource speech translation with data augmentation and ensemble strategies. In *Proceedings of the 20th International Conference on Spoken Language Translation (IWSLT 2023)*, pages 241–250, Toronto, Canada (in-person and online). Association for Computational Linguistics.

Jörg Tiedemann. 2009. *News from OPUS - A Collection of Multilingual Parallel Corpora with Tools and Interfaces*, volume V, pages 237–248.

Xinyuan Zhou, Jianwei Cui, Zhongyi Ye, Yichi Wang, Luzhen Xu, Hanyi Zhang, Weitai Zhang, and Lirong Dai. 2023. Submission of USTC's system for the IWSLT 2023 - offline speech translation track. In *Proceedings of the 20th International Conference on Spoken Language Translation (IWSLT 2023)*, pages 194–201, Toronto, Canada (in-person and online). Association for Computational Linguistics.

A Adapter fine-tuning

We implement the adapters of LORA with package PEFT (Mangrulkar et al., 2022). We set the hyperparameters to rank 8, alpha 32, dropout 0.1, and bias as 'lora_only'. To add adapters for all layers in the encoder and decoders of SeamlessM4T, the target modules are "q_proj, v_proj, linear_q, linear_v".

B Tunisian ASR training

In our first endeavor, we gathered all available Arabic data to fine-tune our model. The dataset used for training is detailed in Table 2. To augment the availability of dialectal data for training, we adopted two approaches: utilizing default validation splits or selecting 0.15% of the training data for validation. Subsequently, we combined the validation sets, retaining only 1,500 utterances for validation, and incorporating the remainder into our training data. We applied the same methodology to other Arabic datasets. Thus, our consolidated validation sets comprised a total of 3,000 utterances, with 50% representing dialectal speech. This model underwent training with early stopping set to five epochs, with results documented as A3 in Table 3.

Subsequently, we implemented various strategies further to enhance the model's performance on dialectal speech. In iteration A4, we conducted additional fine-tuning using solely dialectal data. We experimented with further fine-tuning the A3 model with exclusive Tunisian dialectal data and a LORA module in A5. However, given the lack of promising results and Tunisian's exclusion from the challenge, we discontinued further investigation into this approach.

C North Levantine training

For the A2 North Levantine ASR model, we continued fine-tuning the entire model from A3. We assume starting from the fine-tuned ASR models could alleviate the need for training data. As we only have the validation set, fine-tuning utilizes 90% of the validation set for training and reserves the remaining for validating and early stopping. Upon achieving convergence at a training epoch number, we use the same hyperparameters to conduct a new fine-tuning from A3, utilizing the whole validation set for training and stopping with the same epoch number. This approach brings a risk of overfitting to the validation set but could make full use of the available data for training.

For the E2E ST system, we implement the same training strategy as the ASR systems but start from the pre-trained SeamlessM4T model.

	apc_valid	aeb_valid	aeb_test
A1	-	27.4/62.9	31.1/68.4
A2	39.9/56.9	23.7/46.5	27.6/53.6
A3	49.6/75.7	23.1/47.4	29.6/58.9
A4	46.4/72.7	18.6/38.3	26.1/52.2
A5	-	23.1/47.0	28.7/57.0

Table 5: ASR results without normalization

D Tunisian and North Levantine ASR scores without normalization

For comparison with ASR systems from previous years, we report ASR scores with normalization in Table 3d. Here, we report the scores with normalization in Table 5.

Empowering Low-Resource Language Translation: Methodologies for Bhojpuri-Hindi and Marathi-Hindi ASR and MT

Harpreet Singh Anand and **Amulya Ratna Dash** and **Yashvardhan Sharma**
Dept. of Computer Science and Information Systems
Birla Institute of Technology and Science, Pilani, India

Abstract

This paper presents the methodologies implemented for the Automatic Speech Recognition and Machine Translation for the language pairs Bhojpuri-Hindi and Marathi-Hindi for the Dialectal and Low-Resource shared task proposed by The International Conference on Spoken Language Translation (IWSLT) for 2024. The implemented method uses the transcriptions generated through a fine-tuned Whisper models(for Marathi-Hindi) and vakyansh-wav2vec model (for Bhojpuri-Hindi) and generates the translations using fine-tuned NLLB(No Language Left Behind) Models for both the tasks. The selection of more accurate translation is done through sentence-embeddings generated using the MuRIL(Multilingual Representations for Indian Languages)(Khanuja et al., 2021) model for the Marathi-Hindi task.

1 Introduction

India boasts a vast linguistic variety, with more than 100 official languages and numerous dialects spoken all throughout the nation. Natural Language Generation (NLG) tasks such as automated speech recognition (ASR) and machine translation (MT), are greatly hampered by the tremendous variety. For millions of Indians who do not speak English or other commonly spoken languages, ASR and MT can be crucial in bridging the language gap and granting them access to information and services in a multi-linguistic country like India. However, the creation of ASR and MT systems is a challenging endeavour due to the inherent features of Indian languages, such as rich morphology, the occurrence of code-switching, and borrowing from other languages.

The 'Dialectal and Low-Resource Track'proposed by IWSLT 2024 requires the participants devise creative approaches to leverage the disparate resources available for 8 dialectal and low-resource languages. The participants are required to submit under two conditions - namely constrained and unconstrained. The constrained condition should contain systems that are trained only on the datasets provided by the organizers while the unconstrained condition can contain systems trained with any resource including pre-trained and multilingual models. Our team participated in the unconstrained condition for the language pairs - Marathi to Hindi and Bhojpuri to Hindi. This paper will discuss the implementation details of our ASR and MT systems for the above-mentioned language pairs.

2 Related Work

Automatic Speech Recognition(ASR) and Machine Translation(MT) in low-resource languages have been the subject of extensive research in recent years. Several approaches have been proposed to address the challenges associated with low-resource languages in ASR and MT. For instance, multilingual training has been identified as an effective approach for compensating for the limited amount of data in low-resourced ASR (Madikeri et al., 2020). Additionally, transfer learning methods have been used to develop end-to-end ASR systems for low-resource languages, demonstrating their influence in addressing the challenges of low data levels (Mamyrbayev et al., 2022). Furthermore, the use of self-supervised speech recognition models has been hindered by the requirement for considerable labeled training data, which poses a challenge for their application to low-resource languages (Hameed et al., 2022).

In the context of MT, the scarcity of parallel data for low-resource languages has been identified as a significant challenge (Gao et al., 2020). Neural Machine Translation (NMT) systems, which require large amounts of training data, face difficulties in creating high-quality systems for low-resource languages (Neubig and Hu, 2018). However, research efforts have been directed towards improv-

Proceedings of the 21st International Conference on Spoken Language Translation (IWSLT 2024), pages 277–282
August 15-16, 2024 ©2024 Association for Computational Linguistics

ing low-resource NMT, with studies exploring techniques such as teacher-free knowledge distillation to enhance performance in low-resource languages (Zhang et al., 2020). The encoder-decoder framework for NMT has also been found to be less effective for low-resource languages, highlighting the need for specialized approaches to address the challenges of low-resource machine translation (Zoph et al., 2016).

The use of transfer learning has shown effectiveness in addressing the challenges of low-resource NMT, particularly in scenarios where parallel data is limited (Ji et al., 2019). Additionally, the development of multilingual NMT systems has contributed to improving the quality of translation, especially for low-resource language pairs, enabling zero-shot translation and allowing the translation of language pairs never seen in training (Escolano et al., 2021).

Automatic Speech Recognition (ASR) and Machine Translation (MT) for Indian languages have gained significant attention in recent years. The development of ASR systems for Indian languages has been a focus of research, with studies addressing low-resource challenges (Sailor et al., 2018), multilingual and code-switching ASR systems (Diwan, 2021), and the impact of multilingual representations on ASR and keyword search (Cui et al., 2015). Research has also been conducted on ASR for specific Indian languages such as Hindi, Marathi, Bengali, and Oriya (Dash et al., 2018). Furthermore, the potential of ASR to aid individuals with speech disabilities, such as dysarthria, has been explored (Shahamiri and Salim, 2014). In the realm of MT, efforts have been made to improve the quality of translations for Indian languages through techniques such as transliteration and part-of-speech tagging ((Durrani et al., 2014; Ameta et al., 2013). Moreover, the development of MT systems for Indian languages and their approaches have been a subject of interest (Saini and Sahula, 2015; Godase and Govilkar, 2015). Research has also delved into rule-based machine translation and inflection rules for specific Indian languages like Marathi (Kharate and Patil, 2021). The significance of ASR and MT for Indian languages is underscored by the need to break language barriers and facilitate inter-lingual communication (Godase and Govilkar, 2015). Furthermore, the development of ASR and MT systems for Indian languages is crucial for addressing the diverse linguistic landscape of the country and enabling access to information and services for non-English speakers.

In conclusion, the research on ASR and MT for Indian languages has made substantial progress, addressing challenges related to low-resource settings, multilingualism, and specific language requirements. These advancements are pivotal in enabling effective communication, accessibility, and inclusivity for Indian language speakers.

3 Datasets

We utilized the datasets provided by the track organizers as indicated below:

3.1 OpenSLR

OpenSLR(Open Speech and Language Resources) is a site devoted to hosting speech and language resources, such as training corpora for speech recognition, and software related to speech recognition. This data set[1](He et al., 2020) contains transcribed high-quality audio of Marathi sentences recorded by volunteers. The data set consists of .wav files, and a TSV file (line-index.tsv). The file line-index.tsv contains an anonymized FileID and the transcription of audio in the file. Following are some details about the dataset:

Identifier: SLR64

Summary: Dataset which contains recordings of native speakers of Marathi

Category: Speech

License: Attribution-ShareAlike 4.0 International

3.2 Common Voice

We used the Common Voice 11.0 dataset(Ardila et al., 2020) (Marathi) for the fine-tuning of Whisper. Common Voice is an open-source, multi-language dataset of voices that anyone can use to train speech-enabled applications. The dataset consists of a unique MP3 and corresponding text file. The dataset is available on the HuggingFace Datasets Hub[2] and can be directly imported from there.

3.3 Samanantar

We have used the Indic2Indic part of the Samanantar(Ramesh et al., 2022) dataset which is the largest publicly available parallel corpora collection for Indic languages.

[1]https://www.openslr.org/64/

[2]https://huggingface.co/datasets/mozilla-foundation/common_voice_11_0

4 Methodology

4.1 Marathi - Hindi

For the Marathi-Hindi track(unconstrained condition), we have utilized a cascaded approach consisting of two fine-tuned Whisper models for ASR and a fine-tuned NLLB(NLLB Team et al., 2022) model for MT.

4.1.1 ASR

In our submission, we have fine-tuned the Whisper-small(Radford et al., 2022) pre-trained checkpoint(244M parameters and Multilingual)[3] to obtain two fine-tuned models for ASR in Marathi. The first model was obtained after fine-tuning on the Common Voice 11.0 dataset while the second model was generated after fine-tuning on the OpenSLR dataset(SLR 64). We will call these models as "whisper-ft-cv" and "whisper-ft-slr" respectively. The following hyper-parameters were used during training of both the models:
Learning Rate: 1e-05
Train Batch Size: 16
Eval Batch Size: 8
Seed: 42
Optimizer: Adam with betas=(0.9,0.999)
LR scheduler type: linear
LR scheduler warmup steps: 500
Training Steps: 4000
Mixed Precision Training: Native AMP

We trained both the ASR models for 4000 steps since during experimentation, we found that there was not significant reduction in WER after 4000 steps. Table 1 below shows the results that we obtained on the evaluation dataset(in terms of WER score) after fine-tuning Whisper on the common voice dataset.

Step	Epoch	Training Loss	WER
1000	4.07	0.0658	46.3542
2000	8.13	0.004	44.7295
3000	12.2	0.0004	43.5046
4000	16.26	0.0002	43.3628

Table 1: Training results for whisper-ft-cv

Table 2 below shows the results that we obtained on the evaluation dataset(in terms of WER score) after fine-tuning Whisper on the OpenSLR dataset.

Step	Epoch	Training Loss	WER
1000	12.66	0.0018	16.6181
2000	25.32	0.0005	14.6303
3000	37.97	0.0002	14.4977
4000	50.63	0.0001	14.33917

Table 2: Training results for whisper-ft-slr

4.1.2 MT

For the Machine Translation of the transcriptions generated by the ASR model, we are using a fine-tuned NLLB model (600M-distilled)[4] trained on the Samanantar (Indic2Indic) dataset in the Marathi-Hindi direction.The fine-tuned model is then used to translate transcriptions obtained through both whisper-ft-cv and whisper-ft-slr. Following were the training arguments that were used to fine-tune both the NLLB models:
Learning Rate : 2e-5
Batch Size : 16
Weight Decay : 0.01
Epochs : 5
The model was fine-tuned for 5 epochs only since during experimentation we found out that the training loss and BLEU scores plateaued after 5 epochs.

4.1.3 Choice of Translation

The sentence embeddings of both the transcriptions and their respective translations are generated using MuRIL(Khanuja et al., 2021). The cosine-similarity of these translations with their respective transcriptions are then compared and the pair with higher value of cosine similarity is chosen as the more accurate transcription and translation.

4.2 Bhojpuri - Hindi

For the Bhojpuri-Hindi track(unconstrained condition), we have utilized cascaded approach consisting of a pre-trained wav2vec model(for ASR) and a fine-tuned NLLB model(for MT).

4.2.1 ASR

In our submission, we have used vakyansh-wav2vec2-bhojpuri-bhom-60[5](Chadha et al., 2022; Gupta et al., 2021) model for generating the transcriptions in Bhojpuri. It is a pre-trained wav2vec model available on HuggingFace.

[3]https://huggingface.co/openai/whisper-small

[4]https://huggingface.co/facebook/nllb-200-distilled-600M

[5]https://huggingface.co/Harveenchadha/vakyansh-wav2vec2-bhojpuri-bhom-60

4.2.2 MT

We translate the transcriptions generated in the previous step using NLLB (1.3B)[6] model with Bhojpuri as the source language and Hindi as the target language.

5 Results

The results of ASR have been calculated using WER and CER scores while those of MT are calculated using BLEU(Papineni et al., 2002) and chrF2(Popović, 2015; Zoph et al., 2016) metrics respectively.
Word Error Rate (WER) and Character Error Rate (CER) indicate the amount of text that was misread by the model. WER recognizes three different types of mistakes: substitutions, deletions, and insertions. It is possible to see mispredicted terms from word-level mistakes which can illustrate frequent word-level errors made by a model.Its formal definition is percentage of word-level mistakes in candidate text.Another statistic that measures correctness of a candidate text with regards to substitutions, deletions and insertions is Character Error Rate. Word-level errors focus on mispronounced words or wrong phonemes while character level mistakes help point out such mispronunciations.The number of character level mistake present in a candidate text is called CER. BLEU score measures the quality of predicted text, referred to as the candidate, compared to a set of references. BLEU score is a precision based measure and it ranges from 0 to 1. The closer the value is to 1, the better the prediction.

5.1 Marathi-Hindi

Table 3 below shows the results of our ASR System in which we are using fine-tuned models of Whisper-small. Here, "contrastive1" refers to the model fine-tuned on the Common Voice dataset whereas "contrastive2" refers to the model fine-tuned on the OpenSLR dataset.We chose "contrastive2" as our primary submission for ASR.

Submission	WER	CER
contrastive1	62.9	17.5
contrastive2	69.3	21.2
primary	69.3	21.2

Table 3: Results of our ASR System for Marathi-Hindi

[6]https://huggingface.co/facebook/nllb-200-distilled-1.3B

Table 4 shows the results of our Speech Translation(ST) system (i.e ASR+MT). Here, "contrastive1" refers to ASR using "contrastive1" ASR system and MT using the fine-tuned NLLB model whereas "contrastive2" refers to ASR using "contrastive2" ASR system and MT using the fine-tuned NLLB model. Our "primary" submission consists of the translations which have higher cosine similarity to their respective transcriptions (from their respective ASR models).

Submission	BLEU	chrF2
contrastive1	25	50.1
contrastive2	19	44.8
primary	21.3	48.1

Table 4: Results for our ST System for Marathi-Hindi

5.2 Bhojpuri - Hindi

Table 5 below shows the results for our primary ST system for Bhojpuri-Hindi which consists of a vakyansh-wav2vec model for ASR and NLLB-1.3B distilled model for MT.

Submission	BLEU	chrF2
primary	12.9	41.1

Table 5: Results for our ST System for Bhojpuri-Hindi

6 Conclusion and Future Work

In this paper, we have presented our Speech Translation Systems for the dialectal and low-resource track of IWSLT 2024 employing a cascaded approach using fine-tuned models for both ASR and MT. Our submission trailed by a chrF2 score of 20 in comparison to the best submission in Marathi-Hindi task(unconstrained). In Bhojpuri-Hindi task(unconstrained) our submission trailed the best submission by a chrF2 score of 8.4 .
Our future work will comprise of using data-augmentation techniques and fine-tuning multiple pre-trained multilingual models and exploring more speech translation models for Low-Resource Indian Languages.

References

J. Ameta, N. Joshi, and I. Mathur. 2013. Improving the quality of gujarati-hindi machine translation through part-of-speech tagging and stemmer assisted transliteration. *International Journal on Natural Language Computing*, 2:49–54.

R. Ardila, M. Branson, K. Davis, M. Henretty, M. Kohler, J. Meyer, R. Morais, L. Saunders, F. M. Tyers, and G. Weber. 2020. Common voice: A massively-multilingual speech corpus. In *Proceedings of the 12th Conference on Language Resources and Evaluation (LREC 2020)*, pages 4211–4215.

Harveen Singh Chadha, Anirudh Gupta, Priyanshi Shah, Neeraj Chhimwal, Ankur Dhuriya, Rishabh Gaur, and Vivek Raghavan. 2022. Vakyansh: Asr toolkit for low resource indic languages. *Preprint*, arXiv:2203.16512.

J. Cui, B. Kingsbury, B. Ramabhadran, A. Sethy, K. Audhkhasi, X. Cui, E. Kislal, L. Mangu, M. Nußbaum-Thom, M. Picheny, Z. Tüske, P. Golik, R. Schlüter, H. Ney, M. Gales, K. Knill, A. Ragni, H. Wang, and P. Woodland. 2015. Multilingual representations for low resource speech recognition and keyword search.

D. Dash, M. Kim, K. Teplansky, and J. Wang. 2018. Automatic speech recognition with articulatory information and a unified dictionary for hindi, marathi, bengali and oriya.

A. Diwan. 2021. Multilingual and code-switching asr challenges for low resource indian languages.

N. Durrani, H. Sajjad, H. Hoang, and P. Koehn. 2014. Integrating an unsupervised transliteration model into statistical machine translation. *Proceedings of the 14th Conference of the European Chapter of the Association for Computational Linguistics, Volume 2: Short Pa.*

C. Escolano, M. Costa-jussà, J. Fonollosa, and C. Segura. 2021. Enabling zero-shot multilingual spoken language translation with language-specific encoders and decoders.

L. Gao, X. Wang, and G. Neubig. 2020. Improving target-side lexical transfer in multilingual neural machine translation.

A. Godase and S. Govilkar. 2015. Machine translation development for indian languages and its approaches. *International Journal on Natural Language Computing*, 4:55–74.

Anirudh Gupta, Harveen Singh Chadha, Priyanshi Shah, Neeraj Chimmwal, Ankur Dhuriya, Rishabh Gaur, and Vivek Raghavan. 2021. Clsril-23: Cross lingual speech representations for indic languages. *Preprint*, arXiv:2107.07402.

A. Hameed, I. Qazi, and A. Raza. 2022. Towards representative subset selection for self-supervised speech recognition.

Fei He, Shan-Hui Cathy Chu, Oddur Kjartansson, Clara Rivera, Anna Katanova, Alexander Gutkin, Isin Demirsahin, Cibu Johny, Martin Jansche, Supheakmungkol Sarin, and Knot Pipatsrisawat. 2020. Open-source Multi-speaker Speech Corpora for Building Gujarati, Kannada, Malayalam, Marathi, Tamil and Telugu Speech Synthesis Systems. In *Proceedings of The 12th Language Resources and Evaluation Conference (LREC)*, pages 6494–6503, Marseille, France. European Language Resources Association (ELRA).

B. Ji, Z. Zhang, X. Duan, M. Zhang, B. Chen, and W. Luo. 2019. Cross-lingual pre-training based transfer for zero-shot neural machine translation.

Simran Khanuja, Diksha Bansal, Sarvesh Mehtani, Savya Khosla, Atreyee Dey, Balaji Gopalan, Dilip Kumar Margam, Pooja Aggarwal, Rajiv Teja Nagipogu, Shachi Dave, et al. 2021. Muril: Multilingual representations for indian languages. *arXiv preprint arXiv:2103.10730*.

N. G. Kharate and V. Patil. 2021. Inflection rules for marathi to english in rule based machine translation. *IAES International Journal of Artificial Intelligence (IJ-AI)*, 10:780.

S. Madikeri, B. K. Khonglah, S. Tong, P. Motlíček, H. Bourlard, and D. Povey. 2020. Lattice-free maximum mutual information training of multilingual speech recognition systems. *Interspeech 2020*.

. Mamyrbayev, K. Alimhan, . , A. Bekarystankyzy, and B. Zhumazhanov. 2022. Identifying the influence of transfer learning method in developing an end-to-end automatic speech recognition system with a low data level. *Eastern-European Journal of Enterprise Technologies*, 1:84–92.

G. Neubig and J. Hu. 2018. Rapid adaptation of neural machine translation to new languages.

NLLB Team, Marta R. Costa-jussà, James Cross, Onur Çelebi, Maha Elbayad, Kenneth Heafield, Kevin Heffernan, Elahe Kalbassi, Janice Lam, Daniel Licht, Jean Maillard, Anna Sun, Skyler Wang, Guillaume Wenzek, Al Youngblood, Bapi Akula, Loic Barrault, Gabriel Mejia-Gonzalez, Prangthip Hansanti, John Hoffman, Semarley Jarrett, Kaushik Ram Sadagopan, Dirk Rowe, Shannon Spruit, Chau Tran, Pierre Andrews, Necip Fazil Ayan, Shruti Bhosale, Sergey Edunov, Angela Fan, Cynthia Gao, Vedanuj Goswami, Francisco Guzmán, Philipp Koehn, Alexandre Mourachko, Christophe Ropers, Safiyyah Saleem, Holger Schwenk, and Jeff Wang. 2022. No language left behind: Scaling human-centered machine translation.

Kishore Papineni, Salim Roukos, Todd Ward, and Wei-Jing Zhu. 2002. Bleu: a method for automatic evaluation of machine translation. In *Proceedings of the 40th Annual Meeting on Association for Computational Linguistics*, ACL '02, page 311–318, USA. Association for Computational Linguistics.

Maja Popović. 2015. chrF: character n-gram F-score for automatic MT evaluation. In *Proceedings of the Tenth Workshop on Statistical Machine Translation*, pages 392–395, Lisbon, Portugal. Association for Computational Linguistics.

Alec Radford, Jong Wook Kim, Tao Xu, Greg Brockman, Christine McLeavey, and Ilya Sutskever. 2022.

Robust speech recognition via large-scale weak supervision. *arXiv preprint*.

Gowtham Ramesh, Sumanth Doddapaneni, Aravinth Bheemaraj, Mayank Jobanputra, Raghavan Ak, Ajitesh Sharma, Sujit Sahoo, Harshita Diddee, Divyanshu Kakwani, Navneet Kumar, et al. 2022. Samanantar: The largest publicly available parallel corpora collection for 11 indic languages. *Transactions of the Association for Computational Linguistics*, 10:145–162.

H. Sailor, M. Krishna, D. Chhabra, A. Patil, M. Kamble, and H. Patil. 2018. Da-iict/iiitv system for low resource speech recognition challenge 2018.

S. Saini and V. Sahula. 2015. A survey of machine translation techniques and systems for indian languages. *2015 IEEE International Conference on Computational Intelligence Amp; Communication Technology*.

S. R. Shahamiri and S. S. Salim. 2014. A multi-views multi-learners approach towards dysarthric speech recognition using multi-nets artificial neural networks. *IEEE Transactions on Neural Systems and Rehabilitation Engineering*, 22:1053–1063.

X. Zhang, X. Li, Y. Yang, and R. Dong. 2020. Improving low-resource neural machine translation with teacher-free knowledge distillation. *Ieee Access*, 8:206638–206645.

B. Zoph, D. Yüret, J. May, and K. Knight. 2016. Transfer learning for low-resource neural machine translation.

Recent Highlights in Multilingual and Multimodal Speech Translation

Danni Liu and **Jan Niehues**
Karlsruhe Institute of Technology, Germany
{danni.liu, jan.niehues}@kit.edu

Abstract

Speech translation has witnessed significant progress driven by advancements in modeling techniques and the growing availability of training data. In this paper, we highlight recent advances in two ongoing research directions in ST: scaling the models to **1)** many translation directions (multilingual ST) and **2)** beyond the text output modality (multimodal ST). We structure this review by examining the sequential stages of a model's development lifecycle: determining training resources, selecting model architecture, training procedures, evaluation metrics, and deployment considerations. We aim to highlight recent developments in each stage, with a particular focus on model architectures (dedicated speech translation models and LLM-based general-purpose model) and training procedures (task-specific vs. task-invariant approaches). Based on the reviewed advancements, we identify and discuss ongoing challenges within the field of speech translation.

1 Introduction

Speech translation (ST) is the task of automatically converting speech in a source language into its equivalent in a target language. Recently, there has been significant interest in *multilingual* models (Di Gangi et al., 2019; Inaguma et al., 2019; Li et al., 2021; Le et al., 2021; Radford et al., 2023) that serve a broad range of translation directions, as well as *multimodal* models (Inaguma et al., 2023; Rubenstein et al., 2023; Seamless Communication et al., 2023b) that not only generate text translations but can also synthesize speech output.[1] Both developments are crucial steps towards making ST technologies more inclusive. By expanding language coverage and offering diverse output modalities, these advancements make ST models accessible to a wider range of users, allowing them to interact with the technology in their preferred language and format. Besides the practical relevance, multilingual and multimodal translation are instances of multi-task learning (Caruana, 1997), a central machine learning challenge.

In this paper, we aim to review recent advancements in multilingual and multimodal ST. We structure the review by the stages in a model's development lifecycle, as illustrated in Figure 1. These stages consist of model coverage and architecture selection, training procedures, evaluation methodologies, and deployment considerations. In the review of current model architectures (§3), besides discussing dedicated models for translation, we review emerging models in adapting text-based large language models (LLMs) for speech processing. Given the inherent multi-task learning nature of both multilingual and multimodal ST, we put special emphasis on the learning procedure (§4). Specifically, we take two perspectives from task-specific and task-invariant modeling, and discuss their roles in terms of the trade-off between interference and transfer.

While prioritizing direct ST, we also review related multilingual and multimodal techniques in automatic speech recognition (ASR) and text-to-text machine translation (MT), as they often are extendable to ST tasks. We also note that this work is not an exhaustive survey, but rather aims to highlight directions of recent developments and provide context for open challenges.

2 Training Resources

Determining training resources is one of the initial steps when building a speech translation model. This section provides a brief overview of the language and modality coverage (§2.1) in existing training resources, followed by discussions on scaling datasets by augmentation or mining (§2.2).

[1]Here we restrict our discussion to the two modalities of speech and text. We acknowledge the relevance of additional modalities, such as vision, and leave them for open questions.

Proceedings of the 21st International Conference on Spoken Language Translation (IWSLT 2024), pages 283–301
August 15-16, 2024 ©2024 Association for Computational Linguistics

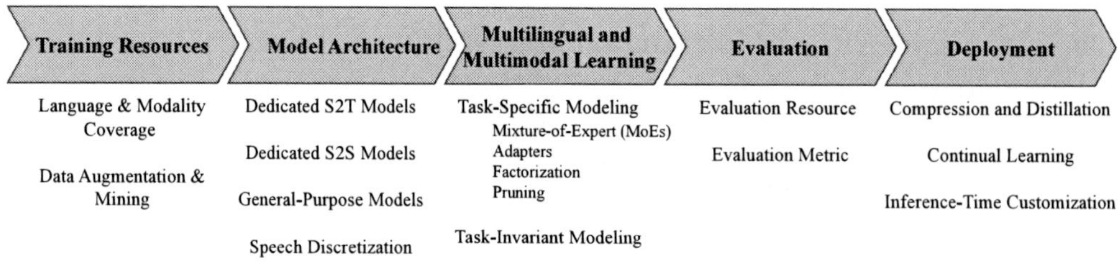

Figure 1: Overall structure of the paper, following sequential stages of model development lifecycle.

Dataset	Directions	Modality & Type	# Lang. Pairs	Total Hours
MuST-C (Di Gangi et al., 2019; Cattoni et al., 2021)	en→X	S2T	14	0.4k
Europarl-ST (Iranzo-Sánchez et al., 2020)	X→X	S2T	12	0.5k
CoVoST 2 (Wang et al., 2021b)	en→X, X→en	S2T	36	3k
mTEDx (Salesky et al., 2021)	X→X	S2T	13	0.4k
VoxPopuli (Wang et al., 2021a)	X→X	S2T/S, interpretation	210	17k
CVSS (Jia et al., 2022b)	X→en	S2T/S, synthesized	21	2k
SpeechMatrix (Duquenne et al., 2023a)	X→X	S2T/S, mined	136	418k

Table 1: Overview of popuplar speech translation training resources.

2.1 Language and Modality Coverage

Curating datasets for speech translation is labor-intensive. Popular training resources often rely on contributions from volunteers on platforms like TED and Common Voice, or are sourced from governmental bodies. Table 1 provides an overview of commonly used speech translation datasets. A trend towards broader language coverage is evident, with datasets like Europarl-ST and mTEDx covering non-English translation directions. Moreover, there has also been growing availability of translation resources with speech output, exemplified by VoxPopuli, CVSS, and SpeechMatrix.

2.2 Augmenting and Mining Data

Speech translation models suffer from the scarcity of parallel data. To address this challenge, several data augmentation approaches have emerged. One approach is to leverage pretrained MT models to convert ASR data into synthetic speech translation pairs (Pino et al., 2020). Text-to-speech (TTS) systems can also be employed to create augmented training data from existing text resources (Jia et al., 2019a, 2022b). Another way to tackle data scarcity is to mine parallel data in large unpaired data collections. In general, these approaches typically invovle learning a multilingual or multimodal sentence embedder, where distances within the embedding space can be used to identify potential parallel data points (Schwenk, 2018). The effectiveness of this method on ST was demonstrated by Duquenne et al. (2021), who showed that mined speech-to-text data can improve the performance of direct speech translation models. This line work was extended with the creation of SpeechMatrix (Duquenne et al., 2023a), a large-scale speech-to-speech translation corpus built using mined data.

2.3 Outlook

Understanding the Impact of Data Quality and Style The increasing volume of ST training resources comes with a risk on data quality. While scaling up training data volume offers obvious benefits, noisy data could hinder model performance. To the best of our knowledge, there is currently no established best practice for data filtering in speech translation. Current research presents conflicting findings on the impact of data quality. For example, Ouyang et al. (2022) observed no improvement in model performance when removing misaligned parallel data from the training set, while Gaido et al. (2022) demonstrated gains by filtering out such misalignments. Meanwhile it also remains unclear whether data filtering best practices are language-specific. Besides data quality, a deeper understanding of training data style's impact on ST performance is also beneficial. In the related field of MT, Maillard et al. (2023) showed gains by using small amounts of professionally-translated data. In ST, Ko et al. (2023) observed that interpretation-style data facilitates simultaneous translation models. Inspired by this finding, Sakai et al. (2024) pro-

Model	# Param	S2T X→en (21 lang.)	S2T en→X (15 lang.)	S2S X→en (21 lang.)	Learning
Speech-to-Text					
XLS-R (Babu et al., 2022)	2B	22.1	27.8	–	self-supervised + supervised FT
MAESTRO (Chen et al., 2022b)	0.6B	25.2	–	–	self-supervised + supervised FT
Whisper Large (Radford et al., 2023)	1.6B	29.7	–	–	(weakly) supervised
ComSL Large (Le et al., 2023)	1.3B	31.5	–	–	(weakly) supervised
AudioPaLM (Rubenstein et al., 2023)	8B	35.4	–	–	supervised FT
↪ + PaLM 2 (Anil et al., 2023)	8B	37.8	–	–	supervised FT
ZeroSWOT Large (Tsiamas et al., 2024)	1.7B	–	31.2	–	zero-shot combination pretrained ASR & MT
Speech-to-Text/Speech					
AudioPaLM S2ST (Rubenstein et al., 2023)	8B	36.2	–	32.5	supervised FT
SeamlessM4T Large (Seamless Communication et al., 2023b)	2.3B	34.1	30.6	36.5	self-supervised + supervised FT
↪ v2 (Seamless Communication et al., 2023a)	2.3B	36.6	31.7	39.2	self-supervised + supervised FT

Table 2: Performance overview of selected recent models for speech-to-text (S2T; BLEU↑; on **CoVoST 2**) and speech-to-speech translation (S2S; ASR-BLEU↑; on **CVSS**).

pose augmenting existing datasets with synthetic targets that mimic the style of interpretation data. Overall, exploring other data styles relevant to specific speech translation tasks could be promising for further performance improvements.

Targeted Resources for Low-Resource Languages The training resources in Table 1 primarily cover high-resource languages. For truly low-resource languages, readily available internet data may be scarce or non-existent. In such cases, collaboration with local communities becomes essential for data collection. The AmericasNLP speech translation shared task (Ebrahimi et al., 2021) is a successful example of this approach. The initiative focused on gathering speech translation data for indigenous languages of the Americas, demonstrating the feasibility of community-driven data collection for low-resource languages.

3 Model Architecture

In this section, we first review dedicated model architectures for speech-to-text (S2T; §3.1) and speech-to-speech (S2S; §3.2) translation, with a focus on the use of foundation models. Afterwards, we discuss recent developments in adapting general-purpose LLMs (§3.3) for encoding or generating speech.

3.1 Dedicated S2T Translation Models

Integrating Foundation Models Foundation models have become essential resources for training. Reflecting this trend, since 2022, a selection of (often massively multilingual) audio and text foundation models are allowed in the constrained data condition[2] in IWSLT (Anastasopoulos et al., 2022). However, as most current speech foundation models are either unsupervised/encoder-only (Baevski et al., 2020; Chung et al., 2021a; Chen et al., 2022a) or supervised with a limited translation directions (Radford et al., 2023), further adaptation is typically needed on specific speech translation tasks. A promising direction has been to pair pretrained audio encoders with text decoders, as frequently used in recent IWSLT system submissions (Gállego et al., 2021; Pham et al., 2022; Huang et al., 2023). In this process, additional lightweight adapters often are injected to bridge the audio and text representations (Li et al., 2021; Gállego et al., 2021; Zhao et al., 2022). For a focused survey of foundation models in S2T translation, we refer the readers to Gaido et al. (2024).

Representative Models and Trends Table 2 presents a chronological overview of some recent S2T translation models. Examining benchmark results on the CoVoST 2 dataset, a substantial performance improvement (+15.7 BLEU) is observed for X→en directions over the last two years. However, the picture for en→X directions remains less clear due to the limited number of data points. Nonetheless, when also considering the speech-

[2]as opposed the unconstrained data condition with no restrictions on training data and resources

to-text/speech results, we clearly see the progress in en→X is far behind X→en (22.1→36.6 BLEU vs. 27.8→31.7 BLEU). Regarding the learning paradigm, a trend emerges from developing new self-supervised representation learning schemes (XLS-R, MAESTRO) towards directly using pre-trained models (ComSL, AudioPaLM), in particular the plug-and-play combination of pretrained modules (Tsiamas et al., 2024) in zero-shot conditions.

3.2 Dedicated S2S Translation Models

Challenges of Generating Speech Speech generation presents unique challenges compared to text generation. First, the inherent longer length of audio signals poses significant computational demands for conventional autoregressive approaches. Moreover, capturing long-range dependencies within these extended sequences becomes more difficult for the model. Second, speech generation is often an under-specified problem. Unlike text, speech can be produced with various voice characteristics for the same content. This ambiguity creates a larger space of possible outputs that the model must handle.

Textless Models An advantage of speech-to-speech translation is the possibility to circumvent intermediate written text. Indeed, there has been growing interest in textless models (Jia et al., 2019b; Tjandra et al., 2019; Zhang et al., 2021b; Lee et al., 2022; Jia et al., 2022a), which do not rely on intermediate text representations and are especially suitable for S2ST of languages without standard writing systems. In general, these approaches first create discrete representations with unsupervised acoustic unit discovery by clustering or autoencoding (Tjandra et al., 2019; Zhang et al., 2021b; Hsu et al., 2021). The learned inventory of acoustic units could be viewed as learned phonemes. The input speech are then mapped to the discrete units, after which a unit-to-speech model is responsible for creating the output speech. Discretization of speech is further discussed in §3.4. Another advantage of textless models is the potential of preserving source voice characteristics. In particular, SeamlessExpressive (Seamless Communication et al., 2023a) is a recent model dedicated to voice characteristic preservation. Expressivity embeddings are extracted from the source speech and integrated in the output speech generation. Specifically, the model disentangles semantic and expressivity components from the source speech by learning speech reconstruction.

Representative Models and Trends In the lower section of Table 2, we list recent models supporting both S2T and S2S translation: AudioPaLM S2ST (Rubenstein et al., 2023) and SeamlessM4T (Seamless Communication et al., 2023b,a). AudioPaLM S2ST, in contrast to its variant lacking speech generation capabilities, is additionally trained on TTS and S2S translation data. The inclusion of additional modalities not only enables speech generation as an output, but also improves S2T translation performance (35.4→36.2 BLEU). Similar to its text generation counterpart, AudioPaLM S2ST fuses AudioLM (Borsos et al., 2023a) and the text-based PaLM model (Anil et al., 2023). The model has a joint vocabulary for both audio and text inputs. The audio tokens are created by an upgraded version of the USM encoder (Zhang et al., 2023b), which discretizes and downsamples the speech input. Speech tokenization is further discussed in (§3.1). Unlike AudioPaLM, **SeamlessM4T** utilizes an encoder-decoder architecture primarily fine-tuned from NLLB (NLLB Team et al., 2022). Its encoder additionally can additionally process speech inputs based on w2v-BERT representations (Chung et al., 2021b). Both AudioPaLM S2ST and SeamlessM4T achieve speech generation by optionally chaining a speech generation module after the text generation stage. AudioPaLM S2ST first converts audio tokens to SoundStream tokens (Zeghidour et al., 2022), which are then used by a vocoder to synthesize audio waveforms. SeamlessM4T, on the other hand, employs a text-to-unit encoder-decoder model followed by a vocoder.

3.3 General-Purpose Models

Adapting LLMs to Encode and Generate Speech Driven by the recent advancements in LLMs, there has been a surge of interest in adapting them for speech translation tasks. However, most publicly available LLMs, such as those in the LLaMA family (Touvron et al., 2023a,b), only support the text-to-text modality. To enable speech translation, these models require additional adaptation for both speech encoding and generation. A common approach for speech encoding involves discretizing and downsampling the audio input. This process transforms the continuous audio signal into a sequence of discrete tokens that the LLM can readily ingest. On the output side, typically discrete audio

Model	Speech Tokenization	Backbone LLM	Generation Module	Evaluated on ST
AudioPaLM (Rubenstein et al., 2023)	USM encoder (variant)	PaLM (8B)	SoundStorm	✓
PolyVoice (Dong et al., 2024)	HuBERT	GPT-2 (1.6B)	SoundStream (variant)	✓
SALMONN (Tang et al., 2024)	Window-level Q-Former	Vicuna (13B)	–	✓
NExT-GPT (Wu et al., 2023)	ImageBind	Vicuna (7B)	AudioLDM	✗
CoDi-2 (Tang et al., 2023)	ImageBind	LLaMA 2 (7B)	AudioLDM 2	✗
AnyGPT (Zhan et al., 2024)	SpeechTokenizer	LLaMA 2 (7B)	SoundStorm (variant)	✗

Table 3: Selected recent works adapting LLMs for speech processing and their components (speech tokenziation module, backbone LLM, and speech generation module).

tokens are generated similarly to text tokens. Afterwards, a synthesizer, for instance SoundStorm (Borsos et al., 2023b), converts these tokens to speech waveforms.

Representative Models and Trends In Table 3, we summarize recent works in LLMs for encoding and generating speech. Regarding the *speech tokenization* modules, common choices include ImageBind (Girdhar et al., 2023), SpeechTokenizer (Zhang et al., 2023a), HuBERT (Hsu et al., 2021), and the encoder of USM (Zhang et al., 2023b). For the *backbone LLMs*, the surveyed models mostly choose use small LLM variants (<10B parameters). For the *audio generation* module, popular choices are diffusion-based AudioLDM (Liu et al., 2023a), vector-quantization-based SoundStream (Zeghidour et al., 2022) and SoundStorm (Borsos et al., 2023b). As many of the reviewed models in Table 3 are not evaluated on speech translation, currently it is still difficult conclusively compare them to more conventional architectures.

3.4 Speech Tokenization

As introduced earlier, speech tokenization offers benefits in various applications, including textless translation and integration with text-based LLMs. Table 4 provides an overview of prominent approaches for speech tokenization and their underlying techniques. A common thread among these methods is the use of residual vector quantization (RVQ) (Barnes et al., 1996), which partitions the latent space into a finite number of subsets. While HuBERT employs k-means clustering, similar to RVQ in its objective of latent space partitioning, it differs in its implementation of offline clustering in a separate stage. In contrast to the other methods, ImageBind (Girdhar et al., 2023) directly encodes audio by transforming the spectrogram by Vision Transformer (ViT) (Dosovitskiy et al., 2021). It is worth exploring whether this approach carries sufficient fine-grained information for speech transcription or translation. The window-level Q-Former used in SALMONN (Tang et al., 2024) is also inspired by image processing. A sliding window of fixed size is applied on the speech features, where each window is processed by a Q-Former (Li et al., 2023), which creates a fixed number of token embeddings. These audio tokens embeddings are later ingested by the backbone LLM.

Model	Technique
HuBERT (Hsu et al., 2021)	k-means clustering
SoundStream (Zeghidour et al., 2022)	RVQ
SoundStorm (Borsos et al., 2023b)	RVQ
SpeechTokenizer (Zhang et al., 2023a)	RVQ
ImageBind (Girdhar et al., 2023)	spectrogram + ViT
Win.-level Q-Former (Tang et al., 2024)	sliding-window + Q-Former

Table 4: Common speech tokenization techniques.

3.5 Outlook

More Unified Speech and Text Generation As reviewed in this section, current speech and text generation approaches primarily rely on sequential processing or separate model branches. This raises the question of whether a more unified approach could be beneficial. Circumventing sequential processing could be particularly beneficial under real-time constraints.

Comparison between Architecture Paradigms Given the recency of some reviewed model types, especially those leveraging LLMs for general-purpose tasks (§3.3), a clear understanding of their performance compared to established architectures is still missing. Comprehensive benchmarking efforts targeting these recently emerged approaches could bridge this gap.

Identifying Scaling Law Prior works have examined how increasing model size affects model performance in MT (Fernandes et al., 2023). As the reviewed approaches in this work primarily focus on smaller LLMs, similar investigations for ST, particularly considering the foundation model size, could yield valuable practical insights.

How far will Transformers take us? A broader open question is whether alternative architectures can challenge the dominance of Transformers. State-space models (Gu et al., 2022a; Gu and Dao, 2023) could be a promising candidate, as their strength lies in capturing long-range dependencies, a crucial aspect for effective ST due to the inherent sequential nature of speech.

4 Multilingual and Multimodal Learning

Both multilingual and multimodal speech translation are instances of multi-task learning, where each translation direction in one input-output modality pair corresponds to one task. As also observed in general multi-task learning (Caruana, 1997), a key goal here is to maximize the transfer while minimizing the interference between tasks, while maintaining an efficient trade-off (Arivazhagan et al., 2019b). Given a defined model architecture (§3), different training procedures control the learned representations. In this section, we will discuss the relevant approaches in detail, taking two perspectives from task-specific (§4.1) and task-invariant modeling (§4.2).

4.1 Task-Specific Modeling

A central question when adding task-specific capacity is determining the optimal allocation between shared and task-specific components. Early works use hand-picked sharing strategies of sub-networks, such as language-specific decoders (Dong et al., 2015), attention heads (Zhu et al., 2020), and layer norm/linear transformation (Zhang et al., 2020). Recently, research interests shifted towards learning to balance between task-specific and shared capacity. We summarize representative approaches in the following categories: **1)** mixture-of-experts, **2)** adapters, **3)** factorization, and **4)** pruning, as illustrated in Figure 2. While these approaches may share similar end goals, the categorization helps to outline their specific computational approaches.

Mixture-of-Experts (MoEs) Compared to their dense counterparts, MoE networks (Eigen et al., 2014; Shazeer et al., 2017; Lepikhin et al., 2021) incorporate multiple expert subnets and use a gating mechanism to selectively activate the expert modules. Besides increasing model capacity, this approach also provides a neat framework for balancing between task-specific and task-agnostic modules. MoEs can be seen as neural architecture search (Baker et al., 2017), where the search space is the combination of the parallel expert modules.

For multilingual applications, a common configuration of MoE is to reserve one universal expert shared by all languages, while keeping the remaining experts language-specific. The importance of each expert module is learned by a gating mechanism. The final output is a mix between language-specific and shared ones. The overall amount of language-specific capacity can be controlled by a budget (Zhang et al., 2021a). There have been works applying MoEs in both multilingual ASR (Gaur et al., 2021; Kwon and Chung, 2023; Hu et al., 2023; Wang et al., 2023b) and MT (Zhang et al., 2021a; NLLB Team et al., 2022; Pires et al., 2023). In direct ST, there are fewer works using MoE. One work (Berrebbi et al., 2022) uses the MoE gating mechanism to balance different acoustic features to improve ST robustness.

Adapters Like MoEs, adapters (Rebuffi et al., 2017; Houlsby et al., 2019; Bapna and Firat, 2019) is another of form conditionally activated network. They can be seen as a restricted case of MoE with hard gating and fixed routing[3]. In this case, how the adapters are allocated to tasks needs to be decided a priori. A variety of allocation schemes have been explored, for example by language pairs (Bapna and Firat, 2019), single languages (Philip et al., 2020), and language families (Chronopoulou et al., 2023). In multilingual ST, language-specific adapters have been shown to improve over monolithic multilingual models and achieve comparable results to full fine-tuning (Le et al., 2021). Besides adding capacity, a more common use-case of adapters in speech translation is to bridge speech and text representations (Li et al., 2021; Escolano et al., 2021; Zhao et al., 2022), especially when coupling pretrained ASR and MT models (Gállego et al., 2021; Tsiamas et al., 2024). Further discussions on this are in §4.2.

Factorization Another perhaps less explored line of work uses factorization to balance language-specific and shared parameters. By decomposing originally shared parameters into (low-rank) factors that are either language-specific or shared, factorization enables a learned task allocation of

[3]Fusion between adapters (Pfeiffer et al., 2021) is an exception.

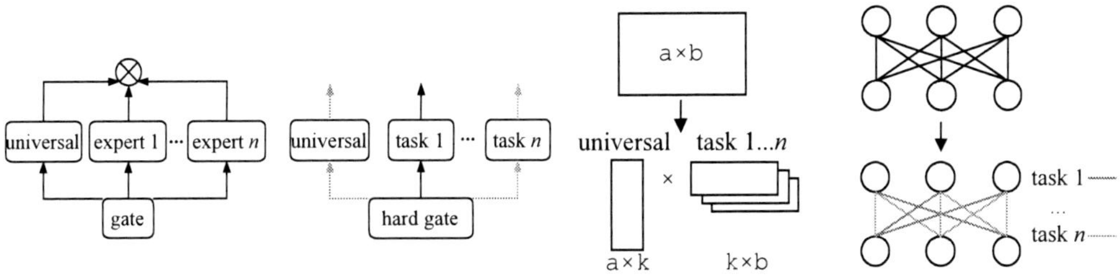

(a) MoEs (b) Adapters (c) Factorization (d) Pruning

Figure 2: Representative approaches for task-specific modeling.

parameters. This approach has seen applications in multilingual ASR (Pham et al., 2021) and MT (Xu et al., 2023). Compared to MoEs or adapters, an advantage of factorized models is their fewer total parameters, especially under large language coverage (Pham et al., 2021; Xu et al., 2023).

Pruning Pruning also leads to sparse sub-networks, similar to with MoEs. The difference is that pruning starts with a trained model, and then finetunes the selected sub-network. This therefore does not increase model capacity like MoEs. For multilingual models, per-language pruning results in a partially shared network, fostering a learned distribution of language-specific and shared capacities. This approach has demonstrated effectiveness in multilingual ASR (Lu et al., 2022; Yang et al., 2023b) and MT (Lin et al., 2021; Koishekenov et al., 2023; He et al., 2023). The pruned sub-networks are shown to correspond to language relatedness (Lin et al., 2021; He et al., 2023), suggesting the validity of the learned sharing patterns.

4.2 Task-Invariant Modeling

As introduced in §4.1, task-specific modeling often helps to alleviate interference in supervised conditions. One the other hand, language- or modality-invariant representations are often beneficial in zero-shot or low-resource data conditions as well as retrieval tasks.

Aligning Speech and Text Representations Many prior works (Liu et al., 2020b; Dinh et al., 2022; Ye et al., 2022; Wang et al., 2022; Ouyang et al., 2023; Duquenne et al., 2022, 2023b) seek to align speech and text representations, such that semantically similar sentences are represented similarly irrespective of their source modality (speech or text). A semantically-aligned multimodal latent space has at least the following benefits: **1)** It could facilitate the plug-and-play use of pretrained unimodal models (Duquenne et al., 2023b; Yang et al., 2023a; Tsiamas et al., 2024). **2)** Text representations are often more robust than speech due to more training data, where cross-modal alignment can help distill from the resource-richer text-based task (Liu et al., 2020b; Tang et al., 2021). Indeed, multiple works showed that enforcing cross-modal universal representations improves low-resource (Dinh et al., 2022; Ouyang et al., 2023) and zero-shot ST (Wang et al., 2022; Duquenne et al., 2022; Tsiamas et al., 2024). A major challenge in the alignment of speech and text is the length mismatch, where speech sequences are often factors longer than text. Therefore some shrinking mechanism is often necessary, e.g., by CTC-based downsampling (Liu et al., 2020b; Gaido et al., 2021), CNN-based length adapters (Gállego et al., 2021), or learning to aggregate the representations from both modalities to fixed sizes (Duquenne et al., 2022, 2023b).

Language-Invariant Modeling Another form of task-invariant modeling is to enforce similar representations for different languages, thereby establishing a language-agnostic semantic latent space. In multilingual MT, such approaches (Arivazhagan et al., 2019a; Pham et al., 2019; Liu et al., 2021) are shown effective on zero-shot translation of new language pairs not included in training. Another application where language-invariant modeling helps is similarity search, where multilingual sentence encoders (Artetxe and Schwenk, 2019; Duquenne et al., 2023b) are used to mine parallel data (Schwenk et al., 2021; Duquenne et al., 2023a) for translation training corpora.

4.3 Outlook

Synergy between Languages and Modalities Multi-task learning inherently faces a tradeoff between knowledge sharing and negative interference. This becomes particularly challenging to investigate in recent LLM-based models capable of handling a wide range of modalities (§3.3). A deeper understanding of the interactions between tasks will enable targeted solutions to mitigate interference and promote knowledge sharing.

Efficiently Adding Languages and Modalities While in this paper we primarily focuses on the two modalities of speech and text, expanding modality coverage is a natural next step. For new modalities, vision offers significant potential for real-world applications, including sign language translation (Müller et al., 2023) and lip reading (Afouras et al., 2020). Recent foundation models like Audio-Visual BERT (Shi et al., 2022) demonstrates the feasibility of multimodal processing that incorporates vision. An additional interesting direction is the continual learning of trained ST systems. The key challenge would be to integrate additional languages or modalities into the model without compromising its existing performance.

5 Evaluation

The evaluation of multilingual and multimodal ST models relies on more resources than their bilingual and unimodal counterparts. Here we outline relevant developments in evaluation resources (§5.1) and metrics (§5.2).

5.1 Evaluation Resources

The evaluation of multilingual and multimodal ST models heavily rely on multiway parallel evaluation data, such as the FLoRes evaluation set (Goyal et al., 2022; NLLB Team et al., 2022) and its speech-based extension FLEURS (Conneau et al., 2022). Meanwhile, the increasing training data scale of large foundation models introduces significant risks of data contamination. A very alarming example is the inclusion of the FLoRes-200 evaluation data (NLLB Team et al., 2022) in the training corpus of BLOOMZ (Muennighoff et al., 2023), leading to highly inflated performance scores on this specific set (Zhu et al., 2023), and rendering downstream models based on BLOOMZ untestable by this benchmark. As any Internet content could be ingested in LLM training, developing new, unpublished test sets becomes even more essential. The recent initiative of test suites in WMT (Kocmi et al., 2023) as well as in IWSLT is a significant step forward in addressing this challenge.

5.2 Evaluation Metric

Speech-to-Text Evaluation While the translation community is gradually moving beyond BLEU (Papineni et al., 2002) to neural metrics better calibrated to human ratings (Freitag et al., 2022) such as COMET (Rei et al., 2020), language coverage remains a challenge for very low-resource languages. For instance, COMET supports 109 languages at the time of writing[4], whereas evaluation on extremely low-resource languages often rely on match-based scores like chrF (Popović, 2015). Noteworthy are initiatives like AfriCOMET (Wang et al., 2023a) to scale neural metrics to lower-resource languages.

Speech-to-Speech Evaluation For evaluation of speech-to-speech translation, the emergence of similar neural metrics like BLASER (Chen et al., 2023) as replacement of ASR-BLEU is also encouraging. For expressive speech, evaluation on voice preservation primarily has been relying on basic acoustic features such as the fundamental frequency (Akuzawa et al., 2018) or pitch and energy (Jeuris and Niehues, 2022), which do not account for speech naturalness. Recently, Seamless Communication et al. (2023a) propose AutoPCP and a rhythm evaluation toolkit to measure prosody.

5.3 Outlook

Reliably Measuring Progress As discussed in §5.1, the advent of LLM also introduces higher risks of test data leakage. Besides calling for more rigorous documentation by model developers and critical evaluation by practitioners applying these models to downstream tasks, this also presents a crucial research question: how to effectively create representative testing scenarios to properly measure progress. Recent targeted evaluation datasets (Salesky et al., 2023) and community-driven creation of test suites (Kocmi et al., 2023) are excellent examples of such efforts. Only with such robust testing methodologies can we ensure the generalizability of observed performance improvements.

6 Deployment

In this section, we review three aspects relevant to model deployment: compression and distillation for serving the models (§6.1), continual learning of new capabilities (§6.2), and inference-time customization (§6.3).

[4]https://github.com/Unbabel/COMET?tab=readme-ov-file#languages-covered

6.1 Compression and Distillation

While tight-integrated multi-task models offer the advantage of a compact and unified structure that simplifies deployment, the growing trend of incorporating large pretrained components can negate part of this initial benefit. Recent works in pruning massively multilingual MT models (Mohammadshahi et al., 2022; Koishekenov et al., 2023) show successful model compression while maintaining translation quality. Another related direction is to distill larger models into to smaller student models (NLLB Team et al., 2022).

6.2 Continual Learning

Given a deployed model, one use-case is to add more languages or modalities to the existing system. A trade-off here is maintaining performance on existing tasks and achieving optimal adaptation to the new task. While continual learning for adding languages has been explored in multilingual ASR (Li et al., 2022; Pham et al., 2023) and MT (Gu et al., 2022b; Sun et al., 2023; Liu et al., 2023b) its application in direct ST remains less investigated. Recent advancements in parameter-efficient finetuning approaches, such as LoRA (Hu et al., 2022), offer an alternative modular approach. By training only the newly added parameters, inherently, one can naturally decouple the new knowledge from previously acquired information.

6.3 Inference-Time Customization

Deployed models sometimes require customization to meet additional constraints specific to the use case. An example is real-time applications, such as simultaneous translation, where speech input needs to be decoded before it is complete. While other approaches involve designing separate models for online scenarios, repurposing offline models for online use cases (Liu et al., 2020a; Papi et al., 2022, 2023) has been shown to be a competitive alternative. This is particularly advantageous on foundation models (Papi et al., 2024) where retraining the model for specific use-cases is infeasible.

6.4 Outlook

Retrieval-Augmented Generation For both continual learning and inference-time customization as reviewed above, retrieval-augmented generation could be a promising approach. For instance, a separate data store could house continual learning data points, allowing for model updates without modifying the deployed model itself. Retrieval-augmented translation has demonstrated success in the text domain (Zhang et al., 2018; Xu et al., 2020; Cai et al., 2021; Hoang et al., 2023; Hao et al., 2023). In the context of ST, Du et al. (2022) explored kNN-MT (Khandelwal et al., 2021) for domain adaption using a joint speech and text input model with a text-based data store. However, it remains unclear how speech-based retrieval can benefit ST performance. Methods for efficiently incorporating speech data into the retrieval process is an interesting direction of future research.

7 Conclusion

In this paper, we presented a selection of recent advancements in multilingual and multimodal speech translation. We zoom into individual stages of the lifecycle of building a system: from determining model coverage and architecture, training procedures, to evaluation, and eventually deployment. This work is not an exhaustive survey, but rather a snapshot of ongoing developments related to multilingual and multimodal speech translation. We welcome the community's feedback on any relevant omitted works in the current version.

Acknowledgement

We thank the anonymous reviewers for constructive and insightful feedback. We also thank Annika Sauer for helpful pointers. This paper has received funding from the European Union's Horizon research and innovation programme under grant agreement No 101135798, project Meetween (My Personal AI Mediator for Virtual MEETtings BetWEEN People). Part of this work was supported by funding from the pilot program Core-Informatics of the Helmholtz Association (HGF).

References

Triantafyllos Afouras, Joon Son Chung, and Andrew Zisserman. 2020. ASR is all you need: Cross-modal distillation for lip reading. In *2020 IEEE International Conference on Acoustics, Speech and Signal Processing, ICASSP 2020, Barcelona, Spain, May 4-8, 2020*, pages 2143–2147. IEEE.

Kei Akuzawa, Yusuke Iwasawa, and Yutaka Matsuo. 2018. Expressive Speech Synthesis via Modeling Expressions with Variational Autoencoder. In *Proc. Interspeech 2018*, pages 3067–3071.

Antonios Anastasopoulos, Loïc Barrault, Luisa Bentivogli, Marcely Zanon Boito, Ondřej Bojar, Roldano

Cattoni, Anna Currey, Georgiana Dinu, Kevin Duh, Maha Elbayad, Clara Emmanuel, Yannick Estève, Marcello Federico, Christian Federmann, Souhir Gahbiche, Hongyu Gong, Roman Grundkiewicz, Barry Haddow, Benjamin Hsu, Dávid Javorský, Věra Kloudová, Surafel Lakew, Xutai Ma, Prashant Mathur, Paul McNamee, Kenton Murray, Maria Nădejde, Satoshi Nakamura, Matteo Negri, Jan Niehues, Xing Niu, John Ortega, Juan Pino, Elizabeth Salesky, Jiatong Shi, Matthias Sperber, Sebastian Stüker, Katsuhito Sudoh, Marco Turchi, Yogesh Virkar, Alexander Waibel, Changhan Wang, and Shinji Watanabe. 2022. Findings of the IWSLT 2022 evaluation campaign. In *Proceedings of the 19th International Conference on Spoken Language Translation (IWSLT 2022)*, pages 98–157, Dublin, Ireland (in-person and online). Association for Computational Linguistics.

Rohan Anil, Andrew M. Dai, Orhan Firat, Melvin Johnson, Dmitry Lepikhin, Alexandre Passos, Siamak Shakeri, Emanuel Taropa, Paige Bailey, Zhifeng Chen, Eric Chu, Jonathan H. Clark, Laurent El Shafey, Yanping Huang, Kathy Meier-Hellstern, Gaurav Mishra, Erica Moreira, Mark Omernick, Kevin Robinson, Sebastian Ruder, Yi Tay, Kefan Xiao, Yuanzhong Xu, Yujing Zhang, Gustavo Hernández Ábrego, Junwhan Ahn, Jacob Austin, Paul Barham, Jan A. Botha, James Bradbury, Siddhartha Brahma, Kevin Brooks, Michele Catasta, Yong Cheng, Colin Cherry, Christopher A. Choquette-Choo, Aakanksha Chowdhery, Clément Crepy, Shachi Dave, Mostafa Dehghani, Sunipa Dev, Jacob Devlin, Mark Díaz, Nan Du, Ethan Dyer, Vladimir Feinberg, Fangxiaoyu Feng, Vlad Fienber, Markus Freitag, Xavier Garcia, Sebastian Gehrmann, Lucas Gonzalez, and et al. 2023. Palm 2 technical report. *CoRR*, abs/2305.10403.

Naveen Arivazhagan, Ankur Bapna, Orhan Firat, Roee Aharoni, Melvin Johnson, and Wolfgang Macherey. 2019a. The missing ingredient in zero-shot neural machine translation. *CoRR*, abs/1903.07091.

Naveen Arivazhagan, Ankur Bapna, Orhan Firat, Dmitry Lepikhin, Melvin Johnson, Maxim Krikun, Mia Xu Chen, Yuan Cao, George F. Foster, Colin Cherry, Wolfgang Macherey, Zhifeng Chen, and Yonghui Wu. 2019b. Massively multilingual neural machine translation in the wild: Findings and challenges. *CoRR*, abs/1907.05019.

Mikel Artetxe and Holger Schwenk. 2019. Massively multilingual sentence embeddings for zero-shot cross-lingual transfer and beyond. *Transactions of the Association for Computational Linguistics*, 7:597–610.

Arun Babu, Changhan Wang, Andros Tjandra, Kushal Lakhotia, Qiantong Xu, Naman Goyal, Kritika Singh, Patrick von Platen, Yatharth Saraf, Juan Pino, Alexei Baevski, Alexis Conneau, and Michael Auli. 2022. XLS-R: Self-supervised Cross-lingual Speech Representation Learning at Scale. In *Proc. Interspeech 2022*, pages 2278–2282.

Alexei Baevski, Yuhao Zhou, Abdelrahman Mohamed, and Michael Auli. 2020. wav2vec 2.0: A framework for self-supervised learning of speech representations. In *Advances in Neural Information Processing Systems 33: Annual Conference on Neural Information Processing Systems 2020, NeurIPS 2020, December 6-12, 2020, virtual*.

Bowen Baker, Otkrist Gupta, Nikhil Naik, and Ramesh Raskar. 2017. Designing neural network architectures using reinforcement learning. In *5th International Conference on Learning Representations, ICLR 2017, Toulon, France, April 24-26, 2017, Conference Track Proceedings*. OpenReview.net.

Ankur Bapna and Orhan Firat. 2019. Simple, scalable adaptation for neural machine translation. In *Proceedings of the 2019 Conference on Empirical Methods in Natural Language Processing and the 9th International Joint Conference on Natural Language Processing (EMNLP-IJCNLP)*, pages 1538–1548, Hong Kong, China. Association for Computational Linguistics.

C.F. Barnes, S.A. Rizvi, and N.M. Nasrabadi. 1996. Advances in residual vector quantization: a review. *IEEE Transactions on Image Processing*, 5(2):226–262.

Dan Berrebbi, Jiatong Shi, Brian Yan, Osbel López-Francisco, Jonathan D. Amith, and Shinji Watanabe. 2022. Combining spectral and self-supervised features for low resource speech recognition and translation. In *Interspeech 2022, 23rd Annual Conference of the International Speech Communication Association, Incheon, Korea, 18-22 September 2022*, pages 3533–3537. ISCA.

Zalán Borsos, Raphaël Marinier, Damien Vincent, Eugene Kharitonov, Olivier Pietquin, Matthew Sharifi, Dominik Roblek, Olivier Teboul, David Grangier, Marco Tagliasacchi, and Neil Zeghidour. 2023a. Audiolm: A language modeling approach to audio generation. *IEEE ACM Trans. Audio Speech Lang. Process.*, 31:2523–2533.

Zalán Borsos, Matthew Sharifi, Damien Vincent, Eugene Kharitonov, Neil Zeghidour, and Marco Tagliasacchi. 2023b. Soundstorm: Efficient parallel audio generation. *CoRR*, abs/2305.09636.

Deng Cai, Yan Wang, Huayang Li, Wai Lam, and Lemao Liu. 2021. Neural machine translation with monolingual translation memory. In *Proceedings of the 59th Annual Meeting of the Association for Computational Linguistics and the 11th International Joint Conference on Natural Language Processing (Volume 1: Long Papers)*, pages 7307–7318, Online. Association for Computational Linguistics.

Rich Caruana. 1997. Multitask learning. *Mach. Learn.*, 28(1):41–75.

Roldano Cattoni, Mattia Antonino Di Gangi, Luisa Bentivogli, Matteo Negri, and Marco Turchi. 2021. Must-c: A multilingual corpus for end-to-end speech translation. *Comput. Speech Lang.*, 66:101155.

Mingda Chen, Paul-Ambroise Duquenne, Pierre Andrews, Justine Kao, Alexandre Mourachko, Holger Schwenk, and Marta R. Costa-jussà. 2023. BLASER: A text-free speech-to-speech translation evaluation metric. In *Proceedings of the 61st Annual Meeting of the Association for Computational Linguistics (Volume 1: Long Papers)*, pages 9064–9079, Toronto, Canada. Association for Computational Linguistics.

Sanyuan Chen, Chengyi Wang, Zhengyang Chen, Yu Wu, Shujie Liu, Zhuo Chen, Jinyu Li, Naoyuki Kanda, Takuya Yoshioka, Xiong Xiao, Jian Wu, Long Zhou, Shuo Ren, Yanmin Qian, Yao Qian, Jian Wu, Michael Zeng, Xiangzhan Yu, and Furu Wei. 2022a. Wavlm: Large-scale self-supervised pre-training for full stack speech processing. *IEEE J. Sel. Top. Signal Process.*, 16(6):1505–1518.

Zhehuai Chen, Yu Zhang, Andrew Rosenberg, Bhuvana Ramabhadran, Pedro J. Moreno, Ankur Bapna, and Heiga Zen. 2022b. MAESTRO: Matched Speech Text Representations through Modality Matching. In *Proc. Interspeech 2022*, pages 4093–4097.

Alexandra Chronopoulou, Dario Stojanovski, and Alexander Fraser. 2023. Language-family adapters for low-resource multilingual neural machine translation. In *Proceedings of the The Sixth Workshop on Technologies for Machine Translation of Low-Resource Languages (LoResMT 2023)*, pages 59–72, Dubrovnik, Croatia. Association for Computational Linguistics.

Yu-An Chung, Yu Zhang, Wei Han, Chung-Cheng Chiu, James Qin, Ruoming Pang, and Yonghui Wu. 2021a. w2v-bert: Combining contrastive learning and masked language modeling for self-supervised speech pre-training. In *IEEE Automatic Speech Recognition and Understanding Workshop, ASRU 2021, Cartagena, Colombia, December 13-17, 2021*, pages 244–250. IEEE.

Yu-An Chung, Yu Zhang, Wei Han, Chung-Cheng Chiu, James Qin, Ruoming Pang, and Yonghui Wu. 2021b. w2v-bert: Combining contrastive learning and masked language modeling for self-supervised speech pre-training. In *IEEE Automatic Speech Recognition and Understanding Workshop, ASRU 2021, Cartagena, Colombia, December 13-17, 2021*, pages 244–250. IEEE.

Alexis Conneau, Min Ma, Simran Khanuja, Yu Zhang, Vera Axelrod, Siddharth Dalmia, Jason Riesa, Clara Rivera, and Ankur Bapna. 2022. FLEURS: few-shot learning evaluation of universal representations of speech. In *IEEE Spoken Language Technology Workshop, SLT 2022, Doha, Qatar, January 9-12, 2023*, pages 798–805. IEEE.

Mattia A. Di Gangi, Roldano Cattoni, Luisa Bentivogli, Matteo Negri, and Marco Turchi. 2019. MuST-C: a Multilingual Speech Translation Corpus. In *Proceedings of the 2019 Conference of the North American Chapter of the Association for Computational Linguistics: Human Language Technologies, Volume 1 (Long and Short Papers)*, pages 2012–2017, Minneapolis, Minnesota. Association for Computational Linguistics.

Mattia Antonino Di Gangi, Matteo Negri, and Marco Turchi. 2019. One-to-many multilingual end-to-end speech translation. In *IEEE Automatic Speech Recognition and Understanding Workshop, ASRU 2019, Singapore, December 14-18, 2019*, pages 585–592. IEEE.

Tu Anh Dinh, Danni Liu, and Jan Niehues. 2022. Tackling data scarcity in speech translation using zero-shot multilingual machine translation techniques. In *IEEE International Conference on Acoustics, Speech and Signal Processing, ICASSP 2022, Virtual and Singapore, 23-27 May 2022*, pages 6222–6226. IEEE.

Daxiang Dong, Hua Wu, Wei He, Dianhai Yu, and Haifeng Wang. 2015. Multi-task learning for multiple language translation. In *Proceedings of the 53rd Annual Meeting of the Association for Computational Linguistics and the 7th International Joint Conference on Natural Language Processing (Volume 1: Long Papers)*, pages 1723–1732, Beijing, China. Association for Computational Linguistics.

Qianqian Dong, Zhiying Huang, Qiao Tian, Chen Xu, Tom Ko, yunlong zhao, Siyuan Feng, Tang Li, Kexin Wang, Xuxin Cheng, Fengpeng Yue, Ye Bai, Xi Chen, Lu Lu, Zejun MA, Yuping Wang, Mingxuan Wang, and Yuxuan Wang. 2024. Polyvoice: Language models for speech to speech translation. In *The Twelfth International Conference on Learning Representations*.

Alexey Dosovitskiy, Lucas Beyer, Alexander Kolesnikov, Dirk Weissenborn, Xiaohua Zhai, Thomas Unterthiner, Mostafa Dehghani, Matthias Minderer, Georg Heigold, Sylvain Gelly, Jakob Uszkoreit, and Neil Houlsby. 2021. An image is worth 16x16 words: Transformers for image recognition at scale. In *9th International Conference on Learning Representations, ICLR 2021, Virtual Event, Austria, May 3-7, 2021*. OpenReview.net.

Yichao Du, Weizhi Wang, Zhirui Zhang, Boxing Chen, Tong Xu, Jun Xie, and Enhong Chen. 2022. Non-parametric domain adaptation for end-to-end speech translation. In *Proceedings of the 2022 Conference on Empirical Methods in Natural Language Processing*, pages 306–320, Abu Dhabi, United Arab Emirates. Association for Computational Linguistics.

Paul-Ambroise Duquenne, Hongyu Gong, Ning Dong, Jingfei Du, Ann Lee, Vedanuj Goswami, Changhan Wang, Juan Pino, Benoît Sagot, and Holger Schwenk. 2023a. SpeechMatrix: A large-scale mined corpus of multilingual speech-to-speech translations. In *Proceedings of the 61st Annual Meeting of the Association for Computational Linguistics (Volume 1: Long Papers)*, pages 16251–16269, Toronto, Canada. Association for Computational Linguistics.

Paul-Ambroise Duquenne, Hongyu Gong, Benoît Sagot, and Holger Schwenk. 2022. T-modules: Translation modules for zero-shot cross-modal machine translation. In *Proceedings of the 2022 Conference on Empirical Methods in Natural Language Processing*, pages 5794–5806, Abu Dhabi, United Arab Emirates. Association for Computational Linguistics.

Paul-Ambroise Duquenne, Hongyu Gong, and Holger Schwenk. 2021. Multimodal and multilingual embeddings for large-scale speech mining. In *Advances in Neural Information Processing Systems 34: Annual Conference on Neural Information Processing Systems 2021, NeurIPS 2021, December 6-14, 2021, virtual*, pages 15748–15761.

Paul-Ambroise Duquenne, Holger Schwenk, and Benoît Sagot. 2023b. SONAR: sentence-level multimodal and language-agnostic representations. *CoRR*, abs/2308.11466.

Abteen Ebrahimi, Manuel Mager, Adam Wiemerslage, Pavel Denisov, Arturo Oncevay, Danni Liu, Sai Koneru, Enes Yavuz Ugan, Zhaolin Li, Jan Niehues, Monica Romero, Ivan G Torre, Tanel Alumäe, Jiaming Kong, Sergey Polezhaev, Yury Belousov, Wei-Rui Chen, Peter Sullivan, Ife Adebara, Bashar Talafha, Alcides Alcoba Inciarte, Muhammad Abdul-Mageed, Luis Chiruzzo, Rolando Coto-Solano, Hilaria Cruz, Sofía Flores-Solórzano, Aldo Andrés Alvarez López, Iván V. Meza-Ruíz, John E. Ortega, Alexis Palmer, Rodolfo Zevallos, Kristine Stenzel, Thang Vu, and Katharina Kann. 2021. Findings of the second americasnlp competition on speech-to-text translation. In *NeurIPS 2022 Competition Track, November 28 - December 9, 2022, Online*, volume 220 of *Proceedings of Machine Learning Research*, pages 217–232. PMLR.

David Eigen, Marc'Aurelio Ranzato, and Ilya Sutskever. 2014. Learning factored representations in a deep mixture of experts. In *2nd International Conference on Learning Representations, ICLR 2014, Banff, AB, Canada, April 14-16, 2014, Workshop Track Proceedings*.

Carlos Escolano, Marta R. Costa-jussà, José A. R. Fonollosa, and Carlos Segura. 2021. Enabling zero-shot multilingual spoken language translation with language-specific encoders and decoders. In *2021 IEEE Automatic Speech Recognition and Understanding Workshop (ASRU)*, pages 694–701.

Patrick Fernandes, Behrooz Ghorbani, Xavier Garcia, Markus Freitag, and Orhan Firat. 2023. Scaling laws for multilingual neural machine translation. In *International Conference on Machine Learning, ICML 2023, 23-29 July 2023, Honolulu, Hawaii, USA*, volume 202 of *Proceedings of Machine Learning Research*, pages 10053–10071. PMLR.

Markus Freitag, Ricardo Rei, Nitika Mathur, Chi-kiu Lo, Craig Stewart, Eleftherios Avramidis, Tom Kocmi, George Foster, Alon Lavie, and André F. T. Martins. 2022. Results of WMT22 metrics shared task: Stop using BLEU – neural metrics are better and more robust. In *Proceedings of the Seventh Conference on Machine Translation (WMT)*, pages 46–68, Abu Dhabi, United Arab Emirates (Hybrid). Association for Computational Linguistics.

Marco Gaido, Mauro Cettolo, Matteo Negri, and Marco Turchi. 2021. CTC-based compression for direct speech translation. In *Proceedings of the 16th Conference of the European Chapter of the Association for Computational Linguistics: Main Volume*, pages 690–696, Online. Association for Computational Linguistics.

Marco Gaido, Sara Papi, Dennis Fucci, Giuseppe Fiameni, Matteo Negri, and Marco Turchi. 2022. Efficient yet competitive speech translation: FBK@IWSLT2022. In *Proceedings of the 19th International Conference on Spoken Language Translation (IWSLT 2022)*, pages 177–189, Dublin, Ireland (in-person and online). Association for Computational Linguistics.

Marco Gaido, Sara Papi, Matteo Negri, and Luisa Bentivogli. 2024. Speech translation with speech foundation models and large language models: What is there and what is missing? *CoRR*, abs/2402.12025.

Gerard I. Gállego, Ioannis Tsiamas, Carlos Escolano, José A. R. Fonollosa, and Marta R. Costa-jussà. 2021. End-to-end speech translation with pre-trained models and adapters: UPC at IWSLT 2021. In *Proceedings of the 18th International Conference on Spoken Language Translation (IWSLT 2021)*, pages 110–119, Bangkok, Thailand (online). Association for Computational Linguistics.

Neeraj Gaur, Brian Farris, Parisa Haghani, Isabel Leal, Pedro J. Moreno, Manasa Prasad, Bhuvana Ramabhadran, and Yun Zhu. 2021. Mixture of informed experts for multilingual speech recognition. In *IEEE International Conference on Acoustics, Speech and Signal Processing, ICASSP 2021, Toronto, ON, Canada, June 6-11, 2021*, pages 6234–6238. IEEE.

Rohit Girdhar, Alaaeldin El-Nouby, Zhuang Liu, Mannat Singh, Kalyan Vasudev Alwala, Armand Joulin, and Ishan Misra. 2023. Imagebind one embedding space to bind them all. In *IEEE/CVF Conference on Computer Vision and Pattern Recognition, CVPR 2023, Vancouver, BC, Canada, June 17-24, 2023*, pages 15180–15190. IEEE.

Naman Goyal, Cynthia Gao, Vishrav Chaudhary, Peng-Jen Chen, Guillaume Wenzek, Da Ju, Sanjana Krishnan, Marc'Aurelio Ranzato, Francisco Guzmán, and Angela Fan. 2022. The flores-101 evaluation benchmark for low-resource and multilingual machine translation. *Trans. Assoc. Comput. Linguistics*, 10:522–538.

Albert Gu and Tri Dao. 2023. Mamba: Linear-time sequence modeling with selective state spaces. *CoRR*, abs/2312.00752.

Albert Gu, Karan Goel, and Christopher Ré. 2022a. Efficiently modeling long sequences with structured state spaces. In *The Tenth International Conference on Learning Representations, ICLR 2022, Virtual Event, April 25-29, 2022*. OpenReview.net.

Shuhao Gu, Bojie Hu, and Yang Feng. 2022b. Continual learning of neural machine translation within low forgetting risk regions. In *Proceedings of the 2022 Conference on Empirical Methods in Natural Language Processing*, pages 1707–1718, Abu Dhabi, United Arab Emirates. Association for Computational Linguistics.

Hongkun Hao, Guoping Huang, Lemao Liu, Zhirui Zhang, Shuming Shi, and Rui Wang. 2023. Rethinking translation memory augmented neural machine translation. In *Findings of the Association for Computational Linguistics: ACL 2023*, pages 2589–2605, Toronto, Canada. Association for Computational Linguistics.

Dan He, Minh-Quang Pham, Thanh-Le Ha, and Marco Turchi. 2023. Gradient-based gradual pruning for language-specific multilingual neural machine translation. In *Proceedings of the 2023 Conference on Empirical Methods in Natural Language Processing*, pages 654–670, Singapore. Association for Computational Linguistics.

Cuong Hoang, Devendra Sachan, Prashant Mathur, Brian Thompson, and Marcello Federico. 2023. Improving retrieval augmented neural machine translation by controlling source and fuzzy-match interactions. In *Findings of the Association for Computational Linguistics: EACL 2023*, pages 289–295, Dubrovnik, Croatia. Association for Computational Linguistics.

Neil Houlsby, Andrei Giurgiu, Stanislaw Jastrzebski, Bruna Morrone, Quentin de Laroussilhe, Andrea Gesmundo, Mona Attariyan, and Sylvain Gelly. 2019. Parameter-efficient transfer learning for NLP. In *Proceedings of the 36th International Conference on Machine Learning, ICML 2019, 9-15 June 2019, Long Beach, California, USA*, volume 97 of *Proceedings of Machine Learning Research*, pages 2790–2799. PMLR.

Wei-Ning Hsu, Benjamin Bolte, Yao-Hung Hubert Tsai, Kushal Lakhotia, Ruslan Salakhutdinov, and Abdelrahman Mohamed. 2021. Hubert: Self-supervised speech representation learning by masked prediction of hidden units. *IEEE ACM Trans. Audio Speech Lang. Process.*, 29:3451–3460.

Edward J. Hu, Yelong Shen, Phillip Wallis, Zeyuan Allen-Zhu, Yuanzhi Li, Shean Wang, Lu Wang, and Weizhu Chen. 2022. Lora: Low-rank adaptation of large language models. In *The Tenth International Conference on Learning Representations, ICLR 2022, Virtual Event, April 25-29, 2022*. OpenReview.net.

Ke Hu, Bo Li, Tara Sainath, Yu Zhang, and Françoise Beaufays. 2023. Mixture-of-Expert Conformer for Streaming Multilingual ASR. In *Proc. INTERSPEECH 2023*, pages 3327–3331.

Wuwei Huang, Mengge Liu, Xiang Li, Yanzhi Tian, Fengyu Yang, Wen Zhang, Jian Luan, Bin Wang, Yuhang Guo, and Jinsong Su. 2023. The xiaomi AI lab's speech translation systems for IWSLT 2023 offline task, simultaneous task and speech-to-speech task. In *Proceedings of the 20th International Conference on Spoken Language Translation (IWSLT 2023)*, pages 411–419, Toronto, Canada (in-person and online). Association for Computational Linguistics.

Hirofumi Inaguma, Kevin Duh, Tatsuya Kawahara, and Shinji Watanabe. 2019. Multilingual end-to-end speech translation. In *IEEE Automatic Speech Recognition and Understanding Workshop, ASRU 2019, Singapore, December 14-18, 2019*, pages 570–577. IEEE.

Hirofumi Inaguma, Sravya Popuri, Ilia Kulikov, Peng-Jen Chen, Changhan Wang, Yu-An Chung, Yun Tang, Ann Lee, Shinji Watanabe, and Juan Pino. 2023. UnitY: Two-pass direct speech-to-speech translation with discrete units. In *Proceedings of the 61st Annual Meeting of the Association for Computational Linguistics (Volume 1: Long Papers)*, pages 15655–15680, Toronto, Canada. Association for Computational Linguistics.

Javier Iranzo-Sánchez, Joan Albert Silvestre-Cerdà, Javier Jorge, Nahuel Roselló, Adrià Giménez, Albert Sanchis, Jorge Civera, and Alfons Juan. 2020. Europarl-st: A multilingual corpus for speech translation of parliamentary debates. In *ICASSP 2020 - 2020 IEEE International Conference on Acoustics, Speech and Signal Processing (ICASSP)*, pages 8229–8233.

Pedro Jeuris and Jan Niehues. 2022. LibriS2S: A German-English speech-to-speech translation corpus. In *Proceedings of the Thirteenth Language Resources and Evaluation Conference*, pages 928–935, Marseille, France. European Language Resources Association.

Ye Jia, Melvin Johnson, Wolfgang Macherey, Ron J. Weiss, Yuan Cao, Chung-Cheng Chiu, Naveen Ari, Stella Laurenzo, and Yonghui Wu. 2019a. Leveraging weakly supervised data to improve end-to-end speech-to-text translation. In *ICASSP 2019 - 2019 IEEE International Conference on Acoustics, Speech and Signal Processing (ICASSP)*, pages 7180–7184.

Ye Jia, Michelle Tadmor Ramanovich, Tal Remez, and Roi Pomerantz. 2022a. Translatotron 2: High-quality direct speech-to-speech translation with voice preservation. In *International Conference on Machine Learning, ICML 2022, 17-23 July 2022, Baltimore, Maryland, USA*, volume 162 of *Proceedings of Machine Learning Research*, pages 10120–10134. PMLR.

Ye Jia, Michelle Tadmor Ramanovich, Quan Wang, and Heiga Zen. 2022b. CVSS corpus and massively multilingual speech-to-speech translation. In *Proceedings of the Thirteenth Language Resources and Evaluation Conference*, pages 6691–6703, Marseille, France. European Language Resources Association.

Ye Jia, Ron J. Weiss, Fadi Biadsy, Wolfgang Macherey, Melvin Johnson, Zhifeng Chen, and Yonghui Wu. 2019b. Direct Speech-to-Speech Translation with a Sequence-to-Sequence Model. In *Proc. Interspeech 2019*, pages 1123–1127.

Urvashi Khandelwal, Angela Fan, Dan Jurafsky, Luke Zettlemoyer, and Mike Lewis. 2021. Nearest neighbor machine translation. In *9th International Conference on Learning Representations, ICLR 2021, Virtual Event, Austria, May 3-7, 2021*. OpenReview.net.

Yuka Ko, Ryo Fukuda, Yuta Nishikawa, Yasumasa Kano, Katsuhito Sudoh, and Satoshi Nakamura. 2023. Tagged end-to-end simultaneous speech translation training using simultaneous interpretation data. In *Proceedings of the 20th International Conference on Spoken Language Translation (IWSLT 2023)*, pages 363–375, Toronto, Canada (in-person and online). Association for Computational Linguistics.

Tom Kocmi, Eleftherios Avramidis, Rachel Bawden, Ondřej Bojar, Anton Dvorkovich, Christian Federmann, Mark Fishel, Markus Freitag, Thamme Gowda, Roman Grundkiewicz, Barry Haddow, Philipp Koehn, Benjamin Marie, Christof Monz, Makoto Morishita, Kenton Murray, Makoto Nagata, Toshiaki Nakazawa, Martin Popel, Maja Popović, and Mariya Shmatova. 2023. Findings of the 2023 conference on machine translation (WMT23): LLMs are here but not quite there yet. In *Proceedings of the Eighth Conference on Machine Translation*, pages 1–42, Singapore. Association for Computational Linguistics.

Yeskendir Koishekenov, Alexandre Berard, and Vassilina Nikoulina. 2023. Memory-efficient NLLB-200: Language-specific expert pruning of a massively multilingual machine translation model. In *Proceedings of the 61st Annual Meeting of the Association for Computational Linguistics (Volume 1: Long Papers)*, pages 3567–3585, Toronto, Canada. Association for Computational Linguistics.

Yoohwan Kwon and Soo-Whan Chung. 2023. Mole : Mixture of language experts for multi-lingual automatic speech recognition. In *IEEE International Conference on Acoustics, Speech and Signal Processing ICASSP 2023, Rhodes Island, Greece, June 4-10, 2023*, pages 1–5. IEEE.

Chenyang Le, Yao Qian, Long Zhou, Shujie Liu, Yanmin Qian, Michael Zeng, and Xuedong Huang. 2023. Comsl: A composite speech-language model for end-to-end speech-to-text translation. In *Advances in Neural Information Processing Systems 36: Annual Conference on Neural Information Processing Systems 2023, NeurIPS 2023, New Orleans, LA, USA, December 10 - 16, 2023*.

Hang Le, Juan Pino, Changhan Wang, Jiatao Gu, Didier Schwab, and Laurent Besacier. 2021. Lightweight adapter tuning for multilingual speech translation. In *Proceedings of the 59th Annual Meeting of the Association for Computational Linguistics and the 11th International Joint Conference on Natural Language Processing (Volume 2: Short Papers)*, pages 817–824, Online. Association for Computational Linguistics.

Ann Lee, Peng-Jen Chen, Changhan Wang, Jiatao Gu, Sravya Popuri, Xutai Ma, Adam Polyak, Yossi Adi, Qing He, Yun Tang, Juan Pino, and Wei-Ning Hsu. 2022. Direct speech-to-speech translation with discrete units. In *Proceedings of the 60th Annual Meeting of the Association for Computational Linguistics (Volume 1: Long Papers)*, pages 3327–3339, Dublin, Ireland. Association for Computational Linguistics.

Dmitry Lepikhin, HyoukJoong Lee, Yuanzhong Xu, Dehao Chen, Orhan Firat, Yanping Huang, Maxim Krikun, Noam Shazeer, and Zhifeng Chen. 2021. Gshard: Scaling giant models with conditional computation and automatic sharding. In *9th International Conference on Learning Representations, ICLR 2021, Virtual Event, Austria, May 3-7, 2021*. OpenReview.net.

Bo Li, Ruoming Pang, Yu Zhang, Tara N. Sainath, Trevor Strohman, Parisa Haghani, Yun Zhu, Brian Farris, Neeraj Gaur, and Manasa Prasad. 2022. Massively multilingual asr: A lifelong learning solution. In *ICASSP 2022 - 2022 IEEE International Conference on Acoustics, Speech and Signal Processing (ICASSP)*, pages 6397–6401.

Junnan Li, Dongxu Li, Silvio Savarese, and Steven C. H. Hoi. 2023. BLIP-2: bootstrapping language-image pre-training with frozen image encoders and large language models. In *International Conference on Machine Learning, ICML 2023, 23-29 July 2023, Honolulu, Hawaii, USA*, volume 202 of *Proceedings of Machine Learning Research*, pages 19730–19742. PMLR.

Xian Li, Changhan Wang, Yun Tang, Chau Tran, Yuqing Tang, Juan Pino, Alexei Baevski, Alexis Conneau, and Michael Auli. 2021. Multilingual speech translation from efficient finetuning of pretrained models. In *Proceedings of the 59th Annual Meeting of the Association for Computational Linguistics and the 11th International Joint Conference on Natural Language Processing (Volume 1: Long Papers)*, pages 827–838, Online. Association for Computational Linguistics.

Zehui Lin, Liwei Wu, Mingxuan Wang, and Lei Li. 2021. Learning language specific sub-network for multilingual machine translation. In *Proceedings of the 59th Annual Meeting of the Association for Computational Linguistics and the 11th International Joint Conference on Natural Language Processing (Volume 1: Long Papers)*, pages 293–305, Online. Association for Computational Linguistics.

Danni Liu, Jan Niehues, James Cross, Francisco Guzmán, and Xian Li. 2021. Improving zero-shot translation by disentangling positional information. In *Proceedings of the 59th Annual Meeting of the Association for Computational Linguistics and the 11th International Joint Conference on Natural Language Processing (Volume 1: Long Papers)*, pages 1259–1273, Online. Association for Computational Linguistics.

Danni Liu, Gerasimos Spanakis, and Jan Niehues. 2020a. Low-Latency Sequence-to-Sequence Speech Recognition and Translation by Partial Hypothesis Selection. In *Proc. Interspeech 2020*, pages 3620–3624.

Haohe Liu, Zehua Chen, Yi Yuan, Xinhao Mei, Xubo Liu, Danilo P. Mandic, Wenwu Wang, and Mark D. Plumbley. 2023a. Audioldm: Text-to-audio generation with latent diffusion models. In *International Conference on Machine Learning, ICML 2023, 23-29 July 2023, Honolulu, Hawaii, USA*, volume 202 of *Proceedings of Machine Learning Research*, pages 21450–21474. PMLR.

Junpeng Liu, Kaiyu Huang, Hao Yu, Jiuyi Li, Jinsong Su, and Degen Huang. 2023b. Continual learning for multilingual neural machine translation via dual importance-based model division. In *Proceedings of the 2023 Conference on Empirical Methods in Natural Language Processing*, pages 12011–12027, Singapore. Association for Computational Linguistics.

Yuchen Liu, Junnan Zhu, Jiajun Zhang, and Chengqing Zong. 2020b. Bridging the modality gap for speech-to-text translation. *CoRR*, abs/2010.14920.

Yizhou Lu, Mingkun Huang, Xinghua Qu, Pengfei Wei, and Zejun Ma. 2022. Language adaptive cross-lingual speech representation learning with sparse sharing sub-networks. In *IEEE International Conference on Acoustics, Speech and Signal Processing, ICASSP 2022, Virtual and Singapore, 23-27 May 2022*, pages 6882–6886. IEEE.

Jean Maillard, Cynthia Gao, Elahe Kalbassi, Kaushik Ram Sadagopan, Vedanuj Goswami, Philipp Koehn, Angela Fan, and Francisco Guzman. 2023. Small data, big impact: Leveraging minimal data for effective machine translation. In *Proceedings of the 61st Annual Meeting of the Association for Computational Linguistics (Volume 1: Long Papers)*, pages 2740–2756, Toronto, Canada. Association for Computational Linguistics.

Alireza Mohammadshahi, Vassilina Nikoulina, Alexandre Berard, Caroline Brun, James Henderson, and Laurent Besacier. 2022. SMaLL-100: Introducing shallow multilingual machine translation model for low-resource languages. In *Proceedings of the 2022 Conference on Empirical Methods in Natural Language Processing*, pages 8348–8359, Abu Dhabi, United Arab Emirates. Association for Computational Linguistics.

Niklas Muennighoff, Thomas Wang, Lintang Sutawika, Adam Roberts, Stella Biderman, Teven Le Scao, M Saiful Bari, Sheng Shen, Zheng Xin Yong, Hailey Schoelkopf, Xiangru Tang, Dragomir Radev, Alham Fikri Aji, Khalid Almubarak, Samuel Albanie, Zaid Alyafeai, Albert Webson, Edward Raff, and Colin Raffel. 2023. Crosslingual generalization through multitask finetuning. In *Proceedings of the 61st Annual Meeting of the Association for Computational Linguistics (Volume 1: Long Papers)*, pages 15991–16111, Toronto, Canada. Association for Computational Linguistics.

Mathias Müller, Malihe Alikhani, Eleftherios Avramidis, Richard Bowden, Annelies Braffort, Necati Cihan Camgöz, Sarah Ebling, Cristina España-Bonet, Anne Göhring, Roman Grundkiewicz, Mert Inan, Zifan Jiang, Oscar Koller, Amit Moryossef, Annette Rios, Dimitar Shterionov, Sandra Sidler-Miserez, Katja Tissi, and Davy Van Landuyt. 2023. Findings of the second WMT shared task on sign language translation (WMT-SLT23). In *Proceedings of the Eighth Conference on Machine Translation*, pages 68–94, Singapore. Association for Computational Linguistics.

NLLB Team, Marta R. Costa-jussà, James Cross, Onur Çelebi, Maha Elbayad, Kenneth Heafield, Kevin Heffernan, Elahe Kalbassi, Janice Lam, Daniel Licht, Jean Maillard, Anna Y. Sun, Skyler Wang, Guillaume Wenzek, Al Youngblood, Bapi Akula, Loïc Barrault, Gabriel Mejia Gonzalez, Prangthip Hansanti, John Hoffman, Semarley Jarrett, Kaushik Ram Sadagopan, Dirk Rowe, Shannon Spruit, Chau Tran, Pierre Andrews, Necip Fazil Ayan, Shruti Bhosale, Sergey Edunov, Angela Fan, Cynthia Gao, Vedanuj Goswami, Francisco Guzmán, Philipp Koehn, Alexandre Mourachko, Christophe Ropers, Safiyyah Saleem, Holger Schwenk, and Jeff Wang. 2022. No language left behind: Scaling human-centered machine translation. *CoRR*, abs/2207.04672.

Siqi Ouyang, Rong Ye, and Lei Li. 2022. On the impact of noises in crowd-sourced data for speech translation. In *Proceedings of the 19th International Conference on Spoken Language Translation (IWSLT 2022)*, pages 92–97, Dublin, Ireland (in-person and online). Association for Computational Linguistics.

Siqi Ouyang, Rong Ye, and Lei Li. 2023. WACO: Word-aligned contrastive learning for speech translation. In *Proceedings of the 61st Annual Meeting of the Association for Computational Linguistics (Volume 1: Long Papers)*, pages 3891–3907, Toronto, Canada. Association for Computational Linguistics.

Sara Papi, Marco Gaido, Matteo Negri, and Luisa Bentivogli. 2024. Simulseamless: Fbk at iwslt 2024 simultaneous speech translation. *Preprint*, arXiv:2406.14177.

Sara Papi, Marco Gaido, Matteo Negri, and Marco Turchi. 2022. Does simultaneous speech translation need simultaneous models? In *Findings of the Association for Computational Linguistics: EMNLP 2022*, pages 141–153, Abu Dhabi, United Arab Emirates. Association for Computational Linguistics.

Sara Papi, Matteo Negri, and Marco Turchi. 2023. Attention as a guide for simultaneous speech translation. In *Proceedings of the 61st Annual Meeting of the Association for Computational Linguistics (Volume 1: Long Papers)*, pages 13340–13356, Toronto, Canada. Association for Computational Linguistics.

Kishore Papineni, Salim Roukos, Todd Ward, and Wei-Jing Zhu. 2002. Bleu: a method for automatic evaluation of machine translation. In *Proceedings of the 40th Annual Meeting of the Association for Computational Linguistics*, pages 311–318, Philadelphia, Pennsylvania, USA. Association for Computational Linguistics.

Jonas Pfeiffer, Aishwarya Kamath, Andreas Rücklé, Kyunghyun Cho, and Iryna Gurevych. 2021. AdapterFusion: Non-destructive task composition for transfer learning. In *Proceedings of the 16th Conference of the European Chapter of the Association for Computational Linguistics: Main Volume*, pages 487–503, Online. Association for Computational Linguistics.

Ngoc-Quan Pham, Tuan-Nam Nguyen, Thai Binh Nguyen, Danni Liu, Carlos Mullov, Jan Niehues, and Alexander Waibel. 2022. Effective combination of pretrained models - kit@iwslt2022. In *Proceedings of the 19th International Conference on Spoken Language Translation, IWSLT@ACL 2022, Dublin, Ireland (in-person and online), May 26-27, 2022*, pages 190–197. Association for Computational Linguistics.

Ngoc-Quan Pham, Tuan-Nam Nguyen, Sebastian Stüker, and Alex Waibel. 2021. Efficient weight factorization for multilingual speech recognition. In *Interspeech 2021, 22nd Annual Conference of the International Speech Communication Association, Brno, Czechia, 30 August - 3 September 2021*, pages 2421–2425. ISCA.

Ngoc-Quan Pham, Jan Niehues, Thanh-Le Ha, and Alexander Waibel. 2019. Improving zero-shot translation with language-independent constraints. In *Proceedings of the Fourth Conference on Machine Translation (Volume 1: Research Papers)*, pages 13–23, Florence, Italy. Association for Computational Linguistics.

Ngoc-Quan Pham, Jan Niehues, and Alex Waibel. 2023. Towards continually learning new languages. In *Proc. INTERSPEECH 2023*, pages 3262–3266.

Jerin Philip, Alexandre Berard, Matthias Gallé, and Laurent Besacier. 2020. Monolingual adapters for zero-shot neural machine translation. In *Proceedings of the 2020 Conference on Empirical Methods in Natural Language Processing (EMNLP)*, pages 4465–4470, Online. Association for Computational Linguistics.

Juan Pino, Qiantong Xu, Xutai Ma, Mohammad Javad Dousti, and Yun Tang. 2020. Self-Training for End-to-End Speech Translation. In *Proc. Interspeech 2020*, pages 1476–1480.

Telmo Pires, Robin Schmidt, Yi-Hsiu Liao, and Stephan Peitz. 2023. Learning language-specific layers for multilingual machine translation. In *Proceedings of the 61st Annual Meeting of the Association for Computational Linguistics (Volume 1: Long Papers)*, pages 14767–14783, Toronto, Canada. Association for Computational Linguistics.

Maja Popović. 2015. chrF: character n-gram F-score for automatic MT evaluation. In *Proceedings of the Tenth Workshop on Statistical Machine Translation*, pages 392–395, Lisbon, Portugal. Association for Computational Linguistics.

Alec Radford, Jong Wook Kim, Tao Xu, Greg Brockman, Christine McLeavey, and Ilya Sutskever. 2023. Robust speech recognition via large-scale weak supervision. In *International Conference on Machine Learning, ICML 2023, 23-29 July 2023, Honolulu, Hawaii, USA*, volume 202 of *Proceedings of Machine Learning Research*, pages 28492–28518. PMLR.

Sylvestre-Alvise Rebuffi, Hakan Bilen, and Andrea Vedaldi. 2017. Learning multiple visual domains with residual adapters. In *Advances in Neural Information Processing Systems 30: Annual Conference on Neural Information Processing Systems 2017, December 4-9, 2017, Long Beach, CA, USA*, pages 506–516.

Ricardo Rei, Craig Stewart, Ana C Farinha, and Alon Lavie. 2020. COMET: A neural framework for MT evaluation. In *Proceedings of the 2020 Conference on Empirical Methods in Natural Language Processing (EMNLP)*, pages 2685–2702, Online. Association for Computational Linguistics.

Paul K. Rubenstein, Chulayuth Asawaroengchai, Duc Dung Nguyen, Ankur Bapna, Zalán Borsos, Félix de Chaumont Quitry, Peter Chen, Dalia El Badawy, Wei Han, Eugene Kharitonov, Hannah Muckenhirn, Dirk Padfield, James Qin, Danny Rozenberg, Tara N. Sainath, Johan Schalkwyk, Matthew Sharifi, Michelle Tadmor Ramanovich, Marco Tagliasacchi, Alexandru Tudor, Mihajlo Velimirovic, Damien Vincent, Jiahui Yu, Yongqiang Wang, Vicky Zayats, Neil Zeghidour, Yu Zhang, Zhishuai Zhang, Lukas Zilka, and Christian Havnø Frank. 2023. Audiopalm: A large language model that can speak and listen. *CoRR*, abs/2306.12925.

Yusuke Sakai, Mana Makinae, Hidetaka Kamigaito, and Taro Watanabe. 2024. Simultaneous interpretation corpus construction by large language models in distant language pair. *CoRR*, abs/2404.12299.

Elizabeth Salesky, Kareem Darwish, Mohamed Al-Badrashiny, Mona Diab, and Jan Niehues. 2023. Evaluating multilingual speech translation under realistic conditions with resegmentation and terminology. In *Proceedings of the 20th International Conference on Spoken Language Translation (IWSLT 2023)*, pages 62–78, Toronto, Canada (in-person and online). Association for Computational Linguistics.

Elizabeth Salesky, Matthew Wiesner, Jacob Bremerman, Roldano Cattoni, Matteo Negri, Marco Turchi, Douglas W. Oard, and Matt Post. 2021. The Multilingual TEDx Corpus for Speech Recognition and Translation. In *Proc. Interspeech 2021*, pages 3655–3659.

Holger Schwenk. 2018. Filtering and mining parallel data in a joint multilingual space. In *Proceedings of the 56th Annual Meeting of the Association for Computational Linguistics (Volume 2: Short Papers)*, pages 228–234, Melbourne, Australia. Association for Computational Linguistics.

Holger Schwenk, Guillaume Wenzek, Sergey Edunov, Edouard Grave, Armand Joulin, and Angela Fan. 2021. CCMatrix: Mining billions of high-quality parallel sentences on the web. In *Proceedings of the 59th Annual Meeting of the Association for Computational Linguistics and the 11th International Joint Conference on Natural Language Processing (Volume 1: Long Papers)*, pages 6490–6500, Online. Association for Computational Linguistics.

Seamless Communication, Loïc Barrault, Yu-An Chung, Mariano Coria Meglioli, David Dale, Ning Dong, Mark Duppenthaler, Paul-Ambroise Duquenne, Brian Ellis, Hady Elsahar, Justin Haaheim, John Hoffman, Min-Jae Hwang, Hirofumi Inaguma, Christopher Klaiber, Ilia Kulikov, Pengwei Li, Daniel Licht, Jean Maillard, Ruslan Mavlyutov, Alice Rakotoarison, Kaushik Ram Sadagopan, Abinesh Ramakrishnan, Tuan Tran, Guillaume Wenzek, Yilin Yang, Ethan Ye, Ivan Evtimov, Pierre Fernandez, Cynthia Gao, Prangthip Hansanti, Elahe Kalbassi, Amanda Kallet, Artyom Kozhevnikov, Gabriel Mejia Gonzalez, Robin San Roman, Christophe Touret, Corinne Wong, Carleigh Wood, Bokai Yu, Pierre Andrews, Can Balioglu, Peng-Jen Chen, Marta R. Costa-jussà, Maha Elbayad, Hongyu Gong, Francisco Guzmán, Kevin Heffernan, Somya Jain, Justine Kao, Ann Lee, Xutai Ma, Alexandre Mourachko, Benjamin Peloquin, Juan Pino, Sravya Popuri, Christophe Ropers, Safiyyah Saleem, Holger Schwenk, Anna Y. Sun, Paden Tomasello, Changhan Wang, Jeff Wang, Skyler Wang, and Mary Williamson. 2023a. Seamless: Multilingual expressive and streaming speech translation. *CoRR*, abs/2312.05187.

Seamless Communication, Loïc Barrault, Yu-An Chung, Mariano Coria Meglioli, David Dale, Ning Dong, Paul-Ambroise Duquenne, Hady Elsahar, Hongyu Gong, Kevin Heffernan, John Hoffman, Christopher Klaiber, Pengwei Li, Daniel Licht, Jean Maillard, Alice Rakotoarison, Kaushik Ram Sadagopan, Guillaume Wenzek, Ethan Ye, Bapi Akula, Peng-Jen Chen, Naji El Hachem, Brian Ellis, Gabriel Mejia Gonzalez, Justin Haaheim, Prangthip Hansanti, Russ Howes, Bernie Huang, Min-Jae Hwang, Hirofumi Inaguma, Somya Jain, Elahe Kalbassi, Amanda Kallet, Ilia Kulikov, Janice Lam, Daniel Li, Xutai Ma, Ruslan Mavlyutov, Benjamin Peloquin, Mohamed Ramadan, Abinesh Ramakrishnan, Anna Y. Sun, Kevin Tran, Tuan Tran, Igor Tufanov, Vish Vogeti, Carleigh Wood, Yilin Yang, Bokai Yu, Pierre Andrews, Can Balioglu, Marta R. Costa-jussà, Onur Celebi, Maha Elbayad, Cynthia Gao, Francisco Guzmán, Justine Kao, Ann Lee, Alexandre Mourachko, Juan Pino, Sravya Popuri, Christophe Ropers, Safiyyah Saleem, Holger Schwenk, Paden Tomasello, Changhan Wang, Jeff Wang, and Skyler Wang. 2023b. Seamlessm4t-massively multilingual & multimodal machine translation. *CoRR*, abs/2308.11596.

Noam Shazeer, Azalia Mirhoseini, Krzysztof Maziarz, Andy Davis, Quoc V. Le, Geoffrey E. Hinton, and Jeff Dean. 2017. Outrageously large neural networks: The sparsely-gated mixture-of-experts layer. In *5th International Conference on Learning Representations, ICLR 2017, Toulon, France, April 24-26, 2017, Conference Track Proceedings*. OpenReview.net.

Bowen Shi, Wei-Ning Hsu, Kushal Lakhotia, and Abdelrahman Mohamed. 2022. Learning audio-visual speech representation by masked multimodal cluster prediction. In *The Tenth International Conference on Learning Representations, ICLR 2022, Virtual Event, April 25-29, 2022*. OpenReview.net.

Simeng Sun, Maha Elbayad, Anna Sun, and James Cross. 2023. Efficiently upgrading multilingual machine translation models to support more languages. In *Proceedings of the 17th Conference of the European Chapter of the Association for Computational Linguistics*, pages 1513–1527, Dubrovnik, Croatia. Association for Computational Linguistics.

Changli Tang, Wenyi Yu, Guangzhi Sun, Xianzhao Chen, Tian Tan, Wei Li, Lu Lu, Zejun MA, and Chao Zhang. 2024. SALMONN: Towards generic hearing abilities for large language models. In *The Twelfth International Conference on Learning Representations*.

Yun Tang, Juan Pino, Xian Li, Changhan Wang, and Dmitriy Genzel. 2021. Improving speech translation by understanding and learning from the auxiliary text translation task. In *Proceedings of the 59th Annual Meeting of the Association for Computational Linguistics and the 11th International Joint Conference on Natural Language Processing (Volume 1: Long Papers)*, pages 4252–4261, Online. Association for Computational Linguistics.

Zineng Tang, Ziyi Yang, Mahmoud Khademi, Yang Liu, Chenguang Zhu, and Mohit Bansal. 2023. Codi-2: In-context, interleaved, and interactive any-to-any generation. *CoRR*, abs/2311.18775.

Andros Tjandra, Sakriani Sakti, and Satoshi Nakamura. 2019. Speech-to-speech translation between untranscribed unknown languages. In *2019 IEEE Automatic Speech Recognition and Understanding Workshop (ASRU)*, pages 593–600.

Hugo Touvron, Thibaut Lavril, Gautier Izacard, Xavier Martinet, Marie-Anne Lachaux, Timothée Lacroix, Baptiste Rozière, Naman Goyal, Eric Hambro, Faisal Azhar, Aurélien Rodriguez, Armand Joulin, Edouard Grave, and Guillaume Lample. 2023a. Llama: Open and efficient foundation language models. *CoRR*, abs/2302.13971.

Hugo Touvron, Louis Martin, Kevin Stone, Peter Albert, Amjad Almahairi, Yasmine Babaei, Nikolay Bashlykov, Soumya Batra, Prajjwal Bhargava, Shruti Bhosale, Dan Bikel, Lukas Blecher, Cristian Canton-Ferrer, Moya Chen, Guillem Cucurull, David Esiobu, Jude Fernandes, Jeremy Fu, Wenyin Fu, Brian Fuller, Cynthia Gao, Vedanuj Goswami, Naman Goyal, Anthony Hartshorn, Saghar Hosseini, Rui Hou, Hakan Inan, Marcin Kardas, Viktor Kerkez, Madian Khabsa, Isabel Kloumann, Artem Korenev, Punit Singh Koura, Marie-Anne Lachaux, Thibaut Lavril, Jenya Lee, Diana Liskovich, Yinghai Lu, Yuning Mao, Xavier Martinet, Todor Mihaylov, Pushkar Mishra, Igor Molybog, Yixin Nie, Andrew Poulton, Jeremy Reizenstein, Rashi Rungta, Kalyan Saladi, Alan Schelten, Ruan Silva, Eric Michael Smith, Ranjan Subramanian, Xiaoqing Ellen Tan, Binh Tang, Ross Taylor, Adina Williams, Jian Xiang Kuan, Puxin Xu, Zheng Yan, Iliyan Zarov, Yuchen Zhang, Angela Fan, Melanie Kambadur, Sharan Narang, Aurélien Rodriguez, Robert Stojnic, Sergey Edunov, and Thomas Scialom. 2023b. Llama 2: Open foundation and fine-tuned chat models. *CoRR*, abs/2307.09288.

Ioannis Tsiamas, Gerard I. Gállego, José A. R. Fonollosa, and Marta R. Costa-jussà. 2024. Pushing the limits of zero-shot end-to-end speech translation. *CoRR*, abs/2402.10422.

Changhan Wang, Morgane Riviere, Ann Lee, Anne Wu, Chaitanya Talnikar, Daniel Haziza, Mary Williamson, Juan Pino, and Emmanuel Dupoux. 2021a. VoxPopuli: A large-scale multilingual speech corpus for representation learning, semi-supervised learning and interpretation. In *Proceedings of the 59th Annual Meeting of the Association for Computational Linguistics and the 11th International Joint Conference on Natural Language Processing (Volume 1: Long Papers)*, pages 993–1003, Online. Association for Computational Linguistics.

Changhan Wang, Anne Wu, Jiatao Gu, and Juan Pino. 2021b. CoVoST 2 and Massively Multilingual Speech Translation. In *Proc. Interspeech 2021*, pages 2247–2251.

Chen Wang, Yuchen Liu, Boxing Chen, Jiajun Zhang, Wei Luo, Zhongqiang Huang, and Chengqing Zong. 2022. Discrete cross-modal alignment enables zero-shot speech translation. In *Proceedings of the 2022 Conference on Empirical Methods in Natural Language Processing*, pages 5291–5302, Abu Dhabi, United Arab Emirates. Association for Computational Linguistics.

Jiayi Wang, David Ifeoluwa Adelani, Sweta Agrawal, Ricardo Rei, Eleftheria Briakou, Marine Carpuat, Marek Masiak, Xuanli He, Sofia Bourhim, Andiswa Bukula, Muhidin Mohamed, Temitayo Olatoye, Hamam Mokayed, Christine Mwase, Wangui Kimotho, Foutse Yuehgoh, Aremu Anuoluwapo, Jessica Ojo, Shamsuddeen Hassan Muhammad, Salomey Osei, Abdul-Hakeem Omotayo, Chiamaka Chukwuneke, Perez Ogayo, Oumaima Hourrane, Salma El Anigri, Lolwethu Ndolela, Thabiso Mangwana, Shafie Abdi Mohamed, Ayinde Hassan, Oluwabusayo Olufunke Awoyomi, Lama Alkhaled, Sana Sabah Al-Azzawi, Naome A. Etori, Millicent Ochieng, Clemencia Siro, Samuel Njoroge, Eric Muchiri, Wangari Kimotho, Lyse Naomi Wamba Momo, Daud Abolade, Simbiat Ajao, Tosin P. Adewumi, Iyanuoluwa Shode, Ricky Macharm, Ruqayya Nasir Iro, Saheed S. Abdullahi, Stephen E. Moore, Bernard Opoku, Zainab Akinjobi, Afolabi Abeeb, Nnaemeka C. Obiefuna, Onyekachi Raphael Ogbu, Sam Brian, Verrah Akinyi Otiende, Chinedu Emmanuel Mbonu, Sakayo Toadoum Sari, and Pontus Stenetorp. 2023a. Afrimte and africomet: Empowering COMET to embrace under-resourced african languages. *CoRR*, abs/2311.09828.

Wenxuan Wang, Guodong Ma, Yuke Li, and Binbin Du. 2023b. Language-Routing Mixture of Experts for Multilingual and Code-Switching Speech Recognition. In *Proc. INTERSPEECH 2023*, pages 1389–1393.

Shengqiong Wu, Hao Fei, Leigang Qu, Wei Ji, and Tat-Seng Chua. 2023. Next-gpt: Any-to-any multimodal LLM. *CoRR*, abs/2309.05519.

Haoran Xu, Weiting Tan, Shuyue Li, Yunmo Chen, Benjamin Van Durme, Philipp Koehn, and Kenton Murray. 2023. Condensing multilingual knowledge with lightweight language-specific modules. In *Proceedings of the 2023 Conference on Empirical Methods in Natural Language Processing*, pages 1575–1587, Singapore. Association for Computational Linguistics.

Jitao Xu, Josep Crego, and Jean Senellart. 2020. Boosting neural machine translation with similar translations. In *Proceedings of the 58th Annual Meeting of the Association for Computational Linguistics*, pages 1580–1590, Online. Association for Computational Linguistics.

Jichen Yang, Kai Fan, Minpeng Liao, Boxing Chen, and Zhongqiang Huang. 2023a. Towards zero-shot learning for end-to-end cross-modal translation models. In *Findings of the Association for Computational Linguistics: EMNLP 2023*, pages 13078–13087, Singapore. Association for Computational Linguistics.

Mu Yang, Andros Tjandra, Chunxi Liu, David Zhang, Duc Le, and Ozlem Kalinli. 2023b. Learning ASR pathways: A sparse multilingual ASR model. In *IEEE International Conference on Acoustics, Speech and Signal Processing ICASSP 2023, Rhodes Island, Greece, June 4-10, 2023*, pages 1–5. IEEE.

Rong Ye, Mingxuan Wang, and Lei Li. 2022. Cross-modal contrastive learning for speech translation. In *Proceedings of the 2022 Conference of the North American Chapter of the Association for Computational Linguistics: Human Language Technologies*, pages 5099–5113, Seattle, United States. Association for Computational Linguistics.

Neil Zeghidour, Alejandro Luebs, Ahmed Omran, Jan Skoglund, and Marco Tagliasacchi. 2022. Soundstream: An end-to-end neural audio codec. *IEEE ACM Trans. Audio Speech Lang. Process.*, 30:495–507.

Jun Zhan, Junqi Dai, Jiasheng Ye, Yunhua Zhou, Dong Zhang, Zhigeng Liu, Xin Zhang, Ruibin Yuan, Ge Zhang, Linyang Li, Hang Yan, Jie Fu, Tao Gui, Tianxiang Sun, Yugang Jiang, and Xipeng Qiu. 2024. Anygpt: Unified multimodal LLM with discrete sequence modeling. *CoRR*, abs/2402.12226.

Biao Zhang, Ankur Bapna, Rico Sennrich, and Orhan Firat. 2021a. Share or not? learning to schedule language-specific capacity for multilingual translation. In *9th International Conference on Learning Representations, ICLR 2021, Virtual Event, Austria, May 3-7, 2021*. OpenReview.net.

Biao Zhang, Philip Williams, Ivan Titov, and Rico Sennrich. 2020. Improving massively multilingual neural machine translation and zero-shot translation. In *Proceedings of the 58th Annual Meeting of the Association for Computational Linguistics*, pages 1628–1639, Online. Association for Computational Linguistics.

Chen Zhang, Xu Tan, Yi Ren, Tao Qin, Kejun Zhang, and Tie-Yan Liu. 2021b. Uwspeech: Speech to speech translation for unwritten languages. In *Thirty-Fifth AAAI Conference on Artificial Intelligence, AAAI 2021, Thirty-Third Conference on Innovative Applications of Artificial Intelligence, IAAI 2021, The Eleventh Symposium on Educational Advances in Artificial Intelligence, EAAI 2021, Virtual Event, February 2-9, 2021*, pages 14319–14327. AAAI Press.

Jingyi Zhang, Masao Utiyama, Eiichro Sumita, Graham Neubig, and Satoshi Nakamura. 2018. Guiding neural machine translation with retrieved translation pieces. In *Proceedings of the 2018 Conference of the North American Chapter of the Association for Computational Linguistics: Human Language Technologies, Volume 1 (Long Papers)*, pages 1325–1335, New Orleans, Louisiana. Association for Computational Linguistics.

Xin Zhang, Dong Zhang, Shimin Li, Yaqian Zhou, and Xipeng Qiu. 2023a. Speechtokenizer: Unified speech tokenizer for speech large language models. *CoRR*, abs/2308.16692.

Yu Zhang, Wei Han, James Qin, Yongqiang Wang, Ankur Bapna, Zhehuai Chen, Nanxin Chen, Bo Li, Vera Axelrod, Gary Wang, Zhong Meng, Ke Hu, Andrew Rosenberg, Rohit Prabhavalkar, Daniel S. Park, Parisa Haghani, Jason Riesa, Ginger Perng, Hagen Soltau, Trevor Strohman, Bhuvana Ramabhadran, Tara N. Sainath, Pedro J. Moreno, Chung-Cheng Chiu, Johan Schalkwyk, Françoise Beaufays, and Yonghui Wu. 2023b. Google USM: scaling automatic speech recognition beyond 100 languages. *CoRR*, abs/2303.01037.

Jinming Zhao, Hao Yang, Gholamreza Haffari, and Ehsan Shareghi. 2022. M-Adapter: Modality Adaptation for End-to-End Speech-to-Text Translation. In *Proc. Interspeech 2022*, pages 111–115.

Wenhao Zhu, Hongyi Liu, Qingxiu Dong, Jingjing Xu, Lingpeng Kong, Jiajun Chen, Lei Li, and Shujian Huang. 2023. Multilingual machine translation with large language models: Empirical results and analysis. *CoRR*, abs/2304.04675.

Yun Zhu, Parisa Haghani, Anshuman Tripathi, Bhuvana Ramabhadran, Brian Farris, Hainan Xu, Han Lu, Hasim Sak, Isabel Leal, Neeraj Gaur, Pedro J. Moreno, and Qian Zhang. 2020. Multilingual Speech Recognition with Self-Attention Structured Parameterization. In *Proc. Interspeech 2020*, pages 4741–4745.

Word Order in English-Japanese Simultaneous Interpretation: Analyses and Evaluation using Chunk-wise Monotonic Translation

Kosuke Doi[1], Yuka Ko[1], Mana Makinae[1], Katsuhito Sudoh[1, 2], Satoshi Nakamura[1, 3]

[1]Nara Institute of Science and Technology,
[2]Nara Women's University, [3]The Chinese University of Hong Kong, Shenzhen
{doi.kosuke.de8, sudoh, s-nakamura}@is.naist.jp

Abstract

This paper analyzes the features of monotonic translations, which follow the word order of the source language, in simultaneous interpreting (SI). Word order differences are one of the biggest challenges in SI, especially for language pairs with significant structural differences like English and Japanese. We analyzed the characteristics of chunk-wise monotonic translation (CMT) sentences using the NAIST English-to-Japanese Chunk-wise Monotonic Translation Evaluation Dataset and identified some grammatical structures that make monotonic translation difficult in English-Japanese SI. We further investigated the features of CMT sentences by evaluating the output from the existing speech translation (ST) and simultaneous speech translation (simulST) models on the NAIST English-to-Japanese Chunk-wise Monotonic Translation Evaluation Dataset as well as on existing test sets. The results indicate the possibility that the existing SI-based test set underestimates the model performance. The results also suggest that using CMT sentences as references gives higher scores to simulST models than ST models, and that using an offline-based test set to evaluate the simulST models underestimates the model performance.

1 Introduction

Simultaneous interpreting (SI) is the task of translating speech from a source language into a target language in real time. SI is cognitively demanding, and human simultaneous interpreters employ such strategies as segmentation, summarization, and generalization (He et al., 2016). Maintaining word order in a source language is another important strategy, especially for language pairs whose word order differs (*e.g.*, English and Japanese), to shorten delays and reduce cognitive load. Because of these features, SI sentences are different from offline translation sentences, although most automatic SI studies (Oda et al., 2014; Ma et al., 2019; Liu et al., 2020; Papi et al., 2023) have used offline translation corpora (*e.g.*, MuST-C; Di Gangi et al., 2019) for both training and evaluatng models due to the limited amount of simultaneous interpretation corpora (SICs).

For English-Japanese language pairs, several SICs have been constructed (Toyama et al., 2004; Shimizu et al., 2014; Matsushita et al., 2020; Doi et al., 2021). Based on the NAIST Simultaneous Interpretation Corpus (NAIST-SIC; Doi et al., 2021), Zhao et al. (2024)[1] created an automatically-aligned parallel SI dataset: NAIST-SIC-Aligned. Since its sentences are aligned at the sentence level, they can be used for model training. Actually, Ko et al. (2023) and Zhao et al. (2024) trained SI models using SI data from NAIST-SIC-Aligned. Their model performances were evaluated through automatic evaluation metrics such as BLEU (Papineni et al., 2002) using a small test set curated based on SI sentences generated by professional human simultaneous interpreters.

Although the scores reported in Ko et al. (2023) and Zhao et al. (2024) were relatively low, the test set used in both studies might have underestimated the model performance. Since human simultaneous interpreters use such strategies as summarization and generalization, phrases that do not affect the main idea are not necessarily translated into the target language. If an SI model generates translations for phrases that a human interpreter did not, the output sentence might not be evaluated properly, even when it is a *correct* translation.

Fukuda et al. (2024) pointed out the difficulty for SI models to learn which phrases in source speech are less important and advocated constructing SI models that only employ a strategy that maintains the word order in a source language. As a first step, they created the NAIST English-to-

[1]The dataset was released in 2023 (see version 3 of the paper).

Proceedings of the 21st International Conference on Spoken Language Translation (IWSLT 2024), pages 302–312
August 15-16, 2024 ©2024 Association for Computational Linguistics

Source	(1) The US Secret Service, / (2) two months ago, / (3) froze the Swiss bank account / (4) of Mr. Sam Jain right here, / (5) and that bank account / (6) had 14.9 million US dollars in it / (7) when it was frozen.
Offline	(1) 米国のシークレットサービスは / (2) 2ヶ月前に / (4) サム・ジェイン氏の / (3) スイス銀行口座を凍結しました / (5) その口座には / (6) 米ドルで1490万ドルありました [The US Secret Service / two months ago / Mr. Sam Jain's / froze the Swiss bank account / that bank account / had 14.9 million US dollars]
SI	(1) アメリカのシークレッドサービスが、/ (3) スイスの銀行の口座を凍結しました。 / (4) サムジェインのものです。 / (5) この銀行口座の中には、 / (6) 一千四百九十万ドルが入っていました。 [The US Secret Service / froze the Swiss bank account / it is Sam Jain's one / in this bank account / had 14.9 million dollars]
CMT	(1) アメリカ合衆国シークレットサービスは、 / (2) 2ヶ月前に、 / (3) スイスの銀行口座を凍結しました、 / (4) ここにいるサム・ジェイン氏の口座です、 / (5) そしてその銀行口座には / (6) 490万米ドルが入っていました、 / (7) 凍結された時。 [The US Secret Service / two months ago / froze the Swiss bank account / the account of Mr. Sam Jain right here / and that bank account / had 14.9 million US dollars in it / when it was frozen]

Table 1: Comparison of target sentences in each translation mode. Examples of offline, SI, and CMT are respectively from subtitles of TED talks, NAIST-SIC, and NAIST English-to-Japanese Chunk-wise Monotonic Translation Evaluation Dataset. "/" shows boundaries of chunks. Numbers preceding chunks in source sentence represent appearance order. Numbers preceding chunks in target sentences correspond to numbers in source sentence.

Japanese Chunk-wise Monotonic Translation Evaluation Dataset[2]. The source sentences in the test set used in Ko et al. (2023) were automatically segmented into chunks, each of which was translated in a way that did not include the content of subsequent chunks. Unlike in SI sentences by human interpreters, where not all the information in the source sentences is translated, chunk-wise monotonic translation (CMT) sentences[3] were translated so that all the information is translated (Table 1)[4]. Fukuda et al. (2024) have investigated the quality of the CMT sentences in their dataset through human evaluation, although they have not analyzed its characteristics. Nor have they conducted any evaluation experiments in which model outputs are evaluated on their dataset.

In this paper, we qualitatively and quantitatively analyze CMT sentences in the NAIST English-to-Japanese Chunk-wise Monotonic Translation Evaluation Dataset. In the process of generating CMT sentences for the dataset, it was allowed to `repeat`, `defer`, and `omit` phrases in the source sentences to maintain the translation's fluency. We assume the presence of factors (*e.g.*, syntactic structures) that prevent monotonic translation if phrases were `repeated`, `deferred`, or `omitted` in the CMT sentences since they were translated without time constraints. In addition, we evaluate the output from an existing speech translation (ST) model and two simultaneous speech translation (simulST) models (See 5.2). Both the ST[5] and simulST models are used to investigate the differences in scores when evaluating translations with different characteristics. The contributions of this paper are as follows:

- We analyze CMT sentences and show that they tend to be longer than offline translations primarily because of `repetition`.
- We investigate what causes the phrases in source sentences to be `repeated`, `deferred`, and `omitted` and show that most cases occur because of particular grammatical structures. When a phrase in a chunk is a dependent of a phrase in the preceding chunk, the head phrase is typically `repeated` or `deferred`.
- We evaluate the output from three different models on the NAIST English-to-Japanese Chunk-wise Monotonic Translation Evaluation Dataset: (1) an ST model trained on offline data, (2) a simulST model trained on offline data, and (3) a simulST model trained on both offline and SI data. The results suggest that the existing SI-based test set (Ko et al., 2023; Zhao et al., 2024) underestimates the model performance. The results also suggest that using CMT sentences as references gives higher scores to simulST models than ST models, while using an offline-based test set for evaluating simulST models underestimates the model performance.

[2] https://dsc-nlp.naist.jp/data/NAIST-SIC/Aligned-Chunk_Mono-EJ/

[3] CMT refers to the task of segmenting a source sentence into chunks and translating it in the order of the chunks. A CMT sentence is a target sentence generated through CMT.

[4] Precisely, omissions that maintained the fluency of the sentence were allowed. See Section 3.1 for the details about the dataset.

[5] A ST model generates translations after the utterances are completed.

2 Related Work

2.1 Simultaneous Interpretation Corpora

SICs are valuable resources both for developing automatic SI models and analyzing SI's characteristics. For English-Japanese language pairs, several SICs are publicly available (Toyama et al., 2004; Shimizu et al., 2014; Matsushita et al., 2020; Doi et al., 2021), although the amount of such corpora is very limited compared to offline translation corpora.

Using these corpora, SI sentences have been analyzed from various perspectives, such as strategies and interpreting patterns used by interpreters, latency, translation quality, and word order (Tohyama and Matsubara, 2006; Ono et al., 2008; Cai et al., 2018, 2020; Doi et al., 2021). SI models have also been developed using SICs (Ryu et al., 2004; Shimizu et al., 2013; Ko et al., 2023).

2.2 Word Order in Simultaneous Interpreting

When dealing with language pairs whose sentence structures are different, including English and Japanese (SVO/head-initial vs. SOV/head-final), reducing the word order differences between the source and the target languages is crucial for minimizing delays.

Murata et al. (2010) segmented source sentences into semantically meaningful units with a maximum length of 4.3 seconds and translated those units from an SI viewpoint. He et al. (2015) designed syntactic transformation rules for Japanese-English simultaneous machine translation. By applying the rules to target language sentences (*i.e.*, English), they generated more monotonic translations, while preserving the meaning of source sentences and maintaining the grammaticality of the target language. In English-Japanese SI, Futamata et al. (2020) reordered Japanese sentences to make the word order closer to the original English sentences. They further applied style transfer to increase the fluency and obtained sentences close to SI sentences by human interpreters. Han et al. (2021) proposed an algorithm to reorder and refine the target sentences so that the target sentences were aligned largely monotonically. They trained SI models for four language pairs, including English-Japanese. Nakabayashi and Kato (2021) segmented sentences into chunks and created bilingual pairs of such chunks with explicit annotations of context information. The SI model trained on the data translated the source sentences while referencing the preceding chunks although naturally connecting chunks remained a challenge. Higashiyama et al. (2023) constructed a large-scale English $\leftrightarrow$ Japanese SIC with the information of chunk boundaries in source and target sentences and phrases that can be omitted in target sentences. The NAIST English-to-Japanese Chunk-wise Monotonic Translation Evaluation Dataset (Fukuda et al., 2024), which is similar to Higashiyama et al.'s (2023), is relatively small and intended for the evaluation purposes.

The word order differences among different translation modes have also been investigated. Okamura and Yamada (2023) quantitatively compared the degree to which the word order of the source sentences was maintained and found that SI sentences retained the order better than consecutive interpreting and offline translation sentences. Cai et al. (2020) found syntactic and non-syntactic factors that affect interpreters' word order decisions through the statistical analyses of an SIC. In this paper, we analyze what makes monotonic translation difficult. While Cai et al. (2020) analyzed the actual SI data generated by human simultaneous interpreters, we use CMT sentences, which were generated without time constraints, and in which all the information in the source sentences is translated into target sentences.

3 Chunk-wise Monotonic Translation

In SI between language pairs with different sentence structures, interpreters segment source sentences into chunks and translate them from chunk to chunk[6] (Okamura and Yamada, 2023). This section describes the details of the NAIST English-to-Japanese Chunk-wise Monotonic Translation Evaluation Dataset, which is used in our analyses.

3.1 Data

The NAIST English-to-Japanese Chunk-wise Monotonic Translation Evaluation Dataset consists of 511 pairs of source sentences and their corresponding chunk-wise monotonic translation (CMT) sentences with information of chunk boundaries in the source and target sentences. Source (*i.e.*, English) sentences, which were used as the test set in Ko et al. (2023), were segmented following the five rules that reflected the interpreter's strategies[7]

[6] Reordering may occur within a chunk.

[7] See the original paper or the code for chunking: `https://github.com/ahclab/si_chunker`

Data	Sum	Per Sent.±SD
# sentence pairs	511	–
# chunks	1,677	3.28±2.12
# source words	8,104	15.86±10.16
# target words	13,981	27.36±18.55

Table 2: Statistics for chunk-wise monotonic translation data. Standard deviations and number of words in target sentences were calculated by us. Other values are cited from Fukuda et al. (2024).

based on the syntactic analysis results from spaCy. The source sentences come from eight TED talks.

Translators were provided with source sentences with chunk boundaries and asked to (1) translate them in the order of the chunks while (2) naturally connecting the chunks and (3) not including the content of subsequent chunks. They were allowed to (1) `repeat`, (2) `defer`, and (3) `omit` phrases in the source sentences to keep translation fluency, although they were instructed to minimize their use of the operations with larger number as much as possible (*e.g.*, `defer` should not be used when `repeat` can handle the situation) . Data statistics are shown in Table 2.

4 Data Analysis

Fukuda et al. (2024) have examined the quality of CMT sentences through human evaluation but have not analyzed the characteristics of them. We suppose that factors exist that prevent monotonic translation if a phrase in the source sentences is `repeated`, `deferred`, or `omitted` since the CMT sentences were generated without time constraints. Therefore we qualitatively and quantitatively analyze the CMT sentences with these operations and reveal such factors.

To better understand the characteristics of the CMT sentences, we also compare them with SI sentences from NAIST-SIC and NAIST-SIC-Aligned as well as offline translation sentences from the subtitles of TED talks. Since the SI sentences in NAIST-SIC were not aligned at the sentence level, we manually align them. Some source sentences did not match across the datasets, and we excluded those ten sentences from the analyses. In addition, 25 sentences were not translated in NAIST-SIC[8], which were also excluded from the analyses. As a result, 476 sentences were used for our analyses.

4.1 Annotations

To analyze the characteristics of the CMT sentences, we annotated tags to the source and CMT sentences. The list of tags is shown in Table 3. Prior to the annotations, we tokenized the English sentences using spaCy[9] and the Japanese sentences using MeCab (Kudo et al., 2004) with unidic. Then, we concatenated the source and CMT sentences with a special token `[SEP]` and annotated them using an open-source data labeling tool, doccano.[10]

We identified spans (*i.e.*, words or phrases) that are `repeated`, `deferred`, or `omitted` and annotated the span tags. In addition, we annotated `ahead`, `add`, and `error` tags for analyses of problematic translations. The corresponding span tags in the source and CMT sentences were associated using relation tags. Annotation examples are shown in Figure 1.

The first and second authors collaboratively annotated the first 50 examples while discussing their decisions. Since sufficient agreement was assumed, the remainder of the data were just annotated by the first author.

4.2 Analysis Results

4.2.1 Comparison among Different Translation Modes

We compared the sentence lengths of the four datasets. Fukuda et al. (2024) also conducted similar comparisons based on the number of characters. However, since variations in spelling and differences in transcription systems (*e.g.*, numbers) were found, we made comparisons based on the number of words segmented by MeCab.

Table 4 shows that the CMT sentences were the longest, followed by offline, NAIST-SIC, and NAIST-SIC-Aligned. These results matched those reported in Fukuda et al. (2024). Long translated sentences can pose some problems. As discussed in Fukuda et al. (2024), the lenght may increase the cognitive load on the listeners/readers of the translations. In addition, longer output may cause a delay even though CMT aims to reduce it.

4.2.2 Factors that Lengthen CMT Sentences

To reveal what factor lengthened the CMT sentences, we first analyzed them qualitatively. Our analyses suggest that (1) CMT sentences contain

[8]For example, due to time constraints, interpreters might have been unable to translate a whole sentence. See Doi et al. (2021).

[9]`https://spacy.io/`

[10]`https://github.com/doccano/doccano`

Type	Tag	Meaning
Span	repeat	Phrases that are repeated
	zero-repeat	Target phrases that are repeated; No corresponding source phrases (*e.g.*, zero that-clause)
	defer	Phrases that are not translated within the current chunk but in a subsequent chunk
	omit	Source phrases that are not translated in the target sentences
	ahead	Target phrases translated using the subsequent chunks
	add	Target phrases that have no corresponding source phrases
	error	Phrases with translation errors
	sep	Boundaries of source and target sentences
Relation	rel-repeat	Connect source and target phrases with `repeat` tags
	repeat_d#	Connect target phrases with `repeat` tags
	defer_d#	Connect source and target phrases with `defer` tags
	ahead_d#	Connect source and target phrases with `ahead` tags
	rel-err	Connect source and target phrases with `error` tags

Table 3: List of tags used for annotations. "d#" (#=1, 2, ...) represents distance between chunks.

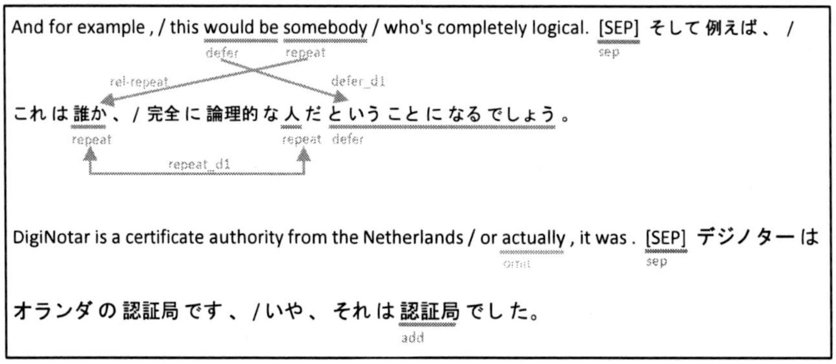

Figure 1: Annotation examples. `Repeat` tags were assigned even if strings did not exactly match but referred to same entity or had same meaning.

Dataset	Sum	Per Sent.±SD
CMT	13,508	28.38±18.66
NAIST-SIC	8,914	18.73±12.08
NAIST-SIC-Aligned	8,072	16.96±11.52
Offline	9,907	20.81±12.62

Table 4: Comparison of number of words in different translation modes

many formulaic expressions for the end of sentences as they are segmented into small chunks, and (2) the words that are often omitted in Japanese (*e.g.*, pronouns) are explicitly translated since translators were instructed to avoid `omitting` phrases in the source language, as in the following examples:

> (En) It's when we warmed it up, / and we turned on the lights / and looked inside the box, / we saw that the piece metal / was still there in one piece.
> (CMT) 私たちがそれを暖めるときです、/電気をつけて、/箱の中を見たときです、/私たちはその金属片を見たんです、/それはまだ一つの塊としてそこにありました。
> (offline) 物体を暖め明かりをつけ 箱の中を見たところ金属片はまだそこに存在していました
>
> (En) He only has use of his eyes.
> (CMT) 彼は目だけを使えます。
> (offline) 目だけしか動かせません

In addition to the above characteristics, we observed many repetitions in particularly *long* sentences. To verify this, we further analyzed particularly *long* and *short* sentences, chosen based on the length ratio of the CMT sentences to the offline ones. The *long* and *short* sentences were defined as those with a length ratio greater/smaller than the average ± 0.5 standard deviations (avg.=1.39, SD=0.43). We subjectively judged whether these sentences contained many repetitions. We also identified sentences whose offline translations were short.

Table 5 shows that *long* sentences contained more repetitions than *short* ones. The offline translation sentences were short, probably because they were originally subtitles, for which limited space was allowed. We also quantitatively checked them

Type	N	Repeat (subjective)	Repeat (tag)	Short offline
Long	131	54 (41.22%)	3.35	53
Short	171	22 (12.87%)	0.81	–

Table 5: Comparison between *long* and *short* CMT sentences. Number of repeat tags is denoted per sentence.

Operation	N
repeat	301
defer	173
omit	36

Table 6: Comparison of number of operations used in CMT sentences

using the number of assigned `repeat` tags and found that the frequency of `repetition` tags was higher in *long* sentences (Table 5).

4.2.3 Omission in SI Sentences

To find techniques for shortening translations, we analyzed the SI sentences in NAIST-SIC. Based on the length ratio of SI sentences to the offline ones, we defined SI sentences that might have reasonable omissions (`omission`; $0.6 \leq$ ratio < 0.9) and SI sentences that probably failed to fully convey the meaning of the source sentences (`undertranslation`; ratio < 0.6), following the criteria in Higashiyama et al. (2023).

Although we expected to identify some trends (*e.g.*, part-of-speech) in the phrases that were omitted, we did not do so. In addition, we found a certain number of *unacceptable* translations in both categories (43.12% and 60.00% for `omission` and `undertranslation`, respectively). The results suggest that human simultaneous interpreters judge the importance of phrases based on context and decide whether to translate them; some judgements are correct, and some are not.

4.2.4 Factors that Make Monotonic Translation Difficult

With the help of tags annotated to the source and CMT sentences, we analyzed the factors that make monotonic translation difficult. Table 6 shows the number of source phrases that were `repeated`, `deferred`, or `omitted`. The values are based on the number of `rel-repeat`, `defer_d#`, and `omit` tags. We counted the relation tags for `repeat` and `defer` because the span tags for those two operations were assigned to both the source and CMT sentences. The results show that the translators used `repeat` most frequently, followed by `defer` and `omit`, as they were instructed (see Section 3.1).

For these phrases, we explored what makes monotonic translations difficult. Our analyses revealed that most cases of `repeat` and `defer` were caused by particular grammatical structures. Table 7 lists the major structures along with their frequencies in the data and examples. In these structures, a phrase in a chunk is typically a dependent of a phrase in the preceding chunk. In the example of a post-modifier (Table 7), the relative pronoun clause is a dependent of the noun phrase *a device*, which is in a preceding chunk. When phrases with a dependency relation exist across multiple chunks, CMT is difficult because Japanese is a strongly head-final language. The examples in Table 7 show how human translators address these structures by repeating or deferring some phrases in subsequent chunks.

Prepositions, post-modifiers, and dependent clauses have also been identified as syntactic factors that affect interpreters' word order decisions in Cai et al. (2020). Human interpreters find these structures challenging for SI and adopt a strategy to maintain the word order of the source language.

In addition, we observed that inappropriate segmentation was addressed by `repeating` and `deferring` the phrases. Most inappropriate segmentation was found in phrasal verbs, verbal gerunds, and to-infinitives.

In the SI data, we also found that human interpreters `repeat` phrases to maintain the word order of the source language. For example, in the example in Table 1, a noun modified by a preposition phrase is `repeated`:

> (En) ... / froze the Swiss bank account / of Mr. Sam Jain right here, / ...
>
> (SI) ... / スイスの銀行の口座を凍結しました。 / サムジェインのものです。 / ...
> [... / froze the Swiss bank account / it is Sam Jain's one / ...]

In addition, Okamura and Yamada (2023) reported that the order of the chunks is shuffled about once on average in an SI sentence. These things suggest that human interpreters address the word order differences that make monotonic translation difficult by `repeating` and `deferring` some phrases.

Structures	# repeat	# defer	Examples
Noun with a post-modifier	88	12	And now we've created a device / that has absolutely no limitations. さて、私たちはデバイスを作り出しました、/ 全く制限のないものです。 [And we've created a device / one that has absolutely no limitations]
Head followed by multiple dependents	35	6	... / allows for deep squats, / crawls and high agility movements. ... / 深いスクワットを可能にし、/ クロールや高い敏捷性の動きを可能にします。 [... / allows for deep squats / allows for crawls and high agility movements]
Dependent conjunction	26	6	... / when he's covered / in four feet of snow. ... / 彼が / 四フィートの雪に覆われてしまっていた時には。 [he / when was covered in for feet of snow]
Chunk boundary before a clause	15	13	... / you know that this isn't / how it normally goes. / あなたは分かるはずです、これは / 通常の進行ではないということが。 [you know that this / isn't how it normally goes]
Chunk boundary before a preposition	10	7	... / providing totalitarian governments with tools / to do this / against their own citizens. ... / 全体主義政府にツールを提供しているということです、/ これを行うための、/ 自国の市民に対してこれを行うためのツールを。 [providing totalitarian governments with tools / to do this / tools to do this against their own citizens]

Table 7: Syntactic factors that prevent monotonic translations. Cases involving multiple structures were classified separately as *compound factors*.

5 Evaluation Using CMT sentences

To investigate the impact of using CMT sentences for evaluating translation quality, we evaluated the output from existing ST and simulST models using the NAIST English-to-Japanese Chunk-wise Monotonic Translation Evaluation Dataset as well as existing test sets.

5.1 Data

We used the following four datasets as references for the automatic evaluation metrics:

- **n-cmt**: CMT sentences from the NAIST English-to-Japanese Chunk-wise Monotonic Translation Evaluation Dataset
- **si_hum**: SI sentences from NAIST-SIC, manually aligned to the source speech
- **si_auto**: SI sentences from NAIST-SIC-Aligned, aligned automatically
- **offline**: offline translation sentences from the subtitles of TED talks.

Because `si_auto` was created by applying automatic alignment and filtering techniques to SI sentences in `si_hum`, it may contain alignment errors. In addition, SI sentences in `si_auto` tend to be shorter than those in `si_hum` (see Table 4). Therefore, we used the two SI-based datasets for our evaluation.

5.2 Speech Translation Models

We used three existing models (*i.e.*, one ST and two simulST models):

- **ST_offline**: an ST model trained on offline data (Fukuda et al., 2023)
- **simulST_offline**: a simulST model trained on offline data (Ko et al., 2023)
- **simulST_si_offline**: a simulST model trained on both offline and SI data (Ko et al., 2023).

All the models were built by connecting two pre-trained models, HuBERT-Large (Hsu et al., 2021) for their speech encoder and the decoder of mBART50 (Tang et al., 2020) for their text decoder. The encoder and decoder were connected by Inter-connection (Nishikawa and Nakamura, 2023) and a length adapter (Tsiamas et al., 2022). Both SimulST models used bilingual prefix pairs extracted using Bilingual Prefix Alignment (Kano et al., 2022) for the model training and employed a decoding policy called local agreement (Liu et al., 2020). For ST_offline, we used a model with checkpoint averaging (`Inter-connection + Ckpt Ave.` in Fukuda et al. (2023)). For simulST_offline and simulST_si_offline, we used the models that satisfy the task requirement of the simultaneous track in the IWSLT 2023 Evaluation Campaign[11], latency measured by Average Lagging (Ma et al., 2019) $\leq$ 2 seconds (`Offline FT` and `Mixed FT + Style` in Ko et al. (2023), respectively).

5.3 Metrics

We evaluated the translation quality of the output from the ST and simulST models (see Section 5.2)

[11] `https://iwslt.org/2023/simultaneous`

Model	BLEU				BLEURT				COMET			
	n-cmt	si_hum	si_auto	offline	n-cmt	si_hum	si_auto	offline	n-cmt	si_hum	si_auto	offline
ST_offline	14.487	8.856	8.637	17.775	0.553	0.447	0.414	**0.538**	**0.838**	**0.797**	**0.781**^{*1}	**0.833**
simulST_offline	15.406†	8.446†	7.773†	**17.907**	0.556	0.442	0.406	0.531	0.826	0.780	0.763	0.821
simulST_si_offline	**15.982**†	**12.031**†	**11.020**†	13.191†	**0.567**	**0.493**^{*1}	**0.460**^{*1}	0.519	0.807^{*2}	0.774^{*3}	0.761	0.789^{*2}

Model	BERTScore (Pre.)				BERTScore (Rec.)				BERTScore (F1)			
	n-cmt	si_hum	si_auto	offline	n-cmt	si_hum	si_auto	offline	n-cmt	si_hum	si_auto	offline
ST_offline	0.801	0.735	0.722	**0.789**	0.769	0.739	0.735	**0.788**	0.784	0.737	0.728	**0.788**
simulST_offline	0.799	0.730	0.717	0.783	0.770	0.738	0.734	0.786	0.783	0.734	0.725	0.784
simulST_si_offline	**0.817**^{*1}	**0.764**^{*1}	**0.746**^{*1}	0.759^{*2}	**0.784**^{*1}	**0.766**^{*1}	**0.760**^{*1}	0.757^{*2}	**0.800**^{*1}	**0.764**^{*1}	**0.752**^{*1}	0.757^{*2}

Table 8: Results of quality evaluation metrics across ST and simulST models. †: significantly different from ST_offline. $*1$: significantly higher than other two. $*2$ significantly lower than other two. $*3$ significantly lower than ST_offline. Significance threshold was set to $p < .05$ for all tests.

using BLEU[12], BLEURT[13] (Sellam et al., 2020), COMET[14] (Rei et al., 2020), and BERTScore[15] (Zhang et al., 2020). BERTScore was calculated using `bert-base-multilingual-cased`. We used the four datasets described in Section 5.1 as references.

5.4 Evaluation Results

Table 8 shows the results of the quality evaluation metrics across the ST and simulST models. For the BLEU scores, we conducted paired significance tests using paired bootstrap resampling (Koehn, 2004). We specified `ST_offline` as the baseline for the significance tests. For the other scores, we conducted a one-way ANOVA, followed by Tukey's multiple comparisons test.

When the translation quality was evaluated using BLEU with `n-cmt` as the reference, `simulST_si_offline` achieved the highest score. On the SI-based test sets (*i.e.*, `si_hum` and `si_auto`), `simulST_si_offline` also had the highest score. On the offline-based test set, in contrast, the models trained on only offline data achieved much higher scores than `simulST_si_offline`. The same tendencies were observed in BLEURT and BERTScore. These results suggest that the models trained on both SI and offline data generated more SI-like translations, and such models perhaps should be evaluated using a reference closer to SI sentences. In addition, using an offline-based test set might underestimate the performance of models trained on both SI and offline data.

Comparing `n-cmt`, `si_hum`, and `si_auto`, the scores were highest for `n-cmt`, followed by `si_hum` and `si_auto` on all the metrics and models. Because `si_hum` is based on SI sentences generated by human simultaneous interpreters, some content in the source speech might be omitted or inadequately translated (under-translation). SI sentences in `si_auto`, which were automatically created based on human SI sentences, might contain less source speech content than those in `si_hum` due to the alignment and filtering techniques applied (see Zhao et al., 2024). In fact, BERTScore precision was higher than recall on `n-cmt`, in which there were almost no omissions, while recall was higher than precision on `si_auto` and precision and recall were almost equal on `si_hum`. These results indicate the possibility that the existing SI-based test sets (Ko et al., 2023; Zhao et al., 2024) underestimate the model performance.

However, the COMET results were different from those on the other metrics (Table 8). On all four test sets, `ST_offline` achieved the highest score, followed by `simulST_offline` and `simulST_si_offline`. One possible reason is that COMET uses source sentences to calculate its scores.

To examine the impact of the source sentences, we also calculated a reference-free COMET-QE using `wmt22-cometkiwi-da` and got similar results (0.813, 0.798, and 0.766 for `ST_offline`, `simulST_offline`, and `simulST_si_offline`, respectively). We further calculated COMET-QE for `n-cmt` and `offline`, regarding them as oracle data, and found that `n-cmt` had a higher score than `offline` (`n-cmt`: 0.832, `offline`: 0.812). Because some translation sentences in `offline` are under-translated, these results suggest that the COMET scores tend to become high when more content in the source sentences is covered in the

[12] BLEU was calculated using sacreBLEU. (Post, 2018) `https://github.com/mjpost/sacrebleu`

[13] `https://github.com/google-research/bleurt`

[14] `https://github.com/Unbabel/COMET`

[15] `https://github.com/Tiiiger/bert_score`

target sentences. This feature does not fit the nature of SI, where human interpreters use sophisticated strategies (see He et al., 2016; Cai et al., 2020, for example). We need to carefully interpret COMET scores when we use them for evaluating simulST models.

6 Conclusion

This paper focused on monotonic translations in English-Japanese SI. Our analyses revealed some grammatical structures that make monotonic translations difficult and that human interpreters/translators address these challenges by repeating or deferring some phrases in source language in the subsequent chunks. The grammatical structures that might cause delays would be useful information for developing segmentation or decoding policies for simultaneous machine translation systems. One possible direction would be predicting whether a phrase in a chunk is the head of a phrase in subsequent chunks.

We also evaluated the output from the existing ST and simulST models on the NAIST English-to-Japanese Chunk-wise Monotonic Translation Evaluation Dataset as well as on existing SI-based and offline-based test sets. The BLEU, BLEURT, and BERTScore results supported using CMT sentences for evaluating simulST models trained using SI data, although the results with COMET were different. Further analysis across various evaluation metrics is necessary. Analyzing how the source and target sentences are aligned monotonically on different types of translations (*e.g.*, Han et al., 2021) would also be useful.

This paper investigated the impact of using CMT sentences for evaluation purposes. A future study would involve using monotonic translation sentences for developing simulST models (Sakai et al., 2024)[16]. It could potentially address the problem that simulST models trained using SI sentences suffered from under-translation (Ko et al., 2023). However, CMT sentences tend to be long. Investigating the trade-offs between longer CMT sentences and the potential cognitive load on listeners/readers might provide further insights.

Acknowledgments

A part of this work was supported by JSPS KAKENHI Grant Numbers JP21H05054 and by JST, the establishment of university fellowships towards the creation of science technology innovation, Grant Number JPMJFS2137.

[16]Published around the same time as the submission of this paper.

References

Zhongxi Cai, Koichiro Ryu, and Shigeki Matsubara. 2018. Statistical analysis of missing translation in simultaneous interpretation using a large-scale bilingual speech corpus. In *Proceedings of the Eleventh International Conference on Language Resources and Evaluation (LREC 2018)*, Miyazaki, Japan. European Language Resources Association (ELRA).

Zhongxi Cai, Koichiro Ryu, and Shigeki Matsubara. 2020. What affects the word order of target language in simultaneous interpretation. In *Proceedings of 2020 International Conference on Asian Language Processing (IALP)*, pages 135–140.

Mattia A. Di Gangi, Roldano Cattoni, Luisa Bentivogli, Matteo Negri, and Marco Turchi. 2019. MuST-C: a Multilingual Speech Translation Corpus. In *Proceedings of the 2019 Conference of the North American Chapter of the Association for Computational Linguistics: Human Language Technologies, Volume 1 (Long and Short Papers)*, pages 2012–2017, Minneapolis, Minnesota. Association for Computational Linguistics.

Kosuke Doi, Katsuhito Sudoh, and Satoshi Nakamura. 2021. Large-scale English-Japanese simultaneous interpretation corpus: Construction and analyses with sentence-aligned data. In *Proceedings of the 18th International Conference on Spoken Language Translation (IWSLT 2021)*, pages 226–235, Bangkok, Thailand (online). Association for Computational Linguistics.

Ryo Fukuda, Kosuke Doi, Katsuhito Sudoh, and Satoshi Nakamura. 2024. 原発話に忠実な英日同時機械翻訳の実現に向けた順送り訳評価データ作成 [Creation of Evaluation Data for Monotonic Translation toward the Realization of Simultaneous English-Japanese Machine Translation Faithful to the Source Speech]. In *Proceedings of the 259th meeting of Special Interest Group of Natural Language Processing (IPSJ-SIGNL), 2024-NL-259(14)*, pages 1–6. (in Japanese).

Ryo Fukuda, Yuta Nishikawa, Yasumasa Kano, Yuka Ko, Tomoya Yanagita, Kosuke Doi, Mana Makinae, Sakriani Sakti, Katsuhito Sudoh, and Satoshi Nakamura. 2023. NAIST simultaneous speech-to-speech translation system for IWSLT 2023. In *Proceedings of the 20th International Conference on Spoken Language Translation (IWSLT 2023)*, pages 330–340, Toronto, Canada (in-person and online). Association for Computational Linguistics.

Kosuke Futamata, Katsuhito Sudoh, and Satoshi Nakamura. 2020. 英日同時通訳システムのための疑似同時通訳コーパス自動生成手法の提案[Proposal of a Method for Automatically Generating Pseudo-simultaneous Interpretation Corpora for English-Japanese Simultaneous Interpretation Systems]. In *Proceedings of the 26th Annual Meeting of the Association for Natural Language Processing*, pages 1281–1284. (in Japanese).

HyoJung Han, Seokchan Ahn, Yoonjung Choi, Insoo Chung, Sangha Kim, and Kyunghyun Cho. 2021. Monotonic simultaneous translation with chunk-wise reordering and refinement. In *Proceedings of the Sixth Conference on Machine Translation*, pages 1110–1123, Online. Association for Computational Linguistics.

He He, Jordan Boyd-Graber, and Hal Daumé III. 2016. Interpretese vs. translationese: The uniqueness of human strategies in simultaneous interpretation. In *Proceedings of the 2016 Conference of the North American Chapter of the Association for Computational Linguistics: Human Language Technologies*, pages 971–976, San Diego, California. Association for Computational Linguistics.

He He, Alvin Grissom II, John Morgan, Jordan Boyd-Graber, and Hal Daumé III. 2015. Syntax-based rewriting for simultaneous machine translation. In *Proceedings of the 2015 Conference on Empirical Methods in Natural Language Processing*, pages 55–64, Lisbon, Portugal. Association for Computational Linguistics.

Shohei Higashiyama, Kenji Imamura, Masao Utiyama, and Eiichiro. Sumita. 2023. GCP 同時通訳コーパスの構築[Construction of GCP Simultaneous Interpretation Corpus]. In *Proceedings of the 29th Annual Meeting of the Association for Natural Language Processing*, pages 1405–1410. (in Japanese).

Wei-Ning Hsu, Benjamin Bolte, Yao-Hung Hubert Tsai, Kushal Lakhotia, Ruslan Salakhutdinov, and Abdelrahman Mohamed. 2021. Hubert: Self-supervised speech representation learning by masked prediction of hidden units. *IEEE/ACM Transactions on Audio, Speech, and Language Processing*, 29:3451–3460.

Yasumasa Kano, Katsuhito Sudoh, and Satoshi Nakamura. 2022. Simultaneous neural machine translation with prefix alignment. In *Proceedings of the 19th International Conference on Spoken Language Translation (IWSLT 2022)*, pages 22–31, Dublin, Ireland (in-person and online). Association for Computational Linguistics.

Yuka Ko, Ryo Fukuda, Yuta Nishikawa, Yasumasa Kano, Katsuhito Sudoh, and Satoshi Nakamura. 2023. Tagged end-to-end simultaneous speech translation training using simultaneous interpretation data. In *Proceedings of the 20th International Conference on Spoken Language Translation (IWSLT 2023)*, pages 363–375, Toronto, Canada (in-person and online). Association for Computational Linguistics.

Philipp Koehn. 2004. Statistical significance tests for machine translation evaluation. In *Proceedings of the 2004 Conference on Empirical Methods in Natural Language Processing*, pages 388–395, Barcelona, Spain. Association for Computational Linguistics.

Taku Kudo, Kaoru Yamamoto, and Yuji Matsumoto. 2004. Applying conditional random fields to Japanese morphological analysis. In *Proceedings of the 2004 Conference on Empirical Methods in Natural Language Processing*, pages 230–237, Barcelona, Spain. Association for Computational Linguistics.

Danni Liu, Gerasimos Spanakis, and Jan Niehues. 2020. Low-Latency Sequence-to-Sequence Speech Recognition and Translation by Partial Hypothesis Selection. In *Proceedings of Interspeech 2020*, pages 3620–3624.

Mingbo Ma, Liang Huang, Hao Xiong, Renjie Zheng, Kaibo Liu, Baigong Zheng, Chuanqiang Zhang, Zhongjun He, Hairong Liu, Xing Li, Hua Wu, and Haifeng Wang. 2019. STACL: Simultaneous translation with implicit anticipation and controllable latency using prefix-to-prefix framework. In *Proceedings of the 57th Annual Meeting of the Association for Computational Linguistics*, pages 3025–3036, Florence, Italy. Association for Computational Linguistics.

Kayo Matsushita, Masaru Yamada, and Hiroyuki Ishizuka. 2020. An overview of the Japan National Press Club (JNPC) Interpreting Corpus. *Invitation to Interpreting and Translation Studies*, 22:87–94. (in Japanese).

Masaki Murata, Tomohiro Ohno, Shigeki Matsubara, and Yasuyoshi Inagaki. 2010. Construction of chunk-aligned bilingual lecture corpus for simultaneous machine translation. In *Proceedings of the Seventh International Conference on Language Resources and Evaluation (LREC'10)*, Valletta, Malta. European Language Resources Association (ELRA).

Akiko Nakabayashi and Tsuneaki Kato. 2021. 同時機械翻訳のための文脈を考慮したセグメントコーパス[Context-Aware Segment Corpus for Simultaneous Machine Translation]. In *Proceedings of the 27th Annual Meeting of the Association for Natural Language Processing*, pages 1659–1663. (in Japanese).

Yuta Nishikawa and Satoshi Nakamura. 2023. Inter-connection: Effective Connection between Pre-trained Encoder and Decoder for Speech Translation. In *Proceedings of INTERSPEECH 2023*, pages 2193–2197.

Yusuke Oda, Graham Neubig, Sakriani Sakti, Tomoki Toda, and Satoshi Nakamura. 2014. Optimizing segmentation strategies for simultaneous speech translation. In *Proceedings of the 52nd Annual Meeting of the Association for Computational Linguistics (Volume 2: Short Papers)*, pages 551–556, Baltimore, Maryland. Association for Computational Linguistics.

Yuki Okamura and Masaru Yamada. 2023. 「順送り訳」の規範と模範 同時通訳を模範とした教育論の

試論 [Norms and Canon of Progressive Translation - An Exploratory Study on Educational Theories Using Simultaneous Interpretation as a Canon]. In Hiroyuki Ishizuka, editor, *Word Order in English-Japanese Interpreting and Translation: The History, Theory and Practice of Progressive Translation*, pages 217–250. Hitsuji Syobo. (in Japanese).

Takahiro Ono, Hitomi Tohyama, and Shigeki Matsubara. 2008. Construction and analysis of word-level time-aligned simultaneous interpretation corpus. In *Proceedings of the Sixth International Conference on Language Resources and Evaluation (LREC'08)*, Marrakech, Morocco. European Language Resources Association (ELRA).

Sara Papi, Marco Turchi, and Matteo Negri. 2023. AlignAtt: Using Attention-based Audio-Translation Alignments as a Guide for Simultaneous Speech Translation. In *Proceedings of INTERSPEECH 2023*, pages 3974–3978.

Kishore Papineni, Salim Roukos, Todd Ward, and Wei-Jing Zhu. 2002. Bleu: a method for automatic evaluation of machine translation. In *Proceedings of the 40th Annual Meeting of the Association for Computational Linguistics*, pages 311–318, Philadelphia, Pennsylvania, USA. Association for Computational Linguistics.

Matt Post. 2018. A call for clarity in reporting BLEU scores. In *Proceedings of the Third Conference on Machine Translation: Research Papers*, pages 186–191, Brussels, Belgium. Association for Computational Linguistics.

Ricardo Rei, Craig Stewart, Ana C Farinha, and Alon Lavie. 2020. COMET: A neural framework for MT evaluation. In *Proceedings of the 2020 Conference on Empirical Methods in Natural Language Processing (EMNLP)*, pages 2685–2702, Online. Association for Computational Linguistics.

Koichiro Ryu, Atsushi Mizuno, Shigeki Matsubara, and Yasuyoshi Inagaki. 2004. Incremental japanese spoken language generation in simultaneous machine interpretation. In *Proceedings of Asian Symposium on Natural Language Processing to Overcome language Barriers*, pages 91–95.

Yusuke Sakai, Mana Makinae, Hidetaka Kamigaito, and Taro Watanabe. 2024. Simultaneous Interpretation Corpus Construction by Large Language Models in Distant Language Pair. *arXiv*. ArXiv:2404.12299.

Thibault Sellam, Dipanjan Das, and Ankur Parikh. 2020. BLEURT: Learning robust metrics for text generation. In *Proceedings of the 58th Annual Meeting of the Association for Computational Linguistics*, pages 7881–7892, Online. Association for Computational Linguistics.

Hiroaki Shimizu, Graham Neubig, Sakriani Sakti, Tomoki Toda, and Satoshi Nakamura. 2013. Constructing a speech translation system using simultaneous interpretation data. In *Proceedings of the 10th International Workshop on Spoken Language Translation: Papers*, Heidelberg, Germany.

Hiroaki Shimizu, Graham Neubig, Sakriani Sakti, Tomoki Toda, and Satoshi Nakamura. 2014. Collection of a simultaneous translation corpus for comparative analysis. In *Proceedings of the Ninth International Conference on Language Resources and Evaluation (LREC'14)*, pages 670–673, Reykjavik, Iceland. European Language Resources Association (ELRA).

Yuqing Tang, Chau Tran, Xian Li, Peng-Jen Chen, Naman Goyal, Vishrav Chaudhary, Jiatao Gu, and Angela Fan. 2020. Multilingual translation with extensible multilingual pretraining and finetuning. *arXiv*, arXiv:2008.00401.

Hitomi Tohyama and Shigeki Matsubara. 2006. Collection of simultaneous interpreting patterns by using bilingual spoken monologue corpus. In *Proceedings of the Fifth International Conference on Language Resources and Evaluation (LREC'06)*, Genoa, Italy. European Language Resources Association (ELRA).

Hitomi Toyama, Shigeki Matsubara, Koichiro Ryu, Nobuo Kawaguchi, and Yasuyoshi Inagaki. 2004. CIAIR Simultaneous Interpretation Corpus. In *Proceedings of Oriental COCOSDA*.

Ioannis Tsiamas, Gerard I. Gállego, Carlos Escolano, José Fonollosa, and Marta R. Costa-jussà. 2022. Pretrained speech encoders and efficient fine-tuning methods for speech translation: UPC at IWSLT 2022. In *Proceedings of the 19th International Conference on Spoken Language Translation (IWSLT 2022)*, pages 265–276, Dublin, Ireland (in-person and online). Association for Computational Linguistics.

Tianyi Zhang, Varsha Kishore, Felix Wu, Kilian Q. Weinberger, and Yoav Artzi. 2020. Bertscore: Evaluating text generation with bert. In *International Conference on Learning Representations*.

Jinming Zhao, Yuka Ko, Kosuke Doi, Ryo Fukuda, Katsuhito Sudoh, and Satoshi Nakamura. 2024. NAIST-SIC-Aligned: Automatically-Aligned English-Japanese Simultaneous Interpretation Corpus. *arXiv*. ArXiv:2304.11766, version 4.

Leveraging Synthetic Audio Data for End-to-End Low-Resource Speech Translation

Yasmin Moslem
Bering Lab

Abstract

This paper describes our system submission to the International Conference on Spoken Language Translation (IWSLT 2024) for Irish-to-English speech translation. We built end-to-end systems based on Whisper, and employed a number of data augmentation techniques, such as speech back-translation and noise augmentation. We investigate the effect of using synthetic audio data and discuss several methods for enriching signal diversity.

1 Introduction

Resource scarcity and the scattered nature of the data are crucial challenges for low-resource languages (Lankford et al., 2021; Haddow et al., 2022; Lovenia et al., 2024). In this sense, Irish is considered a low-resource language and significantly lacking in speech and language tools and resources (Barry et al., 2022; Lynn, 2022). Researchers have been employing various data augmentation techniques to improve the quality of low-resource textual machine translation (MT) systems. Among these techniques is using synthetic data generated by back-translation (Sennrich et al., 2016; Edunov et al., 2018; Dowling et al., 2019; Poncelas et al., 2019; Haque et al., 2020), or large language models (Moslem et al., 2022). Similarly, in the area of speech, Lee et al. (2023) showed that models trained solely on synthetic audio datasets can generalize their performance to human voice data. Nevertheless, Guo et al. (2023) revealed a consistent decrease in the diversity of the outputs of language models trained on synthetic textual data. We observe that leveraging synthetic audio data generated by text-to-speech (TTS) models can be beneficial for training speech translation models, especially for low-resource languages. However, it can lack the diversity found in authentic audio signals in terms of pitch, speed, and background noise.

Speech translation systems can be cascaded systems or end-to-end systems (Agarwal et al., 2023). Cascaded systems use two models, one for automatic speech recognition (ASR) and one for textual machine translation (MT). End-to-end speech translation systems use one model for the whole process; hence, it is more challenging. In this work, we present end-to-end speech translation models.

In addition to describing our system submitted to IWSLT 2024, this work presents the following contributions:

- Showcasing "speech back-translation" as an effective data augmentation technique for speech translation. In other words, just as back-translation can improve the output quality of text-to-text MT, generating source-side synthetic audio data can considerably enhance the performance of speech translation systems, especially for low-resource languages.
- Introducing a collection of datasets for Irish-to-English speech translation, three of which comprise 196 hours of synthetic audio.
- Exploring diverse training settings and data processing techniques such as noise augmentation and voice audio detection (VAD).
- Releasing versions of Whisper models, specifically fine-tuned for Irish-to-English speech translation.

2 Authentic Data

The organizers of the IWSLT shared task, provided the IWSLT-2023 dataset, which consists of training, dev, and test portions. We used both the training and dev portions for training, and the test portion for evaluation. We also used the Irish portion of the FLEURS datasets. Moreover, we employed the bilingual audio-text data available at the Bitesize website for teaching Irish.[1]

[1] https://huggingface.co/datasets/ymoslem/BitesizeIrish-GA-EN

Proceedings of the 21st International Conference on Spoken Language Translation (IWSLT 2024), pages 313–321
August 15-16, 2024 ©2024 Association for Computational Linguistics

Dataset	Audio	Translation	Train Hours (H:M)	Train Segments	Test Segments
IWSLT-2023	Authentic	Authentic	8:25	8,598	347
FLEURS	Authentic	Authentic	16:45	3,991	0
Bitesize	Authentic	Authentic	5:15	6,149	0
SpokenWords	Authentic	MTed	3:02	10,925	0
EUbookshop	Synthetic	Authentic	159:45	67,268	0
Tatoeba	Synthetic	Authentic	2:39	3,966	0
W Wikimedia	Synthetic	Authentic	34:23	15,090	0
Authentic ()			33:27	29,663	347
Synthetic (w)			196:47	86,324	0
Authentic () + Synthetic (w)			70:29	48,719	347
Authentic () + Synthetic (w)			229:14	115,987	347

Table 1: Data Statistics: "Audio" and "Translation" columns refer to whether the data is human-generated or machine-generated. "Train Hours" and "Train Segments" refer to the size of the training data in terms of duration and number of utterances, respectively. Finally, "Test Segments" refer to the number of utterances in the test dataset.

3 Synthetic Data

This section explains diverse approaches for creating synthetic data for speech translation. We describe each approach, as well as its advantages and disadvantages.

3.1 Machine Translation

When both audio and transcription are available, but there is no translation, forward MT can be useful as a data augmentation technique. However, there is the risk of feeding incorrect target translations into the training process. Forward MT is more sensitive to the quality of the system used to produce the synthetic data. Compared to back-translation, biases and errors in synthetic data are intuitively more problematic in forward-translation, since they directly affect the gold labels (Bogoychev and Sennrich, 2019). Hence, the used MT system must be of high quality.

We automatically translated the Irish portion of the Spoken Words dataset into English using the Google Translation API. For quality considerations, we decided to use this dataset for training only, but not for evaluation. The dataset consists of 10,925 utterances. Some words are spoken by multiple narrators.[2]

3.2 Synthetic Audio Data

OPUS (Tiedemann, 2012) hosts several bilingual textual datasets. We extracted portions of the Tatoeba, Wikimedia, and EUbookshop datasets, comprising 1,983, 7,545 and 33,634 segments, respectively. We extensively filter the datasets based on the following criteria: removing duplicates, removing segments longer than 30 words,[3] language detection with fastText (Joulin et al., 2017) (both sides), and Seamless toxicity filtering (Barrault et al., 2023). Finally, we used Azure Speech service to generate two sets of audio data, one with a female voice (OrlaNeural) and the other with a male voice (ColmNeural). As an outcome of this process, we introduce three new datasets, Tatoeba-Speech-Irish,[4] Wikimedia-Speech-Irish,[5] and EUbookshop-Speech-Irish,[6] which together comprise 196 hours of synthetic audio. Table 1 illustrates the statistics of our datasets.

3.3 Audio Signal Processing Augmentation

Synthetic audio data generated by TTS models can have different characteristics than authentic audio. In addition to quality considerations, we observe that among the features that distinguish data generated by TTS systems from authentic data are: 1) lack of noise, and 2) silence differences.

Lack of noise: TTS systems try to mimic studio settings, and produce very clean audio signals.

[2] https://huggingface.co/datasets/ymoslem/SpokenWords-GA-EN-MTed

[3] https://github.com/ymoslem/MT-Preparation

[4] https://huggingface.co/datasets/ymoslem/Tatoeba-Speech-Irish

[5] https://huggingface.co/datasets/ymoslem/Wikimedia-Speech-Irish

[6] https://huggingface.co/datasets/ymoslem/EUbookshop-Speech-Irish

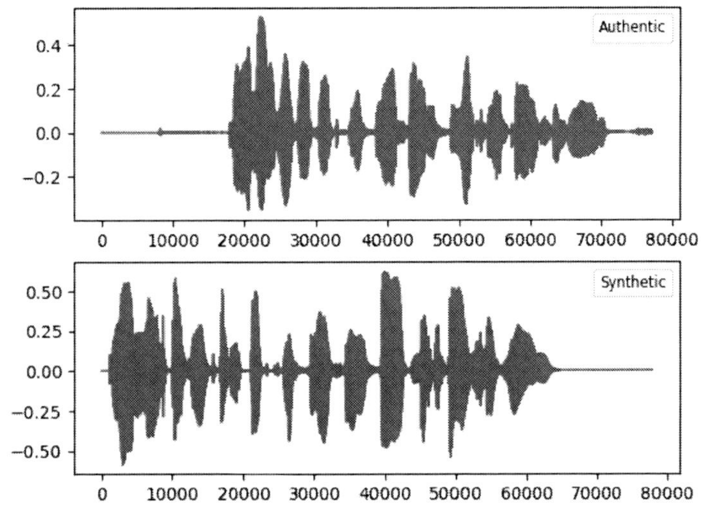

Figure 1: Comparing authentic (top) and synthetic (bottom) audio signals

However, authentic audio signals can include all sorts of environmental noise, ranging from white noise to background voices of people and cars. Even in studio settings, some breath signals can occur unless the audio is extensively edited.

Silence variances: All the synthetic audio signals we generated start at a similar point, with almost no silence at the beginning of the audio (probably to facilitate mixing tracks). However, authentic audio signals can start at any point depending on the recording and processing settings, or whether a signal is truncated from a longer one.

Figure 1 illustrates an example sentence from the Common Voice dataset uttered by a human female (non-studio settings) and its synthetic equivalent generated by Azure TTS system.[7] The Irish sentence represented here is "*Go raibh maith agaibh as ucht na fíorchaoin fáilte a d'fhear sibh romham.*" It can be translated into English as "*Thank you all for that very generous welcome.*" The authentic signal has more noise (both white background noise and sounds of starting/stopping the recording software), while the synthetic signal does not show any noise occurrence. Moreover, unlike the authentic signal, the synthetic data starts almost immediately. Another observation is that this specific authentic signal has a lower volume than synthetic signals.

[7]Voice name: "*Microsoft Server Speech Text to Speech Voice (ga-IE, OrlaNeural)*"

3.3.1 Voice Activity Detection

One of the most common audio preprocessing techniques is Voice Audio Detection (VAD). The main idea of VAD is to remove low-amplitude samples from an audio signal. Low-amplitude samples might represent science or noise samples of audio signals, which usually occur at the beginning and end of an audio signal, but can also happen in the midst of longer audio signals. In its basic form, this can be achieved by removing any sample below an absolute value of a threshold (e.g. ± 0.001). However, advanced models like *Silero VAD*[8] can be used as part of the *torchaudio* framework, and include more sophisticated options (e.g. minimum silence duration) to avoid removing important low-amplitude samples like breath and natural silent durations.

During training, data processed with VAD can either substitute the original data or augment it, i.e. both processed and unprocessed data can be used during training. In one of our experiments (cf. Section 4), we used basic VAD with a threshold of ± 0.001 as a data augmentation technique. When basic VAD is used (i.e. without taking a minimum silence duration into account), this can also speed up the audio signal; in other words, the utterance is spoken faster. At inference time of all the models, we used Silero VAD within Faster-Whisper based on CTranslate2 (Klein et al., 2020).

[8]https://github.com/snakers4/silero-vad

3.3.2 Noise Augmentation

Mimicking the effect of white noise can take diverse forms, ranging from using real noise to generating random arrays. To simulate light white noise, we generated a random array with a distribution scale 0.002 and added it to all the audio signals in the dataset.

4 Experiments

Our experiments fine-tune Whisper (Radford et al., 2022) for the task of Irish-to-English speech translation. We experiment with a number of data augmentation techniques, such as speech back-translation (source-side synthetic audio data generation), and audio data augmentation with noise and VAD.

4.1 Speech Back-Translation

By the term "speech back-translation", we refer to generating source-side synthetic audio for data augmentation of speech translation systems, in the same manner that back-translation is employed in text-to-text MT systems. Section 3.2 explains how we created these synthetic audio datasets. In this set of experiments, we built 3 systems by fine-tuning Whisper Medium. We use different types of datasets as outlined by Table 1.

- **Model A**: It uses the authentic data only, namely IWSLT-2023 dataset, FLEURS, Bite-size, and SpokenWords.
- **Model B**: It uses the same authentic data used in Model A as well as two synthetic audio datasets, namely Tatoeba-Speech-Irish, and Wikimedia-Speech-Irish.
- **Model B++**: In addition to the authentic and two synthetic datasets used in the aforementioned models, Model B++ uses a third synthetic dataset, namely EUbookshop-Speech-Irish.

4.2 Noise and VAD Augmentation

- **Model C**: It uses the same data as Model B, as well as two versions of the data augmented with basic VAD, and white noise. In other words, we fine-tuned Whisper-Medium on all the authentic data and two synthetic data as well as two augmented datasets, one with low-amplitude sample removal, and one with noise augmentation, as described in Section 3.

4.3 Training Arguments

We tried different learning rates and warm-up values. Specifically, we experimented with warm-up ratios 0%, 1%, and 3% out of 3000 steps, which corresponds to 0, 30, 90 warm-up steps, respectively. As Table 5 and Table 4 demonstrate, when fine-tuning Whisper Small, changing the warm-up ratio does not seem to lead to a consistent improvement for the first two sizes of data used in Model A and Model B. However, increasing the warm-up ratio to 3% when the size of data is larger as in Model C, seems to slightly improve the performance. For the learning rate, we used 1e-4 across all the experiments for the sake of consistency. The batch size was decided based on the compute capacity of one A100-SXM4-80GB GPU. Hence, we used a batch size of 64 examples when fine-tuning Whisper Small and a batch size of 16 examples when fine-tuning Whisper Medium. The max length of generation was set to 225. As this is an Irish-to-English translation task, both the tokenizer language and model generation language were set to English. We train the main models with Whisper Medium for at least two epochs, and save the best performing checkpoint based on the chrF++ score on the validation dataset. Section 5 elaborates on the results of these experiments.

4.4 Training Epochs

As we reported in the previous section, we used 3000 steps for all the experiments with Whisper Small, as further training did not seem to improve the output quality when more than one epoch of data is already reached. However, Whisper Medium was trained with a smaller batch size due to computing constrains. We wanted to see the effect of training for at least two epochs. Hence, we report different step milestones in Table 6. In deep learning training in general, it is a common practice to use early stopping. However, for low-resource languages, a smaller value for early stopping can result in the model not seeing the whole data, which can affect the robustness of the model. This is especially true if we are not sure if the validation dataset is well-representative of the task that the model will be actually required to tackle in the real world. While there is no one rule that applies to all cases, we recommend taking this point into consideration when training generic models for low-resource languages.

Whisper	Model	Datasets	Data Size	BLEU ↑	chrF++ ↑	WER ↓	Semantic 1 ↑	Semantic 2 ↑
Medium	A	authentic	29,663	32.38	48.95	58.85	62.09	63.28
	B	A + synthetic (2d)	48,719	36.34	54.08	53.35	68.31	69.93
	B++	A + synthetic (3d)	115,987	**38.41**	**57.18**	**51.10**	**69.72**	**71.13**
	C	B + augmented	146,157	34.09	51.40	55.83	64.26	65.56

Table 2: Evaluation Results: Model B++ that uses both authentic data and 3 synthetic audio datasets achieved the best results across all the systems. The results show that augmenting the training data with synthetic audio (i.e. Model B and Model B++) outperforms using authentic data only (Model A), while further signal processing augmentation with white noise and VAD (Model C) did not help. Moreover, increasing the amount of high-quality synthetic audio data in Model B++ resulted in better quality than Model B that uses a less amount of synthetic data.

5 Evaluation and Results

To evaluate our systems, we calculated BLEU (Papineni et al., 2002), chrF++ (Popović, 2017), and TER (Snover et al., 2006), as implemented in the sacreBLEU library[9] (Post, 2018). For semantic evaluation, we used an embedding-based approach, calculating and comparing cosine similarity between the vector embeddings of each reference and the equivalent translation generated by the model. We report the average of semantic similarity across utterances. We used two models with Sentence-Transformers (Reimers and Gurevych, 2019), *"all-mpnet-base-v2"* (Semantic 1) and *"all-MiniLM-L12-v2"* (Wang et al., 2020) (Semantic 2). As we fine-tuned all the models for approximately two epochs, we report the evaluation of the best performing checkpoint.

For inference, we used Faster-Whisper [10] with the default VAD arguments. We also compared the results without VAD, and found that applying VAD at inference time is better for all the models (cf. Appendix A). We used 5 for "beam size" and 2 for "no repeat ngram size".

As Table 2 shows, after fine-tuning Whisper Medium on both the authentic and synthetic audio data (Model B), there are consistent improvements across all metrics compared to when we fine-tuned it on the authentic audio data only (Model A). Moreover, Model B++ that uses three synthetic datasets outperforms Model B that uses only two synthetic datasets. This demonstrates that augmented authentic audio data with high-quality synthetic audio data can enhance end-to-end speech translation systems, especially for low-resource languages like Irish.

Model C uses the same training data as Model B as well as two augmented versions, one version that applies basic VAD, removing low-amplitude samples (cf. Section 3.3.1) and another version that injects white background noise into the data (cf. Section 3.3.2). Although Model C that uses noise and VAD augmented data still outperforms Model A that uses authentic training data only, both Model B and B++ that combines authentic data with synthetic data outperform Model C.

While the choice of augmentation techniques were based on manual observation of the characteristics of the authentic data and the synthetic data, the achieved improvements encourage further investigation. In the future, we would like to conduct more experiments that employ other data augmentation techniques. Moreover, we would like to measure the effect of adding synthetic audio data compared to augmenting the authentic data only. Finally, as the main purpose of this research is to understand the best practices of using synthetic audio data (i.e. data generated by TTS models) to improve speech translation quality, we will conduct further study on mimicking authentic data characteristics to enhance the effect of data augmentation with synthetic audio data.

[9] https://github.com/mjpost/sacrebleu

[10] https://github.com/SYSTRAN/faster-whisper

References

Milind Agarwal, Sweta Agrawal, Antonios Anastasopoulos, Luisa Bentivogli, Ondřej Bojar, Claudia Borg, Marine Carpuat, Roldano Cattoni, Mauro Cettolo, Mingda Chen, William Chen, Khalid Choukri, Alexandra Chronopoulou, Anna Currey, Thierry Declerck, Qianqian Dong, Kevin Duh, Yannick Estève, Marcello Federico, Souhir Gahbiche, Barry Haddow, Benjamin Hsu, Phu Mon Htut, Hirofumi Inaguma, Dávid Javorský, John Judge, Yasumasa Kano, Tom Ko, Rishu Kumar, Pengwei Li, Xutai Ma, Prashant Mathur, Evgeny Matusov, Paul McNamee, John P. McCrae, Kenton Murray, Maria Nadejde, Satoshi Nakamura, Matteo Negri, Ha Nguyen, Jan

Niehues, Xing Niu, Atul Kr. Ojha, John E. Ortega, Proyag Pal, Juan Pino, Lonneke van der Plas, Peter Polák, Elijah Rippeth, Elizabeth Salesky, Jiatong Shi, Matthias Sperber, Sebastian Stüker, Katsuhito Sudoh, Yun Tang, Brian Thompson, Kevin Tran, Marco Turchi, Alex Waibel, Mingxuan Wang, Shinji Watanabe, and Rodolfo Zevallos. 2023. FINDINGS OF THE IWSLT 2023 EVALUATION CAMPAIGN. In *Proceedings of the 20th International Conference on Spoken Language Translation (IWSLT 2023)*, pages 1–61, Toronto, Canada (in-person and online). Association for Computational Linguistics.

Loic Barrault, Andy Chung, David Dale, Ning Dong (ai), Paul-Ambroise Duquenne, Hady Elsahar, Hongyu Gong, Kevin Heffernan, John Hoffman, Christopher Klaiber, Peng-Jen Chen, Daniel Licht, Jean Maillard, Alice Rakotoarison, Kaushik Ram Sadagopan, Guillaume Wenzek, Abinesh Ramakrishnan, Alexandre Mourachko, Amanda Kallet, Ann Lee, Anna Sun, Bapi Akula, Benjamin Peloquin, Bernie Huang, Bokai Yu, Brian Ellis, Can Balioglu, Carleigh Wood, Changhan Wang, Christophe Ropers, Cynthia Gao, Daniel Li (fair), Elahe Kalbassi, Ethan Ye, Gabriel Mejia Gonzalez, Hirofumi Inaguma, Holger Schwenk, Igor Tufanov, Ilia Kulikov, Janice Lam, Jeff Wang (pm Ai), Juan Pino, Justin Haaheim, Justine Kao, Prangthip Hasanti, Kevin Tran, Maha Elbayad, Marta R Costa-jussa, Mohamed Ramadan, Naji El Hachem, Onur Çelebi, Paco Guzmán, Paden Tomasello, Pengwei Li, Pierre Andrews, Ruslan Mavlyutov, Russ Howes, Safiyyah Saleem, Skyler Wang, Somya Jain, Sravya Popuri, Tuan Tran, Vish Vogeti, Xutai Ma, and Yilin Yang. 2023. SeamlessM4T—Massively Multilingual & Multimodal Machine Translation. *Meta AI*.

James Barry, Joachim Wagner, Lauren Cassidy, Alan Cowap, Teresa Lynn, Abigail Walsh, Mícheál J Ó Meachair, and Jennifer Foster. 2022. gaBERT — an Irish Language Model. In *Proceedings of the Thirteenth Language Resources and Evaluation Conference*, pages 4774–4788, Marseille, France. European Language Resources Association.

Nikolay Bogoychev and Rico Sennrich. 2019. Domain, Translationese and Noise in Synthetic Data for Neural Machine Translation.

Meghan Dowling, Teresa Lynn, and Andy Way. 2019. Leveraging backtranslation to improve machine translation for Gaelic languages. In *Proceedings of the Celtic Language Technology Workshop*, pages 58–62, Dublin, Ireland. European Association for Machine Translation.

Sergey Edunov, Myle Ott, Michael Auli, and David Grangier. 2018. Understanding Back-Translation at Scale. In *Proceedings of the 2018 Conference on Empirical Methods in Natural Language Processing*, pages 489–500, Brussels, Belgium. Association for Computational Linguistics.

Yanzhu Guo, Guokan Shang, Michalis Vazirgiannis, and Chloé Clavel. 2023. The Curious Decline of Linguistic Diversity: Training Language Models on Synthetic Text. In *Proceedings or the Annual Conference of the North American Chapter of the Association for Computational Linguistics*, Mexico City, Mexico.

Barry Haddow, Rachel Bawden, Antonio Valerio Miceli Barone, Jindřich Helcl, and Alexandra Birch. 2022. Survey of Low-Resource Machine Translation. *Computational Linguistics*, 06:1–67.

Rejwanul Haque, Yasmin Moslem, and Andy Way. 2020. Terminology-Aware Sentence Mining for NMT Domain Adaptation: ADAPT's Submission to the Adap-MT 2020 English-to-Hindi AI Translation Shared Task. In *Proceedings of the 17th International Conference on Natural Language Processing (ICON): Adap-MT 2020 Shared Task*, pages 17–23, Patna, India. NLP Association of India (NLPAI).

Armand Joulin, Edouard Grave, Piotr Bojanowski, and Tomas Mikolov. 2017. Bag of Tricks for Efficient Text Classification. In *Proceedings of the 15th Conference of the European Chapter of the Association for Computational Linguistics: Volume 2, Short Papers*, pages 427–431, Valencia, Spain. Association for Computational Linguistics.

Guillaume Klein, François Hernandez, Vincent Nguyen, and Jean Senellart. 2020. The OpenNMT Neural Machine Translation Toolkit: 2020 Edition. In *Proceedings of the 14th Conference of the Association for Machine Translation in the Americas (Volume 1: Research Track)*, pages 102–109, Virtual. Association for Machine Translation in the Americas.

Seamus Lankford, Haithem Alfi, and Andy Way. 2021. Transformers for Low-Resource Languages: Is Féidir Linn! In *Proceedings of Machine Translation Summit XVIII: Research Track*, pages 48–60, Virtual. Association for Machine Translation in the Americas.

Jihyun Lee, Yejin Jeon, Wonjun Lee, Yunsu Kim, and Gary Geunbae Lee. 2023. Exploring the Viability of Synthetic Audio Data for Audio-Based Dialogue State Tracking. In *Proceedings of IEEE Workshop on Automatic Speech Recognition and Understanding*, Taipei, Taiwan.

Holy Lovenia, Rahmad Mahendra, Salsabil Maulana Akbar, Lester James V Miranda, Jennifer Santoso, Elyanah Aco, Akhdan Fadhilah, Jonibek Mansurov, Joseph Marvin Imperial, Onno P Kampman, Joel Ruben Antony Moniz, Muhammad Ravi Shulthan Habibi, Frederikus Hudi, Railey Montalan, Ryan Ignatius, Joanito Agili Lopo, William Nixon, Börje F Karlsson, James Jaya, Ryandito Diandaru, Yuze Gao, Patrick Amadeus, Bin Wang, Jan Christian Blaise Cruz, Chenxi Whitehouse, Ivan Halim Parmonangan, Maria Khelli, Wenyu Zhang, Lucky Susanto, Reynard Adha Ryanda, Sonny Lazuardi Hermawan, Dan John Velasco, Muhammad Dehan Al Kautsar, Willy Fitra Hendria, Yasmin Moslem, Noah Flynn, Muhammad Farid Adilazuarda, Haochen Li, Johanes Lee, R Damanhuri, Shuo Sun, Muhammad Reza Qorib, Amirbek Djanibekov, Wei Qi

Leong, Quyet V Do, Niklas Muennighoff, Tanrada Pansuwan, Ilham Firdausi Putra, Yan Xu, Ngee Chia Tai, Ayu Purwarianti, Sebastian Ruder, William Tjhi, Peerat Limkonchotiwat, Alham Fikri Aji, Sedrick Keh, Genta Indra Winata, Ruochen Zhang, Fajri Koto, Zheng-Xin Yong, and Samuel Cahyawijaya. 2024. SEACrowd: A Multilingual Multimodal Data Hub and Benchmark Suite for Southeast Asian Languages.

Teresa Lynn. 2022. Report on the Irish Language. Technical report, European Language Equality.

Yasmin Moslem, Rejwanul Haque, John Kelleher, and Andy Way. 2022. Domain-Specific Text Generation for Machine Translation. In *Proceedings of the 15th biennial conference of the Association for Machine Translation in the Americas (Volume 1: Research Track)*, pages 14–30, Orlando, USA. Association for Machine Translation in the Americas.

Kishore Papineni, Salim Roukos, Todd Ward, and Wei-Jing Zhu. 2002. Bleu: a Method for Automatic Evaluation of Machine Translation. In *Proceedings of the 40th Annual Meeting of the Association for Computational Linguistics*, pages 311–318, Philadelphia, Pennsylvania, USA. Association for Computational Linguistics.

Alberto Poncelas, Gideon Maillette de Buy Wenniger, and Andy Way. 2019. Adaptation of Machine Translation Models with Back-Translated Data Using Transductive Data Selection Methods. In *Proceedings of the 20th International Conference on Computational Linguistics and Intelligent Text Processing CICLing 2019: Computational Linguistics and Intelligent Text Processing*, pages 567–579, La Rochelle, France. Springer Nature Switzerland.

Maja Popović. 2017. chrF++: words helping character n-grams. In *Proceedings of the Second Conference on Machine Translation*, pages 612–618, Copenhagen, Denmark. Association for Computational Linguistics.

Matt Post. 2018. A Call for Clarity in Reporting BLEU Scores. In *Proceedings of the Third Conference on Machine Translation: Research Papers*, pages 186–191, Brussels, Belgium. Association for Computational Linguistics.

Alec Radford, Jong Wook Kim, Tao Xu, Greg Brockman, Christine McLeavey, and Ilya Sutskever. 2022. Robust Speech Recognition via Large-Scale Weak Supervision.

Nils Reimers and Iryna Gurevych. 2019. Sentence-BERT: Sentence Embeddings using Siamese BERT-Networks.

Rico Sennrich, Barry Haddow, and Alexandra Birch. 2016. Improving Neural Machine Translation Models with Monolingual Data. In *Proceedings of the 54th Annual Meeting of the Association for Computational Linguistics (Volume 1: Long Papers)*, pages 86–96, Berlin, Germany. Association for Computational Linguistics.

Matthew Snover, Bonnie Dorr, Rich Schwartz, Linnea Micciulla, and John Makhoul. 2006. A Study of Translation Edit Rate with Targeted Human Annotation. In *Proceedings of the 7th Conference of the Association for Machine Translation in the Americas: Technical Papers*, pages 223–231, Cambridge, Massachusetts, USA. Association for Machine Translation in the Americas.

Jörg Tiedemann. 2012. Parallel Data, Tools and Interfaces in OPUS. In *Proceedings of the Eighth International Conference on Language Resources and Evaluation (LREC'12)*, pages 2214–2218, Istanbul, Turkey. European Language Resources Association (ELRA).

Wenhui Wang, Furu Wei, Li Dong, Hangbo Bao, Nan Yang, and Ming Zhou. 2020. MINILM: deep self-attention distillation for task-agnostic compression of pre-trained transformers. In *Proceedings of the 34th International Conference on Neural Information Processing Systems*, number Article 485 in NIPS'20, pages 5776–5788, Red Hook, NY, USA. Curran Associates Inc.

A Appendix: Arguments

A.1 Inference VAD

Argument	Type	Value	Argument	Type	Value
threshold	float	0.5	min_silence_duration_ms	int	2000
min_speech_duration_ms	int	250	window_size_samples	int	1024
max_speech_duration_s	float	float("inf")	speech_pad_ms	int	400

Table 3: Default VAD values of *Faster-Whisper*.

A.2 Training Warm-up Ratio

Whisper	Model	Datasets	Data Size	Warm-up	BLEU	chrF++	WER	Semantic 1	Semantic 2
Small	A	authentic	29,663	0.00	**31.49**	45.59	59.66	58.23	60.35
				0.01	30.97	46.19	**59.57**	59.69	61.09
				0.03	31.43	**46.71**	61.14	**60.48**	**61.59**
	B	A + synthetic	48,719	0.00	34.09	**50.79**	**55.47**	**65.64**	**66.66**
				0.01	31.92	47.32	58.31	62.56	63.57
				0.03	**34.15**	49.81	56.87	65.09	66.43
	C	B + augmented	146,157	0.00	30.75	45.87	61.37	60.51	61.98
				0.01	32.82	48.31	57.95	63.26	64.72
				0.03	**35.07**	**50.23**	**56.73**	**63.33**	**64.80**

Table 4: **Comparing diverse values of warm-up ratio at training time.** Ratios are out of 3000 steps. Hence, 0.01 and 0.03 correspond to 30 steps and 90 steps, respectively. The results here are **with VAD at inference time**, using the default VAD arguments of *Faster-Whisper*. The highest score in each group is displayed in a bold font.

Whisper	Model	Datasets	Data Size	Warm-up	BLEU ↑	chrF++ ↑	WER ↓	Semantic 1 ↑	Semantic 2 ↑
Small	A	authentic	29,663	0.00	29.14	43.34	**60.51**	56.96	58.14
				0.01	30.66	**45.41**	62.09	**58.69**	**59.79**
				0.03	**30.68**	45.36	62.09	57.82	59.29
	B	A + synthetic	48,719	0.00	**32.05**	**48.32**	**58.44**	**62.51**	63.72
				0.01	31.94	46.81	59.93	61.57	62.36
				0.03	31.61	47.74	59.16	62.49	**64.09**
	C	B + augmented	146,157	0.00	30.51	44.52	63.48	59.6	60.71
				0.01	**32.58**	47.65	**59.39**	**62.86**	**63.72**
				0.03	31.89	**48.83**	59.84	62.32	63.17

Table 5: **Comparing diverse values of warm-up ratio at training time.** Ratios are out of 3000 steps. Hence, 0.01 and 0.03 correspond to 30 steps and 90 steps, respectively. The results here are **without VAD at inference time**. The highest score in each group is displayed in a bold font.

A.3 Training Epochs

Whisper	Model	Datasets	Data Size	Warm-up	Steps	Epoch	Best Epoch	BLEU ↑	chrF++ ↑	WER ↓	Semantic 1 ↑	Semantic 2 ↑
Medium	A	authentic	29,663	0.03	2,000	1.08	1.02	29.14	47.03	63.17	60.78	62.11
				cont.	4,000	2.16	1.83	32.38	48.95	58.85	62.09	63.28
	B	A + synthetic (2d)	48,719	0.03	4,000	1.31	1.22	36.02	53.73	53.26	66.86	68.16
				cont.	7,000	2.30	2.27	36.34	54.08	53.35	68.31	69.93
	B++	A + synthetic (3d)	115,987	0.03	4,000	0.55	0.55	**38.41**	**57.18**	**51.10**	**69.72**	**71.13**
				cont.	8,000	1.10	0.55	~	~	~	~	~
				cont.	15,000	2.07	0.55	~	~	~	~	~
	C	B + augmented	146,157	0.03	4,000	0.44	0.38	33.46	50.72	57.59	63.01	64.56
				cont.	10,000	1.09	1.05	34.09	51.4	55.83	64.26	65.56
				cont.	19,000	2.08	1.05	~	~	~	~	~

Table 6: Investigating the effect of training for 1-2 epoch(s). It seems that smaller amounts of training data can benefit from training for 2+ while larger amounts of data can benefit from training for only 1 epoch or less. The first row of each section starts the training with warm-up ratio 0.03, then the next 1 or 2 row(s) continues training for more steps without changing any training arguments. The reported scores are for the best step, based on training validation with 100-step intervals. That is why some rows are marked with the "~" sign, as the best step was still the same as the one reported in the previous row.

HW-TSC's Simultaneous Speech Translation System for IWSLT 2024

Shaojun Li, Zhiqiang Rao, Bin Wei, Yuanchang Luo, Zhanglin Wu ,
Zongyao Li, Hengchao Shang, Jiaxin Guo, Daimeng Wei, Hao Yang
Huawei Translation Service Center, Beijing, China
{lishaojun18, raozhiqiang, weibin29, luoyuanchang1, wuzhanglin2,
lizongyao, shanghengchao, guojiaxin1, weidaimeng, yanghao30}@huawei.com

Abstract

This paper outlines our submission for the IWSLT 2024 Simultaneous Speech-to-Text (SimulS2T) and Speech-to-Speech (SimulS2S) Translation competition. We have engaged in all four language directions and both the SimulS2T and SimulS2S tracks: English-German (EN-DE), English-Chinese (EN-ZH), English-Japanese (EN-JA), and Czech-English (CS-EN). For the S2T track, we have built upon our previous year's system and further honed the cascade system composed of ASR model and MT model. Concurrently, we have introduced an end-to-end system specifically for the CS-EN direction. This end-to-end (E2E) system primarily employs the pre-trained seamlessM4T model. In relation to the SimulS2S track, we have integrated a novel TTS model into our SimulS2T system. The final submission for the S2T directions of EN-DE, EN-ZH, and EN-JA has been refined over our championship system from last year. Building upon this foundation, the incorporation of the new TTS into our SimulS2S system has resulted in the ASR-BLEU surpassing last year's best score.

1 Introduction

This paper delineates the HW-TSC's contributions to the SimulS2T and SimulS2S Translation task at IWSLT 2024. Presently, research on SimulS2T translation from a systems architecture standpoint can be segregated into two categories: cascade and end-to-end. Cascade systems traditionally encompass a streaming Automatic Speech Recognition (ASR) module and a streaming text-to-text machine translation (MT) module, with an additional option of integrating correction modules. Despite the complexity of module integration, training each unit with ample data resources can yield significant results. On the other hand, an end-to-end approach for SimulS2T is feasible, where translations are directly procured from a unified model with speech input. It's worth mentioning, however, that bilingual speech translation datasets, indispensable for end-to-end models, remain scant.

Present efforts in simultaneous SimulS2T focus on the development of dedicated models customised for this task. This approach, nonetheless, comes with certain limitations, such as the need for an extra model, often accompanying a more complex training and inference process, augmented computational demands, and potential performance decrement when employed in an offline environment.

Our methodology for SimulS2T encompasses the use of a reliable offline ASR model and a robust offline MT model as the system's bedrock. We have adapted the onlinization approach of (Polák et al., 2022) and introduced an improved technique suitable for integration into the cascade system. On the official development set, our SimulS2T achieved a comparable level to the offline models under stringent latency constraints without any alterations to the original models. The disparity between offline and cascade has been further reduced compared to our last year's system. For the new CS-EN language pair, we submitted the end-to-end (E2E) system. We anticipate that future research will further enhance the E2E system's performance. Lastly, for SimulS2S, our system from the previous year had a low-performing TTS model. Hence, we updated the SimulS2S TTS model and integrated it with our latest SimulS2T system.

Our achievements is as follows:

- We further explored the upper limit of incremental decoding on our last year's champion SimulS2T system, and the BLEU value has been further improved compared to last year.
- We tried to extend our cascade SimulS2T method to the end-to-end system, and achieved the same effect with small losses between the offline and simultaneous system.

Proceedings of the 21st International Conference on Spoken Language Translation (IWSLT 2024), pages 322–327
August 15-16, 2024 ©2024 Association for Computational Linguistics

- Our method can be naturally extended to the SimulS2S system, and after SimulS2T reduced minor error propagation, SimulS2S achieved greater improvements.

2 Models

All models used by our system are offline models and do not use special streaming strategies. The following is an introduction to each model.

2.1 Offline ASR

In all our cascade system, Our system uses the U2 (Wu et al., 2021) framework as the ASR (Automatic Speech Recognition) module because it is flexible and supports streaming and non-streaming ASR. U2's key features include dynamic chunk training, CTC decoder, and autoregressive attention decoder. It's capable of conditional training with different chunk sizes and allows for multiple decoding strategies. We use "attention_rescoring" for re-scoring CTC generated texts.

2.2 Offline MT

The Machine Translation (MT) module of our system is the Transformer (Vaswani et al., 2017), a very common tool used in machine translation (Wei et al., 2021; Li et al., 2022). To improve this, we use multiple training strategies like multilingual translation (Johnson et al., 2017) for English to German, Chinese, and Japanese, forward translation (Wu et al., 2019) for generating synthetic data (Nguyen et al., 2020), and generation from an ASR model to reduce the domain gap.

2.3 Offline S2T

For CS-EN direction, We used the offline SeamlessM4T (Seamless Communication, 2023) as our end-to-end SimulS2T model. SeamlessM4T integrates a deep learning framework with a self-supervised speech representation learned from 1 million hours of open speech audio data using w2v-BERT 2.0. The speech to text model employs a audio encoder and text decoder. Open-sourced for community development, SeamlessM4T includes robust safety measures to mitigate harmful content and is designed to be adaptable for various applications, from international communication to content creation.

2.4 Offline TTS

The Text-to-Speech (TTS) module is vital for generating high-quality speech from translated text. We use the VITS (Kim et al., 2021) model for this, a state-of-the-art tool that can produce natural, fluent speech. The process is efficient, only needing the generated text to create the raw audio waveform. This makes the TTS module faster and improves the user experience.

3 Methods

3.1 Cascaded SimulS2T

For EN-DE, EN-JA, EN-ZH, we followed last year's model (Guo et al., 2023). Regarding the incremental decoding strategy, we added vad segmentation and chunk padding on the ASR side to achieve smaller delays, and added an ensemble strategy on the MT side to achieve better MT stability.

Onlinization Incremental Decoding is the main way to make an offline model into a real-time one. Translation tasks might need reordering or more information, which isn't clear until the source sentence ends. Offline models work best when they can process the whole sentence at once, but this can cause delays in real-time mode. A possible solution is to break the source sentence into smaller pieces and translate each piece separately. This lessens the processing time while keeping the translation quality. By using incremental decoding with these smaller pieces, we can speed up the translation process a lot, which is perfect for real-time situations.

In incremental inference, we break the input sentence into set-sized chunks and decode each chunk as it comes in. Once a chunk is chosen, its predictions are locked in and aren't changed anymore to avoid distractions from constantly changing guesses. The decoding of the next chunk depends on the locked-in predictions. In reality, decoding for new chunks can either continue from a saved decoder state or start after forced decoding with the locked-in tokens. In either situation, the source-target attention can cover all available chunks, not just the current one.

Prefix Vad Incremental decoding can pose challenges with longer sentences. As the sentence lengthens and the prefix extends, the decoding process tends to slow down, relying progressively on extensive contexts. Consequently, this requires waiting for more chunks to output translation results, which in turn affects our decoding delay. To mitigate this, we propose incorporating vad (Tong et al., 2014) detection and trimming excessively long prefixes once the input reaches a sufficient length. This strategy helps to minimize the streaming delay and reduce computational overhead for the model. Simultaneously, to ensure decoding quality, it's crucial to maintain adequate context. Therefore, when detecting vad, we consider the current vad position's distance from the sentence's start and end. Balancing this length setting with overall performance is a key aspect of our approach.

Chunk Padding During the ASR streaming decoding process, we observed instability with decoding the final few frames of the audio features. This instability presumably results from the model's insufficient edge handling during the convolution process. This issue consequently disrupts the beam search of streaming ASR, leading to inconsistent or sometimes erroneous outcomes. These errors are then carried over to the MT model, negatively impacting the streaming translation's stability. However, by appending blank padding to the end of each streaming chunk, we can notably enhance the decoding stability for the stream's last few words.

MT Ensemble In cascaded systems, the elimination of error propagation is often challenging. The erroneous ASR inputs that the MT system processes often lead to more significant errors. Moreover, our MT system has certain constraints due to its use of various strategies for domain adaptation and fine-tuning, resulting in an overfitting risk. To address these issues, we have incorporated MT models trained with diverse strategies into this year's system. By employing ensemble (Sagi and Rokach, 2018) methods, we aim to enhance the model's fault tolerance while simultaneously mitigating the risk of overfitting in the field.

3.2 E2E SimulS2T

For the newly introduced language direction this year, CS-EN, we utilized the pre-trained seamlessM4T as our end-to-end SimulS2T model. We attempted to fine-tune the seamlessM4T using the officially provided data. Concurrently, we implemented the aforementioned cascaded SimulS2T decoding strategy to seamlessM4T, aiming to attain a streaming effect.

3.3 Cascaded SimulS2S

In a cascaded speech-to-speech translation system, the TTS module plays a critical role in rendering high-quality speech output from translated text. To this end, we utilize the state-of-the-art VITS (Kim et al., 2021) model, which is pretrained on massive amounts of data and incorporates advanced techniques such as variational inference augmented with normalizing flows and adversarial training. This model has been shown to produce speech output that is more natural and fluent compared to traditional TTS models.

The inference process involves providing the VITS model with the generated text, after which the model generates the raw audio waveform. This process is highly efficient and requires no additional input from the user. By leveraging the VITS model, we are able to streamline the TTS module and deliver high-quality speech output in a fraction of the time traditionally required by other systems. This results in a more seamless and intuitive user experience, enabling our system to be used by a wider range of individuals and applications.

4 Experiments Setup

4.1 Dataset

We used four datasets to train the ASR (Automatic Speech Recognition) module: LibriSpeech V12, MuST-C V2, TEDLIUM V3, and CoVoST V2. Each dataset contains different types of data, like audio book recordings, TED talks, and open-domain content. LibriSpeech doesn't have punctuations in its texts, but MuST-C and CoVoST do.

For training the machine translation (MT) model, we collected all available parallel corpora that were similar to the MuST-C domain, then trained a multilingual MT baseline model. We also incrementally trained the model based on data from each language direction.

4.2 Model

ASR We used 80-dimensional Mel-Filter bank features from audio files to create the ASR training corpus, and Sentencepiece for ASR texts tokenization. The ASR model has different configurations for encoder layers, decoder layers, heads, hidden dimensions, and FFN. For training, we used a batch size of up to 40,000 frames per card and trained the model on 4 GPUs for 50 epochs. To improve accuracy, we augmented all audio inputs with spectral augmentation and normalized with utterance cepstral mean and variance normalization. We also apply prefix vad and chunk padding in the asr decoding metioned in Section 3.1.

System	Language Pair	BLEU	AL	AP	DAL
IWSLT23 Best	EN-DE	33.54	1.88	0.83	2.84
Our System	EN-DE	**34.24**	1.94	0.84	2.94
IWSLT23 Best	EN-JA	17.89	1.98	0.83	2.89
Our System	EN-JA	**17.94**	1.93	0.84	2.82
IWSLT23 Best	EN-ZH	27.23	1.98	0.83	2.89
Our System	EN-ZH	**27.63**	1.88	0.83	2.82
Our System	CS-EN	19.03	1.96	0.91	3.67

Table 1: Final systems results of SimulS2T on tsc-Common v2.0/dev

Model	Language Pair	ASR_BLEU	StartOffset	EndOffset	ATD
IWSLT23 Best	EN-DE	26.7	2.33	5.67	-
Our System	EN-DE	**27.09**	1.86	4.17	3.06
IWSLT23 Best	EN-JA	14.53	1.59	2.96	2.76
Our System	EN-JA	**15.55**	2.32	3.15	2.89
IWSLT23 Best	EN-ZH	20.19	1.77	2.98	2.93
Our System	EN-ZH	**22.92**	1.76	3.0	2.79
Our System	CS-EN	17.12	1.48	4.11	4.09

Table 2: Final systems results of SimulS2S on tsc-Common v2.0/dev

MT We used the Transformer deep model architecture for our MT model experiments. The configuration of this model includes encoder layers, decoder layers, heads, hidden dimensions, FFN, and pre_ln. The model was trained using 8 GPUs, with a batch size of 2048, a parameter update frequency of 32, and a learning rate of 5e-4. During inference, we used a beam size of 8 and set the length penalties to 1.0. We selected 2 MT models for ensemble mentioned in Section 3.1.

S2T We finetuned seamlessM4T-medium with the official data, BLEU improved by two points but did not exceed seamlessM4T-large-v2. Finally, we submitted the seamlessM4T-large-v2 model as our E2E model. We used the same decoding strategy as the cascade, using a beam_size of 5 and setting no_repeat_ngram_size.

TTS For EN-DE direction, we utilize the open-source Espnet (Watanabe et al., 2018) for inference. For EN-JA/ZH and CS-EN, we use the pretrained models in huggingface. The pretrained models are VITS (Kim et al., 2021) architecture, which adopts variational inference augmented with normalizing flows and an adversarial training process.

5 Results

5.1 SimulS2T

From Table 1, we can see that the our systems work well on various language pairs. And our systems even beat the best IWSLT23 systems of ourselves with methods mentioned in Section 3. EN-DE has improved the most. Since the gap between EN-DE offline and streaming is much larger than that of EN-JA and EN-ZH, we found that there is still a big gap between the MT results of cascaded streaming and ASR golden. In subsequent research, we may focus on this point.

5.2 SimulS2S

From Table 2, we observed that the improvement of S2S is greater than that of S2T. For EN-DE, most of the improvement is mainly due to our replacement of the TTS model, while for EN-JA and EN-ZH, thanks to the more stable SimulS2T, we spread to The TTS error is smaller, so the improvement of SimulS2S is more obvious than SimulS2T, which also illustrates the impact of error propagation on cascade system.

5.3 Ablation Study on Decoding Strategies

Decoding strategies	BLEU
Baseline	34.24
IWSLT23 Best	33.54
- Prefix Vad	33.91
- Chunk Padding	34.02
- Ensemble	33.86

Table 3: Ablation Study on Decoding Strategies

We separately studied the impact of today's newly introduced decoding strategies on translation quality: prefix vad, chunk padding, ensemble. It is evident from Table 3 that these decoding strategies can effectively improve the overall quality of the system.

6 Conclusion

In summary, this paper presents our efforts for the IWSLT 2024 Simultaneous Speech-to-Text and Speech-to-Speech Translation competition. We improved upon our previous system, achieved better translation accuracy and successfully integrated a novel Text-to-Speech model. Our system uses reliable offline models, and we managed to enhance the simulated conversation translation system's quality. Our experiments demonstrated that our system performs well across different language pairs. Future work will pay more focus on end-to-end systems.

References

Jiaxin Guo, Daimeng Wei, Zhanglin Wu, Zongyao Li, Zhiqiang Rao, Minghan Wang, Hengchao Shang, Xiaoyu Chen, Zhengzhe Yu, Shaojun Li, Yuhao Xie, Lizhi Lei, and Hao Yang. 2023. The HW-TSC's simultaneous speech-to-text translation system for IWSLT 2023 evaluation. In *Proceedings of the 20th International Conference on Spoken Language Translation (IWSLT 2023)*, pages 376–382, Toronto, Canada (in-person and online). Association for Computational Linguistics.

Melvin Johnson, Mike Schuster, Quoc V. Le, Maxim Krikun, Yonghui Wu, Zhifeng Chen, Nikhil Thorat, Fernanda B. Viégas, Martin Wattenberg, Greg Corrado, Macduff Hughes, and Jeffrey Dean. 2017. Google's multilingual neural machine translation system: Enabling zero-shot translation. *Trans. Assoc. Comput. Linguistics*, 5:339–351.

Jaehyeon Kim, Jungil Kong, and Juhee Son. 2021. Conditional variational autoencoder with adversarial learning for end-to-end text-to-speech. In *Proceedings of the 38th International Conference on Machine Learning, ICML 2021, 18-24 July 2021, Virtual Event*, volume 139 of *Proceedings of Machine Learning Research*, pages 5530–5540. PMLR.

Shaojun Li, Yuanchang Luo, Daimeng Wei, Zongyao Li, Hengchao Shang, Xiaoyu Chen, Zhanglin Wu, Jinlong Yang, Zhiqiang Rao, Zhengzhe Yu, Yuhao Xie, Lizhi Lei, Hao Yang, and Ying Qin. 2022. HW-TSC systems for WMT22 very low resource supervised MT task. In *Proceedings of the Seventh Conference on Machine Translation (WMT)*, pages 1098–1103, Abu Dhabi, United Arab Emirates (Hybrid). Association for Computational Linguistics.

Xuan-Phi Nguyen, Shafiq R. Joty, Kui Wu, and Ai Ti Aw. 2020. Data diversification: A simple strategy for neural machine translation. In *Advances in Neural Information Processing Systems 33: Annual Conference on Neural Information Processing Systems 2020, NeurIPS 2020, December 6-12, 2020, virtual.*

Peter Polák, Ngoc-Quan Pham, Tuan-Nam Nguyen, Danni Liu, Carlos Mullov, Jan Niehues, Ondrej Bojar, and Alexander Waibel. 2022. CUNI-KIT system for simultaneous speech translation task at IWSLT 2022. In *Proceedings of the 19th International Conference on Spoken Language Translation, IWSLT@ACL 2022, Dublin, Ireland (in-person and online), May 26-27, 2022*, pages 277–285. Association for Computational Linguistics.

Omer Sagi and Lior Rokach. 2018. Ensemble learning: A survey. *Wiley interdisciplinary reviews: data mining and knowledge discovery*, 8(4):e1249.

Yu-An Chung Mariano Coria Meglioli David Dale Ning Dong Mark Duppenthaler Paul-Ambroise Duquenne Brian Ellis Hady Elsahar Justin Haaheim John Hoffman Min-Jae Hwang Hirofumi Inaguma Christopher Klaiber Ilia Kulikov Pengwei Li Daniel Licht Jean Maillard Ruslan Mavlyutov Alice Rakotoarison Kaushik Ram Sadagopan Abinesh Ramakrishnan Tuan Tran Guillaume Wenzek Yilin Yang Ethan Ye Ivan Evtimov Pierre Fernandez Cynthia Gao Prangthip Hansanti Elahe Kalbassi Amanda Kallet Artyom Kozhevnikov Gabriel Mejia Robin San Roman Christophe Touret Corinne Wong Carleigh Wood Bokai Yu Pierre Andrews Can Balioglu Peng-Jen Chen Marta R. Costa-jussà Maha Elbayad Hongyu Gong Francisco Guzmán Kevin Heffernan Somya Jain Justine Kao Ann Lee Xutai Ma Alex Mourachko Benjamin Peloquin Juan Pino Sravya Popuri Christophe Ropers Safiyyah Saleem Holger Schwenk Anna Sun Paden Tomasello Changhan Wang Jeff Wang Skyler Wang Mary Williamson Seamless Communication, Loïc Barrault. 2023.

Seamless: Multilingual expressive and streaming speech translation.

Sibo Tong, Nanxin Chen, Yanmin Qian, and Kai Yu. 2014. Evaluating vad for automatic speech recognition. In *2014 12th International Conference on Signal Processing (ICSP)*, pages 2308–2314. IEEE.

Ashish Vaswani, Noam Shazeer, Niki Parmar, Jakob Uszkoreit, Llion Jones, Aidan N. Gomez, Lukasz Kaiser, and Illia Polosukhin. 2017. Attention is all you need. In *Advances in Neural Information Processing Systems 30: Annual Conference on Neural Information Processing Systems 2017, December 4-9, 2017, Long Beach, CA, USA*, pages 5998–6008.

Shinji Watanabe, Takaaki Hori, Shigeki Karita, Tomoki Hayashi, Jiro Nishitoba, Yuya Unno, Nelson Enrique Yalta Soplin, Jahn Heymann, Matthew Wiesner, Nanxin Chen, Adithya Renduchintala, and Tsubasa Ochiai. 2018. Espnet: End-to-end speech processing toolkit. *CoRR*, abs/1804.00015.

Daimeng Wei, Zongyao Li, Zhanglin Wu, Zhengzhe Yu, Xiaoyu Chen, Hengchao Shang, Jiaxin Guo, Minghan Wang, Lizhi Lei, Min Zhang, Hao Yang, and Ying Qin. 2021. Hw-tsc's participation in the WMT 2021 news translation shared task. In *Proceedings of the Sixth Conference on Machine Translation, WMT@EMNLP 2021, Online Event, November 10-11, 2021*, pages 225–231. Association for Computational Linguistics.

Di Wu, Binbin Zhang, Chao Yang, Zhendong Peng, Wenjing Xia, Xiaoyu Chen, and Xin Lei. 2021. U2++: unified two-pass bidirectional end-to-end model for speech recognition. *CoRR*, abs/2106.05642.

Lijun Wu, Yiren Wang, Yingce Xia, Tao Qin, Jianhuang Lai, and Tie-Yan Liu. 2019. Exploiting monolingual data at scale for neural machine translation. In *Proceedings of the 2019 Conference on Empirical Methods in Natural Language Processing and the 9th International Joint Conference on Natural Language Processing, EMNLP-IJCNLP 2019, Hong Kong, China, November 3-7, 2019*, pages 4205–4215. Association for Computational Linguistics.

UoM-DFKI submission to the low resource shared task

Rishu Kumar[◇] **Aiden Williams*** **Claudia Borg*** **Simon Ostermann**[◇]

[◇]DFKI, *University of Malta
rishu.Kumar@dfki.de, aiden.williams.19@um.edu.mt
claudia.borg@um.edu.mt, simon.ostermann@dfki.de

Abstract

This system description paper presents the details of our primary and contrastive approaches to translating Maltese into English for IWSLT 24. The Maltese language shares a large vocabulary with Arabic and Italian languages, thus making it an ideal candidate to test the cross-lingual capabilities of recent state-of-the-art models. We experiment with two end-to-end approaches for our submissions: the Whisper and wav2vec 2.0 models. Our primary system gets a BLEU score of 35.1 on the combined data, whereas our contrastive approach gets 18.5. We also provide a manual analysis of our contrastive approach to identify some pitfalls that may have caused this difference.

1 Introduction

In this paper, we describe the UoM-DFKI submission to the Dialectical and Low-Resource track of the IWSLT 2023 evaluation campaign, focusing on the unconstrained approach for the Maltese to English track. Maltese is considered a hybrid language, with most vocabulary coming from Arabic, Italian, and English. While there is a major overlap with Arabic, Maltese data uses Latin instead of Arabic script. Our main focus for this submission is using publicly available multilingual models to exploit the multilingual capabilities of models, given the interesting mixture of vocabulary in the Maltese language.

For this paper, we focus on end-to-end approaches for spoken language translation (SLT), namely with Whisper (Radford et al., 2022) and wav2vec 2.0 xls-r (Baevski et al., 2020; Babu et al., 2021). We use the Whisper-based model as our primary submission and the wav2vec 2.0 model as the contrastive approach. The Whisper system is pre-trained on 680,000 hours of speech data using an encoder-decoder method. A substantial amount of the training data, nearly one-fifth, is English audio, and 9,000 hours is Maltese. (Radford et al., 2022) claim that with 41 hours of Maltese translation data, the Whisper model is able to achieve roughly 14 BLEU points. In this paper, we use the data released for this task to fine-tune the Whisper model further. There are various Whisper models with varying parameter sizes. (Williams et al., 2023b) shows how, with larger parameters, the Whisper architecture performs better in the ASR setting for Maltese ASR. For this work, we decided to use the most recent Whisper model; the largest model is Whisper-large-v3. Our approach for wav2vec 2.0-based models also consisted of using an encoder-decoder approach, namely SpeechEncoderDecoder framework (Chan et al., 2015; Wang et al., 2021), as made available on HuggingFace (Wolf et al., 2020). We worked with three different models as our decoder for our contrastive approaches, namely BERT (Devlin et al., 2019) and mBART fine-tuned for machine translation from different languages into English (Tang et al., 2020).

2 Literature Review

The IWSLT Low-resource and Dialectical shared task increased the number of language pairs they released data for in 2023. In the 2022 edition of the workshop, (Anastasopoulos et al., 2022) released the data for teams to develop systems to transcribe and translate the low-resource language pairs of Tamasheq-English and Tunisian Arabic-French. In the 2023 edition of the task, however, Agarwal et al. (2023) extended the task to include the language pairs Irish-English, Maltese-English, Pashto-French and Quechua-Spanish.

In 2022, three teams submitted models for Tamasheq-English: ON-TRAC (Zanon Boito et al., 2022), TalTech and GMU. ON-TRAC also submitted to the Tunisian Arabic-French pair, like CMU (Yan et al., 2022) and JHU (Yang et al., 2022) did. In 2023, GMU submitted models

Proceedings of the 21st International Conference on Spoken Language Translation (IWSLT 2024), pages 328–333
August 15-16, 2024 ©2024 Association for Computational Linguistics

for Irish-English, Marathi-Hindi, Pashto-French and Tamasheq-French (Mbuya and Anastasopoulos, 2023), Alexa AI submitted models for Marathi-Hindi and Tamasheq-French (Shanbhogue et al., 2023), ON-TRAC submitted for Tamasheq-French and Pashto-French (Laurent et al., 2023), NAVER submitted for Tamasheq-French and Quechua-Spanish (Gow-Smith et al., 2023), BUT (Kesiraju et al., 2023) and SRI-B (Radhakrishnan et al., 2023) submitted only for Marathi-Hindi, QUESPA submited for Quechua-Spanish (E. Ortega et al., 2023) and UM-DFKI submitted for Maltese-English (Williams et al., 2023a).

These teams employed various techniques, ranging from traditional cascade systems to various end-to-end architectures. Many teams leveraged large pre-trained models, including XLS-R, mBART, Wav2Vec 2.0 and HuBERT. The Alexa AI team tried an interesting approach by focusing on data augmentation, ensemble modelling and post-processing techniques to improve their results. Transformer models for MT were popular across the board. The NAVER submissions obtained particularly good results in their respective language pairs by using pre-trained ASR and MT models from the NLLB project (Team et al., 2022), which include both Tamasheq and Quechua in their training, showing the importance of language diversity in multilingual models.

3 Dataset

In this section, we briefly describe the dataset used to fine-tune our systems. We include a description of the dataset used to fine-tune the mBART50 many-to-one model (Tang et al., 2020) and the dataset released for this shared task.

mBART50 many-to-one (Tang et al., 2020) utilized and released the ML50 dataset for fine-tuning the mBART model for translating in 50 languages. It uses English as a pivot language to collect parallel data for 49 other languages from sources such as IWSLT, TED, WAT, etc. It is also noted that the 49 languages selected for the dataset are based on language family, available mono-lingual data and parallel data. This, in turn, means that the dataset is not balanced and results in better performance improvements for high-resource languages compared to low-resource languages.

We used the data released for this shared task to fine-tune our models. Namely, the two training sets created from the Common Voice and MASRI Maltese speech corpora. Subsets from these larger corpora were extracted, 5 hours and 11 minutes from the verified Common Voice data and 6 hours and 39 minutes from the MASRI-Headset corpus. The transcription of each sample was translated. Fine-tuning Whisper for speech translation requires audio for input and the transcription of that audio in sentence form as a target. We pre-processed the input text so that numbers were written in words and no punctuation or capitalization was included.

Given how they were acquired, we note the difference between the subset released from the MASRI corpus and the CommonVoice dataset. While the MASRI corpus provides clean and nearly noise-free audio samples, CommonVoice samples vary in terms of different noises and the quality of audio-capturing devices.

4 Experiments

In this section, we briefly describe different experiments we conducted for our submissions, including those we did not submit for evaluation. First, we describe our experiments with the wav2vec2-xls-r (Babu et al., 2021) model, followed by the Whisper-based (Radford et al., 2022) models. We utilized HuggingFace (Wolf et al., 2020) libraries for our experiments.

4.1 SpeechEncoderDecoder models

A SpeechEncoderDecoder model is an encoder-decoder-based model used for spoken language translation or transcription, where the encoder is used to process the speech, and a language model as a decoder generates the text in the target language. In our experiments, we use the wav2vec2-xls-r model with 2B parameters as our encoder, with BERT (Devlin et al., 2019), and mBART50 (Tang et al., 2020) as the decoder following the approach in Wang et al..

4.1.1 BERT based decoder

We utilize the base BERT (Devlin et al., 2019) model as our baseline model for our SpeechEncoderDecoder approach. Namely, we use `bert-large-uncased`[1] as our language model for the decoding since the evaluation strategy does not factor in casing or punctuations. For training and inference, we add cross attention to our decoder using the `BertConfig` class from the transformers

[1] https://huggingface.co/google-bert/bert-large-uncased

Submission Name	BLEU	ASR WER
KIT.st-unconstrained-Primary	58.9	0.0835
KIT.st-unconstrained-Contrastive1	55.2	
KIT.st-unconstrained-Contrastive2	56.2	
UM.st-unconstrained-Primary	52.4	0.1431
UM.st-unconstrained-Contrastive1	52.4	0.1431
UM.st-unconstrained-Contrastive2	52.3	0.1431
UM.e2e-unconstrained-Primary	35.1	
UM.e2e-unconstrained-Contrastive1	18.5	

Table 1: Official results for the IWSLT'24 shared task, as released by organizers.

library. We did not submit results from this experiment as the models failed to produce any output during inference.

4.1.2 mBART based decoder

For our mBART-based decoding approach, we utilize the model fine-tuned for translating from 49 languages to English as released by (Tang et al., 2020). Since Maltese has a large vocabulary that is shared with Arabic and Italian, we decided to use this model instead of the vanilla mBART model. We indicate outputs from this system as the contrastive system for our work.

4.2 Whisper model

For our main system, we fine-tuned the `whisper-large-v3` model on the released dataset. As mentioned in previous sections, we also utilize several pre-processing steps for our dataset while fine-tuning.

5 Results & Discussion

In this section, we discuss the results from both submissions. As per the participation instruction, the results are reported individually for the CommonVoice subset, MASRI subset and the combined testset.

Table 1 provides the official results for different submission to the Maltese->English track for the IWSLT Low-Resource SLT shared task. Our `whisper` based submission performed consistently better than our `SpeechEncoderDecoder` model based on wav2vec2-xls-r (Babu et al., 2021) and mBART (Tang et al., 2020).

A rudimentary manual analysis of our constrained system shows a common theme of repeated phrases across some bad translations. For example, for the file MSRTS_M_03_TS_00016.wav, our contrastive system produced "`our words are not 'as it were', the people's words are not 'as they should be', our words are not 'as they should be'`", whereas for the file MSRTS_M_09_TS_00008.wav, it produced "`and he comes running`" repeated 8 times. We did not find any conclusive pattern of this repetition based on the output text length, as in some instances, we find that only a sub-phrase is repeated one or more times towards the end of the output. We experimented with different output token lengths while debugging this behaviour, but it did not yield any conclusive reason, as it was present while using different inference strategies as well. Another approach to fix this behaviour would be a post-fix approach where we automatically fix the output with repeated substring search. In this study, we did not utilize such an approach and left it for future work.

We analyzed the performance of our primary submission method using speech in a code-switched conversation (Hindi and English) and found Whisper auto-translating the Hindi part to English in a few instances when we put the input language as "en". The nature of these fixes is not deterministic in this preliminary experiment, as we saw different segments translated in different runs. However, due to the end-to-end nature of our approaches, we are uncertain if this is the case with our model as well. We attribute the improved performance of the Whisper model to the increased pre-training of the model on more data than wav2vec2-xls-r. However, without inspection of the data and the high domain sensitivity in Maltese, it remains difficult to quantify the effect.

We also note that our models' performance on the testset closely resembles the results we obtained on the dev set during our training. Our primary model scored **35.9** on the dev set, whereas it scored **35.1** on the testset; similarly, our contrastive model scored **18.5** on both dev and test splits.

6 Conclusion & Future work

In our end-to-end translation system experiments, we report that the Whisper-based model outperforms our SpeechEncoderDecoder model. The performance of our contrastive model is much worse for the MASRI subset than that of the CommonVoice subset. We report that multi-lingual pre-training and fine-tuning can provide good-quality translation output in an end-to-end approach. We also report that since Whisper is already trained in a semi-supervised manner, the model output had to be re-processed to produce the ideal results for this work. Overall, the results are much better compared to Williams et al. (2023a) for IWSLT 2023. However, we note that in the previous edition, the test dataset drastically differed in quality and domain compared to the test set for this year's shared task. However, it is not possible to draw a parallel for this comparison as the test set in the IWSLT'23 edition consisted of a podcast episode, which is more colloquial in nature. It also suffered from poor ASR outputs as there were instances of speakers talking over each other. Another hypothesis is that while much of the training data for the MT part of the previous submission contains legal domain data, which has more influence from Italian, the colloquial speak has more influence from Arabic.

Based on the performance of our SpeechEncoderDecoder model, we hypothesize that data augmentation and combining parallel data from Arabic and Italian may improve the models' performance. We aim to extend this study with an analysis of gain/drop in performance when using a fine-tuned mBART50 as a translation system from Arabic and Italian to English, compared to using the same model as the decoder in this encoder-decoder setting. We also aim to investigate the auto-translation capabilities of Whisper-based models by using them in a pipeline-based approach as well.

Furthermore, using language-specific adapters to leverage models trained only on ASR or NMT data enables SLT in low-resource contexts. Previous work on this area (Escolano et al., 2021), (Le et al., 2021), including previous submissions to IWLST (Gow-Smith et al., 2023) achieved high BLEU scores and found that this method works particularly well in low-resource contexts. We also aim to explore this approach in the future with related languages such as Italic and Arabic, as it shows promise for Maltese-English SLT.

Acknowledgments

We acknowledge the LT-Bridge Project (GA 952194).

References

Milind Agarwal, Sweta Agrawal, Antonios Anastasopoulos, Luisa Bentivogli, Ondrˇej Bojar, Claudia Borg, Marine Carpuat, Roldano Cattoni, Mauro Cettolo, Mingda Chen, William Chen, Khalid Choukri, Alexandra Chronopoulou, Anna Currey, Thierry Declerck, Qianqian Dong, Kevin Duh, Yannick Esteve, Marcello Federico, Souhir Gahbiche, Barry Haddow, Benjamin Hsu, Phu Mon Htut, Hirofumi Inaguma, David Javorsky, John Judge, Yasumasa Kano, Tom Ko, Rishu Kumar, Pengwei Li, Xutai Ma, Prashant Mathur, Evgeny Matusov, Paul McNamee, John P McCrae, Kenton Murray, Maria Nadejde, Satoshi Nakamura, Matteo Negri, Ha Nguyen, Jan Niehues, Xing Niu, Atul Kr Ojha, John E Ortega, Proyag Pal, Juan Pino, Elijah Rippeth, Elizabeth Salesky, Jiatong Shi, and Matthias Sperber. 2023. FINDINGS OF THE IWSLT 2023 EVALUATION CAMPAIGN.

Antonios Anastasopoulos, Loïc Barrault, Luisa Bentivogli, Marcely Zanon Boito, Ondřej Bojar, Roldano Cattoni, Anna Currey, Georgiana Dinu, Kevin Duh, Maha Elbayad, Clara Emmanuel, Yannick Estève, Marcello Federico, Christian Federmann, Souhir Gahbiche, Hongyu Gong, Roman Grundkiewicz, Barry Haddow, Benjamin Hsu, Dávid Javorský, Věra Kloudová, Surafel Lakew, Xutai Ma, Prashant Mathur, Paul McNamee, Kenton Murray, Maria Nădejde, Satoshi Nakamura, Matteo Negri, Jan Niehues, Xing Niu, John Ortega, Juan Pino, Elizabeth Salesky, Jiatong Shi, Matthias Sperber, Sebastian Stüker, Katsuhito Sudoh, Marco Turchi, Yogesh Virkar, Alexander Waibel, Changhan Wang, and Shinji Watanabe. 2022. Findings of the IWSLT 2022 Evaluation Campaign. In *Proceedings of the 19th International Conference on Spoken Language Translation (IWSLT 2022)*, pages 98–157, Dublin, Ireland (in-person and online). Association for Computational Linguistics.

Arun Babu, Changhan Wang, Andros Tjandra, Kushal Lakhotia, Qiantong Xu, Naman Goyal, Kritika Singh, Patrick von Platen, Yatharth Saraf, Juan Miguel Pino, Alexei Baevski, Alexis Conneau, and Michael Auli. 2021. Xls-r: Self-supervised cross-lingual speech representation learning at scale. In *Interspeech*.

Alexei Baevski, Henry Zhou, Abdelrahman Mohamed, and Michael Auli. 2020. wav2vec 2.0: A framework for self-supervised learning of speech representations. *Preprint*, arXiv:2006.11477.

William Chan, Navdeep Jaitly, Quoc V. Le, and Oriol Vinyals. 2015. Listen, attend and spell: A neural network for large vocabulary conversational speech recognition. *2016 IEEE International Conference on Acoustics, Speech and Signal Processing (ICASSP)*, pages 4960–4964.

Jacob Devlin, Ming-Wei Chang, Kenton Lee, and Kristina Toutanova. 2019. BERT: Pre-training of deep bidirectional transformers for language understanding. In *Proceedings of the 2019 Conference of the North American Chapter of the Association for Computational Linguistics: Human Language Technologies, Volume 1 (Long and Short Papers)*, pages 4171–4186, Minneapolis, Minnesota. Association for Computational Linguistics.

John E. Ortega, Rodolfo Zevallos, and William Chen. 2023. QUESPA Submission for the IWSLT 2023 Dialect and Low-resource Speech Translation Tasks. In

Proceedings of the 20th International Conference on Spoken Language Translation (IWSLT 2023), pages 261–268, Toronto, Canada (in-person and online). Association for Computational Linguistics.

Carlos Escolano, Marta R. Costa-jussà, José A. R. Fonollosa, and Carlos Segura. 2021. Enabling Zero-shot Multilingual Spoken Language Translation with Language-Specific Encoders and Decoders. ArXiv:2011.01097 [cs].

Edward Gow-Smith, Alexandre Berard, Marcely Zanon Boito, and Ioan Calapodescu. 2023. NAVER LABS Europe's Multilingual Speech Translation Systems for the IWSLT 2023 Low-Resource Track. In *Proceedings of the 20th International Conference on Spoken Language Translation (IWSLT 2023)*, pages 144–158, Toronto, Canada (in-person and online). Association for Computational Linguistics.

Santosh Kesiraju, Karel Beneš, Maksim Tikhonov, and Jan Černocký. 2023. BUT Systems for IWSLT 2023 Marathi - Hindi Low Resource Speech Translation Task. In *Proceedings of the 20th International Conference on Spoken Language Translation (IWSLT 2023)*, pages 227–234, Toronto, Canada (in-person and online). Association for Computational Linguistics.

Antoine Laurent, Souhir Gahbiche, Ha Nguyen, Haroun Elleuch, Fethi Bougares, Antoine Thiol, Hugo Riguidel, Salima Mdhaffar, Gaëlle Laperrière, Lucas Maison, Sameer Khurana, and Yannick Estève. 2023. ON-TRAC Consortium Systems for the IWSLT 2023 Dialectal and Low-resource Speech Translation Tasks. In *Proceedings of the 20th International Conference on Spoken Language Translation (IWSLT 2023)*, pages 219–226, Toronto, Canada (in-person and online). Association for Computational Linguistics.

Hang Le, Juan Pino, Changhan Wang, Jiatao Gu, Didier Schwab, and Laurent Besacier. 2021. Lightweight Adapter Tuning for Multilingual Speech Translation. ArXiv:2106.01463 [cs].

Jonathan Mbuya and Antonios Anastasopoulos. 2023. GMU Systems for the IWSLT 2023 Dialect and Low-resource Speech Translation Tasks. In *Proceedings of the 20th International Conference on Spoken Language Translation (IWSLT 2023)*, pages 269–276, Toronto, Canada (in-person and online). Association for Computational Linguistics.

Alec Radford, Jong Wook Kim, Tao Xu, Greg Brockman, Christine McLeavey, and Ilya Sutskever. 2022. Robust speech recognition via large-scale weak supervision. *Preprint*, arXiv:2212.04356.

Balaji Radhakrishnan, Saurabh Agrawal, Raj Prakash Gohil, Kiran Praveen, Advait Vinay Dhopeshwarkar, and Abhishek Pandey. 2023. SRI-B's Systems for IWSLT 2023 Dialectal and Low-resource Track: Marathi-Hindi Speech Translation. In *Proceedings of the 20th International Conference on Spoken Language Translation (IWSLT 2023)*, pages 449–454, Toronto, Canada (in-person and online). Association for Computational Linguistics.

Akshaya Vishnu Kudlu Shanbhogue, Ran Xue, Soumya Saha, Daniel Zhang, and Ashwinkumar Ganesan. 2023. Improving Low Resource Speech Translation with Data Augmentation and Ensemble Strategies. In *Proceedings of the 20th International Conference on Spoken Language Translation (IWSLT 2023)*, pages 241–250, Toronto, Canada (in-person and online). Association for Computational Linguistics.

Y. Tang, C. Tran, Xian Li, Peng-Jen Chen, Naman Goyal, Vishrav Chaudhary, Jiatao Gu, and Angela Fan. 2020. Multilingual translation with extensible multilingual pretraining and finetuning. *ArXiv*, abs/2008.00401.

NLLB Team, Marta R. Costa-jussà, James Cross, Onur Çelebi, Maha Elbayad, Kenneth Heafield, Kevin Heffernan, Elahe Kalbassi, Janice Lam, Daniel Licht, Jean Maillard, Anna Sun, Skyler Wang, Guillaume Wenzek, Al Youngblood, Bapi Akula, Loic Barrault, Gabriel Mejia Gonzalez, Prangthip Hansanti, John Hoffman, Semarley Jarrett, Kaushik Ram Sadagopan, Dirk Rowe, Shannon Spruit, Chau Tran, Pierre Andrews, Necip Fazil Ayan, Shruti Bhosale, Sergey Edunov, Angela Fan, Cynthia Gao, Vedanuj Goswami, Francisco Guzmán, Philipp Koehn, Alexandre Mourachko, Christophe Ropers, Safiyyah Saleem, Holger Schwenk, and Jeff Wang. 2022. No Language Left Behind: Scaling Human-Centered Machine Translation. *arXiv preprint*. ArXiv:2207.04672 [cs].

Changhan Wang, Anne Wu, Juan Miguel Pino, Alexei Baevski, Michael Auli, and Alexis Conneau. 2021. Large-scale self- and semi-supervised learning for speech translation. In *Interspeech*.

Aiden Williams, Kurt Abela, Rishu Kumar, Martin Bär, Hannah Billinghurst, Kurt Micallef, Ahnaf Mozib Samin, Andrea DeMarco, Lonneke van der Plas, and Claudia Borg. 2023a. UM-DFKI Maltese Speech Translation. In *Proceedings of the 20th International Conference on Spoken Language Translation (IWSLT 2023)*, pages 433–441, Toronto, Canada (in-person and online). Association for Computational Linguistics.

Aiden Williams, Andrea Demarco, and Claudia Borg. 2023b. The applicability of Wav2Vec2 and Whisper for low-resource Maltese ASR. In *Proc. 2nd Annual Meeting of the ELRA/ISCA SIG on Under-resourced Languages (SIGUL 2023)*, pages 39–43.

Thomas Wolf, Lysandre Debut, Victor Sanh, Julien Chaumond, Clement Delangue, Anthony Moi, Pierric Cistac, Tim Rault, Remi Louf, Morgan Funtowicz, Joe Davison, Sam Shleifer, Patrick von Platen, Clara Ma, Yacine Jernite, Julien Plu, Canwen Xu, Teven Le Scao, Sylvain Gugger, Mariama Drame, Quentin Lhoest, and Alexander Rush. 2020. Transformers: State-of-the-art natural language processing.

In *Proceedings of the 2020 Conference on Empirical Methods in Natural Language Processing: System Demonstrations*, pages 38–45, Online. Association for Computational Linguistics.

Brian Yan, Patrick Fernandes, Siddharth Dalmia, Jiatong Shi, Yifan Peng, Dan Berrebbi, Xinyi Wang, Graham Neubig, and Shinji Watanabe. 2022. CMU's IWSLT 2022 Dialect Speech Translation System. In *Proceedings of the 19th International Conference on Spoken Language Translation (IWSLT 2022)*, pages 298–307, Dublin, Ireland (in-person and online). Association for Computational Linguistics.

Jinyi Yang, Amir Hussein, Matthew Wiesner, and Sanjeev Khudanpur. 2022. JHU IWSLT 2022 Dialect Speech Translation System Description. In *Proceedings of the 19th International Conference on Spoken Language Translation (IWSLT 2022)*, pages 319–326, Dublin, Ireland (in-person and online). Association for Computational Linguistics.

Marcely Zanon Boito, John Ortega, Hugo Riguidel, Antoine Laurent, Loïc Barrault, Fethi Bougares, Firas Chaabani, Ha Nguyen, Florentin Barbier, Souhir Gahbiche, and Yannick Estève. 2022. ON-TRAC Consortium Systems for the IWSLT 2022 Dialect and Low-resource Speech Translation Tasks. In *Proceedings of the 19th International Conference on Spoken Language Translation (IWSLT 2022)*, pages 308–318, Dublin, Ireland (in-person and online). Association for Computational Linguistics.

HW-TSC's submission to the IWSLT 2024 Subtitling track

Yuhao Xie, Yuanchang Luo, Zongyao Li, Zhanglin Wu, Xiaoyu Chen, Zhiqiang Rao, Shaojun Li, Hengchao Shang, Jiaxin Guo, Daimeng Wei, Hao Yang
Huawei Translation Service Center, Beijing, China
{xieyuhao2, luoyuanchang1, lizongyao, wuzhanglin2, chenxiaoyu35, raozhiqiang, lishaojun18, shanghengchao, guojiaxin1, weidaimeng, yanghao30}@huawei.com

Abstract

This paper introduces HW-TSC's submission to the IWSLT 2024 Subtitling track. For the automatic subtitling track, we use an unconstrained cascaded strategy, with the main steps being: ASR with word-level timestamps, sentence segmentation based on punctuation restoration, further alignment using CTC or using machine translation with length penalty. For the subtitle compression track, we employ a subtitle compression strategy that integrates machine translation models and extensive rewriting models. We acquire the subtitle text requiring revision through the CPS index, then utilize a translation model to obtain the English version of this text. Following this, we extract the compressed-length subtitle text through controlled decoding. If this method fails to compress the text successfully, we resort to the Llama2 few-shot model for further compression.

1 Introduction

In recent years, the demand for subtitles across various media platforms has surged, driving the need for efficient and high-quality subtitling solutions. Two main approaches have emerged for automatic subtitle generation: cascaded strategies and end-to-end models.

Cascaded Strategies Traditional cascaded strategies involve a multi-step pipeline (Bentivogli et al., 2021), where each component handles a specific subtask. This typically begins with an Automatic Speech Recognition (ASR) system that transcribes the audio into text. The transcribed text is then segmented into subtitles, accounting for timing constraints and reading speeds. Finally, the segmented subtitles may undergo text compression to ensure they fit within spatial limitations while retaining critical information.

End-to-End Strategies In contrast, end-to-end models (Berard et al., 2016) aim to directly generate subtitles from audio or audio-visual inputs using a single unified framework, typically leveraging recent advances in deep learning and sequence-to-sequence modeling. Such models can jointly learn and optimize all subtitling tasks, mitigating error propagation issues.

In this paper, we employ a cascaded strategy. Due to Whisper (Radford et al., 2023)'s remarkable achievements across multiple domains, the cascaded strategy is expected to perform well. At the same time, it allows us to leverage our existing text-to-text machine translation capabilities.

In the process of automatic subtitle generation discussed above, regardless of the method employed, subtitle compression emerges as a pivotal element. This is due to the restricted display space for subtitles, and the necessity of adapting subtitles to the playback speed of the video, as well as the reading speed of the audience. Consequently, once the automatic generation of the subtitle file is finalized, it becomes essential to compress content for overly long subtitles. By retaining the basic information and meaning, this compression significantly enhances the quality of the subtitles.

Traditional text compression strategies encompass Deletion-oriented approach (Moran, 2009) and Substitution-oriented approach (Yang et al., 2010). In addition to the aforementioned methods, training sequence-to-sequence models with parallel data of both the original and compressed text can enhance efficiency in text compression while more effectively preserving semantic integrity (Angerbauer et al., 2019).

In this paper, we leverage a model generation approach to accomplish the task of subtitle compression. Uniquely, in the absence of extensive parallel data of original and compressed text for model training, we deviate from traditional model compression methods. Instead, we employ a machine translation model to execute the task. This requires the compression and reformation of text, and the deployment of large language models to

Proceedings of the 21st International Conference on Spoken Language Translation (IWSLT 2024), pages 334–338
August 15-16, 2024 ©2024 Association for Computational Linguistics

manage the compression task on certain texts that pose challenges for rewriting.

2 Automatic Subtitling

We propose a Whisper-based cascaded automatic subtitling strategy, with the details as follows:

2.1 Automatic Speech Recognition (ASR)

Whisper is a general-purpose speech recognition model. It is trained on a large dataset of diverse audio and is also a multitasking model that can perform multilingual speech recognition, speech translation, and language identification. We use the large-v3 version of Whisper for ASR, and output word-level timestamps, which will help with re-segmentation after punctuation restoration.

2.2 Punctuation-Restoration-Based Segmentation

Bert-restore-punctuation[1] model is a punctuation restoration model for the general English language. Through punctuation restoration, we can obtain sentence segmentation information that is more semantically consistent, thereby obtaining better segments. Aided by the word-level timestamps from the previous step, we perform sentence segmentation at the predicted punctuation marks (commas, periods, exclamation marks, question marks), and generate corresponding timestamps.

2.3 CTC-Alignment

We use wav2vec2-large-960h-lv60[2] for forced alignment, which is pretrained and fine-tuned on 960 hours of Libri-Light and Librispeech on 16kHz sampled speech audio.

2.4 Machine Translation

Since the timestamps generated by the ASR system are good enough, when generating subtitles, we only translate the English into the target language, keeping the timestamps unchanged.

This track contains two language directions: English to German and English to Spanish, with the details as follows:

2.4.1 Data

The training data includes domains such as travel, subtitles, applications, and technology. The data size is shown in Table 1.

[1]https://huggingface.co/felflare/bert-restore-punctuation

[2]https://huggingface.co/facebook/wav2vec2-large-960h-lv60

	en2de	en2es
Baseline Data	5.8M	8.4M
Subtitle Data	1.3M	1.1M

Table 1: Data sizes of MT corpus.

2.4.2 Baseline models

We directly employ the en2de model we trained for the IWSLT 2024 Offline track and we employ our online-server en2es model. The training strategies include the following steps:

Regularized Dropout Regularized Dropout (R-Drop) (Wu et al., 2021) improves performance over standard dropout, especially for recurrent neural networks on tasks with long input sequences. It ensures more consistent regularization while maintaining model uncertainty estimates. The consistent masking also improves training efficiency compared to standard dropout. Overall, Regularized Dropout is an enhanced dropout technique that often outperforms standard dropout.

Back Translation Augmenting parallel training data with back-translation (BT) (Sennrich et al., 2016; Wei et al., 2023) has been shown effective for improving NMT using target monolingual data. Numerous works have expanded the understanding of BT and investigated various approaches to generate synthetic source sentences. Edunov et al. found that back-translations obtained via sampling or noised beam outputs tend to be more effective than those via beam or greedy search in most scenarios. For optimal joint use with FT, we employ sampling back-translation (ST)

Forward Translation Forward translation (FT) (Abdulmumin, 2021) uses source-side monolingual data to improve model performance. The general procedure of FT involves three steps: (1) randomly sampling a subset from large-scale source monolingual data; (2) using a "teacher" NMT model to translate the subset into the target language, thereby constructing synthetic parallel data; and (3) combining the synthetic and authentic parallel data to train a "student" NMT model.

2.4.3 Domain Adaptation Models

We used domain data to fine-tune the baseline model to achieve domain adaptation. The domain data came from three sources: 1. Directly crawled from the internet. 2. Obtained domain data from general domain data through curriculum learning.

Curriculum Learning A practical curriculum

learning (CL) (Zhang et al., 2019) approach for NMT should address two key issues: ranking training examples by difficulty, and modifying the sampling procedure based on ranking. For ranking, we estimate example difficulty using domain features (Wang et al., 2020). The domain feature is calculated as:

$$q(x, y) = \frac{\log P(y|x; \theta_{in}) - \log P(y|x; \theta_{out})}{|y|} \quad (1)$$

Where θ_{in} is an in-domain NMT model, while θ_{out} is an out-of-domain model. The subtitle domain is treated as in-domain.

We fine-tune the model on the validation set to get the teacher model and select top 40% of the highest scoring data for fine-tuning.

2.4.4 Settings

In the training, each model undergoes training utilizing 8 NPUs. The encoder-decoder layers is 25-6. The batch size remains fixed at 6144, the update frequency is 2, the dropout is 0.1, and the learning rate is maintained at 5e-4. A total of 4000 warmup steps are executed, and the model is saved every 2000 steps. Additionally, λ is set to 5 for R-Drop. During inference, the beam size is set to 5 for both models.

2.5 Experiment

We conduct our experiments on the IWSLT 2023 development data (including itv, peloton and TED), and calculate the SubER (Wilken et al., 2022), shown in Table 2 and Table 3. Here are the systems we submitted:

Pipeline We used the strategies mentioned in sections 2.1, 2.2, and 2.4.

Length-Penalty In addition to the pipeline system, we incorporated a length penalty when performing machine translation. We set the length normalization parameter to 10 and the word penalty parameter to 15.

CTC-alignment In addition to the pipeline system, we performed CTC-alignment on the transcription results.

SubER-en2de	itv	peloton	TED	avg
Matesub	73.11	79.72	67.70	73.51
AppTek	71.40	71.90	64.30	69.20
FBK	83.70	79.10	69.40	77.40
Pipeline	74.41	78.92	72.03	75.10
+Length-Penalty	74.32	78.77	65.52	**72.86**
+CTC-alignment	74.21	79.30	71.24	74.91

Table 2: SubER in en2de

SubER-en2es	itv	peloton	TED	avg
Matesub	71.25	74.87	45.94	64.02
AppTek	82.10	79.00	48.80	69.97
FBK	82.20	80.30	52.50	71.67
Pipeline	71.87	79.98	52.49	68.11
+Length-Penalty	69.18	78.31	49.03	**65.50**
+CTC-alignment	71.41	80.27	51.27	67.62

Table 3: SubER in en2es

3 Subtitle Compression

In the task of subtitle compression, our explicit objective is to rewrite the original subtitle text, leveraging its content to fulfill the parameters of characters per second (CPS (Papi et al., 2023)) and BLEURT (Sellam et al., 2020) indicators to the highest degree possible.

3.1 Strategy

Given the constraints that only the original subtitle file can be utilized and its timestamp information remains unalterable, our compression strategy is confined to sentence-level rewriting tasks. It implies that compression needs to retain the original semantics, but sentence-level fusion compression is unfeasible.

In the absence of large volumes of parallel data comprising original and compressed text, and the presence of substantial bilingual data, we suggest a subtitle compression approach that blends machine translation model rewriting and large model rewriting. Our subtitle compression framework is delineated in Figure 1.

We employ the same training data and strategies used for automatic subtitles to train the bidirectional translation model between English and German, and between English and Spanish. For large language models, we utilize Llama2 to accomplish the subtitle text rewriting task.

3.2 Experiment

We performed exploratory studies on the IWSLT 2023 development data and computed CPS and BLEURT, utilizing the compressed subtitle text as the benchmark reference. The computation details are presented in Table 4. We have listed below the systems submitted for consideration:

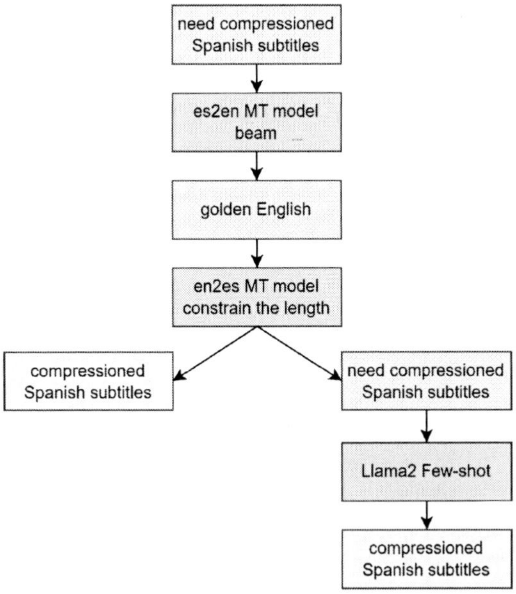

Figure 1: The subtitle compression framework

Reformulation using the machine translation model(system A) Within the inference architecture of the machine translation model, two parameters exist that can potentially constrain the length of the generated text:

1. the length normalization parameter: Divide translation score by pow(translation length, arg)

2. the word penalty parameter: Subtract (arg * translation length) from translation score

We also carry out the task of subtitle compression based on this feature. Using Spanish subtitle files as an example, we first utilize the CPS index to identify subtitle texts that do not conform to the required length specifications and, therefore, need compression. These texts are then processed through the Spanish-to-English translation model to generate golden English. These English versions are then subjected to re-translation back into Spanish, but we apply a length penalty during this translation to yield a compressed subtitle text. In this study, the length normalization parameter is set to 10 while the word penalty parameter is set to 15.

Revision based on the Llama2(systems B) The large-scale model exhibits robust reasoning capabilities, which can also be harnessed to accomplish the task of rephrasing subtitle text. Although Llama2 may not have been specifically trained for text condensation tasks, we adopt a few-shot methodology during inference. More precisely, a number of subtitle texts are chosen at random, and the condensed text is achieved through the aforementioned approach based on machine translation model rephrasing. During each inference, the large-scale model is initially presented with these instances, and then permitted to carry out the condensation and rephrasing assignment. The specific guidelines are as follows:

Tienes una gran capacidad de reescritura. Ahora necesitas reescribir el español en oraciones más concisas y cortas manteniendo la mayor cantidad posible de semántica del texto original.

1. Texto original: - ¿Cómo ayudará este impuesto a Europa a salir de la crisis económica? Texto después de reescribir: - ¿Cómo ayudará este impuesto a Europa a salir de la crisis?

2. Texto original: - Al fin y al cabo es un gesto político, nada más. Texto después de reescribir: - Al final es un gesto político, nada más.

3. Texto original: - Creo que la realidad es que, con sólo 11 países en el mundo, han adoptado este impuesto de manera efectiva Texto después de reescribir: - Creo que la realidad es que, con sólo 11 países efectivos en el mundo, adoptan este impuesto

Revision strategy utilizing machine translation models and large model amalgamation(systems A and B) Given that the machine translation model's output is derived from the golden English text, it holds a higher BLEURT score juxtaposed with Spanish, implying lesser semantic loss. Therefore, the initial consideration is leveraging a machine translation model for rewriting. However, for texts that pose higher rewriting complexities, a rewriting approach based on the Llama2 model is explored. Despite the potential for some semantic loss, this strategy ensures compliance with the prescribed length requirements for subtitle text.

System	CPS	CPS_mean	BLEURT
System A	75.3	19.9	0.78
System B	71.8	19	0.71
Systems A and B	81.2	18.6	0.62

Table 4: CPS and BLEURT in Spanish dev set

4 Conclusion

Although our performance in the experiment did not achieve best results, the comparison between our own systems can also illustrate some issues:

1. In automatic subtitling track, the results of machine translation with length penalty performed the best, indicating that compared to real subtitles, machine translation results tend to be longer.

2. In the subtitle compression track, the machine translation model produces rewritten text with a low BLEURT loss. However, the mean CPS value is 19.9, higher than the mean value of 19 from Llama2-based rewrites. This suggests that the machine translation model prioritizes translation quality and struggles to compress long sentences significantly. On the other hand, rewrites from Llama2 show lower CPS but higher BLEURT loss, indicating that the larger model possesses stronger reasoning abilities and can tackle challenging compression tasks effectively with prompts, albeit at the cost of potentially losing some sentence semantics.

References

Idris Abdulmumin. 2021. Enhanced back-translation for low resource neural machine translation using self-training. In *Information and Communication Technology and Applications: Third International Conference, ICTA 2020, Minna, Nigeria, November 24–27, 2020, Revised Selected Papers*, volume 1350, page 355. Springer Nature.

Katrin Angerbauer, Heike Adel, and Ngoc Thang Vu. 2019. Automatic compression of subtitles with neural networks and its effect on user experience. In *Interspeech*, pages 594–598.

Luisa Bentivogli, Mauro Cettolo, Marco Gaido, Alina Karakanta, Alberto Martinelli, Matteo Negri, and Marco Turchi. 2021. Cascade versus direct speech translation: Do the differences still make a difference? In *Proceedings of the 59th Annual Meeting of the Association for Computational Linguistics and the 11th International Joint Conference on Natural Language Processing (Volume 1: Long Papers)*, pages 2873–2887, Online. Association for Computational Linguistics.

Alexandre Berard, Olivier Pietquin, Christophe Servan, and Laurent Besacier. 2016. Listen and translate: A proof of concept for end-to-end speech-to-text translation. *ArXiv*, abs/1612.01744.

Sergey Edunov, Myle Ott, Michael Auli, and David Grangier. 2018. Understanding back-translation at scale. In *Proceedings of the 2018 Conference on Empirical Methods in Natural Language Processing*, page 489. Association for Computational Linguistics.

Siobhan Moran. 2009. *The effect of linguistic variation on subtitle reception*. York University Toronto.

Sara Papi, Marco Gaido, Alina Karakanta, Mauro Cettolo, Matteo Negri, and Marco Turchi. 2023. Direct speech translation for automatic subtitling. *Transactions of the Association for Computational Linguistics*, 11:1355–1376.

Alec Radford, Jong Wook Kim, Tao Xu, Greg Brockman, Christine McLeavey, and Ilya Sutskever. 2023. Robust speech recognition via large-scale weak supervision. In *International Conference on Machine Learning*, pages 28492–28518. PMLR.

Thibault Sellam, Dipanjan Das, and Ankur P Parikh. 2020. Bleurt: Learning robust metrics for text generation. *arXiv preprint arXiv:2004.04696*.

Rico Sennrich, Barry Haddow, and Alexandra Birch. 2016. Improving neural machine translation models with monolingual data. In *54th Annual Meeting of the Association for Computational Linguistics*, pages 86–96. Association for Computational Linguistics (ACL).

Wei Wang, Ye Tian, Jiquan Ngiam, Yinfei Yang, Isaac Caswell, and Zarana Parekh. 2020. Learning a multi-domain curriculum for neural machine translation. In *Proceedings of the 58th Annual Meeting of the Association for Computational Linguistics*, pages 7711–7723.

Daimeng Wei, Zhanglin Wu, Hengchao Shang, Zongyao Li, Minghan Wang, Jiaxin Guo, Xiaoyu Chen, Zhengzhe Yu, and Hao Yang. 2023. Text style transfer back-translation. In *Proceedings of the 61st Annual Meeting of the Association for Computational Linguistics*, pages 7944–7959, Toronto, Canada.

Patrick Wilken, Panayota Georgakopoulou, and Evgeny Matusov. 2022. SubER - a metric for automatic evaluation of subtitle quality. In *Proceedings of the 19th International Conference on Spoken Language Translation (IWSLT 2022)*, pages 1–10, Dublin, Ireland (in-person and online). Association for Computational Linguistics.

Lijun Wu, Juntao Li, Yue Wang, Qi Meng, Tao Qin, Wei Chen, Min Zhang, Tie-Yan Liu, et al. 2021. R-drop: Regularized dropout for neural networks. *Advances in Neural Information Processing Systems*, 34:10890–10905.

Jie Chi Yang, Chia Ling Chang, Yi Lung Lin, and M Shih. 2010. A study of the pos keyword caption effect on listening comprehension. *SL Wong et al.*

Xuan Zhang, Pamela Shapiro, Gaurav Kumar, Paul McNamee, Marine Carpuat, and Kevin Duh. 2019. Curriculum learning for domain adaptation in neural machine translation. In *Proceedings of NAACL-HLT*, pages 1903–1915.

Charles Locock, Lowcock or Lockhart? Offline Speech Translation: Test Suite for Named Entities

Maximilian Awiszus[1], **Jan Niehues**[2], **Marco Turchi**[1], **Sebastian Stüker**[1], **Alex Waibel**[3]

[1]Zoom Video Communications, [2]Karlsruhe Institute of Technology, [3]Carnegie Mellon University

{maximilian.awiszus, marco.turchi, sebastian.stueker}@zoom.us, jan.niehues@kit.edu, waibel@cs.cmu.edu

Abstract

Generating rare words is a challenging task for natural language processing in general and in speech translation (ST) specifically. This paper introduces a test suite prepared for the Offline ST shared task at IWSLT. In the test suite, corresponding rare words (i.e. named entities) were annotated on TED-Talks for English and German and the English side was made available to the participants together with some distractors (irrelevant named entities). Our evaluation checks the capabilities of ST systems to leverage the information in the contextual list of named entities and improve translation quality. Systems are ranked based on the recall and precision of named entities (separately on person, location, and organization names) in the translated texts. Our evaluation shows that using contextual information improves translation quality as well as the recall and precision of NEs. The recall of organization names in all submissions is the lowest of all categories with a maximum of 87.5% confirming the difficulties of ST systems in dealing with names.

1 Introduction

Generating rare words is a big challenge for several natural language processing (NLP) tasks such as machine and speech translation and speech recognition. Rare words are those terms that have a low frequency in the training data and include, among others, named entities (NE), i.e. names of persons, organizations, and locations, acronyms and abbreviations, and domain-specific terms. These words carry a huge amount of the information of a sentence (Li et al., 2013) and their wrong realization in a text can significantly impact the user's understanding and experience.

In machine translation (MT), there has been a significant effort in making the translation system able to translate better the rare words (Sennrich et al., 2016; Koehn and Knowles, 2017; Niehues and Cho, 2017). This becomes crucial when translations serve as a base for upstream tasks like summarization, errors in those named entities can introduce wrong attributions or overall misleading information. To improve the accuracy of translating named entities correctly one could either integrate a knowledge graph (Mota et al., 2022; Xie et al., 2022) or use NE tags in the source sentence to make the NMT system aware of the NEs (Ugawa et al., 2018; Dinu et al., 2019; Zhou et al., 2020).

For automatic speech recognition (ASR) the problem with rare words and NEs is even harder since with speech the system has to handle an additional modality. Similar to NMT there is a lack of training data for those entities and in addition to that, the pronunciation of named entities is often different compared to other words. Current state-of-the-art approaches tackle this problem using contextual biasing (Sathyendra et al., 2022) where the ASR system is provided with contextual information which can be a list of named entities. The work is usually distinguished in a shallow-fusion, where the actual ASR model is untouched and only modifications are added at inference time (Wang et al., 2023) and a deep-fusion approach, where a context mechanism is trained and later used as a black-box (Munkhdalai et al., 2023; Zhou et al., 2023; Huber et al., 2021; Sathyendra et al., 2022; Bruguier et al., 2019).

In speech translation (ST), addressing the modality problems encountered in ASR and the lack of alternative translations for NEs in neural machine translation simultaneously increases the complexity of the problem. There is already existing work exploring the capability of ST system handling NEs (Gaido et al., 2021). Similar to their work also this test suite concentrates on evaluating the accuracy of translating named entities for person, organization and location names. Additional to Gaido et al. also the precision in translating named entities of the systems is evaluated. Furthermore contextual information is given per talk as a list of named entities

Proceedings of the 21st International Conference on Spoken Language Translation (IWSLT 2024), pages 339–345
August 15-16, 2024 ©2024 Association for Computational Linguistics

to evaluate if a system can utilize this information for the translation task.

It has been shown that the main factors for a cascaded system might be the frequency of words occurring in the training and foreign words with different pronunciations (Gaido et al., 2022). They suggest tackling the first factor by using more data, synthetic data, or fine-tuning on in-domain data. The second factor is tackled by using multilingual speech data to increase the variety seen for phoneme-to-grapheme mappings during training. Additionally, there has been work incorporating a list of named entities into a direct ST model to improve the accuracy for NE translation (Gaido et al., 2023) based on the CLAS approach for contextual ASR (Pundak et al., 2018).

We proposed a test suite for the Offline ST shared task at IWSLT to draw attention to the problem of NE translation in speech translation. The test suite was used to evaluate the ability of ST systems to translate NEs in the English-German TED test set accurately. The test suite provides contextual information in the form of a list of source language NEs that may or may not be present in the source spoken audio. The aim is to assist the ST system in improving translation quality. This paper introduces the test suite and examines the performance of different submitted ST systems on our test. Our findings indicate that ST systems encounter difficulties when translating NEs, but the list of NEs can help enhance the performance when utilized.

2 Test Suite

2.1 Task

This test suite has been developed to check the capability of a speech-translation system to leverage source language textual knowledge to improve the translation of specific aspects (i.e. named entities), and properly translate named entities.

For this reason, in addition to the classic test audio for the English into German translation direction, contextual information is available in textual form. This information might be used to mitigate translation errors on these contextual terms.

The context information was given as a list of entities per English audio file. To emulate real scenarios, where large lists can be used without any adaptation to specific audio, some entities that were not present in that audio were added as distractors. The goal of each participant and system is to distill the correct information from the list and use it to improve translation quality.

2.2 Data

As a test corpus we use 27 English TED talks with translations into German used as one of the evaluation sets in the Offline task.

A state-of-the-art multilingual fined-tuned named-entity-recognition (NER) model based on BERT (Kenton and Toutanova, 2019)[1] is used to annotate NEs in our test corpus for English as well as for German. The NER tagger outputs different name entity classes – in the following, we will concentrate on the most frequent classes which are person names, locations, and organization names.

Additionally, in the first post-processing step, some miss-classified words were manually removed and statistics of tagged words were calculated to get a consistent tagging of all words. In the second step, the correspondence for the named entities from English and German is estimated since we are only interested in named entities which occur in the reference as well as in the target. As an heuristic we construct a graph where each named entity is represented by a node. In the graph, there is only an edge between two nodes if the character edit distance of two named entities of the two different languages was below a specific threshold. To finally estimate the correspondence a maximum bipartite matching (Hopcroft and Karp, 1973) is calculated between the named entities of German and English per segment.

Finally, the lists for each segment were merged per talk resulting in a list of named entities with corresponding entities in English resp. German.

Exemplary excerpts of a talk can be examined in table 1.

Table 1: Exemplary corresponding *named entity* in the test corpus tagged by a NER model.

English Transcription
a. The Company and *Jan Pieterszoon Coen*, its Governor-General b. In 1971, *East Pakistan* seceded
German Translation
a. Das Unternehmen und *Jan Pieterszoon Coen*, sein Generalgouverneur b. 1971 spaltete sich *Ostpakistan* ab

[1]The cased version of BERT is used because also the transcripts resp. translations are provided cased.

The same procedure as described above was applied to nearly 400,000 sentences from other TED talks to extract named entities. In the final step for each English audio in the test set distractors were sampled from these entities to add at least one distractor per audio but a maximum reach of 20% distractors per audio (c.f. table 2). This results in a final named entity list containing 153 words in total (including distractors).

Table 2: Excerpt of the final context list containing named entities. One line corresponds to one whole audio of the utterance in table 1. The list was artificially augmented by adding **distractors (bold)**.

a. Banda, Banda Islands, Bandanese, Coen, **David Brin**, Europe, Jan Pieterszoon Coen, Verenigde Oostindische Compagnie
b. **Alex Kipman**, Assam, Bangladesh, Bengal, Calcutta, Delhi, Dhaka, East Pakistan, Hindus, India, Jawaharlal Nehru, Karachi, Kashmir, Lahore, Mohandas Gandhi, Muhammad Ali Jinnah, Pakistan, Punjab, **Shree Bose**

2.3 Metric

The submitted hypotheses were automatically resegmented based on the reference translation.

Since the hypothesis-reference sentence alignment might not always be correct in the following evaluation the named entity measurements are calculated per audio. A named entity in the hypotheses translations is considered a hit if an exact case-sensitive match in the reference is found and a miss otherwise. Those hits and misses per audio are then used to calculate the recall.

Furthermore the same procedure as described in section 2.2 was applied to all submitted translations. By finding a match of the detected named entities in the reference, the precision of translated named entities can be calculated which is reported as NE-Precision.[2]

The translation quality is computed using the COMET score (Rei et al., 2020).

3 ST Models

All tested systems are cascaded systems that first transcribe the audio by an ASR system and translate the transcript with an NMT system. That might be due to the fact that cascaded systems performed better than end-to-end systems for Offline ST in the last years' evaluations (Agarwal et al., 2023; Anastasopoulos et al., 2022, 2021). There exist three different data conditions[3]: Firstly constrained, where the systems are only allowed to be trained on a fixed amount of data, secondly constrained + LLM where in addition a list of allowed large language model (LLM) can be used and thirdly unconstrained to allow training the system and a large amount of training data.

The only system incorporating the contextual information is the submission of the Karlsruhe Institute of Technology (KIT). Their cascaded system uses a LoRA (Hu et al., 2021) fine-tuned LLM to 1) post-edit the ASR transcript incorporating the N-best list and 2) to post-edit the MT output on document-level. Only their primary (prm) submission injects contextual information in the second step by including the words into their LLM prompt. The first contrastive submission (ctr1) only applies the ASR post-edit step and for ctr2 both LLM corrections are used but without injecting the contextual information.

All unconstrained systems use a multilingual ASR model - namely Whipser-large-v3 (Radford et al., 2023) - for transcription.

As stated above also the Huawei Translation Service Center (HW-TSC) and Carnegie Mellon University (CMU) submitted a cascaded approach.

4 Results

All systems' results are reported in table 3 grouped by the aforementioned data condition (c.f. section 3). It can be observed that unconstrained systems are performing better on the general ST metric, COMET, as well as on the named entity recall and precision. Because the unconstrained systems are trained on more data, also the number of named entities might be higher, which directly is related to predicting named entities correctly (Gaido et al., 2022). Additionally the multilingual ASR component of the unconstrained cascaded ST systems might be beneficial for the translation of named entities because often names originate from different languages than the actual source language (English in our case). This observation is also au-pair with other investigations (Gaido et al., 2022). Also, we

[2]We want to note that this metric depends on the performance of the NER model used for extracting NEs on the different translation submissions.

[3]For more details visit the webpage of IWSLT-2024 offline track: `https://iwslt.org/2024/offline`

Table 3: Systems evaluated using general MT metric COMET as well as recall (NE-Recall) and precision (NE-Precision) of named entities per category person (per), location (loc) and organization (org) evaluated in the target language (German) and number of predicted distractors (DT).

System	COMET	NE-Recall [%]				NE-Precision [%]				DT
		ALL	per	loc	org	ALL	per	loc	org	
Data Condition: Unconstrained										
NYA (prm)	0.8339	88.68	**84.44**	97.78	75.00	75.15	76.36	**82.05**	57.89	-
NYA (ctr1)	0.8329	**91.51**	**84.44**	**100.00**	**87.50**	**74.56**	**78.18**	78.75	58.33	-
NYA (ctr2)	0.8330	**91.51**	**84.44**	**100.00**	**87.50**	74.55	77.36	78.48	57.14	-
NYA (ctr3)	0.8332	**91.51**	**84.44**	**100.00**	**87.50**	73.10	**78.18**	77.78	54.05	-
CMU (prm)	**0.8596**	83.96	80.00	93.33	68.75	64.61	65.08	72.15	47.50	-
CMU (ctr1)	0.8542	83.02	80.00	91.11	68.75	61.96	65.08	71.43	42.55	-
CMU (ctr2)	0.8358	83.96	80.00	93.33	68.75	63.74	65.57	75.64	42.55	-
HW-TSC (prm)	0.8461	88.68	**84.44**	95.56	81.25	71.76	75.41	76.71	54.05	-
HW-TSC (ctr)	0.8472	88.68	**84.44**	95.56	81.25	73.21	76.67	55.56	**78.08**	-
Data Condition: Constrained										
HW-TSC	0.8376	87.74	**84.44**	93.33	**81.25**	**73.91**	76.27	76.06	**60.61**	-
Data Condition: Constrained + LLM										
KIT (prm)	0.8283	87.74	**86.67**	93.33	75.00	68.75	73.68	78.08	42.42	0
KIT (ctr1)	0.8245	83.96	80.00	93.33	68.75	64.85	60.32	**79.45**	40.62	-
KIT (ctr2)	0.8260	85.85	84.44	93.33	68.75	66.47	67.80	78.38	40.54	-
HW-TSC	**0.8490**	**89.62**	**86.67**	**95.56**	**81.25**	**73.78**	**79.63**	74.36	**60.61**	-

might suspect a data leakage problem since the Whisper model was released in November 2023 and some TED talks from the test set are publicly available since 2013.

Furthermore the recall and precision for locations archives the highest score, followed by persons and then organization names. That might be related to the main factor of frequency of words occurring in the training which likely is higher for location names compared to person and organization names.

Looking closer at the unconstrained submissions one can observe that CMU's primary submission is the best-performing submission for COMET, but NYA's contrastive submissions achieve a better NE-Recall as well as NE-Precision.

Comparing HW-TSC's primary submission on the constrained data to the condition with LLM, it achieves the highest precision for named entities in general and also has a competitive performance for the recall.

From the results for KIT's primary (prm) and second contrastive (ctr2) submission, it can be seen that the overall recall and precision of NEs as well as the scores for person and organization names increased. This indicates that the provided context information can be useful to not only increase the general COMET score but also the translation for NEs.

Additionally, the number of appearing distractors (DT) in the translations was measured. Only KIT's primary submission used the provided context information and is therefore prone to copying a wrong-named entity from the provided list. Nevertheless, 0 distractors were copied from the provided context list.

Table 4: Exemplary misses for the person *named entity* (*Charles Locock*) as well as one correct translation of four German hypotheses translations of unconstrained - NYA (prm) and CMU (prm) - and constrained systems with a LLM - HW-TSC and KIT (ctr2).

Reference	
Mediziner wie Sir *Charles Locock*	
Hypotheses	
NYA (prm)	Ärzte wie Sir *Charles Lowcock*
CMU (prm)	Ärzte wie Sir *Charles Lockhart*
HW-TSC	Ärzte wie Sir *Charles Lowcock*
KIT (ctr2)	Ärzte wie Sir Charles Locock

In table 4 an example of a person-named entity that was mistranslated by most of the tested systems can be examined. In that example, only KIT's submissions translated the name *Charles Lo-*

cock correctly. Other systems translated the last name as *Lockhart*, *Lowcock*, or *Lowcock*. All miss-translations are close to the actual name *Locock* but might raise confusion when reading the translation without having access to the original audio.

Table 5: Two exemplary misses for the organizational *named entity* (*WARIF*) as well as two correct translations in four German hypotheses translations of unconstrained - NYA (prm) - and constrained systems - KIT (ctr2), KIT (prm) and HW-TSC.

Reference	
Internationale Stiftung für Frauen in Gefahr, *WARIF*, gegründet	
Hypotheses	
NYA (prm)	Women at Risk International Foundation, *WAR*
KIT (ctr2)	Women at Risk International Foundation (*WRIF*) gegründet
KIT (prm)	Women at Risk International Foundation (*WARIF*) gegründet
HW-TSC	Women at Risk International Foundation, *WARIF*

Additionally translations of an abbreviation resp. an organizational named entity, namely *WARIF* which is short for *Women At Risk International Foundation*, are reported in table 5. The NYA's primary resp. KIT's second contrastive system is missing the NE and translates it with only *WAR* resp. *WRIF*. Also, it's worth noting that when injecting the contextual information the KIT's primary system is translating this organizational NE correctly. For completes: also the HW-TSC's primary submission was translating this NE correctly without using any contextual information. Especially for organization terms, it's important to translate them correctly. In this example, it can be seen that a hallucinated abbreviation also introduces confusion and makes it hard to understand the meaning of the translation.

5 Conclusions

In our test suite, we explored the translation of named entities for English-German ST. Named entities are translated correctly with a recall of approx. 92% and a precision of approx. 75% in an unconstrained, approx. 88% resp. 74 % in a constrained data condition without LLMs and approx. 90% resp. 81% in a constrained data condition with using a LLM. Firstly this indicates that LLMs comprise contextual knowledge about named entities which is useful to translate named entities. But secondly that also suggests that there is still a gap in translating named entities correctly, especially looking at the category of organization names where when additionally using a LLM the precision and recall was not improved. Furthermore that might indicate that the capabilities of LLM of improving the quality of named entity translation is limited due to the fact that some misreconized named entities can not be corrected without the access to audio information in a cascaded system.

The given contextual information (list of named entities) improved the overall COMET score as well as the recall and precision of NE translation. We are looking forward having more systems using a context list for ST to see more benefits from using provided contextual information or LLMs using audio information for translation directly.

References

Milind Agarwal, Sweta Agrawal, Antonios Anastasopoulos, Luisa Bentivogli, Ondřej Bojar, Claudia Borg, Marine Carpuat, Roldano Cattoni, Mauro Cettolo, Mingda Chen, William Chen, Khalid Choukri, Alexandra Chronopoulou, Anna Currey, Thierry Declerck, Qianqian Dong, Kevin Duh, Yannick Estève, Marcello Federico, Souhir Gahbiche, Barry Haddow, Benjamin Hsu, Phu Mon Htut, Hirofumi Inaguma, Dávid Javorský, John Judge, Yasumasa Kano, Tom Ko, Rishu Kumar, Pengwei Li, Xutai Ma, Prashant Mathur, Evgeny Matusov, Paul McNamee, John P. McCrae, Kenton Murray, Maria Nadejde, Satoshi Nakamura, Matteo Negri, Ha Nguyen, Jan Niehues, Xing Niu, Atul Kr. Ojha, John E. Ortega, Proyag Pal, Juan Pino, Lonneke van der Plas, Peter Polák, Elijah Rippeth, Elizabeth Salesky, Jiatong Shi, Matthias Sperber, Sebastian Stüker, Katsuhito Sudoh, Yun Tang, Brian Thompson, Kevin Tran, Marco Turchi, Alex Waibel, Mingxuan Wang, Shinji Watanabe, and Rodolfo Zevallos. 2023. FINDINGS OF THE IWSLT 2023 EVALUATION CAMPAIGN. In *Proceedings of the 20th International Conference on Spoken Language Translation (IWSLT 2023)*, pages 1–61, Toronto, Canada (in-person and online). Association for Computational Linguistics.

Antonios Anastasopoulos, Loïc Barrault, Luisa Bentivogli, Marcely Zanon Boito, Ondřej Bojar, Roldano Cattoni, Anna Currey, Georgiana Dinu, Kevin Duh, Maha Elbayad, Clara Emmanuel, Yannick Estève, Marcello Federico, Christian Federmann, Souhir Gahbiche, Hongyu Gong, Roman Grundkiewicz, Barry Haddow, Benjamin Hsu, Dávid Javorský,

Věra Kloudová, Surafel Lakew, Xutai Ma, Prashant Mathur, Paul McNamee, Kenton Murray, Maria Nădejde, Satoshi Nakamura, Matteo Negri, Jan Niehues, Xing Niu, John Ortega, Juan Pino, Elizabeth Salesky, Jiatong Shi, Matthias Sperber, Sebastian Stüker, Katsuhito Sudoh, Marco Turchi, Yogesh Virkar, Alexander Waibel, Changhan Wang, and Shinji Watanabe. 2022. Findings of the IWSLT 2022 evaluation campaign. In *Proceedings of the 19th International Conference on Spoken Language Translation (IWSLT 2022)*, pages 98–157, Dublin, Ireland (in-person and online). Association for Computational Linguistics.

Antonios Anastasopoulos, Ondřej Bojar, Jacob Bremerman, Roldano Cattoni, Maha Elbayad, Marcello Federico, Xutai Ma, Satoshi Nakamura, Matteo Negri, Jan Niehues, Juan Pino, Elizabeth Salesky, Sebastian Stüker, Katsuhito Sudoh, Marco Turchi, Alexander Waibel, Changhan Wang, and Matthew Wiesner. 2021. FINDINGS OF THE IWSLT 2021 EVALUATION CAMPAIGN. In *Proceedings of the 18th International Conference on Spoken Language Translation (IWSLT 2021)*, pages 1–29, Bangkok, Thailand (online). Association for Computational Linguistics.

Antoine Bruguier, Rohit Prabhavalkar, Golan Pundak, and Tara N Sainath. 2019. Phoebe: Pronunciation-aware contextualization for end-to-end speech recognition. In *ICASSP 2019-2019 IEEE International Conference on Acoustics, Speech and Signal Processing (ICASSP)*, pages 6171–6175. IEEE.

Georgiana Dinu, Prashant Mathur, Marcello Federico, and Yaser Al-Onaizan. 2019. Training neural machine translation to apply terminology constraints. In *Proceedings of the 57th Annual Meeting of the Association for Computational Linguistics*, pages 3063–3068, Florence, Italy. Association for Computational Linguistics.

Marco Gaido, Matteo Negri, Marco Turchi, et al. 2022. Who are we talking about? handling person names in speech translation. In *Proceedings of the 19th International Conference on Spoken Language Translation (IWSLT 2022)*, pages 62–73. Association for Computational Linguistics (ACL).

Marco Gaido, Rodríguez Susana, Matteo Negri, Luisa Bentivogli, and Marco Turchi. 2021. Is" moby dick" a whale or a bird? named entities and terminology in speech translation. In *Proceedings of the 2021 Conference on Empirical Methods in Natural Language Processing*, pages 1707–1716. Association for Computational Linguistics.

Marco Gaido, Yun Tang, Ilia Kulikov, Rongqing Huang, Hongyu Gong, and Hirofumi Inaguma. 2023. Named entity detection and injection for direct speech translation. In *Proceedings of ICASSP 2023-2023 IEEE International Conference on Acoustics, Speech and Signal Processing (ICASSP)*, pages 1–5. IEEE.

John E Hopcroft and Richard M Karp. 1973. An n^5/2 algorithm for maximum matchings in bipartite graphs. *SIAM Journal on computing*, 2(4):225–231.

Edward J Hu, Yelong Shen, Phillip Wallis, Zeyuan Allen-Zhu, Yuanzhi Li, Shean Wang, Lu Wang, and Weizhu Chen. 2021. Lora: Low-rank adaptation of large language models. *arXiv preprint arXiv:2106.09685*.

Christian Huber, Juan Hussain, Sebastian Stüker, and Alexander Waibel. 2021. Instant one-shot word-learning for context-specific neural sequence-to-sequence speech recognition. In *2021 IEEE Automatic Speech Recognition and Understanding Workshop (ASRU)*, pages 1–7. IEEE.

Jacob Devlin Ming-Wei Chang Kenton and Lee Kristina Toutanova. 2019. Bert: Pre-training of deep bidirectional transformers for language understanding. In *Proceedings of NAACL-HLT*, pages 4171–4186.

Philipp Koehn and Rebecca Knowles. 2017. Six challenges for neural machine translation. In *Proceedings of the First Workshop on Neural Machine Translation*, pages 28–39, Vancouver. Association for Computational Linguistics.

Haibo Li, Jing Zheng, Heng Ji, Qi Li, and Wen Wang. 2013. Name-aware machine translation. In *Proceedings of the 51st Annual Meeting of the Association for Computational Linguistics (Volume 1: Long Papers)*, pages 604–614, Sofia, Bulgaria. Association for Computational Linguistics.

Pedro Mota, Vera Cabarrao, and Eduardo Farah. 2022. Fast-paced improvements to named entity handling for neural machine translation. In *Proceedings of the 23rd Annual Conference of the European Association for Machine Translation*, pages 141–149, Ghent, Belgium. European Association for Machine Translation.

Tsendsuren Munkhdalai, Zelin Wu, Golan Pundak, Khe Chai Sim, Jiayang Li, Pat Rondon, and Tara N Sainath. 2023. Nam+: Towards scalable end-to-end contextual biasing for adaptive asr. In *2022 IEEE Spoken Language Technology Workshop (SLT)*, pages 190–196. IEEE.

Jan Niehues and Eunah Cho. 2017. Exploiting linguistic resources for neural machine translation using multi-task learning. In *Proceedings of the Second Conference on Machine Translation*, pages 80–89.

Golan Pundak, Tara N Sainath, Rohit Prabhavalkar, Anjuli Kannan, and Ding Zhao. 2018. Deep context: end-to-end contextual speech recognition. In *2018 IEEE spoken language technology workshop (SLT)*, pages 418–425. IEEE.

Alec Radford, Jong Wook Kim, Tao Xu, Greg Brockman, Christine McLeavey, and Ilya Sutskever. 2023. Robust speech recognition via large-scale weak supervision. In *International Conference on Machine Learning*, pages 28492–28518. PMLR.

Ricardo Rei, Craig Stewart, Ana C Farinha, and Alon Lavie. 2020. Comet: A neural framework for mt evaluation. In *Proceedings of the 2020 Conference on*

Empirical Methods in Natural Language Processing (EMNLP), pages 2685–2702.

Kanthashree Mysore Sathyendra, Thejaswi Muniyappa, Feng-Ju Chang, Jing Liu, Jinru Su, Grant P Strimel, Athanasios Mouchtaris, and Siegfried Kunzmann. 2022. Contextual adapters for personalized speech recognition in neural transducers. In *ICASSP 2022-2022 IEEE International Conference on Acoustics, Speech and Signal Processing (ICASSP)*, pages 8537–8541. IEEE.

Rico Sennrich, Barry Haddow, and Alexandra Birch. 2016. Neural machine translation of rare words with subword units. In *Proceedings of the 54th Annual Meeting of the Association for Computational Linguistics (Volume 1: Long Papers)*, pages 1715–1725, Berlin, Germany. Association for Computational Linguistics.

Arata Ugawa, Akihiro Tamura, Takashi Ninomiya, Hiroya Takamura, and Manabu Okumura. 2018. Neural machine translation incorporating named entity. In *Proceedings of the 27th International Conference on Computational Linguistics*, pages 3240–3250, Santa Fe, New Mexico, USA. Association for Computational Linguistics.

Weiran Wang, Zelin Wu, Diamantino Caseiro, Tsendsuren Munkhdalai, Khe Chai Sim, Pat Rondon, Golan Pundak, Gan Song, Rohit Prabhavalkar, Zhong Meng, et al. 2023. Contextual biasing with the knuth-morris-pratt matching algorithm. *arXiv preprint arXiv:2310.00178*.

Shufang Xie, Yingce Xia, Lijun Wu, Yiqing Huang, Yang Fan, and Tao Qin. 2022. End-to-end entity-aware neural machine translation. *Machine Learning*, 111(3):1181–1203.

Leiying Zhou, Wenjie Lu, Jie Zhou, Kui Meng, and Gongshen Liu. 2020. Incorporating named entity information into neural machine translation. In *Natural Language Processing and Chinese Computing: 9th CCF International Conference, NLPCC 2020, Zhengzhou, China, October 14–18, 2020, Proceedings, Part I 9*, pages 391–402. Springer.

Shilin Zhou, Zhenghua Li, Yu Hong, Min Zhang, Zhefeng Wang, and Baoxing Huai. 2023. Copyne: Better contextual asr by copying named entities. *arXiv preprint arXiv:2305.12839*.

Fixed and Adaptive Simultaneous Machine Translation Strategies Using Adapters

Abderrahmane Issam
Yusuf Can Semerci
Jan Scholtes
Gerasimos Spanakis
Department of Advanced Computing Sciences
Maastricht University
{abderrahmane.issam, y.semerci, j.scholtes, jerry.spanakis}@maastrichtuniversity.nl

Abstract

Simultaneous machine translation aims at solving the task of real-time translation by starting to translate before consuming the full input, which poses challenges in terms of balancing quality and latency of the translation. The wait-k policy offers a solution by starting to translate after consuming k words, where the choice of the number k directly affects the latency and quality. In applications where we seek to keep the choice over latency and quality at inference, the wait-k policy obliges us to train more than one model. In this paper, we address the challenge of building one model that can fulfil multiple latency levels and we achieve this by introducing lightweight adapter modules into the decoder. The adapters are trained to be specialized for different wait-k values and compared to other techniques they offer more flexibility to allow for reaping the benefits of parameter sharing and minimizing interference. Additionally, we show that by combining with an adaptive strategy, we can further improve the results. Experiments on two language directions show that our method outperforms or competes with other strong baselines on most latency values. [1]

1 Introduction

Simultaneous machine translation (SiMT) aims at reducing the latency of translation systems. In scenarios with low latency demands, such as conferences or lectures, translating with minimum delay is crucial. In order to reduce the latency, SiMT models start translating before consuming the full input sentence, which improves the latency but affects the quality of the translation, because of limited access to enough source context to make a correct prediction. SiMT techniques design a strategy to decide when to make a READ (i.e. wait for more source tokens) or WRITE (i.e. output a new token) action. The strategy has to balance the trade-off between quality and latency by making more READ or WRITE actions. Making more READ actions will lead to improved quality but will hinder the latency, while the opposite is true for making more WRITE actions. Fixed policies design a strategy that is detached from whether there is sufficient context to make a WRITE action (Ma et al., 2019; Elbayad et al., 2020; Zhang and Feng, 2021). For instance, the wait-k policy (Ma et al., 2019) trains the model to make k number of READ actions before every WRITE action. The value of k has a direct impact on the quality and latency of the translation and since it is decided during training, wait-k models have to be trained with latency in mind, which means that in order to support multiple latency levels, we need to train multiple models. The multi-path training (Elbayad et al., 2020) was introduced to solve this issue by sampling the value of k randomly during training, which results in a model that supports multiple latency levels. This technique was shown to benefit the inference at lower wait-k values by improving the results, but it neglects that parameter sharing between all the wait-k values might introduce interference. Zhang and Feng (2021) addressed the interference issue by using Mixture-of-Experts (MoE), where each head of the multi-head attention is treated as an expert and is trained on different wait-k values. This has proven to be a successful technique, but the number of wait-k experts we can introduce depends on the number of heads in the Transformer model, which limits the flexibility in terms of balancing parameter sharing and interference between the wait-k paths. Our method relies on inserting lightweight adapters (Rebuffi et al., 2017; Houlsby et al., 2019) for this purpose. The number of the adapters and their capacity can be easily adjusted depending on the wait-k values we intend to support and the complexity of the language direction.

Dynamic strategies have gained increased atten-

[1] Code is available at: https://github.com/issam9/Adapters-SiMT

Proceedings of the 21st International Conference on Spoken Language Translation (IWSLT 2024), pages 346–358
August 15-16, 2024 ©2024 Association for Computational Linguistics

tion in recent years (Gu et al., 2017; Zheng et al., 2019, 2020; Ma et al., 2020; Zhang and Feng, 2022; Zhao et al., 2023) due to their effectiveness. Dynamic strategies strive to strike a balance between latency and quality by making as much READ actions as necessary and as much WRITE actions as possible. The decision to read or write is made dynamically based on the context (which can be the received input and the previous target tokens) at each decoding step. Although dynamic strategies achieve state-of-the-art results, they often require specialized training techniques (Gu et al., 2017; Ma et al., 2020; Zhang and Feng, 2022) that can balance between latency and quality when generating READ/WRITE actions, or even require the training of multiple models (Zheng et al., 2020; Ma et al., 2020) to support multiple latency levels. In order to take advantage of the dynamic wait-k strategies, we adopt a strategy that composes multiple wait-k models during inference (we refer to this as Adaptive Wait-k (Zheng et al., 2020)) to work with wait-k adapters instead. This brings efficiency and cost benefits as only one model is required to satisfy multiple latency levels and also improves performance compared to other strong baselines including Adaptive Wait-k.

In summary, our main contributions are the following:

- We introduce lightweight adapters as a flexible solution to balance parameter sharing and interference in multi-path training.
- We show that by combining adapters with a simple adaptive strategy (i.e. Adaptive Wait-k) we can further improve the results.
- We show that our technique outperforms or competes with other strong baselines on most latency levels.

2 Related Works

2.1 Adapters for Machine Translation

Adapters (Rebuffi et al., 2017; Houlsby et al., 2019) are typically small modules that are used in order to efficiently adapt a pre-trained model to a downstream task, where the pre-trained model can be either frozen (Houlsby et al., 2019), or trained jointly with the adapters (Stickland and Murray, 2019).

Adapters have been used for efficient multi-task fine-tuning (Stickland and Murray, 2019), where each set of adapters is trained on a specific task. Pfeiffer et al. (2021) added AdapterFusion on top of the adapters as a way to compose the representations of different tasks. Pfeiffer et al. (2022) used adapters as language-specific parameters in order to address the curse of multilinguality in multilingual pre-training, where the adapter modules are introduced during pre-training instead of post-hoc.

For Neural Machine Translation (NMT), Bapna and Firat (2019) introduced a simple formulation of adapters to learn language-pair specific parameters, where they showed that it improves performance on high resource languages in Multilingual Translation. Chronopoulou et al. (2023) trained language-family adapters to address negative interference while allowing for parameter sharing between similar languages, which improved performance on low resource languages. Zhao and Calapodescu (2022) fine-tuned adapters on multimodal noise, then added a fusion layer in order to improve generalization to other types of noise. Adapters were also explored for other motivations like Zero-shot NMT and unsupervised domain adaptation (Philip et al., 2020; Malik et al., 2023).

2.2 Simultaneous Machine Translation

SiMT systems can be divided into fixed and adaptive policies. Fixed policies rely on predefined rules for READ/WRITE decisions. Ma et al. (2019) proposed the wait-k policy, where the model starts by reading k tokens then alternates between reading and writing one token. Elbayad et al. (2020) introduced multi-path training, where one model is trained to support multiple wait-k values by sampling k randomly during training. Zhang and Feng (2021) addressed interference in multi-path training by using Mixture-of-Experts. Zhang et al. (2021) used Knowledge Distillation from a Full-Sentence Transformer to embed future information into the SiMT model. For adaptive policies, Gu et al. (2017) trained a Reinforcement Learning agent to decide READ/WRITE actions, where the reward function is designed to consider both quality and latency. Zheng et al. (2019) generated supervised READ/WRITE actions then trained a classification model to predict the action based on encoder and decoder representations. Zheng et al. (2020) introduced a heuristic strategy to compose wait-k models into an adaptive policy based on their uncertainty. Zhang and Zhang (2020) trained a sentence segmentation model to predict complete sentences and feed them through a full-sentence translation model. Arivazhagan et al. (2019) introduced MILK, where they modified the attention mechanism to learn a Bernoulli variable to decide READ/WRITE actions. Ma et al. (2020) adapted MILK to the transformer architecture. Zhang and Feng (2022) proposed ITST, which quantifies the transported information from source to target then generates a token when the quantity is deemed sufficient. Zhao et al. (2023) trained a supervised policy network based on automatically generated divergence between the predicted distribution of partial and full sentence input.

The majority of the techniques outlined require training multiple models to accommodate different latency levels. Our approach focuses on the efficient training of a single model that can support various latency levels at inference time.

3 Background

3.1 Adapters

Adapters are lightweight modules that can be inserted into a model for the purpose of task or domain adaptation (Houlsby et al., 2019; Bapna and Firat, 2019). They offer an efficient solution for fine-tuning the model and limiting catastrophic forgetting (Houlsby et al., 2019).

Formally, for a set of N tasks and a model M, the adapter parameters A are introduced. We assume that for each task we have a dataset D_n. The model parameters can be frozen or jointly trained with the adapters. For a frozen model, the model M is pre-trained and the objective function for task $n \in \{1, ..., N\}$ can be defined as:

$$A_n \leftarrow \underset{A_n}{argmin}\, L_n(D_n; M, A_n) \quad (1)$$

The parameters A_n are randomly initialized for each task, then they are trained on the dataset D_n in order to minimize the loss function L_n. This results in N adapters that can specialize the model representations to each task n.

In the case of jointly training the model and the adapters, the model parameters M can be randomly initialized or frozen. The objective function can be defined as:

$$M' \leftarrow \underset{M,A}{argmin} \left(\sum_{n=1}^{N} L_n(D_n; M, A_n) \right) \quad (2)$$

where M' is both the parameters of the model M and the adapters A_n for $n \in \{1, ..., N\}$. The parameters A_n are activated during training depending on the task n.

3.2 Wait-k Policy

The wait-k policy (Ma et al., 2019) trains a model to start translating after receiving k source tokens. The model then alternates between writing and reading a new token. It is a fixed policy, where the k value has to be chosen during training and inference. The model reads $g_k(t)$ number of source tokens from the source sentence $x = (x_1, ..., x_m)$ when generating the target token y_t, where $g_k(t)$ is defined as:

$$g_k(t) = min\{|x|, t + k - 1\} \quad (3)$$

Instead of training the model for a specific wait-k value, Elbayad et al. (2020) introduced the multi-path training, which samples k uniformly from $[1, ..., |x|]$ for each batch during training. This enables the model to support multiple wait-k values and allows for information sharing between different wait-k paths. While it was shown that the multi-path training improves the results over the wait-k policy, it does not offer a solution to balance between parameter sharing and interference that we aim at solving by introducing adapters.

4 Method

Our method is composed of two steps: first we train a single model that can support multiple fixed wait-k values by using wait-k adapters, then we rely on the probability that the model assigns to the most likely token in order to build an adaptive strategy, where we decide a READ or WRITE action based on a predefined probability threshold.

4.1 Multi-path Training with Adapters

Multi-path training is highly advantageous as an efficient alternative to the wait-k policy, where we need to train multiple models to support more than one latency at inference, but might introduce interference between wait-k paths due to parameter sharing. In order to provide the ability to balance between parameter sharing and interference, we introduce adapters into each decoder layer and we activate adapters according to the wait-k paths they are meant to support. Figure 1 shows an illustration of this. During training, the wait-k value for each batch is sampled uniformly from $[1, ..., |x|]$ following the multi-path training (Elbayad et al., 2020) and based on that, the model decides which adapter will be activated. We set the adapter lagging K_A as a list of equally spaced positive integers in increasing order, where each integer specifies the minimum wait-k value supported by each adapter. We insert one adapter for each value in K_A. Since the train wait-k is randomly sampled from $[1, \ldots, |x|]$, we train each adapter on values starting from its minimum wait-k up until the minimum wait-k of the next adapter. For example, we can set $K_A = \{1, 5, 9, 13\}$ and this will indicate adding 4 adapters, where each adapter will handle 4 wait-k values (starting from each integer in K_A until the next), except the fourth adapter (k_A = 13), which will handle values starting from 13 up until the length of the input sequence $|x|$. We follow Bapna and Firat (2019) implementation and insert the residual adapter modules after the feed-forward layer. Algorithm 1 shows the pseudo-code for computing the decoder hidden states at decoding step t using Adapters Wait-k, where H^0 is considered to be the input embeddings of the decoder, and $g_k(t)$ is computed based on equation 3.

Algorithm 1 Adapters Wait-k Policy

Input: Encoder output Z, Decoder hidden states H_t, Adapter lagging K_A, Test lagging k_{test}
Output: Hidden states H_t^L
  if is_training **then**
    $k \leftarrow$ Sample from $[1, \ldots, |Z|]$
  else
    $k \leftarrow k_{\text{test}}$
  end if
  for k_A in K_A **do**
    if $k \geq k_A$ **then**
      $A^l = A^l_{k_A}$ for $l \in [1, \ldots, L]$
    end if
  end for
  for $l \leftarrow 1$ to L **do**
    $H_t^l = Decoder^l(H_t^{l-1}, Z_{\leq g_k(t)})$
    $H_t^l = A^l(H_t^l) + H_t^l$
  end for
  Return H_t^L

4.2 Adaptive Adapters

We follow Zheng et al. (2020) to build an adaptive strategy by using adapters instead of different models for each wait-k value, which can be computationally expensive and less efficient. At each decoding step, we activate one adapter based on the lagging behind the current generation step, which is calculated as $k = |x| - |y|$, where $|x|$ is the number of input tokens and $|y|$ is the number of generated tokens. At the beginning of generation, $|x| = 1$ and $|y| = 0$, which means k starts from 1. Then, we rely on the probability of the most likely token to decide whether to write or read a new token. If the probability is less than a threshold ρ_k, we read a new token, otherwise, we write. The possible values of k are between k_{min} and k_{max} that we determine during inference. If k is lower than k_{min}, we force the model to read, if it is higher or equal to k_{max}, we force the model to write, which means that the choice of k_{min} and k_{max} also impacts the trade-off between latency and quality (as we analyze in Section 6.1). When the whole input sequence is consumed (i.e. $x_{|x|}$ = </s>), we set k to k_{max} and generate the rest of the target sequence. Algorithm 2 shows the pseudo-code of this method using adapters.

Algorithm 2 Uncertainty based Adaptive Policy

Input: Two integers k_{min} and k_{max} and a sequence of thresholds ρ_k for $k_{\text{min}} \leq k \leq k_{\text{max}}$.
Output: Predicted sequence y
  while $x_{|x|} \neq$ </s> and $y_{|y|} \neq$ </s> **do**
    $k \leftarrow |x| - |y|$
    if $k < k_{\text{min}}$ **then**
      $x \leftarrow x \circ$ READ()   ▷ READ action
    else
      $y_{\text{top}}, p_{\text{top}} \leftarrow P_k(M, A_k, x, y)$
      if $k < k_{\text{max}}$ and $p_{\text{top}} < \rho_k$ **then**
        $x \leftarrow x \circ$ READ()   ▷ READ action
      else
        $y \leftarrow y \circ y_{\text{top}}$ ▷ WRITE action
      end if
    end if
  end while
  while $y_{|y|} \neq$ </s> **do**
    $y_{\text{top}}, p_{\text{top}} \leftarrow P_{k_{\text{max}}}(M, A_{k_{\text{max}}}, x, y)$
    $y \leftarrow y \circ y_{\text{top}}$ ▷ WRITE action
  end while
  return y

5 Experiments

In this section, we describe the datasets we used to evaluate the models and the baselines that we compare against along with the evaluation setup. We also provide the main results of our experiments.

5.1 Datasets

We evaluate our method on two public datasets: the En-Vi dataset for Transformer-Small and De-En for both Transformer-Base and Transformer-Big.

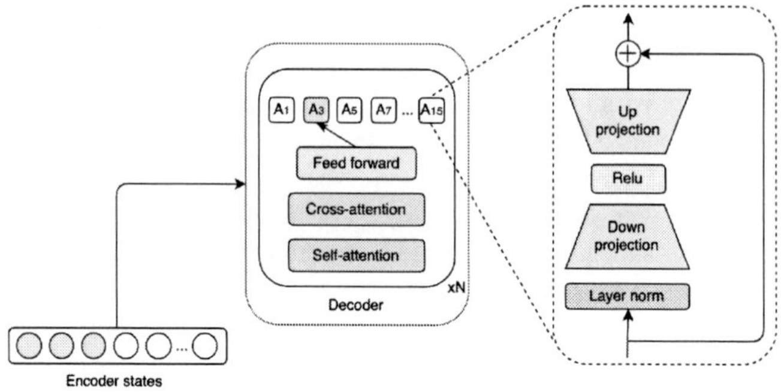

Figure 1: Transformer Decoder with Adapters Wait-k, we illustrate an example where 8 adapters are inserted with $K_A = \{1, 3, 5, 7, 9, 11, 13, 15\}$, the generation step is $t = 0$, and A_3 is activated because $k = 3$.

IWSLT15[2] English → Vietnamese (133K pairs) (Cettolo et al., 2015). We follow the settings of Raffel et al. (2017) and Ma et al. (2020). We use TED tst2012 (1553 pairs) as the validation set and TED tst2013 (1268 pairs) as the test set. We replace tokens with frequency less than 5 with $< unk >$. The final vocabulary sizes are 17K and 7.7K for English and Vietnamese respectively.

WMT15[3] German → English (4.5M pairs) We follow the settings of Ma et al. (2019). We use newstest2013 (3000 pairs) as the validation set and newstest2015 (2169 pairs) as the test set. We apply BPE (Sennrich et al., 2016) with 32K merge operations jointly on the source and target to construct a shared vocabulary.

5.2 System Settings

We conduct experiments on the following systems:

Full Sentence: (Vaswani et al., 2017) Standard Transformer model that takes the full sentence as input before starting to translate.

Wait-k: (Ma et al., 2019) A simple policy that waits for k source tokens before starting to alternate between writing a target token and reading a source token.

Multi-path Wait-k: (Elbayad et al., 2020) Trains a model to support multiple wait-k policies by randomly sampling k during training, then the k value is fixed during inference.

Adaptive Wait-k: (Zheng et al., 2020) It is a method for composing multiple wait-k models during inference in order to build an adaptive strategy. The model is selected based on the lagging behind the generation step, and the decision to write or read is based on the output probabilities.

MoE Wait-k: (Zhang and Feng, 2021) Mixture-of-Experts Wait-k is similar to Multipath Wait-k but applies experts to learn different wait-k policies to avoid interference.

MMA: (Ma et al., 2020) Monotonic multi-head attention (MMA) jointly learns a Bernoulli variable that is used to decide READ/WRITE action.

Adapters Wait-k: Our method as described in Section 4.1.

Adaptive Adapters: Our method as described in Section 4.2.

All implementations are based on the original Transformer architecture (Vaswani et al., 2017) and are using the Fairseq library (Ott et al., 2019). We apply Transformer-Small (4 heads) for En-Vi and both Transformer-Base (8 heads) and Transformer-Big (16 heads) for De-En. The encoder is made unidirectional to avoid encoding the source input each time a new token is added.

The evaluation is performed using BLEU (Papineni et al., 2002) for translation quality and Average Lagging (AL)[4] (Ma et al., 2019) for latency. AL measures by how many tokens the system is lagging behind an ideal policy (a wait-k policy with $k = 0$). Given $g(t)$, AL is computed as:

$$AL_g(x, y) = \frac{1}{\tau_g(|x|)} \sum_{t=1}^{\tau_g(|x|)} g(t) - \frac{(t-1)}{|y|/|x|} \quad (4)$$

where x and y are the source and target sentences respectively, while $\tau_g(|x|) = \min\{t \mid g(t) = |x|\}$ is the decoding step where the source sentence finishes.

We set the adapter lagging to $K_A = \{1, 3, 5, 7, 9, 11, 13, 15\}$ for our experiments,

[2]nlp.stanford.edu/projects/nmt/

[3]www.statmt.org/wmt15/

[4]github.com/SimulTrans-demo/STACL

which means that 8 adapters are inserted into the model and we specify the adapter bottleneck size as 64. In Table 1, we report the number of parameters of each method and the number of models required to achieve the latency levels reported in the results section. Adapters Wait-k policy introduces 79.94M parameters into Transformer-Big, but still has the advantage of using one model to support multiple latency levels. In Section 6.3, we experiment with other settings of K_A in order to shed light on how much sharing is best between wait-k values during the multi-path training.

Model	#Parameters	#Models
Full Sentence	209.91M	1
Wait-k	209.91M	5
Adaptive Wait-k	209.91M	13
Multipath	209.91M	1
MMA	222.51M	7
MoE Wait-k	209.91M	1
Adapters Wait-k	289.85M	1
Adaptive Adapters	289.85M	1

Table 1: The number of parameters of the models for Transformer-Big on De-En along with the number of models required to achieve different latency levels.

The adaptive strategy requires three parameters to be specified at inference, namely, k_{min}, k_{max}, and the probability threshold ρ_k. For En-Vi experiments, k_{min} and k_{max} are set to 1 and 9 respectively, while for De-En, we lower k_{max} to 5, which we have found to improve the results in low latency. We analyze this effect in Section 6.1. ρ_k decreases as a function of the lagging k, since we want the model to be more aggressive when k is low and more conservative when k is high. We set $\rho_{k_{min}}$ and $\rho_{k_{max}}$ and compute the threshold as: $\rho_k = \rho_{k_{min}} - d.(k-1)$, where $k_{min} \leq k \leq k_{max}$ and $d = (\rho_{k_{min}} - \rho_{k_{max}})/(k_{max} - k_{min})$. In order to vary the latency, we test the following values of $\rho_{k_{min}}$ and $\rho_{k_{max}}$: $\rho_{k_{min}} \in \{0.2, 0.4, 0.6, 0.8, 1.\}$, $\rho_{k_{max}} = 0.$, and $\rho_{k_{min}} = 1.$, $\rho_{k_{max}} \in \{0.2, 0.4, 0.6, 0.8\}$.

5.3 Main Results

In Figure 2, we compare our methods to previous adaptive and fixed strategies on two language directions. We find that our method improves or competes with other strategies while using a single model. MMA, Wait-k, and Adaptive Wait-k require the training of multiple models in order to support different latency levels (as seen in Table 1), while our method is more efficient in this regard. Adapters Wait-k is competitive with other strong fixed strategies like MoE Wait-k and Multipath Wait-k and it brings further improvements to combine it with the adaptive strategy.

Our method does not support higher latency on De-En because we are using a k_{max} value of 5 (as seen in Figures 2b and 2c), which we have found to improve results for low latency. However, we show the results for higher k_{max} and compare them with Adaptive Wait-k on De-En in Section 6.1.

Using adapters alone is competitive with other methods, especially on En-Vi (as seen as in Figure 2a). Compared to Multi-path Wait-k, our method achieves better results on most latency levels, which shows the importance of minimizing interference between different lagging values. Combining our method with an adaptive strategy further improves the results, especially in low latency. In comparison to Adaptive Wait-k, where wait-k policy models are trained and composed during inference, we find that our method is better in all latency levels while being more efficient.

Compared to MoE Wait-k, which also aims at minimizing interference introduced by multi-path training (Zhang and Feng, 2021), we find that our method is better in all latency levels on En-Vi and De-En with Transformer-Big (as seen in Figures 2a and 2c), while achieving competitive results when using Transformer-Base (as seen in Figure 2b). Our method is more flexible in terms of balancing the trade-off between parameter sharing and interference, as we can choose the number of wait-k values supported by each adapter and we can also manipulate the capacity of the adapters by adjusting the bottleneck size. This can bring further improvements but requires more experimentation to find the appropriate hyperparameters.

6 Analysis

In this section, we look into how the performance changes in response to varying the value of k_{max}, then we provide a wall-clock time comparison between Adapters Wait-k and Multi-path Wait-k. Moreover, we experiment with how balancing between parameter sharing and interference by adjusting the adapter lagging impacts the performance, and also experiment with varying the bottleneck size in order to discern the impact of the complexity of the adapters. At last, we analyze the L2-norm of the adapter representations to discover which

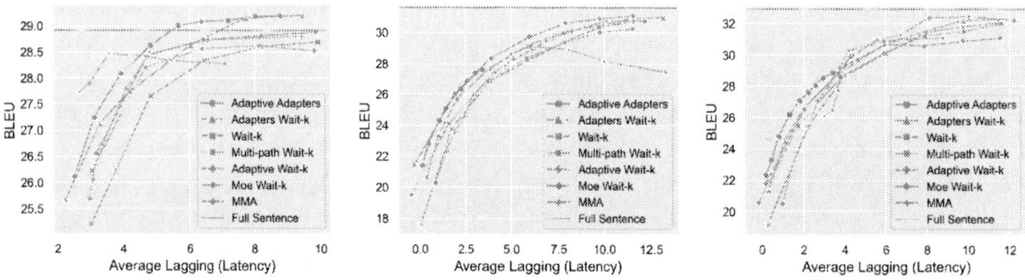

a En-Vi, Transformer-Small b De-En, Transformer-Base c De-En, Transformer-Big

Figure 2: Translation quality (BLEU) against latency (AL) of our methods (Adaptive Adapters, Adapters Wait-k) and previous adaptive (MMA, Adaptive Wait-k) and fixed (Wait-k, MoE Wait-k, Multi-path Wait-k) strategies on En-Vi and De-En.

adapter layers are involved in the prediction.

6.1 Ablation

We found that lowering the value of k_{max} for the adaptive strategy improves the results in low latency, which we believe is the priority in SiMT, but a lower k_{max} value also limits the ability of supporting high latency. In Figure 3, we show that by increasing the value of k_{max} we can support high latency and get better quality translations. We compare to Adaptive Wait-k and show that we still achieve better results for all the values of k_{max}. A lower k_{max} forces the model to be more aggressive, which in some cases can improve the results in lower latency. The fact that forcing the model to be more aggressive improves the performance signifies that the adaptive strategy decides to wait in cases where the model is able to make a correct prediction, which suggests that the adaptive strategy based on the probability threshold can still be improved by a better strategy.

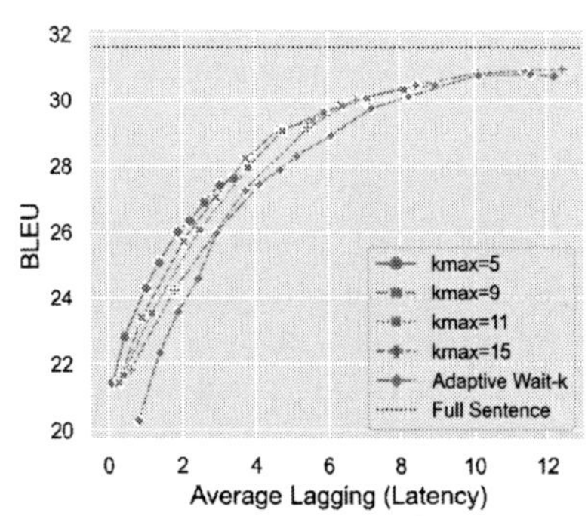

Figure 3: Results of increasing the value of k_{max} on De-En. Lower k_{max} values achieve better BLEU score in low latency, but it is necessary to increase the value of k_{max} in order to support high latency.

6.2 Inference Time

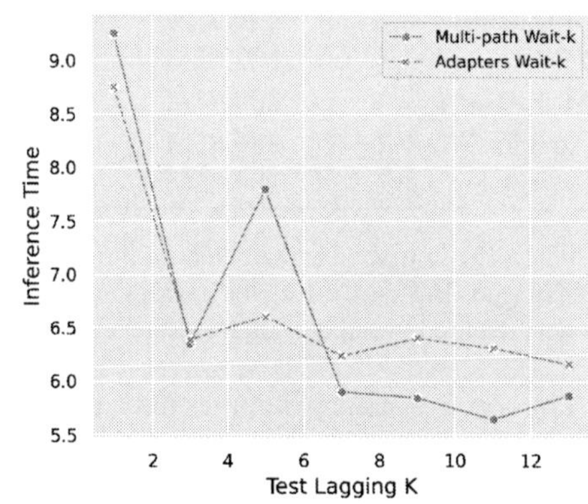

Figure 4: Wall-clock time comparison between Adapters Wait-k and Multi-path Wait-k averaged over 5 runs on En-De.

Although our method has more parameters than the baseline Multi-path Wait-k due to the additional adapters, the effect on the inference time is not proportional to the number of adapters because only one adapter is activated at a time. To illustrate this, we compare the wall-clock inference time (averaged over 5 runs) of Adapters Wait-k and Multi-path Wait-k in Figure 4. It seems that adapters are faster in low k values which could be due to over generation by the Multi-path model (where the model generates longer sequences than it should), while starting from a k value of 7, Multi-path Wait-k is better and the difference fluctuates between 0.29s and 0.66s.

6.3 Adapter Lagging

The adapter lagging K_A specifies the number of wait-k values that one single adapter will support

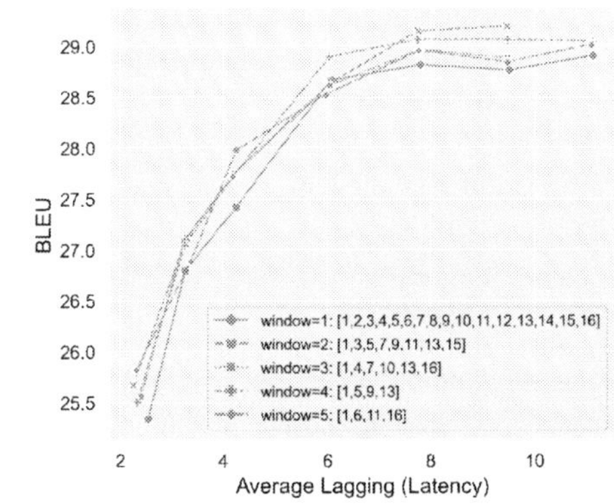

Figure 5: Results of varying the window sizes of the adapter lagging between 1 and 5 on En-Vi.

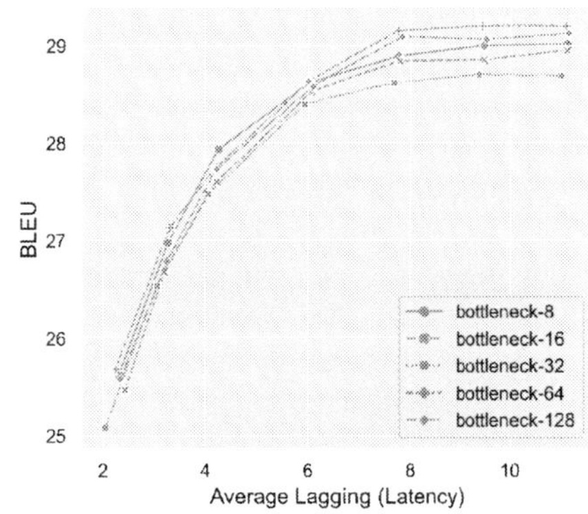

Figure 6: Results of doubling the bottleneck size of the adapters on En-Vi.

and also the number of adapters that we will use. We vary the adapter lagging window between 1 and 5, while maintaining the range between 1 and 16. The results are shown in Figure 5. The wait-k values supported by an adapter controls the amount of sharing and interference between the values. For example, for $K_A = \{1, 5, 9, 13\}$, adapter A_1 will be trained on $k \in \{1, 2, 3, 4\}$. We note that although it has more parameters, a window of 1 achieves the worst results, which signifies that parameter sharing between wait-k values is crucial. Adapter lagging with window 4 and 5 are competitive especially in low latency, which indicates that lower wait-k values benefit more from sharing. This is consistent with the fact that wait-k models achieve better results when tested on lower wait-k values (Zhang and Feng, 2021).

6.4 Adapter Bottleneck

The adapter's bottleneck size can be used to tune the representation capacity of the adapters and can be interesting to tune depending on the language pair and the adapter lagging. In Figure 6, we experiment with doubling the adapter's bottleneck size from 8 to 128, which can be regarded as increasing the representation capacity of the adapter network. We found that the bottleneck size impacts the performance but not in a consistent way - as in larger size results in better performance - but it seems to interact with other hyperparameters (e.g. adapter lagging) to improve or hinder the performance, especially in high latency, where the gap in performance is larger.

6.5 Adapter Representation Norm

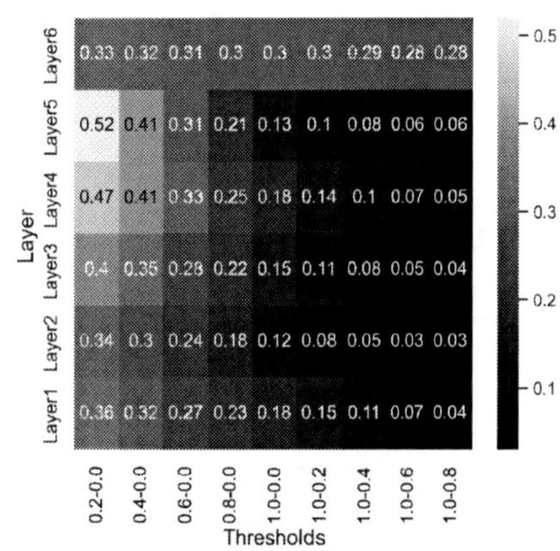

Figure 7: Confusion matrix of the average norm of the adapter representations in each layer of the decoder by the values of $\rho_{k_{min}}$ and $\rho_{k_{max}}$ on En-Vi.

We compute the L2-norm of the adapter representations in order to discover which adapter layers are involved in the representations (Liu et al., 2020; Zhu et al., 2021). We measure the L2-norm during inference for $k_{min} = 1$ and $k_{max} = 9$ while varying the value of $\rho_{k_{min}}$ and $\rho_{k_{max}}$, as described in Section 5.2. As depicted in Figure 7, the norm for all layers except layer 6 decreases as we increase $\rho_{k_{min}}$ or $\rho_{k_{max}}$, which correlates with making the adaptive strategy more conservative because the threshold for making a write action is higher. This shows that the adapters are more involved in the prediction when the model is forced to be more aggressive. Only layer 6 is stably invested in adapting the model representations at all the threshold values, which seems to indicate that only low threshold predictions are complex enough to recruit all the adapter layers. Based on this observation, we experiment with inserting adapters only in the last layer (i.e. layer 6). We show in Figure 8 the results of comparing between inserting adapters in all layers and inserting the adapters only in the last layer, where we see a drop in performance only in lower latency levels. This shows that we can make the model more efficient by removing lower layer adapters with a small drop in performance.

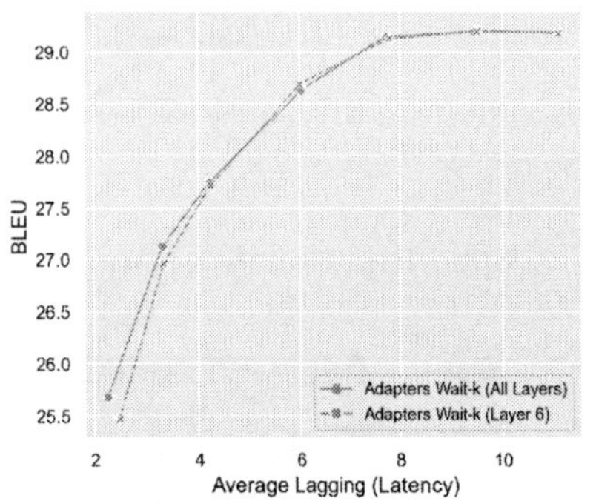

Figure 8: Comparison of the results of inserting adapters in all layers vs. only the last layer on En-Vi. We witness a drop in performance only in low latency levels.

7 Conclusion

In this paper, we employ adapters to build a SiMT model that can support multiple latency levels at inference. We use the multi-path training and show that by adding wait-k adapters we can flexibly balance parameter sharing and interference between the wait-k paths. Furthermore, we adopt a simple adaptive strategy and show that it further improves the results. By comparing against strong adaptive and fixed strategies, we find that our method achieves better or competitive results on most latency levels.

8 Limitations

The two datasets we used are common in SiMT research and were selected to compare against other baselines, but evaluating on only two language directions can be a limiting factor for the generalization of our results. Although Vietnamese is from a different language family, it deploys a similar word order (i.e. Subject-Verb-Object) to English and German and we believe that more challenges might emerge when dealing with language directions with a different word order. Additionally, we evaluate latency using common SiMT latency metrics such as AL, which are sentence-level and do not reflect the nature of a streaming scenario (Iranzo-Sánchez et al., 2021). Furthermore, in this work, we only evaluated on offline data, while evaluating on real interpretation data might offer more realistic results (Zhao et al., 2021).

Acknowledgements

The research presented in this paper was conducted as part of VOXReality project[5], which was funded by the European Union Horizon Europe program under grant agreement No. 101070521.

References

Naveen Arivazhagan, Colin Cherry, Wolfgang Macherey, Chung-Cheng Chiu, Semih Yavuz, Ruoming Pang, Wei Li, and Colin Raffel. 2019. Monotonic infinite lookback attention for simultaneous machine translation. In *Proceedings of the 57th Annual Meeting of the Association for Computational Linguistics*, pages 1313–1323, Florence, Italy. Association for Computational Linguistics.

Ankur Bapna and Orhan Firat. 2019. Simple, scalable adaptation for neural machine translation. In *Proceedings of the 2019 Conference on Empirical Methods in Natural Language Processing and the 9th International Joint Conference on Natural Language Processing (EMNLP-IJCNLP)*, pages 1538–1548, Hong Kong, China. Association for Computational Linguistics.

Mauro Cettolo, Jan Niehues, Sebastian Stüker, Luisa Bentivogli, Roldano Cattoni, and Marcello Federico. 2015. The IWSLT 2015 evaluation campaign. In *Proceedings of the 12th International Workshop on Spoken Language Translation: Evaluation Campaign*, pages 2–14, Da Nang, Vietnam.

Kyunghyun Cho and Masha Esipova. 2016. Can neural machine translation do simultaneous translation? *CoRR*, abs/1606.02012.

Alexandra Chronopoulou, Dario Stojanovski, and Alexander Fraser. 2023. Language-family adapters for low-resource multilingual neural machine translation. In *Proceedings of the The Sixth Workshop on Technologies for Machine Translation of Low-Resource Languages (LoResMT 2023)*, pages 59–72, Dubrovnik, Croatia. Association for Computational Linguistics.

Maha Elbayad, Laurent Besacier, and Jakob Verbeek. 2020. Efficient Wait-k Models for Simultaneous Machine Translation. In *Proc. Interspeech 2020*, pages 1461–1465.

[5]https://voxreality.eu/

Jiatao Gu, Graham Neubig, Kyunghyun Cho, and Victor O.K. Li. 2017. Learning to translate in real-time with neural machine translation. In *Proceedings of the 15th Conference of the European Chapter of the Association for Computational Linguistics: Volume 1, Long Papers*, pages 1053–1062, Valencia, Spain. Association for Computational Linguistics.

Neil Houlsby, Andrei Giurgiu, Stanislaw Jastrzebski, Bruna Morrone, Quentin De Laroussilhe, Andrea Gesmundo, Mona Attariyan, and Sylvain Gelly. 2019. Parameter-efficient transfer learning for NLP. In *Proceedings of the 36th International Conference on Machine Learning*, volume 97 of *Proceedings of Machine Learning Research*, pages 2790–2799. PMLR.

Javier Iranzo-Sánchez, Jorge Civera, and Alfons Juan. 2021. Stream-level latency evaluation for simultaneous machine translation.

Xuebo Liu, Houtim Lai, Derek F. Wong, and Lidia S. Chao. 2020. Norm-based curriculum learning for neural machine translation. In *Proceedings of the 58th Annual Meeting of the Association for Computational Linguistics*, pages 427–436, Online. Association for Computational Linguistics.

Mingbo Ma, Liang Huang, Hao Xiong, Renjie Zheng, Kaibo Liu, Baigong Zheng, Chuanqiang Zhang, Zhongjun He, Hairong Liu, Xing Li, Hua Wu, and Haifeng Wang. 2019. STACL: Simultaneous translation with implicit anticipation and controllable latency using prefix-to-prefix framework. In *Proceedings of the 57th Annual Meeting of the Association for Computational Linguistics*, pages 3025–3036, Florence, Italy. Association for Computational Linguistics.

Xutai Ma, Juan Miguel Pino, James Cross, Liezl Puzon, and Jiatao Gu. 2020. Monotonic multihead attention. In *International Conference on Learning Representations*.

Bhavitvya Malik, Abhinav Ramesh Kashyap, Min-Yen Kan, and Soujanya Poria. 2023. UDAPTER - efficient domain adaptation using adapters. In *Proceedings of the 17th Conference of the European Chapter of the Association for Computational Linguistics*, pages 2249–2263, Dubrovnik, Croatia. Association for Computational Linguistics.

Myle Ott, Sergey Edunov, Alexei Baevski, Angela Fan, Sam Gross, Nathan Ng, David Grangier, and Michael Auli. 2019. fairseq: A fast, extensible toolkit for sequence modeling. In *Proceedings of the 2019 Conference of the North American Chapter of the Association for Computational Linguistics (Demonstrations)*, pages 48–53, Minneapolis, Minnesota. Association for Computational Linguistics.

Kishore Papineni, Salim Roukos, Todd Ward, and Wei-Jing Zhu. 2002. Bleu: A method for automatic evaluation of machine translation. In *Proceedings of the 40th Annual Meeting on Association for Computational Linguistics*, ACL '02, page 311–318, USA. Association for Computational Linguistics.

Jonas Pfeiffer, Naman Goyal, Xi Lin, Xian Li, James Cross, Sebastian Riedel, and Mikel Artetxe. 2022. Lifting the curse of multilinguality by pre-training modular transformers. In *Proceedings of the 2022 Conference of the North American Chapter of the Association for Computational Linguistics: Human Language Technologies*, pages 3479–3495, Seattle, United States. Association for Computational Linguistics.

Jonas Pfeiffer, Aishwarya Kamath, Andreas Rücklé, Kyunghyun Cho, and Iryna Gurevych. 2021. AdapterFusion: Non-destructive task composition for transfer learning. In *Proceedings of the 16th Conference of the European Chapter of the Association for Computational Linguistics: Main Volume*, pages 487–503, Online. Association for Computational Linguistics.

Jerin Philip, Alexandre Berard, Matthias Gallé, and Laurent Besacier. 2020. Monolingual adapters for zero-shot neural machine translation. In *Proceedings of the 2020 Conference on Empirical Methods in Natural Language Processing (EMNLP)*, pages 4465–4470, Online. Association for Computational Linguistics.

Colin Raffel, Minh-Thang Luong, Peter J. Liu, Ron J. Weiss, and Douglas Eck. 2017. Online and linear-time attention by enforcing monotonic alignments. In *Proceedings of the 34th International Conference on Machine Learning*, volume 70 of *Proceedings of Machine Learning Research*, pages 2837–2846. PMLR.

Sylvestre-Alvise Rebuffi, Hakan Bilen, and Andrea Vedaldi. 2017. Learning multiple visual domains with residual adapters. In *Advances in Neural Information Processing Systems*, volume 30. Curran Associates, Inc.

Rico Sennrich, Barry Haddow, and Alexandra Birch. 2016. Neural machine translation of rare words with subword units. In *Proceedings of the 54th Annual Meeting of the Association for Computational Linguistics (Volume 1: Long Papers)*, pages 1715–1725, Berlin, Germany. Association for Computational Linguistics.

Asa Cooper Stickland and Iain Murray. 2019. BERT and PALs: Projected attention layers for efficient adaptation in multi-task learning. In *Proceedings of the 36th International Conference on Machine Learning*, volume 97 of *Proceedings of Machine Learning Research*, pages 5986–5995. PMLR.

Ashish Vaswani, Noam Shazeer, Niki Parmar, Jakob Uszkoreit, Llion Jones, Aidan N Gomez, Ł ukasz Kaiser, and Illia Polosukhin. 2017. Attention is all you need. In *Advances in Neural Information Processing Systems*, volume 30. Curran Associates, Inc.

Ruiqing Zhang and Chuanqiang Zhang. 2020. Dynamic sentence boundary detection for simultaneous translation. In *Proceedings of the First Workshop on Automatic Simultaneous Translation*, pages 1–9, Seattle, Washington. Association for Computational Linguistics.

Shaolei Zhang and Yang Feng. 2021. Universal simultaneous machine translation with mixture-of-experts wait-k policy. In *Proceedings of the 2021 Conference on Empirical Methods in Natural Language Processing*, pages 7306–7317, Online and Punta Cana, Dominican Republic. Association for Computational Linguistics.

Shaolei Zhang and Yang Feng. 2022. Information-transport-based policy for simultaneous translation. In *Proceedings of the 2022 Conference on Empirical Methods in Natural Language Processing*, pages 992–1013, Abu Dhabi, United Arab Emirates. Association for Computational Linguistics.

Shaolei Zhang, Yang Feng, and Liangyou Li. 2021. Future-guided incremental transformer for simultaneous translation. *Proceedings of the AAAI Conference on Artificial Intelligence*, 35(16):14428–14436.

Jinming Zhao, Philip Arthur, Gholamreza Haffari, Trevor Cohn, and Ehsan Shareghi. 2021. It is not as good as you think! evaluating simultaneous machine translation on interpretation data.

Libo Zhao, Kai Fan, Wei Luo, Wu Jing, Shushu Wang, Ziqian Zeng, and Zhongqiang Huang. 2023. Adaptive policy with wait-k model for simultaneous translation. In *Proceedings of the 2023 Conference on Empirical Methods in Natural Language Processing*, pages 4816–4832, Singapore. Association for Computational Linguistics.

Yuting Zhao and Ioan Calapodescu. 2022. Multimodal robustness for neural machine translation. In *Proceedings of the 2022 Conference on Empirical Methods in Natural Language Processing*, pages 8505–8516, Abu Dhabi, United Arab Emirates. Association for Computational Linguistics.

Baigong Zheng, Kaibo Liu, Renjie Zheng, Mingbo Ma, Hairong Liu, and Liang Huang. 2020. Simultaneous translation policies: From fixed to adaptive. In *Proceedings of the 58th Annual Meeting of the Association for Computational Linguistics*, pages 2847–2853, Online. Association for Computational Linguistics.

Baigong Zheng, Renjie Zheng, Mingbo Ma, and Liang Huang. 2019. Simpler and faster learning of adaptive policies for simultaneous translation. In *Proceedings of the 2019 Conference on Empirical Methods in Natural Language Processing and the 9th International Joint Conference on Natural Language Processing (EMNLP-IJCNLP)*, pages 1349–1354, Hong Kong, China. Association for Computational Linguistics.

Yaoming Zhu, Jiangtao Feng, Chengqi Zhao, Mingxuan Wang, and Lei Li. 2021. Counter-interference adapter for multilingual machine translation. In *Findings of the Association for Computational Linguistics: EMNLP 2021*, pages 2812–2823, Punta Cana, Dominican Republic. Association for Computational Linguistics.

A Hyperparameters

We list the hyperparameters of our experiments in Table 2.

B Numeric Results

In Tables 3, 4 and 5, we report the numeric results of our methods. We report the BLEU score for quality, while for latency we used Average Lagging (AL), Consecutive Wait (CW) (Gu et al., 2017), Average Proportion (AP) (Cho and Esipova, 2016) and Differentiable Average Lagging (DAL) (Arivazhagan et al., 2019). Below we provide the definition of CW, AP and DAL. $g(i)$ constitutes the number of tokens read when predicting y_i, while $|x|$ and $|y|$ refer to the number of source and target tokens respectively.

Consecutive Wait (CW) Computes the average number of consecutive tokens read between two predicted tokens.

$$CW = \frac{\sum_{i=1}^{|y|}(g(i) - g(i-1))}{\sum_{i=1}^{|y|}\mathbb{I}_{g(i)-g(i-1)>0}} \quad (5)$$

Average Proportion (AP) Computes the proportion of tokens read to make every prediction.

$$AP = \frac{1}{|x||y|}\sum_{i=1}^{|y|} g(i) \quad (6)$$

Differentiable Average Lagging (DAL) Is a differentiable version of the Average Lagging metric.

$$g'(i) = \begin{cases} g(i) & \text{if } i = 1 \\ \max\left(g(i), g'(i-1) + \frac{|x|}{|y|}\right) & \text{if } i > 1 \end{cases} \quad (7)$$

$$DAL = \frac{1}{|y|}\sum_{i=1}^{|y|} g'(i) - \frac{i-1}{|x|/|y|} \quad (8)$$

Hyperparameter	IWSLT15 En→Vi	WMT15 De→En (Base)	WMT15 De→En (Big)
Encoder layers	6	6	6
Encoder attention heads	4	8	16
Encoder embed dim	512	512	1024
Encoder FFN embed dim	1024	2048	4096
Decoder layers	6	6	6
Decoder attention heads	4	8	16
Decoder embed dim	512	512	1024
Decoder FFN embed dim	1024	2048	4096
Dropout	0.3	0.3	0.3
Optimizer	Adam	Adam	Adam
Adam-β	(0.9, 0.98)	(0.9, 0.98)	(0.9, 0.98)
Clip-norm	0.	0.	0.
Learning rate (lr)	5e-4	5e-4	5e-4
LR scheduler	inverse sqrt	inverse sqrt	inverse sqrt
Warm-up updates	4000	4000	4000
Warm-up init LR	1e-7	1e-7	1e-7
Weight decay	1e-4	1e-4	1e-4
Label smoothing	0.1	0.1	0.1
Max tokens	16000	8192×4	4096×4×2

Table 2: System Hyperparameters

IWSLT15 English→Vietnamese Transformer-Small						
	K	CW	AP	DAL	AL	BLEU
Adapters Wait-k	1	1.16	0.59	3.32	2.25	25.68
	2	1.17	0.64	4.13	3.30	27.13
	3	1.22	0.68	4.91	4.21	27.75
	5	1.44	0.75	6.63	6.01	28.63
	7	1.87	0.81	8.36	7.74	29.15
	9	2.56	0.85	10.05	9.45	29.20
	$(\rho_{k_{min}}, \rho_{k_{max}})$	CW	AP	DAL	AL	BLEU
Adaptive Adapters	(0.2, 0.0)	1.37	0.60	3.89	2.52	26.12
	(0.4, 0.0)	1.73	0.63	5.04	3.13	27.24
	(0.6, 0.0)	2.19	0.67	6.14	3.92	28.09
	(0.8, 0.0)	2.66	0.71	6.95	4.80	28.62
	(1.0, 0.0)	2.71	0.74	7.58	5.65	29.00
	(1.0, 0.2)	3.08	0.76	8.40	6.36	29.08
	(1.0, 0.4)	3.33	0.79	9.10	7.20	29.10
	(1.0, 0.6)	3.34	0.82	9.55	8.01	29.18
	(1.0, 0.8)	3.11	0.84	9.87	8.78	29.19

Table 3: Numerical results for En-Vi with Transformer-Small.

WMT15 German→English Transformer-Base						
	K	CW	AP	DAL	AL	BLEU
	1	1.15	0.52	1.79	0.36	20.72
	2	1.19	0.55	2.49	1.00	23.37
	3	1.21	0.59	3.32	2.03	25.73
	5	1.37	0.66	5.19	3.85	27.71
Adapters Wait-k	7	1.69	0.73	7.11	5.86	29.17
	9	2.16	0.78	8.98	7.76	30.05
	11	2.77	0.82	10.78	9.65	30.45
	13	3.52	0.85	12.49	11.46	30.90
	15	4.43	0.88	14.10	13.17	31.01
	$(\rho_{k_{min}}, \rho_{k_{max}})$	**CW**	**AP**	**DAL**	**AL**	**BLEU**
	(0.2, 0.0)	1.52	0.52	2.61	0.12	21.42
	(0.4, 0.0)	1.78	0.53	3.19	0.45	22.83
	(0.6, 0.0)	1.95	0.55	3.68	1.03	24.30
	(0.8, 0.0)	2.05	0.57	4.04	1.39	25.09
Adaptive Adapters	(1.0, 0.0)	1.91	0.59	4.31	1.90	26.00
	(1.0, 0.2)	2.02	0.60	4.66	2.23	26.34
	(1.0, 0.4)	2.03	0.62	4.90	2.60	26.89
	(1.0, 0.6)	1.94	0.63	5.06	3.03	27.41
	(1.0, 0.8)	1.74	0.65	5.16	3.41	27.62

Table 4: Numerical results for De-En with Transformer-Base.

WMT15 German→English Transformer-Big						
	K	CW	AP	DAL	AL	BLEU
	1	1.18	0.52	1.84	0.31	21.37
	2	1.19	0.55	2.55	1.09	24.53
	3	1.22	0.59	3.40	2.06	26.70
	5	1.38	0.66	5.24	3.88	28.98
Adapters Wait-k	7	1.68	0.73	7.15	5.93	30.70
	9	2.16	0.78	9.02	7.85	31.50
	11	2.77	0.82	10.82	9.73	32.21
	13	3.52	0.85	12.52	11.50	32.31
	15	4.44	0.88	14.12	13.16	32.44
	$(\rho_{k_{min}}, \rho_{k_{max}})$	**CW**	**AP**	**DAL**	**AL**	**BLEU**
	(0.2, 0.0)	1.50	0.52	2.56	0.18	22.30
	(0.4, 0.0)	1.78	0.53	3.11	0.44	23.30
	(0.6, 0.0)	1.99	0.55	3.60	0.79	24.79
	(0.8, 0.0)	2.08	0.57	4.02	1.31	26.18
Adaptive Adapters	(1.0, 0.0)	1.94	0.59	4.29	1.82	27.05
	(1.0, 0.2)	2.03	0.60	4.66	2.22	27.60
	(1.0, 0.4)	2.06	0.62	4.92	2.58	28.05
	(1.0, 0.6)	1.99	0.63	5.09	2.94	28.52
	(1.0, 0.8)	1.77	0.65	5.20	3.41	28.85

Table 5: Numerical results for De-En with Transformer-Big.

IWSLT 2024 Indic Track system description paper: Speech-to-Text Translation from English to multiple Low-Resource Indian Languages

Deepanjali Singh, Ayush Anand, Abhyuday Chaturvedi and **Niyati Baliyan***
Department of Computer Engineering
National Institute of Technology Kurukshetra
Haryana, India, 136118
⋆niyatibaliyan@nitkkr.ac.in

Abstract

Multi-Language Speech-to-Text Translation (ST) plays a pivotal role in bridging linguistic barriers by converting spoken language into written text across different languages. This project aims to develop a robust ST model tailored for low-resource Indian languages, specifically targeting the Indo-Aryan and Dravidian language families. The dataset used consists of speeches from conferences and TED Talks, along with their corresponding transcriptions in English (source language) and translations in Hindi, Bengali, and Tamil (target languages). By tackling the lack of data and disparities in attention within low-resource languages, the paper strives to create an efficient ST system capable of real-world deployment. Additionally, existing resources in related languages are leveraged and word-level translation resources are explored to enhance translation accuracy.

1 Introduction

Multi-Language Speech-to-Text Translation (ST) is indispensable for facilitating communication across diverse linguistic contexts. While recent advancements have shown remarkable progress, many dialects and low-resource languages still lack sufficient parallel data for effective supervised learning. Creative approaches are essential to overcome this challenge, such as leveraging resources from related languages or utilizing word-level translation resources and raw audio. This work aims to address these gaps by developing an End-to-End (E2E) or Cascaded ST model for low-resource Indian languages, including Hindi, Bengali, and Tamil.

2 Motivation

The scarcity of translators proficient in multiple languages, especially in low-resource settings, highlights the urgent need for ST systems supporting multiple languages. In regions like India, characterized by a multitude of languages, the development of dedicated models for Indian languages is essential for effective communication. This task aims to advance ST technology for a wide range of languages. Our ultimate goal is to foster inclusively and accessibility through the creation of robust ST models. This research work is fueled by a strong commitment to address significant challenges in speech translation, with a particular focus on languages spoken in India. In modern interconnected society, the capacity to communicate across various languages is crucial. However, the shortage of translators who can handle multiple languages in resource-constrained areas, presents a major obstacle.

3 Related Work

Prior research in ST has primarily focused on high-resource languages, leaving many dialects and low-resource languages underserved. The lack of parallel data poses a significant challenge in training supervised learning models for these languages. However, recent efforts have demonstrated the effectiveness of leveraging existing resources from related languages and employing innovative approaches to enhance translation accuracy[5]. The 20th International Conference on Spoken Language Translation (IWSLT) organized shared tasks targeting nine scientific challenges in spoken language translation (SLT). These tasks covered a wide spectrum. This encompasses simultaneous and offline translation, automatic subtitling and dubbing, speech-to-speech translation, multilingual translation, translation of dialects and low-resource languages, and formality control. The conference witnessed substantial interest with a total of 38 submissions from 31 teams, evenly distributed between academia and industry [1]. The focal point of the 2023 IWSLT Evaluation Campaign was offline SLT, which involved translating audio speech from one language to text in another language without time constraints. It com-

Proceedings of the 21st International Conference on Spoken Language Translation (IWSLT 2024), pages 359–364
August 15-16, 2024 ©2024 Association for Computational Linguistics

prised three sub-tasks for translating English into German, Japanese, and Chinese. Participants were given the flexibility to utilize either cascade architectures, which combine automatic speech recognition (ASR) and machine translation (MT) systems, or E2E approaches that directly translate input speech [1]. Principal objectives were twofold: firstly, to gauge the performance disparity between cascade and end-to-end systems, and secondly, to evaluate SLT technology's competence in handling intricate scenarios like simultaneous overlapping or concurrent speakers. The introduction of new test sets, encompassing ACL presentations and press conferences/interviews, aimed at a comprehensive assessment of system efficacy [1]. Training data conditions spanned from constrained to unconstrained, offering varying levels of access to training resources. Development data encompassed TED talks, ACL presentations, and interviews from the European Parliament Multimedia Centre. System evaluations were conducted employing BLEU and COMET metrics, supplemented by human assessment of the top-performing entries [4]. Ten teams partook in the offline task, collectively submitting 37 runs. A plethora of techniques were employed across these submissions, including cascade and direct models, leveraging large language models, multimodal representations, data augmentation, ensemble methods, and advanced training strategies. Evaluation criteria emphasized the attainment of high translation quality across diverse language pairs and challenging scenarios [1].

4 System Overview

4.1 Key Components of the App

4.1.1 Audio Processor and Transcription Module

- Responsible for cleaning audio file
- Uses ResembleAI for Noise reduction, Restoring distortion, enhancing speech bandwidth
- Uses OpenAI's Whisper [1] model for transcription [3].

4.1.2 Input Module

- Responsible for receiving audio files
- Validates and preprocesses the input data for further processing.

[1]https://openai.com/index/whisper/

4.1.3 Translation Module - English to Hindi

- Integrates the Helsinki model for achieving translation of the transcribed text
- Fine tuning of pretrained translator model to enhance the result quality [2].

4.1.4 Translation Module - English to Tamil

- Integrates Facebook's mBART model for achieving translation of the transcribed text
- Fine tuning of pretrained translator model to enhance the result quality [2].

4.1.5 Translation Module - English to Bengali

- Integrates Facebook's mBART model for achieving translation of the transcribed text
- Fine tuning of pretrained translator model to enhance the result quality [2].

4.1.6 Output Module

- Performs syntax correction and eliminates any detectable hallucination by the model
- Delivers the translated text to users in their desired format, such as text files

4.2 SacreBLEU scores

Table 1 contains self assessment `SacreBLEU` scores of different model tested. Models selected are:
Whisper and Helsenki [3] for English-to-Hindi.
Whisper and mBART for English-to-Tamil
Whisper and mBART for English-to-Bengali

4.3 Implementation Pillars

4.3.1 translate.py

- It imports various functions from different modules to perform tasks like transcribing audio, translating text, breaking lines, saving files, and post-processing text.
- It sets up the starting time to measure how long the code takes to execute.

Language Pair	Model Used	Score
`en-hi`	whisper/helsenki	24.21
`en-bn`	whisper/helsenki	14.18
`en-bn`	whisper/mBART	16.18
`en-ta`	whisper/helsenki	7.1
`en-ta`	whisper/mBART	10.79

Table 1: SacreBLEU Scores

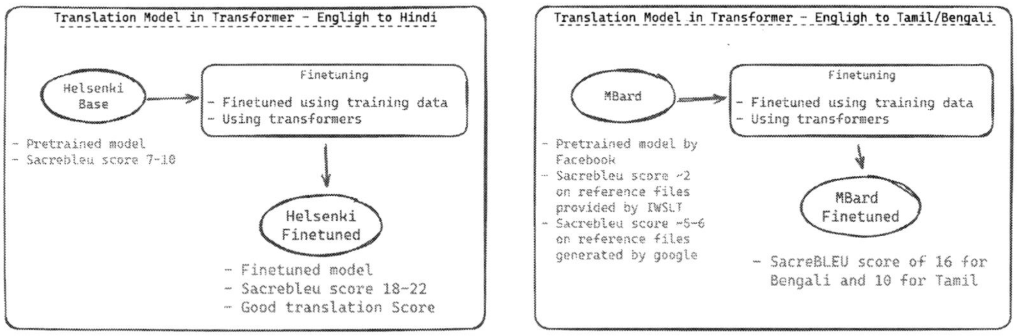

Figure 1: (a):English-to-Hindi by Helsenki (b):English-to-Tamil/Bengali by mBART

- It transcribes audio files present in the specified folder in English text, optionally based on a YAML file that specifies line changes.
- It translates the transcribed English text into Hindi and saves it.
- It translates the transcribed English text into Tamil and Bengali using Facebook's mBART translation service, then saves them.
- Finally, it prints the time it takes for execution.

4.3.2 transcriber.py

- It imports necessary libraries/modules such as `os`, `yaml`, `pydub`, `logging`, and a pipeline from the `transformers` library.
- It sets the logging level for the `transformers` library to `ERROR` to suppress unnecessary output, except for any errors.
- It defines a function `transcribe_audio(filePath)` that takes the path of an audio file, uses the OpenAI Whisper model via the Hugging Face Transformers library to transcribe the audio, and returns the transcribed text [3].
- It defines another function `transcriber(audios_dir, yaml_file_path)` that takes the directory containing audio files and the path to a YAML file as inputs. This function loads audio segments from the YAML file, iterates through audio files in the specified directory, extracts segments based on the information in the YAML file, transcribes each segment using the `transcribe_audio` function, and returns a list of transcribed texts.
- Enables selective use of YAML-based chunks to force line changes in the result.

4.3.3 translator.py

- Figure 1(a) shows English-to-Tamil translation workflow of `translator.py` module, it imports necessary functions from the `transformers` library to utilize pretrained translation models.
- It defines a function called `translatorModel`, which takes two arguments: `lines`, representing the text to be translated, and `target`, indicating the target language for translation.
- Inside the function, it loads a pretrained translation model and tokenizer specific to the target language using the Helsinki-NLP library.
- It iterates through each line in the input lines.
- For each non-empty line, it tokenizes the text using the tokenizer, prepares the input for the model, generates the translation, and decodes the translated output.
- It appends the translated text to a result array.
- It returns an array of translated text lines.

4.3.4 fbtranslate.py

- Figure 1(b) shows English-to-Tamil and English-to-Bengali translation workflow of `fbtranslate.py` module ,it defines a function called `fbtranslate(lines)`, which takes a list of input text lines as its argument.
- Inside the function, it initializes a translation pipeline using the `pipeline` function. This pipeline is configured to use the model named `"facebook/mbart-large-50 -many-to-many-mmt"` for translation tasks.

- It initializes an empty list named `result` to store the translated text lines.
- It iterates through each line in the input lines.
- For each non-empty line, it translates the text from English (source language: `"en_XX"`) to Tamil (target language: `"ta_IN"`) using the translation pipeline.
- It extracts the translated text from the output of the translation pipeline and appends it to the `result` list.
- Finally, it returns the list containing the translated text lines.

4.4 Fine Tuning Logic Overview

4.4.1 Importing Libraries

We import necessary libraries including `Dataset`, `DatasetDict`, `AutoTokenizer`, `AutoModelForSeq2SeqLM`, `DataCollatorForSeq2Seq`, `Seq2SeqTrainingArguments`, `Seq2SeqTrainer`, and `load_metric`.

4.4.2 Loading Metric

We load the `SacreBLEU` metric for evaluating translation quality.

4.4.3 Model Checkpoint and File Paths

- The pretrained model checkpoint `"Helsinki-NLP/opus-mt-en-hi"` is specified.
- Paths for English (`train.en`) and Hindi (`train.hi`) training data files are defined.

4.4.4 Reading Data

English and Hindi sentences are read from their respective files.

4.4.5 Creating Dataset

- The English and Hindi sentence pairs are organized into a dictionary format.
- A `Dataset` object is created from this dictionary.

4.4.6 Creating DatasetDict

A `DatasetDict` object is created containing the train dataset.

4.4.7 Initializing Tokenizer

The tokenizer is instantiated using the specified model checkpoint.

4.4.8 Defining Preprocessing Function

- A function `preprocess_function` is defined to prepare input data for training.
- Inputs and targets are tokenized, and input IDs and labels are generated.

4.4.9 Mapping Preprocessing Function

The `preprocess_function` is applied to the train dataset using the `map` function.

4.4.10 Model Initialization

The pretrained model for sequence-to-sequence learning is instantiated.

4.4.11 Defining Training Arguments

- Evaluation strategy, learning rate, batch size, etc., are defined using `Seq2SeqTrainingArguments`.
- A data aggregator is developed for sequence-to-sequence assignments.

4.4.12 Defining Post-processing Function

A post-processing function for predictions and computing metrics is defined.

4.4.13 Training Configuration

A `Seq2SeqTrainer` is initialized with the model, training arguments, datasets, data collator, tokenizer, and compute metrics function.

4.4.14 Training Loop

The `train` method of the trainer object is called to initiate training.

4.4.15 Saving the Model

After successful execution of above logic, we have a fine-tuned model saved as a `.safetensors` file.

5 Workflow

Figure 2 shows basic workflow of the application. At first, there is Input Processing, where users upload audio files or provide input through supported channels. This serves as the gateway for input data, ensuring its integrity and validity. The Input Module undertakes the crucial task of verifying and preprocessing the audio data, preparing it for subsequent processing stages by addressing any inconsistencies.

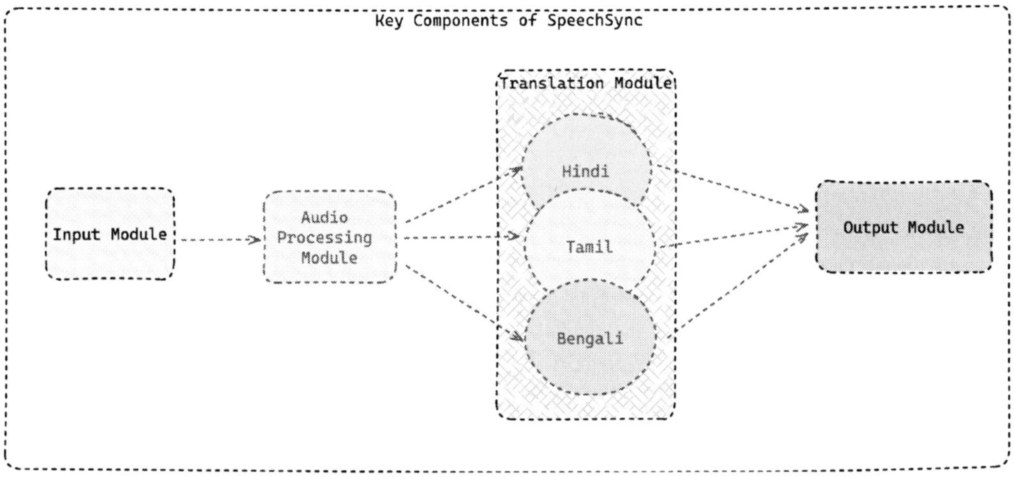

Figure 2: Basic flow of SpeechSync System

Next, Transcription and Translation enable transformation of audio content into translated text. The Transcription Module uses advanced algorithms to convert audio files into text, maintaining high accuracy and reliability. Meanwhile, the Translation Module leverages Helsinki model to translate transcribed text into specific languages, ensuring linguistic precision and preserving contextual nuances to facilitate communication across languages.

Once the transcription and translation processes are complete, the Output Delivery stage takes over, presenting the translated text to users through the Output Module. This enables seamless access and utilization of the translated content, offering users the flexibility to download the text or integrate it directly into their workflows. By providing a user-friendly interface and facilitating easy dissemination of translated content, the application empowers users to overcome language barriers and engage in effective cross-cultural communication.

5.1 Environment Settings

5.1.1 Prerequisites

- Python 3.11
- `ffmpeg` (command-line tool)

5.1.2 Installing ffmpeg

- **Ubuntu:** `sudo apt update && sudo apt install ffmpeg`
- **MacOS:** `brew install ffmpeg`
- **Windows:** `choco install ffmpeg`

5.1.3 App Installation

1. **Clone the repository**[2]

```
git clone git@github.com:
ayushannand/SpeechSync.git
```

2. **Create a virtual environment**

```
python3 -m venv env
```

3. **Activate the virtual environment**

```
source env/bin/activate
```

5.1.4 Install Rust

```
curl --proto '=https' --tlsv1.2
-sSf https://sh.rustup.rs | sh
```

6 Baseline vs. Results

The baseline `SacreBLEU` scores is provided by INDIC Track. For each language pair we have a different baselines.

6.0.1 English-to-Hindi

For language pair `en-hi` baseline is `5.23` and we get a score of `24`.

6.0.2 English-to-Bengali

For language pair `en-bn` baseline is `5.86` and we get a score of `16`.

[2]https://github.com/ayushannand/SpeechSync

6.0.3 English-to-Tamil

For language pair `en-ta` baseline is `1.9` and we get a score of `10`.

7 Limitations

While we acknowledge the significant challenges ahead, such as the shortage of multilingual individuals and insufficient data for certain languages, we are determined to find innovative solutions. Our input module currently supports only one language, so if the audio file contains multiple languages, the application ignores languages other than primary language. Currently, the other limitation is the time taken by the models to produce output. We may try out various optimisations and configurations to achieve faster results. For language pair - English to Bengali, we are barely crossing the baseline, so our primary goal is to achieve better score for Bengali language.

8 Conclusion

In summary, our key contributions lie in rigorous experimentation conducted to identify effective models for speech translation. We perform extensive preprocessing of data performed to ensure quality and suitability for training. The proposed solution establishes a robust pipeline including code development and workflow setup. The training and experimentation is focused on one language for an in-depth analysis. We perform close monitoring of performance metrics and numerical evaluations for model assessment.

This paper is committed to advancing ST technology for low resource languages. Through the creation of dedicated datasets and the development of robust models, our aim is to facilitate seamless communication and accessibility across diverse linguistic communities, ultimately promoting inclusivity and empowerment.

References

[1] Milind Agarwal, Sweta Agrawal, Antonios Anastasopoulos, Luisa Bentivogli, Ondřej Bojar, Claudia Borg, Marine Carpuat, Roldano Cattoni, Mauro Cettolo, Mingda Chen, William Chen, Khalid Choukri, Alexandra Chronopoulou, Anna Currey, Thierry Declerck, Qianqian Dong, Kevin Duh, Yannick Estève, Marcello Federico, et al. 2023. Findings of the iwslt 2023 evaluation campaign. In *Proceedings of the 20th International Conference on Spoken Language Translation (IWSLT 2023)*, pages 1–61, Toronto, Canada. Association for Computational Linguistics.

[2] Raymond Li, Wen Xiao, Lanjun Wang, Hyeju Jang, and Giuseppe Carenini. 2021. T3-Vis: visual analytic for training and fine-tuning transformers in nlp. In *Proceedings of the 2021 Conference on Empirical Methods in Natural Language Processing: System Demonstrations*, pages 220–230, Online and Punta Cana, Dominican Republic. Association for Computational Linguistics.

[3] Alec Radford, Jong Wook Kim, Teng Xu, Greg Brockman, Conor McLeavey, and Ilya Sutskever. 2023. Robust speech recognition via large-scale weak supervision. Technical Report arXiv:whisper, OpenAI.

[4] Elizabeth Salesky, Kareem Darwish, Mohamed Al-Badrashiny, Mona Diab, and Jan Niehues. 2023. Evaluating multilingual speech translation under realistic conditions with resegmentation and terminology. In *Proceedings of the 20th International Conference on Spoken Language Translation (IWSLT 2023)*, pages 62–78, Toronto, Canada. Association for Computational Linguistics.

[5] Elizabeth Salesky, Marcello Federico, and Marine Carpuat. 2023. Proceedings of the 20th international conference on spoken language translation (iwslt 2023). In *Proceedings of the 20th International Conference on Spoken Language Translation (IWSLT 2023)*, Toronto, Canada. Association for Computational Linguistics.

Author Index